HITLER'S HOME FRONT

Hitler's Home Front

Württemberg under the Nazis

Jill Stephenson

hambledon
continuum

Hambledon Continuum, a Continuum imprint
The Tower Building, 11 York Road, London SE1 7NX, UK
80 Maiden Lane, Suite 704, New York, NY 10038, USA

First Published 2006

ISBN 1 85285 442 1

A description of this book is available from the
British Library and from the Library of Congress.

Typeset by Egan-Reid Ltd, Auckland, New Zealand.
Printed in Great Britain by MPG Books Ltd, Cornwall.

Contents

Illustrations

Plates

Between Pages 240 and 241

Maps

In memory of Steve,
with gratitude

Introduction

This book aims to portray the experience of small town and rural Württemberg, with its distinctive heritage and traditions, under the Nazis. It addresses the problems faced by the rural population in wartime and this population's attitudes and responses to the demands and pressures imposed by the Nazi regime. Not surprisingly, there was considerable continuity from the prewar period into the war years. It will doubtless seem, therefore, that, for a book which purports to be about 'Hitler's Home Front' in wartime, there is a great deal of preamble about the prewar years. In defence it can be said that the war years cannot be fully understood without some knowledge – and sometimes detailed knowledge – of what preceded them. In particular, some understanding of the socio-economic and political background of interwar Württemberg, and, from 1933, of the relationship between the Nazi Party and the state there, is essential. The fundamentals and application of Nazi racial policy, and the relationship between the churches and the Nazi state before the war, are also required context. In addition, to understand the experience of those in the countryside requires some appreciation of that of the urban population, the townees.

Some will undoubtedly regard my approach as one that dwells excessively on the trials and tribulations experienced by Germans. It is, however, worth noting that those who were most immediately targeted as victims *within* Nazi Germany were themselves overwhelmingly Germans. In addition, most Germans who were not Jews, who were not classed as opponents or delinquents liable to be consigned to a concentration camp, and who were not potentially or actually vulnerable to Nazi policies such as sterilisation or 'euthanasia', experienced hardship and suffering during the Second World War. A few million were killed through combat, bombing and invasion; many more experienced the death of family members and friends, and possibly the destruction of home and livelihood as well. This is a matter of historical fact. Historians and others may argue about the extent to which the 'Aryan', 'politically reliable' and 'socially responsible' population of Germany *deserved* to suffer, but it is incontrovertible that the overwhelming majority of them did, in one way or another, during the war and especially in its later stages. Denying or de-emphasising this assumes – erroneously – that acknowledgement of suffering is a zero-sum game. That is to say, if one draws attention to the suffering of 'Aryan' Germans one is – whether consciously or not – either diminishing the suffering of Nazism's most obvious victims or distracting attention from their experience. It is a matter for debate whether that is a greater distortion than refusing to recognise the hardship and suffering faced in the Second World War by those Germans who were not the targeted victims of the Nazi regime. To argue that they brought suffering upon themselves does not negate the validity of documenting it.

The violent and antidemocratic character of the NSDAP was clearly evident before Hitler came to power in 1933. The brutal and discriminatory nature of his dictatorial regime was unmistakable during the 1930s. Those who accepted it, or failed to resist it – in Germany and abroad – did not necessarily welcome all of its methods and policies, any more than most people in a democratic polity agree wholeheartedly with all of the policies of the political party that they support at elections. Those who supported or simply tolerated the Nazi regime in the 1930s, as well as those who resented or detested it, could not predict the character of the Second World War and could not predict the Holocaust – any more than could Nazism's opponents or targeted victims. The Holocaust was indeed, as Hans Mommsen has said, 'the realisation of the unthinkable'.[1] Certainly, it has been clear for many years that the Nazi system could not have functioned as it did, and its functionaries could not have perpetrated violence and murder on a huge scale, without the participation of substantial numbers of people who had not necessarily been NSDAP members or even voters in January 1933. Many of them were in key positions in business and industry, or as technocrats, or as members of the professions, especially in the bureaucracy, law, medicine and teaching. Many more obeyed their orders, as well as those given by army officers who directed the slaughter of prisoners of war and civilians in – with a few notorious exceptions – eastern Europe.

It is, however, self-evident that small-scale farmers, artisans and their families in rural communities in Württemberg were, under Nazi rule, not in a position to influence government policy or its implementation. Unless they belonged to the relatively small numbers of NSDAP activists in rural areas, they could merely respond to government demands through obedience or evasion, or a combination of the two. The evidence suggests that their responses were for the most part motivated by parochial self-interest and adherence to traditional practice rather than by any appreciation of government strategic thinking or ideological imperatives. It can be argued – as a commentator contended at the German Studies Association conference in 2000, in response to my paper on foreign workers in Württemberg – that farmers, artisans and their families in small communities in Württemberg were the relatives of men who were committing atrocities on the eastern front. Whether they were or not, attributing guilt by association is a dubious exercise.

Recognition that the maintenance of the Nazi system involved a much wider range of Germans than merely a restricted group of party criminals, and that the perpetration of crimes in that system's name depended on the collaboration of substantial numbers of both civilians and soldiers, has resulted in overcompensation. The pendulum has swung dangerously close to the immediate postwar position of blaming 'the Germans' as an undifferentiated whole for the crimes of the Nazi period. Arguing that the majority 'backed Hitler' legitimately recognises the power of the 'Hitler Myth', but it also implies a degree of political awareness and engagement that is resonant more of the multimedia information world of the early twenty-first century than of even well-educated and technologically advanced society in Germany's towns in the 1930s and 1940s.[2] It also underestimates the effects of a system where the message of only one faction is publicly, relentlessly purveyed. Yet in the countryside, and especially in Württemberg, the spread of technology was limited and the reach of the message tended to be only as great as the numbers, ability and enthusiasm of NSDAP functionaries and ordinary members afforded. To say all of this is not to attribute particular virtue to the rural population of Württemberg but rather to recognise both the 'limits of Hitler's power' and the modest standard of living, restricted horizons and adherence to the familiar that characterised the members of that population and informed their attitudes and responses.[3]

Acknowledgements

A book that takes as long to write as this one leaves the author with an accumulation of debts. In the first place, the project would have been impossible without the resources of archives and libraries, especially the Hauptstaatsarchiv Stuttgart; the Staatsarchiv Ludwigsburg; the Bundesarchiv (formerly in Koblenz, now in Berlin); the former Berlin Document Center; the Institut für Zeitgeschichte in Munich; the Forschungsstelle für Zeitgeschichte in Hamburg; the United States Holocaust Memorial Museum in Washington, DC; and the German Historical Institute, London. Special mention is due to Mr J.C. Robertson of Cockburnspath, who – many years ago – generously sent me his copies of the SOPADE (German Social Democratic Party in Exile) reports. The initial research for the book was supported by the Wolfson Fund of the British Academy, and the Arts and Humanities Research Board (now Council) funded study leave which enabled me to make much progress with writing. The University of Edinburgh provided matching study leave, and the University Library's staff have been unfailingly helpful. I am deeply grateful to all of them.

A great many friends and colleagues have provided assistance and encouragement. My interest in 'war and society' was first stimulated by my undergraduate special subject, 'The War and the Welfare State in Britain' taught by Arthur Marwick. During the later stages of my first research project, on women in Nazi Germany, I developed an interest in the effects of the Second World War on German society. It became clear that a regional study would be more manageable than a national one, especially in the days of a divided Germany. Michael Kater kindly took a keen interest in my plans and advised me to study Württemberg during the Second World War. At an early stage of my research, Jerry Kleinfeld invited me to speak at the German Studies Association conference in Denver, and was a generous host in Tempe, Arizona. I owe gratitude also to the late Charles and Kay Burdick, to Bruce and Caroline Frye, and to Charles McClelland for their hospitality when I gave papers in San José, Fort Collins and Albuquerque, respectively. Michael Kater invited me to present some of my findings on a DAAD-funded panel at the GSA in Los Angeles, and John J. Delaney invited me to join panels at the AHA in Washington and the GSA in Houston. Thanks to Gerhard Hirschfeld, Ulrich Herbert and Hans-Günther Hockerts, I gave papers at the Bibliothek für Zeitgeschichte in Stuttgart, Albert-Ludwigs-Universität

Freiburg and Ludwig-Maximilians-Universität in Munich. In Britain, too, various university history departments have, over many years, had the dubious pleasure of hearing my thoughts on war and society in Württemberg. Beyond that, for many years I have benefited from the encouragement of that most collegial of scholars, Ian Kershaw, who read the entire text in draft and offered valuable comments. Neil Gregor also generously read the text and provided perceptive suggestions. Donald Bloxham, from whose acute insights and scholarly rigour I have tried to benefit, read Chapter Four and volunteered to act as an additional proof-reader. My thanks to them is poor recompense for the precious time that they have devoted to my work.

Among the many others who have given me help and encouragement I would particularly like to thank Frank Bajohr, Mary Buckley, Roger Chickering, Harry Dickinson, Mary Fulbrook, Jim McMillan, Hans Mommsen, Jeremy Noakes, Paul Sauer, Thomas Schnabel, Kevin Spicer. The Rutgers Center for Historical Analysis, led by John W. Chambers III, welcomed me as a Visiting Fellow in autumn 1994 and gave me the opportunity to write and to participate in its seminar programme. In addition, I benefited greatly from the insights and collegiality of John J. Delaney and the other members of the fortnight's Summer Research Workshop on 'Forced Foreign Laborers, POWs and Jewish Slave Workers in the Third Reich: Regional Studies and New Directions', held at the United States Holocaust Memorial Museum in August 2003. My publisher, Martin Sheppard, has been involved, patient and understanding in ways that one scarcely expects from publishers in these days of large conglomerates. He, and others named above, have advised me about errors or infelicities in the text. Those that remain are entirely my responsibility.

When I was in the later stages of writing the book my husband, Steve, became seriously ill; he died in April 2004. His patience, love and selfless encouragement sustained me for almost four decades. There can be no substitute, but in his absence I have been supported unstintingly by friends and colleagues, including particularly Margaret McLelland, Enid Larkin, Edith Vaughan, Patsy Iddison, Rosemary and Hugh Gentleman, Irene and James McCulloch, Sandra and Christopher Kempston, Gill and Jim McNeillage, Sylvia and Alex Ritchie, Brenda and Dennis Carmichael, Fiona Douglas and Jeremy Crang, Bernard and Andy Ginsborg, Rosalind and Alex Ungar, Elizabeth and Bruce Hobson, Anne and Graham Runnalls, John Kelly, Donald Bloxham, Sarah Williams, Jim McMillan, Richard Mackenney, Alvin Jackson, John and Katherine Gooding, Rhodri and Mary Jeffreys-Jones, Tony and Jackie Goodman, Frank and Mimi Cogliano. Chloë (tabby and white) and Zoë (black and white) have demonstrated customary self-centred but unconditionally affectionate loyalty. These cats are not alone on this list in being oblivious to how much I value their presence in my life.

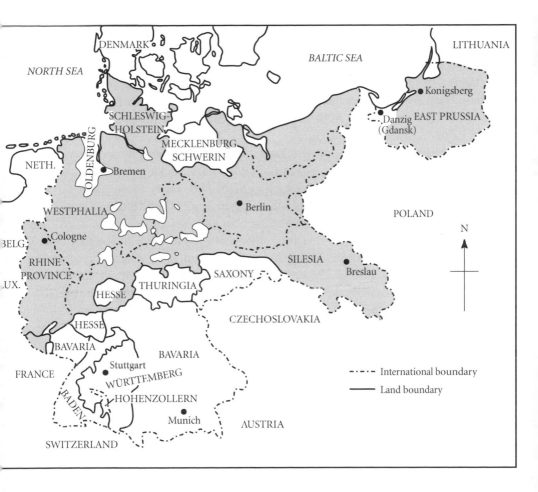

Germany in 1937. The shaded area is Prussia.

EXPLANATORY NOTE

Württemberg was a *Land* (federal state) of Germany. In the Nazi party's
organisational structure, *Gau* (region) Württemberg-Hohenzollern included
both Württemberg and Hohenzollern – comprising the districts of Hechingen and
Sigmaringen – which was a small hereditary Prussian possession and remained so
until the dissolution of Prussia in 1947. The Catholics in Hohenzollern – 94.4 per
cent of the population – belonged, with Catholics in Württemberg and Baden,
to the archdiocese of Freiburg.[4] In *Reichstag* elections, Hohenzollern belonged
with Württemberg to electoral district 31.[5]

Württemberg: showing the new districts dating from 1938. The names of the new districts are in roman type, with the exception of the area around Friedrichshafen, where the district's name was *Tettnang*.

1

Town and Country

The effects of twentieth century wars on major industrialised powers, including Germany, have generally been considered from the point of view of urban civilians.[1] These effects are normally measured in terms of casualties, armaments production, resources for that production – both human and material – as well as the dislocation of civilian life, the destruction of plant and buildings, and the disruption of communications. The weapons used in these wars were produced in industrial concerns, generally in an urban environment, and the most terrifying aspect of the Second World War, from the civilian point of view, was aerial bombardment, mostly of urban areas. As the post-war mayor of Stuttgart, Arnold Klett, said, 'the cities have carried the major burdens of the war, and they will have to carry the major burdens of the peace'.[2] The contribution made by the rural population to the waging of modern war – directly, through being subject to conscription into the armed forces and war industry, and indirectly, through food production for those who produce armaments, as well as for themselves – was regarded as vital. The other effects of war on rural society can, however, seem trivial in comparison with the suffering in bomb damaged towns and cities. In the Second World War, for example, on 30 May 1942, the first thousand bomber raid by the RAF (Royal Air Force) on Cologne cost 469 people their lives. More than 5000 others were injured, some 13,000 homes were destroyed, and 45,000 people were left homeless.[3] In 'Operation Gomorrha', when Hamburg was mercilessly bombed during ten days from 25 July to 3 August 1943, around 34,000 civilians were killed, some 125,000 were injured and over 255,000 dwellings were destroyed. By the end of the war, 902,000 Hamburgers had lost all their possessions, most of them during 'Operation Gomorrha'.[4] By contrast, in Britain a quarter of a million homes were destroyed in the full six years of war.[5]

Incontrovertibly, bombing bore disproportionately heavily on urban populations. In Württemberg, from 1943 the capital, Stuttgart, as well as the towns of Heilbronn, Ulm and Friedrichshafen, in particular, experienced the horrors of what the Nazi regime called 'terror bombing'. This was, similarly, endured in virtually all towns and cities in northern and western Germany, in neighbouring Bavarian cities such as Munich and Nuremberg, and ultimately in cities of eastern Germany as well, with Dresden now a symbol of what it entailed.[6] In the countryside, it is true, there was occasional damage caused by bombers, but this was mostly either incidental or else to achieve a limited strategic objective – for example, the disruption of a rail line – until the final campaigns to subdue all of Germany at the end of the war. For the most part, it was only in the last month or so of the war that military operations became a reality in rural Württemberg, one of the last areas of Germany to be brought under undisputed Allied control. Hitler's insistence on fighting to defend every last village, street and house was not observed everywhere, but, when his underlings tried to implement it, it sometimes caused the nearest thing to popular rebellion that there was in the Third Reich, and it stirred folk memories of the devastation of the Thirty Years War in the seventeenth century.[7]

Although many rural areas were spared the devastation of bombing, modern war affected rural society in many intrusive ways. For example, small communities generally experienced heavier losses of young men in military action than they had sustained during the First World War. In addition, significant numbers of men became prisoners of war or were listed as 'missing'.[8] The conscription of rural civilians into the armed forces and armaments manufacture, and away from the land, caused acute problems on farms. The denuding of farms of German male labour – as well as of machinery and draught animals – which was virtually complete by 1944, was also regarded as serious by the urban authorities, less because of the immediate burdens which it entailed for the remaining rural population than because of its damaging effects on *urban* society.[9]

This was because a decline in domestic food production, together with an enemy blockade to prevent imports, could, as had been the case with Germany in the First World War, be catastrophic in towns, with radical political as well as social consequences.[10] The disaster of the 'turnip winters' in 1916–17 and 1917–18, which were widely believed to have contributed to the German armies being 'stabbed in the back' by the home front, both contributed to the development of strategies for 'total war' in the 1920s and 1930s and made Adolf Hitler determined that in any future war Germany's food supply would be safeguarded.[11] The motive was to maintain popular morale and thus minimise any risk of disaffection or rebellion. The Nazi leadership assumed it as self-evident that any such threat would come from the *urban* population, especially from members of the urban working class among whom the Social Democratic Party (SPD) had long had substantial but far from overwhelming support. The founding of a Communist Party (KPD) in Germany at the end of 1918, and the electoral success which it enjoyed in urban areas in the great depression during the years 1930 to 1933, seemed to add flesh to this spectre.

By contrast, there was no fear of a peasant revolt. In the aftermath of the Bolshevik Revolution of 1917 in Russia, modern, twentieth-century rebellions were likely, it was generally believed, to be Marxist-inspired, and would therefore originate in the 'proletariat', with its political and trade union organisations. To combat this, in the Third Reich stringent measures of both surveillance and terror were deployed to neutralise and contain working-class opposition.[12] Peasants, however, and especially peasant proprietors, were overwhelmingly anti-Marxist. Accordingly, recent peasant protests had been successfully mobilised in northern areas such as Schleswig-Holstein by the National Socialists – rather than against them – during the agrarian crisis whose origins predated the onset of the great depression in 1929. While middle-class support for the Nazi party is no longer regarded as the overwhelming reason for its success, it nevertheless remains the case that many of the party's earliest supporters were to be found in rural areas (whether or not they were 'middle-class') and that agrarian distress drew many to a party that demagogically promised to put the interests of rural Germany first.[13]

This promise was not met, because where the interests of rural and urban Germany conflicted – as they frequently did in the Third Reich, especially in wartime – the interests of urban Germany were given priority.[14] The Nazi party has often been characterised as being 'reactionary' and 'fascist', and therefore hostile to the working class; yet the party's leadership was above all concerned to maintain at least the quiescence, if not the acquiescence, of the 'proletariat', the group that, by staffing essential heavy industries, played a key role both in rebuilding Germany's industrial strength after the depression and in preparing Germany for war. It may be true that many urban workers were so discontented with the conditions and restrictions imposed upon them by the Nazi system that they withheld their cooperation.[15] Yet it is clear that some workers found a comfortable niche in the Third Reich, not least because of their privileged place in its racial hierarchy. Whatever workers' attitudes to it, from the regime's perspective the imperative was not simply to terrorise and incarcerate working-class activists but also to conciliate the mass of the politically passive working class, as the leader of the German Labour Front, Robert Ley, for one, understood.[16]

This meant adopting policies which helped to render many rural Germans profoundly disaffected with the regime, provoking them not only into withholding cooperation from its functionaries before and during the war but even into positively obstructing their efforts in a variety of areas. In wartime these included, crucially, the maintenance of an orderly food supply and prohibitions on fraternisation with 'aliens', in the shape of coerced foreign workers. Rural obstruction meant avoiding involvement in Nazi organisations and a tenacious loyalty to the local church. Ultimately, it would mean a refusal to work tooth and nail to block the western Allies' inexorable advance through southern Germany in 1945. These manifestations of obstruction were pragmatic – rather than either political or ideological – in both intent and effect, but they embraced a variety of areas, and a culture of illicit activity and disobedience developed. Indeed, the intrusive demands of the Nazi leadership cast many peasants involuntarily in the role of miscreants, petty opponents or even criminals who were judged to be undermining the war effort. Disobedience only increased as the war dragged on, and as the mounting difficulties and final crises of wartime intensified. The villagers' interdependence strengthened community loyalties in ways that thwarted the centralising pretensions of the National Socialist regime, to the frustration of its more diehard adherents in the localities.

This was perhaps the central area of failure, as far as the Nazi regime's integrative policies were concerned. In its election campaigns before 1933, the NSDAP had promised to bring back a sense of national unity to a Germany that was torn by political strife and deeply socially divided. The concept of *Volksgemeinschaft* – of an allegedly genuine 'people's ethnic community' – was central to the NSDAP's appeal to communal solidarity as opposed to 'liberal individualism', the alleged scourge of German society after the First World War as epitomised by social and political developments during the Weimar Republic. Social resentments, political divisions, cultural innovations and even economic catastrophes were characterised in Nazi propaganda as having their roots in the blinkered selfishness of intrinsically decent individuals. These were men and women who had been duped by parliamentary politicians into pursuing personal advantage and material gratification at the expense of patriotism, self-control and consciousness of an overriding responsibility for the health and prosperity of the 'racial body' (*Volkskörper*) of the ethnically pure nation as a total entity. In the Third Reich, the regime's leaders aimed for nothing less than a complete reorientation of individuals' attitudes and conduct. Those who were judged by the regime's officers, often highly subjectively, to be 'Aryan', 'politically reliable' and 'socially responsible' were praised and flattered. They were beguiled by the invented traditions of festivals and spectacles in which they were important extras – with the starring roles reserved for the self-regarding nonentities who had been catapulted to power as slavish adherents of the charismatic leader, Hitler.[17]

The language used by the regime's leaders was one of egalitarianism, but that did not mean the abolition of class distinctions. The only serious redistribution of wealth was from Jews to 'Aryans', especially in the later 1930s. It was simply the case that the NSDAP had to compete in an age of mass politics, with both parliamentary democrats and Marxian socialists – both reformist and revolutionary – crying their wares before they were abruptly prevented from doing so in the first half of 1933. For Nazis, 'equality' meant not the levelling of class and income differentials but their transcendence by the allegedly more fundamental and vital values of 'German Socialism'.[18] This was portrayed as being completely different from Marxian Socialism, its criteria for equal status being rooted in nationality and 'race'. By this analysis, the humblest German 'Aryan' worker who eschewed 'the false idol of Marxism' and lived a productive and thrifty life was inherently superior to the most gifted, qualified or wealthy person in an 'inferior' race.[19] He or she was 'superior' in the only way that – according to this analysis – mattered: in terms of 'racial value'. The class and income differentials that continued to exist among the 'valuable' could be mitigated in small and piecemeal ways, both through acts of communal charity and through targeted government grants to those who were both needy and – by the regime's criteria – deserving. Class and wealth, however, were portrayed as secondary attributes – more significant in a materialist than in an allegedly idealistic culture. Therefore they should not preoccupy citizens who were assured of a favoured status by virtue of the alleged nobility of their 'blood'.

The ideal of the *Volksgemeinschaft* was perhaps not fully put to the test between 1933 and 1939, with sources of actual and potential opposition neutralised and kept suppressed. Yet there were signs that it was failing to penetrate the consciousness of the mass of the politically unobjectionable population to an extent that would make more than a small minority of them voluntarily adjust their expectations and behaviour to accord with National Socialist norms. Exercises such as the *Winterhilfswerk* (Winter Aid Scheme), which were publicised as providing help for needy fellow citizens from collections made among the community at large, had some practical effect – although increasingly the funds were siphoned off corruptly for more general Nazi purposes – but there is little evidence that they also changed people's perceptions of, and attitudes to, groups in society outside their own. Increasingly, to the disgust of NSDAP loyalists, ordinary people tired of the ceaseless round of collections, especially those made by the NSV (*Nationalsozialistische Volkswohlfahrt* – NS People's Welfare).[20]

In fact, the contrary applied. There is growing evidence that traditional attitudes on the part of one class or group towards others did not change. Even before 1939, the gulf between rhetoric and reality had been evident. The Bavarian Political Police complained in 1936 about farmers having 'apparently a special conception of *Volksgemeinschaft* ... which in their opinion only came into play if benefits were to be gained for themselves'.[21] In the village of Oberschopfheim in Baden, despite evidence to the contrary, 'many villagers *believed* Nazi claims that they had levelled the nation socially – somewhere else'.[22] The Second World War, in which national solidarity was regarded as the *sine qua non* of victory, subjected the Nazi boast of having created a 'people's community' to the closest examination, and, in the southern *Land* (federal state) of Württemberg, as in neighbouring Bavaria, found it to be unjustified. The *Gendarmerie* in one Bavarian district complained in 1941 that 'egoism' was more evident than patriotism and that 'One can't talk about a *Volksgemeinschaft* ... For the farmer, his own property is his only fatherland'.[23] The Nazis' favoured, if spurious, slogan of 'the common good before self-interest' (*'Gemeinnutz vor Eigennutz'*) had cut little ice in rural southern Germany.[24]

There is nothing remarkable about individuals acting self-interestedly and selfishly, particularly in time of hardship and shortage. This had certainly been evident during the First World War, the memory of which was still fresh in the minds of many Germans a couple of decades later.[25] Beyond that, during the Second World War there probably was no European belligerent or occupied country which did not have a black market in scarce goods or 'under the counter' transactions, which defied rationing restrictions. Such dealings were clearly not regarded as criminal by the wide range of participants: this was certainly the case in Britain, to say nothing of countries occupied by German forces in both western and eastern Europe.[26] In Germany, however, after six peacetime years of Nazi rule, while recovery from the depression and the quest for autarky had perhaps brought benefit to some urban workers, in terms of the availability of jobs and the recreational facilities of the KdF (*Kraft durch Freude* – Strength through Joy) project, it had also led to periods of acute shortages of essential supplies, such as food and fuel.[27] As far as the rural population was concerned, in the early years of the Third Reich Hitler's government had provided help for farmers who were deep in debt and had recently endured difficult times. By the end of the 1930s, however, the industry-led recovery was inflicting severe pressure on rural society, not least because it had provided new opportunities in the towns, which encouraged farmers' sons and daughters, to say nothing of rural hired labour, to seek their fortune there and escape from the arduous, restrictive and physically draining life of a peasant.[28]

This was yet another wave of the migration from the countryside to the towns and rapidly growing cities that had been one of the major effects of Germany's massive development as a formidable industrial power from the mid nineteenth century, particularly after the founding of the German Empire in 1871. For example, in a mere thirty years, between 1875 and 1905, Berlin's population more than doubled, to just over two million, while that of both Dortmund and Munich almost trebled, to 175,000 and 530,000, respectively. At the same time, the populations of Hamburg, Frankfurt and Düsseldorf had more than trebled, to almost 800,000, to 330,000 and to 250,000, respectively. That of Leipzig had almost quadrupled, to over half a million, while Essen's more than quadrupled, to 230,000. The capital city of Württemberg, Stuttgart, experienced somewhat more modest but still massive growth, from 107,000 in 1875 to almost a quarter of a million in 1905. By the latter year, several of Württemberg's prominent towns accommodated more than ten thousand inhabitants, among them, in descending order of size, Ulm, Heilbronn, Esslingen, Ludwigsburg, Tübingen, Tuttlingen and Aalen.[29] Stuttgart also increased its physical size by absorbing some surrounding small towns and villages, including Gaisburg in 1901, Canstatt in 1905, Degerloch in 1908, Botnang, Kaltental, Obertürkheim and Hedelfingen in 1922, and Rotenberg, Münster and Zuffenhausen in 1931. Further waves of incorporation of surrounding communes into the city of Stuttgart followed in

1933, 1936, 1937 and, even in wartime, in 1942. Other Württemberg towns, for example Heilbronn and Tübingen, also extended their boundaries to incorporate adjacent communes.[30]

With industrialisation and urbanisation came the development of modern facilities in the towns, including piped water supplies, sewage disposal, gas and electrical power supplies, and telephone lines. Streets were blacktop or laid with stone setts, while tramlines were laid and tram services operated within towns, and even beyond. For example, Stuttgart city trams served the village of Hedelfingen from 1910, over a decade before its incorporation into the capital. In addition, rail services both ran within towns and linked towns to each other and to some outlying villages. As early as 1846, the railway linked the nearby farming commune of Zuffenhausen to Stuttgart.[31] In the 1920s and 1930s bus services also developed, sometimes serving small country towns and even – though less commonly – villages. With urbanisation, mass entertainment became more varied and widespread. In addition to traditional concert halls, theatres and music halls, the new medium of cinema became especially popular in the towns in the 1920s and 1930s, while the even newer medium of radio afforded home entertainment in the form of the 'wireless set', provided that one had access to an electricity supply.

These facilities were already being taken for granted in much of German urban society by the 1930s, but in many rural communes in Württemberg they were largely non-existent. In the purely rural area around Creglingen, in Mergentheim district in Württemberg's far north, the purchase of radios as well as clocks was said to be 'very minimal' both before and during the Second World War.[32] Malmsheim, a commune in Leonberg district, similarly had very few radio owners at this time.[33] These examples were far from exceptional. Those who acquired the cheap short-wave radios – the 'people's receivers' – introduced in the Third Reich might find that they worked poorly or not at all. The Württemberg SD (*Sicherheitsdienst* – Security Service of the SS) reported in April 1939 that half of all those sold were defective.[34] To bring the Nazi message to those who either were without a radio set of their own or preferred not to tune in to government propaganda, the installation of loudspeakers in public places was used from the start of the Third Reich. Yet this, too, mainly affected urban areas, including the small country town of Mühlacker.[35] Even in November 1941, the SD was still considering the merits of establishing the 'community radio', via loudspeakers, in all communes so that important broadcasts could be heard by everyone. With mayors of communes responsible for raising the funds for loudspeakers and arranging their installation, the SD was anxious to canvass opinion before any action was taken.[36] In wartime, however, there were already many other demands on communes' resources; in villages close to towns or facilities such as a rail line which might be bombed, maintaining the local fire brigade had a higher priority than the installation of loudspeakers. The broadcast Nazi message did not reach substantial numbers of rural inhabitants.

Beyond this there was in the towns an explosion of retail outlets, some of them large department stores but most of them specialist shops. Services such as laundries and dry cleaners, as well as early labour saving devices including the first vacuum cleaners, also led to an expectation of higher standards of personal and domestic cleanliness. All of this meant that the daily experience of urban dwellers diverged increasingly sharply from that of those who remained in the countryside, where the labour-intensive nature of work on small farms involved a relationship with dirt and dung that was increasingly alien to urban dwellers. First generation townspeople soon became accustomed to those urban facilities which they could afford to enjoy; for second and third generation townspeople, by the 1930s rural life was either remembered through the prism of their parents' or grandparents' recalled experience or envisaged as either a dark and primitive world or a romantic idyll.

While there have been differences of experience and perceptions between those in towns and those in the countryside for as long as there have been towns, these differences were given sharper focus in countries which became urbanised rapidly and extensively. While Britain had undergone this transformation during the nineteenth century, albeit at a more leisurely pace, in the later nineteenth and earlier twentieth centuries few – if any – countries experienced the process as intensively as Germany. By 1914, a majority of Germans lived in a town, with country dwellers increasingly feeling that their work and cultural norms were undervalued. The fact that it was possible for some people from the countryside to work or shop in towns while continuing to live in a village brought them into contact with urban facilities and attitudes without their being able to share fully in the benefits of urban life. Many returned home along dirt roads to accommodation without a piped water supply or electricity. Economic prosperity, too, centred on the towns, with small farms continuing to operate on a traditional and labour-intensive basis, at a time when rural labour was draining away to the towns where wages were higher and conditions less arduous. Yet unlike Britain, where agriculture had been relegated to a minor role in the economy by 1914, in Germany – as in eastern and southern Europe, as well as in France – agricultural production remained a substantial and significant sector of the economy, after the First World War as before it.

The increasing differences in experience and lifestyle between many urban and rural dwellers were perhaps scarcely noticeable to most people in the towns – and of less concern to government authorities – in time of peace than they would become in time of war. Nevertheless, by the later 1930s both the SD in Württemberg and the German Labour Front's research unit, in a survey of Württemberg, expressed anxiety about the lower incomes and lower standard of living in rural areas which had scarcely been affected by developments in technology and economies of scale. This meant rural communities remote from a prosperous urban hinterland that could boost the wealth of a district as a whole. The Labour Front's research unit's investigation also exploded the myth of rural areas benefiting from lower living costs.[37] The SD was particularly concerned about the viability of small-scale family farming in Württemberg, and cited consciousness of the low esteem in which the rural lifestyle was held by townspeople as a reason for demoralisation over and above the impoverishment that many farmers were experiencing. The way in which urban priorities and urban preoccupations seemed to dominate government policy, an impression reinforced by the output of the new mass media, were seen by the SD as an additional irritant.[38]

Part of the reason for the increased dominance of urban perspectives in the 1930s lay in the distribution of the effects of the great depression. The depression was a crisis of modern economies which had its most dramatic impact on heavy industrial sectors such as construction and the metal industries. Small-scale agriculture was already in deficit in many parts of Germany, yet its slide into the economic doldrums was relatively long term and gradual. Industry's crisis was, by contrast, sudden and its consequences affected also the non-industrial modern sectors of the economy, such as white-collar and professional work. The ramifications of the industrial crisis for broad swathes of urban German society accounted for the huge numbers affected and therefore for the urgency with which Hitler's government attended to the need for industrial recovery, which also accorded with its rearmament and foreign policy agenda.

This was a continuation of the NSDAP's political strategy, which had focused on the misery of the millions of casualties of the depression. Especially from 1930, the adoption of new and effective campaigning methods had enabled the National Socialists to challenge, on equal terms, the self-appointed representatives of the newer, modern forces in society, the urban classes spawned by industrialisation. The depression gave Marxists hope that this 'crisis of capitalism' would be the harbinger of revolution in Germany. Yet while the communists in the KPD and its affiliated societies did win adherents in the depression years, the other political party with a Marxist constitution, the SPD, steadily lost ground in Germany as a whole. In Württemberg, it saw its share of the vote more than halved between 1919 and 1933.[39] Altogether, neither the political parties and trade unions of the left nor the political parties and associations of the middle classes could match the dynamism and appeal of the NSDAP in the fevered political arena of a Germany sunk in depression. Disarmed and demoralised workers and disillusioned or opportunistic bourgeois were easy prey, less able to withstand the Nazi appeal and, from 1933, to resist Nazi demands than were 'backward' rural sections of society, who might be insecure and volatile in time of agricultural depression, but whose traditional community relationships were much more difficult to infiltrate or subvert.

Attempts to 'integrate' rural communities into the new system of the Third Reich, in a way that is alleged to have occurred throughout society with the creation of a *Volksgemeinschaft*, or to force them to change their habits or recognise new allegiances, often met a kind of guerrilla warfare in which groups and whole communities persistently undermined Reich, *Land* or NSDAP policies at the most local level.[40] In addition, a sense of disillusionment developed among some of the regime's own foot soldiers, especially when they had their roots in the community which they now informed on, ordered, or policed.[41] In towns, with their shifting populations, individual party or state officials might not have had roots in the community in which they operated, so that their loyalty might well have been unswervingly to the regime's leadership and ideology – give or take bribes and blandishments offered by individuals for favours. The Nazi regime also made a point of quickly replacing the mayors of cities as well as those in towns who were regarded as being politically unacceptable; but, in the first instance, at least, this applied to only a small minority of mayors of Württemberg's villages.

There were certainly Württembergers whose commitment to Hitler and National Socialism was unquestioning. They tended, however, to be relatively few in number. Enough of them had the intelligence and political skills to organise their followers and, from 1933, to maintain a dictatorial system in Württemberg, always with the power of the party's national leadership to reinforce their authority. At local level, however, the party was uncomfortably dependent on a small number of enthusiasts, mainly those members who had joined the NSDAP before 1933. Few of them had the requisite character and aptitude for office.[42] In small communes there might or might not be an active Nazi presence. In theory, all of Württemberg was covered by the party's organisation. In practice, there were communes where there was no party organisation, and communes where a small minority of the inhabitants were party members and a small number of these members were activists. Nevertheless, with the power of party and state behind them, they had disproportionate authority and influence. Nowhere was this more evident than in their role in enforcing segregation between Jews and 'Aryans', in the relatively small number of Württemberg's communes where Jews lived and worked.[43]

The weakness of the Württemberg NSDAP before and after 1933 is one of the reasons for Württemberg's distinctiveness. There can be little doubt that only the party's success in other regions of Germany brought it to power there after Hitler's appointment as Chancellor on 30 January 1933. On its own, the Württemberg NSDAP would not have achieved power.[44] The relative lack of enthusiasm for the party, beyond a hard core of fanatics whose numbers were augmented from 1933 by opportunists who could see advantages in party membership, together with the shortcomings of the party's leadership both in Stuttgart and in Württemberg's districts, ensured that winning over the hearts and minds of the public at large would be an uphill struggle. The lack of talent in the Württemberg NSDAP was particularly obvious when compared with the high levels of qualifications and qualities required of professional civil servants. In fact, as long as they were not actually Jews, Communists or Social Democrats, civil servants in post in 1933 were retained in office and had a fair amount of room for manoeuvre.[45] Beyond that, in the countryside, where conflicts developed between the regime and the community, NSDAP and local government officials might find their loyalties divided: it was not so much a case of going native as of *being* native.[46] Being native meant, in Württembergers' self-perception, being thrifty, tenacious, inventive and modest.[47] Württembergers took 'pride in the slow-moving, thoughtful, shrewd character of "die dummen Schwaben" [the simple Swabians]'.[48]

There was a substantial Catholic population in Württemberg, but it remained in a clear minority in a *Land* whose cultural values were dominated by Lutheran Protestantism of a distinctly Pietist variety. This contrasted with the Catholic majorities in the other two south German states, Bavaria and Baden, which flanked Württemberg. Nevertheless, from 1928 to 1933 the Württemberg State President (head of government) was Eugen Bolz of the Catholic Centre Party, which was a member of the governing coalition.[49] The Catholic communities of Württemberg remained distinctive, true to their heritage and peculiarly resistant to the demands made by the Nazi state, particularly in their relative imperviousness to penetration by Nazi ideology. Women, who comprised an increasingly high proportion of wartime civilian society, were particularly strong adherents of the church in Catholic areas. The rise of the NSDAP led Catholic priests to warn in early 1933 of a new *Kulturkampf* (cultural struggle).[50] Without doubt, Catholic defensiveness in the face of a Protestant majority was enhanced by the increasingly evident antagonism towards Catholicism on the part of Württemberg's Nazi leaders, including some NSDAP district leaders. Yet while most active Nazis were either practising or nominal Protestants, until the official campaign for resignation from church membership in the later 1930s, the Evangelical (Protestant) Church in Württemberg was neither emasculated nor coopted into the Nazi system in the way in which other *Land* or provincial Evangelical churches were. This gave its leaders unusual room for manoeuvre in criticising policies of the regime to which they took exception. They availed themselves of this only selectively.[51]

In economic terms, Württemberg was not a centre of the heavy industries which had dominated the first phase of Germany's industrial revolution in the mid-to-later nineteenth century and had transformed the towns of the Ruhr, in particular. Industrial development in Württemberg focused first on textiles and then on light and specialised industries, and was restricted to relatively few urban centres which remained small in size. Esslingen, with its textile industry, and Friedrichshafen, which became the main centre of aero-engine development, were examples of this. It followed that, while Württemberg had a fairly strong and well-organised working class, it was not on the scale of the massive concentrations of industrial workers in big cities, Ruhr towns or even Bavarian towns.[52] The capital, Stuttgart, dwarfed the other significant towns in Württemberg, yet it was not large in comparison with other *Land* capitals such as Berlin, Munich or Leipzig, even if it was larger than Karlsruhe, the capital of neighbouring Baden.[53] In spite of migration to the towns, both before and after the depression, the rural population of Württemberg remained significant in size and relatively backward in both its methods of working and the distribution of its produce. The many small towns in Württemberg remained the focus of local loyalties and activities, for both their own inhabitants and those of the rural areas which surrounded them.

Although Württemberg's small-town character persisted, it was nevertheless a centre of both advanced specialised industry in Stuttgart and Friedrichshafen and innovation in medical sciences. The medical faculty at Tübingen University was a specialist centre for neurological, reproductive and gynaecological sciences. Medical doctors and university researchers in Tübingen, such as Robert Gaupp, Hermann Hoffmann, Ernst Kretschmer, Wilhelm Gieseler and Robert Ritter, were in the vanguard of developments in what they termed 'racial hygiene'. By 1924, there was sufficient interest in combating the alleged 'deterioration of our race' for the establishment of a branch of the 'Society for Racial Hygiene' – founded in 1904 – in Tübingen. Against this background, the sterilisation of some women who were considered qualitatively 'inferior' was performed in the Tübingen gynaecology clinic, covertly and completely illegally, in the 1920s.[54] This anticipated the legislation of 14 July 1933 which introduced a government policy of sterilising those with physical or mental 'deficiencies', in particular the 'feeble-minded', if necessary using coercion.[55] In wartime, the anatomy department in the Tübingen medical faculty examined the corpses of Red Army prisoners of war who had died of malnutrition or exposure while forced labourers in Germany.[56]

High-tech industry and innovative, if sinister, medical advances were a world away from the countryside. The rural population of Württemberg consisted to a large extent of those living and working in small communes of a few hundred people – generally those with not more than about two thousand inhabitants. The word 'commune' is a more accurate rendering of the German administrative term *Gemeinde* than 'village' (*Dorf*) would be. Around 1930, there were 1829 communes in Württemberg. While some were coterminous with villages, others embraced a central village and one or more small satellite villages which might be called *Teilgemeinden* (partial communes). For example, in Crailsheim district in north-eastern Württemberg, the village of Hengstfeld was the '*Mutterort*' (literally, 'mother place') in the commune of the same name, but the adjacent hamlets of Rossbürg and Schönbronn, which were described as '*Teilorte*' (literally, 'part places'), also belonged to the commune of Hengstfeld. These three villages had separate boundaries and identities, but for administrative purposes Hengstfeld, Rossbürg and Schönbronn belonged together in the commune of Hengstfeld and were administered by a single *Bürgermeister* (mayor) whose office was in Hengstfeld village.[57] The inhabitants of Württemberg's communes were largely endogamous, with close networks of blood relationships, which meant that homegrown local officials of the Nazi system might suffer from a conflict of loyalties: that is, whether to serve their politicial masters, or to accommodate the sometimes subversive aspirations of their own community. It is hard to estimate how often loyalty to the system came first, but it is clear that there were conspicuous occasions when loyalty to the community took precedence – for example, on the part of *Bürgermeister*, officials of the *Reichsnährstand* (Reich Food Estate) or even functionaries of the NSDAP itself.

The majority of the inhabitants of Württemberg's communes were small-scale farmers and rural artisans, members of a community who were to a great extent mutually interdependent and self-sufficient, if perhaps becoming less so by the 1930s. Their work on the land was highly labour intensive, conducted with the assistance of family members, of hired labour – often on a seasonal basis – and of animals, with few machines; certainly, there were very few tractors in rural Württemberg before 1950.[58] Many were engaged in mixed farming, growing cereals, vegetables, sugar beet and fruit such as apples, soft berries, and grapes for winemaking, as well as keeping various animals. Cows were kept for milk, while beef cattle and pigs provided meat, and there were various kinds of poultry, such as chicken, ducks and geese, with egg production often a significant part of a small farmer's output. Some small farmers kept rabbits or bees. Horses or cattle served as draught animals, the former for the better off, the latter for less substantial farmers; it followed that the possession of horses was also a status symbol.

This was, at any rate, true where horses were in use in rural areas, for example in much of eastern Württemberg. The amount of land worked by individual farmers generally reflected the number of horses that were owned. In parts of the north east, larger farmers, with perhaps 20 hectares of land, might have three or more horses, while medium farmers had no more than two. Smaller farmers, with land holdings of less than 10 hectares, worked the land with cows. In one commune in the area, the largest farmer had 37 hectares of land and five horses.[59] Further south, in 1939 there were fifty-three working horses in the commune of Türkheim, two-thirds of which were requisitioned by the army. The resulting compensation was sufficient to enable a group of four farmers to buy a tractor as an innovative joint venture.[60] In western Württemberg, farmers in the commune of Münchingen regarded having to surrender horses to the army as a great hardship, although they, too, were paid compensation for them.[61] In other areas, however, horses were of much less value because of the nature of the land, with river valleys with steep ravines, for example. Equally, horses were of little practical use where wine growing was conducted on terraced hills, as, for example, in the commune of Burgbach, in the Remstal area near Stuttgart, although some farmers there possessed cows as draught animals for wagons containing produce.[62]

On the whole, these people did not fit an urban idealised image of the rural past, nor yet the vision, held by 'agrarian romantic' Nazis and others, of a 'clean nature' – 'a utopian Germany in which the classes and the generations were reunited along "racial lines" and the economy was based on the harmonious integration of technology into the landscape'.[63] By contrast, these peasants' reality was distinctly mucky, with the most rudimentary plumbing – and in some cases none at all – and dirt or gravel roads. It was not unknown for farm animals to share the family's accommodation, as part of the rural household, although most farmers had barns or stalls for their livestock. The piles of manure stacked up in front of the dwelling houses could serve as a status symbol – the larger the pile, the more prosperous the farmer – as well as being of obvious practical value.[64] These features were superseded by more modern facilities only *after* the Second World War, generally in the years between 1950 and 1970, although there were vestiges of this older lifestyle even beyond that time.[65] At the same time, traditional community networks persisted and enabled the inhabitants to insulate themselves against some aspects of National Socialist intrusiveness from 1933, in particular those which challenged communal customs and practices. In some respects these community networks even survived the upheavals of the Third Reich and the Second World War. This is endorsed by the work of social anthropologists who investigated life in Württemberg villages circa 1970, even after the massive upheavals of the Second World War and its aftermath.[66] Yet if material conditions and working methods changed little in Württemberg's communes in the interwar years, political allegiances became increasingly fluid, especially in the years 1928–33. For example, a growing number of former conservative, liberal, peasant party and, to a lesser extent, Centre Party adherents supported the NSDAP in elections in these years.[67]

If the Nazis seem to have had a curious, apparently contradictory, attitude to rural society, the explanation is probably that, as with so much of Nazi ideology, there were several conflicting views within the leadership. In particular, there remained an apparent mismatch between the misty-eyed nostalgia of the 'agrarian romantics', who included Reich Farmers' Leader (*Reichsbauernführer*) Darré and SS leader Himmler, when they contemplated their idealised view of peasant society, and the Nazi leaders, technocrats and militarists who sought ever more efficient ways of controlling society and, ultimately, killing both domestic and foreign enemies. That Himmler had a prominent place in both groups indicates that this was less of a mismatch than two sides of the same coin. It has been argued that the aim of creating an 'agrarian state' remained a priority with some Nazi grandees, who nevertheless also accepted the need for greater industrial and technological progress in order to achieve the leadership's power-political objectives.[68] This aim was entirely unrealistic in the context of twentieth century Germany.

It seems, therefore, clear that 'blood and soil' propaganda remained just that, and that the demands of the military and heavy industry were given priority over a promised regeneration of the rural sector.[69] This was hardly surprising when the leading Nazis at national level tended to be the product of urban rather than rural society. Key figures, such as Goebbels, Göring – whose interest in the countryside was confined by the limits set by his passion for hunting – and Speer, were concerned only with what the countryside could produce for the towns, while Hitler himself did not identify with rural society, seeing its members as having a utilitarian role to play in his grand scheme of things rather than a destiny of their own to fulfil.[70] By contrast, in Württemberg at least some of the leading men in the Third Reich derived from a rural background, even if they had, by 1933, become acclimatised as townspeople.[71]

Nevertheless, much of Nazi propaganda lauded the German peasant farmer as the salt of the earth, the backbone of society. With their simple lifestyle and above average birth rate, small farmers were acclaimed as an example to those who had been uprooted by industrialisation and thrust, friendless and disorientated, into teeming urban centres, where Marxist agitators, it was said, tried to supplant their innate industriousness and inherent national pride with subversive ideas about class warfare and revolution. Agriculture had a special place in both Nazi ideology and Nazi art, with romantic images of simple, undemanding, hardworking peasant folk nurturing large families who would work selflessly to feed the nation. The NSDAP's harvest thanksgiving rally at Bückeberg, held annually at Michaelmas from 1933 to 1937, was a massive demonstration of this idealised view of farming communities. At local level, officials of the *Reichsnährstand* laboured to identify peasant families who had farmed the same plots of land for several generations. Photographs of aged peasants in traditional costume, and of their farmhouses, were published in the party's local press to broadcast the image of this sturdy, self-reliant backbone of the nation.[72] All of this, at any rate, was the conception of Himmler, Darré and other 'agrarian romantics' within the party's leadership.

Nazi propaganda towards and about farmers assumed particular importance because of the regime's policy of autarky, or self-sufficiency, in food and essential raw materials, which was an article of faith with some NSDAP leaders even before 1933. Once again, this harked back to the desperate days of the 1914–18 war, when the failure to ensure that domestic food production was anywhere near self-sufficiency level became disastrous once the British blockade of Germany's North Sea coast was complete. The image of the simple peasant also conveyed the essence of another element of autarky, that of consumer self-restraint. Idealising peasant life, with its natural rhythms of recycling and avoiding waste, was intended to be instructive to townspeople for whom the lure of consumerism was, by the later 1930s, once the depression had receded, increasingly attractive. The Nazi regime's objective was to throttle back consumption by all possible means, to concentrate resources on industry and rearmament, not least because increased consumption would mean a rise in imports. It was a particular cause of concern to the Nazi regime, as well as to conservatives of all kinds, including peasants, that a hunger for material possessions and other aspects of a growing Americanisation of German popular culture had become evident in the 1920s and persisted in the 1930s.[73] There was also criticism of 'nudity and bedroom scenes ... [and] lecherousness' in French films.[74] This was an urban problem. Rural people preferred marionette or puppet shows based on traditional German stories to foreign films.[75]

On the face of it, Nazi nostalgia for an idealised rural past – before the development of industrialisation and large-scale urbanisation – appears little different from that which allegedly led to the decline of the industrial spirit in Britain in the nineteenth and twentieth centuries.[76] Yet if the Nazis' smokescreen of nostalgic pro-peasant rhetoric is penetrated, it is clear that in their ideology the image of the timeless and quietly contented peasant was married to relatively new ideas of biological racism:

> peasant virtue was indissolubly linked to the concept of 'racial renewal'. It may be true to say that the village, with its special social framework, was supposed to embody a sort of microcosmic model of the Nazis' 'people's community' (*Volksgemeinschaft*), which was in turn supposed to replicate on a larger scale the idea of the village society as a system of economic, social and cultural integration'.[77]

Nevertheless, this does not tell the whole story. The defining feature of the *Volksgemeinschaft* was not its inclusiveness but its exclusiveness: it denied the rights and privileges of membership to those who were subjectively deemed to be unworthy. In a sense, the village was exclusive, in its attitude of suspicion or even outright hostility to incomers, to those who did not belong to one of its constituent families or households: this sense of acceptance or exclusion persisted in some Württemberg villages into the 1970s.[78] Beyond that, those who belonged but nevertheless transgressed local norms and customs could face ostracism.[79] Yet while 'village idiots … may have been mocked and stigmatised … they were always supported by the community … and … they were not carted off to the asylum'.[80]

How different this was firstly from the tidier but less humane practice in towns where the mentally impaired could not be left to their own devices and generally were consigned to an asylum. It was even more of a contrast with the practice of the Third Reich in which the systematic exclusion from the *Volksgemeinschaft* of 'racial enemies', in particular Jews and also Romanies, and of the mentally ill and of large and varied numbers of 'asocials', became not merely official policy but even a top government priority.[81] Many people in these categories were certainly ostracised and stigmatised, but their treatment went much further than that, especially in wartime when large numbers were systematically murdered. By contrast, village councils did not order or effect the incarceration and murder of those who had transgressed their code. Far from being part of an organic social tradition, biological racism was a modern construct imposed on communities from outside. That is not to say that no villagers collaborated in the persecution which this entailed, but rather that the congruence between the microcosmic entity of the village and the gigantic entity of the *Volksgemeinschaft* was not only not complete, but was incomplete in a massively important respect.

There is little merit in idealising small rural communities as havens of good will and neighbourliness: for many, living and working conditions were primitive, and attitudes were, accordingly, rough and ready. German rural labourers had long had a hard life, working gruelling hours and often being mistreated by their employers. It was no wonder that so many of them were glad to escape to the towns when they could. But farming families, too, worked long and hard, and the farmer's wife, in particular, shouldered many heavy burdens which aged her rapidly and prematurely. The idealised life of the simple peasant, one of the staples of Nazi propaganda, was divorced from reality, as harder headed party officers were well aware.[82] Even the party's press had the occasional truth to tell. For example, in 1934 the *Völkischer Beobachter* carried a supplement which soberly outlined some of the problems on the land:

> For all rural dwellers, the entire burden of work has increased considerably since the [1914–18] war, with the economic crisis forcing them to reduce the number of full-time employed labourers and to take on the extra work themselves. And this extra burden has in far the greatest measure fallen on the shoulders of the rural woman. It is easy to see the consequences for the health of women and their offspring.[83]

The main concern here was what this implied for birth and survival rates among those deemed to be making proportionately the greatest contribution to population growth. Yet farming families had been among those which had begun to adopt methods of family limitation before the end of the nineteenth century.[84] In 1939 in the Reich as a whole, in communities with fewer than two thousand inhabitants there were 23.0 live births per 1000 of the population, whereas in towns of up to 100,000 inhabitants there were 20.7 and in cities with over 100,000 inhabitants there were 17.5. The corresponding figures for Württemberg showed narrower differentials, with 22.6, 21.8 and 19.4, respectively.[85] These reflect the rural and small-town character of Württemberg, with the last figure applying to Stuttgart alone, as the only city. They also suggest that Nazi faith in the fecundity of rural families was only partly justified by the time Hitler launched his war. In Württemberg, by 1939 the 'one and two-child family', so derided by the Nazis, had become the norm.[86] The SD might report that the proceedings of the League of Large Families' congress in Aalen in June 1939 were 'very gratifying', but this was and remained an unproductive propaganda organisation.[87]

It seems clear that those areas which had not been fundamentally altered by industrial modernisation and consequent class formation were equally not fundamentally altered by National Socialism as a political force and a proselytising creed, although the Second World War, with all its upheavals, certainly brought change. These areas had already survived the upheavals of the First World War, including conscription and carnage, without their fundamental character being transformed. For them, National Socialism of itself was not a structurally revolutionary force. What really changed these areas were two separate and unrelated factors. The first – undoubtedly caused by Nazi policies – was the influx of refugees from eastern Germany and eastern Europe at the end of the Second World War, migrants in far larger numbers and on a longer-term basis than the temporary influx that there had been during the war of POWs, coerced foreign workers and evacuees from neighbouring and northern cities. The second factor was growing prosperity from the 1950s in West Germany, along with a technological revolution, which brought both a renewed flight from the land and a greater degree of mechanisation on farms, including the first experience of mechanisation on many small farms. For as long as agricultural work remained largely labour intensive, overwhelmingly using the labour of people and animals, traditional society retained its fundamental characteristics. In the smaller communities, while there might be some modern facilities such as an adjacent rail line and the private ownership of radios, the major change to a degree of mechanisation of farm work was what altered patterns of working and, ultimately, of life in most of its aspects. In most of Württemberg's small communes, this change came after the war.[88]

It would, nevertheless, be wrong to underestimate the changes wrought by the experience of the Second World War. One was some levelling of class, or perhaps of status, occasioned by requisitioning, rationing and shortages. It has been asserted that Hitler's regime destroyed the foundations of traditional conservative authoritarianism, unintentionally but inexorably effecting a social revolution.[89] Insofar as this occurred, it resulted neither from the regime's invoking the ideal of the *Volksgemeinschaft*, nor from the simple device of designating all those included in it as *Volksgenossen* (citizens – literally, 'national comrades'). It was not the case that the Third Reich displayed a 'classless reality', with the traditional barriers of class and status either broken down or confused by the aggregation of Germans from all kinds of background in a racial community.[90] Those of greatest wealth and status endeavoured for the most part to retain them and the privileges which they brought, until some were dispossessed by either bombing or the border changes at the end of the war. Some survived even that.

Those of middling wealth and status, by contrast, were more likely to be *declassé* – even if only on a temporary basis – as a result of losing the material possessions which indicated their status. The conscription of both vehicles and horses hit some of the wealthier elements in urban and rural society and reduced both their ability to function and their status. The pressure exerted on women of all classes to engage in work during the war may have been hesitating and in many cases unproductive, but it appeared to treat women of all classes similarly – even if enforcement was less successful in the case of middle-class women. Middle-class women in Germany, as in Britain, were said to fear factory work: no doubt part of what they feared was how it would affect their status, if they had to work alongside those whom they regarded as social inferiors or, worse, under the authority of such people. In the Württemberg countryside, none of this was an issue, although in wartime Nazi functionaries became alarmed if a German woman was working under the authority of an 'inferior' foreigner. Rural women worked to maintain their farms as going concerns. Again, the unavailability of commodities, latterly including food in the towns, at any price – or at any but an astronomical price – put the middle and lower classes on a more similar footing. Both groups were largely reduced to bartering whatever they possessed or could lay their hands on, by whatever means. The destruction of homes by bombing left people from different backgrounds similarly homeless. Those who had more domestic possessions had more to lose.

Aerial bombardment was the major factor which caused destruction and havoc within Germany and necessitated physical reconstruction after the war. As we have noted, it particulary affected cities and towns, leaving many rural areas – including some in close proximity to conurbations – untouched. This undoubtedly led some rural inhabitants to view the emergencies of the war in urban areas with less urgency than they might have done if they themselves had been in the firing line. It was to some extent this that made them seem uncooperative and selfish when viewed by desperate people from an urban perspective – the perspective from which historians in the twenty-first century tend to view the past. For example, are we in the least impressed by villagers in

Württemberg being outraged at the requisitioning of their church bells in 1942, as a contribution to Germany's low reserves of raw materials, at a time when thousands of urban Germans were losing their homes and possessions, and perhaps also family members, in bombing raids? Or, when many urban Germans were obliged to leave their homes, to escape the bombing raids, do we sympathise with villagers who resented their arrival as evacuees in the countryside and then complained about their refusal to help out on the farm? After all, to many horrified townees, the countryside was like an underdeveloped foreign country where a foreign language, *Schwäbisch* (Swabian), was spoken, and where the food, while relatively plentiful, was – to the urban palate – at least unappetising and perhaps revolting. Even some Polish forced labourers complained about the fare which they shared with farming families.[91] Or, again, can we identify with devious and selfish peasants who cheated the authorities by surrendering as little of their produce as they could get away with – thus depriving urban consumers of scarce food supplies? The answer is probably 'no', on all three counts: we do not identify with the peasants; rather, we identify with the townees.

Yet we should try to understand the logic of the villagers' position.[92] The effects of the war on rural society did not seem trivial to peasants because they were bound up with the identity and traditions of the village. First, the village church remained a social and devotional centre, and the removal of its bells for recycling was seen not as a minor inconvenience but as an attack on the traditions, and indeed on the very identity, of the village. There was particular resentment when historic bells which had been left in place during the requisitions of the First World War were removed. Removing centuries-old unique bells destroyed part of a village's character. It was also seen – and resented – as part of the regime's campaign against the churches. Secondly, many evacuees from northern cities were seen as ungrateful townees, who did nothing but complain that there was no hot and cold running water in farmhouses and that the village had no cinema.[93] Accordingly, these townees were treated with suspicion and often with contempt – dismissed, perhaps, as some of them were, as 'those loose women from Duisburg'.[94] Thirdly, there was in the countryside little sense of responsibility about working to feed 'the nation' – the godless urban nation which had lured young country people away from their roots, and had imposed restrictions on their own time-honoured practices, notably the bartering of goods and services. Rather, in the last two years of the war, agriculture on small farms became increasingly a matter of subsistence production to meet local needs. Indeed, by 1943–45, village communities felt that they had made nothing but sacrifices for the aims of the urban-based National Socialist government which had conscripted their young men and introduced a new coercive economy reminiscent of that of the First World War. For many, the top priority was to maintain their farm – which had in many cases been held by the same family for several generations – as a going concern in the face of extreme difficulty, until the war was over.

All of this needs to be considered within the context of the pre-war years: neither the impact of Nazi rule nor the circumstances and effects of the war can be understood without an appreciation of what preceded them. This requires examination of society in rural Württemberg before and after the Nazi assumption of power in 1933, including the degree of support for Nazism there. It requires evaluation of the extent of Nazi party control in areas beyond the main towns. Beyond that, it is helpful to view Nazi racial policy and policy towards the churches in Württemberg in wartime within the context of their development from 1933, because these policies did not suddenly commence with the outbreak of war. Taking this longer perspective demonstrates how and why the view from the Württemberg countryside was markedly different from the view from the towns – or, at least, from how that view has been represented. For example, it has been argued that

> The [Nazi] appeal to individual initiative within the context of an overarching responsibility to the *Volk* ... did work. All opinion surveys point to the active participation of the Germans and to the importance of individual initiative in the preparation and the pursuit of war.[95]

Even if this is an accurate appraisal of the attitudes and conduct of urban Germans in general – and that would be a major concession to make – this picture bears little relation to life and work in the south German countryside in the 1930s and 1940s. The premises of the quotation are that the Nazi leadership was dealing with individuals living and operating in modern societal structures, responding with the attitudes that were informed by these structures and by modern media. By contrast, south German peasants generally persisted in operating with no more distant horizons than their traditional community and as members of it.

There has been much argument about whether National Socialism was or was not a modernising force.[96] Yet, in the context of the south German family farm, this dispute is almost irrelevant. More importantly, National Socialism was *perceived* within many rural communities as a force bringing unwelcome changes – changes which were associated by rural people with the life of the towns, changes which threatened traditional village life and culture. Country folk regarded the changes being imposed on them in the Third Reich – and, indeed, earlier – as 'new', as the product of a power elite based in towns and cities whose main concern lay in appeasing the increasingly numerically dominant urban population, as migration from the countryside to the towns continued. It may well be legitimate to deride farmers for selfishly refusing to supply food to the towns for prices which they regarded as inadequate.[97] Yet the new controls on production, prices and distribution imposed by the Nazi regime, before the war and particularly during it, gave farming communities the impression that the only forms of 'individual initiative' left to them were obstruction and disobedience. This, accordingly, did not lead them to feel any 'overarching responsibility to the *Volk*' – quite the reverse.

In many southern rural areas, traditional familial and community networks and relationships continued to obtain, to a considerable extent, through to the end of the Second World War, with varying degrees of hostility to disruptive outsiders, whether government officials, NSDAP snoopers, evacuees from northern cities or, ultimately, ethnic German refugees from eastern Europe. This was generally a matter of ingrained habit being reinforced by the wartime struggle for survival, but in some respects it was also a manifestation of opposition to – or, at least, a rejection of – Nazi norms, values and demands which threatened to undermine these networks and relationships. For many rural dwellers, the Nazi system in peacetime had brought unexpected and unwelcome change, with centralising demands which made inroads into traditional loyalties and practices and with the establishment of networks of control to try to enforce observance of new normative requirements. The massive demands of modern warfare greatly intensified this development, and – in spite of some determined obstruction by families and groups of individuals – disrupted at least some of the bonds of personal relationships and mutual interest which had traditionally underpinned rural society. In particular, the long lists of men killed, injured or taken prisoner contributed to a massive change, with unprecedented burdens of responsibility thrust upon women, while many in the westward flood of refugees, who would never return to their eastern homes, settled in villages whose identity their presence altered irrevocably.[98] If only by these brutal means, the Nazi era brought an element of radical change to rural outposts. While Hitler's war lasted, however, its exigencies reinforced their ties of mutual interdependence.

2

Before the War

Hitler's rise to power in the later 1920s and early 1930s followed the dual trauma for Germans of defeat in the First World War and the perceived humiliation of the ensuing peace settlement embodied in the Treaty of Versailles between newly Republican Germany and the victorious Allies. It accompanied, and Hitler exploited, Germany's descent into agrarian recession and cataclysmic industrial depression, with acute distress reaching its peak in the winter of 1932–33. These disasters were exacerbated by the peculiarity of Germany's identity: the European continent's foremost industrial power was also a country with a relatively backward agrarian sector.[1] With an abundance of natural resources in some areas, most notably in the Ruhr in western Prussia, intensive industrial development, especially after the founding of the German Empire in 1871, had propelled Germany into the front rank of world military powers by 1914. Industrial progress had massively accelerated urbanisation so that within a few decades the balance of German society was virtually reversed: whereas in 1871 roughly one German in three had lived in a town, by 1914 almost two Germans in three lived in towns, and this at a time of massive population growth, from some 40 million to around 65 million. Urban Germany's achievements in all branches of academic, intellectual and cultural life – especially in the sciences, but also in music and the visual arts – were prodigious, as befitted an advanced European country.[2] Yet by contrast with Britain, Europe's other major industrial power, Germany retained a substantial agrarian sector. In 1914 Britain derived a mere 7 per cent of its income from agriculture, compared with Germany's 23 per cent.[3] Even after the First World War, as the 1925 census results showed, almost 36 per cent of the German population continued to live in communities of two thousand inhabitants or fewer.[4] Even in 1939, after a new wave of migration to the towns, 21 million Germans lived in communities of fewer than two thousand people, or 30 per cent of the total, although by this time a similar number lived in cities of 100,000 people or more.[5]

The First World War imposed severe pressures on the German economy, with industry facing increasing shortages of raw materials as a result of the initially partial British blockade which became total from mid-1916. The blockade, which continued into mid-1919, helped to bring malnutrition and disease to German towns and cities. German agriculture was less productive during the war than in normal times because men were conscripted away from the land and into the armed forces, and because the demand for workers in war industry had led to attractive wage levels being offered there, which induced even more people to leave the land. In addition, the commandeering of the lion's share of produce for the army's consumption contributed to shortages at home which occasioned the 'turnip winters' of 1916–17 and 1917–18, when urban civilians were reduced to eating animal fodder beets and, if they were lucky, potato peelings. On the thriving black market, only the rich could afford the peeled potatoes, as well as a multiplicity of otherwise unavailable goods. Government attempts to regulate the production and distribution of food, to ensure that supplies reached the towns, resulted in the *Zwangswirtschaft* (coercive economy), in which the prices of agricultural produce were fixed, at a time of rising inflation. Farmers' reluctance to sell under these conditions led, in the winter of 1917–18, to troops being detailed to requisition food from farms.[6] Worse, so it seemed to bitterly aggrieved farmers, the controls continued beyond the end of the war, until as late as 1922.[7] But there were two sides to this: long after the war, in 1928, the citizens of Württemberg's capital city, Stuttgart, retained bitter memories of the alleged selfishness of farmers and rural traders in the years during and immediately after the war, when the urban population was suffering severe shortages of food and bearing the brunt of the losses of the great inflation which reached its peak in autumn 1923.[8]

Whatever animosities between town and country there were, in Württemberg, as elsewhere in Germany, there was also the persistence of particularism, of local and regional loyalties, and of hostility to outsiders that set limits to interregional understanding and tolerance. Above all, Württembergers, like other south Germans, possessed both strong pride in their own traditions and institutions and deeply-rooted hostility to northern Germany, especially Prussia. Much as in 1917 army chaplains in the Royal Württemberg Army reported hearing civilians saying that 'it doesn't matter whether we become French or remain German', or that it would be preferable to be French than Prussian, so in Bavaria anti-Prussian feeling was heightened during the later stages of the war.[9] These sentiments reflected long-standing hostility. At the beginning of the nineteenth century, Württemberg had fought on Napoleon's side against Prussia, while in the early 1860s King Wilhelm I of Württemberg is reputed to have said: 'Better be an ally of France than the vassal of Prussia'. This attitude was more typical than exceptional, and it persisted well into the twentieth century; after the First World War, many Württembergers remained no fonder of Prussians.[10] In 1932, during the depression, the Württemberg Minister of Economics, Reinhold Maier, a liberal, admitted that there was 'a grain of truth' in the local complaint that 'laws are made in Prussia, read in Bavaria, and implemented in Württemberg'.[11] The last Nazi Minister of Justice in Württemberg, Jonathan Schmid, complained in

January 1935 about centralising attempts to turn 'Württemberg into a Prussian colony', for which he carefully blamed the 'power-hungry Prussian bureaucracy' rather than their political masters.[12] In the 1930s and early 1940s, the experience of both Nazi centralising policies and wartime evacuation left northerners and southerners as mutually resentful as ever.[13]

Yet Württemberg's identity had been forged not merely in opposition to Prussian power and pretensions but as a positive attribute of integration within its own territory. This consisted, after Napoleon's reordering of the map of Germany, of most of the pre-1806 dukedom of Württemberg, the Swabian lands (*Schwabenland*), along with a few imperial free cities from the old Holy Roman Empire and the region of Hohenlohe-Franken in the north.[14] In population terms, the Swabians accounted for around three-quarters of the total. While in the 1930s there was some special pleading about the 'uncommonly happy and organically evolved ... union of two million Swabians and 700,000 Franks', around 1970 the inhabitants of the Hohenlohe region still spoke of 'pig-headed Swabians' as opposed to 'amiable Franks', while the majority population tended to refer to the inhabitants of Württemberg as a whole as 'Swabians'.[15] Accordingly, while no doubt 'it could well be argued that' the years 1938–42 were 'the first time when a majority of Germans experienced their Germanness', it all depends on what individuals and communities perceived as being 'German'.[16] Even the NSDAP's press officer in Gau Württemberg-Hohenzollern wrote, in 1938 in a work of propaganda entitled *Das Buch der deutschen Gaue* (*The Book of German Gaus*),

> overwhelmingly about Swabian people ... Only in the last two sentences was there reference, albeit in typical form, to respect for National Socialism: 'Thus did we in Gau Württemberg-Hohenzollern as good Swabians become better Germans. And that is the achievement of our Swabian leader [*Schwabenführer*] Wilhelm Murr'.[17]

'Germanness' was perceived through the prism of their Swabian identity, and indeed through that of different kinds of Swabianness. Undoubtedly the idea of 'Germanness' was different in Bavaria, in Berlin, in the Rhineland or in Hamburg, or elsewhere. With specific reference to Württemberg in Imperial Germany, it has been persuasively argued that 'Germans imagined nationhood as a form of localness'.[18] Even if modern communications and military service, followed by war service, eroded this perception in the first half of the twentieth century, in some areas of rural Württemberg this frame of reference persisted into the 1970s, and perhaps beyond that.[19] Yet for some of those who remained at home, the demands of war – including particularly the billeting of northern evacuees in Württemberg's communes – generated an image of the nation that was different and alien.

At the end of the First World War, German cities were in revolutionary turmoil. A massive demonstration in Stuttgart on 9 November 1918 led to the proclamation of a republic, whereupon the constitutional monarch, King Wilhelm II of Württemberg, who had presided over a raft of liberalising reforms since his accession in 1891, abdicated.[20] Württemberg remained one of the three south German political entities, now *Länder* (federal states) in the new German Republic (see Map 1), retaining its own *Land* government and *Landtag* (state parliament). Württemberg's confessional profile remained similar to that of the Reich as a whole, with two-thirds of its inhabitants Evangelical Christians (Protestants) and almost one-third Roman Catholic. Württemberg had a below average number of citizens who belonged to other Christian denominations or had no religious affiliation. Its proportion of religious Jews was, at 4.2 per 1000 of the population, less than half of the Reich average of 9; in 1930, after a century of migration to the towns, only slightly more than 20 per cent of Württemberg's Jews lived in the countryside.[21] Catholics were in a strong majority in southern Württemberg, accounting for 75 per cent or more of the population in most districts, while Evangelicals dominated central and northern areas, again with the allegiance of 75 per cent or more of the inhabitants in many districts.[22] Evangelicals in Württemberg belonged to a tradition where their church enjoyed independence from state control or interference, a Protestant tradition which was significantly influenced by Pietism, where the accent was on personal faith based on individual devotion and adherence to scripture.[23] In general, religious affiliation was stronger than in some other parts of Germany, reflecting the fact that, during the 1920s and 1930s, Württemberg continued to consist largely of rural or small town communities.

By the later 1930s, as much as 37.5 per cent of Württemberg's 2,896,920 inhabitants lived in communities of fewer than two thousand people, while altogether 59 per cent of the population lived in communities of fewer than 10,000 inhabitants. The numbers of inhabitants of the four largest towns were Stuttgart 420,533, Heilbronn 68,953, Ulm 62,472, and Esslingen 43,089.[24] Dwarfing the other three, and the only city, Stuttgart, housed almost 16 per cent of the entire population of Württemberg.[25] In terms of population density, Württemberg was quite sparsely inhabited, particularly in comparison with the large urban agglomerations of north-western Germany, although it was roughly comparable with its southern neighbours, less densely-populated Bavaria and more densely-populated Baden.[26]

In the period between the 1933 and 1939 censuses, the population of Württemberg had increased by 7.5 per cent, ahead of the Reich average of 5 per cent. This was due mainly to an increase in the birth rate, along with lower rates of infant mortality, apparently confirming Nazi assumptions that rural and small town areas were more fecund than larger towns and cities. In addition, around 80,000 migrants had moved to Württemberg, overwhelmingly to recovering industrial areas, with an exceptional rise in population of 37 per cent in the aero-engine centre of Friedrichshafen in six years. Pressure on accommodation in the town was such that many industrial workers were obliged to live in nearby villages, contributing to social change there. The town of Böblingen saw an increase of 27 per cent, while Ludwigsburg's population rose by 17 per cent and Waiblingen's by 13 per cent in the same period. At the same time, the rural districts of Öhringen, Künzelsau, Saulgau, Ehingen, Wangen and Biberach saw a small decline in their population, while in other chiefly agricultural districts such as Calw, Mergentheim and Münsingen there was a miniscule rise. These developments intensified the extent to which Württemberg's inhabitants were unevenly distributed: seven districts in the north east and six across the southern central area, along with Wangen in the extreme south east (see Map 2) had a population density of less than one hundred people per square kilometre, while, at the other end of the scale, three adjacent districts in west central Württemberg – Stuttgart, Ludwigsburg and Esslingen – had a density of over 300 inhabitants per square kilometre. Esslingen was the most densely populated, with 394.9 inhabitants per square kilometre, while Münsingen, in southern Württemberg, was the least dense with only 47.8. The Hohenzollern enclave in the south, consisting of the districts of Hechingen and Sigmaringen, was also sparsely populated.[27]

Württemberg's agriculture was based on the peasant proprietor with only a small proportion of its farms, 6.8 per cent in 1925, in the hands of tenants.[28] The proprietors were overwhelmingly male – 83 per cent in 1939 – while 82 per cent of the 'assisting family members', who did not receive a formal wage for their labours, were female.[29] The farms operated as family concerns, with only small numbers of hired agricultural workers. Yet this did not mean that Württemberg's small farms were mechanised, in the sense of having motorised vehicles and implements. On the contrary, cheap family labour prevailed up to the Second World War, with virtually all of the work on small farms carried out by hand or with draught animals; even the proprietors of medium-sized farms tended not to have the means to acquire machines.[30] There was one experiment in the commune of Häusern where the proprietors of larger farms together bought a tractor for communal use, but when this did not reduce their overall costs they abandoned it.[31] In Burgbach, in the Remstal, it was only after the Second World War that 'a large number of tractors were acquired rather suddenly' by the farmers.[32]

Württemberg had more than its share of marginal small-holdings. Around 1930, the average size of farms in hectares was: Württemberg, 4.6; Bavaria, 8.7; East Prussia, 14.3. The Reich average was 7.2. Altogether 35 per cent of Württemberg's agricultural land – twice as much as in the Reich as a whole – was farmed in units of less than five hectares.[33] Whereas in Prussia landowners with holdings of less than 20 hectares were in a clear minority in 1937, in Württemberg only 26 per cent of all landowners had holdings of 20 hectares or more.[34] Some areas had particularly fragmented holdings because of the tradition of partible inheritance, which resulted in parcels of land being divided among several heirs: 'whatever had been gathered up and held together despite all obstacles in one generation had to be divided up every time among the next'. The relatively few women who were proprietors usually lived in communities where partible inheritance applied.[35] These were to be found in most of the western half of the *Land*, in the regions of the Black Forest and the Neckar valley, whereas in almost all of eastern and southern Württemberg property was transmitted to a single heir. Accordingly, land holdings tended to be larger in the latter areas than in the former.[36]

Even in the nineteenth century, the disadvantages of partible inheritance had become evident. Emigration to the United States, from as early as the mid eighteenth century, had eased the pressure on the land at a time of population growth, and it intensified from the 1840s to the 1890s.[37] Those who remained often faced a stark choice between chronic poverty and becoming wage earning employees in local – or even distant – industries or trades.[38] This allowed them to retain both their small parcel of land and their identity as members of the community, while earning a living wage. Even so, partly because of competition from producers abroad and partly because the owners of small, splintered plots of land could not avail themselves of new labour-saving machines, the position had become so acute by the interwar years that some communes decided to change to single-heir inheritance. In 1930, the transition from partible to single-heir inheritance had begun in 130 of Württemberg's communes.[39] Nevertheless, industry was able to develop in areas where partible inheritance fragmented landholdings, whereas in eastern Württemberg, where impartible inheritance tended to apply, family farms remained viable as economic concerns for longer into the twentieth century – only to be dismissed as 'backward' once the mechanisation and motorisation of farming, along with a new surge of industrial expansion, had occurred from the 1950s. Indeed it was still possible in the early 1970s to refer to 'the industrial "backwardness" of … North Württemberg as a whole'. In the five north-eastern districts of Württemberg, 'as late as 1961, the number of persons engaged in the region's agriculture was as high as it had been in 1882'.[40]

The administrative structure of Württemberg derived from the post-Napoleonic settlement. The *Land* was divided into sixty-one *Oberämter* (counties), which were renamed *Kreise* (districts), on the Prussian model, in 1934 by central order. This was resented in Württemberg, and the usage 'Oberamt' persisted in some quarters until the reform of 1938 which, more or less in accordance with the prescriptions of the Reich Minister of the Interior, created instead thirty-seven

Kreise (districts) of somewhat more equal population size and economic capacity. Nevertheless, while the aim was to create districts of between 60,000 and 100,000 inhabitants each, in Württemberg the districts of Göppingen, Heilbronn and Ludwigsburg, as well as the relatively massive city of Stuttgart, each had over 100,000 inhabitants. At the same time, nineteen of the new districts had fewer than 60,000, with the largely agricultural districts of Künzelsau, Öhringen, Mergentheim, Ehingen, Münsingen, Horb and Leonberg each having between 22,000 and 40,000 inhabitants. The counties, and later the districts, were composed of *Gemeinde* (communes), some of which were *Stadtgemeinde* (towns) while the majority were *Landgemeinde* (rural communes). The communes were largely self-governing in local matters – for example, in having the right to enact bylaws, to raise local taxes, and to adjudicate in matters relating to the distribution of local property. Local government comprised a directly elected community council (*Gemeinderat*), headed by a directly elected *Bürgermeister* (mayor). Of the thirty-seven new districts created by administrative reorganisation in 1938, there were three *Stadtkreise* (urban districts) – Stuttgart, Heilbronn and Ulm – and thirty-four *Landkreise* (provincial districts) (see Map 2). Of the latter, fifteen were classed as 'agricultural', 'predominantly agricultural' or 'more agricultural', fourteen were described as 'mixed', and eight were regarded as 'industrial':[41]

Industrial Districts	Mixed Districts	Agricultural Districts
Stuttgart	Aalen	Biberach
Heilbronn (town)	Backnang	Crailsheim
Ludwigsburg	Balingen	Ehingen
Ulm (town)	Böblingen	Hall
Tettnang*	Calw	Heilbronn (environs)
Heidenheim	Esslingen	Horb
Göppingen	Freudenstadt	Künzelsau
Reutlingen (8)	Gmünd	Leonberg
	Nürtingen**	Mergentheim
	Rottweil	Münsigen
	Tübingen	Öhringen
	Tuttlingen	Ravensburg
	Vaihingen	Saulgau
	Waiblingen (14)	Ulm (environs)
		Wangen (15)

* formerly Friedrichshafen

** Nürtingen was not listed. It belongs in the 'mixed' category

Across Württemberg, farming conditions varied according to a landscape where 'fertile pastures alternate with arid ground; boggy areas alternate with woodlands'.[42] The Hohenlohe region in the north and also central Württemberg were mostly favoured with good soil, although some of the land was waterlogged and relatively unproductive; other areas of eastern Württemberg as well as much of the western side were less well endowed.[43] Hilly terrain and deep river valleys with steep bends formed an inhospitable environment for both arable cultivation and farm machinery, but animal husbandry enjoyed some success and a variety of good quality fruit – apples, pears, plums, cherries, for example, as well as soft fruit – was produced in quantities that led Reinhold Maier to claim in 1932 that 'Württemberg is the real fruit garden of Germany'.[44] In Stuttgart itself and in the Remstal area to its east, as well as in several other areas, including Heilbronn district, vineyards were planted on steep terraces.[45] There were broad variations in income, with farmers on small or dwarf holdings in areas of partible inheritance earning meagre amounts while those with larger holdings were able to earn nearer the Reich average for farmers. Nevertheless, in 1927 Württemberg farmers had on average a lower income than their south German neighbours in Baden and Bavaria, to say nothing of the more prosperous farmers further north in Prussia, Saxony and especially Mecklenburg.[46] One purpose of the administrative reform of 1938 was to try to create districts in Württemberg in which relatively unproductive or impoverished rural areas were balanced by areas of greater wealth-creating capacity, through industry or trades. This was only partially realised.[47]

Uneconomic agriculture bred the part-time farmer, whose main employment was in local industry or trade; in 1925, 15 per cent of all workers in these economic sectors in Württemberg ran a part-time farm, compared with the Reich average of almost 11 per cent.[48] In Gosheim in south-west Württemberg, a commune of 978 inhabitants in 1933, the production of 'screws, nuts and bolts, spindles shafts, ratchets, cogs and time pieces' within the village itself was facilitated in the 1930s by the purchase of a lathe. Nevertheless, it was still the case in the 1960s that the vast majority of native Gosheim families continued to have a connection of some kind with farm work.[49] In Kiebingen, in the Neckar valley, a commune of almost 740 inhabitants, some 140 people were daily commuters to work in factories or on building sites in the mid 1920s, but the vast majority of the inhabitants gained their main income from farm work.[50] Commuters who lived on their part-time farm and went elsewhere to work still accounted in 1939 for 14 per cent of the employed population in Württemberg.[51] Some of them remained resident in the village through choice, but others remained because they could not afford to live in the town where they worked. The existence which this dictated for these daily commuters in the 1930s was regarded by the German Labour Front, the Nazis' sham trade union organisation, as a social problem.[52] Yet there were also areas where agriculture remained the full-time occupation of almost all of the inhabitants. Until the Second World War, in two communes in the Hohenlohe region in the north, over 90 per cent of the workforce was involved in family farming, with no-one engaged in work outside the commune. Some hired labourers were brought in; they lived with their employers. Even in 1961, only 7 per cent and 10 per cent of those employed in each of these communes worked outside it, although this changed considerably after that date.[53] In Burgbach, a village with 1600 inhabitants in 1935, there was before the Second World War 'a relatively simple human community ... The business of Burgbach was land, vegetables, fruits, cows, pigs, milk, and, above all, the production of high-quality grapes for wine and the making of wine'.[54]

If agriculture continued to be structured largely on traditional, unmechanised lines on smaller farms in Württemberg during the inter-war years, this was reflected in the maintenance of the village commune as the most important basic unit of rural society. This was the case even when some members of the community had ceased to work within the village, and perhaps ceased to work in agriculture as a full-time occupation. In the village of Körle (Hesse), for example, after the First World War, where most villagers had abandoned farming during the 1920s, traditional relationships persisted.[55] As long as the part-time 'worker-peasants' resided in their commune, it seems that local ties of family, neighbours and church had first call on their loyalty.[56] Even in the later twentieth century, according to an ethnologist who had studied a village near Tübingen,

> the village – even this village, where there were scarcely any farmers left and people worked mostly in the surrounding towns – still possesses the strength to defend itself against inquisitive strangers and pushy newcomers. The village still exists, now as before, as a communicative structure with its own domestic and foreign policies, and ... one should have no illusions about its effectiveness.[57]

Around 1930, even some of the small towns in Württemberg maintained their former rural character. For example, in Mühlacker, a country town of some 6000 inhabitants in north-western Württemberg, many of the workers in small industrial concerns or crafts retained a garden or smallholding where they worked in their free time and produced various vegetables. However, the proportion of Mühlacker's inhabitants engaged in agriculture was judged to be unusually high for a town.[58]

In this predominantly agrarian *Land*, 'industry' had traditionally meant crafts such as those of the blacksmith, carpenter, wheelwright, baker and shoemaker which were practised in individual workshops in small towns or even villages.[59] The fitters and turners of Gosheim were a case in point.[60] Large-scale factory industry had developed only slowly and on a smaller scale than elsewhere in Germany, not least because of the absence of both local raw materials for heavy industry and established trading and transportation routes.[61] Modern industrial

development, from the later nineteenth century dispersed among a variety of
centres in Württemberg, led to the production of textiles, luxury goods, and
vehicles of various kinds, including bicycles, motor cars and airships, but without
the growth of the kind of large industrial concerns involved in mining, iron and
steel and other heavy industries.[62] As Reinhold Maier said in December 1932,
there were 'thousands of specialist products: from linen to accordions, to surgical
knives and clocks, from soft toys to Bosch fuses, Salamander shoes, Daimler cars,
and so on and so on, to Zeppelin airships, everything …' Furthermore, these
products were fashioned in businesses in which either the owner or a manager
appointed by him was in control, unlike 'the mammoth factories of the typical
industrialist, or the major banks'.[63] For these kinds of specialist and technical
occupation, members of Württemberg's industrial workforce tended to undergo
lengthy periods of training from which an unusually high proportion of them
emerged as skilled workers.[64]

All of these factors combined to ensure that Württemberg suffered less from
the direct effects of the world economic crisis around 1930 than almost any
other area of Germany. Before 1932, Württemberg hardly felt the stresses of the
depression, but as Reinhold Maier said in December of that year, 'Württemberg
first felt the full force of the effects of the crisis relatively late, but today is
suffering grievously from the crisis. In no sense is Württemberg an "oasis"'.[65]
In Maier's – perhaps typically Swabian – view, Württemberg's ills had largely
been caused by a crisis of confidence which was a direct result of the economic
and financial policies pursued by the Reich government in Berlin from the mid
1920s.[66] Even so, in 1932 Württemberg's unemployment rates were relatively low:
133,604 unemployed represented 50 per thousand of the population, compared
with 76 in neighbouring Baden and 92 as the Reich average.[67] Yet even these lower
levels represented a catastrophe for many individuals and families. In Mühlacker
in 1930, increasing numbers of the unemployed were unable to pay their
electricity and gas bills, while by the end of the year the small unemployment
office there simply could not cope with the large numbers of those needing to
have their benefit cards stamped each day.[68] In occupations related to machine
construction, instrument making and electronics, only half as many people in
Württemberg were employed in January 1933 as there had been in 1928. In some
areas, significant numbers working reduced hours, along with both private and
organised charitable relief work, camouflaged the true extent of the problem.[69]
During the depression, the number of commuters from village communities
also fell by around 25,000 as some lost employment in nearby urban centres
and 'silently vacated their jobs in the town and held nobody responsible for
their plight save themselves and their families … withdraw[ing] to the village
and its opportunities for self-support through farming'. But, in keeping with the
tradition of both inclusiveness and exclusiveness, it was only those members of

the army of the unemployed who had a current or previous connection with the village who were allowed to fall back on it in time of crisis; impecunious strangers were not welcome.[70]

There can be no doubt that the small rural communes maintained much of their traditional character in the inter-war years and into the 1940s, and that in some of them conditions remained relatively primitive. In Crailsheim district, for example, perhaps 90 per cent of the communes were not linked to a piped water supply, while in Ulm district the farmhouses generally had one living room that could be heated and bedrooms whose walls had not been plastered.[71] Yet many small communes had assimilated some of the features offered, or imposed, by their urban neighbours. For example, the effects of industrialisation – most notably high-speed transport – transformed some aspects of rural life but left others untouched. The small town of Mühlacker had had the character of a largely self-contained village around 1900, but the coming of the railway had transformed it into an important transport hub, and in 1930 a radio transmitter had been erected.[72] Whereas two neighbouring communes in the Hohenlohe region of Crailsheim were eight kilometres from the nearest railway station and had only gravel or dirt roads until the 1960s, in Kiebingen, by contrast, already in the 1920s, some inhabitants owned telephones and automobiles, and from 1925 there was a domestic electricity supply. From 1927 there was a piped water supply system and a petrol station. The villagers could travel to the nearby towns of Tübingen and Rottenburg by rail and, from 1927, by bus.[73] The commune of Metzingen, too, became linked to Stuttgart and Reutlingen by bus in February 1934.[74] Members of some previously self-contained villages could now use the railway as a means of commuting to a nearby town, to work or to shop. Reciprocally, the railway made the countryside more accessible to townspeople, as tourists or as itinerant salesmen. The frustrated urban shoppers in Württemberg who, in the summer of 1941, travelled out to the countryside by rail to buy fruit and vegetables direct from the farmers, demonstrated this accessibility.[75]

Nevertheless, partly because of the same unevenness of terrain that helped to determine the nature of agriculture, in the 1930s the extent of railway development in Württemberg was below the Reich average: the figures for length of track per 100,000 inhabitants were 86 kilometres in Württemberg and 101 in the Reich. Some areas were more favoured than others. Not surprisingly, Stuttgart was a major hub for railway lines from Bavarian towns to the Neckar valley, Baden and Hesse, and further afield. The urbanised central area of Württemberg was particularly well served by the rail network, to the benefit of nearby villages and their commuters. By contrast, in eastern Württemberg railway lines were thin on the ground, in both north and south. For example, apart from the main line between the major centres of Ulm, on the Bavarian border, and Friedrichshafen on the Bodensee, there were only two branch lines in Biberach district. Further north, growing industry in Schwäbisch Hall was stunted because the absence of branch lines prevented potential commuting workers from reaching it. Also in the north, in the districts of Künzelsau and Öhringen there was a gap in the major railway line in the area which meant that each autumn farmers had to spend precious time on transporting their harvest of sugar beet to the nearest railway stop some six kilometres distant.

On the other hand, Württemberg was well served by a road network whose density, at 543 kilometres per 100,000 inhabitants, was much greater than the Reich average of 322.[76] This may have owed something to the location, from the mid 1920s, of the production of Daimler-Benz motor cars at Untertürkheim and of its body plant at Sindelfingen, both in the Stuttgart area. On the other hand, it seems more likely that it was the building of motorways (*Autobahnen*), not least to stimulate the economy in the depression, that gave impetus to the automobile market.[77] In the 1930s, there were plans to build three *Autobahnen*. Two were to run from east to west: one would link Stuttgart to Karlsruhe and Munich; another, further north, would link Crailsheim and Neckarsulm to Nuremberg in the east and Bruchsal in the west. The third was to run from north to south, linking Stuttgart and Heilbronn to Würzburg.[78] Parts of these routes were operational before the war. For example, on 5 November 1938, *Gauleiter* Murr together with his counterpart from Baden, Robert Wagner, opened the new stretches from Stuttgart to Pforzheim and from Stuttgart to Ludwigsburg.[79] To facilitate the movement of goods, plans were developed in 1939 for feeder roads to the *Autobahnen*, while trunk roads were extended and improved. There were also several projects for improving local roads between individual communes and for renovating bridges.[80] Yet while these measures undoubtedly opened up some rural areas, in many others roads were not blacktop and transport continued to be overwhelmingly powered by draught animals until after 1945.[81] In some areas, however, goods and people could also be transported by water. The Bodensee in the south, with the major industrial town of Friedrichshafen on its shore, provided one opportunity. In the north, the stretch of the Neckar Canal between Heilbronn and Mannheim was completed in 1935, with part of the route from Heilbronn to Ulm under construction before Hitler launched his war in 1939.[82]

While modern facilities, particularly transport, impinged on rural areas and brought some of them clear benefits, nevertheless the main beneficiaries of rail and motorised transport, electricity supplies, domestic water and sanitation services, and cinema, the telephone and radio – an innovation in the 1920s – were those who lived in towns.[83] Yet rural dwellers did not anathematise these new inventions in the obscurantist way in which Pobedonostzev, Procurator of the Holy Synod in late Imperial Russia, saw 'the works of the devil everywhere, in telegraphs, telephones and railways'.[84] Farmers and their families were, for example, eager to make use of the railway where they could. They did, however, complain that some of the items produced by the mass media were alien and threatening. There were accusations 'that too many films are shown which bear no relation to reality and only encourage the flight from the land', by glamorising urban life, while

> the rural population never stops criticising the radio station in Stuttgart for broadcasting jazz music which they cannot begin to understand. They say that insufficient consideration is given to the entertainment of the farmer and farm labourer, who want to hear popular songs, popular music (Swabian) and marches.[85]

The commuting phenomenon, in particular, brought many rural inhabitants into contact with at least some of these facilities and demonstrated to them that the priorities of governments and businesses were dictated by the interests of the urban population. This impression reinforced a rural outlook that had already formed in opposition to government taxation and expenditure on a welfare system geared to meeting the needs of urban dwellers.

Even in the decades before 1914, the German rural population – diverse as it was – had perceived its fortunes to be declining in comparison with those of the urban population, while the effects of the First World War and its aftermath worsened the position of agriculture generally.[86] It was to this increasingly disaffected constituency, with its greatest concentrations in the south and east but with significant representation also in northern areas, that the National Socialists directed strong propaganda appeals, especially from 1928. This included a revision of Point 17 of the 'unalterable' NSDAP programme of 24 February 1920, which stated: 'We demand a land reform suitable to our national requirements, the passing of a law for the expropriation of land for communal purposes without compensation; the abolition of ground rent, and the prohibition of all speculation in land'. With its echoes of Marxist 'common ownership of the means of production', this had had something of a deterrent effect as far as the rural population was concerned. So, claiming that it had been distorted by 'false interpretations on the part of our opponents', in April 1928 Hitler issued a 'clarification' of Point 17:

> Since the NSDAP accepts the principle of private property, it is self-evident that the phrase 'confiscation without compensation' refers simply to the creation of possible legal means for confiscation, when necessary, of land acquired illegally or not managed in the public interest. It is, therefore, aimed primarily against Jewish companies which speculate in land.[87]

Thereafter the NSDAP began to make inroads into the rural vote generally, although less so in Württemberg than elsewhere. While it was at one time customary to argue that the rural inhabitants of Schleswig-Holstein and Pomerania were exceptional in their enthusiasm for Nazism, more recent studies have shown that the NSDAP managed to make significant headway in other rural areas, for example in Baden.[88]

The reasons for the NSDAP's growing success in rural areas probably had much less to do with the 'clarification' of Point 17 than with mounting agrarian distress in the later 1920s.[89] The effects of the world economic crisis, which compounded the prevailing agrarian recession, had a disastrous effect on small farmers in particular. For example, 'from Württemberg came accounts of financial collapse among peasants, due to high interest rates and lack of liquid resources. Agitation was now said to be rife "even amongst otherwise calm people"'.[90] Seeking to capitalise on worsening rural distress, in 1930 the NSDAP's leadership created the *Reichsamt für Agrarpolitik* (Central Department for Agricultural Policy), which devised the party's policy on agriculture and offered the promise of agricultural renewal and solutions to the problems of struggling farmers, in order to try to win their support for the NSDAP in elections. Its leader was a newcomer to the party, R.W. Darré; soon to become one of its leading 'agrarian romantics', he was a 'blood and soil' theoretician who subscribed wholeheartedly to the NSDAP's racist ideology.

Darré devised a plan for the creation of an *agrarpolitischer Apparat* (Agrarian Policy Apparatus). Its machinery would include local and regional officials, ultimately responsible to himself, who would give leadership to farmers in their area and impress on them the importance and desirability of the NSDAP's programme for agriculture. The result was an intricate bureaucracy of the complex and hierarchical kind typical of Nazi institutions. Initially, it had its greatest impact in northern Germany, where it successfully challenged some of the existing farmers' associations, but it also enjoyed some success further south, in Baden and Franconia, in 1931. Hitler's own contribution to this was characteristically propagandistic: 'The Third Reich will be a peasant Reich or it will pass like those of the Hohenzollern and the Hohenstaufen'.[91] In addition, local NSDAP speakers toured rural areas, promising, in typical Nazi fashion, to give indebted and struggling farmers what they wanted: 'No peasant would be driven from his land, mortgage debts would be taken over by the State, interest would be abolished'.[92] Within a couple of years, the Agrarian Policy Apparatus, spreading its tentacles across much of rural Germany, had made significant headway in infiltrating existing local rural interest groups.[93]

It has been suggested that the NSDAP should have enjoyed success in Württemberg because of its social structure and confessional allegiances. Certainly, with two-thirds of the population Protestant, the party could perhaps have hoped for greater than average popular support.[94] Yet in neighbouring Baden, where 58 per cent of the population was Catholic, the National Socialists enjoyed better electoral fortunes than in Württemberg.[95] Several reasons can be adduced to explain the Nazis' relatively unimpressive electoral performance there. The liberal tradition, the success of the parliamentary system at *Land* level, the ability of the region's economy to weather the depression, and, not least, the ineffectual and factious regional and local NSDAP leadership all contributed.[96] In addition, Württemberg's Protestants belonged to an identifiable social milieu which was strongly characterised by Pietism, which inhibited the spread of National Socialism's militant creed of xenophobia and violence.[97] Many of Württemberg's Protestants already had well-established political allegiances: while there was strong localised support during the 1920s for national political parties such as the SPD and the German Democratic Party (DDP) – the latter with strongholds in the towns of Heilbronn and Reutlingen, for example – there was also a regional political party, the Bauern-und Weingärtnerbund (Farmers' and Winegrowers' Association – BWB), which had been founded in 1893 and appealed especially to Protestant small farmers.

The BWB was particularly strong in Evangelical areas of north-eastern Württemberg, and from 1924 it was a member of the *Land*'s governing coalition; its stance was one of opposition to national political parties and to the government in Berlin, reflecting the parochialism of its target constituency. The BWB was explicitly opposed to socialism of any kind, as its election campaign literature demonstrated; some of its political propaganda was also emphatically antisemitic. In the 1928 *Land* elections, in communities of fewer than 2000 people the BWB was the most popular party with 34 per cent of the vote, compared with the Centre's 30 per cent and the SPD's 14 per cent. At this time, the BWB campaigned energetically against the NSDAP, whose leaders hoped to make inroads into its support.[98] It also challenged the Centre for the Catholic rural vote, with some success.[99] Nevertheless, while it mustered between 17 and 20 per cent of the vote consistently between 1920 and 1928, thereafter the BWB's support declined sharply, to 11 per cent in the *Landtag* election of April 1932 and to 7 and 8 per cent in the July and November *Reichstag* elections, respectively.[100] Participation in the *Land* government, which was capable of doing little to mitigate the severe crisis of the early 1930s, may well have cost it some support. There can be no doubt that, in the years after 1928, some of the BWB's erstwhile voters transferred their support to the Nazis, particularly in 1932–33. The national parties which fared best in the Württemberg-Hohenzollern electoral district were the SPD and the Centre Party. The SPD's votes came mainly, although not exclusively, from the towns whereas the Centre's appeal was strongly conservative and particularly oriented towards rural Catholics. With 30 per cent of Württemberg's population Catholic, the Centre easily amassed between 19 and 23 per cent of the vote in all Reich and *Land* elections between 1924 and 1932, confirming the persistence of a traditional allegiance.[101] Yet in 1928 it lost rural votes to the BWB, as some voters felt the need to be represented as farmers or rural traders rather than as Catholics.[102] If Württemberg Catholics' loyalty to the Centre was diminishing by the later 1920s – with 72 per cent of them supporting it in 1924 and 60 per cent in 1928 – these figures were still well in excess of the Reich average for Catholic support for the Centre.[103]

Only with the Landtag election in April 1932 did the NSDAP become the most popular party in Württemberg. In the 1928 elections its impact there had been negligible, at a time when the Protestant rural vote for the conservative German Nationalists (DNVP) was collapsing nationally.[104] While it made progress after that, its performance lagged well behind its Reich average. In neither the Reichstag nor the Landtag elections in 1928 could the NSDAP muster quite 2 per cent of the vote in Württemberg as a whole, while, out of the thirty-five German electoral districts, the NSDAP's worst results of all in the 1930 Reichstag election were in district 31, Württemberg and Hohenzollern. Additionally, whereas it obtained almost 10 per cent of the vote in Stuttgart and between 13 and 22 per cent of the vote in the towns of Ulm, Esslingen, Tübingen and Ludwigsburg, it could attract barely 8 per cent of the vote in communities of 2000 or fewer and only 6 or 7 per cent in the towns of Heilbronn, Göppingen, Gmünd and Reutlingen.[105] In April 1932, however, the NSDAP won 26.4 per cent of the vote, entitling it to twenty-three out of the eighty seats in the Landtag, whereas previously it had held none. As recently as the Reichstag election of September 1930 it had secured only 9 per cent of the vote in Württemberg, but in April 1932 the NSDAP emerged as the strongest force in thirty-one of the sixty-two electoral districts.

The 1932 Landtag election was, therefore, a landmark for the Württemberg NSDAP, particularly in witnessing its belated breakthrough in rural areas: it made its greatest gains in communes with fewer than 2000 inhabitants. This was a reward for its strongly targeted propaganda which spoke in apocalyptic terms of Hitler rescuing the peasantry and of 'the disdain for the peasantry in the present-day German state'. It has been argued that the particularly acute effects of the depression in rural eastern Württemberg contributed to this success. Certainly, animal husbandry in the north east was working at very low profit margins, and sometimes even at a loss, whereas in north-western rural areas, which were closer to the main industrial centres, conditions were better and support for the NSDAP accordingly lower. Both of these regions were predominantly Protestant, suggesting that religion was not of itself a major factor. Nevertheless, in many places the BWB's losses were the NSDAP's gains, while the Centre Party scored solidly, maintaining its number of Landtag seats at seventeen. For example, in Wangen, in the south east, one of its strongholds, the Centre received 70 per cent of the votes.[106]

The BWB blamed its eclipse, from sixteen seats in the Landtag to nine, on 'uncommonly spiteful and forceful agitation by the National Socialists'. Particularly galling was that the NSDAP overtook it in some areas which had been BWB strongholds, especially in north-eastern districts where in some cases more than half of the BWB's supporters transferred their allegiance to the NSDAP. For example, in Gerabronn county, 53 per cent of electors voted for the NSDAP in April 1932.[107] Nevertheless, the BWB was not the only party to lose ground to the NSDAP: the SPD and the liberal and nationalist parties also sustained losses, with the KPD the only other party able to improve its position, from six to seven *Landtag* seats. Further, in some electoral districts in north-western Württemberg the BWB managed not only to hold off the challenge from the NSDAP but to do so by an appreciable margin. Above all, the NSDAP failed to 'drive the regional peasant party out of the villages' as it had done in some other parts of Germany; it also failed to dislodge the Centre from Catholic villages. In communes of fewer than 2000 inhabitants, the BWB attracted, on average, over 20 per cent of the vote, the Centre Party almost 30 per cent, and the NSDAP some 25 per cent.[108]

Even in the two *Reichstag* elections of 1932, where the NSDAP obtained 37 and 33 per cent of the vote nationally, in Stuttgart the figures were as low as 27 and 23 per cent, while the figures for Württemberg as a whole were 30 and 26 per cent, respectively.[109] By this time, however, some overwhelmingly Evangelical rural counties in Württemberg were giving the NSDAP a majority of their votes. In July 1932, these included Gerabronn with 64 per cent, Nagold with 52 per cent, and Crailsheim with 51 per cent. Calw, Gaildorf and Öhringen each gave the NSDAP 50 per cent of their votes.[110] This was similar to Protestant rural areas elsewhere: in Stade, in the electoral district of Hanover East, for example, the NSDAP scored 59.5 per cent and 51.5 per cent of the valid votes cast in July and November 1932.[111]

In these two elections, however, the Centre could still score around 20 per cent of the vote in Württemberg.[112] Where a town such as Sigmaringen, in Hohenzollern, which was more than 90 per cent Catholic, gave the NSDAP strong support – its 19 per cent of the vote there was a good result for the NSDAP in 1930 – this was one of the exceptions that proved the rule that strongly Catholic areas were relatively resistant to the Nazi appeal. In July 1932, the counties of Ellwangen, Spaichingen and Schwäbisch Gmünd, for instance, gave the NSDAP only between 14 and 17 per cent of their votes.[113] In the Hohenzollern administrative district, where almost 95 per cent of the population was Catholic, while the NSDAP scored 22 per cent of the vote in the *Reichstag* election of July 1932, this looked less than impressive against the Centre Party's 61 per cent.[114] The strength of the Centre in Württemberg was illustrated by its consistent participation in the *Land* government and by the presence in the office of State President of the leading Centre Party politician, Eugen Bolz, from 1928 to 1933.[115] Only in the election of March 1933 did Württemberg's Catholics vote for the NSDAP in significant numbers. In the thirteen overwhelmingly Catholic counties, it won at least 37 per cent of the vote, against a *Land* average of 42 per cent. At the same time, however, a higher turnout enabled the Centre to increase its absolute number of votes, although its share of the vote sank to 16.9 per cent.[116]

If the NSDAP's electoral fortunes in Württemberg lagged behind those in most other areas of Germany up to 1933, the party membership's sluggish growth seemed to confirm that, comparatively, the party's history in Württemberg was one of relative failure.[117] Although Protestants – the majority – were more susceptible to the Nazi appeal than Catholics, nevertheless Württemberg was not a *Hochburg der Bewegung*, a stronghold of the movement. On the contrary, together with Baden, Württemberg has been described as a 'first stronghold of liberalism' in Germany.[118] The fact that in the 1920s the NSDAP was permitted to organise freely there, by contrast with some other *Länder*, testifies to liberalism – similar to that of the Russian Provisional Government of 1917 – rather than any sympathy for Nazism.[119] It was certainly true that large numbers of Württembergers were economically active as proprietors in agriculture and small commercial enterprises, along with their 'assisting family members'.[120] But to suggest that this predisposed them to Nazism is to subscribe to the now discredited thesis that there was overwhelming lower middle-class support for the NSDAP.[121] Apart from the fact that it is unhelpful to call farmers, rural artisans and their families 'lower middle-class', it is clear that their traditions and lifestyle predisposed them rather to Christian conservatism.

This helps to account for the slow growth of the NSDAP's organisation in Württemberg. The founding of local branches of the NSDAP in Stuttgart in 1920, Geislingen and Göppingen in 1922, and in Tübingen and Vaihingen, among other towns, in 1923, as well as the establishment of a unit of the SA in Tübingen in 1923, along with the early financial backing provided for Hitler by the Geislingen industrialist Heinrich Becker, proved to be a false start.[122] After the failed Munich *Putsch* of 9 November 1923, the prohibition of the NSDAP gave new life to other radical groups which were opposed to the political left, including the National Socialist German Freedom Movement (NSDFB). In Württemberg 'only the Stuttgart local branch aligned itself "unconditionally" behind' Hitler.[123] But, although the ban on the party nominally lasted until 1930, by the later 1920s the NSDAP had established branches in many of Württemberg's towns, including Esslingen, Geislingen, Nagold and Ulm, and in 1929 it acquired its first seat in the Württemberg *Landtag*. This seat was awarded to Christian Mergenthaler, an early NSDAP recruit who had, after the *Putsch*, become the Württemberg leader of the NSDFB and a member of the *Landtag* in that capacity, but who had in 1927 rejoined the NSDAP.[124]

Even if there were several lively NSDAP branches in the towns, until 1930 there was little coordination among the individual local branches, which were able to operate relatively independently.[125] In addition, there was very little Nazi penetration of Catholic and rural areas. At the beginning of 1932, in four southern Catholic counties there were 532 NSDAP members out of a total of some 120,000 inhabitants. They were organised in twelve overwhelmingly urban local branches.[126] And, while there tended to be a higher party membership in Evangelical counties, farmers were significantly underrepresented even in strongly Protestant rural areas. Clearly, the NSDAP was signally unsuccessful in recruiting members in the smallest communities, those of 2000 and under.[127] It may well have been true that 'tradition-minded South German farmers needed time in which to develop trust in a movement that had originated in a big city and was said to appeal to workers'.[128] Yet it does not seem that any growing 'trust' was translated into active membership of the party. Certainly, by the time of the *Reichstag* election in July 1932, there were almost 21,000 NSDAP members in Württemberg, organised in 430 local branches.[129] Yet the party's records showed, in 1935, that almost 80 per cent of *Gau* Württemberg-Hohenzollern's then NSDAP members had joined *after* the *Machtübernahme* (takeover of power) on 30 January 1933, making them the fourth most opportunist *Gau* party membership in Germany. Farmers, accounting for 37 per cent of Württemberg's population, joined in, bringing their share of the *Gau* party to just under 8 per cent in 1935, compared with 6 per cent on 30 January 1933, and 4 per cent in September 1930.[130] Nevertheless, not all of those who actively supported the NSDAP were members of it. For example, in July 1931 the local branch leader in Geislingen claimed to have over a hundred women working for the party, scarcely twenty of whom were members or would – in the straitened circumstances of the depression – be able to pay a subscription to join.[131]

Certainly, there were active local NSDAP branches in Württemberg before 1933, including Geislingen and Esslingen, the home base of *Gauleiter* Murr. In the relatively underdeveloped north east, the heavily Protestant Gerabronn county could in mid 1932 claim to have thirty-two local branches with around 900 party members.[132] At the opposite end of the *Land*, in the small country town of Trossingen in the south west, the proprietor of a thriving paper products firm, Fritz Kiehn, founded and led a local NSDAP branch in May 1930, and actively supported it with both his time and his money; for a time, he also served as the leader of the NSDAP in Tuttlingen district, to which the Trossingen local branch belonged. It was a great advantage to the party that, for the 1930 *Reichstag* election campaign, Kiehn's printing works produced NSDAP leaflets for the whole of *Gau* Württemberg-Hohenzollern. Yet Kiehn was an exception. Württemberg's employers, large and small, tended to remain aloof from the NSDAP, and his local branch remained before 1933 a small affair, with members coming largely from his own firm and a leadership in which his own family, including his wife, Berta, was strongly represented. Trossingen was one of the few pockets of firm support for the NSDAP in Württemberg, closely shadowing the party's electoral performance at national – rather than *Land* – level before 1933.[133]

After its national electoral successes in July and – rather less so – November

1932, the NSDAP was given its chance by conservatives keen to instal an authoritarian system. Yet, even after Hitler's *Machtübernahme* in Berlin on 30 January 1933, there seemed to be nothing inevitable about a Nazi takeover in Stuttgart. Certainly, the local Nazis were jubilant, but the caretaker government of Eugen Bolz – having lost its majority in 1932 – kept its nerve, refusing, for example, to implement in Württemberg the Law for the Protection of the People and the State of 28 February 1933 which abrogated fundamental liberties including freedom of speech, the press and association.[134] Nevertheless, after a bitter election campaign, in which *Land* government leaders including Bolz and Reinhold Maier fearlessly attacked the National Socialists, the results of the *Reichstag* election of 5 March 1933 narrowly gave the NSDAP and its allies over half of the votes cast. A spectacular rise in the NSDAP's vote in Württemberg, to 42 per cent, from 26.5 per cent in November 1932, was partly because the party waged a ruthless and propagandistically adroit campaign, using state radio – including public loudspeakers, even in some smaller communes – to get its message across. This seems to have brought out the vote to an unprecedented extent. The turnout in Württemberg had been several percentage points below the Reich average in the 1932 elections, but in March 1933 it was, at almost 86 per cent, a mere 2 per cent below it. One result of the increased turnout was that, for the first time, the NSDAP made significant gains in Catholic districts. While the Centre increased its vote, it saw its share of the vote decline from almost 20 per cent to barely 17 per cent. The impecunious BWB, which aligned itself with the NSDAP and the DNVP against parties such as the Centre with which it had served in government, lost both credibility and voters. In Gerabronn county – an extreme case – the NSDAP won almost 72 per cent of the vote.[135]

Three days after the election, the Reich government, acting under the terms of the Law for the Protection of the People and the State, appointed as emergency Reich Commissioner in Württemberg Dietrich von Jagow, NSDAP *Reichstag* member for Esslingen and leader of the Württemberg SA. He instituted a reign of terror in which his SA attacked and incarcerated opposition activists and Jews, with two hundred members of the KPD arrested in one night alone. The premises and property of the SPD and the KPD, in particular, were seized, and in Stuttgart Jagow organised a boycott of businesses owned by Jews. His SA established a concentration camp at Heuberg in southern Württemberg where, as early as April 1933, 1902 persons were held in 'protective custody'. Within nine months, the numbers incarcerated had risen to around 15,000, of whom forty died in custody as a result of torture and maltreatment.[136] By this time, a new National Socialist order had been installed in Stuttgart. With the KPD deputies barred from the *Landtag* after the *Reichstag* Fire on 27 February, and in the face of opposition from SPD deputies and abstentions by liberals and the Centre, Wilhelm Murr was elected State President on 15 March 1933.[137] Under the terms of the Law for the *Gleichschaltung* (coordination) of the *Länder* with the Reich of 31 March 1933, the membership of the *Landtag* – which had been elected in April 1932 – was forcibly altered to accord with the results of the *Reichstag* election of March 1933, which gave the NSDAP a much higher proportion of the seats. Indeed, with the KPD banned, this gave the NSDAP an outright majority. On 14 July, a law decreed that 'the National Socialist German Workers' Party constitutes the only political party in Germany'. All other national political parties had by this time been dissolved, although the BWB did not formally dissolve itself until 13 August 1933, a month later.[138] In October the *Landtag* itself was disbanded, and in December 1933 the political police in Württemberg were brought under the authority of Heinrich Himmler. In 1935 the administration of justice was removed from the *Länder* and centralised in the hands of the Reich Minister of Justice, Franz Gürtner; in the case of Württemberg, this was in the face of a protest by the incumbent Nazi Minister of Justice, Jonathan Schmid.[139]

The prickly Murr was not only an implacable foe of his political adversaries: he was also reluctant to hand over significant power to those NSDAP colleagues whom he regarded as rivals. But the shortcomings of leading National Socialists in Württemberg were obvious even to him, and, in the first instance, he retained under his own control the Interior and Economics ministries while handing over the *Kultministerium*, which embraced the portfolios for Education and Culture, including the churches, as well as the Ministry of Justice to the man he detested and feared, Christian Mergenthaler. Two months later, a redistribution left Mergenthaler as Minister President and *Kultminister*, with the Interior Ministry going to Dr Jonathan Schmid, who remained in that post until 1945 while also holding the Justice portfolio from 1933 to 1935 and the Economics portfolio from 1936 to 1945. The Nationalist, Dr Alfred Dehlinger, who had been Finance Minister in the Bolz government, retained his post until 1942, when he was succeeded by Karl Wilhelm Waldmann, who was from 1933 to 1945 State Secretary to Murr in his role as *Statthalter*. Murr and Mergenthaler felt that they were so short of experts that they even held exploratory talks with one of their most outspoken opponents, Reinhold Maier – whose wife was non-'Aryan' – with a view to offering him the Economics portfolio. But there were those in the party who felt that Murr himself was not a fit and proper person for the role of Württemberg's leader. The NSDAP district leader in Murr's home base, Esslingen, wrote to Murr in these terms, at the same time resigning from his post.[140]

Many who had voted for the NSDAP in the elections of 1932–33 had been desperately seeking a panacea for Germany's problems, and in particular, and most immediately, for the ravages of the depression. But there were other scars on the German body politic. The outcome of the First World War continued to rankle, partly because of the loss in international status that Germany was perceived to have suffered as a result, and partly because many Germans believed that, because their armies had not been decisively defeated in the field, Germany had been unjustly cast in the role of the vanquished power. Accordingly, one of the major attractions of the NSDAP's propaganda was the emphasis which it placed on 'national renewal'; there was also an equally attractive appeal to the idea of the 'national community'. Post-war Germany was a deeply divided country, with middle-class memories of attempted revolution in 1918–19 promoting paranoia in some quarters. Some groups of industrial workers demonstrated at times a militancy which was more than matched by the hardline stance of their employers. Many non-proletarians, not least in rural Germany, were affronted by the Weimar Republic's 'social state' (*Sozialstaat*), in which trade unions had a degree of power and a high profile, while taxation was raised to fund social welfare benefits, which mainly accrued to urban workers, and – it was often complained – a swollen bureaucracy to administer these and much else.

The rise of the KPD in the depression years was a source of acute anxiety to the God-fearing, law-abiding, property-owning classes – including small farmers – while the prominence of the SPD, with its Marxist programme, generated fears disproportionate to its lack of genuine radicalism. The Evangelical and Roman Catholic churches were both outspoken in their hostility to the parties of the left and shrill and persistent in their warnings about the perceived threat of a communist insurrection in Germany of the kind that had been staged in Russia in October 1917. On the left, there certainly were fears of 'fascism', but for an increasing number of non-proletarians, and for some proletarians also, the ideal of a 'national community', in which differences would allegedly be resolved without class warfare, was desperately welcomed. For many of the casualties of the depression their last hope was that the populist Hitler could work the kind of miracle that Republican politicians, even when using authoritarian powers in the years 1930–33, had signally failed to produce.[141]

One fundamental Nazi policy which was at least implicit, and often explicit, in its propaganda about 'national renewal' was racial antisemitism. There can be no doubt that this attracted some members and voters to the NSDAP, although during the crisis of the depression there were more desperate material reasons for the NSDAP's appeal. In Württemberg, there was a degree of antisemitism in the rural north east, particularly; this area was, before 1933, both a stronghold of the BWB and severely economically depressed. Antisemitism there has been attributed to 'the important role played [by] the considerable number of Jewish livestock dealers'. Yet when the regime attempted to prevent Württemberg's farmers from trading with Jews, it encountered disobedience. In the towns with the largest Jewish populations – Göppingen, Heilbronn and Stuttgart – antisemitism was insignificant. The poor showing of the NSDAP in elections there, including the election in March 1933, seemed to confirm that. Even in the Nazi stronghold of Gerabronn, in December 1931 a Jew received the highest vote in an election to a local agricultural trades association. Nevertheless, there were antisemitic demonstrations in the Hohenlohe region in March 1933, demonstrations which some individual members of the clergy attempted to stop.[142]

Nationally, the outbreak of uncontrolled violence by the SA, in particular, in the months following Hitler's takeover of power focused on known members of the SPD and KPD, and on Jews. The official boycott of Jewish shops and businesses on 1 April 1933 was primarily intended to canalise the activism of the zealots. Within a week of it, a law was passed which targeted political opponents and most Jews in the public service: they were to be summarily dismissed.[143] These events occurred even before the creation of the one party state in July 1933. Many other acts of discrimination against and harassment of Jews followed, including the infamous Nuremberg Laws of September 1935.[144] By these means and many others, including the 'Aryanisation' of businesses owned by Jews, the exclusion of Jews from Nazified associational life and the exclusion of Jewish children from schools attended by other Germans, Jews were progressively marginalised and segregated from 'Aryan' German society. At local level in Württemberg, NSDAP functionaries harassed Jews and threatened gentiles who associated with them or transacted business with them. Many Jews, particularly in the younger age groups, saw no alternative to emigration; this was particularly true in Württemberg's rural areas where, by the later 1930s, mainly the elderly remained.[145]

The solution of the perceived 'Jewish problem' was an explicit and constant aim of the NSDAP, although what form it would take had not been conceived by the time Hitler became Chancellor. Equally, it was not clear in 1933 what kind of relationship the Nazi regime would have with the churches. Initially, the regime aimed to subvert the Evangelical Church by sponsoring the strongly pro-Nazi group of self-styled German Christians – with their creed of 'positive Christianity' – within it. Those who congregated in their ranks in the early 1930s believed that National Socialism and Christianity were naturally symbiotic, and that the devolved Evangelical Church, which existed as a confederation of twenty-eight Landeskirchen (Land churches), should be centralised in one Reich church under a single leadership, in keeping with the Nazi Führerprinzip (leadership principle). Styling themselves 'the SA of Jesus Christ', German Christians fully accepted the authoritarian and racial premises of the NSDAP, rejecting both the Old Testament and the apostle Paul as 'Jewish', and adopting an 'Aryan paragraph' which stated: 'He who is not of Aryan descent or who is married to a person not of Aryan descent may not be called as clergyman or official of the general church government'.[146] During 1933, another group of Evangelical pastors took a stand against the German Christians' perversion of church doctrine, and especially against the 'Aryan paragraph'. They formed the Confessing Church, which maintained Evangelicals' traditional doctrines and theological training of pastors in the face of German Christian politicising encroachments.[147] While the Evangelical *Landeskirchen* were rent by these divisions, the Catholic Church was more monolithic, as an international church which had, in Germany up to July 1933, its own national political party, the Centre. Nevertheless, there were divisions of opinion within its ranks: for example, many in the Catholic clergy were content to see the Centre Party sacrificed in the negotiations between Hitler's regime and the Vatican that resulted in the Reich Concordat in July 1933.[148]

At first, high profile members of the clergy, hoping to roll back the tide of secularism which had been rampant since 1918, believed that the common interest in suppressing the left that they shared with the National Socialists would help to ensure protection for the churches. The incautious welcome given to the advent of the Nazi regime in general, and to the assumption of the education portfolio by Minister President Mergenthaler in particular, by the Catholic teachers' association in Württemberg seems in retrospect to epitomise the naïvety of some Christians in the face of an unashamedly dictatorial party.[149] As Evangelical church president in Württemberg, Bishop Wurm, an elderly conservative nationalist, and a former representative of the German National People's Party in the Württemberg *Landtag*, at first gave the National Socialists the benefit of the doubt.[150] In the vote within the Evangelical Church for a Reich bishop, a centralising innovation, in May 1933, he even supported Ludwig Müller, a leading German Christian, against his anti-centralist opponent, Bodelschwingh, in the hope of achieving peace and harmony in the church in Württemberg, where German Christians were proving a disruptive force. He could hardly have been more deluded. Eventually realising this, in March 1934 he, together with Evangelical Bishop Meiser of Bavaria, refused further cooperation with Reich Bishop Müller, who wanted nothing less than the *Gleichschaltung* of the independent *Land* churches into a centralised Reich church. When a vote was taken on this issue in September 1933, 82 per cent of Württemberg's pastors supported Wurm's anti-centralising stance. Only 8 per cent opposed him, with the remaining 10 per cent undecided.[151] This ensured that the Evangelical Church in Württemberg would retain its independent identity and that, by contrast with the churches of the Old Prussian Union and the Evangelical Church in Saxony and Thuringia, it would not be dominated by the German Christians.

Wurm's initial desire to conciliate the German Christians was misplaced – as he came to realise – on two counts. First, the German Christians would not compromise. Their allegiance to Hitler, their acceptance of the racist precepts of National Socialism and their ambition to oust Evangelical leaders who did not subscribe to these views were non-negotiable and were reinforced by the readiness of the *Gestapo* to act against dissidents.[152] Secondly, however, in Württemberg the German Christians were far from being the powerful force that they were further north. In Trossingen, for example, there were only some twenty to thirty German Christians.[153] In Tübingen, an Evangelical stronghold, the German Christians initially enjoyed a prominent position, not least because of pressure from the *Gau* and *Kreis* NSDAP leaderships. Yet this was quickly eroded by power struggles within their ranks which led to a loss of confidence in the local leadership. By autumn 1933, a moderate group of Tübingen pastors was distancing itself from the factious German Christian leadership, resulting in the secession of a number of the most prominent clerics and theologians in the district, several of whom even joined the new Pastors' Emergency League, the nucleus of the Confessing Church, if only temporarily. This did not, however, signify disenchantment with Hitler's regime; it was solely a result of the incompetence and infighting in the German Christian camp.[154]

In the Catholic Church, the complacency with which the conclusion of the Reich Concordat between the Vatican and the Nazi regime in July 1933 was regarded by many of the clergy was badly shaken when the regime hastened to violate the Concordat's terms.[155] The total claim of the Nazi state on 'Aryan' Germans was entirely at odds with the concessions made to the Catholic Church, which permitted the continued existence of Catholic non-political organisations at a time when *Gleichschaltung* was effecting the dissolution or Nazi takeover of both secular social and cultural groups and the Evangelical youth groups.[156] On 7 February 1934 the Württemberg Evangelical youth organisations were absorbed into the HJ.[157] While some were opposed to this, others welcomed it enthusiastically, mostly because they believed Nazi promises that they would retain their identity and enjoy a leading role in national youth work.[158] It would soon become evident that this was a false prospectus. With the Protestants apparently neutralised, local Nazi activists felt empowered to harass or dissolve forcibly Catholic social groups, especially church youth associations. Neither anticlerical *Kreisleiter* nor members of the *Gau* leadership were inclined to rein them in.[159]

While there was a limited preview of future Nazi policies towards both Jews and the churches in 1933–34, the burning priority for Hitler's government was to provide remedies to the problems caused by the depression, and, in particular, to offer more than election promises to the millions of Germans who were unemployed. Even if its chosen policy for agriculture was 'to grant [it] a position of preference and encouragement, easing its burden of debt and interest and promoting it in every possible manner', the regime's immediate priority was to find a way of working millions of men – especially men rather than women – into jobs, and above all into jobs in the areas worst hit by the depression, which included the construction industry and the iron and steel trades.[160] After three years of Nazi rule, and by means that were sometimes at least unconventional and possibly even fraudulent, the unemployment figures had been reduced to pre-1930 levels; in 1938, indeed, there was effectively full employment, with staff shortages in some areas.[161] While the industrial recovery may have brought Hitler's government more or less grudging acceptance even from some formerly neutral or hostile urban workers, criticism was soon aired about the government's policies towards the chronic problems facing agriculture. It was not that agriculture was viewed as being marginal to the leadership's power-political objectives.[162] On the contrary, it was precisely the indispensability of the food-producing sector, as a support service for the urban population, that made the government determined to exert central control over agricultural production and distribution virtually from the start, with increasing state intervention, under the Four Year Plan of 1936, to promote autarky and prepare Germany to withstand the domestic strains of war, always with the memory of the unrest in the last two years of the First World War in mind.[163]

The Nazi regime's chosen instrument of control in this area was the *Reichsnährstand* (RNS – Reich Food Estate), which was founded on 13 September 1933 under the leadership of the NSDAP's *Reichsbauernführer* (Reich Farmers' Leader), Walther Darré, who had already become Reich Minister for Food and Agriculture in June. By September 1933, Darré had brought under his control the existing agricultural organisations – which had in many areas been thoroughly infiltrated by his Agrarian Policy Apparatus – as part of the new regime's *Gleichschaltung* of all political and organisational life under Nazi leadership. In their place, he had already established regional offices of the RNS, the *Landesbauernschaften* (LBS – regional farmers' groups). In Württemberg, Alfred Arnold from Künzelsau district, the new *Landesbauernführer* (LBF – *Land* farmers' leader) of the LBS Württemberg and Hohenzollern, which had been established in June 1933, attended the final congress of the BWB on 13 August 1933, after which it was announced that 'henceforth the only professional organisation for farmers is the *Landesbauernschaft*'.[164] Many small farmers welcomed the creation of the RNS. They hoped that it would provide them with a strong and unified pressure group to represent their interests and enhance the profile of agriculture in a way that had been sorely lacking in the decades of rapid industrialisation. Darré certainly gave the impression that this was his intention – and perhaps it genuinely was – but the priorities of the regime, in particular the securing of self-sufficiency in food supplies, ensured that the RNS would be less a champion of farmers' interests than an instrument for controlling them.[165]

From 1 January 1934, membership of the RNS was obligatory for all farmers and proprietors engaged in forestry, fishing, hunting, viticulture and horticulture in Württemberg, along with their 'assisting family members' and employees, as well as members of trade associations and anyone involved in the processing, wholesale or retailing of agricultural produce.[166] The RNS was, therefore, given a monopoly which encompassed all of those involved in agricultural production and distribution in a mammoth corporation envisaged as the rural counterpart of the German Labour Front, the mass organisation into which urban workers from different political and trades union traditions – and from none – had been forcibly merged in May 1933. This was, however, a recipe for characteristic Nazi jurisdictional disputes between the two combines. In the Württemberg Labour Front organisation, for example, one of around twenty 'occupational sections' was for 'agriculture'.[167] This was a direct challenge to the LBS's competence. There was also rivalry between the Nazi women's organisation (*NS-Frauenschaft* – NSF) and the RNS, with the NSF's leadership in no doubt that its brief was to organise German women as a whole and the RNS claiming the right to organise women engaged in agriculture and rural trades.[168]

Also characteristic of the Nazi system was the organisational asymmetry caused by the division of the RNS into nineteen LBS, whereas there were seventeen *Länder* in the Reich and, until 1938, thirty-two *Gaue* of the NSDAP. Similarly, while there were sixty-one (from 1938, thirty-seven) administrative districts in Württemberg, the LBS Württemberg-Hohenzollern was divided into fifteen, and later twenty, *Kreisbauernschaften* (KBS – district farmers' groups), each with three or four subdivisions.[169] Darré's intention may have been to safeguard the RNS's organisational autonomy, but the chief effects of this asymmetry were a multiplication of the bureaucratic structures of the Third Reich and the potentiation of jurisdictional infighting. The LBS Württemberg and Hohenzollern (soon to drop the 'Hohenzollern' from its title) quickly developed a mammoth bureaucracy and a modern managerial style, with its own corporate identity, logo and two versions of headed notepaper. The exhaustive detail of both office procedures and the language of written communication demonstrated the Nazi obsession with hierarchical structures. For example, written messages directed 'to a superior office will be called "reports", to an office of equal status "communications", and to an inferior office a "decree" or an "order". Superior and equivalent offices will be "requested", inferior offices "required"'. The use of the official stamp, bearing the words 'Reichsnährstand, Landesbauernschaft Württemberg', was restricted to a small group of elite LBS managers who were responsible for ensuring that it was not used inappropriately.[170]

The LBS had its own press and radio officers, its own publications' unit and an archive and library. Its sections included 'The Man', with subsections for farmers large and small, foresters, gardeners, winegrowers and fishermen, as well as employees of various kinds. There was also 'The Woman', who was 'the guardian of the peasant's bloodline' and 'the guardian of the peasant's spiritual heritage', as well as being responsible for promoting village culture. There were separate subsections for young men and young women, for settlers and for both vocational training and ideological instruction. In pride of place, in section one, subsection one of the LBS's organisation, whose leader had a doctorate, was the 'blood and soil' question, which encompassed research into peasant lineages as well as peasant cultural issues. There was also an officer deputed to devise ways of honouring the peasant as the life blood of the nation. All aspects of growing crops, tending animals and marketing produce had their own trade associations; these figured as subsections with specialist officials in the LBS office. There were also subsections for agricultural machines and buildings, and for the conservation of woods. The section for 'home economics' in rural households challenged the monopoly of the NSF over women's activities, but it was regarded as an integral aspect of farming life.[171]

The individual trade associations, too, were dense bureaucracies with sections and subsections, each with a dedicated staff. The LBS's Livestock Trade Association, for example, had a governing council based in Stuttgart. Its members and their deputies were appointed from the various interest groups for producers, livestock wholesalers, retailers, consumers, butchers and fat processors. The Livestock Trade Association had its own price commission, composed of appointees from the groups of producers, slaughterers, distributors and consumers. There was, similarly, a marketing council.[172] The members of these commissions and councils were closely politically vetted by the relevant NSDAP *Kreisleiter* to ensure that they were utterly reliable. This applied even to NSDAP members who were nominated for such functions. For example, in February 1938 Arnold confirmed that the Stuttgart *Kreisleiter* had approved the appointment of a particular party member 'as representative of consumers on the council of the marketing association'.[173] Under such conditions, how 'representative' he was of consumers is a matter for extreme doubt. By 1936, the trade association's leader presided over the district leaders of the various interest groups who belonged to the KBS offices in Württemberg. By 1943, the hierarchy reached down to the subsections of the KBS, where there were 'liaison officers'.[174] There were trade associations for producers of other kinds, including the Württemberg Milk and Fats Trade Association and the Württemberg Egg Trade Association. These trade associations were responsible for supervising all aspects of production and distribution, and for ensuring that farmers met the production quotas imposed on them. This would become a particularly vital concern during the war.

The RNS was given specific priorities. Ideologically, its aim was to protect and strengthen the 'German peasant'. From the point of view of the NSDAP's population policies, 'the peasants [were] valued as the "chief promoters of racial and hereditary health". Economically, they contributed to the achievement of "nutritional autarky", and from the military point of view they were regarded as the "backbone of armed strength"'.[175] The RNS was charged with encouraging Germans to settle on the land and to become productive farmers, protecting farmers against foreclosure for indebtedness, and setting official prices for their produce, to ensure that small farmers could count on a reliable income. The second and third of these were practical measures which relieved many small farmers of the pressures under which they had laboured in the depression. This bolstering of the small farmer was geared to guaranteeing production in order to make Germany less reliant on – and if possible independent of – foreign imports and save precious foreign currency. It was not all rhetoric: in the first two years of Nazi rule, agricultural prices rose markedly. The result was that, although industry in Württemberg had suffered less from the economic crisis than elsewhere in the Reich and had recovered more quickly, in 1936 industrial workers felt keenly the higher prices which they had to pay for food, which amounted to 'a reduction in real wages'. Yet the price rises varied from one commodity to another, rarely reaching the level of real prices before the First World War. Forestry was an exception, as the prices for wood rose markedly, while the sale of animals, and particularly of sheep's wool, was clearly profitable.[176]

The *quid pro quo* for government support for agriculture was government intervention in agricultural production, and in rural life generally. One aspect of this was the law of entailment, the *Reichserbhofgesetz* of 29 September 1933, which enforced single-heir inheritance on the farms involved and outlawed both the alienation and the mortgaging of a family's land: the family was to hold the land in perpetuity, thus safeguarding the numbers of the 'healthy peasants' who were the backbone of the nation. On the other hand, siblings of the single heir were effectively disinherited, with the latter not permitted to borrow money – using the farm as collateral – at a time when the effects of the depression meant that they had no other means of compensating siblings for losing all rights to the farm. Women, whether wives or daughters, were at a clear disadvantage under the new law, although their position was slightly ameliorated under modifications made to the original law during the following ten years. Those owners eligible to become *Erbhofbauer* (hereditary farmers) had – in theory, at least – to own farms of between 7.5 and 125 hectares, the majority of which were in northern and eastern Germany.[177] In Baden, only 16.6 per cent of farms were large enough to qualify as 'hereditary farms'; in the small village of Oberschopfheim, for example, no farm was eligible.[178] The *Erbhof* law had greater applicability in Bavaria, where it caused massive rural discontent.[179] In Württemberg, by mid 1938, 16,366 farms of between 7.5 and 20 hectares and 7325 farms of between 20 and 125 hectares, as 55.2 per cent and 93.5 per cent of those in these two categories of size, respectively, had become *Erbhöfe*.[180]

However impressive these figures may seem, it was nevertheless the case that, under the letter of the law, large numbers of farms in Württemberg were disqualified, including both the small or dwarf holdings of part-time farmers and the fragmented farms of those in areas of partible inheritance. Yet it seems that size did not necessarily matter. For example, some 400 farms in the KBS Künzelsau were considered ineligible, more than 80 per cent of them on the grounds that they were uneconomic concerns, although they mostly met the minimum size requirement.[181] By contrast, in the KBS Stuttgart in July 1939, the Stuttgart-Amt section had eleven *Erbhöfe*, only two of which were over 7.5 hectares, at 13 and 15 hectares. The remainder were between 5.5 and seven hectares in size, significantly below the legal minimum. Similarly, in the Esslingen section of the KBS Stuttgart, the *Erbhöfe* weighed in at between five and twenty-three hectares, with the vast majority at between five and 7.5 hectares.[182] On the other hand, in Hochmössingen, in Rottweil district, during the war there were farms of eight hectares whose proprietors remained *Landwirte* (farmers) as opposed to *Bauern* (peasant farmers), the term of honour officially reserved for those with an *Erbhof*.[183]

The other planks of Darré's reform programme for agriculture involved controls on the production and distribution of farm produce, under the supervision of a corps of farmers' leaders who were directly responsible to the RNS through chains of command based on the *Führerprinzip* (leadership principle), a system of 'line management'.[184] The RNS's regional leadership was drawn from the Agrarian Policy Apparatus, and the 'hierarchy continued on down through *Land*, *Kreis* and local farm leaders. Thus Darré concentrated in his hands the vocational, state and party control of agriculture'.[185] In Württemberg, the twenty *Kreisbauernführer* reported to *Landesbauernführer* Arnold and were themselves in authority over large numbers of *Ortsbauernführer* (OBF – local farmers' leaders), who were, at least nominally, responsible for the implementation of Nazi agricultural policy at local level.[186] This meant advising farmers in their locality and also policing them to ensure that they complied with the state's requirements. Yet OBF were members of a commune, even if their remit made them responsible for more than one commune. In many cases they remained sensitive to the needs of the rural population and the rhythms of their life. For example, in Nürtingen the local branch NSDAP leader sent a reminder on 24 May 1935 to the leaders of all Nazi formations in his branch about the requirement that they submit to him on the twenty-third of each month their plan of events for the following month. The OBF in Nürtingen replied that, as he had previously indicated, there would be no special *Reichsnährstand* events in the six summer months – that is, the growing season – apart from two field inspections which did not, in any case, have to be reported.[187]

The RNS was prepared to offer farmers assistance with land improvement, always with the aim of raising productivity. The poor quality of some of Württemberg's soil was attributable to a shortage of water in some places and an excess of it in others. The *Sicherheitsdienst* (SD – Security Service) reported in April 1939 that 'the first problem for Württemberg is its shortage of water', mentioning that projects were under way to divert water from the upper Danube or upper Iller into the River Neckar in order to make good the deficit in some agricultural communes.[188] In north-eastern Württemberg, the Hohenlohe Water Supply Group tried to provide enough water for thirty-one communes and several satellite communes in the districts of Crailsheim and Mergentheim with agricultural land amounting to 33,000 hectares. The need for a reliable water supply was particularly pressing because of the high density of farm animals in the region. It was estimated that there were over 28,000 cattle, more than 3000 horses, almost 25,000 pigs and some sheep. Here, the farmers could not themselves afford to install a piped water supply, and so the communes, together with the LBF, tried to ensure that at least a basic water supply was available.[189] This was bound to be a major operation that would take time, and after ten years of Nazi rule it was still the case that around 90 per cent of the communes in Crailsheim district were not linked to a piped water supply.[190]

Elsewhere, however, particularly in the south east, there were communes with boggy ground which required to be drained. The RNS provided both advice and small grants to help with this, sometimes paying for workers to carry out drainage projects, but sometimes depending on the cheap labour of the men's Labour Service. In January 1939, the RNS office in Ehingen gave its approval for the draining of an area of 15.9 hectares – about half and half meadow and field – belonging to eight hereditary farmers in one commune in Biberach district. This would allow the area to be cleared of the grasses and weeds to which a damp environment was hospitable, so that crops such as animal fodder and potatoes could flourish instead. The inspection of the area had been led by the chief of the Ehingen RNS office and the commune's OBF. The total cost of the project was estimated at 14,000 marks, of which the RNS would contribute a grant of 3500 marks. The balance would be paid by the farmers, who would borrow what they needed at a reasonably favourable rate. As they were proprietors of 'middling and large agricultural concerns', however, they would be able to reduce their costs by providing some of the labour for the project; otherwise, workers would be hired.[191] In a neighbouring commune, approval was given in March 1939 for the drainage of a comparable piece of land, which was owned by nineteen farmers – six of whom were hereditary farmers – and was regularly subject to flooding. This project was regarded as urgent because of the damage wrought by flood water on fodder crops in a commune with a substantial number of cattle on the land. The farmers here were clearly less prosperous, with the RNS sanctioning a 50 per cent grant, a long term loan – for twenty-eight and a half years – and the deployment of the Labour Service for the necessary work.[192]

To stimulate farming communities' consciousness of their heritage, Ortsbauernführer were encouraged to seek out pictures of old peasant dwellings, and aged peasant men and women in traditional dress were photographed for propaganda publications. Devising the elaborate ceremonies to honour families that had been settled on the same land for at least two hundred years was, however, not left to the discretion of lowly local officials. The RNS leadership itself decreed the conditions which families had to fulfil, inevitably including their 'German blood' and 'hereditarily healthy stock'. The provision of a family tree was obligatory. In addition, there had to be evidence that the family would continue to hold the land in the future, through an absence of debt and the presence of heirs. Families that qualified would be presented with a plaque – to be displayed prominently in the farmhouse thereafter – at a ceremony attended by Darré himself, if possible, and by dignitaries including the *Gauleiter*. The RNS was gratified that in 1935 the LBS Württemberg had been able to nominate 135 families from one commune, Neenstetten in Ulm district. Publicising the ceremony to honour these families attracted further applications from Württemberg. Other areas, however, had shown greater interest: none had provided more than Bavaria, with its 871 honoured families. A particularly memorable ceremony had also been held in Pomerania when an entire village had been honoured.[193] The families were encouraged to invite all of their relations, including those living in towns, to the ceremony, and to provide for display documents and artefacts attesting to their ancient lineage.[194]

LBS and KBS officials conscientiously dated their letters with Germanic instead of Latinate names for the months – 'Brachmond' for June, 'Heumond' for July, 'Ernting' for August, for example – although they often added the modern name in brackets.[195] The party at local level also manufactured or hijacked 'traditional' events and festivals, particularly at significant dates in the rural calendar, for example *Sonnenwendfeier*, the celebration of the summer solstice. The annual harvest festival, too, was commandeered as a national NSDAP event, with the massive Bückeberg rally held at Michaelmas in the years 1933–37; hundreds of thousands of villagers in regional costume were brought annually by trains of the Labour Front's 'Strength Through Joy' project to this cosmetic display near Hanover, until rumours of war led to its being cancelled in 1938.[196] The corollary of this was that alternative harvest festivals were banned. There were also official village events, at which every effort was made to ensure that the party's formations were assigned a leading role, with young people from the *Hitlerjugend* (HJ – Hitler Youth) and *Bund Deutscher Mädel* (BDM – League of German Girls), as well as the NSDAP local branch leader and the OBF, prominent.[197] In Trossingen, Fritz Kiehn's daughter, Gretl, played a leading role as BDM leader and 'May Queen'.[198] The filming in some places of such events engendered great interest.[199]

After a brief honeymoon period in which farmers saw the prices for their produce rise, the full implications of Nazi management of agriculture became apparent. It might be too much to say that they amounted to a new *Zwangswirtschaft* in peacetime, yet coercion was inherent in the system and was explicitly to be used against recalcitrants. Those who breached the prices, production quotas or quality standards set by the RNS could be fined or sent to prison. The RNS also had the authority to close down shops or businesses.[200] This was the essence of the *Marktordnung* (market regulation), which was resented and sometimes resisted by farmers. In Stade district, all kinds and conditions of farmers were to be found among recalcitrants who failed to make the required deliveries of vegetables to the state collection depots: 'small farmers, large farmers or hereditary farmers, party members, mayors or even *Ortsbauernführer*, all contravened the delivery quotas that had been laid down'.[201] The delivery quotas of themselves were irksome to farmers who expected to be able to trade freely with consumers. They would, however, probably not have generated as much discontent among farmers in many parts of Germany had not the prices of vegetables, milk, eggs and other produce been fixed by the RNS at what farmers regarded as an intolerably low level.[202] Yet this was entirely within the logic of the regime's priorities, in a way that the *Erbhof* system was not. The aim of increasing the number of small and medium-sized farms, both through the *Erbhof* system and through encouragement to new settlers on the land, ran contrary to the requirements of both a modern industrial economy and a society with large numbers of urban dwellers for whom food needed to be produced efficiently and as cheaply as possible. The *Marktordnung*, on the other hand, complemented the urban economy by holding down food prices at a time of rising economic activity. This was intended to facilitate the maintenance of wage restraint in industry, which was a major government objective, yet the expansion of industrial production in Württemberg in the 1930s meant that holding down wages was possible only in sectors of the economy not directly related to rearmament.[203]

The RNS enjoyed some success in the 1930s, both in stemming the tide of rural misery and disaffection for a time and in imposing controls on farmers. Yet, at the same time, the priority given by industry to armaments production inhibited the manufacture of agricultural machinery that might have made small farms more cost effective.[204] The same priority meant that, as soon as the worst of the depression was over and industrial production expanded, there was a renewed migration from the countryside to the towns, with the result that the single most pressing problem on the land from the mid 1930s was a growing shortage of labour.[205] By the later 1930s, in some respects, the Nazi government was becoming the victim of its own success in combating the depression of the early 1930s. Whereas the most traumatic and intractable problem in January 1933, when Hitler was appointed Chancellor, had been unemployment levels running at well over six million, and perhaps as high as eight million, by contrast a potentially serious shortage of labour was already apparent in Germany *before* Hitler's regime launched the Second World War. This was particularly marked in Württemberg, where by 1939 average annual industrial growth rates for the period since 1933 stood at 12 per cent. An important reason for this was massive growth in the armaments industries, for example at the Dornier aircraft works in Friedrichshafen.[206] In the winter of 1938–39, employers in Württemberg's seasonal industries either sent their workers on paid holiday until the weather improved, or else had them undertake casual work, such as clearing snow, because they could not utilise them for normal purposes in winter conditions but were reluctant to lay them off and thus risk losing them altogether to another employer.[207] This was a far cry from the position in spring 1934, when persistently high levels of unemployment had led to jobless workers from Stuttgart being sent to rural areas to occupy themselves by helping out on the land.[208]

Recovery from the depression centred on the modern industrial sectors of the economy and brought little benefit to rural areas. For example, rural local authorities in Württemberg did not enjoy the post-depression upturn in tax receipts which accrued to the urban local authorities. They therefore remained impoverished, unable to mitigate hardship in their area and therefore unable to win popular support for the Nazi system.[209] Above all, recovery denuded rural communities of labour, to a disastrous extent, with the result that, by the later 1930s, communities of small farmers were under severe pressure, with remaining male and female agricultural workers, recognising their own scarcity value, holding out for higher wages.[210] As early as July 1936, the president of the regional Employment Office in south-west Germany reported to the Württemberg Interior Ministry that 'the shortage of labour in agriculture is this year extraordinarily acute'.[211] Further, in April 1937 it was reported that in Württemberg agriculture was short of 4000 permanent workers with a further 4000, in addition, likely to be needed at harvest time. It was a measure of this desperate situation that not only the Labour Service but also workers seconded from industry – in spite of the growing shortage of labour there – provided the majority of these temporary workers, while the *Wehrmacht* also helped out at harvest time.

The fundamental problem was the shortage of permanent, full-time workers on the land. The Württemberg Interior Ministry believed that the only solution was 'to arrest the flight from the land', particularly in the case of young people. Yet this was to be done chiefly by exhortation and propaganda campaigns by the party, the HJ and other Nazi formations, whose effectiveness in rural areas was limited. Beyond that, the 3000 youngsters who were, reportedly, waiting for vacancies for apprentices to occur in the metal industry in spring 1937 'are just sitting around at home. These people cannot be prevailed on to go into agriculture'.[212] As a result, the labour problem on the land became increasingly acute. In June 1939, it was estimated that German agriculture was short of 800,000 workers, with particularly large migrations from rural to urban communities in 1938. The losses were not spread evenly across agricultural concerns of all kinds and sizes; rather, the highest proportion came from small family farms. On farms of between five and 20 hectares, there were 38 per cent fewer males and 27 per cent fewer females in 1938 than there had been in 1935.[213]

The industrial upswing impinged more directly on some small communities than on others. For example, in the area around Friedrichshafen on the Bodensee, some villages saw their population increase. But this was not the result of an increase in the farming population; rather, skilled workers from all over Germany had been attracted by new opportunities in industries there. The shortage of housing in Friedrichshafen meant that these new workers had to find accommodation in villages and become commuters. At the same time, some inhabitants of these villages staged a 'flight from the land' without moving: they abandoned the struggle to try to make a living as small-scale proprietors in agriculture and became employees in someone else's business. Some workers in industry commuted huge distances, which made for a very long working day. The result was that wife and children were left to look after the small agricultural holding that most of them possessed. For example, between twenty-five and thirty workers made a daily round trip of 160 to 170 kilometres by bus from a commune in rural Biberach to Friedrichshafen. By the later 1930s, they were by no means exceptional. Where commuters lived at some distance from a bus stop or rail station, the distance that they had to walk or cycle only added to the length of their day. There was little respite: the chances were that they would take their annual holiday at harvest time to allow them to work full time on their holding at agriculture's busiest time of year.[214]

Government initiatives, such as military service for young men and Labour Service, as well as various other Nazi service schemes for both young men and young women, for example, *Landdienst* (Land Service), *Pflichtjahr* (year of compulsory service for girls), among others, only exacerbated the problems of agriculture by providing rural young people with both new perspectives and opportunities for escape from rural drudgery. It seemed that, once young people from rural society had tasted an alternative, they 'absolutely do not want to go back to the land and try every tactic to avoid agricultural work'. This was not peculiar to Württemberg, but it had particularly damaging effects on smallholders' prospects there. The SD reported sceptically in April 1939 the 'great success' that the Hitler Youth claimed to have been enjoying in recruiting young people into its *Landdienst* project, which accommodated them in camps in rural areas and sent them to work on farms for a year at a time. Forty-eight *Landdienst* camps had been opened in Württemberg, in which there were 530 boys and 296 girls, of whom a staggering 60 per cent were said to have agreed to remain in agriculture.[215] By July 1939, the Hitler Youth claimed that some 20,000 youngsters across Germany had volunteered for *Landdienst*. Given the kind of pressure exerted by Hitler Youth leaders on their charges to conform, the 'voluntary' nature of this recruitment needs to be viewed with considerable scepticism.[216] At the very same time, the SOPADE (Social Democratic Party in exile) was reporting that 'the result of intensive propaganda for the *Landdienst* is small. In the past year only 18,000 boys and girls [throughout Germany] volunteered for it. This year the deadline for recruitment was extended, and still there were no more than 25,000 recruits'.[217] In any case, the *Landdienst* could not accommodate even half of the numbers that the HJ claimed to have attracted because of a shortage of 'suitable leaders, especially for the girls' camps'. This was a sensitive issue because there had been frequent complaints about 'discipline leaving a lot to be desired' in the girls' camps, to the extent that parents in Ulm and Biberach districts had removed their daughters from them.[218]

For those adolescent girls not prepared to volunteer for, or to be pressured into, the *Landdienst* or the women's Labour Service, which also had problems of insufficient accommodation and leaders, the *Pflichtjahr*, introduced in February 1938, threatened them with conscription. There was little escape for those who had not married by the age of twenty-five, which was the upper age limit, although it was not unknown for a teenager to evade service on the pretext that keeping a window box or a garden vegetable patch amounted to cultivation of the land.[219] In February 1939, the SD expressed the hope that the introduction of the *Pflichtjahr* would bring at least some relief for the overburdened farmer's wife.[220] Two months later, however, they reported that eligible girls and their parents were using a variety of tactics to avoid a placement in a farmer's household and to obtain one in a home with only a few children. Parents made private arrangements with acquaintances, or advertised in the press for what they regarded as 'suitable' homes. The 'so-called better classes' were particularly adept at bending the system to their requirements.[221] As a result, the SD estimated that only about 3000 of the 6500 girls enrolled in the *Pflichtjahr* were employed in agriculture, although the intention had been to place two in every three there. The true position was even less favourable, because the employment offices counted placements in all rural households, including those of teachers, businessmen and government officials, as being 'in agriculture'. Any return accruing to farming communities from these kinds of 'national service' was of much less value than full-time workers would have been, while some rural young women, particularly, saw volunteering for Labour Service as a way of escaping from the drudgery of life as an 'assisting family member' on a farm.[222] The shortfall in agricultural labour was to be met by continuing to dragoon school and university students into helping with the harvest, while the SA was enlisted to help in some places and there was talk of seconding men from the Labour Service, the armed forces and even SS military units to agriculture at harvest time.[223]

The inescapable truth which threatened the very bases of Nazi assumptions was that, increasingly, Germans, and particularly young Germans, had no desire to submit to a life of poorly rewarded toil within an environment that was restrictive in ways that the towns – with their employment choices, facilities and abundant social opportunities – seemed not to be. The Labour Front was in no doubt that the flight from the land was 'predominantly an economic problem', with the incomes of small farmers and agricultural labourers lagging far behind those of industrial workers. Yet, beyond that, the spread of mass communications in the 1930s – even piecemeal to rural areas – afforded some rural dwellers, especially commuters to work in a nearby town, an insight into the breadth of choice and facilities that were available in Germany's towns and cities. For example, they could see how, in summer particularly, urban workers put in shorter hours than rural workers, and how 'working women stroll around in silk stockings and posh little boots, while a farmer's wife has to work her fingers to the bone from dawn till dusk'.[224] The plight of the small farmer's wife, with her long hours of labour-intensive work both on the farm and in the home, highlighted the disadvantages of life on the land, for women in particular.[225] Therefore, as industrial and commercial employment expanded, from the mid 1930s, there was renewed migration from the countryside to the towns; the migrants were mostly young men, but they were also increasingly young women from farming families who could observe the draining and early ageing effects of rural toil on their own mothers.[226] Another sign of the reluctance of young women to become trapped in rural drudgery was their documented unwillingness to marry farmers or their sons.[227] If substantial numbers of Germans remained on the land in 1939, the disillusionment of a conspicuous proportion of the young, especially, with the hard grind and poor rewards there suggested that the days of the small family farm as the basic unit of Württemberg's rural society were numbered. The Nazi regime's attempt to halt the tide by means of the *Erbhof* system was a rearguard action which was unlikely to prevent the continued flight from the land, and, indeed, encouraged it by disinheriting younger siblings.

All of this amounted to a structural flaw in Nazi agrarian policy, which meant that the regime's top priority for agriculture was not realistic. Certainly, self-sufficiency was achieved during the 1930s in cereals, but in other commodities, especially fats, Germany remained uncomfortably dependent on imports. It was this that made Hitler's regime all the more determined to acquire 'living space' in agriculturally rich areas of eastern Europe.[228] The SD in Württemberg actually referred to this prospect as early as April 1939: 'If the Reich can, in the near future, provide its supplies of vegetables and potatoes from the fertile territories of the east (Ukraine) ...'[229] Attempts to halt the flight from the land were ineffective as industry expanded, and in 1939 the SD reported – perhaps extravagantly – that the small Württemberg farmer was becoming a member of an endangered species. This, according to the SD, made the countryside a fertile ground for opponents of the National Socialist state, who 'are increasingly locating their

activities almost exclusively in rural areas' in Württemberg.[230] Yet many farmers
and other rural inhabitants had no more time for opposition, beyond perennial
grumbling, than they had for Nazi Party activities. Labour Front researchers
raised concern about how commuters were not able to avail themselves of the
recreational facilities of its 'Strength through Joy' project. Nor, they added, had
commuters time for political meetings, film shows or other events, or even to
read books or magazines. 'All the efforts of our era to make the achievements of
culture and civilisation available to as broad a range of the population as possible
are illusory in the case of commuters', they lamented.[231]

It was probably not only a shortage of time and energy that prevented more
than a small minority of farmers and commuters in Württemberg from pursuing
the heavily politicised leisure activities mounted by the NSDAP and its associated
agencies. Members of a commune already had, before 1933, an introverted social
life which tended, particularly in Catholic areas, to focus on their church. While
a local inn or tavern, too, might provide a focal point for communal festivities
and recreation, the weekly habits of church attendance and participation in
church associations for men, women and young people, together with the annual
cycle of church-centred festivals deriving from the rhythms of agriculture and
the commune's traditions, gave villagers a sense of belonging to a community
whose values were timeless and whose members were self-reliant but also, in
time of adversity, mutually supportive. During the 1930s, the NSDAP tried to
supplant the churches at local level while at the same time attempting to control
them at Reich and *Land* level. The party regarded the churches as competitors
whose room for manoeuvre should be squeezed to the utmost, especially in
terms of clerical influence over the young. The regime's conduct of a range of
policies gave the clear impression that it was bent on eradicating church influence
from the life of the community, which provoked mounting unease in both of
Württemberg's major denominations. Particularly from the later 1930s, there
was louder criticism of the regime's policies from Württemberg's church leaders,
Theophil Wurm, Evangelical *Landesbischof* (bishop of *Land* Württemberg), and
Joannes Baptista Sproll, the Roman Catholic bishop of Rottenburg, than there
was from most other members of both hierarchies in Germany.[232]

Before the war, the issue that did most to shock Catholics in Württemberg
and beyond was the expulsion of Bishop Sproll of Rottenburg. From 1934, Sproll
was prepared to voice criticism of the regime on a limited range of issues, but the
catalyst for official action against him was his refusal to vote in the plebiscite on
the *Anschluss* with Austria in 1938, not because he disapproved of the *Anschluss*
but because support for it was portrayed by the regime as endorsement of it,
its leaders and its policies. In a sustained campaign in Württemberg's Nazi
newspapers, *Reichsstatthalter* Murr called for his removal.[233] Undoubtedly in
response to this, a crowd of Nazi thugs, including the Reutlingen *Kreisleiter*

(district NSDAP leader), Otto Sponer, attacked Sproll's residence, enabling Murr to expel him from Württemberg on the specious grounds that his presence was a threat to law and order.[234] Endorsing Murr's decision, the Reich Churches' Minister, Hanns Kerrl, characterised Sproll's refusal to vote as 'a provocative example by deliberately refusing to carry out his duties as a citizen'.[235] The Nazi propaganda machine did all that it could to discredit the Catholic Church, including exaggerating out of all proportion a small number of cases of sexual abuse by priests in the Rottenburg diocese. The church's press was progressively closed down and its public activities curtailed, while it and its clergy were vilified in Württemberg's Nazi press.[236] In spite of the sustained efforts of many NSDAP district and local branch leaders, however, it remained the case that a commune's church was central to its identity. This was reinforced in wartime when there were dangers to face and casualties to mourn, as well as further Nazi encroachments on church activities and influence. Above all, the issue of 'euthanasia' alienated many churchgoers and galvanised church leaders in Württemberg.

The confrontation between the Nazi regime in Württemberg and the churches soured relations between the party and the people and added to the tensions that already existed for material reasons. As it turned out, the Third Reich did not create a paradise for the small farmers and their families who had been so exalted in Nazi propaganda. For a start, relatively few came, literally, into their inheritance with the *Erbhof* system. Those who did found that, far from being especially privileged, it was much more difficult for them to acquire credit from a bank than it was for farmers who were not *Erbhofbauer*. Even farmers who were in a position to improve their property by repairing or extending buildings could not obtain the necessary materials, while the machines that might have made small farms more productive were, similarly, unobtainable.[237] It was not only individual farmers who were in an increasingly precarious position. Rural communes, especially those not in the vicinity of a town, became increasingly poor in relative terms as towns and their inhabitants, and to some extent their rural hinterlands, benefited from the economic upswing.[238] In early 1939, the SD in Württemberg reported that 'no one can be in any doubt that agriculture is working at a loss ... Some kind of compensation [must] be found, otherwise the small Württemberg farmer will not be able to hold out for much more than another couple of years'.[239] In the SD's view, the flight from the land was 'dire', the living standard of the agricultural population was 'steadily sinking', and farmers were being left with 'unsustainable' burdens.[240] The approach of war only added to these, with doubt cast on the possibility of the *Wehrmacht* being in a position to help out with the 1939 harvest. More immediately, it was a particular source of unrest on the land in summer 1939 – especially in the districts of Künzelsau, Mergentheim and Crailsheim – that many men had been issued with orders conscripting them for military manoeuvres from the beginning of August, at harvest time.[241]

To add to the labour shortage and the low level of prices for agricultural produce, in 1938 poor weather conditions adversely affected the harvesting of many crops, including grain and fruit, while there was, at the same time, an outbreak of foot and mouth disease which had 'very damaging effects on agriculture'.[242] By January 1939, foot and mouth disease had seriously affected fourteen of Württemberg's thirty-seven districts, with Ulm, Schwäbisch Gmünd and Aalen having by far the largest number of communes where the infection had taken hold. Altogether 183 of Württemberg's communes – around 10 per cent of the total – were affected.[243] While there was an overall reduction in the number of reported cases in January and February 1939, in Ulm district the spread of the infection continued and there were fears that there would be a more general increase in spring 1939, once there was greater movement of livestock.[244] The best that the Württemberg Interior Ministry could do was to increase the number of auxiliary police so that movement orders could be enforced. With financial support from Himmler's office, thirty-one retired policemen were enlisted for this task for periods of between two and four weeks each. In June 1939, the commander of the Württemberg police could report that, with a reduction in the incidence of foot and mouth disease, only four auxiliary policemen were being employed.[245]

The foot and mouth outbreak graphically demonstrated the impotence of the RNS in areas which had a critical effect on farmers. When there was an acute crisis of this kind, the civil and police authorities alone had the power to initiate measures to control the situation. The RNS had begun in 1933 by attempting to improve conditions for farmers, by raising the prices of some farm produce and by helping those who were seriously in debt. Yet by the later 1930s its stock had sunk to a low level in rural Württemberg, not least because its inability effectively to represent the interests of farmers was repeatedly demonstrated. Jurisdictional disputes between party and *Reichsnährstand* officials – who 'are not cooperating as they really ought to be doing nowadays' – only added to the sense of bureaucratic intrusiveness and practical irrelevance.[246] While some of the RNS's initiatives had been designed to help small farmers, it remained the case that measures such as piecemeal land improvement grants or the honouring of a few long-established farming families, for example, had either benefited only tiny numbers of them or else had merely had a transient propaganda effect. They did little to mitigate the fundamental problems faced by the majority of small farmers.

By contrast, the coercive aspects of RNS interference in farming practices, especially through the *Marktordnung*, affected virtually all who worked on the land most of the time. By 1939 the SD, while accepting that regulation was necessary, criticised the *Marktordnung*'s tendency towards cumbersome 'overorganisation' that inhibited the normal mechanisms of the market, making goods more expensive than they needed to be.[247] Beyond that, and critically, the RNS had shown itself to be powerless to stem, far less reverse, the flight from the land. In May 1939 *Landesbauernführer* Arnold informed his KBS offices that using the Labour Service and the *Wehrmacht* 'in the usual way' to bring in the harvest would not suffice in 1939, and that, 'once again', volunteers and employees in trades and industry would have to be enlisted. The *Gau* Labour Front office had agreed that workers would be made available for the hay harvest and, later, also for the grain harvest. Yet, although the KBF and OBF were fully involved in reporting both farmers' needs and the availability of labour for this purpose, their inferior position in terms of both capability and authority were demonstrated when the party's district leaders were assigned the task of coordinating the deployment of labour for the harvest. This included ensuring that, where workers incurred travelling costs, these should be paid by the farmers benefiting from their labour.[248] The lowly status of RNS officers, especially compared with that of the party's political leaders, had its effect, as the SD reported: 'the *Reichsnährstand* is having great difficulty in finding suitable men to act as its officials ... because the kind of people who are suitable are simply refusing to take on these "thankless" posts'.[249]

By the late 1930s, the problems in agriculture ensured that small farmers were struggling to survive and, consequently, that large sections of the farming community were alienated from National Socialism, which was regarded as an urban political force whose policies were geared to the promotion of industry and the demands of urban society. The SD reported from Württemberg in summer 1939 that 'the impression has been given that many measures are applicable only to the conditions of cities and large communes, to the disadvantage of the countryside'. Even before the war, for example, workers in various trades were being 'combed out', to try to release labour from small, uneconomic concerns for industry. This, reported the SD, disregarded conditions on the land, where a tradesman might be the only one of his kind in a village and his family members might serve as agricultural workers in the busy seasons of the year. It was, continued the report, positively damaging to apply urban criteria in such a case.[250] The SD's anxiety was real enough, with problems in farming communities threatening fundamental Nazi policies. For one thing, self-sufficiency became even more chimerical an ideal, which suggested that larger amounts of precious foreign currency would have to be released to pay for imported foodstuffs, precisely what the regime had hoped to avoid. In addition, there were indications that poor prospects on the land were leading to a reduction in family size in the only area of the population which was currently more than replacing itself. This was regarded as very serious, given Nazi ambitions to return to a demographic pattern of high birth rates and large families.[251]

Altogether, the rural population had grounds for discontent, given that other areas of the economy were showing a marked upturn, although the SD did not accept that the criticisms often heard of the *Reichsnährstand* were justified. With something of an air of desperation, it claimed that 'it is not true – as has often been suggested and asserted – that the National Socialist state would gladly abandon the peasantry'.[252] Yet whatever rhetoric was expended by Nazi grandees in exalting the peasantry, there could be no doubt that labour-intensive toil on the land was despised by many Germans and that the undervaluing of agricultural work was damaging to the morale of farmers and their families. The SD's view was that, by whatever means, some support would have to be provided, otherwise 'the small Württemberg farmer will barely be in a position to hold out for another couple of years'.[253] It was with farming communities in Württemberg in these straits that Hitler took Germany into the Second World War.

3

Party and State

The National Socialist German Workers' Party was in a privileged position in the Third Reich. From 14 July 1933 it was formally the sole political party in Germany.[1] More than two months earlier, the various trade union groupings had been forcibly dissolved and a new mammoth combine, the German Labour Front, for 'creative Germans of brain and fist', had been formed to eliminate free collective bargaining and industrial militancy by bringing together workers, employers and representatives of the state.[2] The process of *Gleichschaltung* (coordination), of which these developments were a part, proceeded from Hitler's appointment as Chancellor on 30 January 1933. The question of when *Gleichschaltung* was completed is one to which there is no easy answer. Certainly, the major elements in the Nazis' consolidation of power, including the replacement of relatively autonomous *Land* governments by *Reichsstatthalter* (Reich Governors) responsible to the Reich Minister of the Interior in the spring of 1933 and the securing of a political monopoly, were accomplished quickly. The purge of the SA from 30 June to 2 July 1934, one of whose casualties was the recent President of the Württemberg Political Police, Hermann Mattheiss, won Hitler the loyalty of the army's leadership.[3] The subsequent proclamation of Hitler as supreme leader, on President Hindenburg's death on 2 August 1934, can be viewed as the conclusion to the main political objectives of *Gleichschaltung*. As part of the process, during 1933–34, some individual National Socialists came into their inheritance. At Reich level, Frick, Göring, Goebbels and Darré, for example, became government ministers in 1933, while Ley, the NSDAP's new Reich Organisation Leader, became leader of the Labour Front. Himmler began his ascent to leadership of all German police forces, something which he achieved in June 1936.[4]

Yet the position of the NSDAP itself in the Third Reich was more ambiguous. It may have had no party political rivals, but – unlike the Bolshevik Party in revolutionary Russia – it was not permitted to take over wholesale the functions and the authority of the state. Not only did the civil service in Germany at both Reich and *Land* level remain competent, but, in addition, for the most part those who were sufficiently unobjectionable to survive the initial political purges were generally prepared to work with the Nazi leadership. There was no need to replace the survivors with unqualified party hacks, and there would have been

positive disadvantages in doing so. National Socialists had come to power not
through a revolution but more or less legally, with the electoral consent of a
substantial proportion of the population. This made a considerable degree of
continuity both possible and desirable, to the chagrin of party and SA members
who had expected a (non-Marxian) revolution whose beneficiaries they would
be.[5] Beyond that, in an advanced country like Germany there was perhaps not
the potential, especially in peacetime, for outright coercion – of the 'Aryan',
'valuable' and politically unobjectionable majority of the population, at least
– that there manifestly was in the more primitive circumstances of Lenin's and
Stalin's Soviet Union.[6] In any case, while violence against political adversaries
had certainly characterised the campaigns of some local NSDAP branches and,
particularly, the SA before 1933, by contrast the party's strategy with the majority
of the 'valuable' population had been to try to win them over to the Nazi faith
through propaganda and practical welfare work in the depression. The creation
in the 1930s of a police state was intended to reinforce rather than contradict
that aim by minimising the opportunities for political adversaries to subvert the
ostensibly loyal or neutral majority.[7]

Nevertheless, the NSDAP faced a struggle to impose its will in the many small
communes which had not been susceptible to the Nazi appeal before 1933. The
Württemberg electorate may have given the NSDAP support almost equivalent
to the Reich average in March 1933, but thereafter it became painfully apparent
that voting for the party did not mean that all of these electors subscribed
wholeheartedly to its programme and policies. Beyond that, the party faced
other problems. By 1933, it is true, Hitler's party was more developed and
established than Mussolini's Fascist Party had been when he 'seized' power in Italy
in 1922.[8] Yet this did not mean that the NSDAP's organisation was uniformly
developed across Germany.[9] The party's aim was unequivocally to establish
total control over the whole of Germany, down to the last street and the last
house. This, however, was an easier proposition in regions where before January
1933 there had been strong support for National Socialism, for example eastern
Germany or Schleswig-Holstein – although there could be problems there, too
– than it was in a *Land* whose NSDAP organisation was weak and its leadership
given to strife.[10] Certainly, the Württemberg Nazis were able to displace the
parliamentary system without much difficulty in the spring of 1933, but only
because they had the might of Hitler's central government behind them. Given
its lacklustre pedigree and leadership, the chances of the Württemberg NSDAP
taking over dictatorial power on its own would not have been high; beyond that,
securing authority throughout the *Land* was always going to be a painstaking
process.

In particular, and paradoxically, the party which preached 'blood and soil'
and advocated a return to the simple peasant life – in theory, at least – was

significantly more developed in cities and medium-sized towns than it was in many smaller communities. The logistics of organisation determined this: towns and cities had better communications systems and there were more people in more densely populated communities to be canvassed. In addition, while many town dwellers had their roots in their district, in the 1920s and 1930s there were also many newcomers who were first generation townspeople with neither roots nor connections in the towns. If they lost their job during the depression and exhausted any entitlement to both unemployment benefit and emergency relief, they might be able to return to relatives in the countryside, but equally they might have no one to turn to for support. Especially in the few crucial years preceding 1933, people in this plight might be drawn to a party that offered innovative 'charitable' assistance to casualties of the depression through its soup kitchens and nascent 'Winter Aid' scheme, as local NSDAP branches did, particularly in the towns. Volunteers who had been won over to the cause, not least from among full-time housewives, assisted with these ventures.[11] This was hardly the kind of activity for which a farmer's wife or daughters had time. Beyond that, what struggling farmers needed in the depression was income to pay off debts, not a bowl of soup which could readily be made, even in hard times, with home produce.

Yet, in 1933, even in the towns the number of committed enthusiasts was limited. Therefore, because there was not to be a wholesale takeover by the party of the state, and because enthusiasm had to be manufactured to make citizens receptive to measures introduced by Hitler's government, the party's primary task in the Third Reich became that of *Menschenführung*, or 'political education'. This involved both surveillance and guidance, to condition citizens to respond automatically in the manner desired by the regime's leaders and to ensure that they consistently did so.[12] This would be achieved through the leadership given by the NSDAP's own political organisation, by its formations – including the SS, SA, Hitler Youth (HJ), NSF (NS women's group) – and by its many affiliated organisations, for example the NSV (NS People's Welfare) and NSLB (Nazi Teachers' Association), among many others. The party, its formations and its affiliates would – in theory at least – have a corps of carefully groomed leaders who had passed through a range of training courses, whose skills they, in their turn, would purvey to their members. In the first instance, both before and immediately after January 1933, membership of the NSDAP was open to all except the party's designated enemies. After Hitler's appointment as Chancellor, however, the influx into it became a flood, especially of 'March violets', those who applied to join after the result of the election of 5 March confirmed that Hitler's regime was there to stay.[13] By 1 May 1933, the opportunists had diluted the party's *alte Parteigenossen* (old party members) – those who had joined before 30 January 1933 – by a ratio of two to one. As a result, the NSDAP's leadership, acting in haste, imposed a moratorium on entry that was breached only sparingly until it was partly eased in 1937 and finally lifted in 1939.[14]

By contrast, it was expected that from early 1933 the formations and affiliates would recruit extensively from among the population at large. Through both personal contact and ubiquitous training courses, they would provide the spiritual leadership which would persuade Germans to change their ways from those of the old 'liberal individualistic' ethos to those of the new selfless 'people's ethnic community', whose chief virtue would be 'readiness for sacrifice' (*Opferbereitschaft*) for the common good. At local level, this massive task was delegated to largely honorary (*ehrenamtlich*), unpaid enthusiasts, and – whatever soothing untruths were told about the 'unity of party and state' – it was explicitly intended to be formally separate from the administration of government, although formations and affiliates could be pressed into service for relatively menial state purposes.[15] For example, in August 1939 the Württemberg SA was instructed to deliver questionnaires to all who were deemed to be eligible for military service, while during the war the NSF was charged with distributing ration cards.[16] This, however, depended on there being active formations such as the SA and the NSF in the communes, which was far from being the rule. In some places, it took several years for the formations and affiliates, and sometimes even for the party itself, to develop an activist presence in communes. The result was that all too often the tasks which were handed down the line from the centre to the localities devolved onto a small core of enthusiasts. Even they could weary of continually having to make an effort: in 1939, the SD in Württemberg reported that 'in the Party's organisations, there is an almost universal service fatigue, which is especially noticeable in rural districts'.[17]

On the other hand, while those who dominated the new authoritarian government of both the Reich and its constituent *Länder* were National Socialists, they ruled as state functionaries largely independent of control by the NSDAP's organisation. These state functionaries regarded their internalised construct of National Socialism as being at least as valid as that of full-time NSDAP ideologues or bureaucrats. Indeed, it perhaps seemed more valid because they had to apply National Socialist principles to government, whereas purely party officers were in a position to be less responsible, until the crises of wartime at least. The state functionaries' first loyalty was less to the party as an organisation than to Hitler and the 'idea' of National Socialism, while their second loyalty was to government, as both an authority and a process; this was particularly the case in Württemberg. The potential problems of this dualism of party and state were allegedy averted by Hitler's position as Führer, supreme leader of both party and state, and by the appointment during the *Gleichschaltung* process of several *Gauleiter* to the position of *Reichsstatthalter*, the highest civil officer in their *Land*; in the Prussian provinces, the corresponding post was *Oberpräsident* (provincial president). This 'personal union' of offices penetrated the lower levels of the administration to varying degrees in different *Länder*, but in Württemberg to a rather lesser extent than elsewhere.[18]

Political *Gleichschaltung* took longer in Württemberg than in some other areas, for example Prussia, where Chancellor Papen's illegal authoritarian coup against the caretaker Braun government in July 1932 had broken the back of political opposition. Indeed, in Württemberg *Gleichschaltung* was rather less complete than it was in Prussia.[19] Yet in Württemberg, too, the main objectives of the process had been achieved by the summer of 1934. Like several other *Gauleiter*, Wilhelm Murr became a *Reichsstatthalter* in a 'coordinated' *Land*, while other leading NSDAP officers took control of the levers of power.[20] It would have helped the NSDAP's cause if the party in Württemberg had been able to draw on personnel of greater talent and expertise, if there had been a stronger and more unified party leadership in Stuttgart, and if Murr had been a *Gauleiter* of greater stature, more competence and a more dynamic personality. As it was, the leadership principle ensured that Murr, as Hitler's choice, was unassailable, even if he remained outside Hitler's inner circle of favoured *Gauleiter*.[21] In spite of his relative insignificance among his peers, Murr was one of the longer serving *Gauleiter*, remaining in post until the end, in late April 1945, when he saw no alternative to flight from the Allies who had overrun Württemberg. On 14 May 1945, he and his wife, who were in French captivity in Vorarlberg under assumed names, took lethal doses of poison.[22]

Murr made virtually no impact outside *Gau* Württemberg-Hohenzollern, and the persistent attempts by the *Gau*'s propaganda office to develop a personality cult to exalt him were stunted by the all too obvious colourlessness of his personality.[23] While other long-serving *Gauleiter* – his obsessively anti-Catholic neighbour Robert Wagner in Baden, for example, along with others like Martin Mutschmann in Saxony and Karl Kaufmann in Hamburg, or the notoriously Jew-baiting Julius Streicher in Franconia – tend to figure in works on the Third Reich or the NSDAP generally, Murr has been of little interest to historians of areas other than Württemberg and the German south west. His antisemitism was vicious and unrelenting but it was not in the same revoltingly pornographic class as Streicher's; unlike the Reich Organisation Leader, former *Gauleiter* Robert Ley, Murr was neither brain-damaged nor dependent on alcohol. His wife tolerated his infidelities which were of a minor order compared with those of Wilhelm Kube, *Gauleiter* of Kurmark, to name but one.[24] His corrupt practices are barely worth a mention compared with those of Kaufmann, Erich Koch of East Prussia or Ley, among many others, including Streicher, whose 'Gau and his own living habits were ... cesspools of corruption'.[25] Murr's idea of 'provocative' conduct was the sight of women wearing trousers in public in wartime.[26] His dull character and limited abilities suggest that he would have been entirely devoid of interest but for one crucial fact: he was Hitler's highest representative in the fourth largest *Land*, Württemberg. Any prominence or authority that he enjoyed derived from that.[27]

Wilhelm Murr was born in 1888 in Esslingen. He became a clerical worker and a man of *völkisch* (mystical racist) prejudices, narrow vision, dogmatic disposition and notorious 'Swabian thrift', joining the NSDAP before the Munich *Putsch* attempt on 9 November 1923. On the refounding of the party in 1925, Murr became leader of the Esslingen NSDAP local branch and in 1928 Hitler appointed him *Gauleiter* of Württemberg-Hohenzollern. Murr's 'recipe for the recovery' of Germany after the traumas of the post-1918 period amounted to an amalgam of crude antisemitism and an emotional appeal to the idea of a *Volksgemeinschaft* (people's ethnic community). His retention of his position as *Gauleiter* and subsequent acquisition of further offices was – as was the case with several other senior Nazi officers – undoubtedly the result of his slavish loyalty to Hitler personally. Murr's success in accumulating almost all of the top positions in Württemberg owed much to Hitler's personal decisions, on those occasions when the Führer was asked to choose between him and a rival. Having been 'elected' State President of Württemberg on 15 March 1933 by the newly rigged *Landtag*, on 5 May 1933 Murr was appointed *Reichsstatthalter* in Württemberg. On 1 September 1939 he became Reich Defence Commissioner (*Reichsverteidigungskommissar* – RVK) of Baden as well as Württemberg, although in November 1942 he lost this responsibility in Baden when each *Gauleiter* was appointed the RVK for his own *Gau*.[28] In the spat which Murr had with the Baden *Gau*'s leader for communal policy, when he failed to invite the latter to join his Defence Committee in 1939 in spite of repeated requests that he do so, Murr was both characteristically rigidly adhering to the letter of the law and maintaining the traditional animosity between Württemberg and Baden.[29]

Murr remained unconditionally devoted and obedient to Hitler until the very end, in April 1945. With his refusal to allow both the evacuation of the citizens of central Heilbronn and, in the last hopeless days of the war, the surrender of Stuttgart, he demonstrated a chilling disregard for the safety and survival of Württemberg's 'Aryan' human beings. He followed to the letter the injunctions of his master, at a time when many of his own underlings in the party took a more grimly realistic view of the stark choice between surrender and annihilation.[30] This may have owed something to his weak but inflexible character; it also confirms that he was indeed an 'uncompromising instrument of his Führer's will'.[31] By contrast, Mayor Karl Strölin finally surrendered Stuttgart – in defiance of Murr – before what was left of it after merciless bombing was blown to pieces by the invader.[32] Yet Murr's stance during the war and at its end could hardly have been a surprise: his attitude to National Socialist conformity had been made clear from the start, with threatening utterances, for example 'whoever does not vote in the *Reichstag* election of 12 November 1933 and does not give the government his backing is a traitor guilty of high treason'.[33] Even earlier, Murr had been positively menacing in his much quoted threat, issued during his first speech as State President, on 15 March 1933: 'We don't say: an eye for an eye, a tooth for a tooth; no, if someone puts out one of our eyes, we'll knock his head off; and if someone knocks out one of our teeth, we'll break his jaw'.[34]

Murr's *bête noire* among his Nazi colleagues in Württemberg was Christian Mergenthaler, a physics teacher who liked to be styled 'professor' and who did nothing to disguise his contempt for the much less well-educated Murr. Something of an opportunist, Mergenthaler was also stubborn and implacable in his hatreds. Like Murr, Mergenthaler joined the NSDAP before the 1923 *Putsch* attempt, but thereafter he found a temporary political home in the *völkisch* NSDFB, becoming a *Landtag* member representing it in 1924. The *Landtag* would be his power base even after he rejoined the NSDAP in 1927, and, when it became the largest party there, in April 1932, he became *Landtag* president.[35] With the consolidation of Nazi power in Württemberg in the spring of 1933, Mergenthaler hoped to overtake Murr by becoming State President, an office requiring the kind of leadership abilities with which Murr was not, in the view of several NSDAP activists in Württemberg, endowed. Hitler's personal decision in favour of Murr was, however, irrevocable. Yet Murr could not simply dispense with his rival: given the shortage of leading National Socialists in Württemberg who were capable of mastering a specialised ministerial brief, Murr had no choice but to entrust important ministerial portfolios to him. Accordingly, Mergenthaler became Minister President and *Kultminister* (Minister for Schools and Churches), offices which he held until the end; in addition, he served as Justice Minister from March to May 1933, crucial months in which the Württemberg Nazis consolidated power while assaulting and incarcerating their political adversaries.[36]

For the duration of the Third Reich, Murr and Mergenthaler had to learn to work together, although this did not prevent there being petty disputes between them.[37] Indeed, at times 'they confronted each other like cat and dog'.[38] Working in tandem was forced on them, not least because the proposal by the Nazi Reich Minister of the Interior, Wilhelm Frick, that the offices of *Reichsstatthalter* and Minister President be combined in the hands of the *Gauleiter*, was vetoed by Hitler in the cases of Baden, Thuringia and Württemberg.[39] Beyond this odd couple at the head of the Nazi government of Württemberg from 1933 to 1945, there was a handful of men of ability and professional expertise who undoubtedly gave the NSDAP in Württemberg an appearance of competence and respectability. Chief among these were Jonathan Schmid, Georg Stümpfig and Karl Wilhelm Waldmann, all of whom were farmers' sons, as was Friedrich Schmidt, who in 1933 became deputy *Gauleiter*. Jonathan Schmid was born in Leonberg district while the other three came from Crailsheim; all were still at least nominally members of the Evangelical church in 1933, as were Murr and Mergenthaler, although Friedrich Schmidt adopted the preferred Nazi formula of *gottgläubig* (believing in a deity) in the later 1930s. He belonged to a younger generation than the others. Born in 1902, he had not served in the First World War, nor had Waldmann, whereas the others, including Murr and Mergenthaler, had. Jonathan Schmid, Mergenthaler and Stümpfig had been decorated with the highest military honours, and Murr with the Iron Cross, second class.

The young Friedrich Schmidt was undoubtedly the highest flyer of this group. Trained as an elementary school teacher, he was an ideological diehard who had worked as a speaker and organiser for the Nazi cause in the Hohenlohe region in the late 1920s, as a protégé of the mayor of Wiesenbach, Georg Stümpfig. Before 1933 he moved to Stuttgart, becoming the NSDAP *Gau* propaganda leader and then *Gau* business manager. He seems to have been one of the few Württemberg Nazis for whom *Gauleiter* Murr had a good word, although that may only have been when he was writing a reference that would ensure that Schmidt left Stuttgart for Berlin. Nevertheless, in the early years of the Third Reich, Schmidt remained closer to Murr than most. Schmidt had also acquired powerful patrons in Darré and Himmler, which undoubtedly contributed to his secondment in May 1937 to the NSDAP Reich Organisation Leader's office in Berlin, as Robert Ley's choice to head the party's office for ideological training. He went on to become Ley's representative in occupied Poland and Governor in Lublin, at the very time when the Lublin area was becoming a notorious centre of antisemitic brutality and murder.[40] In February 1942, however, he volunteered for service at the front, apparently to advance his career prospects. Throughout, he remained, at least nominally, deputy *Gauleiter* of Württemberg-Hohenzollern, yet when he achieved his ambition of acquiring a rural estate it was not in Württemberg but at Gut Thansau in Bavaria.[41]

Jonathan Schmid, born in 1888 and a lawyer by training, had joined the NSDAP in 1923 when he was already a local councillor in Leonberg. He was leader of the party's local branch there from 1930 until 1932, when he became an NSDAP *Landtag* member. In some respects a conciliatory figure – or, at least, regarded as such initially by some non-Nazi politicians – Schmid frequently had to act as an intermediary between Murr and Mergenthaler.[42] Appointed Württemberg Minister of the Interior in 1933, a position which he held until the end, it was in his interests to defend his own ministry and also local government officials against the encroachments of NSDAP officers, and he did so effectively. Having succeeded Mergenthaler as Justice Minister in 1933, Schmid was in this post when it was abolished as a result of the centralisation of the administration of justice in Reich Minister Gürtner's hands in 1935. A year later, Schmid became Württemberg Minister of Economics, again a post which he held until 1945. Yet his ministerial posts lost their importance in wartime as Murr became overlord of all aspects of domestic policy, in his capacity as RVK. Schmid took up a position in the military government of occupied France, where he encountered but did not denounce conspirators of the July Plot. Nevertheless, Schmid was implicated in the deportation of Jews from France, and in Württemberg he presided over the ministry which organised the 'euthanasia' programme at Schloss Grafeneck (although, as diabetic, he was himself potentially at risk from those who defined eligibility for 'euthanasia' broadly). Schmid was without doubt an utterly loyal National Socialist, but he was also resistant to centralising measures which threatened to undermine Württemberg's identity.[43]

Similarly, Karl Wilhelm Waldmann, a career civil servant who was already a Nazi functionary and adviser to Murr before 1933, was also jealously intent on guarding Württemberg's independence against centralising aspirations on the part of the government in Berlin.[44] This was a matter of old-fashioned particularism rather than a genuine desire for democratic autonomy, and it has to be seen within the context of his loyalty to the National Socialist dictatorial system, which was graphically illustrated by his adoption of the Hitlerian hair style and moustache. Waldmann became in 1933 State Secretary to the *Reichsstatthalter*, a position which he retained until 1945 in spite of increasing clashes with Murr. Between 1942 and 1945 he was also the Württemberg Finance Minister, in succession to the Nationalist politician Dr Alfred Dehlinger, who held his post until he reached the age of retirement in 1942 without feeling the need to join the NSDAP.[45] Both intensely antisemitic and professionally capable, Waldmann became Murr's right-hand man and played a key role in the administration of Württemberg during the Third Reich. The contradictions in his character were evident: Waldmann was an agrarian romantic whose views were close to Darré's, speaking as he did of the importance of 'a healthy peasantry for the maintenance of the ... racial value of the *Volk*', yet he was also determined to maintain at all levels a professional corps of civil officials which was not compromised by the appointment of unqualified NSDAP hacks. Certainly, he was ruthless in purging the administration of 'politically unreliable' officials and in imposing an authoritarian *Führerstaat*, a state based on the leadership principle, but he preferred general political supervision of the bureaucracy to day to day political interference in the details of administration.[46]

Like his close colleague and friend Waldmann, Georg Stümpfig was a non-graduate career civil servant, but one who – unusually – reached the highest levels of the administration in Württemberg, through dogged ability, political achievement and the patronage of Waldmann. A Nazi activist from 1929, he served from 1932 to 1934 as NSDAP *Kreisleiter* (district leader) of Gerabronn in his home region of the north east and one of Nazism's few pre-1933 bastions in Württemberg. For ten years before joining the party he had been mayor of a commune in Gerabronn county. He joined the SS in 1931 and was a member of the *Landtag* in 1932–33, where his contributions related to his main political preoccupation, the plight of small farmers in the economic crisis, for which he blamed the Republican 'system'. Undoubtedly because Waldmann trusted him implicitly, Stümpfig was given the brief of local government in the Interior Ministry in November 1933. He also became *Gau* Württemberg-Hohenzollern's chief of local government policy in 1934 when the incumbent, Rudolf Abele, was dismissed by Murr. Thus Stümpfig united in his person the authority over local government of both party and state; nevertheless, while he remained devoted to the Nazi cause, he had little time for self-serving or corrupt local Nazis whose ambitions outstripped their abilities. In this he was faithful to the principles of the NSDAP's local government office, which increasingly found itself at odds with the Party Chancellery.[47] Stümpfig was never close to Murr, but he enjoyed the patronage of Friedrich Schmidt as well as Waldmann. Like Jonathan Schmid and Waldmann, Stümpfig was both complicit in the brutality of the Nazi system and intent on maintaining the traditions and standards of both the central and local administration in Württemberg. His control over personnel matters enabled him to enjoy considerable success in this.[48]

With the exception of Friedrich Schmidt, these men who dominated the government of Württemberg in the Third Reich all belonged to the same age group as Adolf Hitler, who was born in 1889. Mergenthaler, born in 1884, was a few years older but the others were born in the years 1888–90. This made them somewhat older than leading Nazis elsewhere, for example in Baden.[49] Eugen Stähle, the chief medical officer in the Ministry of the Interior who was the instigator of the 'euthanasia' policy, was also born in 1890, as was Karl Strölin, mayor of Stuttgart for the duration of the Third Reich; he was a highly decorated war veteran.[50] The brutal and fanatical *Kreisleiter* of Heilbronn, Richard Drauz, was slightly younger, born in 1894. He, too, had served in the First World War before working in both the same factory and the same NSDAP local branch in Esslingen as Murr, who would remain his friend until the end.[51] Even younger was Adolf Mauer, born in 1899 in Bavaria but soon domiciled in Stuttgart, who would rise to the heights of being leader of a main department of the NSDAP in the Party Chancellery in Munich in 1944. As a teenager, he had served in an infantry regiment in the First World War, receiving – like Murr – the Iron Cross, second class. He qualified as an engineer and became an active National Socialist, founding branches of the SA and the Hitler Youth in Heidenheim. He was local branch leader and then district leader there before becoming *Gau* Propaganda Leader, and he served as the Special Political Commissioner in Heidenheim in 1933, during the *Gleichschaltung* period.[52] After the suicide of the Stuttgart *Kreisleiter*, Otto Maier, in July 1934, Murr appointed Mauer to serve as acting *Kreisleiter*, a post which he held from November 1934 until the reorganisation of the districts in July 1937.[53]

Drauz was the most assiduous of this group in promoting Nazi population policy: he and his first wife had three children, and, after a divorce in 1937, Drauz and his second wife had four children.[54] Eugen Stähle, too, was reasonably prolific, with five children.[55] Friedrich Schmidt and his wife had two sons and a daughter, and, while his wife was dying of cancer in 1944 and Schmidt himself was serving in the *Waffen-SS* in The Netherlands, Schmidt's lover gave birth to a son in an SS *Lebensborn* nursing home.[56] Adolf Mauer had three children.[57] By contrast, although Waldmann and Stümpfig each had eleven siblings, some of whom did not survive infancy, Waldmann, with two children, and Mergenthaler, Stümpfig and Murr, with one child each, fell into the 'one and two child family' pattern which was so much derided by Nazi propaganda.[58] Like Hitler, Strölin does not seem to have contributed to population development at all, remaining unmarried, while Jonathan Schmid married but appears to have had no children.[59] In terms of propagating the 'race', most of Württemberg's NSDAP notables signally failed to follow the party's prescriptions. On the whole, the *Kreisleiter* showed more zeal: over half of them had three or more children. One of their number, Erich Waizenegger, was guilty of a dereliction of duty in more than one respect when, accompanied by his lover, he abandoned not only his post as *Kreisleiter* in Saulgau at the end of 1939 but also his pregnant wife and five children.[60]

These leading Württemberg Nazis evidenced the much-vaunted Swabian tenacity and endurance, and some were indeed 'pig-headed Swabians', with rivalry and feuding consuming much of their energies.[61] In a *Land* where it was virtually impossible to achieve a senior administrative position unless one was a Württemberger, it is hardly surprising that, apart from the assimilated Adolf Mauer, they were all natives.[62] Württemberg willingly exported its men of ability, ambition or party connections, for example the German Foreign Minister from 1932 to 1938, *Freiherr* Konstantin von Neurath, the leading SS officer, Gottlob Berger, Karl Wahl, who was *Gauleiter* of Schwaben (western Bavaria) from 1928 to 1945, as well as Friedrich Schmidt and, eventually, Adolf Mauer.[63] There was not a Roman Catholic among them: all, without exception, were – at least nominally – Evangelical Christians, until the later 1930s and early 1940s, when most ostentatiously left the church. This was true also of several of the NSDAP's *Kreisleiter* in Württemberg.[64] Accordingly, those who formed and led the NSDAP in Württemberg-Hohenzollern, at both central and local level, were effectively Protestant natives.

Therefore it seems clear that not only did Württembergers perceive their 'Germanness' through the prism of their Swabian identity, but, in addition, Württemberg's Nazis perceived their commitment to National Socialism as a function of their Swabian identity and as a means of perpetuating their Swabian heritage. To some leading Württemberg Nazis, there appeared to be no contradiction between, on the one hand, the unswerving loyalty which they professed towards Hitler and Nazism and, on the other hand, their at times openly expressed hostility towards attitudes and measures emanating from ministers and ministries in a Nazi government in Berlin. Jonathan Schmid's unvarnished protest when the Reich Minister of Justice assumed jurisdiction over the administration of the law in the *Länder* in 1935, which brought his tenure as Württemberg Justice Minister to an abrupt end, was perhaps more pointed than some responses, but it illustrates the strength of particularist feeling that was harboured in areas remote from the centre.[65] Schmid was no less sharp in his criticism of the Reich Ministry of the Interior for announcing in summer 1939 'a further massive reduction in the communes' income to the benefit of the Reich'.[66]

In a Reich context, although Württemberg was the fourth largest *Land* in terms of its population size, Württemberg-Hohenzollern was only one of thirty-two *Gaue* of the NSDAP in the 1930s, until the absorption of both Austria and the Sudetenland in 1938 and of the Wartheland in 1939 made it one of forty-one and still the last in the alphabetical list. Unlike East Prussia, Silesia, Saar-Palatinate and neighbouring Baden, it was not a border *Gau* and therefore was not assigned responsibility for annexed territory in wartime, as the two eastern *Gaue* were for areas of defeated Poland and as Baden was for Alsace and Saar-Palatinate for Lorraine.[67] Murr did not experience either the rise in status or the expansion of opportunities afforded to Josef Bürckel in Saar-Palatinate or Robert Wagner in Baden, to say nothing of Koch in East Prussia or Josef Wagner in Silesia. Certainly, Murr was able to join the self-styled Nazi elite as an honorary SS officer in the spring of 1934, and was one of the first *Gauleiter* to do so.[68]

It was perhaps not entirely Murr's fault that even in this matter there was controversy and ill will. An officer of the Württemberg SS complained that the SS had had to request the agreement of the SA leadership to Murr's appointment, although the SS's agreement had not been sought when Mergenthaler and Jonathan Schmid had recently been appointed honorary officers in the SA. Part of the SS's grievance was that, although Murr's sponsor in the SS had spoken of the *Gauleiter*'s 'marked preference for the SS', the complaining officer could, 'to my regret, ascertain no marked preference on the part of the Reich or *Land* Württemberg for the SS'. The root of the problem was a credit of two million marks afforded by Württemberg to the SA in 1933, whereas the SS had found 'up to now considerable difficulties in its way', leading to the conclusion that in Württemberg there was a 'marked preference for the SA'. Whether Murr's alignment with the SS was at all connected with Mergenthaler's allegiance to the SA – of which he was a longstanding member – and his 'negative attitude' towards the SS is not clear.[69] The SS was, of course, about to achieve the upper hand, with the liquidation of the SA leadership at the end of June 1934. The

Württemberg SS's attitude to the SA thereafter was illustrated by disparaging remarks about it in the reports of its surveillance branch (*Sicherheitsdienst* – SD) in the late 1930s.[70]

After January 1933, purging the political establishment in Stuttgart was relatively easy, with the full authority of the Reich government behind Murr, but changing the order in the communes was more problematic. Certainly, local government was brought more firmly under the control of the centre – in Württemberg's case, Stuttgart – while officers of the NSDAP frequently interfered with or attempted to subvert the authority of the relevant civil officials. Yet Schmid, Waldmann and Stümpfig were deeply committed to the principle of a professional bureaucracy, even if their overriding loyalty was to the National Socialist 'idea' and Hitler's leadership. In this latter sentiment they were no different from Murr, Mergenthaler and Friedrich Schmidt, although there were perhaps limits to the fanaticism of the first three. Jonathan Schmid's view was that, on the one hand, 'the corps of the civil service of National Socialist Germany must be *united*, that is to say, it must be *National Socialist*'. On the other hand, he believed that the new regime had to work with the grain of the Württemberg bureaucracy, and to resist political initiatives from NSDAP officers who wanted a wholesale purge of it. Similarly, while he fully agreed with the party leadership that political enemies had to be removed from positions of influence in local government, he regarded the removal of apparent political neutrals from positions as *Landräte* or mayors as unnecessary and probably undesirable, particularly if a local NSDAP activist's motive in agitating for this was to release a civil position for himself or for someone dependent on him.[71]

For example, the Trossingen businessman Fritz Kiehn, who had founded the NSDAP local branch there and had been awarded a supervisory position in local government in 1933, tried on more than one occasion to replace existing civil officials with creatures of his own. First, he attempted to displace the *Landrat* in Tuttlingen, who had been in post since 1926, running a scurrilous personal campaign against him, and then in 1934 he actively promoted the candidacy of a local teacher for the vacant post of mayor of Trossingen. In the first case, he was simply unsuccessful, and in the second Schmid's ministry insisted on appointing a professional bureaucrat who was also a party member. The Württemberg Ministry of the Interior's policy was and remained that it would choose 'another professionally suitable candidate instead of a pushy political careerist'.[72] This was the line consistently followed by Stümpfig, who held aloof from 'the radical group around Murr'. Indeed, he managed to redeploy officials – in one case a mayor of a commune – who had been dismissed because they were politically suspect, even finding alternative work for an official who had been a KPD sympathiser.[73]

Nevertheless, during the initial phase of *Gleichschaltung* in 1933–34, twenty-one of the sixty-one *Landräte* were replaced. Five of them were dismissed, including the *Landrat* of Leonberg, a member of the German Democratic Party, who had been sacked in February 1933 on the grounds that he had favoured the SPD while in office. Two *Landräte* were promoted and two retired in the normal way; twelve were prematurely retired, less because they were politically objectionable than because Jonathan Schmid, as Minister of the Interior, wanted to promote middle-ranking bureaucrats after years of stunted promotion prospects during the depression, to bring younger men as 'fresh blood' into local government. Certainly, all but one of the twenty-seven county or district leaders who were newly appointed during the Third Reich were born after 1890, by contrast with the rather older new appointees in neighbouring Baden. A further aim was to create a corps of functionaries in local government who would be loyal to the new regime because it had preferred them. Characteristically, the retirements were effected according to a law relating to civil servants passed in Württemberg on 24 March 1933, rather than according to the terms of the Reich 'Law for the Re-Establishment of the Professional Civil Service' of 7 April 1933.[74] Yet even after the replacements of 1933–34, of the sixty-one *Landräte* in Württemberg, by 1935 only forty-four had joined the NSDAP, and only the *Landrat* in Herrenberg had a membership predating 1933.[75]

Schmid rightly perceived Württemberg civil officials in the bureaucracy, the counties and the towns as professionals who were mostly ready to serve the new order as they had served its predecessor, and he realised that antagonising them as a body by removing some of their fellows for purely political reasons would be counter-productive. For him, continuity was the best guarantee of cooperation. He was more conciliatory than either the abrasive Waldmann or even Stümpfig, criticising the latter in 1939 for being too heavy-handed in his attempts to regiment the *Landräte* of the new districts.[76] Yet whether or not Waldmann was aware of it, he was echoing Prussian Minister of the Interior Göring's sentiments when in June 1933 he said of senior civil servants who had rushed to join the NSDAP that *Reichsstatthalter* Murr

> does not understand why such a large proportion of officials, who are inherently not National Socialist, have in recent weeks felt the need to become members of the NSDAP … The character of an official is to be more highly regarded if he is not a National Socialist and has not taken this step.[77]

This was distinctly disingenuous. No doubt other influential civil officials who were NSDAP members acted as Fritz Kiehn did in Trossingen, putting pressure on their subordinates to join the party in order to safeguard their jobs.[78] While it was possible to retain a senior civil service post without joining the NSDAP, ultimately over 80 per cent of Württemberg's 348 senior bureaucrats did join, half of them in 1933; only a good quarter of these, however, could be classed as party activists.[79]

The tactic of a personal union of offices of party and state that was initially favoured in the Third Reich – with Murr, for example, at the summit of both as *Gauleiter* in *Gau* Württemberg-Hohenzollern and *Reichsstatthalter* in *Land* Württemberg – was deployed sparingly in Württemberg, although, as we have seen, Georg Stümpfig combined from 1934 the roles of officer for local government in the Württemberg Interior Ministry and chief of local government policy for *Gau* Württemberg-Hohenzollern.[80] In 1935, only 5 per cent of NSDAP local branch leaders (*Ortsgruppenleiter*) were civil officials, usually in the office of mayor, contributing to Württemberg-Hohenzollern's being the *Gau* with the second lowest density of party officers in the civil administration. By contrast, in Hesse NSDAP *Kreisleiter* were appointed to the overwhelming majority of district governor positions, while many party local branch leaders were also mayors.[81] The three southern *Länder*, Baden, Bavaria and especially Württemberg, deviated from the Reich pattern of there being substantial numbers of district governors with political rather than professional qualifications, often as NSDAP *Kreisleiter*. In Württemberg there were certainly instances of a *Kreisleiter* who was also mayor of a small town, for example Eugen Vogt in Horb in the 1930s, and Adolf Kölle in Ellwangen/Aalen from 1933 until 1942, when he became *Kreisleiter* full time. Nevertheless, Württemberg was both notable and fairly exceptional in having no *Kreisleiter* appointed to the post of *Landrat*.

Although altogether two-thirds of Württemberg's *Landräte* were newly appointed in the Third Reich, none of them was an 'outsider': they all had full professional – that is, legal – qualifications and training.[82] Nevertheless, as the party's 'special representative for communal affairs' in his district, the *Kreisleiter* possessed considerable latitude through his input into personnel policy and his responsibility for the ideological training of state functionaries. Occasionally, a *Kreisleiter* might be successful in exerting pressure to have a *Landrat* retired prematurely or to prevent an appointment that he opposed. Equally, he might successfully recommend a candidate. Gottfried Dill, at the Ministry of the Interior, claimed in 1941 that the division of duties between *Landrat* and *Kreisleiter* had been uncontentious as long as each had respected the other's jurisdiction. He admitted that, very occasionally, a *Kreisleiter* had interpreted his mission of *Menschenführung* in a way that had infringed the sovereignty of the administration.[83] In some places, this was a mild way of putting it, although Schmid and Waldmann were at pains to ensure that professional competence was the primary criterion for appointment. As a result, the influence of the party over the administration – and in particular over *Landräte* – was much less than in other parts of Germany. Even so, in some areas, the personality and ambition of a local branch leader or *Kreisleiter* could be decisive in influencing policy, as was the case in Heilbronn, where *Kreisleiter* Richard Drauz dominated the governance not only of the town but also of the surrounding provincial district (*Landkreis*) of Heilbronn.[84] This was an extreme case, and even here there were limits to what Drauz could achieve in an administrative culture in which a traditional unpolitical attitude towards the state apparatus persisted, even in the Third Reich.[85] Yet the proviso that *Landräte* and mayors should consult the *Kreisleiter* on any matter with a political aspect enhanced the potential power of the *Kreisleiter* in a system where the 'political' was broadly defined.[86]

On the whole, Schmid and Stümpfig together ensured that *Landräte* were civil functionaries responsible to them rather than to NSDAP officers. Even if the *Deutsche Gemeindeordnung* (German Commune Ordinance) of 1935 deprived the *Landrat* of some of his previous autonomy as leader of his district, in wartime he assumed extra duties which strengthened his position versus the *Kreisleiter*, although the latter retained primary political influence in his district.[87] Further, the reduction in the number of *Landräte* in 1938 from sixty-one to thirty-four, to accord with the rationalisation and enlargement of the districts, was an opportunity for a shakeout of those who were less cooperative, although virtually every *Landrat* in the new districts was continuing in post. Yet some of those who lost their position at this time were clearly not purged; rather, they were merely casualties of the specific reform, under which there were bound to be twenty-seven losers. Several of them were regarded as sufficiently reliable to be deployed as administrators elsewhere, while others were appointed in wartime to replace *Landräte* either conscripted into the *Wehrmacht* (armed forces) or else seconded to the Ministry of the Interior in Stuttgart or to occupied Poland.[88] In the Prussian enclave of Hohenzollern, which was part of *Gau* Württemberg-Hohenzollern, the only two *Landräte*, of Hechingen and Sigmaringen, who had been first appointed in 1924 and 1925, survived, although they were Roman Catholics and had been Centre Party members, as 'fossils from the time of the [Weimar] system' until 1945 and 1946, respectively.[89]

In the revised office plans that the *Landräte* drew up in the aftermath of the reorganisation of 1938, there was scarcely a mention of the NSDAP. The *Landrat* of Böblingen was unusual in listing, as number three of the eleven subject areas for which he had special responsibility, 'cooperation with the NSDAP (general)'.[90] The reorganisation of Württemberg's districts in 1938 confirmed that the office of the *Landrat* was 'the basic authority for all matters of internal administration which do not come within the competence of other authorities [including] the implementation of most laws and the orders of the ministries and the other central authorities'.[91] During the war, at the same time as his staff numbers were depleted through conscription, the *Landrat* was responsible for an increasing range of activities, from air raid protection to ensuring that standards of public sexual morality were maintained, from supervising schools, churches and vets to awarding the Honour Cross of the German Mother, from ensuring that price controls were enforced to regulating property transactions, ensuring that utilities were maintained, and implementing the conscription of both horses and automobiles. There was much more besides all of this, including the thorny issue of enforcing the War Economy Decree relating to the production and distribution of foodstuffs and other controlled items. It was an indication of the relative breadth of manoeuvre enjoyed by the *Landräte* that no two of their office plans were identical. They had freedom to delegate functions to their administrators and clerical workers as they saw fit, even if this freedom was increasingly circumscribed by the depletion of their staff numbers as the demands of the armed forces in wartime inexorably increased. As a result, in some cases, even in the early years of the war, women were allowed to take over positions of responsibility which had previously been reserved for men, although they were sometimes explicitly placed under male supervision.[92]

The *Landräte* were also responsible for supervision of the provincial police forces, including both the *Schutzpolizei* (*Schupo*), the municipal police, and the *Gendarmerie*, the police units in the communes, although the ultimate authority in police matters rested with Himmler. The *Gendarmerie* had three main offices in Württemberg, at Stuttgart, Göppingen and Freudenstadt, as well as local offices throughout the *Land*. By the end of 1939, however, twenty local offices were unstaffed and 280 officers had been transferred to wartime duties outside Württemberg, to add to the 116 vacant positions that there had already been by September 1939. Nevertheless, gendarmes were expected by local authorities to take on extra functions in smaller communities – those of up to 5000 inhabitants – because of the even greater shortages of staff in the *Schupo*. Although the gendarmes were few in number and spread thinly across large rural areas, in wartime they maintained a relatively high profile in enforcing the law. In rural areas, their chief activity lay in uncovering and reporting violations of the War Economy Decree, for example bartering, illegal slaughtering or failure to deliver required quotas of food supplies to state depots.

By 1939, most gendarmes in Württemberg were members of the NSDAP, and many of them were functionaries either in the party itself or in a formation or an affiliated organisation. The police in the communes could therefore be regarded as strongly 'politically reliable' and likely to fulfil the regime's requirements. Nevertheless, the *Gendarmerie* – understaffed as it was – guarded its prerogatives jealously, not least against encroachments by party officers. There was palpable resentment that 'there are still leaders of armed units of the NSDAP and [also] party officials who believe that they have special rights (e.g., relating to closing times and black out measures)'. Further, there were complaints that sometimes members of the *Gestapo* (secret state police) operated in their area without informing them. It was regarded as particularly embarrassing when the first that gendarmes heard of this was when a member of the public told them about it.

On the other hand, relations between the *Gendarmerie* and the criminal police were said to be 'exemplary'.[93]

The *Landrat* was normally the superior authority of the *Bürgermeister* (mayors) of the communes; the reorganisation of 1938, however, created, in addition to the thirty-four *Landkreise* in Württemberg, three *Stadtkreise* (urban districts) whose chief executives continued to be lord mayors (*Oberbürgermeister*) who were not responsible to a *Landrat*. In the cities and larger towns of Germany, where mayors had tended to belong to a political party other than the NSDAP, there were sweeping changes, with seventy mayors replaced in May 1933 alone.[94] In Württemberg, too, most of the larger towns had their leadership replaced by reliable National Socialists, notably in Stuttgart, where Karl Strölin, leader of the NSDAP group on the city council and, since the middle of March 1933, the State Commissioner for Stuttgart, replaced the Social Democrat Lautenschlager as *Oberbürgermeister*.[95] In small communes in Württemberg, however, it had been customary to choose as mayor – through direct popular elections – men with professional qualifications who were not card-carrying party members who could now be dismissed for political reasons. Above all, outside the larger towns, Württemberg's mayors did not belong to the groups first targeted for removal by the Nazis, namely socialists and communists. The result was that, compared with other *Länder*, including Württemberg's southern neighbours, Baden and Upper Bavaria, there was remarkable continuity of local government personnel in Württemberg's communes, and 'three-quarters of all mayors in Württemberg survived the *Gleichschaltung* process unscathed ...'[96] This was partly because a comprehensive pensioning off would have been intolerably expensive. One long-term survivor was a farmer who had been elected mayor of Weinstetten, in Ulm district, in 1926 who served until 1 April 1948, when he resigned.[97]

From 1933, rather than being elected, mayors were appointed by the district's *Landrat*, in cooperation with the NSDAP *Kreisleiter*, and, where there was a lively party organisation, mayors found themselves under pressure both from local Nazis and from the government in Stuttgart. Many sought to protect themselves by joining the NSDAP, to which only one in twenty of Württemberg's mayors – compared with one in five nationally – had belonged in January 1933. The moratorium on entry to the NSDAP imposed from 1 May 1933 worked against them, however, so that in 1935, out of a total of some 1760 mayors in Württemberg almost 700 had not joined the NSDAP, whether or not through choice.[98] Some held out for years, succumbing to pressure to join during the war, allegedly as a contribution to strengthening the 'inner front'. The mayor of the small commune of Rossfeld in Crailsheim district, for example, who had been in post since before the First World War, joined the NSDAP only in 1942.[99] On the other hand, some mayors of small communes were Nazi enthusiasts: for example, the mayor of Hofen, in Aalen district, was said to be an 'ambitious, conceited party supporter' who habitually wore his NSDAP uniform, until the last days of the war when it seemed more prudent to change into army uniform.[100] Where the mayor was not himself a party member, the NSDAP *Kreisleiter* might exert pressure to ensure that a party member was appointed deputy mayor.

In addition, it was increasingly the case that new members of local councils were politically vetted to ensure that only the 'politically reliable' were appointed. This did not necessarily mean that candidates had to be party members, but evidence of previous non-Nazi political activity would generally disqualify them. In Leonberg, the NSDAP's local branch leader wrote to his *Kreisleiter* in November 1938 to nominate six new members of the town council, including a master builder, a hereditary farmer, a manufacturer, a clerk, a lawyer and a tailor's cutter. At the same time, he intimated the resignation of four existing members. One, a Labour Front district official, presumably felt that he had enough to do; another, a shoemaker, was said to have 'wanted to give up his office for a long time'. The third was a master plumber who 'is a real old Leonberger and respected by the craftsmen, but against that [he is] politically agnostic'. The first two may well have genuinely resigned; the third clearly was required to do so. Finally, the local branch leader himself wanted to relinquish his place on the town council 'since there will already be two party officials who are councillors'. It is not clear whether he genuinely favoured a light Nazi touch on the tiller or whether he was concerned about his own workload. [101] The Leonberg *Kreisleiter* appears to have been more cautious, proposing a nominee of his own – a manufacturer who was a party member – no doubt to heighten the Nazi complexion of the council. He also required that the politically acceptable nominees – four of the local branch leader's list of six, with the lawyer and the manufacturer excluded – should each provide a handwritten curriculum vitae.[102]

In the smallest communes, it was the mayor rather than a party official who continued for the most part to play the dominant role: for example, during the war, the mayor was responsible for air raid protection in his commune.[103] Maintaining continuity was important where officials were not dismissed as political or racial 'enemies', so as not to antagonise the politically unobjectionable majority at a time when the consolidation of power was the top priority. As a general rule of thumb, the smaller the commune, the greater were a mayor's chances of retaining his post.[104] In 1935 it was recorded that, while a quarter of Württemberg's urban mayors were not NSDAP members, in rural communes this was true of 39 per cent of mayors. Even if the mayor was a party member, he was usually not a party official – the NSDAP's local branch leader, for example. The mayors of the communes of Ailingen, Waldsee, Setzingen and Weissenstein – with its 800 inhabitants – and were relatively unusual in also being local branch leaders.[105] In 1935, barely 17 per cent of those mayors who had joined the NSDAP were 'political leaders', namely local branch or district leaders of the party, while scarcely 8 per cent were officials in the SA, the SS or the HJ, and over a third belonged to other party formations or affiliates as ordinary members and perhaps often as a matter of lipservice. Of those mayors of Württemberg's communes who were party members in 1935, therefore, almost two in five were classed as 'inactive'; that is, they paid a subscription but took no part in the activities of the NSDAP or its formations or affiliates.[106] These figures indicating a lack of political engagement diminished during the 1930s as mayors served out their time and were generally replaced by NSDAP members in a 'creeping seizure of power'.[107] Yet in small communes, where mayors were frequently appointed on an honorary basis, receiving a sum for expenses while continuing to operate their own smallholding or rural business, their duties would leave them with little time for party activities, even if they were keen to engage in them.

After January 1933, over half of the incumbent mayors of Württemberg's rural communes who were not already NSDAP members had rushed to join the party. Others may have tried to do so but been thwarted by the moratorium on party entry imposed on 1 May 1933. A mayor's membership of the NSDAP might be strategic rather than a matter of conviction: many joined the party in 1933 to be sure of retaining their post, as did many of those who aspired to public office. As the NSDAP's 1935 party census returns showed, 'most opportunists come from rural areas, where a relatively greater proportion of mayors found their way to the party only *after the takeover of power*'. *Gau* Württemberg-Hohenzollern had the distinction of being the most opportunist of all, with a mere 5 per cent of rural mayors joining the party before 30 January 1933; the next most 'negative' was *Gau* Main-Franconia, at barely 8 per cent. This contrasted with the most assiduous *Gaue*, Danzig at 61 per cent and Schleswig-Holstein at 48 per cent.[108] The early wartime mayor of Untermarchtal – a commune of around a thousand inhabitants in Ehingen district – was unusual in having joined the NSDAP in 1931. He had been deputy mayor in the neighbouring commune of Munderkingen as well as acting local branch leader of the NSDAP there before he was appointed honorary mayor of Untermarchtal in September 1935. The mayor of nearby Emerkingen was more typical in having joined the party in 1933 before being appointed honorary mayor in January 1935.[109] Similarly, the mayor of Hochmössingen in Rottweil district had joined the party as a 'March violet' in 1933 and had been appointed mayor of this commune of 900 inhabitants in May 1938.[110]

Even if he was a 'March violet', at least a mayor's party membership gave NSDAP officers some purchase with him. On the other hand, mayors who were not party members were, in theory at least, in constant danger of being replaced.[111] In Sonthofen, in Münsingen district, for example, the 'March violet' mayor eventually applied to retire in 1937 after a sustained campaign against him by local NSDAP members. By contrast, some party officers were anxious not to disturb the balance in small communities. The Biberach *Kreisleiter*,

Franz Zirn, restrained an NSDAP cell leader in the commune of Steinhausen who was in dispute with the mayor because Zirn wanted to avoid reopening old wounds.[112] Similarly, in 1937, the NSDAP officer for communal policy in Nürtingen district warned the party's local branch leader in the commune of Aich, who was agitating for the removal of the mayor, that he would have to be patient. There was apparently no thought of simply sacking the mayor of Aich, and the district officer's view was that it might take a few months for him to be transferred to another post.[113]

It is doubtless true that 'where the leading National Socialists were also members of the village elite, there was usually little potential for conflict'.[114] Yet perhaps a better way of putting it would be that there was usually little potential for conflict where members of the village elite became National Socialists, although that might depend on how enthusiastic or nominal their adherence to the party was. Nevertheless, even after the destruction of the political parties and the declaration of the one party state, on 14 July 1933, in small communes former members of parties such as the Centre and the Democrats were able to remain in office as mayor and, at times, to obstruct the pretensions of local Nazi functionaries.[115] This was, however, not necessarily – and perhaps not often – a matter of resistance to the new regime. It was more likely to result from an impasse, the irresistible force of an assertive party officer meeting the immovable object of a traditional civil official.[116] It may have been true that the communes had noticeably less autonomy during the Third Reich, and that 'Württemberg society [was] partially revolutionised' with 'men from the radicalised petty bourgeoisie' claiming plum positions which had previously been the preserve of professionals and property owners. Certainly, Fritz Kiehn was able to displace the industrialist Ernst Hohner, the 'Harmonica King', as the 'King of Trossingen', the most influential man in the town, by virtue of his NSDAP credentials, although he was hardly – by this time, at least – petty bourgeois, and he was a property owner on a large scale.[117] Yet in small communities as in larger ones, new appointees as mayors were chosen on the basis of both bureaucratic competence – although sometimes this was at rather a low level – and 'political reliability', for which membership of the NSDAP was a sufficient qualification. The SD reported with satisfaction in April 1939 that 'newly-installed mayors generally match the expectations of the party'.[118] Even so, there were constraints which set limits to the extent to which the new party elites could wield effective power in the villages, and therefore to the effectiveness of *Menschenführung*.[119]

In its bid to extend its grasp over areas which had proved resistant to its appeal, in particular strongly Catholic areas, the party faced challenges which necessitated an expansion of the numbers in its lower leadership cadres. The aim was to find men – it went without saying that they were men, other than in the women's organisations – with the requisite leadership ability, ideological commitment and discipline, which meant complete acceptance of instructions from above in keeping with the *Führerprinzip*. This was, however, less straightforward than it had appeared in 1933. In many small communes where there was only a rudimentary party presence, the older members were loyal and enthusiastic but not necessarily capable of providing the kind of leadership that the national and *Gau* leaderships regarded as appropriate. Yet in Württemberg-Hohenzollern there were fewer changes than in many other *Gaue*. In immediate terms, in 1933, existing party officers generally continued in post in Württemberg – compared with massive changes elsewhere – with only eight of the sixty-two district leaderships changing hands between 1933 and 1935. More extensive changes came in 1937 with the reduction in the number of NSDAP districts to thirty-six, anticipating the diminution in the number of civil districts. This was an opportunity to remove from office *Kreisleiter* who had proved difficult or contentious; yet Richard Drauz was one who survived, in spite of the disquiet which his arbitrary leadership style had caused within the party in his Heilbronn district and in spite of the charges of a dissolute and immoral lifestyle that were levelled against him.[120] No doubt his longstanding friendship with *Gauleiter* Murr told in his favour.

There was, however, a structural problem in the NSDAP at local level: as a dictatorial, non-representative system based on the *Führerprinzip*, it was utterly dependent on the commitment and capability of its leaders, at all levels. While some party members jumped at the chance to accede to positions of minor leadership, others were less anxious to devote time and energy unpaid to what was often a thankless task, especially in wartime with its increasingly unpopular pressures. The NSDAP itself – quite apart from its formations and affiliated organisations – may have had an active corps of full-time, paid political leaders at national and *Gau* level, but even at district level there were leaders who were expected to serve *ehrenamtlich*, in an honorary capacity and, like rural mayors, receiving only an expenses allowance. If they were in state employment of some kind, they were likely to be given light duties there or, especially if they were bureaucrats or school teachers, perhaps relieved of their duties altogether while on full pay. The schoolmaster Otto Trefz, *Kreisleiter* of Ludwigsburg, came into this category. Otherwise, becoming a mayor or the editor of the local newspaper – as Richard Drauz was in Heilbronn – was an attractive option, and, with the *Gleichschaltung* of both local government and the press from 1933, there were such opportunities in the towns for some *Kreisleiter*.[121]

The battery of officials that each district NSDAP office in Württemberg could boast gives at first sight an impression of massive activity.[122] Yet there was a limited amount that even enthusiasts could do as part-time volunteers. The district leadership had a heavy workload, not only in coordinating the work of its own officials and supervising the work of its local branches and their leaders. In addition, it also had tasks such as the verification of the 'political reliability' of anyone appointed to a position of leadership in any organisation, including, for example, all the sports clubs in the district. In 1939, the *Kreisleiter* assumed yet another duty when he personally exerted pressure on party officers, state employees and the non-farming population in general to help out on farms at times of greatest need, especially at the harvest. The SD, which aimed to monitor both popular opinion and every aspect of civil life, reported that this approach elicited the best response.[123] While some *Kreisleiter*, for example Otto Hänle, first in Gaildorf and then in Crailsheim, and Otto Bosch in Schwäbisch Hall, were full-time party officers from 1935 and 1938, only in 1943 was it decreed that the *Kreisleiter* must be a full-time official, although even then four of Württemberg's thirty-six district leaders continued to act on a part-time basis.[124] The local branch leaders remained voluntary officials with only a tiny minority finding a berth in local government, while those in small rural communities were often regarded patronisingly by the sophisticated professionals in the SD.[125]

Yet the SD had a point: a lack of leadership ability and administrative competence had characterised the Württemberg NSDAP from the start, and had ensured that, in comparison with many other areas of Germany, the party's progress before 1933 had been slow. This could be compensated for in the towns by the new bureaucratic and professional opportunists who rushed to join the party between 30 January and the moratorium on entry from 1 May 1933. In the countryside it was similar, but only up to a point. While the party's aim was to create in a matter of weeks or, at most, months viable party branches where there was none, the need was for individuals in small communes who could inspire citizens or at least provide them with strong leadership. In the communes, however, both the numbers and the quality of the older members were limited. This provided an opening for many incumbent village leaders – mayors, teachers, even sometimes larger farmers – who sought to protect their position by joining the NSDAP, which undoubtedly accounts for the influx of 'opportunists' among existing mayors that was derided when the party's 1935 census results were published. Yet in many small communes the party had limited room for manoeuvre, especially if there was a priest or pastor who commanded the allegiance of the inhabitants. If it was lucky, there might be a competent local branch leader whose bailiwick embraced a number of communes, of none of which he was likely to be mayor.

NSDAP officials at local level in Württemberg were rarely farmers unless they were lowly officers of the RNS as *Ortsbauernführer*. Whereas in the Reich almost 30 per cent of political leaders of the NSDAP were farmers, in Württemberg the figure was a mere 13 per cent. By contrast, public employees were much more likely to be local Nazi functionaries in Württemberg, with 28 per cent of the total compared with 18 per cent in the Reich as a whole. Where farmers became party functionaries, it seems likely that this was at least sometimes in the hope of material gain. For example, farmers with smaller concerns might hope to benefit materially at the expense of their more prosperous neighbours.[126] Where party officials in rural areas were not public employees, they might be tradesmen, shopkeepers or innkeepers. Frequently they were not equal to the tasks of *Menschenführung*. The small numbers of capable functionaries meant that in many communes Nazi policies were implemented only partially or not at all.[127] For example, in smaller places there was a great shortage of reliable National Socialists who were skilled instructors able to coach local party functionaries in the art of 'politically reliable' public speaking, something to which the party leadership attached great importance.[128] For local Nazi activists, particularly pre-1933 members, the NSDAP remained a campaigning party, after 1933 as before it. Those in the minority of communes where there was a Jewish presence saw themselves as guardians of 'Aryan' supremacy, trying to enforce antisemitic policies of boycott and harassment.[129] This gave them a new purpose in a system where, after the summer of 1933, there were no longer any open political opponents to combat.

The local branch was the lowest level of the party's organisation to embrace only NSDAP members; a local branch was, in theory, composed of up to 1500 members – a figure greater than that of the total population in many of Württemberg's communes – but often it had many fewer. If the commune was very small, the party might establish a base (*Stutzpunkt*), which was not a formal part of the party's hierarchical organisational structure but at least provided a focus for local party activists. In many of Württemberg's communes the party was slow to develop even this kind of foothold. This was particularly the case in old Centre Party strongholds such as Saulgau district in the south, where in 1935 only one in five of the communes had a Nazi organisation; yet even in Stümpfig's overwhelmingly Evangelical Nazi stronghold of Gerabronn county the figure was just below the *Land* average of 50 per cent.[130] After four years of Nazi rule, in 1937 the NSDAP had established local branches in scarcely 800 of Württemberg's communes. In addition, there were bases in around 250 communes. This left over 800 communes without a Nazi presence. In the forty communes in Catholic Wangen district, there were twenty-six Nazi units, half of them local branches and half bases. In the two most northerly districts, Crailsheim and Mergentheim, where electoral support for the NSDAP had been significant before 1933, there were only thirty-four local branches and nine bases in a total of 126 communes. These were not dissident Catholic areas; rather, their confessional profile was almost exclusively Evangelical. They were also strongly agrarian districts.[131]

The party's position was, then, precarious in some rural communities in Württemberg, not least because of the patchy and incomplete nature of the NSDAP's territorial organisation. Yet even in Trossingen, which had given the NSDAP support well above the *Land* average in the elections of 1930 and 1932, but significantly below it in March 1933, there were a few party activists and a small number of unequivocal opponents. The overwhelming majority of the inhabitants were prepared to conform outwardly, but this masked varying degrees of acquiescence, indifference or disaffection. Like Württembergers elsewhere, the good citizens of Trossingen paid lip-service to the new dictatorial order insofar as they were positively required to do so. To the disappointment of the party's activists, and in particular Fritz Kiehn, they showed little interest in the party's projects, events and press. The early electoral support for the party in Trossingen had, it transpired, not been the harbinger of widespread enthusiasm for National Socialism in the town, and any good will that the party had had was dissipated when the contrasts between propaganda and reality became evident, even before the hardships of the war were felt.[132]

Claims made after 1945 that there was scant support for the NSDAP in this or that area tend to arouse scepticism; there can be little doubt that they are sometimes disingenuous. In the Remstal area near Stuttgart, it was said, somewhat dismissively, circa 1970 that 'during the Nazi period the small villages … were not a centre of political action, though some of the inhabitants became Nazis'.[133] In a Catholic village in the Hohenlohe, the picture presented was slightly more nuanced: 'a handful of local farmers' came out in favour of the new regime, with 'a larger group … as passively resistant as possible', while most kept a low profile.[134] In Hausen, a commune of some 400 inhabitants, the party's impact was admitted to have been greater: around 17 per cent of the men joined the NSDAP, although this seems to have been less a matter of ideological conviction than of prudence.[135] Contemporary sources do not necessarily contradict these portrayals, but they do suggest a greater degree of Nazi activism than accounts after the event concede. The extent to which that activism generated a positive popular response can be judged only partially, but the picture that emerges is one in which a limited number of activists strove energetically to implement orders from above and to drum up support for the party's projects, frequently in the face of apathy or muted resentment. The most common form of obstruction of party activities was a refusal to be involved in them, but occasionally there were instances of positive opposition in individual localities. In some places, for example, the Hitler Youth had great difficulty in establishing itself because of the opposition of church youth groups.[136] Both the dictatorial Nazi system and the nature of introverted village communes ensured that piecemeal local acts of obstruction remained just that. Yet, if there was no concerted resistance to attempts at Nazification, that does not detract from the fact that substantial numbers of Württembergers in a variety of communes were resistant to it.

While the membership of local branches and bases consisted solely of party members, local branches were divided into groups of households, regardless of whether the inhabitants were or were not party members. They were designed particularly to mobilise and scrutinise Germans in densely populated areas, but they were also applied to rural communes, with 'consideration given to population density and local conditions'. An example from Freudenstadt district in 1936 shows that, while normally a cell consisted of four to eight blocks, in the Wörnersberg local branch there were two cells – each consisting of two blocks – deriving from three communes. The communes of Wörnersberg and Edelweiler had thirty-six and thirty-seven households, respectively, which constituted three 'house groups' and therefore one block in each. The third commune in the local branch, Grömbach, had 118 households divided into groups of nine to ten houses, comprising two blocks.[137] The local branch leader, a part-time official, therefore had under his authority two communes in which he was not resident – assuming that he was resident in the third. He could not personally keep all three under close surveillance, although he would, in the *Blockleiter* (block leader) and any assistants he might have, effectively have agents in them. For this to work as a surveillance system in villages, there had to be individuals who were ready to inform on their neighbours. This undoubtedly accounts for the bitterness with which former NSDAP members in some smaller communes were regarded after 1945.[138] Nevertheless, apart from the general irritant and the occasional danger of having a party snooper for a neighbour, in rural districts and communes the *Landrat*, the mayor and the *Ortsbauernführer* were, from the point of view of the daily life of the community, the most significant officials. Mayors were frequently assertive in defending their authority in their area, for example against what they perceived to be encroachments by members of the *Gendarmerie*.[139]

By 1933, the NSDAP had made headway in some individual small towns and rural communes, although rather less in the strongly Catholic areas of southern Württemberg. This, however, was something of a lottery, demonstrating that the issue of the quality of leadership was crucial. If there was a local enthusiast who was well enough regarded and sufficiently energetic, there were the makings of a local branch (*Ortsgruppe*). An idealistic activist might inspire individuals or even a group in a neighbouring commune to join his local branch, or even to found their own.[140] If a local notable or businessman was a convert to National Socialism, he might establish his own local branch virtually as his own fiefdom: Fritz Kiehn in Trossingen was a case in point.[141] Alternatively, a mayor or member of a commune's council who commanded respect in his locality might join the party and encourage others to do so. For example, Georg Stümpfig had been a mayor in Gerabronn county for ten years when he joined the NSDAP in 1929. In the following year he became a district leader of the party in the north, taking over the leadership of the new Gerabronn district after the party's territorial reorganisation in 1932. Combining civil and party offices in this way undoubtedly enabled a handful of NSDAP officials to make a strong local impression for the party, especially, in this case, when Stümpfig devoted much of his political activity to championing the farmers in his district.[142] Where there was not the kind of leadership or impetus provided by a local notable, or where NSDAP activists had created a poor impression, communities might be resistant rather than receptive to the Nazi message. Yet a good impression could generate a different response: members of the commune of Gebersheim, which came within the remit of the NSDAP's Leonberg local branch, 'refused to be actively involved [in the party] themselves because, they said, party member Schmid', the Württemberg Interior Minister, who had been born in Gebersheim, 'had already done so much for the general good that there was no need for them to do anything'. For this and other reasons, the local branch leader referred to the Gebersheim cell in 1939 as the 'problem child' of his branch.[143]

In the first flush of success, in 1933, there seemed to be no limit to the number of people rushing to join the party, whether from an access of enthusiasm or because they had a position of some kind to protect and saw joining the party as their best insurance policy. Civil servants and urban professionals and businessmen were more likely to feel exposed in this respect than small farmers, tradesmen or artisans, in the early years of the Third Reich, at least. The latter were less likely to be dependent on party favour in order to maintain their livelihood.[144] The opportunism of Württembergers was well illustrated by the party membership list for the Leonberg local branch, which numbered 178 in 1936. While it recorded that a few members had joined before 1933, including a medical doctor, a lawyer, a businessman and two farmers, the influx of 'March violets' is striking. It included the *Landrat*, the mayor, two policemen, three doctors, a teacher, a judge, seven farmers and an agricultural labourer.[145] It seems, however, from remarks made by the local branch leader in 1939, that the influx of members had not been translated into active enthusiasm for the party. He had, he said, been up against traditional attitudes and allegiances in trying to establish a viable Nazi group. Those inhabitants with deep roots in the commune, 'the Old-Leonbergers ... are very proud of their own efforts and have little interest in anything else. This has led to a certain amount of inbreeding and to resistance to anything modern'. This had its effect on his local branch, where only six out of fifty office-holders were 'Old-Leonbergers', and this pattern was repeated in the affiliated organisations. 'It takes years', he said, 'for one to get "close" to the old established citizens.' As if that had not been enough to contend with, there had been 'quarrels of a personal nature' within the party's ranks, and in the years 1933–36 there had also been disputes between the party members of longer standing and the district leader. This had inhibited the party's activities until about 1937, when, with the easing of the moratorium on membership, there had been an influx of new members.[146]

Some local branches experienced even slower development, with their major growth period occurring during the Second World War, once the moratorium on entry to the party had been lifted. For example, in block two of cell one in the Schorndorf local branch, in *Kreis* Waiblingen, of the eight people who were members in 1942 one had joined in 1932 and two in 1934. In cell four, block one of the same branch, four of the nineteen who were members in 1942 had joined as 'March violets' on 1 May 1933, and none earlier.[147] Similarly, the Böckingen branch, in *Kreis* Heilbronn recorded in 1944 that two of its members had joined the NSDAP in 1933, one in 1934, and two in 1935; these were all men. Two women had joined the NSF in 1935, and one girl had joined the BDM (League of German Girls) in the same year. Even allowing for some turnover, perhaps with earlier members dying or leaving the area, these figures are very low indeed. Beyond them, none of the 1944 members of the party and its formations or affiliates had been members before the easing of the moratorium in 1937, and no men were recorded as being members of the SA, the SS or any affiliated organisation.[148] Yet the SA was active in Heilbronn district, with the Brettach unit consisting of 113 men in July 1935; there were also another twenty-three men on its books who had not, in spite of repeated reminders, paid their subscription. With a few exceptions, the Brettach SA men were classed as farmers – or, at least, they were described as being 'mainly farmers' sons and agricultural labourers'. The 136 men of the Brettach SA did not, however, all belong to the commune of Brettach. On the contrary, a mere seven were from Brettach itself, while the remainder belonged to sixteen other communes to the north of the town of Heilbronn.[149]

In most localities there were at least a few people who, whether out of genuine if misplaced idealism or whether because they clearly saw the main chance and took it, indeed worked 'tirelessly' ('*unermüdlich*') – as party zealots liked to claim – to promote the party's growth and influence in their area. For some of them, *Menschenführung* was an honourable task that could succeed in winning hearts and minds. The Leonberg local branch leader wrote earnestly about the need to strengthen 'even more than hitherto the confidence of the people in the party and its formations'. He believed that he had found a way of doing this, holding block meetings to which every inhabitant of the block was invited both by letter and in person by the block leader. This tactic was employed to improve participation, because many Leonbergers who were not party members 'have still never attended a party function'. It was always the same people, he said, both members and non-members, who attended public meetings, with the rest conspicuous by their absence. This was true even of cultural offerings, although one of the problems there was that Leonberg did not have suitable accommodation for a large event. The block meetings, which had only recently been introduced had, claimed the local branch leader, brought out altogether around 1200 people, something which previously had not been achieved in Leonberg. Among those attending had been 'devout' Christians and former political opponents – 'erstwhile supporters of the KPD and SPD' – including people who had experienced a term of incarceration in the concentration camp at Heuberg. The Leonberg leader believed that these block assemblies showed people that the party was taking an interest in them and was paying attention to their concerns, however small. In his view these assemblies ought in time to be able to fulfil the same purpose as a clergyman's prayer meetings.[150] He did not, however, draw the conclusion that personal invitations might be construed as targeted commands that it could be foolish to ignore. Those who had spent time in a concentration camp might be reluctant to risk repeating the experience.

Sometimes party activists were rewarded with a warm reaction, although this tended to be on a piecemeal basis, in relation to individual projects or events which particularly appealed to people in a specific locality. Sometimes there was grudging involvement, and at other times it was hard enough to persuade even paid up party members, let alone the unorganised population, to participate in NSDAP activities. In Trossingen, the theatre performances mounted by the Labour Front's 'Strength through Joy' project were 'from the point of view of attendance and income, a fiasco'.[151] Elsewhere, the audiences for 'Strength through Joy' performances had to be boosted by mass attendance by members of the Hitler Youth.[152] At the same time, party affiliates could be infiltrated by individuals with dissident political or ideological viewpoints. The Württemberg SD reported in July 1939 that 'democrats' were using not only song societies, bowling clubs and pubs as meeting places but 'seem even to want to make the NSV their own domain'.[153] Certainly, the treasurer of the NSV in Trossingen used his home visits both for NSV business and to deliver literature for the Evangelical Church, which was viewed as a competitor organisation.[154]

There could also be changes in attitude over time: the incessant fund-raising campaigns of the NSV, for example, were an initial novelty that soon wore off, especially as the depression receded and, with it, the numbers of the destitute. In the Leonberg local branch, by 1938 NSV collections were held 'just about every Sunday', with the branch leader clearly displeased that neither the money raised nor the goods donated were distributed in Leonberg district, far less within his local branch itself.[155] This was not an isolated criticism of the NSV. In November 1941, the SD reported that in one rural commune a woman supported by the wartime Winter Aid scheme of the NSV had had her hair permed. The NSV members then complained that 'we've got to pay NSV contributions so that people can have perms'. The mayor of the same commune said, on receiving Winter Aid vouchers from the NSV, 'Tell me, to whom should I give these vouchers? I don't know anyone in my commune who is as needy as that'.[156]

By the later 1930s, while many Germans were satisfied with the achievements of Hitler's government at home and abroad, the NSDAP itself had become in many places an object of dislike or derision.[157] People still queued to join it, but more because of what membership of the party could do for them than for any service which they could render to it; possibly an even greater reason was the negative one that it was often felt to be disadvantageous *not* to be a member.[158] The formations and affiliated organisations, too, had recruited members, but, again, these were often people intent on demonstrating their 'political reliability' at a time when entry to the party itself was restricted.[159] In the Geradstetten local branch in *Kreis* Waiblingen, the party census of 1 October 1938 showed that block four of cell one consisted of forty-three households in four 'house groups'. Altogether, there were 160 inhabitants, of whom 142 were over ten years of age, the minimum age for membership of the junior branches of the HJ, the *Jungvolk* for boys and the *Jungmädel* for girls. Half of this population – eighty-one persons – had joined either the NSDAP, a formation or an affiliated organisation. Only fifteen, however, were party members, of whom three were 'political leaders' who had multiple memberships, as would be expected of enthusiasts. A further eleven people were multiple members, including all but one of the seven SA members and the single members of the Nazi civil servants' association and the war veterans' welfare organisation who belonged also to other groups, as did the seven members of the air raid protection association. Of the thirteen HJ and eight BDM members, three and one, respectively, were members of other party groups, but the five NSF members belonged only to it. Three boys belonged to the *Jungvolk* and nine girls to the *Jungmädel*. The largest memberships were of the German Labour Front, with forty-one, and the NSV, with eighteen. There was no mention on the form of either the *Reichsnährstand* or the *Ortsbauernschaft*, of which farmers and rural traders were obligatory members. No one in Geradstetten belonged to any of the other professional organisations, for doctors, lawyers, engineers, teachers, lecturers or students, nor did anyone belong to the Nazi automobile drivers' association.[160]

By contrast with relatively well-developed branches such as those in Leonberg and Geradstetten, some smaller units of the NSDAP remained underdeveloped to the end. For example, in Massenbachhausen, *Kreis* Heilbronn, there were at least four successive cell leaders between 1933 and 1945. There was a 'propaganda leader', along with ten block officers. The only other organisation was the NSV, which had a cell NSV leader from 1942 to 1945 and five block officers whose function was to make collections.[161] Some local branches did develop their organisation beyond a rudimentary level, but only in the later 1930s, and, even then, the structures put in place could belie the limited nature of their activities. In *Kreis* Waiblingen, for example, the NSDAP local branch in the commune of Beinstein was by 1945 composed of two cells with six relatively small blocks and a total membership of around one hundred, including twenty-one young people in the HJ or BDM. Most of the HJ and BDM members appear to have belonged to families with party members. Several members had also joined other party formations or affiliates, in particular the NSV. All of the women NSDAP members had joined the NSF, and most were apparently married to party members. Certainly, there was a *Schulungsleiter* (training officer), but this role was filled by the local branch leader himself. The 'propaganda leader', in post since 1937, had also been 'culture leader' since 1940. The NSF leader served from 1937 to 1945, as did the leader of cell one, whereas cell two had three different leaders between 1937 and 1945. This may have been partly because a vacancy was caused by wartime conscription, as was the case with the local branch's treasurer, who was conscripted in 1944. The propaganda and culture leader had also taken over the leadership of the NSV in Beinstein in 1940 because his two predecessors had been called up and then become prisoners of war. While Beinstein had the entire panoply of offices, its senior officials admitted that 'given the minimal importance of the commune, several offices existed only partially, or did so in name only, for example the office of the radio and film leader and that of the press officer'. In fact, the role of 'press officer' had been occupied only between December 1938 and February 1939, and the incumbent had in that time written only the one article. Nevertheless, the same *Ortsbauernführer* was in post from 1933 until 1945, suggesting that in this small rural commune this officer was more significant than most.[162]

Again, in Böckingen, in *Kreis* Heilbronn, the easing of the moratorium on party membership in 1937 brought a modest influx of men into the party with eight new members in the years 1937 to 1939. A further nine men joined between 1940 and 1944. There were also new recruits to the formations and affiliates, with the NSF adding to the two members who had joined in 1935 a further four in 1937–39, then five more members during the war. This made it possible to establish a branch of the 'mass' organisation for women, the DFW, which by 1944 had seven members.[163] This inappropriate ratio between the 'elite' NSF and the 'mass' DFW was not unusual.[164] In some districts there were relatively affluent housewives who readily took on the task of NSF district leader on an honorary basis; Fritz Kiehn's wife, Berta, described by her grandson as always a '150 per cent' enthusiast, was appointed NSF district leader in Tuttlingen in 1934 by the *Gau* leadership.[165] NSF leaders were expected to mobilise their members for general party purposes as well as for specifically women's activities. The Geradstetten NSF received special mention in the local branch leader's report in September 1940 for its contribution to the harvesting of local crops.[166]

Yet there were also districts, such as Öhringen, where, contrary to party instructions, in 1937 the district NSF leadership was 'currently unoccupied'. So scarce were women volunteers that sometimes an NSF district leader had to take on responsibility for two or more districts.[167] While all of the district NSF posts were filled by November 1942, one woman had had to assume the leadership of three district NSF offices, those of Ehingen and Münsingen as well as that of Biberach where she was resident. These three districts were overwhelmingly rural. At the same time, the NSF/DFW's section for National Economy/Domestic Economy had representatives in all of the districts except for Ehingen.[168] At local level, NSF leaders were thin on the ground. If there was no district leader, the chances of there being active local branches were slim. Even in 1939, some local branches had no NSF group because no one was prepared to organise one on an honorary basis.[169] In October 1941, the party's National Women's Leadership admitted that 'with the exception of a few *Gaue*, the involvement of rural women in the work of the NSF/DFW has so far had only very limited practical effect'.[170]

The moratorium on entry from 1 May 1933 had to some extent stemmed the tide of opportunists but had neither arrested it completely nor reversed it. The resulting heavy weight of 'inactive members' was an affront to genuine enthusiasts, while the moratorium on entry excluded others who, after careful vetting, might have been potential activists who could inject vitality – as well as cash, through extra subscriptions – into the party in their area. With the announcement that the moratorium would be eased in May 1937, the Stuttgart district leadership warned that 'we do not want a repeat of April 1933 when thousands upon thousands were admitted on the unspoken but clear assumption that they would have fulfilled their duty to the National Socialist movement by simply paying their subscription'. Admission meant that the new entrant 'pledged himself to active service'.[171] As Robert Ley would say in the more desperate circumstances of summer 1944, 'Every party comrade is obliged to cooperate and can be called upon to do so at any time. *There are no such things as political pensioners*'.[172] Ordinary members perhaps saw things differently. In 1939, the Leonberg local branch leader claimed that 'especially among members of the NSDAP, the mood is and was good'. Yet at the same time he admitted that the crisis over Hitler's demand for the Sudetenland in the summer of 1938 'showed that to some extent even [party] members themselves still have much to learn about believing in the Führer; a small number were in complete despair and thought that the whole of Europe was going to go under, and their petty little selves with it'.[173]

The Stuttgart and Leonberg districts were not alone in having problems. The local branch leader in Geradstetten sent a circular in June 1937 to both party members and those on the party's waiting list for membership in which he complained about their reprehensible behaviour:

> It is clear that party members and candidate members still do not understand, or do not want to understand, the spirit and purpose of the NSDAP as an organisation. They believe that they do not need to attend party events or meetings, to the extent that many of them go to the length of viewing parades from the window of their house. This constitutes a breach of discipline and a wilfulness worse than which one cannot imagine.

In future, he said, members who did not have written permission from their block or cell leader to be absent from an event would be reported to the district leader or even the *Gauleiter*, because the party was not interested in those who merely paid their subscription.[174] Excluding party members was facilitated by the requirement that, in order to be valid, a party membership card had to be stamped with a 'control mark' every three months.[175] This was in addition to the membership book in which red stamps were affixed each month – from 1943, each quarter – to indicate payment of the subscription.[176]

From this point onwards, the Geradstetten local branch leader kept a register of his ninety-nine members, to enable him to monitor unauthorised absences. Any member who missed three events without permission was considered to have resigned from the party because of a lack of interest. Membership of the NSDAP, he said, was not like membership of the old associations of the previous era, where members picked and chose when to attend. Apparently unconsciously, however, he hit on the nub of the problem. In requiring of 'every single party member the conscientious collaboration and effort of his whole being for the party and its organisations', in the way that the district leader expected this from his local branch leaders, he overestimated the extent of enthusiasm, as opposed to assent, that the mass of his members felt compared with genuine believers, like himself, who devoted most of their free time to the party.[177] Other local branch leaders, and some leaders of party formations, were similarly reduced to making attendance at meetings and events mandatory for members, either mentioning or implying that attendance had previously been poor. For example, the local branch leader in Nürtingen South summoned all party members to a celebration on 30 January 1939 of the sixth anniversary of Hitler's appointment as Chancellor with the words: 'I expect total participation'.[178] In April 1940, he informed his cell leaders that he required 'all male and female party members' to attend an evening event on 20 April to celebrate Hitler's birthday.[179] Again, the Höfingen local branch in *Kreis* Leonberg announced in the local newspaper that a party meeting would be held at 8.30 on 12 July 1940, a Saturday evening, at which the local branch leader of Merklingen would be the speaker, adding: 'attendance is obligatory for all party members and candidate members'.[180] Also in Leonberg in July 1940, the Eltingen local branch's NSF held a meeting at which a lecture on 'England: The Enemy' was delivered. In announcing this event, the leadership added: 'for members, attendance is compulsory; please bring guests'.[181]

The insistence and urgency with which NSDAP local functionaries tried to goad their members into participation reflected the pressure being imposed on them from above.[182] In the line management culture of Nazi Germany, there always seemed to be someone further up the chain of command who was demanding a report on recent activity, a plan for future activity, a statistical breakdown of events, participants and collections, or the recruitment of more citizens into party formations and affiliates. In February 1938, for example, the

NSF leader in Nürtingen South belatedly sent a typed copy of her 'Activity Plan', with its four scheduled events for that month, to her local branch leader.[183] Once again belatedly, she reported to him in October 1938 on the events which she had planned for that month, which included a speaker whose subject was not mentioned, a session sorting second-hand clothing that had been collected, and a study group on ethnic Germans living outside the Reich.[184] Her branch leader, in his turn, had already reported, on time and on the standard form, to the Nürtingen district leader that his branch would hold four events in February: a joint meeting with the Nürtingen North branch; a training session on 'National Socialism and Socialism in the Third Reich'; a farmers' meeting at which the speaker would be the area farmers' leader from Bissingen; and – presumably for light relief – a members' evening in an inn.[185] The Nürtingen district leader, too, seems to have been under pressure from above. In September 1940 he wrote to all his local branch leaders to remind them that they had not yet given him the information about trainee leaders that he was required to submit in a few days' time to the *Gau* leadership.[186] How many replies he received is not recorded, but one local branch leader responded quickly with a 'nil return'.[187]

Local branch leaders were also summoned to attend district events, for example the one held in Nürtingen on a Saturday afternoon in April 1940. As this was Hitler's birthday, 20 April, there was the incentive that long-service medals would be presented to those who had given ten or fifteen years of service to the NSDAP.[188] These cost virtually nothing while massaging the egos of enthusiasts. Yet extraneous events could impose limits on what local party leaders could achieve. As a result of the outbreak of foot and mouth disease in 1938, those in the worst affected districts were instructed by the *Gau* party leadership to restrict the size of their meetings so as to avoid unnecessary travel. In Roigheim, near Heilbronn, the harvest festival of 1937 was the last event of the year because of the ban on assemblies between mid October 1937 and the middle of March 1938. After the lifting of the prohibition, however, little had been achieved by July 1938 other than preparations for the summer solstice celebrations.[189] In the Kirchhausen local branch, the leader of the culture section reported to the Heilbronn district office that 'major events could not be held in the first half of 1938'. On the brighter side, he announced that a district song had been adopted by all formations and affiliates, as well as by schools and choirs. It had also been possible to hold local celebrations on 1 May, with the HJ prominent.[190]

Pressure was constantly exerted on local officers to enrol ordinary citizens in the party's affiliates, particularly the NSV, which incessantly touted for contributions. In June 1938, cell leaders in the Nürtingen South local branch were summoned to the party office with the instruction that they should bring a list of the NSV members in their cell.[191] A recent membership drive to recruit subscribers in the Nürtingen South local branch had netted ninety new members, of whom fifty-three had been recruited by the cell and block leaders of the NSDAP, thirty-one by the NSV's own local officers, and a derisory three each by the war veterans' association and the NSF.[192] Cell number two of the branch had yielded no new members, whether or not because of a lack of vigour on the part of the cell's leader.[193] The local branch propaganda leader's strategy in this campaign had been to advise the cell and block leaders to look through their register of party members and to enrol in the NSV the substantial number who had newly joined the party, after the lifting of the moratorium. He believed that this included several state employees, who could be targeted relatively easily. The local branch leader was under pressure from the Nürtingen district leader to improve his NSV membership, because the district leader, in turn, had received complaints from the district NSV leader that several local branches in Nürtingen had made no effort at all to drum up support for the NSV. The *Kreisleiter* was clearly embarrassed that, before this 1938 campaign, Nürtingen had improved in the *Gau*'s league table of district NSV membership only from thirtieth to twenty-ninth: 'What's the point of that?', he asked, 'Nürtingen district is accustomed to being in sixth or seventh place in the *Gau*'.[194]

The apparent success of the 1938 campaign in Nürtingen South did not achieve enough to satisfy the *Kreisleiter*. Some fifteen months later, the business manager of Nürtingen district was writing to the Nürtingen South local branch leader to say that his branch, with its 465 NSV members – which meant that about one third of all households in the branch subscribed to the NSV – stood at seventeenth in the district's league table. Appealing to a spirit of competitiveness, he pointed out that the Nürtingen North branch was in first place, with a 65 per cent membership. Therefore the *Kreisleiter* now required half of all households in Nürtingen South to join, although the business manager made it clear that recruitment was to be pursued 'tactfully ... It must not look from the outside as if it is compulsory'. Compulsory, however, it was for some, with the district NSDAP office providing the local branch leader with a list of those in his branch who were to be the first targets, namely those who received recurrent child allowances. These would be the parents of needy large families, whose financial position was likely to be precarious enough without having to make a 'voluntary' donation for the dubious privilege of joining the NSV.[195] Obviously, however, it was easier to exert pressure on those who had something to lose. The business manager added that a list would also be provided of farmers who had in recent years received a grant of any kind from the *Reichsnährstand*, although this list was merely to be used as a guide.[196] Presumably he recognised that it was less easy to cajole those who had at some point in the past received a single grant than those in receipt of recurrent benefit.

The unrelenting pressure on political leaders embraced other areas. For example, the leader of cell one of the Nürtingen South local branch reported in August 1938 that he had recruited five volunteers from among his political leaders to help to bring in the harvest on Saturday, 20 August, including block officials.[197] Block leaders also recruited volunteers in their area for that same weekend, from among both party members and non-members, because of the shortage of labour on the land.[198] On another matter, the *Gau* finance officer contacted the Geradstetten local branch treasurer in May 1938 to ask that he respond to a request that he had made almost a year earlier for information about the money received for scrap metal that had been collected in his area, and how the money had been utilised. If there had been no collection and no proceeds, 'a nil return', he said, 'is required'.[199] The Geradstetten treasurer now replied by return that the war veterans' welfare organisation had carried out the collection and that the sum of 19 marks had been delivered to the district finance office.[200] In Nürtingen, too, the war veterans' welfare organisation was charged with a leading role in collecting scrap metal, with the district economic adviser urging NSDAP local branch leaders to ensure that 'redoubled care, attention, tenacity and industriousness' was expended on this campaign in summer 1939.[201]

Given the pressures and demands, it was hardly surprising that some political leaders felt they were carrying too heavy a burden, and either declined to take on additional responsibilities or asked to be relieved of some of their functions. The Leonberg local branch leader, who was also a district official of both the Labour Front and the NSV, asked to be relieved of his leadership of the district's cultural affairs office, recommending in his place a teacher who was a candidate for party membership.[202] Similarly, *Kreisbauernführer* Schmidgall resigned from the council of the Stuttgart Marketing Association 'because of pressure of work'.[203] Again, Richard Drauz felt unable to take on an extra duty, as a member of the council of the consumers' group of the Association of German Meat Producers.[204] The ever-increasing number of posts and committee memberships in the Third Reich's excessively bureaucratised system became too great for the relatively small number of trusted enthusiasts whose 'political reliability' could be guaranteed. The result was that a broader group of people had to be involved, preferably from among individuals with some expertise in the relevant area. Yet, because expertise was not enough in a dictatorial system, every member of every group had to have his or her 'political reliability' vouched for by a political leader, usually the NSDAP *Kreisleiter*.

If the person in question was a party member, vetting was relatively simple. For example, in 1938 the Stuttgart *Kreisleitung* confirmed the appointment of a party member who had been nominated as the consumers' representative on the Stuttgart Marketing Association's council and who had already served as deputy for the same post. To make doubly sure, however, that this sensitive role was conducted reliably, from the regime's point of view, the district leadership further suggested that a bank official who was also an NSDAP local branch leader should be appointed deputy.[205] By autumn 1940, the deputy had taken over the role of representative in his own right; it seems that this did not result from the conscription of his predecessor.[206] The nomination of a press officer for the *Kreisbauernschaft* Stuttgart in May 1939 was, if anything, an even more sensitive matter. The Leonberg *Kreisleiter* was, accordingly, asked to provide a certificate of 'political reliability' for the chosen candidate.[207] With those who were not party members, more detailed investigation was made. For example, in response to a query from the *Gau* Organisation Leader in November 1942, the Stuttgart *Kreisleitung* sent the following appraisal:

> G.S. is a member only of the NSV, since 1 April 1934. His readiness to contribute to collections leaves a lot to be desired. He is in the RLB [air raid protection association]. Nothing is known here about any previous membership by S. of another political party. In terms of character, citizen S. is fine, and he enjoys a good reputation in his area. There is nothing damaging about him from the political point of view. He is very well disposed towards the church.[208]

These last two remarks were potentially contradictory, given the tense relations between the party and the churches at this time, but his church affiliation does not seem to have disadvantaged the candidate in this case.

Even in as insignificant an area as the women's organisation, references were required. Four women in the Böckingen North local branch were admitted to the *NS-Frauenschaft* in 1939 after having shown exemplary diligence in carrying out every task required of them in the *Deutsches Frauenwerk* and the NSV, according to their NSF local branch leader.[209] In wartime, the strengthening of the 'inner front' became an increasingly greater priority, to try to ensure that faith in the leadership and in its ability to deliver 'final victory' did not waver. In August 1944, even women who were running homecraft training courses in rural areas were required to seek NSDAP accreditation. The Heilbronn *Kreisleitung* found most in its area to be 'politically reliable', but five were rejected. Two were said 'to have no connection with the NSDAP, attend no meetings and have still not abandoned their negative attitude'. Another woman was 'most unforthcoming about all political issues'. She had already had 'a politically undesirable influence' on Land Year girls whom she had trained. A fourth was said to have a very negative attitude towards the party and its formations and affiliates. They were all refused accreditation on the grounds that they could not be trusted to instruct their pupils from the National Socialist point of view. Approval could not be given to the fifth woman because nothing was known about her political attitudes and a report on her was pending.[210]

At the same time, the party was permanently vigilant about the conduct of its members. Those who had committed a criminal offence, such as murder, grievous bodily harm, sexual abuse of children, assisting with an abortion, theft, violation of the War Economy Decree or failure to pay taxes, could be expelled. The same applied to those who had brought the party into disrepute by consorting with a 'racial enemy', selling property to a Jew, using the services of a Jewish lawyer or corresponding with Radio Moscow. There were also various categories of offence against the party itself, including failure to maintain subscription payments – whether 'maliciously' or not – defamation of the Führer, spreading rumours, and the rather vaguer categories of 'un-National Socialist attitude', 'uncomradely behaviour' and 'indiscipline'. Party members accused of these and other similar offences would have their case heard in the party's district court, with the court subsequently making a recommendation to the *Kreisleiter* about whether the supreme sanction of exclusion from the NSDAP, or some lesser penalty, should be imposed.

One of the offences which could result in disciplinary action was if members of the party engaged in quarrels with each other.[211] Yet squabbles and disputes had characterised the Württemberg NSDAP since its inception, and neither Hitler's assumption of power nor the outbreak of war altered that. For example, in Weingarten-Ravensburg, in south-eastern Württemberg, the differences both between party and state agencies and within the party itself were regarded by the SD as being particularly regrettable because the strongly Catholic allegiance of the inhabitants made it 'politically a very difficult area'.[212] Again, in strongly Catholic Wiblingen, near Ulm, the local branch leader was forthright in expressing his anger at an HJ leader's overbearing conduct, not least in 'denigrating the achievements of the rural population'.[213] The Württemberg HJ was involved in damaging jurisdictional disputes with both the SS and the SD, as well as with the NSLB. The SD deplored the attitudes which the HJ fostered in the young, lamenting, as adults do, that 'the young of today lack any proper work ethic and will not take a telling off'. Indeed, so assertive was the HJ that pressure from it in particular, and from the party generally, on the teaching profession had apparently led to a shortage of recruits for teaching in Württemberg, at a time when military service was already depleting the profession. Further, there were outbreaks of 'indiscipline' among HJ members, who were supposed to be showing a good example. With overt *Schadenfreude*, the SD reported in July 1939 that 20 per cent of the 261 sexual offences recorded in Württemberg in the first quarter of 1939 had been committed by members of the HJ – adding that 'happily, the SS is not represented at all'. The SD claimed that its main concern was the adverse effect that this would have on popular opinion, but this was no isolated example of snide comments on its part about the HJ.[214] Beyond that, 'after the seizure of power, rivalry between the SA and the SS was particularly bitter in Württemberg.'[215]

The tensions between the SA and the SS were evident in the Leonberg local branch. The SA unit had been founded in 1923, and, when some of its members had broken away to found a local SS group, they were widely regarded as apostates. In 1939, the local branch leader could still say that the SS had made little headway in Leonberg. Further, in the women's organisation, he admitted, there were regrettable class distinctions 'which will have to be resolved as quickly as possible'. Beyond that, it was a source of grievance to the leadership that even in the later 1930s it did not have a dedicated office of its own, partly because the mayor's staff in the town of Leonberg had been augmented when the district of Eltingen had been absorbed, which meant that the extra office staff had to be housed in the only spare municipal accommodation. Because the part-time local branch leader was also the full-time district officer of the Labour Front, he was able to use Labour Front premises as his local branch office. But 'apart from a typewriter and a very small cupboard, the local branch owned nothing'. This was not unusual in small local branches, with NSDAP officers often reduced to trying to obtain municipal accommodation from a mayor through entreaties or even threats. But what particularly rankled with the Leonberg party leader was that the local NSV 'was growing ... into an ever larger superorganisation' in which increasing numbers of staff were being employed on a full-time basis, while the Hitler Youth in his area was lobbying for a hostel with eighteen rooms at a time when 'the local branch leadership has to content itself with one room'.[216] The contrast with his own position was all too clear.

The sheer size of the HJ gave its leaders and some of its members a self-confidence that many adults – not only teachers – found intolerable. Under the leadership of Baldur von Schirach, from 1933 heavy pressure was exerted on juveniles to conform by joining the appropriate section of the HJ, which brought gratifying returns even if some church youth groups stubbornly refused to dissolve themselves.[217] By 1936, about one half of the relevant age group – ten to eighteen year olds of both sexes – had joined the HJ, BDM, *Jungmädel* or *Jungvolk*, and the law issued in that year making membership compulsory, but without sanctions to enforce compulsion, yielded over seven million members out of a total German constituency of almost nine million, a proportion of 82 per cent of the age group. This degree of success was, however, insufficient for the zealots.[218] With children of school age the easiest members of the population to coerce into a Nazi formation, in March 1939 compulsory membership of the HJ and its subdivisions for all young 'Aryan' Germans up to the age of eighteen was enforced. The majority of juveniles who left school at the age of fourteen were less easy to monitor; nevertheless, it was claimed in 1939 that over 90 per cent of the ten to eighteen age group was enrolled in the HJ and its subdivisions.[219]

Enrolment was, however, not enough. It may have been true that 'the Nazis constructed their own organisations – particularly effectively for the younger generation – and carried them into the deepest provincial hinterland in a way in which political organisations and youth groups had previously failed to do'.[220] Certainly, much as NSDAP political leaders expected NSDAP members to participate enthusiastically in party activities, so the most devout Hitler Youth leaders expected complete commitment from their young charges. In Württemberg, the first problem was that such leaders were thin on the ground. In 1938, the SD reported that the HJ in Württemberg faced not only serious financial difficulties but also a 'shortage of suitable leaders', as a result of the conscription of young men into both the armed forces and the Labour Service. This 'damaged the stability of HJ work', and left units which were deprived of actual and potential leaders 'in crisis, particularly in rural areas', handing the initiative to 'rampant confessional youth' organisations, whose territory had traditionally been 'the deepest provincial hinterland'.[221] In two villages in the Hohenlohe region, where boys aged ten and over mostly joined the Hitler Youth, it was harder for those from the Catholic village because the meetings were held either in the Protestant village or in a nearby town, and sometimes Catholic boys found themselves in trouble with their HJ leader for missing a meeting on a Sunday morning because they had instead attended their church. [222] Holding HJ meetings on a Sunday was part of a deliberate campaign against the churches, with religious education in schools becoming a particular target in 1939, when plans were produced to train teachers in all schools to purvey lessons in Nazi 'ideological training'.[223]

Every effort was made to promote the HJ, including allowing it the privilege of having some 200 full-time officers in the HJ area to which Württemberg belonged. These were reduced by a third in late 1938, with seventy being made redundant at short notice after the suicide of a senior officer who had apparently resorted to creative accounting. Yet far more serious for the NSDAP's future in Württemberg was that 'only a relatively small proportion' of former HJ members who had been conscripted into the armed forces went on to join a party formation or affiliate when they returned to civilian life. Similarly, the SD reported with concern that in 1938, while there were sufficient recruits for the more ostensibly glamorous formations, the SS and the NS Flying Corps, 'only a relatively small proportion of eighteen year olds from the HJ had transferred to the Party, SA and NSKK [NS Automobile Drivers' Corps]' on the traditional reception date of 9 November; this was said to be particularly the case in rural areas, 'where interest in political matters frequently remains extraordinarily slight'. The SD claimed that the HJ itself was at least partly responsible for this because it 'holds onto the good recruits in order to groom them as leaders, and among those who are transferred there is no desire for further service'.[224]

If the boys' groups had difficulties, they were as nothing to those encountered by the girls' groups of the BDM. Given that one of the NSDAP's articles of faith was that women and men should be organised separately, both the BDM and the women's organisation, the NSF – as well as the women's Labour Service – could function only if a corps of suitable female leaders was available. Yet the BDM in Württemberg encountered an even greater shortage of suitable and 'ideologically reliable' leaders than did the HJ; there was an almost total absence of women to develop *Glaube und Schönheit* (Faith and Beauty) groups of the BDM for young women of eighteen to twenty-one years of age outside the major towns. Of 400 such groups in Württemberg, it was estimated that around 150 had effective leaders while the remainder functioned only partially.[225] Before 1933, the women of the NSF had tried to effect a takeover of the BDM, but they had been repulsed.[226] By the later 1930s, it was more than ever clear that the matronly leaders of the NSF were not the kind of women with whom the young of the BDM could identify.[227] Yet part of the problem with the youth organisations was that Schirach's Reich Youth Leadership insisted that 'the young should be led by the young'.[228] This could work well enough in towns where there was a reasonably ready supply of young people who evidenced the required leadership qualities, although there might be problems even there, particularly in the BDM.[229] In smaller communities, however, either there might be no one who was willing to assume the undoubted burdens of leadership, or else an early enthusiast might not have an obvious successor when he or she moved on into adult life.[230] The demands of war added to these problems, with eager HJ and BDM leaders seconded to occupied territories for duties including work among the children of ethnic German settlers and, particularly from 1943, the leadership of camps for German youngsters who had been evacuated from urban areas.[231]

By the time Hitler attacked Poland, therefore, the NSDAP's presence in Württemberg in many small communes remained piecemeal and sometimes virtually non-existent. Two or three small communes might share an NSDAP local branch leader who had many tasks – some of them relatively menial – and yet was not a paid official. These tasks only increased in wartime with, for example, virtually interminable collections of metals and all manner of materials for recycling, as well as collections of clothing for soldiers on the eastern front, and, above all, the party's overriding mission of maintaining morale at a high level, whatever military reverses, bombing and shortages there might be.[232] Such tasks became the more difficult as the party became increasingly unpopular, its trumpeted ideals contradicted by its officers' responses to the realities of wartime. An idealistic SD observer in Württemberg lamented in 1941 that

> in reports about the mood of the people, there is repeated reference to a *reassertion of the old spirit of caste, of snobbery and class divisions*, manifestations which have absolutely nothing in common with the idea represented by National Socialism of a *true people's community. Even in the party and its affiliated organisations*, these ills which have traditionally afflicted the Germans persist.

Instead of leading by example, prominent party leaders and members, as conspicuously selfish individuals, undermined the ideals of the *Volksgemeinschaft*.[233] The popular view, reported the SD, was that

> most party members behave no differently from anyone else. If they're hungry and worried about the physical well-being of their family, then they, like anyone else, forget the saying '*Gemeinnutz vor Eigennutz*' ('The common good before self-interest'). Fine words can't change anything.[234]

At the same time, the overbearing attitude of some party officers alienated some of those who were unquestioningly loyal to the Nazi state. In November 1940, the President of the Supreme Court in Stuttgart complained to the Reich Minister of Justice that some *Kreisleiter* were interfering in the administration of justice. Apparently, in one case where a person had been acquitted by the Stuttgart Special Court, he had been obliged by his *Kreisleiter* to make a contribution to the NSV, by way of a fine. There were also instances of *Kreisleiter* trying to meddle in the sentencing of individuals in a manner that did not correspond with the law. The president added that 'I was told by one *Kreisleiter* that he was the highest judge in his district; another *Kreisleiter* told me that a judgment given in a court did not mean a thing'. What worried him was not so much the effect on individual cases but rather the trend towards marginalising law officers and the legal process. The area in which this was most apparent was in the treatment meted out to women who had – or were suspected of having – consorted with prisoners of war. The arbitrary seizure of such women by party activists, and the head shaving that followed, effectively to brand them as moral degenerates before they had been tried in a court, prejudged the issue in a manner that seemed to the president 'intolerable'.[235]

During the war, both the NSDAP and local government offices were increasingly depleted by conscription or secondment, which contributed to instability in the civil administration. The *Landrat* in Heidenheim was conscripted in November 1940, and the *Landrat* in Böblingen was conscripted twice, from October to December 1939 and from May 1940 until his death in November 1940. After his first tour of duty, he, like the *Landrat* in Schwäbisch Hall, retained his *Landrat*'s expense allowance because he had been absent for less than six months.[236] At least three *Landräte* were seconded to the Württemberg Interior Ministry, presumably to compensate for the conscription of staff from there, and other officials, including *Landräte*, were seconded to occupied Polish territories.[237] Absent *Landräte* were generally replaced in the early stages of the war by men who had lost a *Landrat*'s position in the reform of 1938 or had retired.[238] In June 1943, however, Murr told the Interior Minister that, because of their political sensitivity, vacant *Landrat* posts should be filled by 'old party members ... where their industry and personal qualities fit them for such a responsible position'.[239] The calibre of Württemberg's older party members was hardly sufficient for such an important role. It was difficult enough to find local men who were reasonably 'politically reliable' and more or less competent to replace mayors of communes who had been conscripted.

The party's local branch leaders, too, might be conscripted, although the Party Chancellery was anxious to ensure that the men primarily responsible for maintaining discipline and morale at local level remained in post. *Gau* and district leaderships, too, were reluctant to surrender their local officials. As late as December 1943, the Party Chancellery decreed that in each local branch the leader and five officials should be exempt from conscription. This was unsustainable, when already over 30 per cent of political leaders were in war service of some kind. The conscripted might be replaced by men of lesser ability or those who were less acquainted with a local branch, a cell or a block and its inhabitants.[240] Under these conditions, party functionaries' painstaking attempts to maintain surveillance over, and cultivate close personal contact with, those in their locality were vitiated. By the middle of the war, the male formations and affiliated organisations of the party had virtually ceased to operate because of conscription. SA men were given military training, some of them with horses on loan from the *Wehrmacht*, and many were conscripted.[241] The NSV became virtually entirely involved in the organisation and care of evacuees and victims of bomb damage. As the war dragged on, those in the upper reaches of the party's hierarchy in Württemberg, too, might be conscripted. Altogether seventeen former and current *Kreisleiter* were conscripted during the war.[242] There remained little more than the women's organisation and the Hitler Youth, in those communes where these organisations functioned at all.

The HJ tried to maintain in wartime its normal round of activities but it also had to deputise for adults who were either conscripted into the *Wehrmacht* or engrossed in work on the home front. For example, HJ members had increasingly to undergo training in air raid protection.[243] Again, at local Nazi ceremonies for the casualties of war, a choir consisting of HJ and BDM members might sing, and a speaker from the HJ might give an address if no adult officer of the NSDAP – normally the *Kreisleiter* or local branch leader – was available. Even so, in some places, for example in rural areas of Böblingen and Crailsheim districts, the SD reported that the HJ was 'usually numerically so weak' that its participation in such events was negligible.[244] Nevertheless, there were enthusiasts in the Württemberg HJ, probably none more so than the Fellbach unit leader in *Kreis* Waiblingen, Reutlinger, who involved himself in organising cultural events, booking accommodation for study groups, reminding the local press about precisely how to report his unit's events, liaising with senior BDM officers of similar enthusiasm, and offering the services of his unit to various party affiliates, whose leaders were only sometimes pleased to accept them.[245] His major purpose was to ensure that high standards were maintained in his own area, regardless of circumstances that doubtless inhibited the less assiduous. It might be too much to say that he seemed unaware that there was a war going on, but his stamina, persistence and attention to detail were unstinting, whether in reminding a subordinate – in chiding fatherly tones – of a dereliction of duty, or in politely but insistently reminding parents that their son was obliged to attend HJ meetings on a Sunday, regardless of how hard he had had to work in his father's butcher's business during the week, in the absence of his sick brother.[246] Into these mundane concerns, Nazi ideology effortlessly elided. Schirach's central office decreed that at leadership training courses in April 1943 'the race question' should be discussed. Accordingly, the conscientious Reutlinger tried to enlist a senior district NSDAP officer to give a 'presentation about race'. [247]

A stickler for the rules, Reutlinger could nevertheless show flexibility, as in the case of an overzealous subordinate who held local HJ meetings from eight o'clock until half past ten on weekday evenings. A complaint from one mother, on the grounds that her son had to rise at 5 a.m. to catch a bus for work, led Reutlinger to remonstrate with his underling to the effect that the quality of his meetings was more important than their duration, and that he should make a point of finishing by 9.30 p.m.[248] This compromise, however, perhaps derived from the knowledge that there was a limit to the sanctions that HJ leaders could impose on recalcitrants. For example, in October 1942, one of Reutlinger's subordinates upbraided a youth for not complying with a summons to his local HJ office and ordered him to attend on another occasion. The sternness of his message was vitiated by the rather limp conclusion: 'if you are not going to come, I'd ask you to phone in advance'.[249] Another of Reutlinger's subordinates had to moderate the response of one of his own underlings who had sought to impose a levy of 20 or 30 pfennigs on youths who were absent from meetings without notice, in order to cover the cost of contacting them. 'I have nothing against this', he said, 'but we cannot force a youth who refuses to pay to do so.'[250]

Even more worrying for the HJ leadership was the casual attitude of some of its own leaders who were setting their charges anything but a good example. In August 1944, it came to Reutlinger's notice that a recent Sunday morning's 'war duty', that fifty to seventy boys had been ordered to attend at 7 a.m., had been a fiasco. At the appointed time, a solitary youth had been present. Eventually some twenty-five or thirty boys appeared, but only one of the relevant leaders. Reutlinger was of the view that 'before we can educate the young to a sense of responsibility, we shall first have to punish leaders who disregard their duties'. What form this punishment might take was not vouchsafed.[251] One of the leaders involved in this fiasco was also responsible when, ignominiously, two teams from Fellbach were disqualified from the unit's sports gala in 1944 because they had included two boys who did not belong to the Fellbach HJ.[252] There seems to have been little that Reutlinger could do about the shortcomings of his immediate subordinates, beyond bombarding them with letters remonstrating with them and reminding them of their responsibilities. In wartime, with HJ leaders progressively being conscripted, he had to make the best of the resources at his disposal. It seems clear that his immediate subordinates were aware of this and turned it to their own advantage, allowing themselves considerable leeway, with repeated absences from regular meetings and training courses.[253]

The unsinkably cheerful comradely terms in which Reutlinger and a few of his associates wrote, always using the informal 'Du' with each other, testifies to the success of National Socialism as a messianic creed among some young Germans, even if their constant need to chivvy the mass of others, including those in positions of leadership in the HJ, suggests that they were a relatively rare species. While ostensibly a diligent and responsible leader, Reutlinger accepted unquestioningly the premises of Hitler's creed and the implications of his regime. For example, in autumn 1944 he was recruiting vigorously among youths born in 1928 for volunteers for the *Wehrmacht*, with evident disregard for the welfare of these fifteen and sixteen year olds.[254] At the same time, however, his determination to guard local HJ privileges jealously clearly contradicted the demands of the war effort. First, his unit retained in summer 1943 two motor cycles and several bicycles, at a time when even the police in Württemberg could not obtain motor vehicles and ordinary people could not obtain rubber tyres for bicycles.[255] Secondly, with conscription eating into the HJ leadership in summer 1943, one of Reutlinger's subordinates wrote to a local firm to ask if it would allow an employee to leave work early on Wednesday afternoons for HJ duty.[256] Even in summer 1944, Reutlinger regarded his HJ activities as sufficiently vital to request a local business to release an employee for a whole week to attend a 'training course for HJ leaders'.[257] Thirdly, around the same time, he was instructing a subordinate to ensure that HJ units utilised a hostel under their jurisdiction as frequently as possible to show that it was occupied, because the *Wehrmacht* wanted to take it over.[258] Fourthly, in autumn 1944, Reutlinger was trying desperately to maintain attendance at leadership training courses at a time when Germany's fortunes were unravelling.[259]

The weaknesses of the youth organisations trickled through to the NSDAP itself, especially given that by 1944 HJ and BDM members were automatically transferred to party membership at the age of eighteen. Certainly, the numerical size of the NSDAP was greatly increased in its final years, but there could be no guarantee that these new involuntary members would be activists. The SD, in fact, had reason to believe that many, perhaps most, of them would not be, because

> They are not tied to [the party] through the experience of a political struggle which would illustrate to them that the party had to fight for the present state and thus had won the right to make demands on this state and its people ... Therefore, they have no

inhibitions in being critical of the party just as of every other state institution. *They lack the naturally developed loyalty to the party* of older party members ...[260]

Yet these loyal 'older party members' might belong either to the generation of the pre-1933 members, which was to some extent dying out or growing infirm, or to the minority of zealots in the intakes of 1933 and subsequently. The SD did not mention the ranks of the opportunists and the inactive who also figured among 'older party members'. Whereas the relatively tight knit band of genuine believers who had developed the NSDAP in Württemberg in the *Kampfzeit* might have been quarrelsome and lacking in talent, they had nevertheless been unfailingly loyal to Hitler and the 'idea' of National Socialism. By contrast, the mass party of wartime was full of opportunists, foot draggers and those whose faith in Hitler and his movement was progressively dissolving with the mounting reverses of the last two years of the war. There remained a skeleton corps of NSDAP activists who continued in some districts and local branches to mount events and serve in unpaid posts, although these efforts were increasingly curtailed by both progressive conscription and the emergencies of bombing and evacuation. The disruption of activities caused by these emergencies was particularly acute in urban areas, the very ones where the NSDAP's organisation had been well developed before the war, for example in the Stuttgart district.[261]

The war certainly enhanced the party's sphere of competence, but sometimes in ways that were unwelcome to it. There were relatively simple matters to be dealt with in local branches, such as distributing ration cards periodically, which was the kind of duty that could be delegated to the NSF group – if there was one. In addition, there were more complex and, sometimes, sensitive tasks, such as informing families about the death of a husband or son in combat, enforcing government policy, especially in terms of observance of the War Economy Decree, and, increasingly, dealing with the problems of evacuees and the bombed out.[262] Above all, the mission of *Menschenführung* meant, in wartime, the maintenance of morale in general and faith in the leadership in particular, as well as constant exhortation to even greater effort on the home front. This could, however, misfire: with the hardships of the third winter of the war only too apparent, the Stuttgart State Prosecutor reported 'noticeable mistrust' not only of official propaganda and news management but also 'to some extent of the work of the party'.[263] This was a cautious admission of a larger truth, one which would soon embrace also the decline in Hitler's own popular standing.[264]

In the last weeks and days of the war, local party functionaries were faced with uncomfortable choices about whether to follow to the letter the orders of diehard senior NSDAP and SS leaders about fighting to the last street and the last house or whether to protect the inhabitants of their area from further damage and misery. It was hardly surprising that some who had supported the party in good times now deserted it, at least in spirit. The chronicler of the crisis in Aalen in April 1945 mentioned that the battle of Stalingrad had had a decisive effect on opinion in the town:

> The huge sacrifice of blood on all fronts, the fall of Stalingrad and the pointless sacrifice of a whole army in this city brought home forcefully to many of the more reasonable among sympathisers with the NSDAP the entire madness of Hitler's conduct of the war and quietly aroused in them revulsion at a system which was leading the German people into the abyss. Even in these circles there were soon [those who were] 'politically unreliable'.[265]

Yet, even in the later stages of the war, a hard core of loyalists remained faithful to the cause. Older members were said to regard the oath-taking ceremony by the *Volkssturm* (home guard), on 9 November 1944, as being in 'the spirit of the brown columns from the *Kampfzeit* [which] now embrace the entire people'.[266] This was completely at odds with the despair and derision with which most villagers regarded the *Volkssturm*.

Perhaps incredibly, some activists in relatively minor leadership capacities immersed themselves in their organisations to the extent that they appear to have been oblivious to Germany's increasingly dire fortunes in the war. This may have been displacement activity, yet the ardour of the enthusiasts remained palpable. It was perhaps most graphically illustrated by a *Gau* officer of the NSF, who in March 1945 – with much of Germany under enemy control – complained to the *Land* Food Office in Stuttgart that she had received reports from Ludwigsburg, Mergentheim and Backnang that the Food Office had failed to provide tokens for extra rations for DFW cookery courses, demonstrations and tests for home economics' trainees. The reply she received was polite but firm: as from 15 February 1945, the various dispensations which had permitted training agencies, including the DFW, to claim extra tokens for their courses had been revoked.[267] Nevertheless, the spirit of defiance was alive and well among some: in Bopfingen, at the end of March, girls of the BDM used stones to make a huge victory rune bearing the words, 'We Will Win'.[268]

In the last days of the war, while the party's officers in small communes could prove to be a baleful or even deadly force, imposing resistance to an overwhelmingly superior enemy and ferociously punishing those who disobeyed or, in some cases, merely questioned the wisdom of this course of action, it is striking that in many communes there seems, by 1945, to have been little indigenous party presence. There were, nevertheless, individual victims of Nazi 'justice': for example in Satteldorf, a man was shot 'by SS or Gestapo as an alleged traitor' on 19 April 1945 on the road leading out of the village towards Crailsheim.[269] In these last confused days of the regime, the army, the SS and the police were the final defenders and instruments of retribution against doubters, with many party officers fleeing. Not one Württemberg *Kreisleiter* was in his home base when the enemy arrived, although many had, up to the last minute, cajoled or threatened local civilians into defending their territory against the invader.[270] Some local branch leaders – like many mayors – aligned themselves against these last-ditch defenders and with local inhabitants whose only wish was for an end to the war without further hardship for their communities. Probably nothing did more to discredit Hitler's regime in general, and the NSDAP in particular, in the eyes of ordinary Württembergers than the long drawn out end to the war and its attendant casualties and destruction on their own territory.

4

Racial Health and Persecution

The Nazi struggle for total control over German society involved not only a battle for individuals' allegiance but also a new classification of society's constituent members, with government intervention in many aspects of life. Whereas in the 1920s there were both piecemeal welfare schemes and prejudice against groups regarded as non-conformist, in Nazi Germany there was active official discrimination against targeted groups along with a much more comprehensive welfare system for those regarded as deserving. These policies were entirely complementary, for Nazi notions of health were inextricably bound up with an obsession with 'superior' and 'inferior' races. There was therefore a direct correlation between promoting the health and well-being of the 'Aryan' race and mistreating those who were either non-'Aryan' or 'Aryan' with perceived defects, whether of a mental, physical or behavioural nature.

The criterion of 'racial value' was 'racial health'. To qualify, individuals and whole families had to be of 'Aryan' blood.[1] A new specialty, 'racial biology', was developed in the Third Reich, with history graduates, among others, finding employment in genealogical records offices. These were not archives for people interested in tracing their family history but rather data banks where information about individuals' ancestry was stored in card indexes, to be used to demonstrate – or not – that those applying for either certain jobs or welfare benefits had an irreproachably 'Aryan' pedigree. Jews, in particular, were classified as non-'Aryan', increasingly excluded from both desirable jobs and benefits, and marginalised from 'Aryan' German society until they either emigrated or were, in wartime, deported to incarceration and death in eastern Europe.[2] Other non-'Aryans' included Slavs, Blacks and Roma and Sinti (Romanies), although some of these last were classed as 'racially pure'.[3] Together, these non-'Aryans' were regarded as implacable foes: with their numbers allegedly increasing, they were held to pose a serious threat to the well-being, and even the existence, of the 'Aryan' race.

Yet it was not sufficient to be able to prove one's 'Aryan' ancestry. In addition, citizens had to demonstrate their 'racial value' in terms of both health and conduct. Health, in this context, meant an absence of various conditions which were termed 'hereditary illnesses'. For 'Aryans' failing to meet the regime's criteria of 'fitness', a panoply of social workers, medical officers and Hereditary Health Courts determined who should be encouraged to reproduce – to boost the birth rate – and who should be prevented from reproducing characteristics regarded as flaws.[4] The entire language of 'fitness', 'health' and 'hereditary disease' was predicated on a modern conception of both human development and society. As humans increasingly ceased to be the hapless victims of their environment, some believed that they could aspire to control it. As scientific and medical developments, particularly around 1900, offered techniques for combating disease and prolonging life, it seemed to some that humans would eventually be capable of perfecting their species, progressively eliminating conditions and characteristics regarded as flaws. This belief was not confined to Germany. Its proponents were to be found in the United States, Britain and Scandinavia, among other countries.[5]

According to one theory, society was like a garden.[6] The self-appointed guardians of 'racial purity' assumed the role of the dedicated gardener, who seeks to eradicate arbitrarily-defined weeds which threaten to overwhelm valuable plants. Their task, they believed, was to subjugate 'inferior' races, if necessary destroying them to prevent them from overwhelming 'superior' races by force of numbers. In the 1920s and 1930s, German population pundits and their followers – Nazi and non-Nazi alike – generally regarded Slavs, with their dynamic birth rates which contrasted with Germans' low birth rate, in this light. The particularly low birth rate of German Jews provided no comfort because of German racists' firm belief in an *international* Jewish conspiracy against the 'Aryan' race. The responsible gardener would also cull imperfect specimens of desirable plants, to ensure that the healthy monopolised available resources under optimum conditions. In the human garden, the modern science of eugenics offered the possibility of identifying the flawed and the weak, and of selecting only the strong and allegedly perfect for propagation. These ideas were evident in medical and bureaucratic circles before the First World War, in Germany and elsewhere, and they were intensified after the carnage of 1914–18, when large numbers of those regarded as 'valuable' perished, allegedly distorting the balance of societies in favour of the 'flawed'.

This entire belief system was a product of traditional prejudice overlaid with modern theories of human development and given sharper focus by the evolution of modern urban society. Nazi propagandists undoubtedly exploited the prejudices and superstitions of those of limited education, including peasants; some Nazi activists evidently subscribed to them wholeheartedly. Yet the thought processes and methods of racist thinkers and policy-makers were those of an educated elite beguiled by the new science of eugenics. The ever-increasing expansion of state power in the early twentieth century suggested to them that it would be possible to enforce an improvement in the quality of the species throughout society by disaggregating from the community of the 'valuable' those who were either aliens – the equivalent of weeds in a garden

– or defective specimens of the desirable genus. Medical doctors and university researchers in Tübingen were in the vanguard of developments in what they termed 'racial hygiene'.[7]

The central organs of state power were located in modern urban centres and staffed by people – at the higher levels, almost invariably by men – who had received an advanced education and perhaps also professional training. They presided over huge bureaucracies which gathered and stored data identifying and categorising individuals and families. In Nazi Germany, this information was used to identify those whose pedigree was not congruent with official norms. The expansion of state power throughout society was facilitated by the development of mechanised transport, the spread of literacy, and communications such as radio and the postal and telephone services. When this modern, intrusive state came under Hitler's control in 1933, the identification, monitoring and control of urban dwellers was relatively manageable, and of those in scattered villages increasingly possible.

The power of the state had already, well before 1933, been used against unpopular minorities, such as Romanies. In Württemberg, the interior ministry issued decrees against 'the Gypsy nuisance' in 1903 and 1905, to limit the numbers of itinerants roaming together in bands and to force their children to attend school.[8] Further legislation in Württemberg, in 1919 and 1925, was aimed at discouraging the itinerant lifestyle of Romanies, but without the explicitly punitive aspects of a Bavarian law of 1926 which prescribed confinement in a workhouse for adult Romanies who were not in regular employment.[9] Dr Robert Ritter, head of psychiatry at Tübingen University until 1937, had made a special study of 'Swabian vagabonds, crooks and thieves', from which he concluded that 'pedlars, vagrants, street musicians and the workshy' were 'asocial psychopaths' with little hereditary value. In 1938, a research centre for investigating the racial value of 'Gypsies, vagabonds and *Jenische* [itinerants]' was established in Tübingen.[10]

The Nazis' monstrous project to perfect the 'Aryan' race was, then, already prefigured in the early twentieth-century perversion of the new science of eugenics, which was originally concerned with ideas about and remedies for incurable and distressing physical diseases. The chief remedy was the sterilisation of those affected. By about 1900, the principles of heredity were being applied by some scientists and social commentators in various countries to a wide range of social and behavioural problems. The depression around 1930 gave urgency to the motive which already existed of economising on support for those who required institutional care, in particular the mentally impaired. Some American states had already enacted laws permitting sterilisation, on an allegedly voluntary basis. Such a law was enacted in Vermont in 1931, and there was similar legislation in the four Scandinavian countries during the 1930s.[11] In Prussia in 1932 there was a proposal to permit the voluntary sterilisation of those who were 'hereditarily ill'.[12] By this time, some German medical doctors, including Dr August Mayer of the Gynaecology Clinic at Tübingen University, were already sterilising patients on eugenic grounds, covertly and contrary to the law.[13]

The Nazis exploited these trends and fused the prejudices associated with them into the pseudo-science of 'racial biology', whose proponents denounced as unfit and undeserving not only Jews and other non-'Aryans', but also the mentally impaired, prostitutes, homosexuals and alcoholics. Whole families were classed as 'worthless' because they did not conform to standards of conduct – including industry, temperance, thrift and cleanliness – prescribed by the regime.[14] Official attitudes towards these groups became increasingly implacable. Those who were 'Aryan' but not 'valuable' were branded with the label 'asocial', denied state benefits such as marriage loans and family allowances and, increasingly, threatened with compulsory sterilisation or a spell in a concentration camp, where substantial numbers ended their days.[15]

Central to the modern character of racial policy was the principle of cost-effectiveness.[16] This was evident in Scandinavia and the USA, where the costs of maintaining the 'feeble-minded' were computed and adduced as proof of the need to prevent their reproducing.[17] In Germany, especially in time of shortage – above all, during the war – the Nazi regime went significantly further both quantitatively and qualitatively. Resources were to be allocated as generously as possible to the deserving, at the expense of 'racial enemies' such as Jews and the 'hereditarily unhealthy'. Whether the resources were food, clothing, fuel, housing or money, they were increasingly to be expended virtually exclusively on 'valuable Aryans'. The deliberate starvation of some Slav foreign workers during the war, and of some of the children to whom female coerced workers gave birth in Germany, including Württemberg, was entirely within the logic of this priority, as were the meagre rations decreed for Jews in wartime.[18] The housing shortage made the dispossession of Jews in order to accommodate 'Aryans' increasingly attractive to the regime, especially as bombing destroyed urban housing.[19] Dispossession also coincided with its objective of excluding Jews from 'Aryan' German society and from Germany itself.

In addition, 'useless eaters' – as the mentally impaired were labelled – were removed from long-term institutional care, where standards of treatment had markedly worsened during the 1920s and 1930s.[20] This became an urgent preoccupation in wartime, with an influx of ethnic Germans from eastern Europe who required accommodation, as well as the prospect of large numbers of military casualties requiring hospital treatment.[21] The crises caused by bombing, migration and evacuation made the ejection of the 'worthless' from both private houses and institutions an even greater priority. Racial policy was therefore based on both entrenched prejudice and a grotesquely distorted utopian obsession with perfectibility, but a further motive was the calculated desire to redistribute increasingly scarce resources.

Hitler's government was deeply reluctant to spend money even on domestic projects with a high priority. For example, while promoting 'valuable' large families through propaganda, it was reluctant to assign new expenditure to them, with predictable results.[22] Even if, according to the SD, the awarding of Honour Crosses to mothers of large families in 1938 had been well received by the population at large, most Württembergers contented themselves with one or two children, with only a small minority having several.[23] The regime's preferred alternative was to devote existing expenditure to the 'valuable', while those designated 'less valuable' or 'worthless' were condemned to live on the margins of society, increasingly restricted and denied access to public resources. Various groups of 'asocials' were among the first to be targeted. In 1933, in the depths of the depression, Hitler's government unleashed a campaign against 'beggars', who were allegedly sabotaging the work of the Nazi *Winterhilfswerk* (WHW – Winter Relief Project) by competing for citizens' charitable contributions. In Württemberg, 4818 persons were arrested, of whom over half were incarcerated, 500 of them in the workhouse in Vaihingen. A year later, a further 1069 'beggars' were arrested.

In Stuttgart, welfare recipients were increasingly required to demonstrate their 'value' by working for their money. Men laboured in stone-breaking or timber yards, or on road-building schemes, while childless women sewed garments for the WHW or other Nazi projects. Those refusing to do this lost their benefit and, as 'workshy', might be confined in a workhouse. Included were prostitutes, 'drinkers' and Romanies. As the depression receded, and with labour increasingly scarce, punitive policies towards these unpopular groups intensified. In January 1938, the Racial Policy Office of the NSDAP in *Gau* Württemberg-Hohenzollern created a card index of 'asocials' in the region, using information from mayors of communes, the NSV, local NSDAP leaders, welfare offices, the police and the courts. Those targeted were beggars, intinerants, the sexually promiscuous and drunks, as well as those whose family life was unconventional and those making anti-regime complaints. This culminated in a nationwide round-up in 1938, with most of those arrested sent to concentration camps.[24] The Württemberg SD reported in 1939 that, compared with 1938, the number of 'rootless asocials' had diminished by 62 per cent. This had enabled the authorities to close nineteen hostels for the homeless, with plans to close some of the remaining twenty-three hostels because the costs – which were partly borne by the state – were said to be 'unsustainable'.[25] The disciplining of asocials continued in wartime. In Stuttgart, 'asocial' women who refused forced labour were confined in harsh conditions with minimal rations.[26]

While some 'asocials' who were targeted were Romanies and some were people who were not Roma or Sinti but followed an itinerant lifestyle, from December 1938 the regime pursued a concerted policy of racially segregating Romanies from the 'Aryan' population. This was facilitated by the consistent hostility of much of the population towards both Romanies and vagrants. In Württemberg's rural areas, they were regarded as importunate vendors and beggars whose removal would be entirely welcome.[27] A start had already been made by gathering together all 'Gypsy and Gypsy-like' children who had been in institutional care.[28] Some adult Romanies were subjected to sterilisation.[29] Suddenly, in April 1940, Himmler ordered the arrest of 2500 Romanies in northern and western Germany, who were all to be gathered together in Hohenasperg prison in Württemberg.[30] This included 500 Württemberg Romanies, of whom an estimated 300 were deported to Poland, to forced labour. In May 1944, thirty-nine Romany children living in a Catholic home in Mulfingen were transported to Auschwitz after serving as case studies for Dr Eva Justin's PhD thesis. Only four survived.[31]

While 'racial enemies' were identified and victimised, the condition of the 'valuable' was a constant preoccupation. Even before the war there were reasons to be concerned about Württembergers' health. While the SD noted in April and July 1939 that polio had been all but eradicated, by the end of the year the police were reporting an increase in its incidence, and in cases of diphtheria and scarlet fever. The incidence of tuberculosis and sexually transmitted infections (STIs) remained steady, but the SD mentioned an increase in cases of whooping cough and illnesses among infants which, along with a relatively high rate of infant mortality, was attributed to a lack of resistance to infection among those falling ill. An apparent outbreak of paratyphoid at an NSV meeting in Esslingen in June 1939 had, however, turned out to be a case of mass food poisoning. Over a hundred NSV functionaries had been taken ill after eating a pudding made with ducks' eggs which had not been thoroughly cooked. The basic problem was, said the SD, the catastrophic state of egg supplies to the towns. Farmers sold hens' eggs to anyone who approached them, leaving those who relied on the official distribution system so underprovided that they instead bought ducks' eggs, which they did not know how to cook.[32]

Health promotion was a priority, not least to improve people's efficiency at work. Investigation in Germany into the effects of tobacco smoking produced the connection between cigarettes and lung cancer before this was acknowledged elsewhere.[33] There were active public campaigns, among both adults and young people, to discourage smoking and more than modest consumption of alcohol, because of the detrimental effect that long-term consumption of these substances had on users' productive capacity. One solution proposed was a reduction in the relatively high prices of non-alcoholic drinks and mineral water. Young people were urged to follow the healthy example of the Führer, a total abstainer, and specific warnings were issued to pregnant women and car drivers. By 1939, smoking had been banned on the premises of both party and state offices in Württemberg, although Nazi newspapers, including the SS's *Das Schwarze Korps* which published articles condemning smoking, carried prominent advertisements for tobacco products. The spectacle of women – especially those associated with the NSDAP, who should have been setting a good example – smoking in public was unequivocally deplored.[34] In wartime, women were denied ration tokens for cigarettes, although in October 1942 a concession was made for those under twenty-five or over fifty-five with a husband or son in military service.[35] The physical condition of young conscripts who smoked was regarded as detrimental to the army's capability, and there was particular criticism of patients with tuberculosis who continued to smoke, even when their doctor had forbidden it.[36]

The war brought a progressive deterioration in Germans' diet. To try to ensure the availability of diminishing food supplies for the 'valuable', in November 1941 *Landesbauernführer* Arnold ordered that a range of foodstuffs, including poultry, fish and skimmed milk, be prohibited to Jews, although – remarkably – Jewish children and Jews who were ill could be allowed whole milk if medical doctors provided strong evidence that this was necessary.[37] The 'valuable' who were vulnerable – children, new and expectant mothers, many of the physically ill – were assigned extra rations of relatively scarce foods, such as eggs, butter and whole milk. Among the beneficiaries were those with stomache ulcers, gastro-intestinal problems, liver or kidney disease and diabetes.[38] Yet there remained serious problems of supply, especially of milk, fats and oats.[39] By autumn 1943, there were cases of children who had swollen glands as a result of a shortage of fats being diagnosed with tuberculosis, for which a health official in Freudenstadt was quick to blame farmers for selling unpasteurised milk from tubercular cows. His superior, while castigating him for jumping to sensationalist conclusions, expressed anxiety about such allegedly irresponsible conduct on the part of farmers.[40]

Attempts to protect the 'valuable' at the expense of the 'worthless' were vitiated by the diminishing levels of food supplies, even when Germany was pillaging other countries' resources. The result was discrimination even among the 'valuable'. For example, in Württemberg extra rations were allocated during the war to some units of the youth organisations and service schemes, and to educational institutions.[41] By December 1942, medical doctors were appealing for extra milk rations for their patients, and there was particular anxiety about the nutrition of school children and infants.[42] In Nürtingen, an experiment was conducted to assess the value of providing vitamin C tablets for school-age children.[43] These preoccupations were not peculiar to Nazi Germany. In wartime Britain, infants received free or cheap orange juice and cod liver oil, and seven million children were vaccinated against diphtheria.[44] With nutrition levels sinking in Germany, there was particular concern about the spread of disease, from tuberculosis and diphtheria to STIs.[45]

The Nazi regime itself created the conditions in which disease was likely to flourish in wartime by engineering massive migrations of people. The senior health official in the Württemberg Ministry of the Interior, Dr Eugen Stähle, recognised this, admitting that there was a greater need in wartime to combat disease because of the evacuation of children, the movement of sick people from one institution to another, and the influx of ethnic Germans from apparently more primitive circumstances in eastern Europe. He believed that ethnic Germans contributed as much to the spread of disease as Polish POWs and coerced civilian workers; the delousing of eastern Europeans of all kinds was routine practice. Again, from the middle of November 1940, SS X-ray units examined the population at large to try to detect tuberculosis. There was also a campaign to try to prevent the spread of a variety of communicable diseases, especially diphtheria.[46] Yet government agencies could operate at cross-purposes. The medical officer in Böblingen district complained in October 1940 about an order denying tuberculosis sufferers supplementary soap rations, on the grounds that this could jeopardise containment of the disease.[47]

For a regime obsessed with both health and population increase, STIs remained a major preoccupation, especially at a time when effective medical treatment was rudimentary, and when the movement of people in wartime brought them into contact with new sexual partners. Whereas in 1939 the SD reported that the incidence of STIs remained steady in Württemberg, between 1939 and 1943 there was an increase in the number of patients attending the Tübingen sexual health clinic. Men's numbers actually declined, from 197 in 1939 to 165 in 1942, while, at the same time, women's numbers increased, from 281 to 391. The disparity between the sexes was partly due to the increasing conscription of men, who were treated either by military medical officers or in clinics in garrison towns. While the rising numbers of women – with a projected figure of 450 for 1943 – perhaps indicated greater awareness of the facilities available, they also suggested that more women were finding new sexual partners.[48] The movement of people, including the stationing of army units in Württemberg, as well as the influx of both coerced foreign workers and women evacuees, undoubtedly contributed to this.[49] Attempts to keep track of patients treated for STIs were partially frustrated by health offices' protests about being expected to maintain a separate card index for them, over and above their comprehensive index which carried details of individuals' 'hereditary health'.[50]

The straitened circumstances of a long and draining war adversely affected the maintenance of the health and well-being of the 'valuable'. Assigning the largest share of rations to the 'valuable' nevertheless meant, as we have seen, that these provisions declined in absolute terms, especially from 1942. Similarly, the numbers of medical and technical staff available for civilian health care, at a time when the armed forces and their casualties required increasingly more of them, meant that civilian health care devolved onto smaller numbers of well-qualified personnel whose support services were staffed either by the unskilled or not at all. In March 1942, the Ehingen medical officer, had been able to recruit neither a part-time auxiliary to run the district sexual health clinic nor a laboratory assistant to process blood and smear samples. Accordingly, he warned that the clinic would in future be run only 'as far as conditions permit'.[51] His counterpart in Göppingen warned the Württemberg Interior Ministry that he could not conduct his sexual health clinic without adequate technical support. The woman technician responsible for it had complained that she could not entrust the smallest task to the new female laboratory assistant employed in the Geislingen hospital laboratory, who seemed to have neither interest in nor aptitude for the job.[52] Regardless, in 1943 the district clinics' workload increased, with the closing down of the central Württemberg clinic and the devolution of its tasks to the districts.[53]

If the standards of health promotion as well as rations for the 'valuable' deteriorated during the war, this group was nevertheless cushioned against even greater privation by the pillaging of occupied countries and discrimination at home against those designated 'worthless', with resources of all kinds assigned entirely disproportionately to the 'valuable'. Allocating minimal rations to Jews and forced foreign workers was integral to the attempt to shield the 'valuable' population from the worst effects of food shortages. The political motive was important, with the ever-present fear of a 'stab in the back' similar to that alleged to have caused Germany's defeat in 1918. The racial motive was, however, fundamental: the future of the 'Aryan' race depended on its surviving Hitler's war and prospering. Dispossessing its perceived enemies, and severely restricting their nutrition, both weakened them and provided more resources for the 'valuable'. Ultimately, for large numbers of the anathematised this would mean deprivation of food supplies, accommodation and medical attention, probably accompanied by incarceration. At its most extreme, this government policy would result in starvation or outright murder.

As one of the first of these discriminatory policies, legislation on racist population engineering introduced 'eugenic sterilisation' where 'there is a strong probability that his or her offspring will suffer from serious hereditary defects of a physical or mental nature'. Into this category fell those who were 'hereditarily ill'. According to the 'Law for the Prevention of Hereditarily Diseased Offspring' of 14 July 1933, this meant anyone

who suffers from one of the following illnesses: (a) Congenital feeblemindedness. (b) Schizophrenia. (c) Manic depression. (d) Hereditary epilepsy. (e) Huntington's chorea.

(f) Hereditary blindness. (g) Hereditary deafness. (h) Serious physical deformities ... In addition, anyone who suffers from chronic alcoholism can be sterilised.[54]

On the same day, the 'Law Against the Establishment of Parties' declared the one-party state.[55] This ensured that Hitler's government could legislate by proclamation, without formal political opposition. Further, government control of the media severely reduced critics' ability to function, with the initiative devolving largely onto the Christian churches.

There was, however, support for eugenic sterilisation from all wings of the Evangelical Church, with its charitable auxiliary, the *Innere Mission*, carrying out operations on patients in its own asylums, including those at Schwäbisch Hall and Stetten in Württemberg. The Central Committee of the *Innere Mission* opposed only the use of compulsion. By contrast, the Catholic Church was doctrinally opposed to sterilisation.[56] On 2 February 1934, Württemberg's Bishop Sproll directed the Marienhospital in Stuttgart to refuse to accept individuals destined for sterilisation, on the grounds that a Roman Catholic hospital could not collude in such an operation.[57] Nevertheless, neighbouring Baden, with a Catholic to Protestant ratio of three to two, had one of the highest rates of sterilisation, along with Protestant Hamburg and Thuringia.[58] Württemberg's incidence of sterilisation was relatively low, but by no means negligible.[59] Between 1934 and April 1945 there were at least 11,814 sterilisations there, perhaps more.[60]

At first sight, the sterilisation law appeared to be little different from legislation being enacted in other countries at around the same time. It soon transpired, however, that much larger numbers of people were being targeted in Germany, and that those identified as 'hereditarily ill' were under extreme pressure to submit to sterilisation, to the point of outright compulsion. For example, within the jurisdiction of the Tübingen-Rottweil health office, between 1935 and 1941 there were 583 applications for sterilisation, a mere two of which were initiated by the legal guardian of the person concerned, and one by that person. All others were made by medical doctors.[61] In Württemberg as a whole in the same period, only 4 per cent of cases were initiated by either patients or their legal guardians. Almost half of the men, and almost 60 per cent of the women, were sterilised on grounds of 'feeble-mindeness'. A further quarter of both sexes were 'schizophrenic', while 8 per cent of men and less than half of one per cent of women were sterilised on grounds of severe alcoholism. In one case in every twelve, force was used.[62] A Württemberg police report in early 1940 revealed that in several cases the police had been enlisted to compel individuals to submit to sterilisation.[63]

Candidates for sterilisation were identified in both urban and rural areas.[64] Nazis may have extolled the German peasant as the backbone of the 'Aryan' race, but health officials who visited rural communes could find 'racially inferior' elements there to target for sterilisation. The well-known tendency to inbreeding in Württemberg's rural communes no doubt raised officials' suspicions. Yet it was probably a lottery, given that Württemberg consisted of 1829 communes and staff were in short supply. Schlossberg, in Aalen district, was unfortunate in being visited by Stähle himself in 1934. Although the village was well cared for, he regarded the poor housing conditions and generally low standards achieved in the local school as indicative of 'racial inferiority' rather than of rural poverty. Accordingly, he initiated an investigation into the incidence of 'hereditary illness' there, and ordered that habitual criminality and chronic alcoholism in the village be punished severely. By 1938, seventy-two inhabitants of Schlossberg had been investigated by the Aalen district health office, of whom twenty-six had been sterilised on grounds of 'feeble-mindedness', severe alcoholism or physical deformity. The health office's view thereafter was that it had exhausted the number of possible candidates for sterilisation, countering the Württemberg Interior Ministry's proposal that the marked increase in Schlossberg's population should be curbed by further sterilisations.

Other villages, too, came under scrutiny, with Stähle's deputy for mental health, Dr Otto Mauthe, describing the inhabitants of four of them – Matzenbach, Lautenbach, Unterdeufstetten and Wildenstein – as 'probably asocial and hereditarily inferior' in 1938. Few in these communes were sterilised.[65] Individuals elsewhere, however, fell victim. A thirty-year-old housemaid in Crailsheim district who had three illegitimate children was – like her surviving sister – sterilised in 1935 on grounds of 'feeble-mindedness'.[66] In Oppelsbohm, in Waiblingen district, a man was sterilised in 1937 on grounds of 'schizophrenia'. Yet according to the commune's mayor, writing in 1942, while this man had occasional 'confused days', he held down a job and mostly behaved in an orderly and responsible manner.[67] Some others who were judged at least as harshly escaped sterilisation. In June 1943, two doctors in Stuttgart described 'a really worthless family' whose father was a 'drinker' and a convict; some of the children were at schools for the mentally impaired, while one of the daughters had had three children by different 'worthless' partners and was slovenly. Yet only a brother who was 'feeble-minded and an alcoholic' had been sterilised.[68] In August 1944, a sterilisation order was issued for a Romany in Schorndorf, but this had not been implemented by February 1945 and it perhaps never was.[69] The application of the law was arbitrary, with disastrous results for those who became its victims.

Sterilisation could have fatal consequences. A twenty-one-year-old farmer's daughter from a small commune in Tübingen district was sterilised in 1937 because not only was she 'feeble-minded' but in 1936 she had had an illegitimate child whose father was unknown. The authorities regarded it as further evidence of her 'feeble-mindedness' that she had been 'agitated' and 'gone wild' as she tried to resist the operation, to which they attributed her death from peritonitis after undergoing it. This young woman's father conceded that she was 'somewhat retarded mentally, rather weak at school'. No doubt she would have been treated in her village as a simpleton and perhaps even cruelly mocked as an 'idiot'. Yet she would not have been an outcast from her community because, in her father's words, she could 'replace a male labourer in any branch of agriculture' and was the best worker on his farm.[70] At a time of serious shortage of labour on the land, she made a significant contribution, and was therefore valued and perhaps even respected as a worker in her own community, regardless of her deficiencies. The Nazi view of her as 'worthless' was at odds with the values of village life.[71]

Those classed as 'worthless' might be denied the right to marry, whether or not they had been sterilised. Under the Marriage Health Law of 18 October 1935, those intending to marry were legally required to undergo a medical examination to ascertain their eligibility for the 'Certificate of Suitability for Marriage'.[72] Once again, the application of the law was arbitrary and piecemeal. In practice, only a small proportion of intending spouses was actually examined: in Berlin-Charlottenburg in 1934–40 the figure was a mere 9 per cent of intending couples. These were either applicants for a marriage loan or individuals who had been identified by health or social workers as probably being eugenically 'flawed'.[73] On the eve of war in 1939, the legal requirement to undergo a medical examination was relaxed.[74] In 1941, however, intending spouses had to obtain written certification that there were no objections to their marrying. This confirmation could be refused if answers to a questionnaire suggested that one of them, or a member of their families, was in some way 'flawed'.[75]

In Württemberg, a thirty-six-year-old rural housemaid and a Bavarian shepherd, aged thirty-seven, were refused permission to marry in March 1942. The woman appealed – as was her right – to her local hereditary health court to be allowed to marry in spite of failing to meet the Marriage Health Law's eugenic criteria, having been sterilised in August 1935 on grounds of 'feeble-mindedness'. A further examination in 1938 had confirmed this diagnosis. Yet a more recent medical report, dating from 1942, noted an improvement in her condition to the extent that 'she is actually capable of conducting an orderly household'. In addition, not only was permitting her to marry in the interests of her three illegitimate children, but – a mitigating factor – she had lost one brother at the front, and had another two brothers still at the front. Her prospective husband was, it was said, unlikely to find another bride because of an unsightly scar which distorted his facial features. Further, although he seemed to be acceptable in terms of both his physical and his 'hereditary' health, he was nevertheless not 'an entirely valuable member of the community'. By opting to marry a woman who had been sterilised, he was clearly ignoring official strictures about having a duty to reproduce. Thus his 'racial quality' had been devalued by his social attitude. On reconsideration of the facts of the case, the marriage was allowed to proceed.[76]

Others might be denied the right to marry even if they already had children. A Stuttgart man, who had been denied permission to marry by the Württemberg Interior Minister, appealed to the Reich Minister of the Interior in April 1943. He was, however, refused yet again, on the grounds that he was schizophrenic, for which reason he had been sterilised in 1934. In addition, his family had 'hereditary health' flaws, and he himself had been in and out of hospital with various psychotic episodes, while his 'social attitude' left much to be desired. Among his faults, he had not, it was said, held down a job for any length of time, he consorted with women of ill repute at night, and he was 'wildly extravagant'. Further, his fiancée could 'certainly not be regarded as valuable from the hereditary health point of view', while 'her social demeanour does not seem flawless'. The final judgment was that, although she was unlikely to find a 'valuable' partner, she could not be permitted to marry this man, because it would not be a 'halfway orderly marriage', while the welfare of her illegitimate child might be compromised by association with the man she wished to marry.[77]

Senior doctors in Württemberg, including in wartime a woman doctor, as well as senior bureaucrats, made judgments about individuals' physical attributes, mental capacity and personality traits which were regarded as authoritative and which had the most serious consequences for these individuals. They dismissed men and women as 'psychopaths' and based their opinions on an assessment of a person's appearance, intelligence and conduct. One woman was described in June 1943 as having 'a hint of the Gypsy' about her. Her father's identity was unknown; her mother was allegedly 'from Slovakia' and, like her daughter, 'given to thieving'. She and her fiancé – a 'criminal, excitable psychopath given to drinking' – were denied permission to marry, although they had already been previously married to each other and divorced.[78] Individuals' criminal records and sexual history were scrutinised, as was their track record as employees, to determine whether they were fit to marry, for in Nazi Germany state policy took precedence over personal inclination in matters of marriage and procreation. That, at least, was the theory: shortages of money and personnel ensured that it was only very partially realised.

Sterilising those regarded as 'unfit' to belong to the Nazi 'people's ethnic community', and denying some of the 'unfit' the chance to marry, seemed an appropriate solution to future problems by preventing the reproduction of features and characteristics which were 'worthless'. There remained the problems of the present, namely the existence of both 'racial enemies' and 'unfit' 'Aryans', both in Germany and abroad. These perceived problems were magnified in wartime when there were acute pressures on German resources in terms of people, food and accommodation. Once again, the interests of the 'valuable' were to be safeguarded at the expense of the interests, and even the existence, of the 'worthless'. Those identified as non-'Aryans' were immediate potential candidates for marginalisation, sterilisation and, ultimately, death. This was regarded as urgent because, even in a successful war, there would be casualties: 'valuable' men would be killed in battle or injured, distorting the composition of the population in favour of 'racial enemies'. Stähle, among others, believed that it was worth extinguishing some lives in order to secure the future of the nation in time of emergency.[79]

Beyond that, the injured would require hospital facilities, probably on a large scale, while ethnic German immigrants would require accommodation. One solution – only a partial one – was to seize convents and hospitals belonging to religious orders. For example, a transport of ethnic Germans from Bessarabia and Bukovina, scheduled to arrive in Württemberg in November 1940, was mostly to be housed in sequestrated convents.[80] The more radical solution was to decant from hospitals and asylums patients with incurable conditions, in particular the mentally impaired, those described by policy-makers and bureaucrats as 'useless eaters' – people who were said to consume resources but contribute nothing. In much the same way as birth control had its gradations – from contraception to abortion to infanticide – so eugenic control of the 'quality' of the population had its stages: screening, sterilisation and, in Nazi Germany, murder, whose horror was sometimes cloaked in perversion of the term 'euthanasia', meaning literally 'good death'. The removal of these people to killing centres, such as Grafeneck and Hadamar, and their efficient disposal through gassing and cremation, were anything but merciful and entirely erroneously designated as 'euthanasia'.

The desirability of extinguishing 'worthless' lives had figured in some areas of German medical discourse even before 1933. This gained increasing currency in Nazi political and social policy circles after Hitler's assumption of power.[81] In November 1935, the head of the NSDAP's Racial Policy Office, Dr Walter Gross, spoke to the NS-Frauenschaft (NSF) in Stuttgart about preventing any further increase in the numbers of the 'hereditarily ill' in Germany, on whom 'a thousand million marks are spent. That is more than the entire cost of the state administration'.[82] If that was an exaggeration, it was perpetuated in official circles to justify plans that were already crystallising in policy-makers' minds. By 1939, while numerous political opponents and 'racial enemies' had died at the hands of Nazis, and while conditions in asylums had steadily worsened during the 1930s, there was as yet no systematic programme of state-sponsored murder.[83] During 1939, however, such a programme was developed, with the 'children's euthanasia' – which claimed victims in Württemberg – and with surveys of psychiatric hospitals and their patients and discussion of potential methods of killing.[84] The war provided the opportunity to commence this, first in occupied Poland, where Polish psychiatric patients along with some patients from Pomerania were murdered.[85]

In Germany itself, some of the first experiments in the calculated murder of 'useless eaters' took place in Württemberg, at Schloss Grafeneck in Münsingen district, once Hitler had, in deepest secrecy, given his consent in October 1939.[86] Grafeneck, a remote 'care home for cripples', run by the Samaritan Foundation of Stuttgart, was seized, at Stähle's suggestion, in autumn 1939 by the Berlin instigators of the 'euthanasia' programme, and its patients were transferred elsewhere. The home was converted into a strictly isolated killing site, complete with crematorium and registry office, where 10,654 persons were murdered by gas between January and December 1940, of whom 3884 were from asylums in Württemberg, 4451 from Baden and 1864 from Bavaria.[87] Some had previously been sterilised. Patients from hospitals in Berlin and the Rhineland were also murdered at Grafeneck.[88]

The exigencies of war provided both the pretext for moving asylum patients and the motive for killing them. With the evacuation of western Baden in autumn 1939, in anticipation of a French attack, civilians including asylum patients were moved, many of the latter to hospitals in Württemberg.[89] This undoubtedly accounts for the substantial numbers of patients from Baden who perished at Grafeneck. There was a direct correlation between institutions which had been earmarked as military hospitals or billets for other 'deserving' persons in the event of war and those whose inmates were murdered. Five Württemberg asylums so designated provided a total of 1200 patients for 'euthanasia' at Grafeneck. By 1942, almost half of the beds reserved for Württemberg's psychiatric patients in 1938 had been released in this way for other groups, including military casualties, tuberculosis patients and ethnic German settlers.

The 'euthanasia' programme claimed individuals with a variety of disabilities and from different classes and stations in life. At first, psychiatric patients were targeted. This category covered a range of ailments, including epilepsy, Parkinson's disease and senile dementia. In spite of the surveys of patients carried out in advance, with the aim of establishing who was and who was not capable of working independently, there was little discrimination between those who were mildly disabled and those with severe impairment. The first murders at Grafeneck came early in 1940, when thirteen epileptic patients – chosen alphabetically, not by condition – were transported from the Evangelical asylum at Pfingstweide to Grafeneck. Several days later, the families of some were informed that their relative had contracted influenza or pneumonia and died. To avoid the spread of disease, it was alleged, their bodies, their clothes and their belongings had been cremated.[90] Patients in the Rottenmünster asylum, which was run by nuns from the Untermarchtal convent, were 'transferred quite suddenly to another institution, never to return'. Among them were some valued as workers in the asylum's domestic maintenance and on its farm, as well as the sister of a Rottweil lawyer.[91]

People of all kinds were vulnerable, particularly, but not only, if they were being supported by state funds. A farmer from Tettnang district, who had been injured at work in 1929 and then been confined in a mental asylum, was moved to Grafeneck and murdered in May 1940.[92] A woman who had been imprisoned, after her husband had denounced her for criticising the regime, became depressed and was sent to an asylum. She somehow survived transfer to Grafeneck and a long wait in the barracks adjacent to the gas chamber.[93] Bishop Wurm, Württemberg's senior Evangelical clergyman, would claim, in July 1940, that Württembergers were particularly at risk because 'evidence of degeneration is not uncommon, even in intellectually and morally superior families in our small *Land*', because of endemic inbreeding. The President of the Württemberg Supreme Court had a brother who was a patient in the Stetten asylum. Alerted by a state prosecutor, whose father was an asylum director, about the fate of those transferred to Grafeneck, he asked the asylum's staff to inform him immediately if his brother was put on a transfer list. On the two occasions when this happened, he was able to retrieve his brother and take him home, while other patients were sent to Grafeneck to be gassed.[94] This was probably the same court president, Otto Küstner, who reported in late August 1940 that some patients' relatives had sought to retrieve them from asylums because of uncertainty about which ailments rendered a patient vulnerable to transfer to Grafeneck.[95]

Although medical doctors in Württemberg had a relatively low incidence of NSDAP membership – at 36 per cent compared with a national average of 46 per cent in 1937 – enough of them were willing to participate in the murder of the 'worthless' while lavishing care on the 'valuable'.[96] A lead was given by Stähle, who combined in his person the relevant offices, as leader of the Württemberg doctors' association, representative for medical matters in the Interior Ministry and leader of the section for people's health in the *Gau* leadership. He was utterly implacable in his determination to purge Württemberg's, and Germany's, society of those whom he deemed 'worthless', although he was anxious to maintain the utmost secrecy about the processes of 'euthanasia'.[97] Stähle's deputy, Mauthe, too, drove the motors of persecution and murder, while senior bureaucrats in Department X of the Interior Ministry were implicated in the transportation of targeted psychiatric patients from their asylums to institutions close to Grafeneck.[98]

Influential individuals might, however, perceive eugenic policies differently, welcoming some but opposing others. The Tübingen gynaecologist Dr August Mayer, who had performed illegal sterilisations before 1933 and who was unconcerned when mentally impaired women died in his clinic, opposed the 'euthanasia' programme.[99] Pastor Ludwig Schlaich, the director of the *Innere Mission* asylum at Stetten whose personnel had willingly sterilised inmates, protested about attempts to transfer them to Grafeneck.[100] Karl Mailänder, a welfare expert in the Interior Ministry, having collaborated in the transfer of mentally impaired individuals to their death at Grafeneck, protested to Berlin about the extension of the 'euthanasia' programme to physically disabled and elderly patients in care homes.[101] Minister of the Interior Schmid's deputy, Gottfried Dill, expressed to the authorities in Berlin his disapproval of the 'euthanasia' programme, on the grounds that it had no legal basis.[102] Dill's view was that no one who could maintain a relationship with his family should be transferred to Grafeneck, although he did not object to the removal there of those who were unaware of their surroundings.[103] It was perhaps a morsel of justice that the minister, Schmid, had to listen to medical experts in his ministry debating the merits of 'racial hygiene' measures for dealing with diabetics, such as himself.[104]

The 'euthanasia' policy was referred to as 'the secret Reich affair'. Even officers of the regime were kept in the dark. The Stuttgart State Prosecutor wrote in July 1940 about 'rumours' which had reached him about the 'unnatural death of asylum inmates'.[105] Yet this top secret policy became increasingly common knowledge after the first deaths had been reported. Aware of what a transfer to Grafeneck would entail, the authorities in some asylums run by religious bodies endeavoured to protect their patients. Ludwig Schlaich tried – ultimately unsuccessfully – to obstruct the removal of patients from Stetten to Grafeneck and virtually certain death.[106] In the Mariaberg Evangelical asylum, the authorities tried to protect some of their patients at the expense of others, painstakingly evaluating who was able to work productively and who was not. This condemned some while saving others.

The directors of the Christophsbad asylum in Göppingen found employers for most of its patients, and were thus able to demonstrate to officials from the Interior Ministry, who visited the asylum to collect patients for transfer to Grafeneck, that they were of value – that they were not 'useless eaters'. The doctors had to surrender some patients, but managed to protect the majority.[107] Both Dr Glatzel at Christophsbad and Dr Wrede of the Rottenmünster asylum wrote to government ministers to complain about the loss of precious labour. Patients who had made a significant contribution to the work of farms attached to the asylums had been transferred from both institutions. As both directors pointed out, with a severe shortage of labour on the land, it made no sense to remove workers who could not be replaced. Wrede referred to fifteen 'patients who worked as well or better than labourers' who had been transferred as early as 3 February 1940. In December 1940, Glatzel argued against the removal of further valuable workers in addition to those already transferred to Grafeneck.[108] Basing their arguments on grounds of cost-effectiveness did not necessarily indicate that these men regarded that as their primary consideration. They were, however, well aware that the best hope of persuading policy-makers who thought in terms of 'useless eaters' was to argue that their charges were not 'useless'.

Popular disquiet about the 'euthanasia' programme soon manifested itself. If some relatives colluded in the murder of a family member whom they regarded as a burden, other families were first suspicious and then outraged about the untimely death of a relative who was mentally impaired but in good physical health. Implausible formulaic explanations failed to convince families that their relative had died a natural death, especially when these contained elementary errors about the victim's condition.[109] The parent of a schizophrenic son who was a patient in a Württemberg asylum wrote from Ulm to Reich Minister of Justice Gürtner on 8 July 1940 to express horror at 'absolutely reliable information' about the transfer of mentally ill patients from the asylum to release space for military purposes. Relatives of these patients had, shortly afterwards, been informed of their death and cremation. The writer referred openly to 'murder'.[110] Rumours circulated, as they were bound to, about a policy which the authorities were at pains to cloak in secrecy, commented court president Küstner. Children heard about it in the street, and fears spread that even veterans of the First World War whose mental faculties had been impaired were falling victim to 'euthanasia'. It was said that, once the mentally ill had been dispatched, it would be the turn of the old and infirm. Küstner warned that 'the people's sense of justice' should not be underestimated. They were asking who was responsible for this policy, and whether it had any legal sanction.[111]

The Stuttgart State Prosecutor wrote to Gürtner in October 1940 about the deep anxieties he had encountered, and to ask why there was such secrecy about transferring patients if there was nothing to hide. Rumours about 'a mass murder of patients are circulating like wildfire', he said, with people afraid to allow relatives to be taken into hospital or an asylum, saying 'They're just killing old people'.[112] Some Württembergers refused to undergo the X-ray examination to assess their health, from November 1940, because, they said, they did not want to die in Grafeneck.[113] Grim jokes circulated. 'Keep quiet, or you'll go to heaven through the chimney', was one.[114] Farmers in the vicinity of Grafeneck were reportedly saying, 'Hold your tongue, or you'll be burnt', according to Dill in October 1940.[115] They could see and smell the smoke from the crematorium.[116] Most poignantly, many asylum inmates – who were allegedly mentally incompetent – soon became aware of the fate awaiting those who were assembled and taken to the grey buses which were to convey them to Grafeneck. Pitiful scenes ensued, with those gathered for transfer to their death trying to resist or making a tearful farewell.[117]

Disquiet manifested itself particularly in church circles. Some members of the clergy were among the first to learn of the 'euthanasia' policy, because Grafeneck itself was seized from a religious foundation and because many of the victims had been patients in asylums run by religious charitable bodies of both main denominations, such as the Evangelical Stetten and Mariaberg hospitals.[118] The

Rottenmünster asylum was a Catholic institution which was staffed by Catholic nursing nuns.[119] The Catholic Church was, however, somewhat inhibited in its protests, after the expulsion from Württemberg of Bishop Sproll of Rottenburg in 1938. Yet, contrary to Stähle's claims that its leaders had not protested at all, they had indeed represented their constituency's disquiet and alarm that state-sanctioned murder was being carried out on their territory.[120] Sproll's *locum tenens*, Vicar-General Kottmann, was a co-signatory to the letter of protest sent by the senior Catholic clergyman in south-west Germany, Archbishop Gröber of Freiburg.

In this letter of 1 August 1940 to the Reich Chancellery, they protested about the 'euthanasia' of mentally ill individuals from Württemberg and Baden, arguing that the Catholic Church would willingly bear the costs of maintaining these asylum inmates. Catholic bishops condemned 'euthanasia' as being contrary to both natural justice and God's law. There was particular concern about the victims' immortal souls, because they had apparently died without benefit of a priestly presence. In Grafeneck, there had been no opportunity for religious care, and equally there had been no attempt to obtain relatives' permission for cremation.[121] During the summer of 1940, the local priest at nearby Eglingen had tried several times to achieve agreement with Grafeneck's administrators that he would be called to minister to any Catholic patient who fell seriously ill. Although Stähle himself agreed, when approached, that this was appropriate, it was to no avail. Relatives of patients who had died at Grafeneck were distressed when the priest had to tell them that he had not been called to give the last rites or to conduct a Catholic funeral service. Accordingly, the bishop's office in Rottenburg asked the Württemberg Minister of the Interior on 5 October 1940 for the right to serve the spiritual needs of Grafeneck's inmates. The weasel words of the reply expressed a willingness to allow seriously ill individual patients spiritual comfort if they wished it, although most patients judged competent to understand had allegedly either expressed no desire for spiritual comfort or absolutely refused it, while the admission of a priest to Grafeneck would necessarily be circumscribed by the need to contain disease within the institution.[122]

The Evangelical Church in Württemberg took an incomparably stronger line. It was much more outspoken than the Evangelical Church elsewhere in Germany, although the individual and comprehensive protest in July 1940 by Pastor Paul Gerhard Braune, of the *Innere Mission* in Berlin, was extraordinarily courageous.[123] 'Euthanasia' was the cause which showed the Württemberg church, and in particular its leader, Bishop Wurm, to greatest advantage in Nazi Germany.[124] Wurm wrote about it repeatedly to the authorities in Stuttgart and Berlin. In a lengthy letter of 19 July 1940 to Reich Minister of the Interior Frick, he protested about the taking of life. He demonstrated detailed acquaintance with both the circumstances at Grafeneck and the regime's attitude to economising at the expense of 'the weak and defenceless'. When he received no reply, he wrote again to Frick, on 5 September 1940, in much sharper tones, questioning Germany's claim to be a civilised state and asking in the starkest terms: 'Does the Führer know about this business? Has he approved it?' By this time, he had heard that some elderly inhabitants of care homes had been included in transfers to Grafeneck. He complained bitterly that the prevailing view seemed to be that 'in an efficient population, there cannot be any weak or disabled people'.[125]

From several quarters came warnings that the 'euthanasia' programme was having a deleterious effect on popular opinion. Gröber and Kottmann noted that it was likely to undermine morale in wartime.[126] Wurm, too, referred to its being a severe blow to popular feeling. He had already told Kerrl, the Reich Minister for Church Affairs, on 6 July 1940, that people's confidence in both the state authorities and the medical profession had been 'shattered'.[127] The Stuttgart State Prosecutor echoed this sentiment, saying in October 1940 that confidence in the legal authorities as well as in the political leadership had been 'severely shaken'. He added that no one imagined that 'mass murder of this kind would have happened if it had not been ordered, or at least tolerated, by higher authority'.[128]

Even some NSDAP members showed that their commitment to full-blown Nazi racial ideology was defective. The SD in Württemberg had complained in 1939 about the lack of interest in racial policy shown by members of the party's formations, quite apart from non-members.[129] Some had certainly not comprehended its implications for the mentally impaired. In September 1939, patients from the Kork asylum in Baden were evacuated to the already fully-occupied Stetten asylum, near Waiblingen. Stetten's deputy leader, Jakob Rupp, a long-standing party member, was alarmed when, in May 1940, all of the female patients who had been at Kork for more than five years were carted off in buses with blacked-out windows by highly unprepossessing men and women who made little secret of their mission. Rupp's anxiety about the fate of these patients led him to compose a letter to 'the leading party comrade in whom I had the greatest trust', Rudolf Hess. First, however, he confided to Mauthe, in the Württemberg Interior Ministry, his fear that the patients were to be killed. Mauthe told Rupp that he could imagine what he liked but, if he ever divulged this suspicion to anyone, he could expect the harshest punishment. Rupp nevertheless sent his letter to Hess. The reply from Hess's office was that the letter had been forwarded to Himmler's office. This convinced Rupp that 'for our patients, all was lost'. Yet he continued to believe that Hitler knew nothing about 'these euthanasia matters'.[130]

Other Nazis, too, were shocked by the 'euthanasia' policy. In September 1940, a district NSF leader wrote to her Gau NSF leader in Düsseldorf about the death of a 'colleague' in Göppingen district. This colleague had been a patient in a private psychiatric asylum for five years, at her husband's expense. In early August

1940 she had been transferred 'elsewhere', and her husband had been unable to locate her. He had received a notice from Grafeneck – not far from their home – on 13 August announcing that his wife had died there and been cremated. It transpired that some of her belongings had been removed, and her rings replaced by cheap imitations. The writer added twelve questions about these matters and about why this private patient had been consigned to Grafeneck, asking who was responsible for that and for the arrangements at Grafeneck, including the posting of SS guards at its entrances. Her view was that these questions had to be answered both for the sake of relatives of the sick and to maintain faith in the regime.[131]

Another NSF official, in Böblingen district, Elsa von Löwis, wrote in December 1940 to the wife of the NSDAP's senior judge, Walter Buch, to express her distress about the 'tragedy at Grafeneck'. The absence of any legal basis for the killings, and the murder of those who were only slightly or periodically disturbed, had horrified her, although she probably would not have objected to the killing of severely impaired patients if it had had legal sanction. She was concerned about what this meant for the party's reputation, given that farmers in the area were well aware of what was happening. The arrival of the grey buses and the constant pall of smoke from the crematorium were visible to those working in the fields. People believed, she reported, that Hitler could not know about this, otherwise he would have stopped it. He should, she said, be told about both Grafeneck and people's reaction to it. She mentioned that a young woman, 'a 100 per cent party member' employed in the Racial Policy Office had been distraught about this issue; this was either disingenuous or naïve, given where she worked. Elsa von Löwis was not alone in seeing the 'euthanasia' programme as a good propaganda weapon for the Catholic Church.[132] The Stuttgart State Prosecutor had expressed the same fear.[133]

Nevertheless, Stähle, and higher authorities including Himmler, were determined to maintain the fiction that the 'euthanasia programme' was a secret, threatening those who raised objections about it – such as Dr Gmelin of the Stetten asylum – with dire consequences if they discussed it with anyone.[134] It may have been coincidental that the killings at Grafeneck ceased soon after Buch had written to Himmler, on 7 December 1940, about the von Löwis letter, with its report of popular disquiet. Grafeneck had by this time apparently served its purpose of eliminating most of the 'useless eaters' in Württemberg and Baden. Yet the coincidence is striking. In any event, Grafeneck was restored to its function as a home for the physically disabled in spring 1941, and the 'euthanasia' staff were deployed in other killing centres. The murders continued until the end of the war, and even beyond, with patients from Württemberg – including Jews – among the victims, regardless of the pretence that the policy had been halted in 1941 on Hitler's orders.[135] In some Württemberg institutions, patients were starved to death or despatched individually. Towards the end of 1944, Stähle instructed the directors of asylums to reduce the numbers of their patients, leaving the means of achieving this to medical staff. Most ignored his order, but not those at the Weinsberg asylum, where patients were starved and then injected with poison.[136] Nursing nuns at the Irsee asylum, as well as the local priest, were aware that patients were being given lethal injections. As late as midsummer 1945, American troops discovered in the Kaufbeuren asylum the corpses of patients murdered only hours earlier.[137]

'Euthanasia' provided the regime with lessons about effective techniques of mass murder, especially with the use of gas, which would be deployed in far greater measure in occupied eastern Europe where the vast majority of its victims were Jews. The first of twelve deportations of Jews from Württemberg came on 1 December 1941, when a thousand Jews were rounded up and sent to Riga, to be murdered.[138] The last deportation was as late as 12 February 1945 and included Jews from Heilbronn.[139] As few as 180 of the 2500 deportees survived. These 2500 were a mere quarter of the Jewish population of Württemberg in 1933.[140] Emigration to escape discrimination and persecution, as well as suicides and deaths caused by brutality, had taken their toll. By spring 1945, there were only some 200 Jews living in Württemberg, as partners in marriages with 'Aryans'.[141] In rural areas, most Jews had remained faithful to orthodox Judaism and traditional customs, but not necessarily aloof from their gentile neighbours.[142] There had been some intermarriage between Jews and Christians, but, for the most part, rural Jewish communities were endogamous, rendering them more distinct and therefore more vulnerable from 1933, when official policy targeted them.[143]

After decades of migration to the towns and emigration abroad, by 1933 only small numbers of Jews lived in rural Württemberg; in many communes there were no Jewish inhabitants.[144] By 1936, all 160 Jews in Crailsheim district lived in Crailsheim town, where there was a Jewish congregation, with none in the rural communes. The only remaining Jew in Ehingen district lived in the town of Ehingen. In Böblingen district, there were two Jews in Böblingen town, nine in Sindelfingen and one in Magstadt. In Künzelsau district, the 207 Jews lived in six of the forty-eight communes, including sixty in Künzelsau town and sixty-eight in the small commune of Berlichingen, which had 806 inhabitants.[145] Oberdorf am Ipf, in Ellwangen county, was, like Berlichingen, one of a small minority of communes with a significant Jewish population. In 1871 there were 1159 inhabitants, of whom 351 were Jews. By 1933, there were 1021 inhabitants, including eighty-seven Jews.[146] More typical were Eschenau, in Heilbronn district, with seven Jews in 1933, compared with forty-five in 1886, and Nagelsberg, in Künzelsau district, which had fifty-five Jewish inhabitants in 1886, but only four in 1924. The last two were deported to their death during the war.[147] By 1933 there were perhaps forty Jewish congregations, mostly in the towns. The highest density was in the extreme north, especially in areas around Heilbronn and Mergentheim.[148] These congregations were progressively dissolved; from 1939, only a congregation in Stuttgart remained.[149]

Antisemitism in rural areas long predated the Nazis' assumption of power, with prejudice against Jewish traders – and particularly cattle dealers – evident both before and after the First World War.[150] This was more the rough and traditional antisemitism of relatively primitive and devout Christian communities than the pseudo-scientific racial antisemitism of Nazi theorists. It was insidious, foul-mouthed and sometimes violent prejudice, but not potentially murderous. Antisemitic violence was reported only sporadically in Württemberg's communes before 1933. There were some unpleasant incidents in Tübingen, and in Oberdorf in 1919 some workers accused Jews of hiding stocks of flour at a time of acute food shortage. Both Rottweil and Dünsbach experienced Nazi-inspired antisemitic violence before 1933. These were, however, relatively isolated cases.[151]

If there was sometimes reserve between Jews and Christians, in many communes before 1933 relations between them were said to have been good, and it was not uncommon for a Jew to have a place on a commune's council. Among the many examples of this were Bad Buchau in Saulgau district, Bad Wimpfen in Heilbronn district, Berlichingen in Künzelsau district and Edelfingen in Mergentheim district. Buttenhausen, in Münsingen district, was undoubtedly unique in continuing to have a Jewish member of the commune's council until 1935.[152] In some places, Jews took part in their commune's associational life, but in others they confined themselves to Jewish religious and welfare activities.[153] Although rural Jews were significantly poorer than most urban Jews, they tended to be more prosperous than other country dwellers.[154] In many places, before 1933, a Jewish family provided funds for the poor of their commune. In Buttenhausen, a Jewish endowment paid for a local library and a nursery school.[155]

Jewish rural households frequently employed a Christian maid, and tended to pay higher wages than other employers, perhaps also providing small gifts. In some communes, many families would have been in dire need had there not been Jewish employers to provide work. Half of all earners in Olnhausen, in Heilbronn district, worked for a Jewish employer before 1933. In rural communities, Jews were quicker to embrace modern technology and facilities than gentiles, and many had the means to do so. They were much more likely than gentiles to own a telephone, bicycle, radio or even an automobile. Jewish traders who had once travelled by train found the car ideal for expediting business.[156] Punitive Nazi policies restricting the use of these facilities in 1938–40 were therefore a particular blow to Jews remaining in Germany.[157]

Despite its implacable hostility to Jews, the regime's aim of effecting segregation between 'Aryans' and Jews could not be either easily or quickly achieved. As the faltering response to the boycott of 1 April 1933 demonstrated, many rural Württembergers were characteristically stubborn in putting tradition and self-interest before obedience to the new regime. In Öhringen, and elsewhere, in order to pre-empt the boycott, housewives patronised Jewish-owned shops on the preceding day.[158] Nevertheless, it was not merely individuals' personal inclination that partially sabotaged antisemitic initiatives. Driving Jews – and political opponents – out of the professional public services in time of economic depression conveniently released posts for unemployed 'Aryans', particularly in the towns, but in small communes it transpired that imposing a boycott on Jewish-owned businesses, or trying to drive Jews out of trade, raised more problems than it solved.[159]

In September 1933, the chief of the Württemberg political police, Hermann Mattheiss, admitted that discriminating against Jewish-owned businesses in time of depression exacerbated both unemployment levels and conditions for suppliers, by reducing the number of employers. He concluded that boycotts or other kinds of discrimination should not be mounted against Jews who were law-abiding and orderly.[160] Nevertheless, on 13 December 1933, the Rottweil *Kreisleiter* prohibited NSDAP members in his district from buying in Jewish shops, and exerted extreme pressure to try to isolate Jews from the community.[161] Another *Kreisleiter*, in bowing to instructions to abandon the boycott in April 1934, asserted that 'Nothing in our fundamental attitude to the Jewish question is changed if we give up the boycott in theory. In practice, it is easy enough to give Jewish businesses as little custom as possible'. Yet, according to Reich Economics Minister Schacht in December 1934, NSDAP members who tried to prevent people from shopping at Jewish-owned stores, or who noted the names of those who did so in places such as Ravensburg, were not only jeopardising the economic recovery but also damaging people's faith in the state's ability to maintain public order.[162]

Persistent party propaganda urged 'Aryan' farmers to desist from dealing with Jewish traders, which would have meant breaking with tradition. Much is said about the unpopularity of Jewish cattle traders among farmers, and support for the NSDAP in rural areas is sometimes attributed to this.[163] Yet in Hohebach in Künzelsau district, among other communes, the poorer inhabitants, whose small parcel of land did not afford their families a living, gladly found work locally with a Jewish cattle trader, rather than having to seek work in a town, as either a resident or a commuter. These employees found that the cattle trader paid higher wages and allowed workers greater freedom than local farmers gave their labourers. No doubt there were cases of friction between Jews and their gentile employees. Nevertheless, working for a Jewish trader was regarded by some as providing a better living than could otherwise have been earned on the land.[164]

In Oberdorf, some succumbed to party pressure and ceased to work for a Jewish employer. One man who persisted was abused by local Nazis and summoned on several occasions to be berated by the local party branch leader. In despair, he killed himself.[165]

Contrary to claims that rural Jews were more likely than urban Jews to experience prejudice or assaults after 1933, in rural Württemberg there was little violence in smaller communes before 1938.[166] There were anti-Jewish riots in the Hohenlohe area in March 1933, which were deplored by the dean of Öhringen and a local priest who received no support from his superior.[167] In Schwäbisch Gmünd, the interior of the synagogue was demolished in 1934. The local Catholic and Evangelical clergy protested about this and expressed their solidarity with the Jewish community. In other places, such as Talheim, Catholics, Evangelicals and Jews lived peaceably together, and most examples of anti-Jewish violence were instigated by the NSDAP or its formations. On 25 March 1933, SA men from Heilbronn descended on Niederstetten, in Mergentheim district, using as a pretext an order from the Württemberg Interior Ministry authorising searches of enemies of the regime for offensive weapons. They seriously assaulted several Jewish men. A similar attack had been launched by the SA in Künzelsau on 20 March, leaving a religious teacher badly injured and a shopkeeper dead from heart failure; another Jew committed suicide. The local population's protests to NSDAP leaders were dismissed in a press article thus: 'You can't make an omelette without breaking eggs'. Jews in Öhringen suffered a similar assault, one being so badly beaten that he could no longer work. In Hechingen, in June 1935 HJ members broke up a cultural evening in the synagogue, to the anger of the local population. In Horb, NSDAP members insulted and harassed Jews and terrorised Christians who offered passive resistance to boycott measures.[168]

While the NSDAP and its formations engaged in local antisemitic initiatives, they received encouragement from some mayors of communes but obstruction from others. The mayor of Oberdorf was ringleader of a group of Nazis who managed to achieve the increasing isolation of Jews in his commune. He was not, however, able to incite Oberdorfers to engage in attacks on their Jewish neighbours. By contrast, the mayor of nearby Bopfingen, Ellinger, found work for dispossessed Jews, in spite of unremitting criticism from the local NSDAP.[169] The mayor of Sontheim, Richard Stieglitz, who lost his position after the pogrom in November 1938, was said to have had a 'consistently tolerant and considerate attitude' towards local Jews.[170] In Buttenhausen, Mayor Hirrle 'did everything he could for Jewish members of the community, gave assistance to Jews wishing to emigrate, and offered what official and personal support he could to Jews targeted for deportation during the war'.[171]

In much the same way as some individual party members and state functionaries were horrified by the practical application of Nazi racial theory in the

'euthanasia' programme, so others were – with equal naïvety – distressed by the
local consequences of Nazi antisemitic policy. The position in which Fritz Kiehn,
the Trossingen businessman and founder of the local NSDAP branch, found
himself in 1934 was probably unusual but not unique. A faithful employee, Toni
Hunger, who had long been an NSDAP member, was found to have a Jewish
grandmother, albeit a convert to Christianity. Kiehn protested forcefully when
Hunger was excluded from the party by the *Gau* NSDAP court, and he even
enlisted *Gauleiter* Murr's support. The Trossingen NSF, led by Berta Kiehn,
and the local BDM group, led by Hunger herself, threatened mass resignation,
while various officers of party and state rehearsed her dedication to the party,
especially before 1933, affirming that there was nothing 'unGerman' or 'Jewish'
about her character. Although Hitler stopped short of declaring her an 'Aryan'
– the act of grace and favour which her supporters sought – in 1935 he finally
acceded to requests from Trossingen that Hunger be permitted to remain a party
member.[172]

While attempts to disaggregate Jews from German economic and social life
were increasingly driven from the centre, local contradictions and exceptions
persisted. The Nuremberg Laws of September 1935 banned both marriage and
sexual relations between Jews and 'Aryans', as well as the employment of 'Aryan'
maids aged under forty-five in Jewish households.[173] Yet, in some communes,
gentile housemaids continued to work in Jewish households beyond 1935, and
in some cases even until 1940, in the face of abuse and harassment. One was
working in the Sontheim Jewish care home for the elderly when it was attacked
in November 1938.[174] Another was still employed by a Jewish family in 1942.[175]
In Oberdorf, some villagers persistently disobeyed party strictures about the
segregation of Jews from 'Aryans', sometimes defying explicit warnings from
NSDAP functionaries. One father was denounced by such a person to NSDAP
Kreisleiter Kölle, who ordered him to prohibit his daughter from working for a
Jewish cattle trader. In spite of this, she continued to work as usual.[176]

Other gentiles, too, showed reluctance to alter their habits. In Ludwigsburg, a
retired gentile teacher continued to play the organ in the synagogue after 1933. In
addition, in 1936 many 'benighted' gentiles continued to patronise Jewish-owned
shops there, according to the virulently antisemitic *Flammenzeichen*, which had
been taken over in 1935 by the Württemberg NSDAP as a 'campaigning paper',
similar to Julius Streicher's lurid *Der Stürmer*.[177] Customers of a Jewish textiles
retailer in Laudenbach, in Mergentheim district, took to visiting his premises
only at night, to avoid the SA guards stationed there to deter shoppers during the
day. A member of Massenbach commune's council ostentatiously resigned his
office because *Kreisleiter* Drauz of Heilbronn had in 1936 issued severe warnings
to council members and employees who continued to buy meat and sausage at
a Jewish butcher's shop.[178]

In September 1936, the *Flammenzeichen* reported that a Jewish textiles trader was able to make a good living out of the Catholic population of a village which was allegedly still imbued with the Centre Party's values. Apparently, on Sundays and holidays, farmers' wives thronged his premises where they were plied with coffee. The proprietor was allegedly making so much money that he could afford to deliver the women's purchases to their homes by car. Even worse, claimed the *Flammenzeichen*, some women – the wives of public officials as well as 'farmers' wives who won't take a telling' – seemed delighted to be driven home by the Jew, evidently oblivious of their duty as German 'Aryans' to shun him.[179] Segregation was decreed also at funerals. Yet attendance by 'Aryans' at the funeral of a Jewish neighbour was entirely in keeping with the rural custom of every household being represented at the funeral of a villager. Attempts by local party activists in Oberdorf to prevent this included threats of denunciation and further retribution by the NSDAP local branch leader, often to no avail.[180]

Many farmers apparently preferred Jewish cattle traders and were reluctant to cease dealing with them. They were castigated in the party's press, including *Gauleiter* Murr's mouthpiece, the *NS-Kurier*, and the *Flammenzeichen*, which published scurrilous propaganda to try to deter 'Aryans' from trading with Jews. In October 1936, it carried a notice entitled "They are not ashamed' which complained that it was

> outrageous that a cattle Jew can hang around a village for a week while a succession of dishonourable and ungodly citizens reportedly trade with the descendant of Abraham. Outwardly they celebrate the German harvest festival and want to be regarded as German peasants, but there in the stall at home stands the newly purchased Jew cow!

The paper then named five men and three women from a single village who had allegedly betrayed their fellow-citizens in this way.[181] By contrast, the *Flammenzeichen* noted with approval in August 1936 the exclusion of Jews from the Möckmühl livestock market, rather giving the game away by expressing the hope that it would not be an isolated example.[182] A mayor who tried to ban Jewish cattle traders from his town's market was commended by the *Flammenzeichen*, particularly for standing up to a Jewish trader who complained. Yet the trader was undoubtedly correct in retorting that many farmers had grumbled about the mayor's order excluding Jewish traders.[183]

Other mayors were less ready to ban Jewish traders. In Vaihingen in May 1936, the local NSDAP leadership – incensed by farmers' disregard of repeated strictures about trading with Jews – had hung a banner at the entrance to the town's market with slogans including 'Jews are not wanted here'. The mayor disapproved of this, ordering that there should be no repetition of it. In fact, however, neither the farmers nor the Jewish traders had paid the banner any attention. A large placard with a similar message appeared in the Haigerloch market in May 1937. Neither the commune's authorities nor the *Reichsnährstand* (RNS) had authorised it, and the NSDAP's local branch leader denied that it had been done with his authority or knowledge. In this case, the Jewish traders took one look at the placard and departed Haigerloch for nearby Rangendingen, leaving the farmers who had brought cattle to market in Haigerloch with no one to buy them and much to complain about. The placard was impounded by the police.[184]

To the regime, the continued presence of Jewish cattle traders at livestock markets was an offence. Repeated notices were issued at local level and published in the *NS-Kurier*, to the effect that Jewish cattle traders either had been or would be excluded from the markets. While this was effected in Schwäbisch Hall in 1937, in February 1937 Jews were still operating in the Stuttgart market.[185] Threatening and pillorying individual farmers perhaps influenced some, but in places such as Balingen, Metzingen and Ellwangen enough farmers continued to deal with Jewish traders to sabotage official policy.[186] In a commune in Nürtingen district, a Jewish cattle dealer abandoned the local market in October 1937, preferring instead to trade privately with farmers who visited his premises.[187]

Nazi officials expressed incomprehension at, and condemnation of, farmers' evidently persistent sympathy for the Jews.[188] The problem for the regime was that its propaganda was patently untrue: Jewish traders were not swindling farmers, while 'Aryan' cattle traders were offering neither as good a service nor as good a price.[189] One mayor reported in April 1938 that Jews were still trading – if in greatly reduced numbers – in various markets, and that this was unavoidable because there were too few 'Aryan' cattle traders who were prepared to take the risks involved in dealing with farm livestock.[190] At this late stage, the Württemberg Cattle Trade Association was still contemplating the withdrawal of Jews' trading licences on an *ad hoc* basis. The Württemberg *Gestapo* wrote to the *Landräte* and police chiefs in February 1938 to ask where Jews were still permitted to trade in local markets, because there was no uniformity of practice across the *Land*.[191] As it became apparent that farmers would not boycott Jewish traders while they were in business, the authorities concluded that a formal prohibition of Jewish traders would be the only solution. This was finally implemented in October 1938.[192]

At local level, the pressure exerted by Nazi zealots, particularly SA men, on 'Aryans' to desist from contact with Jews eventually had its effect. However much some farmers and employees showed determination to continue to trade with or work for Jews, piecemeal disobedience by individuals, often for self-interested reasons, ultimately could not protect Jews from marginalisation and harassment. Particularly as the depression receded, increasing pressure was exerted from the centre, with converging orders from a variety of sources constricting Jews' room for manoeuvre in small communities as in the towns. On 12 November 1938, a Reich government decree announced the exclusion of

Jews from German economic life. An order spelling out the mechanics of either 'Aryanising' or liquidating Jewish-owned businesses in Württemberg followed on 14 December 1938.[193] Even before this, with the 'Aryanisation' of Jewish-owned assets increasing exponentially in 1937 and 1938 – and bringing financial benefit to acquisitive 'Aryans' – increasing numbers of Jews saw no alternative to emigration.[194] Mounting pressure on the substantial Jewish community in Rexingen, in Horb district, for example, led a number of its members to emigrate to Palestine from 1937 to found a settlement.[195]

Most of those who emigrated from Württemberg went to the USA, with significant numbers also going to Palestine, Britain, France, Switzerland and Argentina; there was, however, scarcely a country in the world that did not receive some Württemberg Jews.[196] Those who left Württemberg were more likely to be men than women, and from the younger rather than the older age groups. Of the five Jews who left Sontheim in 1934, the three men had been born in Sontheim and the two women elsewhere. One man went to Palestine and the four others to the United States. The oldest had been born in 1899. One man left Sontheim in each of the years 1935, 1936 and 1937, the oldest born in 1904 and all natives of Sontheim. The two Picard brothers, who left in 1936 and 1937, were medical doctors, reflecting the exclusion of Jews from the professions. Their father – Julius Picard, the medical director of the Sontheim home for the elderly, who was born in 1866 – and their mother were the last Jews to emigrate from Sontheim, on 7 December 1940. Like most other Sontheimers, the Picards went to the USA. Of a total of twenty-one Jewish emigrants, one left for Argentina, two for Palestine, two for Africa and the remainder for the USA; three of them, the family Herz, went via Switzerland. Apart from those mentioned as leaving in the years 1934–37, all left after the pogrom of November 1938.[197]

The increasing exclusion of Jews from Württemberg's economic life may have brought benefits to urban dwellers, but it spelled financial disaster for some small communes because, as wealthier members of the communes, Jews had contributed significantly to local tax income. In Oberdorf, the local council noted the commune's decreasing income as a result of the dispossession of Jews, and predicted in December 1937 that, if Jews were banned from dealing in cattle, the position would become substantially worse. When this happened in 1938, the council saw no alternative to raising its local commercial tax by 400 per cent.[198] Other communes, too, including Laupheim and Braunsbach, suffered as a result of the exclusion and emigration of Jewish traders. In neither was there any possible substitute for the taxes which Jews had paid. In both, it was feared that a consequent rise in taxes would drive 'Aryan' businessmen away.[199] Unsurprisingly, none of this was mentioned when the Labour Front reported in 1940 on the poverty of the overwhelmingly rural districts of Württemberg.[200]

Enforcement of antisemitic policies depended on how far local party activists were present in a commune, and how far they were prepared to act against both Jews and disobedient 'Aryans' in their neighbourhood, in conformity with instructions from the centre and pressure from the *Flammenzeichen*. It was claimed that in Olnhausen antisemitism had to be imposed from without and that the villagers were mainly unreceptive to it. In Talheim, in Heilbronn district, too, it was said that Nazis brought hatred of Jews into the commune from outside, so that, after a century of harmonious relations between Jews and Christians, Jews were increasingly isolated and excluded. This was because some inhabitants were won over by Nazi propaganda, while others who were not were cowed by threats. Among those who refused to succumb was a master butcher who was forced off the commune's council in 1937 because he had flouted party officials' ban on trading with Jews.

Others were pilloried or punished for fraternising with Jews. In Schwäbisch Gmünd, a senior public official was reprimanded in November 1935 in the *Flammenzeichen* because he had greeted Jews in the street with a firm handshake and had conversed with them. Also in 1935, the Evangelical pastor in Wiesenbach, in Crailsheim district, had taken lodgings with a prominent Jewish family for two 'Aryan' girls who were visiting the commune. The *Flammenzeichen* expressed its vitriolic disapproval. In Weikersheim, in Mergentheim district, a man who had safeguarded a Jewish woman's belongings in 1938 until such time as she could emigrate had two placards hung on his door bearing the legend: 'Jews can still find protection and accommodation here. Fellow citizens, draw your own conclusions!' He had to pay for the cost of the placards. An old man in the same commune had his WHW payments withdrawn for four weeks because he had assisted a Jewish woman by conveying her effects in his handcart.[201]

The massive antisemitic pogrom on 9–10 November 1938, known as *Kristallnacht* ('the night of broken glass'), denoted a qualitative change in Nazi antisemitic policy, in town and country alike, with concerted violence and destruction. In urban areas, the local SA, sometimes galvanised by NSDAP officials, perpetrated damage and destruction in their own towns, where they were less likely than in the countryside to have personal knowledge of those whose persons and property they were attacking. In Ludwigsburg, the local NSDAP branch leader and the SA commander were ringleaders. The SA and members of other Nazi formations in Öhringen wrecked the inside of the synagogue there, on the orders of the *Kreisleiter*. In Ulm, members of Nazi formations staged riots, set the synagogue on fire and assaulted and incarcerated Jews. Schwäbisch Hall witnessed particularly violent and destructive antisemitic outrages on the part of the local SA, SS and NSKK (Nazi Automobile Drivers' Corps).[202]

In rural areas, by contrast, it was almost invariably SA men from elsewhere who arrived in a commune to wreak havoc: in villages, they were reluctant to foul their own nest. Beyond that, some at least could not face hostile action against people whom they knew well. In Buttenhausen, regarded by some Jews as a haven compared with other communes, the synagogue was set on fire on 9 November by SA men from Münsingen. The blaze was extinguished by the local fire brigade, allowing the mayor to rescue some of the synagogue's religious artefacts. Undeterred, on the following day the Münsingen SA men returned. They detained the mayor in his office, set fire to the synagogue and prevented all attempts to extinguish it. For good measure, they compelled some members of the Buttenhausen SA to assist them.[203] Similarly, on 9 November SA men from Ellwangen descended on Oberdorf and urged the local SA leader, Böss, to fetch petrol and set fire to the synagogue. Böss replied: 'I can't do this in Oberdorf, because I've grown up with these people [Jews], gone to school with them and seen active service with them on the battlefield'. The Ellwangen SA leader, Roos, returned on 10 November and ordered Böss to instruct his men to destroy and plunder the homes of Jews. When Böss refused, he was stripped of his command – but not for long, because no other Oberdorf SA man would assume it. Yet again, on 11 November, SA men from Ellwangen arrived. They broke into the synagogue, destroyed books and papers and left. Local people extinguished the fire which they had started. Although Böss prevented some Jews from being taken into custody by Roos's SA men, others were seized and taken away. Outside the commune, one man was murdered.[204]

Elsewhere, too, SA men perpetrated destruction and violence in communes other than their own. In Mühringen, in Horb district, incomers smashed the windows of Jewish-owned shops and houses, and set fire to the synagogue. The local fire brigade turned out to staunch the blaze. SA men from Sulz, in Horb district, travelled by bus during the night to Haigerloch, which was several kilometres distant. There they demolished the synagogue, the Jewish school and community house, and an inn, the 'Rose', which was owned by a Jew and frequented by gentiles. The Jewish teacher and deputy rabbi, among others, were assaulted, and the windows of Jewish-owned homes were smashed. Several Jews were arrested and held for some weeks in Dachau. The synagogue in Baisingen, in Horb district, was demolished by SA men from Horb town and its environs, led by party functionaries. These incomers then wrecked the homes of thirteen prosperous Jewish families, to the distress of their gentile neighbours, some of whom tried to prevent it. Reluctant to be recognised, the SA men moved through the village in civilian dress with their hats pulled down and their collars turned up.

Other communes where non-native SA or NSDAP men perpetrated the pogrom included Berlichingen, Braunsbach, Freudental and Oedheim.[205] In Buchau, the neo-classical synagogue, which had been inaugurated in 1839 in the presence of King Wilhelm I of Württemberg, was set on fire by SA men from Ochsenhausen, in Ulm district, with help from Saulgau NSDAP members. They fetched the local SA leader from a neighbouring village to point out houses where Jews lived so that they could smash their windows. The local population stood by, helpless, and even Buchau's NSDAP members disapproved of the destruction.[206] In Sontheim, a local SA man confronted the group of masked men who had been sent by *Kreisleiter* Drauz and conveyed by the NSKK to destroy the synagogue. He warned them that a fire in the synagogue would have dire consequences for the adjacent buildings. The incomers desisted, but the local man was expelled from the SA. On that evening he had also ferried some local Jews away from Sontheim and potential danger in his car.[207] By contrast, in Talheim local Nazis gave furtive support to the SA men who came from Sontheim to destroy the synagogue and physically abuse Jews.[208]

According to the SD, on *Kristallnacht* in Württemberg eighteen synagogues were destroyed by fire, and a further twelve had their interiors demolished. Altogether 878 Jews were arrested, of whom forty were still in custody on 1 February 1939. Many had been freed on condition that they emigrate immediately. The violence had left thirteen Jews dead. The events of the pogrom were generally well-received in party circles, but many ordinary Württembergers regarded them with disapproval or incomprehension, saying 'Smashing windows is childish, and not what grown men should be doing' and 'It's no way to treat people'.[209] Some asked why, with an official campaign against waste and encouragement to recycle, so many valuable assets had been damaged or destroyed.[210] The pogrom had a mixed reception among 'Aryan' traders, although they should, said the SD, have been its beneficiaries. Indicative of this was the Stuttgart glaziers' decision to charge a reduced rate for replacing the smashed windows of Jewish-owned property 'because it was not the Jews who had caused the damage'.

Although Bishop Wurm and other Evangelical Church leaders abstained from comment or criticism, ordinary members of the clergy and their flock were vocal in their disapproval, manifesting clear sympathy with the victims and saying 'But the Jews, too, are human beings'. Württemberg's Catholics, on the defensive after Bishop Sproll's expulsion, were less outspoken, evidently fearful that it would be their turn next. It was perhaps to be expected that liberals, who were kept under surveillance by the SD, would sympathise with Jews who were arrested and whose property was damaged. More surprising, perhaps, was the attitude of some conservatives. If much of their criticism derived from disapproval of the waste of resources through the destruction of Jewish-owned property, there were also examples of nationalists and even Nazis who showed compassion for individual Jews. A former *Stahlhelm* member, by 1938 an NSDAP member, sent flowers to a Jew to indicate moral support. In Creglingen, a member of the NSKK helped a Jew who had been arrested to escape. He was supported by the district leader of the Nazi War Veterans' Association, who himself rented accommodation to a Jew.[211]

The pogrom hastened Jewish emigration. Whereas there had been 7046 Jews – by Nazi definition – in Württemberg on 1 October 1938, on 1 March 1939 there were 6089. The SD reported in April 1939 that, contrary to the previous tendency of younger Jews to leave, in the aftermath of *Kristallnacht* older Jews, too, were emigrating. The majority had concluded that their position would be as bad in any future war as in peacetime, because in wartime they would probably starve. The SD had no qualms about describing the mood of hysteria that had engulfed some Jewish men and women, with the hopelessness which they felt being expressed by a woman in Ludwigsburg who said 'that, if she had not had children, she would have taken her own life long ago'.[212] In July 1939, the SD reported that, on average, one hundred and fifty Jews were leaving Württemberg every month.[213] One consequence was the dissolution of the remaining Jewish congregations in Württemberg and the creation of one consolidated congregation in Stuttgart.[214] The congregation in Buchau, for example, dissolved itself on 19 July 1939. By the end of 1940, ninety Jews had left the commune.[215]

According to the census of May 1939, 4780 Jews remained, of whom the clear majority, 2841, were female. There were also 1351 '*Mischlinge*', as those with both Jewish and 'Aryan' antecedents were termed. As in 1933, over half of both Jews and '*Mischlinge*' lived in Stuttgart; a further 360 and 197 Jews lived in two other major towns, Heilbronn and Ulm, respectively.[216] It was less easy for rural Jews to leave if their business was associated with the specific agricultural character of their commune. They might send younger family members abroad, leaving those who remained as a mainly elderly and vulnerable small minority.[217] It is not surprising, therefore, that in wartime many of Württemberg's remaining Jews resided in Jewish homes for the elderly. Such a home was established in Buttenhausen in 1940, comprising several individual houses which had been vacated by Jews who had emigrated. The continuing presence of some Jews in Buttenhausen, and the sympathetic reputation of the commune's mayor, led many Jews from elsewhere to congregate there in autumn 1940 and 1941. It proved only a temporary refuge: in two transports, in April and August 1942, the residents were removed from the home to their death. At least 109 Jews from Buttenhausen were sent to Riga or Theresienstadt, including twenty-two who had been living there in 1933.[218]

In Sontheim, a home founded in 1907 had seventy-eight residents by 1937. After *Kristallnacht*, however, many elderly Jews, including some from Heilbronn, sought refuge there, with the result that rooms had to be shared. A further influx after the outbreak of war, this time from Baden, the Saarland and the Palatinate, brought the number of residents to 150.[219] The incomers were probably trying to evade inclusion in the transportations which were taking place from these areas in 1940 to the camp at Gurs in the French Pyrenees.[220] Then, in mid-November 1940, *Kreisleiter* Drauz ordered the dispersal of the residents either to their place of origin or to other homes for the elderly. As the senior *Gau* official of Himmler's *Volksdeutsche Mittelstelle* (Liaison Office for Ethnic Germans), he had decided to requisition the Sontheim home for ethnic German settlers from eastern Europe.

The elderly Jews were sent to homes in Buttenhausen, Oberstotzingen, Herrlingen and Oberdorf, among others. Johanna Gottschalk, for many years head of the Sontheim home, accompanied the thirty-two bound for Buttenhausen. With them, she was later sent to the Theresienstadt ghetto; she was one of the few survivors. Eighteen residents of the Sontheim home, along with two Jews from Heilbronn, were sent to Heggbach in Biberach district, to be accommodated in a psychiatric asylum whose inmates had been 'transferred' in September and October 1940 on the orders of the Württemberg Ministry of the Interior. This seems to have been a case of patients being targeted for 'euthanasia' in order to release accommodation for Jews, whose surviving members were deported to their death in July 1942.[221]

When the decision was taken to render the towns 'free of Jews', late in 1940, the remaining urban Jews were either ordered to relocate to designated communes in the countryside or forcibly transported there.[222] In Oberdorf, fifty-four urban Jews were billeted on six indigenous Jewish families, which caused hardship for everyone in these households.[223] In other communes, such as Dellmensingen in Ulm district, Eschenau in Heilbronn district and Oberstotzingen in Heidenheim district, an empty Schloss was used. From March 1942, some ninety to a hundred, mostly elderly, Jews were compelled to move to Dellmensingen from towns in both Württemberg and Baden. At Eschenau, the Schloss, which was seized by the *Gestapo* from its owner, Alexander Freiherr von Bernus, accommodated at least eighty-seven Jews, most from a home for the elderly in Stuttgart with others from Heilbronn. In Oberstotzingen, Jews from Herrlingen, in Ulm district, were taken to the Schloss.[224]

The deportation of Jews to the countryside was not intended as a permanent solution. Relocation or transportation within Germany was merely a temporary expedient until all Jews could be removed from Germany. The intention behind the internal deportation of elderly Jews from the towns was to isolate them in what were effectively ghettos which could be closely monitored and controlled by the police or party authorities. This was why several of the locations were communes which had never had a Jewish congregation and which had no Jewish inhabitants in the 1930s. Dellmensingen, Tigerfeld and Oberstotzingen were among them. The isolation was guaranteed by their accommodation in a self-enclosed building in a rural area, such as a Schloss which was remote from the main body of the commune. The Schloss in Weissenstein, in Göppingen district, which was seized from its owner, Count von Rechberg, in 1941 was described 'as a kind of transit camp on the way to deportation and death'. This was similar in intent to the removal in 1940 of mentally impaired persons from a variety of asylums to institutions adjacent to Schloss Grafeneck, before transfer to Grafeneck itself. Thus Jews were separated from acquaintances in their former neighbourhood and then segregated from the local population of the commune to which they had been transported. For example, while the renowned boarding school for Jewish children in Herrlingen was turned into a home for elderly Jews from elsewhere, Herrlingen's own Jews were removed to Oberstotzingen.[225]

Moving Germany's remaining Jews about therefore rendered them anonymous: those brought into a community did not possess the traditional relationships which Jewish families of long standing had in small communes. In Dellmensingen, the Jews in the Schloss were not members of the commune: the NSDAP *Gau* administration, not the local mayor, was responsible for their registration documents. Seventeen of the inmates died in the Schloss between March and September 1942, whether from natural causes or starvation it is not clear.[226] While some Jews were relocated within Württemberg in the years 1940–42, others were sent to different parts of western Germany. Several from Bad Wimpfen were compulsorily moved to Mainz in 1939–40. The twelve remaining in nearby Schluchtern were rounded up in October 1940 and taken in a transport of 6500 Jews from western Germany to Gurs, at the behest of *Gauleiter* Robert Wagner of Baden. A few other Württemberg Jews who were moved to Baden were also transported to Gurs. From there, some were able to emigrate to the USA, but most were subsequently sent to eastern Europe to be murdered.[227] The trauma of forced relocation to an unfamiliar and inhospitable place no doubt took its toll on elderly and infirm individuals. It is hard to gauge how many deaths of Jews ostensibly from natural causes were the result of physical abuse or mental anguish occasioned by discrimination, persecution and forced relocation.[228] Probably as an exception, the urban Jews from Stuttgart and Heilbronn who were forcibly settled in Haigerloch between 1940 and 1942 lived with few restrictions and under the leadership of a native Haigerloch Jew. Yet the end result was the same: in 1941–42, at least 192 Jews were deported from Haigerloch to the camps of the east; eleven returned after the liberation.

The rounding up of Württemberg's Jews for deportation to eastern Europe began in November 1941, on the orders of the Stuttgart *Gestapo*. While the *Gestapo* planned the operation and supervised the arrangements, its officers did not normally assemble Jews in rural areas in preparation for deportation.[229] Sometimes SA men or a gendarme would seize individual Jews and deliver them to a collection point.[230] For the most part, however, the *Gestapo* delegated responsibility to the Jewish Cultural Society of Württemberg, whose leaders had the unenviable task of gathering Jews together and ensuring that their luggage contained all manner of household and other goods, to maintain the illusion that Jews were being resettled, not sent to their death.[231] In Ulm, Resi Weglein was arrested in her home in August 1942, along with her disabled war-veteran husband, by a female guard who was not 'Aryan' but a '*Mischlinge*'. They, together with residents of the Buttenhausen home for the elderly, were destined for Theresienstadt. Much of the Wegleins' luggage was stolen, to be distributed to 'Aryans' whose possessions had been destroyed by bombing.[232] Elderly Jews from Buchau were allowed to take only 50 kilos of luggage and no money. Their homes were sold and their furniture auctioned. On 20 August 1942, the remaining fifty Jews in Buchau were deported to Theresienstadt, leaving ten houses empty. The only exceptions were three Jews who were married to Christians.[233]

In Göppingen, the order for an 'evacuation' of Jews was received by both the town's police bureau and the *Landrat*'s office on 18 November 1941. After being searched by *Gestapo* officers, who seized their money and valuables, and spending a night in a gymnasium, without beds or covers, on 27 November forty-one Jews were sent to Stuttgart, imagining that they were bound for labour service in Poland. The beds, clothing and crockery which they were allowed to take with them became Reich property when they crossed the border into Poland. Those Jews who were rounded up for each deportation spent cramped, uncomfortable and agonising nights at the assembly point at Killesberg in Stuttgart. There, their remaining small items of value were stolen – in the Wegleins' case, a gold watch, *eau de cologne* and chocolate – and they came under the direct authority of the *Gestapo*. From there, some were transported in cattle trucks to the insanitary misery of Theresienstadt, while others were sent directly to their death in Poland or Latvia. The first transport of a thousand Jews to Riga, on 1 December 1941, took three days and four nights in unheated cattle trucks. The captives received water only twice during this hellish journey. Twenty-eight of them were shot on arrival. A further eighteen to twenty froze to death each night in the old barns in which they were confined. Others died of diseases such as typhoid and dysentery.[234]

Some 'Aryans' undoubtedly took pleasure in the miserable conditions to which Jews in their area were reduced. In Göppingen, *Kreisleiter* Baptist and Mayor Dr Pack were at one in their vilification of local Jews. In November 1941, the mayor sent the deportees on their way shouting, 'Go to hell, pack of swine', while street urchins jeered. After the pogrom of 1938, the *Kreisleiter* had publicly excoriated an Evangelical dean who had spoken sympathetically of Jews.[235] Youths in Sontheim gathered to throw stones at the home for elderly Jews on the day after the pogrom, when windows, crockery and much else had already been smashed. Shortly after that, a local teacher brought his pupils to view the destruction in the home. He was followed by two men and a woman, escorted by NSKK men, who took photographs of the individual rooms for the *Flammenzeichen*, apparently on the instructions of *Kreisleiter* Drauz.[236]

The best that can be said of most villagers is that they refused to participate in anti-Jewish activity. In Michelbach, antisemitism was imposed from without and found little resonance in the village. The synagogue escaped destruction in the 1938 pogrom. Nevertheless, the party, it was said, was able to enforce 'strict isolation' of Jews from 1938, not least because they were excluded from economic life. In Massenbach, 'National Socialist hate propaganda had, with a few exceptions, an effect only on the young'. Many adults maintained friendly relations with Jewish neighbours, but their opposition to the party's anti-Jewish initiatives was passive.[237] The same was true of other communes. Yet the disproportionate influence, as well as the menace, exerted by party members and officials in a system where the police were *parti pris* eventually had its effect. It was both brave and foolhardy openly to challenge party authority on the issue which was central to Nazi ideology and which therefore gave local party hacks most latitude for arbitrary action. Individuals in villages who refused to conform to Nazi norms and continued to associate with Jews could be vilified, bullied and punished with impunity. Gentiles in Oedheim who tried to intercede for Jewish neighbours during the pogrom were themselves beaten. There was, certainly by 1938, no hope of redress from the police or the courts. Accordingly, as Nazi authorities at district, *Land* and Reich level progressively marginalised Jews from gentile society – reinforced by the *Flammenzeichen*'s scurrilous vilification of non-conformists – villagers increasingly complied, at least ostensibly, whatever their private views. In both Olnhausen and Talheim during the war, some Christians secretly provided food for severely deprived Jewish neighbours, until they were deported.[238]

By contrast with the 'euthanasia programme', where the alarm of ordinary individuals was harnessed by church dignitaries who gave a powerful lead in protesting about it, those who opposed antisemitic policy – or simply found aspects of it distasteful – were left without a champion. Beyond that, it has been argued that Jews could expect nothing from the Evangelical Church as an institution, and that, until well into the war, they found support only from individual members of the clergy and the laity.[239] The *Innere Mission* in Stuttgart attempted to provide both spiritual and practical support for Jews who had converted to Evangelical Christianity, but increasing restrictions on this group vitiated its efforts.[240] The Catholic Church was blinded by its view of Jews as Christ-killers. Archbishop Gröber, the chief prelate in Baden and Württemberg, said, in a pastoral letter in 1939, that, not only had Jews demanded the crucifixion of Christ, but 'their murderous hatred has continued in later centuries'. Another pastoral letter in the same vein followed in March 1941.[241]

Nevertheless, several members of the clergy protested about anti-Jewish policies, and some courageously hid Jews or helped them to escape. These were highly risky individual initiatives without the protection, far less the encouragement, of church leaders. Evangelical Church pastors who openly criticised aspects of the regime's antisemitic policies were taken to task by the church's leadership for meddling in politics. One such was Pastor Umfrid, who had condemned violence against Jews in the Hohenlohe area in 1933, and had been attacked by Nazis for doing so. The most notable case was that of Pastor Julius von Jan, who preached against the outrages of the 1938 pogrom. He was assaulted by SA men, given a prison sentence by a Special Court, and then expelled from Württemberg. The church authorities managed to prevent his incarceration in a concentration camp, but they also criticised his conduct. The Confessing wing of the Württemberg Evangelical Church, by contrast, expressed support for Jan's protest.[242] Some Evangelical pastors were also active in harbouring Jews. The Krakauers and others found refuge in various pastors' homes in Württemberg during the war. In Schwenningen, pastors and lay members tried to supply Jews with false papers to enable them to escape to Switzerland, which some succeeded in doing.

Bishop Wurm began to evince unease about the treatment of non-'Aryans' – as the last element in a catalogue of complaints, starting with 'euthanasia' – in a letter to Goebbels in November 1941. In it, and in a letter to Hitler of 9 December 1941, he opined that such policies would only fuel the enemy's propaganda machine. In December 1941 he had heard rumours of mass murder in the east, but it would not be until 1943 that he protested about it. In a series of letters – to Gottfried Dill, Murr, Kerrl, Frick, and, finally, to Hitler himself – Wurm expressed his horror at the murder of Jews while also making clear his distaste for the previous extent of Jewish influence in all areas of German life, as he saw it. He was particularly exercised by the position of 'Mischlinge' and those in marriages between Jews and 'Aryans', especially as Nazi policy began to focus on these groups from 1943. He seems eventually to have realised that the silence of leaders such as himself, in the face of discrimination against and persecution of Jews, was a dereliction of the duty of leadership.[243] The churches' introspective concern for matters concerning their doctrine and their own members, albeit in the very difficult circumstances of dictatorship and war, had left little room for concern about others. Both churches reserved their belated concern for Jews who had converted to their denomination of Christianity, for Jews who were married to members of their congregations, and for the offspring of such unions.

The Nazis' preoccupation with redistributing resources from the 'worthless' to the 'valuable' continued to the end.[244] 'Aryanisation' involved a massive forced transfer of property from Jews to 'Aryans'. By 1939, the majority of the agricultural holdings formerly owned by Jews were in 'Aryan' hands. Remarkably, in May 1941, a Jew remained in possession of a choice parcel of land in a Württemberg commune. The Württemberg Economics Minister ordered that it should be sold within two months to 'Aryan' farmers.[245] After patients in asylums had been murdered in Grafeneck and other 'euthanasia' centres, their clothes and other effects – which had allegedly been incinerated to prevent the spread of disease – were given to the NSV for distribution to deserving 'Aryans', including the victims of bomb damage. The property of Jews who were transported to their death was sold off or impounded by the *Gestapo*. The clothes and utensils which Jews had been encouraged to pack for their journey were to be given to bombed out 'Aryans'. The ultimate redistribution came when anything which was of value or could be recycled was scavenged from the bodies of murdered Jews.

5

The Impact of War

The Second World War was the most modern war that could have been fought at the time. The major participants – Germany, Britain, France, the Soviet Union, the United States, Japan and Italy – were the largest of the most highly industrialised countries in the world. The weapons of war were therefore the most technologically advanced available anywhere. They had to be produced in huge numbers, particularly by countries whose participation covered most of the 1939–45 period, and above all by Germany which, in 1944–45, was conducting its war effort virtually alone and against massive odds.[1] Certainly, Germany should have been well prepared for war in 1939, with the introduction of rearmament and conscription in 1935, with a Four Year Plan for the economy in 1936, and with plans for mobilising civilians to prepare for a 'total war' in which the nation's entire resources would be concentrated on achieving victory as quickly as possible.[2] Yet the war Hitler pursued from 1939 increasingly imposed acute pressures on German society that had to be sustained because neither Hitler nor the Nazi political leadership would countenance an end to the war that was anything other than 'final victory' (*Endsieg*). That is to say, if 'the refusal to give in kept Germans fighting long after the war was effectively lost', this was, especially in 1944–45, 'the refusal' of the regime's leaders and not of Germans at large – certainly not of rural Württembergers.[3] While the war lasted, the Nazi regime's persecution and murder of its designated 'enemies' proceeded, with ordinary Germans, both soldiers and civilians, among the perpetrators.

The course of the war for Germany was the mirror-image of what it involved for Britain. Even if civilians in both countries had to submit to conscription, rationing, evacuation and a host of other impositions, the difference was that while Britain was in dire national crisis in 1940, by 1943 its citizens could see the tide turning in their favour.[4] During the last two years of the war, in spite of the continuing losses and hardship, confidence in victory grew steadily, sometimes by leaps and bounds. By contrast, while German civilians were anxious from the start, in September 1939, and while there were even then military casualties, in 1939–42 they could greet troops returning from one victory after another, sometimes with genuine enthusiasm.[5] They also enjoyed a reasonable standard of food and other supplies secured by German pillaging of the many countries which the *Wehrmacht* subjugated. Yet the army's failure to take Moscow in late autumn 1941 was a shock, and thereafter the news from the eastern front was at least worrying and at worst catastrophic, especially when Goebbels at last persuaded Hitler that the truth about the disaster at Stalingrad, which reached its climax at the end of January 1943, should be broadcast to the public. For more than two further years, the nightmare on the eastern front continued and drew ever closer to home, with, in addition, defeat in North Africa and the Allied invasion of Italy from July 1943, even before the D-Day landings in France in June 1944.

Although the tightly controlled German media failed to relay the full horror of slow but inexorable defeat, most Germans knew that their position was steadily worsening, especially if they listened to 'black' (British) radio broadcasts.[6] Their own experience also gave them an idea of the price that Germans were paying: a report on the popular mood in Württemberg of 31 May 1943 – almost two years before the war's end – mentioned that in many communes the number of military deaths had reached or even overtaken the total figure for the First World War.[7] In the commune of Tomerdingen, 'by December 1942 already seven [men] from here had been killed in action'.[8] The commune of Beimbach sent altogether 110 men into military service. Twenty-six died in action, nine were still prisoners of war in October 1948, and six were 'missing'.[9] In Neresheim, by the beginning of 1945 'almost every home had dead, missing or wounded to grieve over'.[10] Altogether, it has been estimated that, whereas 14 per cent of German servicemen died in the First World War, the figure for the Second World War was double that, or 28 per cent.[11]

It was not only the military whose position deteriorated. While Allied bombing had caused sporadic damage in western German towns and cities from May 1940, striking at Berlin for the first time in August 1940, it was only with the beginning of 'area bombing' in March/April 1942, with Lübeck and Rostock as the initial targets, that the full horror of aerial warfare was literally brought home to urban Germans. Thereafter, the Royal Air Force and the United States Air Force pounded an increasing number of German towns and cities ever more intensively in the years 1943–45, with damage, casualties and evacuation leading to a situation that was little short of chaotic.[12] Even when there were no air raids, there were frequent alarms which disturbed nights and disrupted days. For example, in Tübingen – hardly a major Allied target – citizens heard their one hundred and second air raid alarm of the war in March 1944, and on 15 January 1945 the sirens wailed there for the two hundred and fiftieth time.[13] Stuttgarters experienced altogether 900 air-raid warnings, 744 of them in 1944–45.[14] With the shrinking of Germany's European empire in 1944–45, the disruption of transport, utilities and services by bombing, and the never-ending conscription of men and materials, the urban food supply dwindled critically. All in all, as Britain's fortunes improved, Germans' deteriorated: what Britons perceived as light at the end of the tunnel was the brightness of Churchill's 'sunlit uplands'; for Germans, it was the raging inferno in their bombed out towns and cities.[15]

The abnormal circumstances of a second twentieth-century war imposed ever-increasing sacrifices on the citizens of all combatant powers, including the conscription into the armed forces of several million men – many of whom would suffer death, injury or incarceration – and the direction of many of the remaining civilians into essential war work in modern industries.[16] In Germany, these demands contributed to a significant transformation in the composition of the civilian population. First, the removal of well over eleven million men into the armed forces – to say nothing of substantial numbers seconded to the occupied territories – left women, children and elderly men not only to cope with tasks which had previously been either performed by or shared with young and middle-aged men, but even to act as substitutes for men who had carried the responsibility of running an enterprise and bearing the burdens of the heaviest work in labour intensive occupations such as agriculture.[17] There remained a substantial but steadily diminishing body of men eligible for military service but retained in the civil sector – in factories, businesses, farms, trade and commerce, and in government and NSDAP offices – to try to maintain functions and facilities at a level as near as possible to normal for as long as possible, and not least to try to avoid a breakdown of either control or morale on the home front.[18] There was not, however, the clear-cut distinction between men serving in the forces and civilian men that this may imply, especially in the early stages of the war: men would be recruited for tours of duty – for 'manoeuvres' or work on the 'West Wall' even before September 1939 – and then perhaps released, only to be called up again several months later.[19] While this perhaps spread the burden of army service more widely than a once and for all call up of a restricted number of men would have done, it remained a source of confusion to the self-employed, to commercial employers and to government departments and local government officials. In 1943–45, however, most remaining civilian men in an extended category of military recruitment age were conscripted, with government and party officials protected only up to a point.[20]

The other major change in the nature of civilian society in Germany during the war was the influx of foreigners from both western and eastern Europe. In total at least ten million foreigners were brought to Germany, with the largest annual total of 7.6 million in 1944. Some were POWs; some were more, or usually less, voluntary immigrants, and many were sent to Germany as forced labourers to help to compensate for the shortage caused by the withdrawal of German men from the home front into the armed forces. This significantly distorted the balance of the civilian population, as German men aged eighteen to forty-five became increasingly thin on the ground. There was a disproportionately large number of both German women and foreign men, and there were also female forced workers, whose numbers reached a maximum of 1,924,912 in August 1944; they were mainly young, often teenagers, and came overwhelmingly from eastern Europe.[21] Forced foreign workers were widely utilised – and increasingly ruthlessly exploited – in German industrial concerns, but some of them were also deployed in rural areas to provide partial compensation for farmers, agricultural labourers and rural artisans who had been conscripted.[22] While the exploitation of foreign workers enabled some German women to avoid involvement in war work, particularly in the years 1939–43, the numbers of these women have probably been exaggerated; many 'Aryan' women were obliged to assume increasingly heavy burdens, especially in agriculture. Jewish women were exploited as forced labourers in Berlin from May 1940 and throughout the Reich from March 1941, before the deportation of German Jews began in late 1941.[23]

In addition to the withdrawal of German men, and the arrival of foreigners, the threat or imminence of either aerial bombardment or, ultimately, invasion led groups within the indigenous civilian population to change their location. At various points during the war, women and, especially, children were removed from their homes in towns or cities and resettled either in towns that were deemed to be safer or, increasingly, in the countryside. The relationship between these incomers and the indigenous population of villages was sometimes less than harmonious.[24] There were also those who were forcibly removed from their homes to either penal or lethal institutions: disobedient nonconformists might be sent to a concentration camp rather than prison; disabled people and those who were terminally or mentally ill might be taken from a hospital or nursing home to another institution specifically in order to be murdered; and tens of thousands of German Jews were rounded up and deported to concentration or, later, extermination camps 'in the east'. In the second half of the war, as war-related industries were relocated from urban bombing targets to safer non-urban sites, those working in them had to be accommodated in small towns and villages. In the later stages, there were also refugees from former German-occupied territories in eastern Europe, including eventually the eastern regions of Germany itself. In smaller numbers, collaborators from France, too, arrived in Germany. Given these movements of people, it is difficult to exaggerate the chaos that obtained in Germany's towns and cities, but also in some villages, by the last months of the war.[25]

In Hitler's war 'Aryans' on the home front may have been better supplied than in the First World War, given his obsession with avoiding another 'stab in the back'. But the home front was also in the front line to an unprecedented degree, initially as a result of increasingly severe aerial bombardment, but secondly because, with the refusal of Hitler's regime to surrender, the invasion of Germany was of necessity prosecuted to its total defeat.[26] The RAF made attempts to bomb targets in Württemberg from as early as May 1940, but their remoteness from Britain made them less attainable for aircraft than western towns, like Frankfurt, or northern ports like, Hamburg and Bremen, which bore the brunt of bombing in the years 1940–43. Frankfurt, for example, had already had upwards of twenty people killed by June 1940, as well as considerable damage to property.[27] Württemberg's topography, with steep hills and deep valleys, made it less accessible at first. In their initial raids on German towns, RAF crews were not able to aim accurately, often dropping bombs on fields rather than buildings; but, especially from 1942–43, huge raids increasingly damaged installations and destroyed residential districts.[28] Sometimes crews were hoodwinked into bombing faked targets, such as the mock airport which was built close to the rural commune of Rohrau, in the Böblingen district of central Württemberg. Rohrau was bombed as early as November 1940, and again in May 1942 and March 1943.[29] There was also the wooden construction erected on open ground well outside the capital but clearly marked with the name 'Stuttgart Station'. This kind of decoy ceased to be useful once navigation improved and radar came into operation.[30] But in one raid on this particular decoy, in October 1941, around forty houses in the nearby commune of Lauffen were damaged, leading the inhabitants to express forcefully their resentment at the authorities in Stuttgart for, they believed, protecting urban facilities and denizens at the reckless expense of villagers.[31]

Although Württemberg's towns were mostly not high on the RAF's immediate list of bombing priorities, in both Stuttgart and Friedrichshafen there were prizes to be had. Stuttgart was particularly vulnerable, both as an important hub in the rail network and as a prominent industrial centre, having earned the sobriquet of 'the German Coventry'.[32] The Bosch plant in Stuttgart, making generators and injection pumps, was earmarked as a target, but attempts in spring 1942 to hit it missed the mark, while the SKF ball-bearings plant in Stuttgart was targeted in September 1943 in what turned into an extremely expensive and abortive raid for the RAF. Even so, the board of Daimler-Benz heeded the advice of Albert Speer, Minister of Armaments from 1942 to 1945, and the warning signals of damage to industrial plant further north. Slowly at first, it began to plan for the dispersal of its various works in the Stuttgart area, where aero-engines, marine engines and cylinders, camshafts and valves for military vehicles were produced. Yet dispersal brought its own problems, slowing down production and inhibiting assembly once transportation facilities were damaged or destroyed. The ultimate dispersal was to sites underground, after Daimler-Benz plants had been severely bombed in September and October 1944.[33]

Friedrichshafen, in the far south of Württemberg on the northern shore of the Bodensee, was a small town with a remarkable concentration of industrial plants. Among the most important were the huge Zeppelin works – where radar devices were made and later in the war the V-2 rocket was developed – and the Dornier aircraft works, as well as major firms which produced tank engines and gearboxes. These industries were crucial for Germany's war effort, as Speer realised. Although the Allies targeted them, they failed to launch a serious bombing raid until 27 April 1943, when they unleashed 'the most damaging attack ever made on German tank production'. In July 1944, a similarly devastating attack was made on jet aircraft production in Friedrichshafen.[34] Yet while armaments works were hit with increasing accuracy, German builders and technicians were able to restore damaged installations with a speed which sometimes surprised even Speer. Nevertheless, time spent on repair was time lost for new production.[35] Even if German production grew at a massive rate in spite of bombing, between 1942 and 1944, output figures probably failed to reflect accurately the deleterious impact that bombing had on the economy from early in the war.[36]

Germany's military successes in spring 1940 engendered boundless confidence, especially in a region like Württemberg where 'air-raid alarms have not occurred particularly often, English bombing is relatively infrequent'.[37] Preparations had nevertheless been made in Stuttgart in September 1939, with twenty first aid stations ready to receive the injured.[38] The Nazi Party newspaper in Stuttgart, the NS-Kurier, boasted on 31 May 1940 that 'Air-raid protection has exploited Stuttgart's natural physical advantages in many ways; many cellars and air-raid bunkers are in excellent condition, so that in any air attack on Stuttgart no casualties among the civilian population are to be expected'. This was a claim too far: scarcely three months later, on 25 August 1940, Stuttgart experienced its first air raid of the war, which claimed four lives and injured five people. Nevertheless, Stuttgart was not yet a primary target and the next fatalities sustained were in its fourth air raid on 5 May 1942, when thirteen people were killed and a further thirty-seven injured.[39] Other towns, such as Esslingen and Heilbronn, had already sustained raids. But even in 1941 and 1942, Württemberg's towns, including Stuttgart, were considered safe enough for them to receive evacuees from the stricken towns and cities of western and northern Germany, especially Essen, Düsseldorf and Hamburg.[40] Gau Württemberg-Hohenzollern was one of the six Gaue of the NSDAP designated as reception areas for evacuees from Gau Essen.[41]

From 1943, however, the major towns in Württemberg sustained dreadfully damaging bombing raids, with ordinary urban civilians at least as vulnerable as industrial concerns in the Allied 'area bombing' campaign. In Stuttgart, the frequency of the attacks steadily increased, with the eleventh raid on 6 September 1943, the first in daylight (in which the USAF was, for the first time, involved over Stuttgart) claiming 107 dead and 165 injured.[42] Worse was to follow: in four attacks in five days from 25 July 1944, which were characterised as retaliation for recent V-1 flying bombs that had killed 2700 people in London, a total of 1690 RAF bombers utterly destroyed the centre of Stuttgart, killing around

1000 people and rendering some 100,000 homeless. With air raid sirens damaged and out of action, wardens had to tour the city to raise the alarm. Sometimes the bombs arrived before they did. Historic buildings, government offices, shops, utilities, schools and cemeteries were destroyed or seriously damaged. The NSDAP's headquarters in Stuttgart, in Goethestrasse, was burned down, to the amazement of a firewatcher who had believed that the 'the party people would save their premises, whatever the cost. After all, it was obviously a matter of prestige'.[43] If Stuttgart was fortunate not to suffer the large-scale fire storms that had obliterated much of Hamburg a year earlier, qualitatively the experience was nevertheless similar.[44] Earlier, the fourteenth raid, on 21 February 1944, had destroyed the Stuttgart offices of the Reich Authors' Chamber and its parent body, the Reich Chamber of Culture, both of which had been housed in the former *Landtag* building. The premises in Königstrasse into which these offices moved after being bombed out were themselves severely damaged in a raid on the night of 12–13 September 1944, a raid which also seriously disrupted the postal service.[45] The same raid 'completely destroyed' the central offices of the criminal police, leading to the commandeering as a substitute of adjacent buildings used by businesses of less importance to the war effort.[46] Even NSDAP grandees were not immune: in May 1944, the home of the seconded deputy *Gauleiter* of Württemberg-Hohenzollern, Friedrich Schmidt, was 'totally destroyed' in 'the most recent attack on Stuttgart'.[47]

Further serious raids followed, particularly in September 1944. In the twenty-fifth raid, on 5 September, thirty-seven people were killed and seventy injured, while in the twenty-sixth raid, on 10 September, the figures were twenty-eight and 113, respectively. The severity of the damage to communications systems led to Stuttgart's being 'to a certain extent isolated', with rail links, telegraph lines and the postal service seriously disrupted. Office buildings and services, including hospitals and schools, were damaged or destroyed to the extent that large-scale improvisation was required to maintain a semblance of order. The water and sewerage systems were disrupted. By this time, some 100,000 people had left the city, but the authorities reckoned that it would be necessary for still more of the remaining 320,000 inhabitants to evacuate it, given the shortage of housing and air raid shelter capacity. Then, on 19 and 20 October 1944, air raids which delivered more bombs to Stuttgart than ever before killed 338 people, injured 872 and left thirty-eight 'missing'. The city's authorities, under *Oberbürgermeister* Dr Karl Strölin, hoped that most of those who were not obliged to remain in Stuttgart because of their employment would depart, releasing accommodation for the new wave of 25,000 people rendered homeless in these most recent raids.[48] By February 1945, the population of Stuttgart, which in 1939 had stood at 420,000, had, according to the Stuttgart Food Office, been reduced to 292,000.[49] Yet even in the face of the catastrophe which Stuttgart was experiencing, the

NSDAP remained defiant. On 9 December 1944, the day of Stuttgart's thirty-seventh air raid of the war, in which twenty-four people were killed and fifty-five injured, the leader of the NSF in *Gau* Württemberg-Hohenzollern, Anny Haindl, issued a rallying call:

> The German woman ... is determined not to surrender the essence of her world – her family and her home – to the enemy without a fight. On the contrary, she is resolved to defend herself with all her might and with deep fanaticism, even with weapons in her hand, if it comes to that ... Our destiny is in our own hands.

The message was clear: whatever the destruction and suffering, there would be no surrender. Altogether, Stuttgart sustained a total of fifty-three air raids, the last of these being on 19 April 1945, three days before Strölin handed over the city to French forces.[50]

Other Württemberg towns, in particular Heilbronn, Ulm and Friedrichshafen, were severely attacked. For example, in eleven raids on Friedrichshafen from 1943 to 1945, 618 people were killed, 159 of them 'foreigners' who were presumably forced workers in industry. Of the 1082 who were injured in these raids, eighty-one were 'foreigners'. The raids in April and July 1944 were especially severe.[51] That of 27–28 April, in which 1800 aircraft participated, destroyed 40 per cent of all buildings, including 1100 houses, leading two thirds of the inhabitants to flee, and leaving over fifteen cubic metres of rubble for each inhabitant.[52] Ulm, too, suffered badly, with heavy raids on 17 December 1944 and in March 1945.[53] The worst experience of all was in Heilbronn, which had first been attacked on 17 December 1940, with three fatalities, but was by the later stages of the war a fairly predictable target, as a port on the River Neckar. In September 1944 an air raid caused 300 fatalities, but still *Gauleiter* Murr refused to permit the compulsory evacuation of the town centre that had been repeatedly requested by the mayor, the Heilbronn police chief and the NSDAP *Kreisleiter*, Richard Drauz, all of whom lacked the courage of their convictions and refused to act without Murr's consent. Drauz's carefully argued case that an attack on Heilbronn's densely populated historic centre would result in 'heavy losses because no help of any consequence can be brought in' failed to sway Murr but proved to be only too prescient.[54] When the town's centre was completely destroyed on 4 December 1944, around 6000 people were killed. Most of the dead were incinerated, but many others died from carbon monoxide poisoning in cellars intended to protect them.[55]

Smaller Württemberg towns were less obvious bombing targets, although Reutlingen and Göppingen were severely attacked in early 1945.[56] Around the same time, the small country town of Trossingen was bombed; this was attributed less to Trossingen's obviously negligible strategic importance than to Heinrich Himmler's presence in nearby Triberg, where he had established his headquarters as commander of the Rhine defence front.[57] In Heilbronn district in the north, another small country town, Gundelsheim, had been overflown by enemy airplanes in the First World War and was in the Second World War a genuine target. Its situation on the important railway line from Heilbronn to Würzburg, and also on the Neckar shipping route from Heilbronn to Mannheim, had led to its being bombed, without serious effects, in 1940, but in 1944–45 it sustained considerable damage. The heaviest raid was on 27 February 1945, when eight to ten planes attacked and destroyed the rail station and its freight store as well as the houses and other buildings adjacent to it, including the cemetery's chapel, a mustard factory and the town's hospital. The object of the exercise was achieved, with the rail line out of service for a considerable time.[58]

Among Württemberg's more prominent towns, only Tübingen was spared the worst, partly because it was not an industrial centre and also because it was home to several hospitals. Until spring 1944, although it had been attacked and suffered some damage, no one had been killed.[59] In 1944, the presence of 6000 wounded soldiers in the town led to a proposal from a group of local notables, including the senior army doctor in Tübingen, the *Rektor* of the university, the deputy mayor and the NSDAP district leader, that Tübingen be recognised as a 'hospital town' under the terms of the Geneva Convention, to exempt it from bombing raids. But this came to nothing because the Ministry of Armaments would not give an undertaking to refrain from diverting war industry to Tübingen.[60] In fact, as part of the strategy of decentralising vital industries away from major German cities which were prime bombing targets, there were by this time plans to move a branch of the Daimler-Benz works from Sindelfingen, near Stuttgart – which was bombed eleven times from November 1942 – to Rottenburg, near Tübingen, because there was a state prison in Rottenburg whose inmates could be used as labour.[61] In the end, Tübingen did not suffer in the way that northern German cities did, nor as Heilbronn, Friedrichshafen, Ulm and Stuttgart did, but in the last few months of the war forty-four people were killed and there was enough damage to destroy houses and disrupt utilities, at a time when the town was overcrowded with evacuees and those bombed out elsewhere.[62]

Despite both the fact that the authorities in southern Germany had had a clear preview, from the fate of northern towns, of what the bombing of urban areas meant for civilians, and the claims made by the NSDAP's press and by officials like Strölin, the mayor of Stuttgart, about the effectiveness of the regime's plans for air raid protection, the provision of 'shelters, bunkers and tunnels [was] in no way sufficient' in Württemberg's towns.[63] *Gauleiter* Murr was in a position to requisition precious labour resources – both POWs and miners from the Ruhr area – in order to build for himself a bunker fifteen metres deep in the grounds of his official residence in Stuttgart, the Villa Reitzenstein.[64] By contrast, in Ulm the vulnerable old town had 'poor cellars, no tunnels or bunkers'.[65] Small towns were left to provide for themselves. In the minor country town of Musberg, adjacent to the southern outskirts of Stuttgart, municipal leaders had long recognised its vulnerability because of its proximity to Stuttgart airport and had put air raid protection measures in place in the 1930s. For example, volunteers from a first-aid group in neighbouring Leinfelden had been brought in to train 150 young women from Musberg, and every house in the commune had been provided with a check-list of procedures to be adopted in the event of a raid. With the possibility of a gas attack from the air a major concern, the commune's leaders laid in stores of a chemical antidote. Eventually, in November 1942, Musberg was in the firing line of an attack on southern Stuttgart. The main priority thereafter was to restore agricultural properties as quickly as possible so as not to endanger the 1943 harvest. Yet scarcely had the damage been made good when, in March 1944, Musberg sustained an even more destructive raid. This was facilitated by the illumination of Stuttgart airport for returning German aircraft. As a result, 'there was not a single house that was not damaged. 399 people were made homeless'. Farm animals were killed, implements and buildings were destroyed, and the water supply was seriously disrupted, impeding efforts to extinguish fires caused by the bombing. After this raid, the people of Musberg set about constructing a reservoir for the fire service and bunkers financed partly privately and partly by the commune. With no further raids on Musberg, these installations were not put to the test.[66]

It would be difficult to exaggerate the terror and chaos caused in German towns and cities by Allied bombing, especially in the last two years of the war.[67] The resulting hardship was to a small extent mitigated by official relief work organised by the NSV (*Nationalsozialistische Volkswohlfahrt* – NS People's Welfare), which was often carried out by members of the Nazi women's organisation or by the BDM (*Bund deutscher Mädel* – League of German Girls), although there were increasingly limits to what the NSV could achieve in areas of mass destruction.[68] In Musberg the relatively small scale of the destruction wrought by the raid in November 1942 was manageable, and there was gratitude for the six days of assistance provided by the Stuttgart NSV. After the raid there in March 1944, however, during which substantial areas of Stuttgart itself were hit, the NSV's support was chiefly in the form of persuading the Labour Front to build emergency accommodation.[69] To say this is not to belittle the efforts of the NSV, which was entrusted with a great variety of tasks relating to evacuation as well as relief.

In order to try to boost morale after a raid, the Reich Minister of Food and Agriculture decreed that a special allocation of meat should be made to those who had suffered hardship.[70] In addition, local officials sometimes authorised special allocations of extra rations. For example, on 9 September 1944 it was announced that a half bottle of brandy would be issued to everyone over eighteen who had experienced the traumatic series of air raids in Stuttgart in July of that year – on condition that they provided their own bottle. On other occasions, there were allocations of meat, coffee, condensed milk and tobacco.[71] As a different kind of palliative, in summer 1943, Goebbels led a campaign to provide urban authorities with second-hand film projectors to replace those destroyed in bombing raids, because films could serve as a means of escapism in time of acute stress. Such projectors were thin on the ground in Württemberg, but Strölin located one for use in Stuttgart.[72] These kinds of palliative or distraction could, however, scarcely be more than token compensation for the human losses and injuries, the destruction of accommodation and property, and the disruption of services and utilities. By the end of the war, British Bomber Command had certainly achieved Lord Cherwell's aim of 'dehousing' huge numbers of Germans.[73] The post-war mayor of Stuttgart, Arnold Klett, was entirely justified in saying that 'the cities have carried the major burdens of the war'.[74]

By contrast, the large areas of farmland remote from major conurbations were bombing targets only infrequently, and generally only in the later stages of the war. Many villages survived through to April 1945 unscathed by the operations of war, although some suffered damage when the enemy arrived on the ground.[75] Some rural areas were hit incidentally: for example, a major raid on Tübingen in March 1944 caused no fatalities in the town but killed three people in the nearby village of Kusterding, while 'over a hundred mainly agricultural properties were reduced to rubble'. The main official concern about this seems to have related to the adverse effect that it was bound to have on the urban food supply.[76] The priority given to repairing or rebuilding bombed agricultural buildings as well as armaments works was presumably motivated by the same preoccupation.[77] Some rural areas of Württemberg experienced enemy bombing in the last year of the war, especially in the north-eastern district of Crailsheim. For example, on 16 July 1944 the commune of Rossfeld was attacked with the losses sustained amounting to thirteen dwellings, twenty-two barns, nineteen stables, twenty-one sheds and sixty-five carts and wagons completely destroyed, with a further two dwellings seriously damaged. A horse, sixteen cattle, twenty-two pigs, three sheep and many other smaller animals were killed.[78] Nine large bombs were dropped on Rot am See on 20 July 1944, causing damage only to nearby fields. It was not until the invading forces reached the area that the village suffered damage, most seriously on 18 April from artillery fire, with a child killed and six people injured.[79]

Villages adjacent to a rail line were most at risk from bombing. In Stimpfach, this was evidently the target of raids in March and April 1945.[80] The destruction of thirty-eight out of forty-six properties in Oberspeltach on 21 April 1945 was undoubtedly because of the nearby rail line.[81] Similarly, in Böblingen district, the commune of Nufringen was attacked from as early as October 1943 because it was on the main rail line from Stuttgart to Horb, while Herrenberg was bombed several times from July 1944 because it was close to the main rail line from Stuttgart to Tuttlingen.[82] There were also cases of damage caused by bombers randomly jettisoning the unused remainder of their load of bombs before returning home. In Aalen district, in early April 1945, forty-six 'giant craters ... some six metres deep and ten to twelve metres across', were counted in the fields around the commune of Zipplingen.[83] While the post-war mayor of Abstatt in Heilbronn district emphatically reported that there had been '*no air raids*', he added that the satellite commune of Happenbach had had twenty bombs offloaded above it on 20 March 1944, resulting in 'ten explosions', which had, however, caused no damage to property.[84] People in some rural communes became accustomed both to being overflown by enemy aircraft and to the relatively small risk of having bombs jettisoned onto their fields rather than their village. The commune of Biberach was a case in point.[85] It seems either that, for the most part, British and American bombers were at pains not to bomb rural communes inadvertently, or that Württemberg's rural communes – which had no strategic value – were extremely fortunate.

Nevertheless, rural communes close to important urban centres or to airfields were potentially in the firing line. For example, the air raid which destroyed the centre of Heilbronn in December 1944 caused 'great horror' among the population of Eberstadt, which was only ten kilometres distant; there, 'every bomb dropped was clearly audible and made doors and windows quake'.[86] The commune of Münchingen, similarly, was sufficiently close to Stuttgart for raids on the capital to cause damage to its windows and roofs. Then, in the major raids of July 1944, a downed bomber crashed into a horticultural business in Münchingen, inflicting serious damage on a plantation of trees. The inhabitants hastened to construct makeshift bunkers in the earth, on their own initiative and without any financial or other assistance from district or *Land* authorities. The urgency of this was such that 'the heaviest kind of men's work was performed by women of all stations. The French POWs, too, helped by working hard at excavation'.[87]

Further south, the commune of Tomerdingen was adjacent to Ulm but even closer to the small town of Dornstadt, where there was an airfield. In 1944 a warning siren was installed in the commune; it wailed frequently from then onwards. In December 1944, in the wake of the damage inflicted on Ulm, 'the church doors were ripped off and we no longer had windows in the church'. Although Tomerdingen itself was not a target until April 1945, by then, 'it was dangerous to work in the fields during the day' and protective trenches were dug. During April 1945 bombs fell on Tomerdingen, killing a woman sitting on a hay wagon and making 'holes in the ground that were ten metres wide by three or four metres deep'.[88] Yet in southern Württemberg there was relatively little bombing, apart from the heavy raids on Friedrichshafen and some damage to Reutlingen. The attacks on Trossingen from February 1945 were exceptional and, while the five south-eastern districts sustained losses, they were, by the horrific standards of major German towns and cities, minimal.[89]

One effect of the bombing of towns was that the distribution of the population within Württemberg was altered. Whereas the three main towns, Stuttgart, Heilbronn and Ulm, experienced a depopulation of between 16 and 30 per cent in the years between 1939 and 1946, in the surrounding rural areas there was a marked increase in the number of inhabitants, as urban dwellers fled to the safer countryside and, in 1945–46, refugees from the east sought a safe haven. For example, in the north of Württemberg, Aalen district saw its population increase in these years by 39 per cent, Schwäbisch Gmünd by 38 per cent, Künzelsau by 37 per cent and Mergentheim by 31 per cent. By contrast, communes in southern Württemberg experienced much less growth, and in Balingen, Freudenstadt and Rottweil there was even a small decline in the population, with Tettnang, in whose district was Friedrichshafen, losing some 13 per cent of its population between 1939 and 1946.[90] Yet these figures perhaps camouflage the extent of German migration away from the southern areas of Württemberg during the war, because they received substantial numbers of coerced foreign workers to labour in industries, especially in Friedrichshafen.

The widespread damage caused by bombing not only destroyed housing, shops, churches, schools and every other kind of facility. It also disrupted utilities such as gas, water and electricity, and the sewerage system, as well as communications, with telephone lines cut and rail lines and roads out of service until repairs could be made. This contributed to existing problems with food supplies in Württemberg's towns that had been obvious even before September 1939, with shortages of fresh meat, milk products, fats, cheese, coffee and eggs, particularly, in the summer of 1939, and the availability and quality of vegetables, fruit, cereals and flour affected adversely by rain both at harvest time in 1938 and in the spring of 1939. The outbreak of foot and mouth disease in Württemberg in 1938 only added to the problems.[91] Yet 'valuable' 'Aryan', Germans did not starve in the Second World War – as civilians in occupied countries such as Greece, Yugoslavia and The Netherlands did – especially not in a food producing region like Württemberg.[92] Food supplies did, however, dwindle, and there was, from virtually the start of the war, rising discontent about this, with loud complaints in Württemberg's towns about 'the catastrophic state of provisions' as early as summer 1941, at a time when Germany was victorious.[93] Certainly, many goods became either completely unobtainable or only erratically available, and the German diet became increasingly restricted in both size and variety: by the last two years of the war urban Germans' diet consisted overwhelmingly of bread, potatoes and other vegetables, and these were often in short supply.[94] But at no time during the Second World War were there the disastrous shortages of the years 1916–18.[95] It was only after the end of hostilities in 1945 that truly catastrophic food shortages afflicted 'Aryan' Germans in the towns.[96]

Hitler's determination to avoid another 'stab-in-the-back' by aggrieved and undernourished urban consumers succeeded, because it was a top priority with the regime and because various strategies were employed to ensure that 'Aryan' Germans were supplied with a more or less adequate amount of food. German domestic food production was increased during the 1930s, if only marginally.[97] Pre-war experiments with substitute foodstuffs and clothing also helped to reduce Germany's dependence on imports, although there remained serious deficiencies, particularly in the domestic production of fats.[98] In 1939 German agriculture produced 83 per cent of the population's essential foodstuffs, but only 57 per cent of the fats required.[99] A huge propaganda campaign was waged to encourage thrift and acceptance of the new substitutes.[100] In particular, the pre-war 'Campaign against Waste' (*Kampf dem Verderb*) was prosecuted with increased vigour in wartime.[101] These pre-war expedients had variable success, but they showed earnest of the regime's intent. The early years of the war brought military successes which permitted the exploitation of resources in occupied countries, at their inhabitants' expense. This was enforced ruthlessly, 'to an extent which grossly violated international law'.[102] In the last two years of the war, however, this important advantage, which had cushioned German civilians against the worst effects of shortages, was increasingly and inexorably being lost. Even before the attack on Poland was launched, however, the rationing of some foodstuffs and other essentials was introduced, on 27 August 1939.[103]

Other controls were imposed to complement rationing. For example, goods that were not rationed were subject to price controls, to try to ensure that they would not merely be bought up by the highest bidder. Yet enforcing price controls was a labour intensive business, at a time when labour was in increasingly short supply. It was only partially successful, and it was commonly said that 'those who have the money can buy anything'.[104] Restaurants were instructed to observe two 'meatless' days a week, although at the start of the war they were not subject to rationing restrictions.[105] At least in the first half of the war, those who could afford to eat in hotels and restaurants could enjoy plenty of potatoes and vegetables, while ordinary people queued at length and often unsuccessfully for them. Visitors to holiday resorts in Württemberg were said to be offering 'fantastic prices' for fruit, when it was in short supply.[106]

As a temporary measure at the start of the war, before the system of controls was fully in operation, shopkeepers were instructed to compile a list of their regular customers, to try to ensure that individuals did not evade the controls by shopping at several outlets.[107] Yet this was only partly enforced and enforceable, with shopkeepers sometimes colluding with customers. For example, in August 1940 the Württemberg office of the Nazi mass organisation for women, the *Deutsches*

Frauenwerk (DFW), reported to the Stuttgart Food Office a shopkeeper who had not stamped the tokens on his customers' butter ration cards, allowing them to be used repeatedly.[108] While some larger stores issued an informal identity card in 1941 to try to prevent individuals from making excessive purchases of goods that were not controlled, smaller retailers faced greater difficulties in trying to placate their regular customers. One butcher, for example, complained that he had lost business to a competitor who could afford to interpret the amounts of meat rations generously because he could obtain extra supplies illegally.[109] The accusation here was that the second butcher was a party to an illegal slaughtering syndicate.[110]

In addition, hoarding and bartering became punishable offences, along with profiteering and black marketeering. Yet in spite of the planning and the regulations – or perhaps partly because of them – the one issue that probably caused the most consistent discontent among broad sections of society in Württemberg, and bred the greatest resentment against the regime, concerned the provision of essentials, especially food, clothing and fuel, and the regulation of their production and distribution. It has been suggested that the issue that featured most frequently in the regular SD reports on developments and morale on the home front was the conscription – or the failure to enforce conscription – of women for employment.[111] That may have been true for the Reich as a whole, and particularly for largely urbanised areas where the wives of prosperous businessmen, professionals and civil servants had no need to earn a wage and were able to run their homes with the aid of a domestic servant or two.[112] In Württemberg, however, an important food producing area with a substantial urban population dependent on local food producers, whose workforce included many women, food supply was and remained a highly charged and socially divisive issue, much as it had been during the First World War.

As for women's employment, the Stuttgart State Prosecutor sounded a note of satisfaction when he said, in July 1940, that 'here and there one even hears that women have given up work because of the generous level of family support' for wives of conscripted soldiers. At this stage, at least, he was more concerned that the regime should avoid antagonising women and their families than with persuading women into war work.[113] Certainly, one childless young married woman was heard to say, in the summer of 1941, 'the Führer appeals to women to go out to work. Well, if women are able to get the food supplies they need only after wandering about for hours, going out to work is completely impossible for married women'.[114] This may well have been true in the towns, with increased domestic tasks caused by shortages and rationing. Yet in the wartime countryside, women were obliged also to shoulder a much greater weight of the burden of work, particularly in agriculture.[115]

The first ration cards left the Stuttgart Statistical Office at 8 a.m. on 27 August

1939 and were sent by lorry not to local government offices but to NSDAP local branches throughout Württemberg. In the party's local branches, the ration cards were distributed to households by 'helpers' of the organisation of Nazi women, the *NS-Frauenschaft* (NSF). That, at any rate, was the theory. In many small communes, as we have seen, there was no NSF group and no NSDAP office, with the result that the ration cards were stored in and distributed from the mayor's office, as the sole administrative centre in the commune.[116] The seventy-two individual tokens on each card controlled the distribution of meat and meat products, milk and milk products, fats, sugar, jam, and various grains, as well as coffee and tea. Tokens had also been printed for other foodstuffs, including bread, eggs and potatoes, and for household coal and soap, although these commodities were not yet rationed. On 30 November 1939, the NSF distributed clothing cards with tokens covering a whole year. Adults received a hundred tokens which could be exchanged at the rate of twenty for a shirt and five for a pair of socks. Clothing was clearly expected to last a long time. The first allowances of food were relatively generous, at 700 grams of meat per person per week, and one-fifth of a litre of milk per person per day, with more for small children and pregnant women. But a month later the 'normal' meat ration was cut to 500 grams a week, and adults were permitted only skimmed milk. At the same time, rationing was applied to a wider range of foodstuffs, including bread.[117]

During the course of the war, the distribution of rationed food was controlled in four week periods, which allowed fine tuning on a regular basis. For example, for the period from 18 October to 14 November 1943, the bread ration was increased because the harvest had been good, with regional variations in the proportions of rye and wheat. Württemberg, Baden and Berlin were among the areas for which a fifty-fifty ratio was prescribed, with the north east of Germany, where rye was the main cereal crop, allocated 70 per cent of rye to 30 per cent of wheat in its bread.[118] As the war dragged on, rationing was extended to cover an increasing range of commodities, and, overall, rations were inexorably reduced. For example, from April 1942, the 'normal' meat ration was cut to 300 grams a week.[119] Rumours of imminent ration reductions abounded throughout the war, sometimes provoked by enemy propaganda.[120] But from time to time extra rations were distributed, if a particular crop had been good or, as we have seen, to boost morale in an area which had suffered severe bomb damage. In addition, the authorities had quickly realised that the controls facilitated discrimination between different categories of inhabitant, with some receiving extra allowances on a regular basis. These included pregnant women, night shift workers and manual workers in heavy industry.[121] In addition there was discrimination not only between industry's 'heaviest workers' and those expending less energy in the national interest, but also between 'Aryan' Germans on the one hand and Jews and many coerced foreign workers and POWs on the other. This would, it was assumed, enable the regime to insulate the 'Aryan' population from the worst effects of rationing for as long as possible – until victory, it was hoped – and therefore to avoid the kind of disaffection there had been in the later stages of the First World War.[122]

The vanquished populations, especially in eastern Europe, were left with meagre rations, while a relatively rich country like France was looted mercilessly. It was not only the German state and German industrialists who requisitioned rapaciously. German soldiers, too, plundered other countries' assets. For the French under German occupation, shortages and controls became the norm. Those living in towns, and especially in Paris, experienced hunger and cold from the first winter of the occupation, in 1940–41. By 1944, 'the meat ration was so small it could be wrapped up in a Métro ticket', and animal fodder beets 'became a staple in kitchens and near-empty cupboards'.[123] The German government avoided inflicting 'turnip winters', like those of 1916–18, on its own population by inflicting them on the French, and others. There were civilian deaths in France attributable to malnutrition and hardship, but the French mostly survived, if often in the greatest discomfort, not least because of the inextinguishable existence of a lively black market.[124]

If the French suffered, in eastern Europe, with its population condemned in the Nazi world view as 'subhuman', the hardship and deprivation were appreciably greater. For Poles, the alternatives were German occupation or Soviet occupation. German policy was geared to 'depriving Poles of the necessary means of livelihood, and thus biologically weakening and destroying them, and … intellectually depriving them of all necessary schooling and education, bar a minimum required by their German employers'. As a result, the Polish intelligentsia was more than decimated. With Poland required to make food deliveries to the Reich, severe malnutrition became the norm in the towns, especially for Polish Jews.[125] Because the economic exploitation of the empire was a German priority, practised most ruthlessly in Poland and the USSR, a similar picture obtained in the occupied areas of the Soviet Union, moving a senior German official to complain that 'we have made it very easy for Soviet propaganda to increase hatred of Germany and of the National Socialist system'. Yet the Nazi view, expressed characteristically forcefully by Hermann Göring in August 1942, was that 'in all the occupied territories I see the people living there stuffed full of food, while our own people are starving'.[126] This travesty of a judgement reflected the attitude which remorselessly drove German policy towards the vanquished peoples of Europe.

Within Germany, unprivileged groups – Jews, foreign workers, those in penal or mental health institutions – bore the main burden of food shortages. Ration allowances for remaining Jews were significantly smaller than for 'Aryans'. Jews were restricted to shopping at specified times; they had to wait until all 'Aryans' had been served and they were prohibited from buying certain foodstuffs, including fresh fruit and chocolate.[127] The result was that 'many Jews feared starvation almost as much as they feared the Gestapo'.[128] As early as December 1939, the dismissed Jewish professor, Victor Klemperer, noted in his diary: 'All special allowances have been cut out of our new food ration cards. But these special allowances are entirely counterbalanced by reductions in other rations. (E.g. more butter = less margarine.) We are very greatly depressed as a result.'[129] Once the deportations were under way, as remaining Jews tried to avoid being rounded up, obtaining food became both a primary preoccupation and extremely hazardous.[130] At the same time, foreign workers brought to labour in German factories were increasingly ill-nourished. As early as 1942 there was talk of Soviet POWs, who were performing heavy manual work in Württemberg, being in a 'poor nutritional state'.[131] Yet some foreign workers in Württemberg's towns were able to steal bread tokens from unused ration cards sent for recycling, and one Frenchman was even able to deal in bread tokens on the black market.[132] Nevertheless, by the end of the war a number of foreign workers had perished and many others were on the brink of starvation.[133] Yet foreigners' conditions were often less dire than those of prisoners in concentration camps and, especially, those in certain psychiatric institutions where patients were deliberately starved as one of the tactics of the 'euthanasia' programme.[134]

Discrimination, rationing and the other controls were wholly consistent with the regime's objectives. It was believed, first, that the controls would help to conserve goods that were in short supply, by pacing consumption so that scarce commodities did not cease to be available altogether, as had happened in the First World War. It was further hoped that, by their universal application, the controls would create a sense of national solidarity, with everyone, regardless of class or station in life (with the major proviso that they were 'Aryan' and 'valuable') making the same, limited sacrifices. But this entire strategy was based on premises which, as far as Württemberg was concerned, were false. In the first place, there was little sense of 'national community', before or during the war; this was not peculiar to Württemberg.[135] On the contrary, there was particular resentment among agricultural producers, urban consumers and working people generally at the way in which the burdens of war in the area of consumption affected them, and at the way in which other groups – the wealthy, the powerful, the well-connected – seemed to be much less disadvantaged because they were able to pay high prices or exert influence to obtain what they wanted, sometimes without being particularly discreet about it.

Ordinary shoppers, in the queues which soon became an unwelcome and wearisome feature of their daily round, could often see when those with enough money were able to buy up large quantities of scarce goods. Sometimes, however, this was done more covertly: from Göppingen, to the east of Stuttgart, it was reported in summer 1941 that a 'clientèle' of women with 'hats and painted fingernails ... and large purses' had come to a private arrangement with a shop's proprietor, whereby they could obtain substantial quantities of goods and remove them unobtrusively through a private exit, while once again ordinary shoppers queued, only to find that the goods that they wanted were sold out. Complaints were made that 'favourite individual customers' were able to buy fruit 'under the counter', at a cheap rate.[136] The vegetable shortage in Stuttgart in summer 1941 was similarly attributed to illicit sales.[137] Women who did not need to take paid employment could shop – or send a domestic servant to shop – when it suited them and could therefore buy up scarce commodities before working women reached the shops only to find that what they wanted was sold out.[138] The wealthy also had other advantages: for example, in February 1940, it was reported in Württemberg that some of the more prosperous had been able to obtain Christmas food parcels from abroad, bought with foreign currency which they held outside Germany.[139] The availability of money, in spite of war taxation and the government's attempts to encourage high levels of personal savings, ensured that measures to apply price controls were ineffective. For example, in Backnang district, to the north of Stuttgart, women evacuees from northern towns were said to be able to outbid local shoppers for eggs and vegetables which they sent home because supplies were more plentiful in Württemberg than in industrial areas.[140] Although the prices charged by retailers were kept under constant surveillance, it seems to have been impossible to enforce a system of maximum prices, and complaints were voiced throughout the war about the high prices charged for scarce goods.

While the application of rationing and other controls in a piecemeal form at the start of the war caused discontent, because of the inequities involved, and while the advantages to be had by the privileged were a source of anger and complaint on the part of the less fortunate, rationing and shortages per se were deeply resented. 'The little people' (*die kleinen Leute*), as whose champion some SD agents posed, had interpreted promises of 'equity' and 'equality of sacrifice' in the *Volksgemeinschaft* in the customary manner, that is, to mean that there would be more for them, at the expense of the wealthy. They had certainly not expected there to be less than they were accustomed to, even in wartime, nor that they would have to make sacrifices. Housewives expected to be able to purchase the normal range of seasonal fruit and vegetables, war or no war. The mounting discontent when they were disabused of this expectation seems to have been generated partly by the perception that Württemberg's food resources were being 'exported' to other areas of the Reich.

People complained openly about both German and foreign freight trains stopping daily at Stuttgart rail station, packed with foodstuffs which onlookers could identify but not obtain.[141] When Italian potatoes arrived in Stuttgart by

rail, there was resentment that half of the consignment had to be delivered to
the central depot in Frankfurt; even the half that remained could be released
for sale in Stuttgart only when permission had been given by the authorities
in Frankfurt.[142] It was also a source of both astonishment and grievance that
civilians were experiencing straitened circumstances while German armies were
stunningly victorious, with official propaganda embellishing their achievements.
Some were heard to say, in the earliest days of the Russian campaign, that 'we
should bump off more [Red Army soldiers] and take fewer prisoners' because
'we will have even less to eat if we have the Russian rogues by the throat and have
to feed them as well'.[143] Killing some three million Soviet POWs – or leaving
them to starve – became official policy, on the pretext that the USSR had not
signed the Geneva Convention, which had clear prescriptions about how to
treat POWs.[144]

In some ways, the regime did not help its cause. One source of acute
resentment was the way in which government-controlled newspapers gave out
misleading information about the state of food supplies. In the summer of 1941,
a notice which all papers in Württemberg were ordered to print stated that, while
the early crop was small, the later cherry crop would be abundant. Yet already it
was common knowledge that spring frosts had destroyed some 90 per cent of the
entire cherry crop. Consumers complained about the absence of cherries in the
market, in spite of what the papers had said, and in some places they went off to
the countryside to buy direct from the producers. As a result, the growers were
incensed that the press had given the wrong impression, because the consumers
were holding them responsible for being thwarted yet again. It was not only the
press that gave misleading information: the radio programme for housewives
ran an item encouraging an increased consumption of cherries, when there was
none to be had. Of particular concern to the SD, who reported these matters,
was that people from all sections of society were saying that 'you can't believe …
what you read in the press any more'. What, asked the SD, would happen when
the press had truly vital information to impart?[145]

The preoccupations of the different sections of the population were rarely
uniform and varied with the course of the war. Some anxieties did cut across class
and occupational barriers, most obviously the fear experienced by all who had
male family members at the front, especially on the eastern front from mid 1941.
But, apart from that, there were major differences of experience, on the one hand
between those who had either the money or family connections to enable them
to obtain scarce goods and those who did not, and on the other hand between
producers and consumers. In the straitened circumstances of a long and bitterly
fought war, these differences bred discontent, envy, resentment and contempt
between different groups of people who were supposed to be on the same side.
In particular, it caused – as in 1914–18 – mutual hostility between townspeople,

who were utterly dependent on food deliveries from agricultural areas, and the rural population. The last thing that the regime wanted was for comparisons to be made with conditions in the First World War, yet in the towns, even in the years of German victories, these were clearly audible. For example, in summer 1941 a woman waiting in a long queue was heard to say, 'It can't go on … It's the same situation as in 1914–18',[146] while an SD report from 1 September 1941 recorded that

> Women often stand for hours to obtain supplies of fruit, vegetables and, especially, potatoes. Since each woman is allowed only two or three pounds of potatoes at a time, women with larger families can often be seen queuing at several shops in order to obtain a greater supply. The picture of women queuing is very evocative of the [First] World War, when almost every kind of foodstuff was obtainable only in this way, and the comments of women queuing underline that, with most of them actually uttering the words 'just like in the World War' …

Sometimes friction among those in the queues led to public disorder. The same SD report mentioned an instance in Stuttgart where 'in a matter of seconds the women were involved in a huge brawl, and it took several policemen to separate them'.[147]

This indicates that the reticence which might have been expected from ordinary people under a despotic regime did not prevent them from making their voices heard and committing breaches of public order. For example, as early as January 1940, there were reports that the coal shortage had, during a particularly cold spell, led to acts of violence and public demonstrations which had had to be broken up by the police.[148] From Ludwigsburg it was reported in summer 1941 that shortages of fruit and vegetables had led to some 'very unattractive scenes', while in Tübingen each market day brought renewed strife involving wholesalers, retailers and customers. Frustrated consumers took to travelling by rail to the countryside to buy goods direct from the producers, with the result that there was often fighting on the overcrowded trains. Shoppers who commuted to the countryside to satisfy their needs aroused great anxiety among the authorities, as this led to the spread of bartering, which was illegal. Salad oil, pure coffee, or shoes from France were exchanged for fruit and vegetables, as consumer and producer did a direct deal at the source of supply, in open contravention of the wartime controls. Some consumers resorted to theft: increasingly, farmers had to keep a lookout at night because of an epidemic of thieving of fruit and vegetables from the fields where they were growing.[149]

Apprehending miscreants became a growing problem. Even in the first winter of the war there was a shortage of gendarmes – police personnel in the communes – partly because of conscription and partly because of secondments to occupied Poland, which left those in post covering the work of two or three men. In rural areas, this created difficulties because the two or three areas of responsibility might be remote from each other. In the winter of 1939–40, conditions had made dirt roads impassable and therefore precluded the use of the twenty-four cars and eight motorcycles that were available for the thirty-four police districts in Württemberg. The luckless remaining gendarmes, whose average age was fifty, found themselves travelling on foot. This led to a noticeable increase in those reporting in sick and even in cases of prolonged illness.[150] A similar picture obtained with the legal authorities. The Stuttgart State Prosecutor reported as early as April 1940 that conscription and secondments had had a particularly severe effect on his office because they had removed the younger and fitter members of his staff. Those left behind were less resilient, owing to ageing or sickness. He warned that, while it had so far been possible to cover for those who had been withdrawn, sometimes by adopting emergency measures, 'the limits of what are possible have almost been reached'.[151]

Nevertheless, in the *Gendarmerie* some forty-nine retired officers were pronounced fit for duty, and, as experienced policemen, were said to have acquitted themselves satisfactorily. There were, however, problems with the eighty reserve policemen who had little training or experience. Whereas they could be entrusted with relatively simple tasks, such as keeping watch over a food provisions depot or checking that houses were blacked out, they tended not to have the necessary skills for writing reports. They were also often inhibited from taking effective action by operating in their home district where they had personal and business relationships.[152] With its customary directness, the Stuttgart SD reported that they were 'frequently accused of not intervening forcefully enough'. The solution proposed by the SS commander in Württemberg was to move individuals who were susceptible in this way to another location.[153] More practicable was the experiment tried by the *Landrat* in Ludwigsburg of enrolling former police office staff as auxiliary policemen. This kind of expedient was necessary for the foreseeable future, given that the supply of trainees for the *Gendarmerie* had 'as good as dried up'.[154] With the progressive withdrawal of men through conscription, maintaining observance of the law became increasingly difficult. This may be partly why dispensing 'justice' became an increasingly arbitrary matter in the second half of the war.

Even the officers of the Nazi regime were not at one on the matter of law enforcement. SD agents, reporting on the popular mood, urged that the *Kriegswirtschaftsverordnung* (War Economy Decree), issued by the Ministerial Council for the Defence of the Reich on 4 September 1939, should be applied more rigorously and that those caught violating its provisions – whether they were producers, retailers or consumers – should be given exemplary sentences.[155] This was in keeping with the SS leadership's view that violation of the economic controls amounted to sabotage of the war effort.[156] Imposing Draconian penalties was, however, a less simple issue than it appeared at first sight, although some transgressors were punished extremely severely, even with a death sentence.[157] In addition to a shortage of staff in both the police and the judicial system, according to the Stuttgart State Prosecutor, there were also the problems of utility, public order and justice. 'Exemplary' sentences could seem to members of the public positively unjust, and 'in the matter of prison sentences, it is becoming ever more difficult to reconcile the principles of justice with the demands of the war economy'.[158] For example, if a butcher were prosecuted for being a party to illegal slaughtering and punished with a prison sentence, that might lead to dangerous discontent; if he was the only butcher in his community, it might jeopardise its members' already precarious meat supply. As a result, the relevant mayor or NSDAP local branch leader might intercede for deferral of the sentence until after the war.[159] The authorities in Berlin, including the Reich Minister of Justice and Göring, as President of the Ministerial Council for the Defence of the Reich, were aware that punishing the proprietor of a retail business who broke the law, whether through imprisonment or through prohibiting him from trading, 'frequently affected the culprit less than the consumers in a neighbourhood or district'.[160] Factory managers, employment exchanges and the local armaments command, too, would beg that a worker found breaking the law have his or her sentence deferred, because of the acute shortage of labour.[161]

The rationing of food and other commodities – clothing and leather shoes, for example – along with measures to curtail the activities of businesses classed as inessential, such as tobacconists, confectioners and hair stylists, in order to release labour for essential war industries, was deeply unpopular with traders, consumers and proprietors. As early as the spring of 1940, some traders found that they could not obtain fuel for their vehicles or were even having their vehicles requisitioned. At the same time, the military showed not the slightest sense of needing to economise, engaging in journeys that seemed to ordinary citizens unnecessary. Those – including senior bureaucrats and legal officials – who had to stand at a tram stop in the worst kind of weather, waiting to squeeze into an overcrowded tram, did not understand how army officers could be chauffeur-driven to and from where they lived every day.[162] Some took their revenge on those who, they believed, were using approved automobiles or goods vehicles for unauthorised purposes by denouncing them to the police. Investigation frequently showed either that no crime had been committed, or that any offence had been greatly exaggerated.[163]

The inescapable truth was that German resources – even with the addition of those plundered from occupied countries – were not sufficient for German ambitions. Much as the ever-lengthening queues reminded adult Germans of conditions in the First World War, so did the incessant exhortations to scrimp and save, to mend and recycle. This was perhaps less irksome, or merely less relevant, to those in the countryside, where economy and recycling were the norm. The use of animal dung as fertiliser was the most obvious example of recycling. Again, when a pig was slaughtered, the farming family and the butcher hired for the occasion utilised virtually every part of the animal for some purpose.[164] There was not much that was simply disposable in the countryside, which was undoubtedly why the government's recycling campaigns had what were regarded as disappointing results there. In the towns, however, higher levels of consumption produced higher levels of waste. In addition, whereas in the countryside gates, fences and implements of most kinds were generally made of wood, in the towns they were increasingly made of metal.

Recycling had become part of government policy under the Four Year Plan of 1936, with state employees – with green armbands – deputed to collect second-hand goods and waste materials, while members of the youth organisations were sent out to retrieve small items such as bottle caps and pieces of metal tubing.[165] Metals were particularly prized, even before the war, with the single biggest collection of them taking place in early 1937.[166] The zealous *Kreisleiter* of Nürtingen wrote to his local branch leaders detailing the procedure for a massive collection from all business and domestic premises in his district on 15 July 1939. Iron bedsteads, ovens and gates were among the targeted items.[167] While the motive was initially at least partly to raise money, in wartime metals were intrinsically valuable. The major metal collection at the start of the war was in the form of a campaign whose results would be announced on Hitler's birthday on 20 April 1940. In introducing it, Göring, as Plenipotentiary for the Four Year Plan, commented that the collection of metal items in the First World War had begun so late that its results had not sufficed for the country's needs. This time, only a few months into the war, all items made from copper, tin, nickel, lead and their alloys which could be spared by official institutions – schools, libraries, hospitals, central and local government offices – were to be surrendered, although at this stage items of particular cultural or historic value were exempted.[168]

At the end of the initial collection period, on 13 April 1940, the Württemberg Economics Minister announced that in most communes people had shown great enthusiasm for the metals collection, with some making real sacrifices. He complained, however, that in some smaller communes the results had fallen far short of expectations, blaming the authorities there for not having made the required effort.[169] Perhaps it was this accusation that galvanised the party's local branch leader in Nürtingen South into ordering all his block leaders, NSV and Labour Front officers, along with members of the HJ and BDM, to make house to house visits 'to ask yet again that citizens surrender items of metal'.[170] Some understaffed police authorities threw themselves into collecting. The Schramberg police, for example, amassed a total of fifty-three kilos of brass in the 1940 campaign, and the police authorities in Heilbronn collected ninety-two kilos of various metals. By contrast, the police chief in Heidenheim made a 'nil return'.[171] After the campaign was extended into June 1940, the Esslingen police collected a further ten kilos of brass and intimated that their offices had nothing else to contribute. [172]

In spite of the urgency with which this campaign was pursued, in the spring of 1940, with Germany's position apparently unassailable, there seemed no need for extreme sacrifice. In April 1940, assiduous *Landräte* in Ludwigsburg and Böblingen offered table lamps, coat racks and door handles made of brass from their offices. The latter was told, that, if brass door handles were in use, they should be retained.[173] By September 1942, however, changed circumstances meant that metal door handles in any kind of building were to be surrendered as soon as substitutes were available.[174] A year later, pots and pans which were made of copper or copper alloy were simply requisitioned, whether or not they were in use. Even items which were built in, such as copper tanks, were to be surrendered.[175] By this time, rural communes had already made what seemed to many the supreme sacrifice: in 1942, church bells had been requisitioned. This included even some bells which had escaped seizure during the First World War, and some which villagers certainly regarded as being of cultural or historic value. In Aalen district, for example, two bells cast in 1607 and 1782 were removed from the commune of Dalkingen in March 1942, although they had been left there during the First World War because of the value attached to their age. A week earlier, Bopfingen had surrendered bells cast in 1496 and 1618, along with another of unknown age. At the same time, two bells had been removed from the steeple of Bopfingen's town hall. [176] In Suppingen, a bell dating from 1575 was finally surrendered after strenuous attempts to persuade the authorities in Ulm and Stuttgart to leave it in place.[177]

As the war dragged on, the restrictions of the War Economy Decree were tightened, resented and, where possible, evaded. A black market flourished, with hoarding and bartering, and the forging and theft of ration cards and tokens. Unused ration cards, printed in excess of need, were sent as waste paper for recycling. This provided ample opportunity for employees in the Stuttgart Food Office to pocket valid ration cards found in wastepaper baskets or sacks. For example, in January 1943, a cleaner there was jailed for over two years for stealing and using a large number of ration cards, and her friend, who had also used some of them, was jailed for two years. Similarly, in June 1943, one of the Food Office clerks was jailed for eighteen months for stealing ration cards for bread, meat, flour and butter, and his accomplice was jailed for seven months for using most of them.[178] The Stuttgart Food Office's efforts to tighten security were thwarted by the difficulty in obtaining a lockable cabinet, because of the shortage of transport.[179] Workers in factories where the cards were recycled into paper were equally able to remove cards that were still valid, for their own use.

The temptation to do so must have been overwhelming, especially for low paid workers with no other access to extra rations. A denunciation to the criminal police in Heilbronn in March 1942 named a woman who worked in a waste-paper business, accusing her of stealing ration cards from its sacks. Her husband, it was said, had boasted that he had not had to go short of any kind of food. The *Landrat* in Heilbronn had already reported to the Food Office about irregularities involving ration cards which, he suspected, derived from the same firm.[180]

A multitude of stratagems was used to obtain extra rations, including the alteration or forging of ration cards, of which a couple of examples must suffice. In 1942–43, one employer sought to obtain more cheese for his works' canteen by simply adding the figure '0' to the amount allocated, so that it read '40 Kg.' instead of '4 Kg.', or '70 Kg.' instead of '7 Kg.'[181] Some occupations provided the perfect opportunity: an elderly printer with the NSDAP's own newspaper in Stuttgart was jailed for three years in July 1943 for producing a substantial number of forged ration cards over a number of months, using his lunch break when he could be alone in the machine room. The large majority of the cards were for meat, and he had used them at five different butchers' shops to try to avoid detection. He was given an exemplary sentence in spite of his advanced years because he had betrayed the trust implied in his job, and because, by undermining the basis of official food policy, he was 'by his deed, on the side of the enemy'.[182]

The War Economy Decree imposed a special rate of taxation on certain goods classed as luxuries rather than necessities. For example, there was a war tax supplement of 20 per cent on the sale of beer and tobacco products.[183] These items were in any case increasingly difficult to obtain, causing some unrest among industrial workers, who claimed in summer 1941: 'we get as good as no beer at all and now there are no more cigars or cigarettes either, but we've got to slave away from dawn till dusk'. Wine and non-alcoholic drinks were also in short supply, with consignments of wine requisitioned from occupied countries slow in arriving.[184] Part of the problem of supply was the arbitrary way in which conscription was applied. This left some businesses, but not others, without their customary proprietors and workers. With the male proprietor called up, his wife might manage to maintain a family business in his absence for most of the duration of the war, sometimes with the assistance of a domestic servant but often with the help of only one or more adult daughters or elderly parents. Many felt that they were the victims of unfair discrimination. Perhaps the chief grievance, adding insult to the manifold problems already facing small businesses, was that the tax assessors were extremely reluctant to allow against the payment of war taxation the cost of a full wage for family members who were now working full time in the business but who had previously been scarcely involved.[185]

Those with businesses which had benefited from the war through an expansion of demand for their product – for example, coal merchants – and those whose businesses had become more labour intensive through the rationing of foodstuffs or other goods, which involved a mass of paperwork, argued at length with the Württemberg Economics Ministry's Prices Authority about the need to offset the extra wages incurred against the profits which they had undoubtedly made. One coal merchant admitted that his turnover had increased by 50 per cent in the first year of the war, but claimed that he had had to enlist the assistance of his wife and two children in order to cope.[186] Another coal merchant explained that his daughter, aged twenty, who had previously worked elsewhere, had had to replace a full-time male worker, which meant spending much of her time loading and unloading coal wagons.[187] But the Prices Authority's response to such arguments was overwhelmingly negative: it was still apparently assumed that a wife or daughter – even a married daughter living away from the parental home – had a duty to provide whatever assistance a husband or father required, including during his absence, without expecting formal remuneration. The census category of *mithelfende Familienangehörige* (assisting family members) clearly implied that such workers were not, in the early 1940s any more than before the First World War, to be thought of as individuals separate from the head of the family, even if many of them were working full-time in the family business only because of the emergency caused by the war.[188]

The same argument applied if the owner of the business was a woman. In the case of a grocer in Ravensburg district in southern Württemberg, matters were complicated by her not having claimed against tax for payment of her son when he worked in the business, on the grounds that 'sooner or later' he would inherit it. But, she argued, her daughter's position was different, for the latter had come to work in the business only when the son was called up at the end of 1939: 'My daughter replaces a full-time employee; in fact it's more than that because she has to work day and night in order to complete the massive workload'. The proprietor was paying the necessary insurance contributions for her daughter, but had not had her wages allowed against tax in either 1940 or 1941.[189] The Prices Authority's reply rejecting her claim was brusque in its disregard of her argument: 'Your family receives the total profit of the business as a result of not having to pay a wage' to a non-familial hired hand.[190] The proprietor of a smart chocolate shop in Stuttgart tried to argue that her rising staff costs were due not to the war but to an increase in turnover, in the hope that this would allow her to claim her daughter's wages against war taxation. Whereas her married daughter had worked 'for only a few hours a week' in the business in 1938, the subsequent move to larger premises had meant that she was required to work for 'at least eight hours a day'. Therefore paying her daughter at the same rate as she would pay an employee who was not a family member seemed appropriate. Giving the extra fruits of her daughter's work 'to the Reich' seemed to her to be 'undue hardship'.[191] But, try as she might, with the aid of her tax adviser, she received only terse and negative replies from the Prices Authority.[192] Her reluctance to surrender extra 'to the Reich' in wartime was clearly viewed as little short of unpatriotic.

To some proprietors in this plight, there seemed no alternative to closing down the family business for the remainder of the war. In the rural district of Münsingen, one woman who was left in charge of a long-established shop selling foodstuffs and tobacco carried on for two years after her husband's enlistment in the army in June 1940, but with the conscription of her 'last employee' in October 1941 and the imminent birth of a child to her sister-in-law, who had previously helped out, she could see no way of keeping the business open because of the total unavailability of staff. Nor did she expect to reopen it until after the war was over, because she had enough to do with two small children to look after.[193] Her brief notification of the closure of the shop was made to the Württemberg Prices Authority in response to its answer to her husband's previous application, in December 1941, for allowance to be made against taxation for wages for himself, his wife and other members of their family involved in the conduct of a prospering business. He had already tried to enlist the support of his *Landrat* in this, apparently without success.[194] It is therefore probable that financial considerations also played a part in the closing of the business, with the family unwilling to operate it in very difficult circumstances, only to see their profits disappear into the war economy chest, at a time when the wife was receiving an allowance because her husband was in the army and she could therefore survive without the income from the business. Nevertheless, the conscription of artisans and shopkeepers either into the armed forces or for work in war industry could cause businesses to close, leading to hardship in a locality if theirs had been the only business there of its kind. Even if a concern retained enough staff to function, it might have to scale down its operations or close altogether if it could no longer obtain essential raw materials. Beyond that, as in the First World War, the higher wages offered to German workers in the armaments industries attracted those from less well-paid sectors, for example, retailing, artisanal trades and the textile industry – as well as agriculture – while the conscription of skilled workers led to a virtual drying up of opportunities for apprentices.[195]

Some proprietors were tenacious in arguing that their needs constituted a special case. For example, those running luxury businesses claimed that they required supplies above the ration allowances. A breeder of silver foxes for the fur trade in Balingen claimed that the young cubs required plenty of milk, while the proprietor of a smart hotel in Friedrichshafen argued that, since his patrons included prominent NSDAP officials and senior *Wehrmacht* officers, he had to be able to offer the best of provisions.[196] In addition, those at the head of virtually any kind of residential institution for the young argued that their growing charges needed more than the ration allowances permitted, and tried to persuade their *Landrat* to provide tokens for extra rations. The *Landräte* were in a quandary, reluctant to dismiss the requests out of hand, but equally unsure that they had the authority to grant extra rations. The result was a flurry of paper. As institutions' leaders entered special pleas, *Landräte* passed them on to the Stuttgart Food Office, with a request for guidance, and officials – and sometimes *Landesbauernführer* Arnold himself – replied, often in the affirmative.

Most favoured were residential colleges associated with the NSDAP. For example, in November 1939, when the head of a *Napola* (elite college) in Backnang claimed that his teenage boys needed more food than the rationing allowances provided because they were pursuing strenuous physical activities, some extra rations were allocated to him. Even when rations had been progressively reduced, special allocations continued to be made to those attending the two *Napolas* in Württemberg, the other being in Rottweil. The leadership training schools of the Hitler Youth enjoyed similar privileges, as did the BDM's home economics schools and boarding schools for the children of ethnic Germans from abroad.[197] As late as November 1943, the senior SS officer in Württemberg and Baden weighed in to endorse the need for extra rations for teenage boys who were daily undergoing arduous physical training.[198] With no end to the war in sight, they might soon have to take their place in the armed forces. The young were particularly favoured in terms of dwindling rations, and in some districts they were provided with regular doses of vitamin C in winter.[199]

Once word circulated about the success of special pleading in one case, the authorities were inundated with applications from people who claimed that their circumstances, too, were exceptional. For example, those running a BDM skiing course heard about the *Napola*'s success and asked for extra potatoes.[200] In February 1942, the head of a women's teacher training college in Freudenstadt had heard that Women's Labour Service camps and camps for evacuated urban children were supplied regularly with extra bread and milk and claimed that her college's situation was similar. Although the reply which came by return was somewhat dismissive – pointing out that the camps received some extra bread, but extra milk only in the normal way for small children, and that Labour Service recruits did much more physically arduous work than college students – it was conceded that some supplementary bread tokens might be made available.[201] The head of another women's teacher training college, in Hohenzollern, asked that her students be allowed extra skimmed milk from her supplier because, she claimed, he had a surplus that would otherwise be given to the pigs. In an aside, she compared her girls' provisioning unfavourably with that of Labour Service recruits. The Food Office instructed the *Landrat* in Hechingen that there was no question of extra milk being allocated but that, under the terms of an order of 9 February 1943 from Berlin relating to residential schools and colleges, the teacher training college was entitled to supplementary tokens for bread, quark, cereals, jam and sugar, which should be distributed from his office.[202]

Two years later, in February 1945, the Reich Minister of Food and Agriculture issued new rules for institutions in the greatly diminished area of Germany under his jurisdiction, because 'the ration card system needs to be implemented more flexibly on account of the situation regarding both provisions and transport'. Special allocations for weddings and to those running cookery courses were withdrawn, as was the special ration of meat for towns which had experienced particularly severe bombing. On the other hand, those in prisons and concentration camps, as well as POWs and civilian labourers from the USSR, were – if they were in work – to receive normal rations, and if they were among industry's 'heaviest workers' they were to receive the rations stipulated for this category of 'Aryan' employees. Normal rations were by this time much reduced. Nevertheless, this last ditch attempt to fuel the German war effort, by providing the unprivileged with rations that had formerly been denied to them, was scheduled to come into effect on 9 April 1945, when much of Germany, but not yet Württemberg, was already under Allied control.[203]

The many instances of special pleading, of which a few examples have been given, together with the way in which some proprietors determinedly pursued their case – with demands for the payment of war taxation for 1940 frequently still being disputed in 1943 – show that a 'readiness for sacrifice' (*Opferbereitschaft*) for the sake of the nation was not uppermost in ordinary citizens' minds, as businessmen or youth leaders or proprietors, any more than it was when they were consumers.[204] Resentment and recrimination only grew as the war dragged on and the German army's success turned into defeat. In his 'total war' speech on 18 February 1943, the Minister for Propaganda, Goebbels, declared war on those who impeded the war effort in any way, promising an end to toleration of shirkers and spivs, and vowing that all sections of society – including 'especially you, the women' – would have to make sacrifices equitably. With consummate theatricality, Goebbels asked: 'Do you agree that whoever commits a crime in wartime should lose his head?'[205] But this was a rallying cry to an invited audience. It made little difference to the attitudes of the mass of the people, who, whether they were townspeople or country folk, had to endeavour, under the increasing pressures of war, to maintain some vestiges of their own normality regardless of the needs of others.

Many of the highest in the land set anything but a good example. In March 1943, a month after Goebbels made his 'total war' speech, Graf Helldorf, the police president in Berlin, wrote to him to complain about the large deliveries of luxury goods being made by the proprietor of a well-known delicatessen to government ministers – Frick, Ribbentrop, Rust, Darré, Lammers and Funk – as well as to military leaders and other officials, in complete contravention of the

War Economy Decree. This gave the clear impression, said Helldorf, that the restrictions of the War Economy Decree did not apply to 'persons of a certain standing'.[206] There were other examples of 'highly placed personalities' who similarly disregarded the law, as Thierack, the Reich Minister of Justice, reported to Bormann, quite apart from the many instances of corrupt practices among leading officers of the NSDAP.[207] The Nuremberg Chief Prosecutor reported in June 1942 that rumours about the hoarding of food by the mayors of Nuremberg and Würzburg, as well as by the NSDAP *Gauleiter* of Main-Franconia, who was based in Würzburg, were putting in jeopardy 'the conviction that all national comrades must countenance smaller food supplies'.[208] It was small wonder, then, that 'the little people' felt no compunction about violating laws, evading restrictions and complaining interminably about the increasing shortages.

The closing down of 'inessential' small businesses, including tailors and cleaners – which became an explicit objective after the catastrophe of Stalingrad in early 1943 – was widely regarded as 'absurd and uncalled for' by proprietors and customers alike, with restrictions on the numbers of women's hairdressers being particularly contentious.[209] Apparently, the authorities in Württemberg were more assiduous than many elsewhere in implementing these unpopular restrictions.[210] There was, then, perhaps some truth in the old jibe that 'laws are made in Prussia, read in Bavaria, and implemented in Württemberg'.[211] The unconditionally loyalist *Gauleiter* Murr seems, as *Reichsstatthalter*, to have adhered to the letter of orders from the centre more literally than others; yet even he was moved to protest in early 1944 about Speer's insistence on reducing the capacity of the Württemberg textile industry, which, Murr claimed – doubtless after lobbying by employers – damaged its position vis-à-vis its competitors in other parts of Germany.[212] Once again the issue of 'exporting' resources to areas outside Württemberg was raised. Firms in Tübingen protested when a commission from Berlin arrived to recruit their workers for armaments production in the capital.[213] In June 1944 the *Gau* Württemberg-Hohenzollern retail trade association complained that it was 'simply incomprehensible' that household utensils which were made locally were being requisitioned for distribution in distant Thuringia and Upper Silesia, while a firm on the Bodensee was commissioned to make tables for shipment to Magdeburg, for evacuees.[214] There was little sign here that either retailers or their customers in Württemberg were 'experiencing their Germanness'.[215]

The imposition of restrictions on artisans and traders was symptomatic of the deepening crisis into which Germany's leaders had plunged the country. By autumn 1943 shops closed on certain days each week, while clothing ration tokens were no longer issued because any material that was available had to be utilised to help those survivors of bombing who had lost everything.[216] Bombing also exacerbated the housing problem until, in the later stages of the war, there was an accommodation crisis.[217] It was almost impossible to obtain paper, soap and shoes. The 'critical labour situation in the shoemaking trade' had made itself felt even in 1941: by 1943, the only shoes to be had 'were now made of straw and wood'.[218] Food rations were cut, and there were particular difficulties in obtaining sufficient supplies of fats. In what must for many have been reminiscent of the way in which windfall fruit and nuts had to be collected during the First World War, as supplies of conventional foods dried up, in autumn 1942 the Württemberg Milk and Fats Trade Association was reduced to publicising the need to collect beechnuts from which 'as is well known, valuable edible oil can be extracted'.[219] Two years later, 'the problematic state of fats' provision in the sixth year of the war' led to an incentive being offered. Those who delivered a kilo of beechnuts to the appropriate depot would receive a voucher for 200 grams of margarine or oil.[220] In Württemberg, however, the 1944 harvest in beechnuts failed, although other sources of oil, including sunflower seeds, were available.[221]

The last weeks of the war were chaotic, with most of Germany under enemy control and the few remaining redoubts, including Württemberg, seriously overcrowded with evacuees, refugees, retreating German and allied soldiers, and even coerced concentration camp victims homing in on the diminished core of the country. Yet in March 1945 the Wurttemberg authorities still produced an edition of the government gazette which proclaimed that the recent outbreak of foot and mouth disease in Vaihingen district had been eradicated and that 'Württemberg is again disease free'. Appointments to and retirements from government ministries, universities and schools were announced as if normality prevailed. There was a reference to the reduction in the bread ration that had been announced for the seventy-third distribution period; in Württemberg the effect of this was mitigated by the provision that consumers could buy 500 grams of meat or meat products instead of 1000 grams of bread.[222] Other areas were not as fortunate. Yet it was all relative: there were serious shortages in Württemberg, and these had led to an epidemic of thieving of ration cards and tokens. The Württemberg Economics Ministry blamed small retailers for not storing sufficiently securely the tokens they had received; it was considering, in February 1945, punishing them by refusing to allow them the substitutes that would enable them to obtain new supplies.[223] The retailers' group responsible for food shops accepted that there might be cases of negligence among its members, but pointed out that retailers could hardly be held responsible when the thieves broke into their shops. Putting the onus on retailers was clearly a desperate resort at a time when the police – who were not mentioned at all in this correspondence – were so thin on the ground.[224]

Increasingly, especially after the catastrophe at Stalingrad in early 1943, the regime's focus narrowed, with an overwhelming emphasis on maintaining the military effort through releasing labour for essential tasks and on trying to maintain as high a level of morale among the 'Aryan' population as possible. This was done partly by exhortation and, later in the war, partly by terror measures against any who were considered 'defeatist'.[225] By contrast, the early successes of the *Wehrmacht* had brought easy acclaim. The Stuttgart State Prosecutor reported in April 1940 that 'the months of waiting' had reconciled people to the possibility of a long war, which they were facing with calm determination.[226] Yet it is unlikely that many conceived of a 'long war' as one that would last into 1943, let alone into 1945. The victories in the west in April-June 1940 had silenced those who had expressed doubts about Germany's prospects and had brought 'unreserved recognition of the greatness of the Führer and of the successes achieved by National Socialism … even among those who had perhaps not yet wholeheartedly accepted National Socialism'.[227] Although at an early stage any continuation of hostilities beyond summer 1940 was said to be likely to cause disappointment, morale remained at a reasonably high level into 1942, in spite of the failure in 1940–41 either to conclude a peace settlement with Britain, or to defeat it, and in spite of the invasion of the USSR in June 1941.[228] In the autumn of 1940, the President of the Supreme Court in Stuttgart reported that the question which most exercised the 'Swabian population' was the conflict with Britain. After the rapid subjugation of France, people had expected that Britain would be similarly humbled, and there was surprise and unease when, contrary to the regime's propaganda, British aircraft were able to reach Germany and to drop bombs. On the other hand, Württemberg was as yet little affected by this. In late 1940, its population was more greatly exercised by news of the killing of mentally ill persons at Schloss Grafeneck and the lynch law treatment meted out to some women who had consorted with POWs.[229]

Even in early summer 1941, the chief topic of conversation was the flight made by the deputy Führer, Rudolf Hess, to Scotland, of which many seemed to have learned from British sources, mostly no doubt the BBC. This was, however, eclipsed by the *Wehrmacht*'s invasion of the USSR, on 22 June 1941, which came as a complete shock. Many regarded it as a diversion while Britain remained undefeated, and expressed resentment at the undoubted prolongation of the war that this would mean.[230] Even the *Wehrmacht*'s early successes on the eastern front brought a mixed response, with the high casualty rates occasioning depression and doubt. The failure of the *Luftwaffe* to deny British bombers access to German air space and worries about the possibility of America's entering the war led to fears of 'war without end', at the very time when the reduction and uneven distribution of rations was causing discontent. All in all, the Stuttgart State Prosecutor was of the view that the popular mood was 'not entirely gratifying' in the summer of 1941, although the President of the Supreme Court in Stuttgart maintained that 'the desire for victory as well as trust in the

Führer and in the *Wehrmacht* are now as firm ever'.[231] Yet he was aware that popular morale was being depressed by several factors, including the length of the war, with no end being in sight, the unexpectedly stubborn resistance by the Red Army, the perceived threat of a Soviet, British and American alliance against Germany, and, at home, the constraints and perceived injustices of the rationing system. He also mentioned the 'strong misgivings' harboured by loyal churchgoers about the regime's anticlerical policies.[232]

The SD was more pessimistic, in July 1941 reporting 'an increasing deterioration' in the popular mood, which it attributed to the ferocity of the campaign in the east and the rather non-committal army reports about its progress which were causing anxiety among 'women in all sections of society'. Eye-witness reports from the eastern front described the war in the west in 1940 as 'a Strength through Joy outing, or manoeuvres' by comparison. Above all, the much higher German casualty rates in the east, compared with the west, were a source of anxiety and depression: there were 'especially among the women ... loud complaints about "the many, many victims"' of the war who came from Württemberg.[233] Two months later, the SD could report that the popular mood was calmer, but that great anxiety persisted about the high level of casualties. In addition, a moratorium on letters from the front led to the spread of rumours, not least as a result of accounts of 'Bolshevik atrocities' related by wounded soldiers who had been sent home.[234] At the same time, Germany's victories in the east and at sea, with aggressive submarine warfare, brought some relief, but they did not disperse the gloom that characterised the popular mood.[235] By the end of 1941, the fears and discontents had led to 'resignation, war weariness and embitterment', with particular worries about the continuing casualties.[236]

The turn of the year 1942 saw a further deterioration in the popular mood as the *Wehrmacht*'s failure to take Moscow and British resistance in North Africa claimed more lives and demonstrated that German forces were not invincible. The need to hold public collections of warm clothes for soldiers on the eastern front confirmed the occasional pessimistic reports given by wounded soldiers, by soldiers home on leave and by letters from those at the front. Shortages on the home front and the theft of food produce, clothes and bicycles, combined with increasingly brazen black marketeering and some evidence of juvenile delinquency, not only depressed spirits at home but also increased mistrust of the official news media. Ordinary Germans showed their displeasure by refraining from participating in the 'iron savings action', the massive campaign to build up funds for the war effort.[237] The best that could be said in early 1942 was that there was a mood of 'grim determination', in spite of the manifold cares and worries.[238]

Yet these were perhaps winter blues: with spring 1942 came better news from the fronts, especially from the Atlantic, which to some extent boosted spirits.[239]

There was said to be a determination to finish off the Soviets once and for all, and a belief that this would indeed happen in the course of the year.[240] Even in the autumn of 1942, with that goal as far away as ever if not more so, the mood was, 'taken overall, good'. The major reason for this was that favourable grain and potato harvests had led to an increase in rations. Yet German forces were being defeated in North Africa, and the arrival of American reinforcements there had caused some alarm. The President of the Supreme Court in Stuttgart was undoubtedly putting a good face on it when he reported that these developments 'had certainly not shaken confidence in the German leadership and the German armed forces'. Already, Württemberg had experienced the full force of the air war, with the RAF inflicting severe damage on both Heilbronn and Stuttgart.[241] A more realistic assessment of the mood was that it consisted of a combination of 'mounting pessimism ... and exaggerated hopes'.[242]

The turning point for morale, if not necessarily for Germany's military fortunes, came with the regime's admission of the surrender of 90,000 men at Stalingrad at the end of January 1943, a few days after Churchill and Roosevelt had announced that they would accept nothing less than the 'unconditional surrender' of German forces. Goebbels could call, with spurious triumphalism, for 'total war' to ensure that the coalition allies, not the *Wehrmacht*, surrendered, but too many Germans recognised this for the bravado that it was.[243] They were utterly shocked that the allegedly weak, ill-equipped and unprepared Red Army could have inflicted such a defeat on the *Wehrmacht*. Various *Gauleiter* might report to the Party Chancellery that, after the initial shock, the population was 'tougher and more determined than before', and that they were persuaded by party propaganda that the Soviets had managed to win only by bringing in troops from other fronts, where German forces were still victorious.[244] Yet such special pleading only delayed the moment when Germany's leaders and its people would have to face reality.

Gauleiter Murr contributed to the self-delusion of February 1943 by lashing out at 'political wind-bags' who ought to maintain a decent silence. Tellingly, he was referring specifically to NSDAP members who, he said, should be 'punished or thrown out of the party by their superiors' if they peddled gossip. In February 1943 he issued a checklist of tactics for dealing with doom merchants, which included hunting down the sources of rumours that undermined morale. The Catholic Church, disaffected conservatives, the Confessing Church – a group of Protestants who resisted Nazi encroachments on the Evangelical churches – 'Bolshevism', intellectuals and foreign workers were all in his sights. Uncovering these elements should not, he said, be left to chance in the hope that 'such criminals will betray themselves'. He was particularly censorious of those who 'listen to the voice of the enemy [and thus] weaken the defensive and resistance capability of our people', threatening that those discovered would be 'prosecuted and mercilessly punished'. He undoubtedly believed that 'all rumours which weaken the strength of our people and damage the reputation of the Führer, the party, the *Wehrmacht* and the state are obviously untrue, even when they describe incidents and events plausibly in such fine detail'.[245]

Those who 'listen to the voices of the enemy' were not necessarily assuaging their curiosity about the actual course of the war, as opposed to the one portrayed by Nazi propagandists. The relatives of soldiers who were 'missing' on the eastern front, particularly after Stalingrad, might receive anonymous letters telling them them to listen to Radio Moscow for information about them.[246] It was hardly surprising if, at great risk to themselves, they did so. One Party Chancellery briefing mentioned that 'people are doing anything to get some news about the fate of the missing'.[247] The terrible losses at Stalingrad had their effect also on serving soldiers. The same Party Chancellery briefing that included Murr's posturing also contained reports from two *Gaue* about low morale in army barracks in their region: one of these was from Württemberg-Hohenzollern. Some officers there were said to be voicing doubts about Hitler's abilities as a commander-in-chief, while 'time and again, one hears that officers and men are now in a pessimistic frame of mind'.[248]

The ensuing series of reverses during 1943 ensured that morale was set on a downward course, even if it continued to fluctuate until well into 1944. After the disaster at Stalingrad, followed by 'Tunisgrad', final defeat in North Africa came in May 1943.[249] The diminishing success of German submarine warfare, the increasing bombing of towns, without much apparent German response, and the mounting difficulties on the home front were additional blows, none more so than the dreadful loss of men in the field. In many communes, the number of casualties had by this time overtaken those of the entire First World War. With despair and disaffection setting in, at the end of May 1943 the Stuttgart State Prosecutor admitted uncomfortably that

> from a careful analysis of all the surveillance reports, one has to come to the conclusion that, in *Gau* Württemberg-Hohenzollern, in spite of the success in stabilising the eastern front, confidence in victory and trust in the leadership on the part of a numerically not inconsiderable part of the population has now been noticeably shaken.[250]

Civilians increasingly turned in on themselves, borne down by the cares of being related to men at the front, by the increasing obstacles in their daily lives – with utilities and transportation out of service as a result of either bombing or a lack of resources – and by the difficulties in obtaining life's essentials.[251] From time to time thereafter there were military successes which transiently revived the increasingly moribund hope that final victory could still be achieved, but only transiently.

Even the occasional triumph, which served as a straw to clutch at, could be marred by the almost complete lack of confidence that civilians had in the reliability of official news reports. Particularly with paper supplies restricted from summer 1941, and with many newspapers closed down from the beginning of 1943, much news and other information was conveyed by radio to a substantial section of the population: in Württemberg, the number of subscribers for radio transmission had passed the half million mark in autumn 1940.[252] Yet radio became a double-edged weapon, cruelly exposing the gulf between propaganda and the reality experienced by civilians and their relatives in the armed forces. Its mostly private character made it difficult for the authorities – depleted as their functionaries were by war service – to monitor the listening habits of the population and to detect instances of 'treasonable' listening to enemy radio, although some 'illegal listeners' were apprehended and punished.[253] The regime itself had made criminals of its citizens, outlawing 'black listening' while failing to give credible information. As the Württemberg SD reported, people simply felt that they had to listen to other countries' radio stations because German radio had proved so unreliable in telling them anything like the truth.[254] By summer 1943, many in south-west Germany were said to be tuning in to Swiss radio, which was credited with 'extraordinary objectivity'.[255]

The Allied landings in Sicily came as a shock, and led 'even those with a positive attitude' to make comparisons with the position in the previous year, when German forces had 'at the same time [of year] been at the gates of Egypt and deep into Russia'.[256] In south Germany the feeling was that 'Sicily must be held on to under all circumstances, otherwise the enemy will advance into Italy, [and] then south Germany will be a battlefield'.[257] There was even talk of regime change in Germany, as in Italy.[258] A worker's wife spoke for many when she said 'perhaps now Hitler, too, will soon have to go'.[259] The fall of Mussolini's regime in July 1943 merely confirmed those who were already depressed by the turn of events in the view that the war could not be won. The wife of an *alter Kämpfer* was heard to say, 'this is the beginning of the end', while the common popular responses were 'once again it's all in vain', 'now they're really in a mess', and 'they've really let themselves in for it'. The SD noted that it was the women, above all, who had turned defeatist, although they forebore to add that this was another parallel with the second half of the First World War.[260] Yet it was hardly surprising that women's voices were prominent on a home front so depleted of adult men. News of the D-Day landings was said to have 'entirely consumed the attention' of people in Stuttgart, with everyone gathering round radio sets.[261] The 'activists put a good face on it' while many kept their own counsel and simply waited to see what would happen.

In urban areas, there was renewed fear of massive air raids, 'particularly among older women'. Their worst expectations were met in Stuttgart, as we have seen, in the devastating raids in July 1944. With some desperation, people continued to hope – rather than expect – that it would all come right for Germany in the end.[262] Yet the intensification of enemy bombing generated an incremental rise in public pessimism. 'If we are so weak that we cannot prevent the destruction of our transport system, which is essential for our supplies', it was said in Stuttgart in the autumn of 1944, 'then the war is lost.' The regime's propaganda which tried to minimise this impression was dismissed by a population which 'wanted to see action'.[263] By this time, reports from Württemberg to the propaganda ministry were said to have become 'very sceptical', while Hitler's own stock was plummeting.[264] In August 1944, the Stuttgart SD reported that 'even those who up to now have believed unwaveringly ... have lost faith in the Führer'.[265]

It was hardly surprising that the gradual erosion of the German military position in Italy and, in particular, the failure of German submarines to scupper the D-Day invasion, led to 'a section of the population becoming increasingly disappointed'.[266] While there remained fear that either Hitler or the enemy would resort to the use of gas, the main cause of despondency was the certain knowledge that enemy forces far outnumbered German resources in terms of both men and matériel.[267] The only responses that the regime could muster came in the form of 'wonder weapons' and the creation of a home guard, the *Volkssturm*. The 'V' weapons – 'V' for *Vergeltung* (retaliation) – were flying bombs and rockets which would, it was promised, strike at the heart of the enemy and exact revenge for the terror visited on Germany's towns and cities.[268] While V-1 pilotless flying bombs and V-2 rockets were deployed, inflicting some damage on London and killing altogether 9000 Londoners in 1944–45, in military terms this was but a pin-prick compared with the pounding of German cities by Allied bombers by night and by day.[269]

The 'V' weapons could at least wreak damage; the *Volkssturm*, by contrast, was a poor substitute for an army, consisting of old men, boys, the injured and infirm. It was called into service on 25 September 1944 as Allied forces were poised to invade Germany in both the east and the west.[270] These unlikely soldiers were ill-equipped, sometimes even lacking appropriate clothing and footwear. Those in Württemberg who were still sympathetic towards the regime felt that this reserve should have been mobilised without fanfare, in the hope of surprising the enemy.[271] Others feared that the enemy would not regard its members as genuine combatants, which would bode very ill for any who were taken prisoner.[272] The Württemberg SD admitted that the announcement of the creation of the *Volkssturm* had been 'received negatively by the overwhelming majority of the population'. From a rural commune, where its existence was regarded as an admission of Germany's weakness, came the comment, 'Now they've let the cat out of the bag'. In Stuttgart, a grim joke did the rounds: 'now we know what the V2 is – the German *Volkssturm* is the V2'. There was also deep pessimism about the possibility of a rearguard action in a country such as Germany, as opposed to huge and inhospitable Russia. In Stuttgart, it was said that 'even if the will ... were there, this [kind of] resistance would be quickly swept aside. It should not be forgotten that we are in the sixth year of the war and the population is war weary'.[273]

This was a massive understatement. Those who remained on the home front were exhausted. Their nutrition might perhaps have been adequate, by comparison with the last two years of the First World War. It might well have sufficed if restricted amounts of food had been reliably available in urban shops and did not have to be desperately hunted down, if public transport had functioned, and if there had been both the time and the capacity for rest and relaxation. But, particularly from 1942, civilians were required to make superhuman exertions under the most debilitating conditions: with lengthy hours of work, little functioning public or private transport, and greatly reduced supplies of fuel; with shabby, patched clothing and defective shoes, the disruption of normal family and social life, and – in the towns especially – a growing crescendo of air raid alarms, all of which disrupted either the daytime struggles or a precious night's sleep and some of which presaged damage, devastation and death. Even in the countryside there was the threat, and sometimes the reality, of an air attack, while those left to run farms and rural businesses struggled against the elements without the human and mechanical assistance which they required, and perhaps without draught animals which had been requisitioned for the army. There were few who did not have a relative in the *Wehrmacht*, and most Germans by the autumn of 1944 had lost a family member, a friend or a neighbour either at the front or as a result of bombing. The almost universal exhaustion was not merely physical; there was also a pervasive mood of nervousness and anxiety, as postmen delivered death notices and the news – generally circulated unofficially, by word of mouth, or gleaned from enemy radio – was of inexorable military defeat.

One of the major myths of the post-1945 era was that Allied bombing did not break German civilian morale. The truth of this perhaps depends on the criteria used for assessing whether morale was holding up or breaking down. Certainly there was no revolt, concerted or otherwise, but that is not sufficient evidence that morale remained intact. In Württemberg, as in the rest of Germany

> there can surely be little doubt that bombing was a uniquely demoralising experience ... The recollections of its victims are unanimous in expressing feelings of panic, of fear, of dumb resignation ... The last thing on the minds of those living under the hail of bombs was political resistance ... Bombed populations developed an outlook both apathetic and self-centred; each night they hoped that if there had to be bombing, it would be on someone else.[274]

Nevertheless, it is difficult to judge how far bombing on its own achieved demoralisation, because civilians who experienced or feared bombing were also subjected to many other pressures. On the other hand, those who escaped bombing but experienced the other emergencies and exigencies of war were, like the bombed, demoralised by the last stages of the war. The land war certainly played its part in this, particularly once Germany's empire was lost and the enemy was closing in from both east and west. The terrible human losses, of dead, severely wounded and missing, had a massive psychological effect on those at home, whether or not they were in the bombers' sights. Added to that, there was virtually no light relief, with places of entertainment closed down and the little luxuries which might have brightened someone's day, albeit temporarily, completely unavailable. It is, then, little wonder that there were, at the end of the war, 'chocolate hungry Swabians' who quickly established at least superficially friendly relations with the occupying forces, particularly if they were American.[275]

6

War in the Countryside

The impact of the chronic problems with food supply and distribution in Württemberg's towns, which led even in the early days of the war to panic buying in Stuttgart and to 'weeping women standing at the counters of the Food Office because they had received too little food for their small children', was scarcely appreciated in the countryside.[1] Quite simply, in rural areas the wartime controls, which were imposed on producers as an extension of the peacetime *Reichsnährstand* (RNS – Reich Food Estate) restrictions of the *Marktordnung* (market regulation), were regarded as intolerable. There was particular resentment at wartime expedients which involved conscription, requisitioning and increased government requirements of a kind which seemed reminiscent of the most oppressive aspects of the *Zwangswirtschaft* (coercive economy) of the First World War era. As far as Württemberg's rural communes were concerned, the traffic was all in one direction: they made sacrifices of various kinds – human, material, cultural – while an urban-based government exploited their resources, interfered in their businesses and controlled the prices of their produce.

In the first place, and of overwhelming importance, there were the problems caused by the conscription of male members of a farming family and paid male workers. The pre-war haemorrhage of rural labour had created enough problems; now, the progressive withdrawal of able-bodied men, to the extent that by April 1943 'the farms were largely denuded of male labour', left the physically weaker members of a family – women, elderly parents and adolescents – to cope with the heaviest work which had been traditionally performed by men.[2] Compensation, in the form of foreign prisoners of war or forced labour, brought new pressures and controls, as did the arrival of increasing numbers of evacuees from bomb-damaged regions, especially in the last two years of the war. In Bavaria, the often arbitrary way in which conscription was applied was a 'source of anger, bitterness, envy, and corruption, rending many village communities', especially over definitions of 'reserved occupation' which seemed to discriminate unfairly against some and in favour of others whose circumstances were very similar.[3] Above all, the disproportionately high rate of conscription of men from farming communities, into both the armed forces and war industry, was a continuing source of both discontent and genuine hardship on the land.[4] Particularly in areas, including much of Württemberg, where farming was a highly labour intensive occupation, conscription on a large scale contradicted the regime's aim of maintaining the nation's food supplies at a tolerable level.

In Württemberg, the conscription of older farmers in September 1939, 'while younger age groups are still at home', occasioned particular anger.[5] In Türkheim, near Ulm, the removal of farmers and labourers made it difficult to bring in the harvest and carry out the autumn phase of planting. To overcome these problems, farmers in the commune collaborated in sharing draught animals and helping out on each others' farms in a partly organised and partly spontaneous fashion. The arrival of Polish POWs from November 1939 brought them some relief.[6] It was not only farmers and their labourers but also rural tradesmen and artisans who were conscripted, causing considerable problems if there was only one butcher or baker or shoemaker in a commune. For example, the commune of Altingen, near Tübingen, which had some 900 inhabitants, lost its only butcher in 1941. The district NSDAP economic adviser, in reporting this, added that the inhabitants therefore 'have to walk to places several kilometres distant' in order to buy meat. 'It is perfectly obvious how great a hardship this is for countless farmers' wives who have to run their business on their own.' He also mentioned that the commune's only miller was apparently about to be conscripted, which would mean the closure of Altingen's mill. 'This is too much', he complained.[7] Yet this was while German forces were still victorious and before the Russian campaign, in particular, had sucked into the *Wehrmacht* ever larger numbers of civilian men from all kinds of occupation. The Nazi regime, through the agency of the *Reichsnährstand*, might continue to try to ameliorate conditions by offering grants for land improvement schemes, but it could not provide in sufficient numbers the one thing that farms and rural trades needed most of all: adult male labour.[8]

On the eve of the outbreak of war, at harvest time in 1939, the requisitioning by the army of many farm horses was a source of great resentment.[9] In Türkheim, during the night of 26–27 August 1939, fifty-three horses were appraised by the army for requisitioning, and thirty-six of these were chosen. This was regarded in the commune as a 'great sacrifice', with those who had owned horses reduced to using cows or oxen as draught animals, although four farmers were able to join forces to buy a tractor.[10] Similarly, in Münchingen, near Leonberg, all of the commune's horses had to be brought to the centre of the commune on the last Saturday in August. A 'large number of mostly young and valuable horses were taken away and … conveyed to the garrison at Ludwigsburg'. That was the last that the Münchingen farmers saw of these horses, but they were at least paid compensation of between 1000 and 1800 marks per horse.[11] With the conscription of horses, not only were farmers deprived of valuable draught animals, especially in the many areas of rural Württemberg where there were few tractors or other agricultural machines and no other means of transport, but, in addition, conscripting horses removed an indication of a farmer's status which was measured by the numbers of horses and cattle which he possessed. The 'well-to-do horse farmers' were therefore disproportionately disadvantaged.[12] Then, in the last days of the war, desperate army units with little or no equipment might seize horses from communes through which they passed.[13]

Official price levels, the imposition of quotas for produce to be delivered to state collection depots, and controls on the slaughter of farm animals were regarded as intolerable interference in private businesses. As early as October 1938, a law had introduced a system of compulsory annual livestock censuses, to enable the government to monitor and control the numbers of live and slaughtered farm animals in communes and even on individual farms; such censuses were held in December of each year from 1940 to 1944, inclusive.[14] In particular, there were stringent regulations to restrict the slaughter of livestock, so that only limited amounts of meat would come onto the market at a time, to prevent the possibility of an immediate superabundance being followed by severe shortage.[15] Inspectors toured farms to try to ensure that only the permitted quotas of animals were slaughtered in the prescribed period. Nevertheless, violations of these regulations – the illegal slaughtering of livestock, which was known literally as 'black slaughtering' (*Schwarzschlachtung*) – soon came to assume a major part of reported crime in Württemberg.[16] By December 1942, the farm animal census covered horses, cattle, donkeys, sheep, pigs, goats, poultry and bees, with, for the first time, rabbits included.[17] Further controls on agricultural production included surveys of soil types and crops grown, with quotas detailing the delivery requirements for each commodity from each farm to the relevant state depot. Yet while this procedure appeared cut and dried on paper, in practice it could be imperfect. For example, in the commune of Untermarchtal, in the major food producing district of Ehingen, in 1940 there was still neither an egg collection depot nor a designated collector who would act there on behalf of the Egg Trade Association.[18]

These paraphernalia of regulation were geared to securing the urban food supply. Together with the allowance paid to the wife of a serving soldier who was not a farmer, and the state-financed evacuation of urban families to safer rural areas, the regulations were intended to placate the industrial workers who were essential to a twentieth-century war effort and among some of whom, at least, 'Marxism' still had something of a hold, compared with the rural population which was conservative and devout. Indeed, fear of Communism was what had chiefly motivated many of those in rural areas who had voted for the NSDAP in 1932–33.[19] In the spring of 1940 there was talk of paying a flat rate allowance to a farmer's wife who had not been able to recruit a permanent replacement for her conscripted husband, and this was indeed introduced for those on small or middling-sized farms.[20] Yet this allowance was set at such a low level that 'a farmer's wife with four or five children had to make do with between 45 and 60 marks, whereas the childless wife of a white collar worker had about 150 to 180 marks a month at her disposal' from her allowance as the wife of a serving soldier.[21] Apart from anything else, this made little sense in terms of Nazi population policy, particularly when it was still the case that rural families tended to be larger than urban families.

If what looked like more favourable treatment for urban dwellers, together with attempts to regiment farming in unpalatable ways, antagonised the rural population, that was the price to be paid for maintaining order in the towns, where any serious challenge to Nazi authority could be expected. Even if, as we have seen, the regulatory framework and its application caused acute discontent in the towns, its purpose was nevertheless to avert the kind of disaffection that genuinely catastrophic shortages there would have provoked. The overriding preoccupation was with the maintenance and promotion of control by the National Socialist leadership, both as an end in itself and as the essential precondition of 'final victory'. There was therefore greater official concern about urban opinion, greater state control, and the relegation of agriculture in practice to the status of handmaid to the industrial, modern state.[22] For example, in the Friedrichshafen area,

> during the war, agriculture was continually at the disposal of industry. The armaments industry provided labour for agriculture in time of shortage of raw materials, or handed over exhausted or weak 'eastern workers' to be 'nursed back to health', so that they could be called back into service when the need arose.[23]

Industry was given priority, in terms of access to dwindling resources, while the government called the tune, with rules and regulations controlling the production, distribution and pricing of food supplies.

In reality, in wartime farmers and rural tradesmen had a trump card: they produced the food that the townspeople needed, and they produced it in the way that they regarded as most appropriate for their circumstances, which was strongly characterised by the rhythms and methods used by their antecedents and by fellow members of their commune. In Burgbach, for example, even circa 1970, there was still a 'ritual of growing food for one's own table [which] has been ... a persistent block against fully professional specialisation ... [and] is no longer rational, and has not been for some time'.[24] Farmers were not impressed by the strictures of urban-based politicians and bureaucrats who would not have known how to milk a cow or slaughter a pig. Nevertheless, inducing producers to change their attitudes, habits and time-honoured practices to meet the regime's demands would not have been impossible. Stalin had demonstrated in the USSR in the early 1930s that it could be done, even in the face of massive opposition, but only at a monstrous and murderous cost – and, even then, only up to a point.[25] In Germany, while the wartime extermination of millions of non-'Aryans' and the 'worthless' became the uniquely grotesque defining feature of National Socialism in power, starving or deporting to their death millions of peasants for varieties of dissidence and disobedience – as perpetrated in Stalin's USSR – was not an option when those peasants were 'racially valuable' and exalted in Nazi ideology. The Nazi leadership never considered bringing agricultural production under state ownership – as opposed to state control through regulation – for both ideological and practical reasons; so, as in its dealings with urban workers, it relied on a combination of coercion and consent.[26]

In the event, rural producers in Württemberg demonstrated that there were clear limits to what they were prepared to concede to the government. In turn, the authorities in Württemberg, at both central and local level, often showed both a kind of sensitivity towards, and a lack of resolve in coercing, the rural population that seems out of character for a dictatorial regime. Part of the reason was that many district and local officials had at least some empathy with the ordinary citizens of their area because they shared the same roots. They understood the structures and traditions of rural society in their area, and in some cases clearly sympathised with the individual and community loyalties and aspirations which derived from these. The apparently rational answers sought by the regime to problems of supplying food and other resources during the war were, they appreciated, fraught with problems when applied to life on the land as it was experienced by rural inhabitants. Even where mayors, *Landräte* or RNS officials did not actually sympathise with rural miscreants who had violated wartime regulations, they tended to believe that their own position within their community depended at least to some extent on their turning a blind eye to customary practices that had recently been criminalised and tolerating repeated minor abuses of official regulations. The pressures and ever-increasing exigencies of war demonstrated beyond doubt that the ideal of the *Volksgemeinschaft* had not been realised on the land, any more than it had been in the towns.[27] The efforts of central and regional officers of both the NSDAP and the Nazi state – including some of those at the head of the regime in Württemberg – to permeate rural communities with an essentially urban conception of 'German Socialism' may have made some converts in the few, fleeting peacetime years, but by the later 1930s the pressures of industry-led economic recovery on small farms in Württemberg had dissipated much of whatever good will the regime had initially enjoyed. For example, an early post-war memoir from one commune referred to 'Nazism, which had met with such massive disapproval among the farmers because of the *Erbhof* law'.[28]

The problem of problems, however, was and remained the labour shortage on the land, which was already serious in many areas of Germany in the last peacetime years and became increasingly critical on small farms during the war. SD reports in February and March 1942 described at length the difficulties caused in several regions, including Württemberg, by conscription, and particularly by the conscription of farm proprietors and skilled farm workers that was having an adverse effect on food production. In the jurisdiction of the *Landesbauernschaft* Württemberg, some 4000 concerns, accounting for a total of around 67,000 hectares of cultivable land, were without both a proprietor and sufficient labour to tend the fields productively. Some of these conscripted farmers had been sent to Bavaria or Thuringia to act as guards keeping watch over POWs, which meant that they could not even spend their free time on their own farm.[29] The Stuttgart State Prosecutor reported in April 1942 on 'the extraordinary shortage of labour, especially in agriculture' which threatened the cultivation of normally productive land.[30] A year later, the SD reported on the effects which another round of conscription into the *Wehrmacht* and the Labour Service in late autumn 1942, combined with the redeployment of some foreign workers from agriculture into war industry, had had. Not surprisingly, this had left some farms critically understaffed. The SD warned that future rounds of conscription – 'which we have to expect' – were likely to cause 'serious damage to agricultural concerns', because withdrawing labour would make those that were currently viable unable to function as businesses. The result would be an enforced retreat into self-sufficiency, which would have disastrous effects on the urban food supply. This prophecy was realised in the last months of the war.

In the examples given by the SD of farms working at the margins of viability, small concerns in Württemberg featured prominently. From Balingen district in the south-west came the tale of a hereditary farmer (*Erbhofbauer*) and sawmill proprietor whose four sons were in the *Wehrmacht*, leaving him to run the business with his disabled elderly father, his twenty-one year-old daughter and a POW. Attempts had been made to obtain the demobilisation of the eldest son, who had the sight of only one eye, but without success. As a result, the farm faced collapse. From Schwäbisch Gmünd, in central Württemberg, it was reported that another *Erbhofbauer*, who, like his wife, was in his seventieth year and capable only of light work, had a property of 16 hectares with twelve head of cattle and a horse. Of his two sons, the elder had been killed in action and the younger was still at the front. Another farm of comparable size was being run by the farmer's wife, her mother and a frail hired hand, whereas before the war it had been operated by the owner and four male labourers. In the same area, a farm twice as large as these others had one horse, eleven cattle and twenty-five pigs. To manage these there remained only the farmer's wife, a female employee and a POW. The heaviest weight of the pressures caused by conscription had fallen on already overburdened farmers' wives, whose health was noticeably impaired.

In Calw district, in western Württemberg, a young wife who had been trying to maintain a small farm on her own, while her husband was in the army, had died while giving birth to their fourth child. The doctor who attended her said unequivocally that the cause of death was extreme overwork.[31] It was, then, perhaps not much of an exaggeration to say that 'as a result of the constant conscription of men for military service … there was a great shortage of labour here … The women almost worked themselves to death'.[32] Yet functionaries were sometimes either sceptical or unsympathetic about 'the so-called extreme cases'. In Tübingen district, a sick farm proprietor who was a war widow asked for one of her sons to be released from the army because she could not manage her farm of three hectares with only a POW and an *Arbeitsmaid* (Labour Service girl). Although her mayor and local police chief had supported her application, the *Kreisbauernführer* (district RNS official) refused to submit it to the appropriate authorities as a special case, leaving her no alternative but to put the farm up for sale.[33]

Nevertheless, there were attempts to provide some compensation for the men who had been conscripted into the *Wehrmacht* and for the young men conscripted into service schemes. In autumn 1939, the *Wehrmacht* itself was able to provide assistance at harvest time. School students worked in agriculture in the vacations. The men's Labour Service was prohibited from working in agriculture, although its members were sometimes drafted in to meet an emergency, but the women's Labour Service supplied young women to help out on farms and, increasingly, elsewhere. The regime of camp life, however, with an emphasis on indoctrination and communal activities, sometimes left the young women with little time for work on the farms to which they had been allocated, and there were complaints from farmers about both this and the unpredictable and short-term nature of the assistance that was afforded. Young women from the *Pflichtjahr* (year of compulsory service) scheme were thin on the ground, with some allocated to farmers' households but more endeavouring to find a placement in the towns.[34] In some cases, there was genuine fear among urban young women of the farm animals with which they were expected to work.[35] The Reich government recognised that there was an enduring problem, and in March 1942 Göring, as Plenipotentiary for the Four Year Plan, decreed that 'citizens who are fit for agricultural work and are not, or are not fully, employed' could be brought in to work on farms. Yet it transpired that this was to apply restrictively to those living on the land or in country towns, 'especially people who have already been engaged in agriculture', who were to be identified by the *Ortsbauernführer* (OBF – local RNS official) in consultation with the relevant mayor and NSDAP local branch leader. The OBF would decide where the conscripts would be deployed.[36] This plan therefore depended on there being spare labour in rural areas, which was not the case in Württemberg. It also depended on an OBF being prepared to exert authority and, if necessary, to use coercive means within his own community.

The result was that foreign workers, where they were allocated to farms, were generally a more reliable labour resource, not least because those from eastern Europe, particularly, often came from a farming background. At the end of May 1943, the Stuttgart State Prosecutor reported that 'the conscription of almost all able-bodied men' meant that, apart from 'the females who were still available', farm workers were 'almost exclusively ... Poles, Serbs and POWs'.[37] Some foreigners became indispensable members of their hosts' household while others were never reconciled to their role and status in what the regime explicitly intended should be for them an alien environment. Yet even with the coercion of millions of foreigners into working in Germany, many small farms were not allocated a foreign worker; increasingly, as with everything else, industry had first call on their labour. By March 1943, the SD was urging that the recent withdrawal of foreigners from farms in several regions, including Württemberg, should not only cease but should actually be reversed, at the very least for the duration of the spring sowing season. This request applied especially to Serb and French workers, who were much preferred by farmers to those from the USSR, who were accustomed to large collectives in which they were employees without a direct stake in the concern, rather than small family farms.[38]

The draining away of labour from the land was the most serious problem facing both farmers and, consequently, consumers as some farming businesses were progressively reduced to subsistence production. But the rural population faced other constraints. For example, although more tokens for clothing and shoes were distributed in rural areas of Württemberg than in Stuttgart, in July 1941 there were 'ever more complaints' about the inadequate supply of work shoes that were suitable for those engaged in agriculture.[39] This problem became only more acute, and in January 1944 the SD reported that farmers in various areas of Germany were complaining about the unavailability of shoes for work. In Württemberg, they told their NSDAP local branch leaders that they could not work in shoes which were 'old and completely worn out'. Shoes could be purchased only with a special permit, and the mayor of one rural commune in Württemberg claimed to have had sixty urgent applications for new work shoes. The supply of these was so infrequent and inadequate that most of those applying would not receive new shoes during the current winter, with the result that they would simply stop working. Part of the problem was that materials for repairing shoes – nails, for example – were unobtainable.[40] In addition, the number of shoemakers in Württemberg had been depleted even before the war, with many of those who worked on their own being told to retrain as upholsterers for the Volkswagen automotive works in Fallersleben.[41] During the war, remaining shoemakers, like other craftsmen and traders, lost their assistants to the armed forces and could not cope with the backlog of repairs themselves. Sometimes repairs made with substitute materials even led to the wearer sustaining injury, if, for example, he or she wore shoes with smooth soles on slippery terrain.[42]

When it came to the wartime shortage of agricultural machines, fuel and the diminishing availability of men and materials to repair machines, farmers in Württemberg were less disadvantaged than many elsewhere. This was because machines, and particularly agricultural vehicles, were relatively little used in Württemberg, although where there was more extensive farming, for example in the wheat fields of Mergentheim district, there were tractors in use before the war. The farmers there and elsewhere, especially in northern and eastern Germany, were reduced to much greater dependence on manual rather than mechanical work during the war. This to some extent depressed both their working conditions and their levels of efficiency to those of the small Württemberg farmer who worked without labour-saving machinery. It therefore had a corresponding effect on their status within their communities. Of greater interest to a larger number of farmers in Württemberg was the shortage of chemical fertilisers, although many continued to use animal dung rather than commercial nitrogen or phosphorus-based fertilisers. Where commercial fertilisers were available, their prices had risen to reflect their scarcity. The productivity of the soil was also affected by shortages of weedkiller, which resulted in vegetable fields being overgrown with weeds.[43]

In spite of the increasing difficulties which they faced, the rural population would probably have been mollified if the prices for their produce had not been controlled but had been allowed to reach their natural level – namely that dictated by the law of supply and demand. This was precisely what the government could not countenance in wartime. Part of the problem was that the interests of urban consumers and rural producers were – as in the First World War – in conflict. This was probably irresolvable. Consumers sought a ready supply of goods, especially foodstuffs, at a moderate price, while producers felt that they were being exploited in time of shortage: if produce was in short supply then prices should rise to reflect that scarcity value, allowing them to recoup some of the losses which they felt they had suffered ever since 1914. Their attitude did not change with the mere passage of wartime emergency measures. While the Württemberg *Gendarmerie* believed that some price rises were due simply to greed, they accepted that others were the result of ignorance on the part of producers. Where the latter was not the case, the problem for the police was that inflated prices were difficult to detect because violating the law 'makes the vendor and the purchaser punishable and so both keep quiet about it'. While the *Gendarmerie* claimed to be trying to enforce the law, its officers complained that the *Schutzpolizei* (*Schupo* – police in the towns) were not as assiduous, leading to resentment on the land that strict controls were apparently being applied in rural areas but not in the towns.[44] This was not a view with which townspeople would have concurred.

Farmers' particular grievance was that, whereas there were strenuous attempts to control the prices of their produce, the cost of other items was allowed to soar. The law of supply and demand, which was not permitted to operate in the interests of food producers, worked against them when it came to other commodities. Work shoes were a case in point. Even when they could be obtained, they were extremely expensive, with rather shoddy wartime work shoes being highly priced for what they were. Farmers reckoned that in late 1941 a pair of shoes was costing them two to three times what it had cost in peacetime.[45] Tobacco products, which in 1941 were not yet rationed, were in unprecedentedly short supply in rural areas, even with women prohibited in wartime from buying them. Village shopkeepers were able to obtain them from wholesalers only in return for ham, butter or eggs.[46] It added insult to injury that consumers complained about the price of items like potatoes, for which farmers felt they received very little but which were ultimately sold at a price that gave traders and retailers a healthy profit.[47] Accordingly, farmers sought a variety of ways of restoring the balance.

For example, the *Gendarmerie* reported that, early in the war, because Bavaria's top prices for poultry were higher than Württemberg's, slaughtered birds from Württemberg were sold to Bavarian retailers instead of being offered for sale at home, exacerbating shortages there.[48] Later, when the Württemberg Prices Authority introduced price controls for berries and soft fruit in the summer of 1941, because of the pressure of demand, producers were outraged because – they claimed, with some justification – their own costs, especially the price of fertiliser, had risen. In Biberach, in south-eastern Württemberg, they gave the time-honoured response of the stubborn peasant, saying that, rather than sell their strawberries at the official price of 35 Pfennigs per half kilo, they would 'cut them down or let them rot on their stems'.[49] The SD expressed the view that farmers would have to be given a better price for their produce, especially easily perishable items, if necessary at the expense of wholesalers and retailers whose margins would have to be reduced. It was clear, said the SD, that permitting higher prices would 'fundamentally change producers' attitude to cultivation overnight, to the benefit of better provision' of fruit and vegetables.[50] Nevertheless, price controls remained in place, as a vital part of the government's domestic strategy. The regime was unswervingly sensitive to the needs and aspirations of the urban population, and therefore it persisted in endeavouring to regulate production and distribution, and to peg prices. Only through price controls, it believed, could a variety of foodstuffs be made available to the widest possible range of 'Aryan' inhabitants and the errors of 1914–18 avoided. Offering incentives to farmers to produce more was not entertained as an option, in spite of lobbying on farmers' behalf by the SD in its reports.[51] Believing that propaganda reinforced by regulation could encourage farmers to produce enough for the nation's needs, the regime set its face against the one concession that would have persuaded farmers to try to achieve this.

It is true that the RNS continued to try to find solutions for a limited range of farming problems. Chief among these were Württemberg agriculture's chronic problems with water: some areas had difficulty in obtaining the water which they required for farming, while others had an excess of it which left waterlogged soil which, again, had adverse effects on agriculture. This had been a source of concern to the authorities even before the war. During the war, the need to maintain and, if possible, enhance the productivity of the land led to a continuation of attempts to drain land that was either boggy or damp enough to encourage weeds and grasses and to obstruct cultivation. For example, in January 1942, at a time when a German victory still seemed assured, an official of the Württemberg LBS outlined an ambitious plan for the draining of 160,000 hectares of waterlogged land in Ellwangen, in the north-east, a project which he described as 'extraordinarily important'. The prevailing condition of the land in the area had had a detrimental effect on the productivity of agriculture there, and the intention was to deploy Labour Service men who were stationed nearby to work on the project – 'as long as ... the unit is not required for special tasks (armed forces)'.[52] The unevenness of much of Württemberg's agricultural land contributed to the problems of excess water. In May 1942, after a lengthy investigation, approval was given, for instance, to a project for upgrading a rough and narrow road, which was approximately one kilometre in length and used by several farmers to gain access to their fields in the vicinity of a commune in Münsingen. Rainfall resulted in the road's being flooded because there was no drainage, rendering it impassible for farm vehicles and draught animals. The project was to widen the road, even it out and lay gravel. The problem with rainfall was to be solved by building a gutter along the length of the road. The costs of this improvement, which was aimed at improving agricultural productivity in the area, were to be borne by the commune.[53] Even as late as 1944, land improvement projects were being designed and approved.[54]

Yet palliative measures for relatively small numbers of people did not alter fundamental attitudes: the wartime controls on the production and distribution of food supplies were resented per se. Beyond that, however, the controls also failed to take account of existing practice. Where there was a conflict between the two, there was extensive violation of the controls. In this war, as in the First World War, scarce items were increasingly available only on the black market at high and sometimes only at 'fantastic' prices. For example, in July 1941, the SD reported that in the southern district of Saulgau geese were being sold at the extortionate price of 60 *Reichsmark* per bird. Consumers who were anxious to obtain a goose for Christmas were, in the preceding summer, paying 20 marks for 'young geese which have scarcely emerged from their eggs', with a further 40 marks to be paid to the farmer on delivery for fattening the birds in the intervening months.[55] By December 1943, as a tobacconist discovered, the price of a goose had risen to 60 marks plus a sizable consignment of cheroots, cigars and cigarettes.[56] While the money was undoubtedly welcome to the farmer, the tobacco products were, in time of acute scarcity, priceless. For those who punctiliously observed the law, the problem was that goods sold at official prices brought the vendor modest sums of money that were inadequate for obtaining black market or other scarce items. As it turned out, most commodities were regarded as valuable by someone, so that, for many people, acquiring and accumulating goods of whatever kind was more of an objective than saving up small amounts of money insufficient to buy black market goods. Hoarding, like its partner in crime bartering, was illegal. Sometimes, no doubt as a result of a tip-off, the authorities sanctioned house searches to ascertain if goods had been bought up and hoarded. One such search, of a Stuttgart doctor's premises, yielded large quantities of both tea and soap, but the doctor was able to prove that she had been buying in bulk at regular intervals and from the same supplier for several years. As a result, she was exonerated.[57]

While in peacetime, at least, most business in the towns was conducted on the basis of a cash economy, bartering assumed even there increasing importance in wartime. In addition, particularly because of the prevalence of part-time farmers in Württemberg, there was already a deeply ingrained tradition of bartering of both goods and services in rural areas and small country towns. Ordinary urban shoppers would buy up goods that were neither perishable nor rationed, such as detergent or glass preserving jars, which they accumulated and then used to obtain foodstuffs either from a retailer or even directly from a farmer, quite illegally. In Ulm, a housewife who boasted that she had 150 preserving jars at home, and intended to buy a further 150, was regarded by the SD as a typical example of someone investing in goods so as to be able to barter with farming families for food. Farmers' wives, who were too busy at harvest time to go shopping, gladly exchanged their produce for items that were hard to obtain. The mayor of a commune in a food-producing area 20 kilometres distant from Stuttgart reported to the SD in 1941 that there had been a great influx into his commune of townspeople, from the capital and even further afield, who bought up everything regardless of the price. This meant that the growers no longer took their produce to market in the towns because it was easier, and more lucrative, to sell to visitors. This kind of trading was often conducted on the basis of barter. In Biberach, a quarter kilo of coffee beans was exchanged for ten pounds of strawberries, a litre of salad oil for cherries, and fabric and shoes from France or other occupied countries were exchanged for fruit and vegetables.[58] It was especially difficult to police rural retailers who bartered with each other. For example, a butcher and a fruiterer might exchange goods rather than sell them to the public for money.[59]

While farmers bartered with traders and individual consumers, they chiefly bartered among themselves. Large numbers of Württembergers were farmers of one kind or another, and, even if their business on the land was not sufficient to provide them with a living, they would still produce enough of certain foodstuffs to meet their own needs, while carrying on a trade or being employed in a concern outside the home. With some items, like eggs or milk, they might produce a surplus beyond their own needs, which they would either sell locally or else exchange for other goods or services.[60] Under the War Economy Decree, however, these practices not only became unlawful but were characterised in official propaganda as being antisocial and unpatriotic as well. For example, in March 1940, a farmer and tradesman from Brenz, in the eastern district of Heidenheim, was prosecuted by the local *Gendarmerie* for having had illegal dealings in eggs. Although his own part-time farm, with around twenty-five hens, produced eggs, he also received them in return for the kitchen utensils in which he traded, as well as for the repairs which he made to local people's cooking pots: 'people pay me with eggs if they don't have any cash', he explained. He even bought surplus eggs from other small producers in order to sell them – at the same price as he had paid, he somewhat disingenuously claimed – to acquaintances who depended on this source of supply. He disposed of the surplus in a variety of ways, selling some and trading others, for example for a shave or a haircut at a barber's shop in Ulm on his weekly visit there to fetch his supplies. On one occasion, he collected eggs from a neighbour in Brenz which he delivered to the neighbour's sister, an innkeeper in Neu-Ulm, for the celebratory meal to be held after her daughter's confirmation. He was adamant that he did not trade in eggs, but rather that he was merely doing a favour for acquaintances, and had been acting in this way for years. He seems to have escaped with a warning, having undertaken to cease these dealings in eggs and in future to deliver his own surplus eggs to the official collecting depot.[61]

If it was hard for people like this part-time farmer to understand that arrangements which they had reached long ago with neighbours and clients, as a matter of mutual convenience, were now illegal and antisocial, it was even harder to persuade them that they should change their ways, although a brush with the forces of law and order undoubtedly acted as an incentive to do so. At the start of the war there was an attempt to educate and persuade both producers and consumers, with warnings issued for first offences. For example, the Milk and Fats Trade Association sent printed notices to nineteen producers in a commune in Horb district with 'a severe warning' that they were in breach of the law, and that, if they continued to fail to deliver to the state depot the amount of milk which was required from them, they would be punished.[62] Yet infringements like failure to send produce to state depots, illegal slaughtering and the unauthorised purchase of rationed goods continued throughout the war. Part of the problem was that the rational approach to monitoring and distributing produce was markedly at odds with the habits of people such as the trader from Brenz, who, while on his travels, delivered his own and others' eggs to acquaintances in different places in what must have seemed to an outsider an extremely haphazard manner, but one which was completely within the logic of his own network of acquaintances and working patterns.

Further, the *modus operandi* of the Nazi dictatorship could sometimes make the administration of the law more complex for those charged with implementing it. The requirements of the War Economy Decree had been clearly set out in the *Reich Law Gazette* in August and September 1939, and a document was prepared by a government official in Stuttgart in December 1939 to clear up 'questions of doubt' about who was responsible for enforcing them.[63] Nevertheless, the early months of the war yielded cases where there was uncertainty about the application of sanctions against perceived miscreants, indicating the disadvantages for enforcers of the National Socialists' ad hoc style of government.[64] In November 1939, the State Prosecutor of the Rottweil District Court asked the Württemberg Food Office for direction in the case of a works' canteen manager who, with the butcher assigned to supply him, had bought illegally slaughtered meat and had colluded with other butchers by supplying them with the canteen's surplus meat, which they then sold to favoured customers without asking for or receiving meat tokens. He had also supplied a private household with forty pounds of meat and twelve pounds of pork fat, again without tokens. The prosecutor was unsure about how to proceed: which precise charges should he bring, and which penalties should he demand? He had already, apparently, proceeded from a misunderstanding of current legislation in dealing with a case of grain purchases which he had judged to be unauthorised, and he now asked for clarification before drawing up charges in this case 'because important regulations are sometimes not published in the *Reich Law Gazette* but are sometimes issued simply by proclamation of an executive order'.[65] Sometimes it was simply too troublesome to apply the letter of the law. In December 1939, the *Landrat* in Rottweil reported that an innkeeper in the commune of Schramberg had appealed against a fine imposed on him for breaching price controls. The Württemberg Prices Authority replied that the extent of the price rise was so small that there was no point in pursuing the innkeeper.[66] With only fifteen gendarmes designated as special officers for maintaining price controls in Württemberg in the early stages of the war, and fewer still as conscription increasingly took its toll, a great many minor violations escaped their scrutiny.[67]

A more intractable case was that of the businessman Matthias Hohner, whose family firm produced accordions in Trossingen. Although he could claim extra supplies of milk for his pregnant wife and small child, to circumvent the rationing of milk he had bought a cow in September 1939 from a local farmer in order to qualify for the privileges of being 'self-sufficient' in milk. On the strength of this, he could claim the yield of up to four litres a day of full cream milk from the cow. But factory director Hohner did not himself look after the cow: he had left it with the farmer from whom he had bought it, to whom he had handed over a plot of the Hohner firm's land for his own use. The farmer also benefited by receiving any milk that the Hohners did not require. With milk one of the earliest commodities to be rationed, and a vital one for the entire population, this matter was taken up by the State Prosecutor of the Rottweil District Court, who once again asked for direction. He was not clear about whether Hohner was actually breaking the criminal law, although he regarded his conduct as 'morally reprehensible'. A senior official of the Württemberg Milk and Fats Trade Association was of the view that Hohner should not be allowed to masquerade as being 'self-sufficient' in milk under these conditions, and that both he and the farmer should face charges. The official was particularly keen to mount a case involving people from Trossingen because, he alleged, the mayor there was permitting – quite illegally – certain families to claim deliveries of milk from designated cowsheds.[68] This was a mayor who had been the choice of the Württemberg Ministry of the Interior in 1934.[69]

Much as the War Economy Decree was designed to apply rational criteria to the control of egg and milk production and distribution, so attempts to control the slaughtering of farm animals were, similarly, based on a rational system for supplying food to the population at large which paid little regard to the rhythms and rituals involved. As early as September 1940, the SD reported that there was likely to be a shortage of 'meat of all kinds in the immediate future. One can already observe this in the case of pork'. Part of the reason for predicted shortages of beef and veal was said to be the need to export meat to the occupied territories, to feed the large numbers of both military and civilian German personnel there. The SD also suspected that local meat shortages might have resulted from butchers making larger quantities of sausage in order to spin out their meat supplies. The SD's main concern, however, was that its intelligence suggested that the incidence of illegal slaughtering was much higher than was generally admitted, and it urged its agents to be vigilant on this score.[70] Yet, however hard the enforcers of the law tried, they could not stamp out this violation of the law that was deemed to be having a damaging effect on the nation's meat supplies.

By far the greatest number of recorded cases of illegal slaughtering in Württemberg involved pigs, while calves, too, were illegally slaughtered in large numbers. Cattle and sheep figured much less prominently.[71] It was probably easy enough for farmers to conceal some of their small animals, for example chickens or rabbits, when an official enumerator was on his rounds, and it was probably fairly easy to kill such small animals surreptitiously. In Oberschopfheim in neighbouring Baden, 'people hid extra chickens. If a cow happened to give birth to twin calves, one would be declared to the authorities and the extra hidden or, more often, hurriedly killed and eaten'.[72] Concealing cattle or pigs was, however, a different proposition. Cows tended to be kept for milk and were therefore not readily slaughtered, although there were also beef cattle on Württemberg's farms. The official enumerators estimated how much milk each cow should yield, and from that they were able to calculate how much milk each farmer should deliver to the state depot, allowing for some to be held back for the farming family's own use. Pigs, however, were kept solely for their meat. Killing and butchering a pig was not something that could be done covertly and in a couple of hours if the maximum advantage were to be gained. It involved a full day's work for a butcher, while the farmer and members of his family, and perhaps also other helpers, worked with him in physically arduous activity to bleed and clean the pig, to remove its head and hooves, and to prepare its innards for conversion into sausage meat or blood sausage. The carcase was hung outside the house during the day and finally butchered into joints of pork, with some cuts being sent to a smokehouse to be converted into bacon or ham.[73] There was not much about the process that could be kept secret, and the wartime bureaucratic paraphernalia compounded that. An official – usually, in a small commune, the mayor – was responsible for issuing certificates of permission to slaughter, and the local meat inspector had to approve the carcase as being fit for human consumption. A record of these decisions had to be kept, normally in a card index in the mayor's office.[74]

In October 1941, following receipt of a circular from the Reich Minister of Food and Agriculture about the need for 'a speedy and thorough investigation and prosecution of illegal slaughtering', the Württemberg Ministry of the Interior instructed government veterinary officers to ensure that meat inspectors reported immediately every case of actual or suspected illegal slaughtering, because instances of the offence had been increasing.[75] The SD, however, had reservations about these officials and instructed its informants that the 'possible implication of vets or meat inspectors [is] of prime importance'.[76] After almost another year the situation had not improved, leading the Reich Minister of Food and Agriculture to send a sternly worded circular pointing out that illegal slaughtering was to be prosecuted through regular court proceedings 'essentially as a crime'. The criminal police was given responsibility for this, and the Land governments were instructed to hold discussions about how to deal with the problem.[77] Nevertheless, there was little sign of satisfaction in the Württemberg Ministry of Economics that a decline in the numbers of illegally slaughtered animals was recorded in 1941–42, compared with 1940–41. The ministry's view was that this was not because the actual incidence of illegal slaughtering had declined, but rather that more cases were going undetected because, on the one hand, there were fewer supervisory officials as a result of conscription and, on the other hand, illegal slaughterers had become more skilful at concealing their offences. The ever declining number of tip-offs from within farming communities was seen as a further cause.[78] Even with a battery of controls in place – to the extent that, in late 1941, there were complaints that 'the economy is drowning in excessive organisation' – illegal slaughtering, bartering and other private arrangements continued among relatives and acquaintances throughout the war, with those involved clearly regarding the risk of being apprehended and becoming liable to prosecution by the state as one worth taking. [79] This suggests that the chances of being discovered were less than high.

The problem with trying to enforce controls on food supplies was that a large proportion of the rural population – the producers – simply did not wish to make them work. Detecting abuses in scattered villages, often with a network of people involved and with local officials sometimes conniving, was a labour intensive activity, and during the war labour was the commodity in shortest supply. Sending the NSDAP's local branch or district leader, or the local RNS official, round farms to make a spot check on numbers of livestock or the volume of milk obtained from a cow might reveal abuse in a few individual cases, but it seems not to have acted as a deterrent to farmers who fundamentally loathed the wartime controls. The resentment felt in the commune of Tomerdingen even after the war was palpable: 'our farmers were enraged by endless requisitioning. Commissions came to check stables, barns and lofts, [and] there was heavy pressure from the Nazis'.[80] It was far from uncommon for farmers deliberately to underestimate the numbers of their livestock when a census was taking place, and then feel free to slaughter animals when they pleased, in excess of their quota which was based on the census return. In a commune in Ehingen district, for example, the official enumerators discovered, in a follow-up check on 10 December 1940, that a substantial number of cattle and pigs had not been declared at the census which had been held a week earlier.

Yet the ensuing police proceedings were inconclusive because the farmers made excuses about having given the wrong numbers of animals: they had had to make the head count in a hurry; new stock had been born in the week since the census; they had not realised that animals which had been put aside to be sold were eligible to be counted. In the end, it was difficult to prove that they had intentionally made false returns. For a start, the matter had not been brought before the state prosecutor until May 1941, by which time the charge of deliberate falsification was hard to sustain. Then there was the fact that most of the enumerators – who were undoubtedly from the same area as the farmers – had not bothered to count the cattle or pigs during the census but had relied on the farmers' own accounting and simply written down the numbers which the farmers had given them. Yet this was entirely in line with the instructions given to the enumerators; the only firm prescription was that a farmer had to permit enumerators to look round their premises. The SD suggested that the only way both to make farmers conform and to avoid prosecutions which were bound to be unsuccessful because of a lack of hard evidence was for enumerators actually to count the animals.[81] This, however, would undoubtedly have slowed down the whole process and therefore made it even less likely that every farm would be thoroughly inspected, especially as conscription continued to take its toll of the relevant officials. As a result, the authorities were uncomfortably dependent on tip-offs from members of the public. While this could mean that a neighbour was responsible for a farmer's being fined or even imprisoned, the resulting penalty would not be on the same catastrophic scale as the starvation suffered in the early 1930s by villagers in the USSR whose hidden grain supplies were confiscated by Soviet officials after a tip-off from a neighbour.[82]

Some farmers went to ingenious lengths to try to circumvent the effects of the animal census. For example, the State Prosecutor in Tübingen reported to the Württemberg Food Office in August 1942 that, after a follow-up inspection, several farmers had been charged with violating the law on animal censuses. They had claimed in their defence that they had obtained extra chickens after the annual census had been held in the previous December, although they had failed to report this either to their mayor's office or to the local food office, as required. The Württemberg Egg Trade Association was of the view that this constituted an offence under the law.[83] A more serious misdemeanour was committed by a farmer in Balingen district, who was arrested in September 1942 on charges which the criminal police said amounted to 'sabotage' of the regulations governing livestock, a particularly serious charge according to SS guidelines which described 'saboteurs' of the war economy as 'enemies of the people and the state' who ought to be punished accordingly.[84] The farmer had delivered 'eggs from his seventy-eight hens (the exact number of the hens in his holding has not been established)' for the first time in March 1942, and he had failed to declare some twenty-five to thirty ducks and eight sheep at the census held in December 1941. Part of the reason for the offences was that he bred silver foxes, which, from the start of the war until July 1942, he had fed with whole milk obtained from three or four cows. The eggs from his hens had also gone to feed the silver fox cubs. The main concern of the police was, however, how this farmer had been able to withhold deliveries of produce for almost three years, and why the appropriate authorities – presumably the mayor, the local RNS official, the relevant trade associations and perhaps also the *Landrat* – had not taken action against him.[85]

Infringements of the economic controls were certainly difficult to police, especially in small localities. The progressively declining numbers of gendarmes was one factor in this, with fewer reports about law-breaking in rural areas from them in the second half of 1941 than previously. The State Prosecutor in Stuttgart attributed this to the progressive withdrawal of gendarmes for deployment in the occupied east. These officers were either replaced by auxiliary policemen, who were inadequate substitutes, or else they were not replaced at all.[86] Even when the police reported a crime or misdemeanour, they tended not to be in a position to investigate cases in detail, which imposed a heavier burden on the diminishing numbers of staff in the prosecutors' offices.[87] In addition, the nature of the economic controls was such that many ordinary members of the public had temptation put in their way. For example, clerical staff, messengers and cleaners were often in a position to steal food ration cards which were stored in the office of a commune's mayor or the district's *Landrat*, and the temptation to do so was clearly hard to resist. Several people in these categories, from all over Württemberg, were jailed for this offence for periods of between six months and three years, but there were undoubtedly more – probably many more – who escaped detection.[88]

Applying wartime regulations was even more difficult when the official responsible for enforcement was himself implicated in their violation. Jurisdiction over ration cards or slaughtering certificates, for example, either permitted officials to abuse the law for their own personal gain or else provided cover for neighbours who were in a position to abuse the system. Few cases were as multifaceted and tortuous as that of the mayor of a commune in Vaihingen district, who was charged with embezzlement, defamation, bribery and the improper use of both an automobile and ration tokens in a variety of ways. In the end, the mayor justified his conduct in some aspects of the case and it proved impossible to sustain the remaining charges. He was, however, charged with bringing his office into disrepute, but let off with a fine of 150 marks because of his 'service over many years as an able and diligent mayor'. How far the charges were justified and how far they resulted from a malicious denunciation by a named official remains a matter for speculation.[89] Mayors from another commune in Vaihingen and from a commune in Tettnang were charged with the unauthorised possession of food ration cards, while a state employee in Freudenstadt was dismissed from his post with full loss of privileges in 1941 because he had utilised food ration cards to which he was not entitled. He had also made special distributions of goods which were unauthorised. The mayor of a commune in Saulgau district was fined 50 marks for permitting illegal slaughtering, while the mayor of another commune in Tettnang was jailed for three years for aiding and abetting black marketeers by falsifying documents.[90]

These last two cases give an indication of why, when concealment was difficult, illegal slaughtering was the offence which quickly loomed large in the state prosecutor's workload. If an official who was meant to regulate slaughtering connived at a breach of the regulations, it was more difficult to enforce the law. During the summer of 1940, the Stuttgart *Sondergericht* (Special Court), which dealt with cases of violation of the War Economy Decree, found that illegal slaughtering was still the main offence involved. By the end of 1941, however, other offences, for example the theft of ration cards from the offices where they were stored, had assumed a high profile. In fact, by the middle of 1942, violations of the War Economy Decree were providing the largest element in the Special Court's caseload. Although in early 1943 cases involving the theft or illegal sale of raw materials and produce of all kinds were 'increasing steadily' and were said to be of great complexity, nevertheless 'the most prominent concern, as always, is illegal slaughtering'.[91] With its staff severely depleted through conscription, the legal profession found itself increasingly unable to cope with the high volume of litigation involved, especially because, as the State Prosecutor in Stuttgart pointed out in May 1943, the cases were 'frequently rather difficult, opaque and complicated'.[92] This was a euphemism for saying that networks of relationships made getting hard evidence difficult and, perhaps, that local officials were reluctant to be seen as punitive agents in their own community, especially in time of hardship. The *Gendarmerie* certainly believed that this was the case. Even in 1939 they complained that mayors were reluctant to see deterrent penalties imposed and urged the police to give more warnings and exhortations, while at the same time regarding police surveillance in their area as unwarranted interference in their own sphere of competence.[93]

Increasingly, especially in view of the mounting casualties on the fighting fronts, consideration was also given to 'compassionate grounds'. For example, in May 1943 a farmer's wife was brought to trial for the illegal slaughtering of a pig whose meat, she claimed, she intended to use to send extra rations to her sons, one of whom was serving on a submarine while the other two were on the eastern front. The butcher who had colluded with her had already lost one son at the front, as well as sons-in-law, and had another son who had been wounded, with a further two sons still at the front. The State Prosecutor was of the view that 'we can by no means discount the accuseds' sacrifices' in judging such a case.[94] But, generally, compassionate grounds merely mitigated a penalty. A butcher's wife in Ludwigsburg was sentenced to two months in prison in January 1943, in spite of the judges' taking into consideration 'the fact that this concerns the wife of a soldier at the front, who, in an effort to maintain her husband's livelihood, took over and conducted his business conscientiously and has probably transgressed only because the task has become too much for her'. With only an apprentice to help her, she had had to pay another butcher to slaughter animals for meat supplies. She had, however, had a pig slaughtered without obtaining permission and without reporting the slaughter, as she was required to do. She had also failed to collect all the ration tokens that were due from her customers, and she apparently had tried to conceal this in the way that she presented the tokens to the district trade office. It was for the latter offences that she was punished; in the case of the slaughtering of the pig, 'it cannot be established that she maliciously endangered the supply of essential food to the population'. Whether the fact that she was a member of both the Nazi women's organisation and the Red Cross told in her favour is not clear.[95] Martin Bormann, replying from the office of the Führer's Deputy, Rudolf Hess, expressed agreement with the Reich Minister of Economics that NSDAP members should not be given preferential treatment if they had committed serious offences. He nevertheless argued that, in the case of a minor misdemeanour, and particularly when it was a first offence, service to the party should be taken into account as a mitigating factor.[96]

If there was some uncertainty about the application of regulations early in the war, by 1942–43 not only were the requirements clear, if sometimes fiendishly complex, but there was also much greater pressure on both agriculture and food supplies. Even then some rural local government or party officials either would not risk unpopularity by trying to enforce the law, or else they were themselves still so enmeshed in their village community that they tended to put that community's interests and habits before their loyalty to the regime. In November 1942, a case involving the illegal slaughtering of pigs in a commune in Rottweil district was heard before the Stuttgart Special Court, sitting in special session in Rottweil, under its president Hermann Cuhorst, a judge whose reputation for National Socialist fanaticism and implacably 'fearsome justice' went before him.[97] Four additional court officials were also present for the case against four individuals, namely three officials – the mayor of the commune, the *Ortsbauernführer* who was also the local meat inspector, and a clerk in the police service – and the mayor's teenage son. The three adult accused came from a farming background. The mayor was by trade a carpenter, but he also possessed a holding of some eight hectares which was partly mortgaged. He had joined the NSDAP in March 1933, when it had seemed opportune to do so, and in May 1938 he had been appointed mayor of the commune with its 900 inhabitants. Early in the war, he had been recalled to the German navy for a brief period, having served in the Imperial German Navy during the First World War. The OBF, who had only recently assumed this role, was himself a farmer with a similar size of holding. Yet he was not an *Erbhofbauer*, although his farm qualified in terms of size and was not mortgaged. He had served as the commune's meat inspector since 1928, having been a decorated soldier in the First World War. He, too, was briefly recalled to service in 1939. He had joined the NSDAP, again opportunely, in May 1933. The police clerk, who had been in his post since 1906, had a dwarf holding and in November 1941 had become the commune's official in charge of weighing animal carcases. He was not a member of either the NSDAP or any of its affiliated groups.

These three officials were entrusted with the task of working together to ensure that the laws relating to slaughtering were upheld. The mayor, for example, was the officer responsible for granting certificates giving permission to slaughter and registering the weight of the slaughtered animals. The three were also in the optimum position to connive at violations of the law, which they did using the services of the mayor's son, who had been a member of the Hitler Youth before being conscripted into the Labour Service, until he was released because he was suffering from dysentery. Under his father's direction, he worked as a clerk at the commune's issue desk for ration cards in the town hall, performing essential tasks such as entering the records of permissions given for slaughtering in the card index. The youth was acquitted of all offences by the court, on the grounds that he was merely a clerk who followed instructions and had no responsibility for the transgressions of the law. He even had his legal costs paid from the public purse. The three adults, however, were found guilty of depriving the wider community of thousands of kilos of meat, and therefore of 'endangering the provision of meat to the population'. They were, said Judge Cuhorst, guilty also of a gross dereliction of duty, given their positions of trust, and they had clearly behaved maliciously. They were well aware of the legal requirements regarding the slaughtering of animals, yet they had permitted the weighing of large numbers of pigs without the head, entirely contrary to official instructions that only an animal's innards should be removed before weighing. This meant that the youth was instructed to enter in the records an artificially low weight, enabling the owner of the pig to hold back an amount of meat equivalent to the weight of the pig's head. The OBF had, as meat inspector, in the period from November 1939 to October 1941, approved illegal weighing in a staggering 227 cases, sometimes allowing the animal to be weighed without other parts, usually its lower limbs, as well as the head. It was estimated that this had resulted in a shortfall of almost 3000 kilos of pork being delivered to the state depot. The police clerk had been responsible for the weighing of animals from 1941 until his arrest in March 1942. He was deemed to have deprived the depot of some 1170 kilos of pork in similar fashion.

The most serious offences had been committed by the mayor, who was in a position of particular trust and responsibility. It was his duty to supervise 'the orderly implementation of the rationing regulations', and he was responsible for the work of the clerk – his son. Yet he had knowingly tolerated the illegal practices of the others, and had himself registered the underestimated weight of pigs in four cases; he had also weighed the carcases of three of his own pigs illegally, gaining an extra 62 kilos of pork for himself. Along with other irregularities which he had committed, all of this was reckoned to have cost the wider community 5080 kilos of pork. All of the offences were, according to the SS guidelines, both serious and intentional, meriting severe punishment.[98] Further, given the alacrity with which Judge Cuhorst pronounced death sentences in the cases over which he presided, including those concerning violations of the War Economy Decree, the accused must have feared the worst.[99] Yet Cuhorst and his two assessors sent the three accused to prison for relatively moderate terms, sentencing the police clerk to ten months, the OBF to eighteen months, and the mayor to two years, with the time spent on remand deducted from these terms. Whether party membership was an issue in this is not clear. Further, the judges added in mitigation that the OBF, in his role as meat inspector, and the police clerk had given years of 'conscientious and punctilious' service. In addition, the commune's records, which had been scrutinised by a higher authority, showed, he said, that the accused had not gained personal advantage from their acts.

Then, in a remarkable demonstration of sensitivity to the circumstances of life in a village community, the judges made two further points. First, they decided that there was no evidence that the accused were motivated by material gain, either for themselves or for the members of their commune who were involved with them in breaking the law, although those involved incontrovertibly acquired for their own use or sale meat to which they were not legally entitled. Rather, said the judges, 'none of them wanted to break with ingrained erroneous practice, in order to avoid conflict and strife with the farmers in their commune'. Secondly, the judges recognised that the accused

> were – in a small community in which everyone knows everything [that happens], and where they are mostly related to each other by ties of blood or marriage – obviously in a difficult position in trying to fulfil their official duties when there was a conflict of interests.[100]

Judge Cuhorst was the son of a distinguished state prosecutor and had attended schools in Stuttgart before studying law.[101] He was not from a rural community, and could hardly have been expected to feel much empathy with the accused. He was an accredited NSDAP public speaker for *Gau* Württemberg-Hohenzollern.[102]

Further, the Special Court whose president he was condemned others to death for apparently similar misdemeanours. In December 1942, a sixty-year-old man was executed in Stuttgart for illegal slaughtering and 'other kinds of trickery'. At the end of February 1943, the Special Court sentenced a butcher in Stuttgart to death for illegal slaughtering and 'other dishonest practices in his business'. His accomplice, a woman innkeeper, was sentenced to ten years in prison. The butcher had, it was said, been repeatedly punished for similar offences. The Rottweil case came a few days after the execution in Stuttgart of several people who had violated the War Economy Decree, including a textiles wholesaler who had bartered textiles for food.[103] In these there may have been aggravating factors which contributed to the harshness of the sentences; alternatively, those convicted may have been victims of arbitrary Nazi 'justice'.[104]

Yet it may simply have been that, in the more public arena of the capital, judges were singlemindedly intent on making an example of miscreants, as the SS and the Reich Ministry of Food and Agriculture demanded.[105] This would certainly add meaning to the term 'capital offence'. In the districts away from Stuttgart, lawbreakers were – if detected – brought to trial and generally punished, but in a much less Draconian manner.

One reason for relative leniency in rural areas was that sometimes an official might intercede on behalf of a farmer or tradesman who had broken the law. In November 1939, an NSDAP *Kreisleiter* (district leader) asked for a sentence for hoarding to be set aside, because the guilty party 'had not been hoarding in a selfish fashion'. The relevant *Landrat*, in petitioning the Württemberg Prices Authority, endorsed this plea for leniency.[106] In January 1940, the *Landrat* in Horb protested to the Württemberg Milk and Fats Trade Association about a threat which the latter had issued to producers in his area who had failed to deliver their required quotas of milk. He did not deny that the law had been infringed, but he took strong objection to the Milk and Fats Trade Association taking his name in vain. It claimed to be issuing the threat on the basis of information received from the *Landrat*, and its threat was that the *Landrat* would impose penalties on those who did not mend their ways. The *Landrat* denied that he had provided the information, pointed out that he did not have the authority to impose penalties under the criminal law, and objected strongly to both the severity and the tone of the warning which, he claimed, would lead to hostility to the authorities 'which, today more than ever, must be avoided'.[107] It was clearly a matter of concern to him that the inhabitants of his district should not feel that he was taking the enforcers' side against them. Again, in May 1940, the SD reported that a café owner in Trossingen was claiming that the mayor there sympathised with his attempts to sell off all of his stock – without necessarily asking for or receiving ration tokens – because he had been called up for military service and would have to close down his business. Certainly, the mayor had been told about the illegal trading – both in a denunciation by a member of the public and in an oral report from a gendarme – but he had taken no steps to prevent the trader from continuing to sell rationed goods without receiving tokens in return. The accused said, under questioning, that the mayor had told him that he should not do this but had added that he, the mayor, could very well see the trader's point of view.[108]

Probably the largest network of those violating the War Economy Decree uncovered in Württemberg was brought before the Special Court in 1942. Once again, Judge Cuhorst presided. The case was a complex one because it involved a Roman Catholic convent in Ehingen district, the *Kloster* Untermarchtal, which included a hospital and educational facilities for training in nursing and home economics. The convent and its associated houses in other parts of Württemberg cared for the sick, including mentally impaired and deaf mute children, as well as wayward young women. In Nazi Germany, these children were likely to be categorised as 'useless eaters' and 'lives unworthy of life', and the young women as 'asocial'.[109] The care of these vulnerable human beings, who were not regarded as worthy of the support and attention of the NSV, was left to the churches and their charitable affiliates. By the early 1940s, however, the churches themselves were under pressure. In Württemberg, by this time many in the Nazi establishment either had repudiated or – like *Gauleiter* Murr – were in the process of repudiating their lifelong Christian affiliations, however nominal they might have been.[110] Those from an Evangelical tradition, as Murr was, were also likely to be at least suspicious of, and possibly actually hostile towards, the Roman Catholic Church. The alacrity with which Murr seized the property and assets of the *Kloster* Untermarchtal in June 1941, when the criminal police informed him that charges were being brought against its leaders for violations of the War Economy Decree, led many both at the time and afterwards to regard the case against the convent as one that had been manufactured as a matter of political and anticlerical expediency.[111] Yet although Murr's response was disproportionate and opportunistic, the complex details of the convent's infringement of the law were uncovered, if belatedly, by the appropriate officials and the case against the convent's leaders was initiated by the criminal police.

Even if this was an exceptional case, its details illuminate facets of life in the Württemberg countryside in wartime. Certainly, the convent had enviable property. It ran its own farm of some 190 hectares with significant numbers of farm animals and 350 white Leghorn hens, as well as some 850 chicks, and it produced a variety of foodstuffs, including milk, butter, eggs, grain and edible oil. The number of its inmates was normally 300, but by the time of the trial it stood at some 800, not least because it had taken in both the sick and the nursing nuns from its related hospital in Stuttgart, which had already been taken over by Himmler's office for resettling ethnic Germans from eastern Europe. The situation was complicated by significant numbers of short-term visitors to the convent, including evacuees from Baden in 1939–40 and nuns who spent limited periods there, either on spiritual retreat or to recover from an illness. The main charge was that, from the very start of rationing, at the end of August 1939, the convent's administrators had claimed an excessive number of ration cards, and that they had been abetted in this by the mayor of Untermarchtal, who was the official responsible for applying to the district food office for ration cards and distributing them within his own commune. This practice had continued even after there had been an official inspection in 1941 and a report about the convent's irregular conduct had been sent to the district food office.

In addition, however, the convent's leaders had claimed, and the mayor had endorsed their claim, that the convent was 'self-sufficient' in certain foodstuffs, particularly eggs. The court's judgement accepted that neither the nuns nor the mayor – and perhaps not even the *Landrat* in Ehingen, under whose jurisdiction the district food office was – had quite understood the singularly complex legislation enacted in 1940 about there being three different classes of 'self-sufficiency', which entitled only those fully eligible to retain their own produce. The court was of the view that only about sixty of the inmates – those actually engaged in agricultural work – could be considered 'self-sufficient', yet not a single egg from the thousands that were estimated to have been laid by the convent's hens had been delivered to the state depot. Further, the medical doctor who worked in the convent's hospital had erroneously designated 160 of the sick as requiring hospital treatment – with the extra rations that that implied – when the appropriate numbers were judged to be barely eighty. Altogether, this meant that in the period up to November 1941 the hospital had received 8000 eggs more than it merited. In addition, before it was seized, the convent's hospital in Stuttgart had received eggs from Untermarchtal, although it was already fully provided with egg tokens by the Stuttgart Food Office. As the investigation into the convent's affairs had proceeded, necessitating an inspection of the commune of Untermarchtal as a whole, it had become clear that none of the producers in the commune of Untermarchtal had surrendered a single egg to the state depot. Nor had the relevant authorities paid any heed to this: the mayor was implicated in the abuse; the local RNS officials had done nothing; and even the Egg Trade Association 'seems not to have noticed that, from a commune that was without any doubt a massive producer, in the course of more than a year no eggs had been delivered'. Instead, the local egg producers had sold their eggs to the convent. One of the nuns claimed that she had asked the mayor his view of this, to which he had replied, erroneously, that, as long as the trade was with local producers and the official price limits were not breached, he could have no objection. The court estimated that the wider public had been deprived of around 90,000 eggs as a result of these dealings.

A similar picture obtained with the convent's milk production. After allowing it to retain amounts for the sixty deemed to be 'self-sufficient' and others such as the eighty people judged to be sick, the law required that the remainder be sent to the state collection depot. Yet only some 30,000 litres out of a total of almost 190,000 litres had been sent in the period between March 1940 and April 1941. Some of the milk that had been held back had been illegally churned into butter. The convent had also continued to buy milk in wartime, using tokens obtained for it from the district food office by the mayor. Once again, there was a complete failure on the part of the local RNS officials, the Milk and Fats Trade Association and the food office in Ehingen to enquire about these matters, although the trade association presumably knew that the convent was the largest milk producer in the district, and the food office must have been aware that it was issuing milk tokens to the mayor for the convent. The mayor's other offences were that he had issued extra tokens for meat to the convent, although it slaughtered its own animals – in this case, apparently completely legally – thus failing to count the convent's own meat supplies towards its entitlement. The mayor had also handed over cheese tokens, which had allowed the convent to buy an extra 400 kilos of cheese to which it was not legally entitled, as well as tokens for *ersatz* coffee, sugar, flour, noodles and rice. Various shopkeepers and traders had, in addition, provided the convent with supplies of these and other items. All of these individuals appeared on the charge sheet.

In total, twenty-eight people were tried for these offences, including seven nuns and the mother superior from the Untermarchtal convent along with the matrons of two related hospitals. The majority of the accused were, however, lay people, including two mayors, several millers, three traders, two farmers, a clerical worker and a maid. The convent's administrators were found guilty both of accepting the illegal tokens from the mayor of Untermarchtal and of bribing him, particularly at festivals such as Christmas and Easter, with goods that were supposed to be controlled. In particular, he had received from them, without making payment, a pig which was looked after and fattened at the convent. The mayor claimed that he had intended to slaughter the pig for a celebration to be held by the Munderkingen NSDAP local branch, of which he was a member, and this was regarded as a mitigating factor. Nevertheless, the mayor's wife had paid for the pig only after the police had begun their enquiries. Even worse, the mayor had received from the convent's administrators the sum of 100 marks towards a holiday excursion, at the very time when he had provided the convent with unauthorised ration cards which allowed it to acquire 15,000 eggs. Yet the judges were prepared to accept that his 'absolutely unbelievable mismanagement' could be partly attributed to the difficulties which he faced, both as a result of the nature of the convent and its shifting population and as a result of the complexity of the legislation, especially that regarding 'self-sufficiency' and the provisioning of the sick. He had not helped himself by, apparently, failing to read the instructions that undoubtedly had arrived in his office, but the judges also recognised that he had no 'assistants of any value' and that the offices which should have been keeping him informed and giving him support had failed to do so.[112]

The mayor of Untermarchtal's defence was that he had genuinely believed that 'the convent in its entirety, that is with all its inmates, qualifies for Category A self-sufficiency', which entitled it to retain all of its produce for its inmates' use. He claimed that this assumption had not been queried when the convent was inspected in March 1941, and that the responsible food office, in Ehingen, 'evidently was not altogether clear about how far the convent's personnel should be treated as Category A self-providers'. The convent's leaders, he said, had not behaved maliciously with regard to the consumption regulations.[113] They certainly claimed this in their defence; they had, they said, 'acted in good faith' and had assumed that the mayor of Untermarchtal and the other authorities involved in applying the consumption regulations were abiding by the letter of the law 'with regard to its details and frequently changing provisions'. Had any of the responsible authorities queried their failure to deliver consignments of produce, they said, they would have complied immediately. The judges described this pleading as disingenuous, given that the three administrators had been responsible for the convent's management for many years and that 'in terms of both experience and intelligence they were superior not only to the mayor but also to the officials and clerks in the relevant authorities'. Further, not only would they have received all the official literature relating to the war economy decree, but, in addition, 'the accused were certainly far better acquainted with the unreliability of this mayor than were the supervisory authorities'. It was 'completely unbelievable' that these nuns and their lay steward, who had a doctorate, had innocently accepted that they could obtain large quantities of food in wartime either using extra tokens issued by the mayor or else without exchanging ration tokens for them at all, while failing, at the same time, to deliver their own produce to the relevant collection depot. The judges regarded it as no defence that the *Kreisbauernführer*, with whom the lay steward claimed to have been in regular contact, 'either had no idea of the prevailing regulations or else disregarded them'.[114]

Nevertheless, as in the Rottweil illegal slaughtering case, Judge Cuhorst and his assessors made a point of investigating the background and character of the accused, and in their sentencing statements they explicitly cited the shortcomings of individual officials and relevant authorities as mitigating factors. They seem to have endeavoured to find reasons for the accused having failed in their duties. In the case of the – by now former – mayor of Untermarchtal, who was 'one of the older party members in Ehingen district' and had brought both party and state into disrepute, they made the unflattering excuse that, even in the less stressful days of peacetime, he was 'hardly suitable' for his post, and that the demands of war had found him entirely wanting: he had, they said, neither the 'iron industriousness' nor the organisational skills to discharge an administrative office independently. The judges added that the detail and constant modifications of the consumption regulations, which were so complex as to be misunderstood 'even by district and *Land* authorities, left him largely helpless'. They recognised that the case of the convent, as both a producer and a consumer with a large and changing population, was extremely complicated, and that the mayor had had no support from the seriously understaffed food office in Ehingen. The mayor could not, said the judges, be entirely exonerated, but these circumstances should clearly mitigate his punishment which had, nevertheless, to be a custodial one. He was sentenced to three years' imprisonment.

In the case of the two nuns who were, with the lay steward, the convent's leading administrators, the judges – contrary to their own earlier pronouncements – regarded the shortcomings of the various responsible offices and officials as a mitigating factor, although not one which fully exonerated them. No official of either the commune or the district or the relevant trade associations, nor even the OBF or KBF, had thought to investigate why no deliveries were being made to collection depots by what was well known to be by far the largest agricultural concern in the entire district, and a very well managed one at that. This was true even when, at least throughout the whole of 1940, it was common currency that in the Ehingen area, and particularly in the commune of Untermarchtal, there was a 'generous attitude' to egg production and distribution, to the extent that not only the convent but also the other egg producers had been able to avoid sending any eggs to the depot. It was hardly surprising, when this went on under the very noses of the relevant authorities, that the convent's administrators assumed that violation of the law was regarded as not being particularly reprehensible. The way in which the mayor was able to issue 600 egg ration cards to the convent without so much as a query from the Ehingen Food Office gave the clear impression that the food office took a relaxed view of the legal prescriptions.

In their readiness to seek mitigating factors, the judges even showed their appreciation of the special circumstances of 'predominantly rural Ehingen' in the first year of the war in which shortages of milk, eggs, flour and other foodstuffs were not as obvious as they had become by the summer of 1941, when the convent's shortcomings were uncovered. In addition, they said, the convent's administrators lived in a relatively closed world and therefore 'did not have the necessary complete understanding of the economic and political requirements of the *Volksgemeinschaft*' or of the damage which their conduct was causing. One of the two nun-administrators had, said the judges, a distinguished record of service in nursing, especially in the First World War, to the detriment of her own health. She was sentenced to eighteen months in prison. Her colleague received a two year sentence. The lay steward was said to be 'of good character and a hardworking and capable farmer'. He had, commented the judges, perhaps been given the impression by the negligent KBF, whom he saw frequently but who 'did not once remind him about deliveries of milk' to the collection depot, 'that even the responsible authorities set little store by the conscientious fulfilment of delivery requirements'. No doubt anxious to protect his own position as steward, he had refrained from taking issue with the two administrators. He was sentenced to ten months in prison.

Six of the accused were acquitted, including four nuns, a clerical assistant and the proprietor of a dairy in Untermarchtal, on the grounds that their involvement in breaking the law had been involuntary and at the behest of others, in particular the mayor of Untermarchtal. For others, the judges found excuses to mitigate their penalty. For example, the mayor of neighbouring Emerkingen, a miller by trade and a party member, was of good character and had served at the front in the First World War. He had illegally appropriated a large amount of grain, but at a time 'when the provision of grain – and especially in the agricultural area of Ehingen – seemed entirely sufficient, and the endangering of the population by such transgressions was therefore not fully appreciated'. By contrast with the mayor of Untermarchtal, this man had shown himself to be a competent honorary mayor. A sentence of four months in prison was felt to be 'sufficient'. Others received short prison sentences or had fines imposed, with mitigation argued in the case of a miller whose business had suffered after he had been conscripted into the armed forces and a woman who, without both experience and assistance, and with great difficulty, had had to take over her husband's retail business when he was called up.[115]

Once again, the judges of the Special Court had shown themselves to be remarkably sensitive to the reality of life on the land, although they nevertheless punished those who had broken the law. Their strictures about the shortcomings of the various supervisory authorities had their effect: a year after the trial, questions were still being asked about their conduct. There was even talk of prosecuting officials of the Ehingen Food Office on the grounds that the mayor of Untermarchtal and his accomplices could not have broken the law so comprehensively if the relevant authorities had been vigilant and had taken their responsibilities more seriously. The *Landrat* in Ehingen, in defence of those within his own jurisdiction, protested that this was a mistaken argument and that the problems had arisen from the complexity of the regulations for provisioning institutions in the early stages of the war economy, adding that even the *Land* inspector had not complained about the convent's arrangements in 1940, while the Ehingen Food Office was under great pressure with an 'entirely insufficient' staff whose members changed frequently, no doubt as a result of conscription. The *Landrat* was successful in defending these officials who were immediately responsible to him. The local government office in Stuttgart and the Economics Ministry agreed that there should be no prosecutions of individual members of staff and that the outcome of the trial should be unaffected by the judges' comments about negligence on the part of local officials.[116]

The case of the Untermarchtal convent was singular in its scale, with massive amounts of produce and large numbers of people involved. It was also particularly newsworthy because it involved a convent at a time when the Roman Catholic Church, particularly, was on the defensive in Nazi Germany. It would be tempting to extrapolate from it and to stress the number of people in authority in the National Socialist system who were implicated in violations of the law. Certainly, as it and other smaller instances mentioned above demonstrate, mayors and a variety of NSDAP local officials and members were to be found either contravening regulations or failing to enforce them, whether through deliberate disregard of them or through negligence which sometimes derived from incompetence. There were also shortcomings on the part of trade associations and local RNS officials who failed to report those who were withholding produce or claiming ration tokens to which they were not entitled. Yet these failings were probably less because of deliberate attempts to cover up transgressions of the law than because the processes and paperwork were tortuous and time consuming, at a time when staff everywhere were being depleted through conscription. The battery of controls and structures for enforcement that the regime had put in place both before and in the early stages of the war were, it turned out, only as effective as those charged with enforcing them were reliable and competent. While the system worked sufficiently well to avoid severe food shortages on the scale of the years 1916–18, there were nevertheless areas where collusion by authorities and either unwillingness or a lack of capability on the part of enforcers undermined its effectiveness.

On the other hand, there were officials who were apparently determined to uphold the law. Some *Landräte* reported cases of fraud to the Economics Ministry, or even imposed fines on miscreants. Yet it is not clear how far these *Landräte* were actively in pursuit of lawbreakers. Much of the time they seem to have been recommending prosecution, asking for guidance or seeking a specific penalty after an individual had been accused of wrongdoing by another official or by a gendarme. The offences were run of the mill examples of the type already discussed: failing to deliver milk to the state depot; providing meat and sausage without receiving ration tokens; slaughtering a calf without permission; buying fruit direct from the grower; or selling eggs from a 'self-sufficient' allocation without receiving ration tokens. The extent to which *Landräte* were protecting their own backs once an offence had been uncovered by a gendarme or a trade association is not clear.[117] In one case, the accused lodged a complaint against the *Landrat* in Waiblingen, who had imposed a fine on him, on the grounds that he was acting as both prosecutor and judge, 'which contradicts any sense of justice', and because the fruit which he was accused of obtaining from the grower had come from his own patch of land. In an appeal to the emotions, he also claimed that his intention was merely to supply the fruit, at his own expense, to 'wounded soldiers and the sick'. The *Landrat*, however, had been acting on information from a gendarme.[118] Had he not proceeded, no doubt the gendarme would have reported the matter to the State Prosecutor, including the *Landrat*'s failure to act against the accused.

Further, *Landräte*, like mayors, sometimes put in a good word for an accused person. In October 1942, a farmer's wife in Heidenheim district was indicted by the State Prosecutor in Ulm because she had erased the name on a holidaymaker's temporary ration card and entered on it the name of the *Pflichtjahr* girl who had been assigned to help her. The *Landrat* in Heidenheim asked the Württemberg Economics Minister if he was entitled to object to the prosecution. It was not clear, he said, that the farmer's wife had known that what she was doing was illegal, and in any case she had not profited in any way that was contrary to the law.[119] In the case of two visitors from Stuttgart to the countryside in May 1942, there seemed to be some doubt about whether the provisions which they had received were obtained legally or not, although they had been seized by the police. The *Landrat* in Nürtingen pointed out that one had received eggs, meat, sausage and butter as a gift from his brother-in-law, a farmer, on the occasion of a family funeral. The other had received eggs to take back to Stuttgart from his wife when he had visited her on the farm where she worked in a permanent capacity. The *Landrat* was of the view that these were not punishable offences, and asked the Württemberg Food Office to inform the police of this, if it shared his view. An official at the food office replied that, while a gift of the other items might have been within the law, this was not the case with eggs, which had either to be used by the 'self-sufficient' producer or else sent to the state depot. He recommended a fine and a warning in both cases. It seems, then, that the *Landrat* had achieved a mitigated penalty, not least in averting the threat of a custodial sentence for these men.[120] Yet it could work the other way: the *Landrat* in Rottweil expressed his disgust when a local pensioner was acquitted in May 1944 of contravening the consumption regulations, although he had been found in possession of a hundred eggs, which relatives had given him in spite of the requirement that all produce be sent to the nearest collecting depot. He was, further, awarded compensation for the eggs, which had been sent to a local hospital so as not to waste them.[121]

Landräte, mayors, RNS officials and others were in a position of influence in rural society, but in time of regimentation and shortage they were also in an exposed position. In 1941, the SD reported that

> the problem of bribery among officials is increasing in wartime. Several cases have come to light of peasants bringing along eggs, sausage and so on in order to have a request expedited or else favourably influenced. Sometimes the intention is disguised, as when a peasant produces a nice piece of bread in the course of a conversation with an official and offers it to him.

This was, apparently, more likely to be the case in urban areas, presumably because officials in rural areas had less difficulty in obtaining food supplies, but it was by no means unknown in the smaller communities.[122] The mayor of Untermarchtal, who was said to have been bribed by the convent's leaders, was evidently far from being an exception.

The issue of bribery on the part of rural producers and traders reinforced an urban prejudice which held that farming communities were inherently selfish and delinquent. In December 1943, an urban geologist wrote disparagingly to the Württemberg Ministry for Agriculture and Food to complain about farmers' deficient 'morals' and 'selfishness', which, he said, he had observed over a period of more than twenty years. In detailing black market activities which he had encountered on the land, he claimed that 'very many farmers are interested only in their own well-being'. They tended not to listen to 'National Socialist propaganda on the radio', yet he had had to upbraid rural innkeepers for tuning in to foreign stations in countries hostile to Germany before this had been banned. In addition, when he had remonstrated with a rural landlord about illegal dealing in wine – in violation of a recently published decree– the landlord had told him, 'get away with your decrees, who bothers themselves with that sort of thing nowadays'. The landlord had tried to justify his conduct by claiming that he could not buy wine at a reasonable price because 'workers with high wages ... were buying wine from the winegrowers at any price'. The geologist's particular complaint was that potato producers were selling potatoes casually and without receiving ration tokens, with the result that retailers, including his own, did not receive from the producers sufficient supplies to meet their customers' ration allowances. As a self-proclaimed staunch National Socialist, he was outraged when one farmer

> told me that the peasants were stupid if they delivered more milk than was absolutely necessary [to official depots] because they didn't receive what they saw as a reasonable price, and they would rather give any extra milk to their labourers, even to Ukrainian farm workers.

The geologist claimed that his main concern was that black market activity on the land was so widespread that it 'endangered the food resources of the entire nation'. What he characterised as the public adulation which farmers received from the *Reichsbauernführer* would, he said, confirm farmers in the view that the highest authorities either did not know about their illegal practices or else were not exercised by them.[123] The geologist's letter was considered as a matter of urgency at a meeting in the relevant office in the Ministry for Agriculture and Food, at which the participants asserted that 'it is not the case that every farmer is a rogue'. The farming population had, they recognised, delivered food supplies 'on the whole in a satisfactory manner'. Nevertheless, the ministry had already been sufficiently exercised about the provision of potatoes that it was taking steps to try to ensure that potatoes which 'had still not been delivered or had gone astray' were collected without delay.[124] There was, then, clearly more than a grain of truth in what the geologist had said. Further, he undoubtedly reflected the views of many townspeople, who felt that the rural population had, once again, as in the First World War, behaved selfishly at their expense.

Yet to rural communities this seemed a one-dimensional attitude. What, after all, had the towns and their inhabitants done for the countryside? Businesses in the towns had attracted labour away from the land. Authorities based in the towns had imposed restrictions on the production and distribution of food supplies, giving strangers an enforceable right to buy farmers' produce in quantities appropriate to their ration allowance and at a fixed price. At the same time, longstanding relationships between private traders in rural areas had been criminalised, with neighbours prohibited from exchanging goods or even buying from each other at prices negotiated between them. For example, a father and son in Aalen district were tried in spring 1944 for a number of offences, including obtaining rationed goods without the necessary tokens from a neighbouring farmer and bartering with other farmers with whom they were acquainted through their box-making business. The farmers had provided the pair with flour, potatoes and a large quantity of eggs, in return for sacks of sawdust from their sawmill.[125] On the land, this was normal conduct; under the War Economy Decree, it was illegal. At the same time, the complaints of some evacuees about the conditions which they had to endure when removed from their home environment and its facilities to the countryside made it clear that living standards in the towns were significantly higher than in many rural areas, while the refusal of many evacuees to lend a hand on farms where they were billeted demonstrated that working for the good of the nation was a one way obligation. None of this disposed the rural population to regard improving the provisioning of the towns as a matter requiring their urgent effort.

Nevertheless, during the war, and particularly by its end, the rural population was incomparably better off than townspeople in the most vital of areas, the supply of food. There were bound to be shortages in wartime in a country which before the war had partly depended on food imports, especially in 1944–45 when Germany's empire was lost and refugees were flooding into the country. The disruption of transportation systems as a result of bombing, along with shortages of fuel for domestic purposes, meant that, even if food was produced, delivering it to consumers was an increasingly difficult, and sometimes a hazardous, exercise. At the end, urban consumers were, give or take ad hoc allotments or 'war gardens', utterly dependent on the severely dwindling supplies of food from rural areas. Yet while the food producers and their neighbours were not in danger of starving, there were serious threats to their livelihood in the later stages of the war. There had by this time been protracted shortages of artificial fertiliser, fodder, working farm animals and, above all, labour. Annual attempts to attract urban volunteers, for example from the NSDAP's women's or youth organisations, to help at harvest time had rarely evoked much response, showing farmers how little consideration urban fellow citizens had for them.[126] All of this, together with the destruction of transportation systems, disrupted supplies to the towns and encouraged many farmers to leave land fallow and to resort simply to subsistence agriculture.[127]

Their ultimate priority was to maintain their businesses as functioning concerns, at however basic a level.

In the last year or so of the war, small rural communes were increasingly likely to be bombed, although many remained immune through to the end. In Steinenbronn, on 16 April 1945, the farmers were busy in the fields planting seed potatoes when the sirens wailed and enemy bombers flew over the commune.[128] There were particular hazards even where fields rather than houses were bombed. For example, in Musberg after the air raid on 15 March 1944, the OBF ordered that pieces of metal from projectiles which had been scattered across the area should be cleared to prevent injury to draught animals.[129] The real and lasting costs of the war in rural areas were summed up in a post-war report from the small commune of Gaggstatt, which had sustained no civilian losses although it suffered 'great material damage' in the last year of the war. More tellingly, its inhabitants had eighteen military casualties to mourn, along with twenty-five who were POWs or 'missing'. Writing three and a half years after the end of the war, the mayor described in heartfelt terms what this had meant for his commune.

> For the fathers who, at the age of seventy or seventy-four, have to pull a plough or wield a hammer in a workshop, and for the mothers and wives who have not seen their sons and husbands for five or six years, the whole commune asks: give us back the prisoners of war![130]

In labour-intensive agriculture, the sacrifice of men in their physical prime was the greatest price farming families could pay.

7

Party and Church

The conduct of the Christian churches in the Third Reich was scarcely edifying. Some have tried to paint a picture of a 'Nazi persecution of the churches' and of church 'resistance' to the Nazi system, and there were certainly individual clerics who risked life and limb in protesting against some of the regime's policies. Indeed, some individual members of the clergy suffered and died in concentration camps for their principles.[1] In addition, some lay Christians asserted themselves to defend not only church rights and traditions but also humane values against an inhuman regime. The churches as institutions, however, had a more chequered history, especially in the case of the Evangelical Church, the church of the majority of Württembergers. The presence within the Evangelical Church nationally of a substantial number of adherents of the Nazi cause, particularly in the self-styled German Christian Faith Movement, did much to discredit the church as a whole, especially when the German Christians were assigned a leading role in the governance of the Evangelical Church nationally in 1933. That church's reputation was only partly salvaged by the formation within it of another group, the Confessing Church, which was a reaction to the attempted Nazification of church doctrine.[2] The role of the Roman Catholic Church, too, has been scrutinised critically, not least because of the charges of collaboration with the Nazi regime which have been levelled against Cardinal Pacelli, who was Papal Nuncio in Munich from 1917–20 and in the Reich from 1920–29, before his election as Pope Pius XII in March 1939. It is perhaps an exaggeration to call him 'Hitler's Pope', yet Eugenio Pacelli seemed excessively anxious not to offend Hitler's regime, with the result that he consistently declined to criticise Nazi aggression and inhumanity. His predecessor, Pius XI, had already given a lead to Catholics everywhere by recognising Hitler's government and concluding a Concordat with it in July 1933.[3]

Nevertheless, the churches were increasingly on the defensive in the Third Reich. In the case of the Catholic Church, memories of Bismarck's *Kulturkampf* (cultural struggle) in Prussia, and to some extent elsewhere, in the 1870s remained raw, while the church's leaders, including popes, were well aware that Catholicism was the religion of only a minority of Germans – a potentially vulnerable minority, they believed. Even so, after 1918 the Catholic Church in Württemberg had been permitted to open houses for male religious orders, including Franciscans, Benedictines and Jesuits. The Evangelical Church had lost in 1918 the privileged position which it had previously held, in the kingdom of Württemberg as well as in Prussia.[4] For both churches, the secularism and, so it seemed from social and cultural manifestations in some urban centres, the licentiousness of the Weimar years had reinforced their feeling of being under threat. Probably nothing had done more to generate fear and sometimes hysteria within the churches than the success of Marxist revolution in Russia in and after 1917, following which attempted revolution in several parts of Germany, including Berlin and Munich, in 1918–19 brought the threat of communism into the country's citadels. The fact that these insurrections had been easily suppressed did little to reassure those terrified by the attempt. Opportunistically playing on the churches' sense of vulnerability in a modernising and unstable world, the NSDAP's leadership had, immediately before 1933, curbed the excesses of its anti-Christian and pagan elements in order to try to conciliate church leaders and their members, at a time when the political left was the perceived enemy of both the churches and Nazism. In addition, emphasising the promise of support for 'positive Christianity' – vague and undefined as that was – made in point 24 of the 1920 programme of the NSDAP, won adherents within the Evangelical Church in particular, some of whom adopted the title 'German Christians'.[5]

Yet from whichever angle it was viewed, the churches and the party were competitors. It was true that both had consistently opposed both 'Bolshevism' in all its perceived forms, from Soviet communism through Social Democracy, and liberalism. Most of the churches' leaders and many of their members were of a conservative disposition in both political and social terms. Further, the churches' leaders in Württemberg, Theophil Wurm, a Heilbronn pastor who had become Evangelical church president in 1929 and *Landesbischof* in 1933, and Joannes Baptista Sproll, Catholic bishop of Rottenburg from 1927, had pledged their loyalty in 1933 to the NSDAP's proclaimed 'national renewal'.[6] This was, however, a statement of political acceptance which did not make the churches partners with the regime in the manner described by a leading Württemberg German Christian, Eberhard Krauss, who in 1934 proclaimed his credo thus: 'Christ and Hitler. Christianity and National Socialism belong indissolubly together. For National Socialism is Christianity in practice ...'[7] This was absurd, and it was completely unacceptable to the vast majority of Christians, clergy and laity alike, who subscribed to the first commandment: 'I am the Lord thy God ... Thou shalt have no other gods before me'. This uncompromising position was, in its turn, scarcely compatible with the kind of loyalty to Hitler required by the Nazi movement. The infamous Nazi judge, Roland Freisler, was much closer to reality when he said to Count von Moltke, at his charade of a trial in the People's Court after the July Plot in 1944, 'Only in one respect are we and Christianity alike; we demand the whole man!'[8] The NSDAP could not accept the all-embracing spiritual demands made of its members by the churches, while the churches could not accept the party's demand for total faith and commitment. In particular, both were anxious to win and hold the allegiance of the nation's youth. This was partly why Schirach's Reich Youth Leadership was so determined to achieve as close to 100 per cent membership as possible: there was to be no room for church influence over the young.

In one sense, this was not so different from the liberal view, dominant in France and Italy in the later nineteenth century and in Portugal and, fleetingly, Spain in the earlier twentieth century. Liberals challenged the authority of the churches and aimed to create a secular society with the churches – and particularly the Catholic Church – confined to matters spiritual.[9] Bismarck's *Kulturkampf* in the 1870s, too, had been geared towards removing the Catholic Church's influence from temporal matters in Prussia.[10] It has even been argued that the Catholic Church suffered a greater degree of harassment during the *Kulturkampf* than it did in the years of the Third Reich up to 1938, although that leaves open the question of how great the harassment was after 1938.[11] Nevertheless, there was a major qualitative difference between the anticlerical campaigns by liberals and an old Prussian conservative, on the one hand, and, on the other hand, the new ideologies of the twentieth century. As in Soviet Russia, so, it came to seem, in Nazi Germany the churches were to be marginalised, kept under surveillance and, eventually, perhaps hounded out of existence.[12] In Germany, however, although there were individual acts of party bullying and mob violence against particular clergymen, only the Jewish faith experienced systematically the kind of crude direct official physical action that was visited on the Orthodox Church in the Soviet Union in the couple of decades after 1917. The burning down of synagogues in the pogrom of November 1938 was the most obvious manifestation of this.

It may be true that some Nazis saw their political allegiance as a means to defend traditional Christian beliefs and moral certainties which were under attack from newer forces in western society, particularly those associated with the political left.[13] For other Nazis, however, Christianity – like Marxian socialism – was a rival ideological faith to be extirpated. Himmler's SS, in particular, was unremitting in its hostility to Christianity and the Christian faith, and to Catholicism in particular.[14] Yet, from Hitler downwards, in the NSDAP there was at least a grudging admiration for the rituals and authority of the churches, especially those of the Catholic Church. The aim of many Nazi activists was, therefore, not to destroy everything that the churches represented, but rather to supplant the churches' ideology and functions with their own, so that the NSDAP local branch leader could assume the role in a community hitherto fulfilled by a priest or pastor. As an Ulm National Socialist explained in 1938, 'in future, then, the local party officer should – as the clergy have done up to now – accompany the people along their journey in life from the cradle to the grave'.[15] In this spirit, the *Kreisleiter* in Balingen-Hechingen ordered that the party should organise the funeral of any deceased active party member, with the local branch leader taking personal control of the event. If the deceased had broken all ties with the church, then the local branch leader could, 'with the necessary sensitivity', try to conduct a secular service. Where a clergyman was also going to be involved, he said, and there was therefore to be a religious service, it was particularly important that the party should have a high profile, and indeed that the local branch leader should conduct the service.[16]

Beyond this kind of hybrid service, the NSDAP tried to introduce its own ceremonies to replace the sacraments and other church rituals. There was, for example, a National Socialist 'naming ceremony' to replace baptism. The reception of fourteen year olds into the Hitler Youth (HJ) and *Bund Deutscher Mädel* (BDM – League of German girls) was intended as a substitute for confirmation or first communion. From the later 1930s, Mergenthaler, the government minister in charge of both education and the churches, attempted to replace religious education in schools with 'ideological instruction'. The Leonberg local branch leader who hoped that his block assemblies would in time be able to fulfil the same purpose as a clergyman's prayer meeting was clearly typical of NSDAP functionaries who believed that 'National Socialism is a religion'.[17]

Initially, it was hardly surprising that church leaders in Germany regarded a party which was resolutely opposed to communism, socialism and liberalism, and which had promised a 'spiritual renewal' after the alleged moral depravity of the Weimar years, as a potential ally, whatever rough and ready ideas and conduct it had manifested before 1933.[18] Yet the Nazi regime's ambition from the outset was to create a total state similar to that which had ostensibly been established in Mussolini's Italy. Fascist Italy was, however, a false model for both the party and the churches. The degree of Fascist party influence in areas dominated by the Catholic Church was much less both than Fascist propaganda asserted and than that to which the NSDAP aspired. The position of the Catholic Church, as the church of the overwhelming majority of Italians, had enabled it to claim freedoms in the 1929 Concordat between Mussolini's regime and the Vatican which would have been tolerated by neither party nor government in Germany. In return, however, Catholic priests in some areas of Italy worked with the Fascist Party. In Treviso, for example, priests publicised and sometimes participated in the activities of the *Massaie Rurale*, the Fascist organisation for rural women.[19] In Germany, only a small minority of Protestant pastors collaborated to that extent, and most of them were German Christians. Even so, the total claim of the Nazi state was underestimated by leading clergymen. When they agreed, in 1933, to refrain from political activities they were undoubtedly thinking narrowly, in terms of party politics. For Nazi leaders who defined 'political' broadly, any churchman who strayed beyond the purely theological in word or deed was potentially interfering in political matters and therefore risking incurring the sanctions invoked by the state for such interference.

On the other hand, the tradition of the Evangelical Church as a state church – the Prussian, Saxon or Württemberg state as opposed to the German state – left it vulnerable to interference by the regime, especially where it was the church of the majority, as it was in Württemberg. The Nazi regime's purpose in promoting a centralised national church was to make state interference still easier. Mounting resistance to Nazi policies was as difficult for an Evangelical Church accustomed to accepting the authority of the state as it was for a Catholic Church whose members feared a new *Kulturkampf*. Nevertheless, Catholics were – and felt themselves to be – more vulnerable. The first response of many Catholics in Württemberg to the *Kristallnacht* pogrom against Jews in November 1938 was: 'when they've finished with the Jews, then it'll be our turn'. As institutions, therefore, the churches in Germany offered as little provocation as possible, perhaps opposing some individual Nazi policies but explicitly challenging neither the regime itself nor those of its policies which did not directly affect church doctrines or interests. For example, Evangelical Church leaders in Württemberg abstained from public comment about the *Kristallnacht* pogrom although, according to the SD, 'the majority of the clergy and also of the Evangelical population disapproved, on the grounds that "the Jews, too, are human beings" and "you can't set fire to places of worship, it's blasphemy"'.[20]

Nevertheless, although they tried to avoid confronting the regime, the churches increasingly waged guerrilla warfare in areas where they felt both that their essential interests had been infringed and that an official policy to which they took exception could be undermined. Self-interested obstruction and an appreciation of the art of the possible therefore defined the limits of their opposition. Crucially, obstruction was more possible for the churches than for other groups, because, while church associations and the churches' press were under severe pressure by the late 1930s, both major denominations nevertheless retained in them assets which other groups had been denied through coordination. They used these to promote their interests and to defend tenaciously the right which they valued above all others: the right to educate the young in the doctrines of their faith.[21]

The NSDAP and, above all, the SS increasingly regarded the churches at least with suspicion and often enough with hostility, casting the Catholic Church, especially, in the role of an opponent.[22] The Nazi regime's problem was that the churches could not simply be dissolved, as the political parties and the trade unions were in the first half of 1933. One reason for this was that, over and above the mass allegiance which the churches enjoyed from substantial sections of the German population, they both – especially the Catholic Church

– had an international dimension. Proceeding against them was necessary for the regime's ambitions, but it was hazardous while Germany was relatively weak internationally, as it was up to 1935–36. This is why the Concordat of July 1933 was a major bonus: effectively, it instructed Catholics everywhere to accept Hitler's government as the legitimate temporal authority in Germany. Having secured that gesture of apparent approval, and with the Evangelical Church in turmoil as a result of the machinations of the German Christians, both government and party attempted piecemeal but progressively to reduce the major churches to the status of powerless sects, and to replace their local rituals and functions with those of the NSDAP. This project was ambitious enough in peacetime in a nation where the majority of the population not only was regarded as being 'Aryan' and 'valuable' but also was overwhelmingly loyal to their denomination. The Nazi regime would make its goals even less attainable by waging a long and terrible war.

In Württemberg, the issues which caused the greatest friction between the Nazi establishment and the churches, including their many adherents in rural areas, were, in peacetime, the treatment of members of the clergy, the onslaught on church associations and the education of the young. The dispute over the removal of the crucifix from school classrooms, which bedevilled relations between the Catholic population and the NSDAP in Bavaria and elsewhere, was barely an issue in Württemberg, although the SD (*Sicherheitsdienst*) expressed concern in December 1940 that crucifixes and religious pictures, 'sometimes up to a metre in height', could still be found in official buildings in Württemberg, including mayors' offices.[23] This does not, however, mean that competition and friction between the party and the churches in Württemberg were of a lesser order. In wartime, particularly, there were important additional areas of conflict between the churches and the regime, including the treatment of foreign workers, the comforting of the bereaved, and the seizure of church property such as convents, seminaries and hospitals, as well as the removal of church bells as, allegedly, a contribution to the war effort. In many ways, however, the most intractable area proved to be the concerted attempt by Mergenthaler's *Kultministerium* to impose 'ideological instruction' on Württemberg's school pupils and to extinguish religious instruction, as part of the Nazi campaign to wrest control of the young from the churches. The most emotive issue was the officially sanctioned 'euthanasia' of people classed as 'lives unworthy of life' at Schloss Grafeneck in 1940, which caused consternation among the many who were aware of it. As we have seen, this was one issue on which leading churchmen took a clear and principled stand.[24]

The agonising question, which to some extent followed from that, was why the churches failed to give a similarly powerful lead on the very evident marginalisation and persecution of German Jews, from 1933 onwards, although some individual members of the clergy were courageous in protecting Jews.

The inescapable conclusion is that, for most church leaders and members, all of the areas of contention between church and state were inextricably associated with their identity as members of a religious denomination. Much as members of small communes had an ingrained attitude of inclusion of the familiar and exclusion of the unfamiliar, those belonging to one church regarded the wellbeing and fate of other people – including the members of other churches or religious sects – as being neither their concern nor their responsibility. For example, south German Catholics could take a compassionate and concerned approach towards Polish prisoners of war and coerced civilian workers. These were co-religionists, while Jews, unless baptised as Catholics, were not. Some individuals and small groups within the Evangelical Church tried to help Jews who were baptised, for example through Provost Gruber's organisation, Church Aid for Jewish Christians.[25] The theological faculty of Tübingen University recognised baptised Jews as their 'brothers in Christ'.[26] Nevertheless, the Evangelical Church's record nationally on baptised Jews – to say nothing of the unbaptised – was, as we have seen, scarcely honorable.[27]

After Hitler's assumption of power, both major denominations were able to continue to operate openly in Württemberg, although they soon found themselves under pressure. The Catholic Church seemed to have won protection with the Reich Concordat of July 1933, yet it remained the more vulnerable of the two, as a minority church – the church of about one Württemberger in three – and as the church to which few diehard Nazis belonged. In 1933, the majority of leading Württemberg Nazis were members of the Evangelical Church, as were thirty-five of the forty-three *Kreisleiter* who admitted to church membership. Only seven *Kreisleiter* were declared Catholics, along with one who had left the church in 1920. Four of these seven left the Catholic Church during the Third Reich, including Eugen Maier, the Ulm *Kreisleiter*, in 1938. The Ehingen *Kreisleiter*, Richard Blankenhorn, was married in a Catholic church in 1936 and claimed, after the war, that he had left the church in 1937 because the party had forced him to do so. Among the district leaders of the Nazi women's organisation, the NSF, most were Evangelical but three – in Ulm, Geislingen and Biberach – were Catholic. Two of the latter eventually left the Catholic Church, in 1940 and 1942, whereas twelve of the thirty declared Evangelicals left their church, the majority between 1936 and 1939, and three in the 1940s.[28]

There can be little doubt that most of the NSDAP's leaders in Württemberg, along with many of the rank and file, were explicitly hostile to Roman Catholicism. The Evangelical Adolf Kölle, *Kreisleiter* in predominantly Catholic Ellwangen (later, Aalen) district, kept Catholic meetings in Aalen town under surveillance and used the local SS to disrupt or prevent them.[29] Murr himself had apparently demonstrated his anti-Catholicism before 1933, and in 1938 he publicly vilified Bishop Sproll for what he claimed was interference in political affairs. His harassment culminated in the expulsion of Sproll from Württemberg.[30] Murr's alacrity in seizing the property of the Untermarchtal convent in 1941 was another example of his vindictiveness towards the Catholic Church.[31] This certainly accorded with his position as an honorary SS officer, as *Gruppenführer* from 1934 and as *Obergruppenführer* from January 1942.[32]

In the Evangelical Church, membership continued until formal notification of resignation was given: members could not simply allow it to lapse. In Württemberg, anyone intending to resign had first to inform the church authorities, and then, after a month had elapsed, make a formal declaration before a registrar. By contrast with some other *Länder*, in Württemberg this had to be done in person, not by letter.[33] In September 1941, the SS leadership in Württemberg instructed members of the security police and the SD that those who regarded themselves as having left the Evangelical church should make the official declaration without delay. They were not, however, permitted to mention that they belonged to the SS because this kind of information had already been used by 'ideological opponents for propaganda purposes'.[34] From the mid-1930s, a pattern had already emerged as leading Württemberg Nazis gave formal notice that they were leaving the church. They included: in 1935, State Secretary Waldmann; in 1937, Georg Stümpfig, head of communal policy in both party and state, SA leader Dietrich von Jagow and *Kreisleiter* Richard Drauz of Heilbronn; and, at some point between 1937 and 1941, the minister for schools and churches, Mergenthaler – whose first name was, inappropriately, Christian – who had by the later 1930s become the scourge of the churches in Württemberg. It was not until 1942 that both *Reichsstatthalter* Murr and the Württemberg Interior Minister, Jonathan Schmid, formally left the Evangelical Church.[35]

Altogether, twenty-four *Kreisleiter* left the Evangelical Church, mostly between 1936 and 1938.[36] Following this trend, Fritz Kiehn, the Trossingen businessman and assiduous Nazi – who had had his daughter, Gretl, confirmed on Hitler's birthday in 1933 – hoped to lead a mass resignation from the Evangelical Church in 1937 when he and his family demonstratively left it, although a portrait of Luther continued to hang in Fritz and Berta Kiehn's bedroom. Yet only twenty-two inhabitants of Trossingen – including the entire Kiehn family and doubtless some of Kiehn's employees – left the church in that year, compared with the customary steady trickle of some three or four. Kiehn's rival Trossingen grandee, Matthias Hohner, remained loyal to the family's tradition of support for the church, and, when a church dignitary visited Trossingen soon after Kiehn's resignation, between five hundred and a thousand people attended a special church service. It was said to be only newcomers to the town, along with members of the party and the formations, who were likely to break their connection with the church. Even so, not all of those with a party affiliation were reliable in this matter: the treasurer of the NSV in Trossingen distributed church leaflets when he made home visits to promote that Nazi organisation.[37] Some people who left the church later returned to it. In the first half of 1936, as many Württembergers rejoined as resigned. It was no 'paradox' that in Berlin, Hamburg, Vienna, Düsseldorf and Essen a larger proportion of the inhabitants left the church than in Thuringia and Württemberg.[38] Church attendance was normally higher in rural areas, whereas significant numbers in the cities were probably only nominal church members by the mid-1930s.

Even high-profile resignations sent mixed messages: leading Nazis were leaving the Evangelical Church, but not in the immediate aftermath of Hitler's assumption of power, and not as a concerted movement. In particular, the most senior Württemberg Nazis, Murr and Mergenthaler, as well as Jonathan Schmid, resigned from the church neither with great haste nor as a group. When Murr and Mergenthaler together attended the memorial service for King George V in Stuttgart's English Church in February 1936, the remarkable thing was not that they were in a church but – given their mutual antipathy – that they were there together.[39] Deputy *Gauleiter* Friedrich Schmidt, who was more committed to 'blood and soil' ideology than most phlegmatic Swabians, still in 1936 belonged to the Evangelical Church and was rare among Württemberg's senior Nazis in later transferring to the category of '*gottgläubig*' (believing in a deity), the designation for those who were not atheist but who equally were attached to no denomination or sect.[40] By 1941, Schmidt had become an outspoken critic of Christianity, accusing the bishops of provocation and ridiculing even the German Christians for accommodating themselves to 'Middle Eastern teachings' that were 'Jewish through and through'.[41] Murr was less extreme, but he, too, appears to have adopted the designation '*gottgläubig*' after he, together with his wife and son, left the church at the beginning of 1942.[42] His resignation from the church may, however, have been a tactical move, after Reich Organisation Leader Robert Ley had pointed out to him the need for 'a clear, unified ideological-political attitude' in the matter of religion, suggesting in addition that this left something to be desired in Murr's *Gau*.[43]

Throughout the Third Reich, many Protestants had little trouble in reconciling church membership with varying degrees of allegiance to the NSDAP. After six years of Nazi rule, the Leonberg local branch NSDAP leader lamented that 'many party members still believe that they can serve both the church and the party'.[44] Yet by this time the hostility inherent in Nazi policies towards the churches was evident. If this had driven several party members and functionaries to leave their church, it had also led some to leave the party. As early as 1933, the Esslingen NSDAP *Kreisleiter*, Friedrich Kustin, resigned his post and in 1934 he left the party, at least partly because he could not reconcile his enduring religious faith with NSDAP membership. For Catholics, the mismatch between church doctrine and Nazi ideology was nothing new, but explicitly anticlerical policies increasingly made it impossible for individuals to subscribe to both. A Catholic former block NSDAP official in Ulm district finally resigned from the party in 1938, and his wife resigned as local branch NSF leader, reportedly 'because she cannot reconcile our *Weltanschauung* with the dogmas of the Catholic Church'.[45]

The Nazis' preferred Christian group, the German Christians, was beset by internecine strife in Württemberg, mainly between what the SD described as 'the more Christian and the more German' tendencies within it. A change of leadership in April 1939 probably sharpened rather than lessened tensions among them: a few weeks later, a number of lay office holders resigned from their posts and left the German Christian church.[46] Thereafter, the German Christians – already a spent force in Württemberg – increasingly resembled a sect. The exception was Friedrichshafen and the surrounding area, which remained a German Christian stronghold throughout the Third Reich, largely because of the activism of a radical pastor who defied instructions from the Evangelical Church authorities in both Württemberg and Bavaria, where he also recruited supporters. Claiming that God had sent Hitler to save Germany, Pastor Karl Steger was repeatedly reprimanded by church leaders, and just as repeatedly vocally supported by parishioners, with over three hundred signing a petition endorsing him in February 1945.[47] Elsewhere in Württemberg the German Christians' continuing existence owed much to the favours granted to them by Murr who was, nevertheless, at pains to cultivate a working relationship with the mainstream Evangelical Church, and with Bishop Wurm in particular, especially in wartime.[48] This does not, however, mean that the atmosphere between the two was cordial. Indeed, a contemporary pun caught the essence of their relationship: 'Murr hat es gewurmt, weil Wurm gemurrt hat' (roughly, 'it rankled with Murr that Wurm grumbled').[49]

Wurm appears as an ambiguous figure. He is regarded by some as being one of the founders of the Confessing Church, yet he accepted the basic tenets of Nazi racism, including those relating to 'hereditary health', and he was at best ambivalent about the roles played by Jews in German society.[50] He was prepared to uphold principles which he regarded as fundamental to Christian teaching, including defence of the Old Testament and, in 1940, opposition to the regime's policy of 'euthanasia'. Nevertheless, he continued to hope that a *modus vivendi* between church and state in Württemberg could be found, even after he had experienced a brief spell of house arrest on manufactured charges of financial irregularities in 1934, as a response to his public opposition to any centralisation of the church. As late as October 1943, Wurm's view – expressed in a letter to the Reich Minister of the Interior – was that much of the friction between the state and the Evangelical Church would be obviated 'if state and party returned to the fundamental principles which the party publicly propounded in the press and in parliament from its founding up to the year 1933'.[51]

This was an optimistic, even a wilful, misreading of Nazism's 'fundamental principles'. By this time Wurm could have been under few illusions, and, indeed, he had already had contact with Moltke's opposition group, the Kreisau Circle, several of whom were executed after the July Plot to kill Hitler in 1944.[52] In his letter of October 1943, he also complained about the arrest and conditions of incarceration of pastor Wilfried Lempp, whose attempts to minister to ethnic German settlers in Württemberg were classed by the regime as 'criminal incitement'.[53] Defending Württemberg pastors who fell foul of the Nazi authorities, as far as he could, gave Wurm a position of considerable authority and enhanced his personal standing among Evangelical Church clergy and members. His speedy release from house arrest in 1934 had owed much to their public protests on his behalf.[54]

The Catholic Church in Württemberg was hamstrung by the absence of Bishop Sproll. The Vatican refused official requests to replace him as Bishop of Rottenburg, but from August 1938 Sproll was obliged to exercise his responsibilities for his diocese from exile in Bavaria. He returned to Rottenburg only on 12 June 1945.[55] Expulsion from his diocese and his *Land* was a fate which befell no other German Catholic bishop, although two Württemberg priests were exiled after a short period of imprisonment and others suffered violence at the hands of local NSDAP thugs.[56] Within Württemberg's Catholic churches, the response to Bishop Sproll's enforced exile was to include a prayer for him in every service, 'as the only weapon that can be utilised at this time'.[57] While the allegiance of Catholic communities in Württemberg to Sproll as their spiritual leader persisted in his absence, this arbitrary and heavy handed treatment of a bishop only increased the mood of defensiveness among Württemberg's Catholics.

Both the strength and the shortcomings of the two major denominations are particularly evident when contrasted with the vulnerability and courage of smaller groups of Christians, who lacked the strong institutional structures which afforded the major denominations some protection, and who were regarded with either indifference or hostility by the clergy of the Catholic and Evangelical churches. It is true that some of the minority free churches and groups classed as 'sects' by the SD succumbed to the clear threat posed by the Nazi regime and toed the racist line: Baptists, Mormons, Methodists and Seventh Day Adventists excluded Jews in order to try to save themselves. The contrasting heroism of Jehovah's Witnesses and Quakers who rejected Nazi militarism and policies of persecution was demonstrated by the numbers of the former, particularly, who were consigned to concentration camps on account of their 'death-defying fanaticism'.[58] Although they were intrinsically harmless, in political terms, Jehovah's Witnesses in Germany, as members of an independent international faith movement, were pursued remorselessly from as early as April 1933, when their essentially peaceful activities were progressively banned in the various *Länder* under the Law for the Protection of the People and the State of 28 February 1933, a law initially directed against communists. Württemberg was the last *Land* to introduce the ban, on 1 February 1934. Particular pressure was exerted on school children who were required daily to give the 'Heil Hitler' greeting and to participate in the ceremony for the raising of the swastika flag. One youth from a Jehovah's Witness family, the Knöllers, in the Württemberg commune of Simmozheim, tried to avoid the flag ceremony by hiding in the school's toilets during it, until he was apprehended by a teacher and forced both to attend and to give the Nazi salute, to his patent distress. Even meeting together for bible study or prayer meetings could earn Jehovah's Witnesses a prison sentence or, worse, 'protective custody' in a concentration camp.[59]

The pressure on the smallest sects intensified in autumn 1938, with the banning of the 'Möttlingen Friends', as the SD reported, 'to the complete surprise of their members'. Others, for example Mormons, warned their members to cooperate fully with the authorities so as not to offer provocation which might result in their being dissolved.[60] This was to little avail, given the determination of the *Gestapo* in Württemberg to eradicate religious sects. Police pressure, however, led to greater cooperation among the various sects, with the result that the *Gestapo* found to their frustration that, when they forced one group to dissolve, its members would promptly join another group. Nevertheless, exemplary *Gestapo* terror against some groups did discourage others from mounting public events such as meetings or missions, although members of the free churches, including Baptists and Methodists, were among those engaged in overt missionary work in Württemberg during summer 1939.[61] Jehovah's Witnesses, however, were especially vulnerable because of their conscientious objection to military service, which brought them into open conflict with the regime after the introduction of conscription in May 1935. In wartime, refusal to serve in the armed forces was treated as desertion, punishable by up to ten years in prison. In fact, many Jehovah's Witnesses, perhaps as many as two hundred and fifty nationally, were executed. Adolf Zanker, a farmer from *Kreis* Göppingen, and Johann Seibold from Ulm were among them. A seventeen year old from Ulm, Jonathan Stark, a conscript in the Labour Service, was consigned by the *Gestapo* to Sachsenhausen concentration camp in 1943 simply for refusing to take the oath of allegiance to Hitler. A year later, aged eighteen, he was hanged.[62]

By contrast with both the vulnerability and the singlemindedness of Jehovah's Witnesses, the two main denominations could, up to a point, defend themselves. Yet church leaders were so blinkered by their fear of the left and of secularism, compounded by their overwhelming preoccupation with maintaining their institutions and structures in the face of mounting Nazi hostility, that they failed to appreciate how strong the churches' position was in a society where a huge majority of the population had a confessional affiliation, and where a

Gauleiter Wilhelm Murr (left) showing Hitler a model of plans for the rebuilding of central Stuttgart, 1 April 1938. (*Hauptstaatsarchiv Stuttgart*)

2. Harvest thanksgiving in Sigmaringen, 1934. In front of the NSDAP functionaries on the speakers' platform are young farm women. (*Sutton Verlag*)

Reich Minister for Food and Agriculture and *Reichsbauernführer* R. Walther Darré (centre, in uniform and bareheaded) in Stuttgart on 22 April 1939 for the Reich Garden Show. To Darré's left is *Gauleiter* Wilhelm Murr. (*Hauptstaatsarchiv Stuttgart*)

4. Children taking part in a religious procession in Sigmaringen in 1936, beneath swastika flags. (*Sutton Verlag*)

Auenstein (Heilbronn district) in spring 1945: ox and horse yoked together. (*Haus der Geschichte Baden-Württemberg*)

6. NSDAP functionaries officiating as a woman has her head shaved as punishment consorting with prisoners of war, Ulm 1940. (*Stadtarchiv Ulm*)

Württemberg Jews crammed into the transit camp at Killesberg, Stuttgart, prior to deportation to eastern Europe in December 1941. (*Stadtarchiv Stuttgart*)

8. Crailsheim, after bombing and the fierce battle for possession of the town, April 19

regime which did not hesitate to use violence against designated 'enemies' sought the consent of most of that majority. It is true that many church associations – including youth groups – were forced to submit to *Gleichschaltung* or to dissolve, that the churches' press was heavily censored and that both churches' public ceremonies and festivals were sometimes restricted to the physical space of church buildings.[63] This was not, however, the rule: from 1934–38, Bishop Sproll held a series of bishop's meetings in Rottenburg attended by as many as ten thousand of the faithful – mostly young people – at which he spoke of the threat posed to the church by National Socialism.[64] The Württemberg Evangelical Church which, unlike most *Land* churches, had maintained its independence from the Reich Church, was still able in November 1938 to launch publicly a week of bible study, and Bishop Wurm was able to celebrate the Luther Festival in the Stuttgart city hall, in the presence of seven or eight thousand people.[65] In the first few months of 1939, the SD reported that the police had counted forty-two Evangelical youth bible study camps in Württemberg which involved 2143 young people. About half of these camps lasted from four to six days, apparently unmolested by the Nazi authorities.[66]

In addition, while *Land* and local church associations were outlawed piecemeal by state authorities, they assumed a hydra-headed character, with new structures springing up to replace the groups which had been banned. In the first three months of 1939, three Catholic *Land* organisations in Württemberg were prohibited, including the Catholic Young Men's Association. This came as no surprise to the diocesan authorities who, after years of *ad hoc* local harassment, had for some time expected a ban on Catholic youth organisations. Accordingly, alternative arrangements had been put in place which had the advantage of restructuring Catholic youth organisations in Württemberg into parish youth groups which were entirely locally based and were therefore better able to withstand encroachment by the HJ at local level.[67] With the outbreak of war in 1939, the churches were said by the SD to be increasing their activity among the young. One Catholic priest organised separate groups for boys and girls which met either in his own home or in parishioners' houses. The members were said mostly to belong to the HJ or BDM, and also to be active members of the German Red Cross. The activities of these organisations provided cover for their illicit meetings for religious purposes. The young people also made excursions on Sunday afternoons to meet similarly inclined youths in the countryside. The SD was of the view that these groups were successors to Catholic youth organisations which had previously been banned.[68]

There were also Evangelical youth groups in existence, in spite of their formally having been absorbed into the HJ. In March 1940, the SD reported that the Young Men's Christian Association still operated leadership training courses, whose members made visits to the homes of teenagers, liaised with their parents, and held bible study groups and holiday camps. The SD was anxious to learn more about this association's sporting activities and film and theatre performances, as well as about the extent to which it had infiltrated both the Labour Service and the German Labour Front. In particular, it was anxious to know how far HJ leaders were involved in it.[69] The SD concluded that, in order to discover the extent of participation by HJ members and leaders in religious activities, it would have to plant surveillance cells within local HJ groups. It was regarded as a priority that the local HJ groups, including their leaders, should not be made aware of this, because otherwise the success of those charged with surveillance of confessional associations and more informal religious groups would undoubtedly be vitiated.[70] Certainly, in areas where church affiliation was particularly strong, local HJ groups often accommodated themselves to the sympathies and susceptibilities of the communes in which they operated. This had worked well enough in the Catholic commune of Schnürpflingen for as long as a local youth had been the HJ leader. In wartime, however, the HJ branch there withered, with very poor attendance and overt local hostility to an HJ leader from a neighbouring commune who tried to round up boys at the end of a church service in order to hold an HJ meeting on a Sunday evening. Even the NSDAP local branch leader in Schnürpflingen took the part of the local population against this overbearing youth.[71]

Above all, the churches had a major asset in a system that permitted virtually no other non-Nazi organisation to function publicly: they were able to hold weekly meetings, in the form of church services. Groups of citizens of a district or a commune were, therefore, able to meet together on a regular basis for a purpose that – in the overwhelming majority of cases – had no input from the only party that was permitted in the Nazi state. Even if these services were under party or police surveillance, they still occurred on a regular basis, both before and during the war, for as long as bombing permitted. In most small communes, this meant throughout the war. The clergy were therefore able, if they were so minded, to instruct their congregations to participate in or to abstain from activities prescribed by the authorities of party or state, although some felt the full force of Nazi brutality for encouraging dissent.[72] For this reason, clergy and congregations in different districts, and even in different communes within the same district, frequently reacted to events and policies in the Third Reich in an essentially local manner, making it more difficult for the regime to confront 'the churches' as monolithic entities.

At the same time, some NSDAP functionaries were rabidly anti-Christian or, more specifically, anti-Catholic, while others regarded Protestants, but not Catholics, as potential allies. For example, *Kreisleiter* Kölle in Ellwangen put severe pressure on public servants who were Catholics to leave the church, on pain of dismissal from employment, whereas *Kreisleiter* Eugen Maier in Ulm personally recommended an Evangelical pastor for NSDAP membership. In 1936, the Waiblingen *Kreisleiter*, Gustav Dickert, urged the *Gestapo* to act against Alois Dangelmaier, priest in the commune of Öffingen, because, he alleged, the priest was telling lies whose effect was that 'those who are Catholic through and through have greater faith in this priest than in our people'.[73] Dangelmaier had in 1934 been consigned to the concentration camp at Kuhberg for several months for holding a requiem mass in Metzingen in Ulm district, his previous parish, for six communists who had been executed in Cologne. In 1937 he was deprived of the right to teach religious instruction.[74]

Most communes in *Gau* Württemberg-Hohenzollern were either overwhelmingly Evangelical or almost entirely Catholic, although some, such as Gundelsheim in Heilbronn district, like Metzingen, had churches for each of the two main denominations.[75] Some districts were overwhelmingly Evangelical, for example Gerabronn and Öhringen in the north, Freudenstadt and Calw in the west, and Nürtingen in central Württemberg, while most of southern Württemberg, as well as the Hohenzollern provinces of Sigmaringen and Hechingen, were almost exclusively Catholic. There were also mixed areas, such as Mergentheim and Künzelsau in the north and Münsingen, Ulm, Blaubeuren and Göppingen in east central Württemberg. Rottenburg, where the Catholic episcopal see had its seat, was about 60 per cent Catholic.[76] Protestant and Catholic communes frequently coexisted in the same district, as a legacy of the religious settlement of the Peace of Augsburg of 1555 which was modified by the Treaty of Westphalia at the end of the Thirty Years War in 1648. Whereas pre-Napoleonic Württemberg had been largely Protestant, the additional lands acquired after the dissolution of the Holy Roman Empire in 1806 had significant Catholic populations. Yet even there the patchwork effect obtained: for example, of two neighbouring villages in the Hohenlohe, before 1945 one was 100 per cent Catholic and the other was, with the exception of one long established farming family, entirely Evangelical.[77]

By the late 1930s, it was evident that the old allegiances remained remarkably persistent, in both town and country, in spite of the various pressures applied by party and state. The SD in Württemberg reported in July 1939 that, while participation in major Catholic festivals – Trinity Sunday and the Corpus Christi procession, for example – had 'slightly declined' in the towns, in comparison with the previous year, in rural areas the entire Catholic population participated, 'as usual'.[78] This was to be expected: in rural communities, particularly, the church had long been an important focus of loyalty, and the physical premises of the church's buildings were a social as well as a devotional space. Furthermore, local priests and pastors worked hard to maintain their parishioners' loyalty and to win the trust of newcomers to a commune. In July 1938, the *Gau* leadership described how, soon after arriving, newcomers were visited at home by the local clergyman and invited to social events, before the party had a chance to welcome them: 'When the party shows its concern, after attention from the church which is usually very productive, it is often too late, and extraordinary efforts are required to bring back into the German *Volksgemeinschaft* citizens in thrall to the church.' The Catholic Church was particularly effective in ensuring that those who moved from one location to another were put in touch with both the priest and devout parishioners in their new home.[79]

While this arrangement worked well with rural dwellers who moved from one small commune to another, those who uprooted themselves to settle in a town might join the congregation of an urban church, not least to enjoy a sense of fellowship in an alien environment. In Württemberg, they would find lively and committed congregations of both main denominations in the towns, including Stuttgart, Heilbronn and Tübingen. On the other hand, migrants might lose altogether their affiliation to any particular parish church – not least if they moved around in search of a particular line of work – while continuing to identify themselves generically as 'Catholic' or 'Evangelical'. Württembergers who remained in the countryside generally retained their attachment to their local church and its priest or pastor, in a fellowship which did much to define and reinforce the communal nature of their relationships. The result was that, while the advance of secularism had had some impact in the towns, especially after the First World War, this was barely perceptible in many small communes. There, in particular, the churches continued to enjoy devotion and loyalty of the kind that, for the most part and beyond a hard core of fanatics, the NSDAP could only dream about. In addition, the kind of pressure that could be exerted on those in public employment to conform by breaking with their church applied overwhelmingly to townees, with perhaps only the mayor and the school teacher vulnerable in small communes.[80] Local party organisations might try to emulate the churches' ability to provide a welcoming environment for existing and new parishioners alike, but their most assiduous efforts could be quickly undermined if unpopular policies were imposed on communities, especially if these policies adversely affected the churches.

The regime kept both the churches and the smaller sects under close surveillance. For example, in January 1939 the Leonberg NSDAP *Kreisleiter*, following a directive from Hess's office, instructed all of his local branch leaders to report on the number and location of new church buildings which had been erected since July 1937, and on any plans that existed for new church buildings.[81] Leonberg was a problematic district for the party because it was home to a number of free churches and sects as well as to both major denominations. In June 1938, after the Methodists had celebrated their bicentenary in Leonberg, the NSDAP district propaganda leader wrote to the Leonberg local branch leader asking for details about the propaganda, events, participants, representatives from foreign

Methodist groups and preachers involved in the celebrations. He was also anxious to know whether local communes or associations had provided support for them.[82] Methodists and sects were particularly strong in Gebersheim commune, Jonathan Schmid's birthplace and the cell regarded as the 'problem child' within the Leonberg NSDAP local branch's organisation. The local branch leader was particularly concerned about the consistently high levels of attendance – of men and women, young and old – achieved by revivalist meetings there and elsewhere in Leonberg in December 1938, not least because attendance by non-members at party events was derisory by comparison. His alternative strategy, the block assembly, did attract some of 'the devout' after a personal invitation had been issued. This enabled the party, he believed, to demonstrate that it – rather than a pastor or priest – could provide a sympathetic ear for their concerns.[83]

The Nürtingen *Kreisleiter*, too, regarded party functions as a substitute for those of the church. In June 1939 he instructed all of his local branches to hold a summer solstice festival, taking care to propagate it as a party event. All NSDAP members were to participate, while the party's formations were to assume a high profile in the celebrations. Nevertheless, while the festival was to follow the guidelines laid down at Reich level, its character was 'to correspond with local circumstances'. Completely without irony, the *Kreisleiter* stressed that the summer solstice festival was to be organised with the greatest care, 'so that it becomes a religious experience'. Winning over the mass of the people to the party's alternative ideology was a major preoccupation. In Nürtingen district, the first priority was to detach party members from the church, before trying to wean non-members away. This meant instructing NSDAP members who were parents that they should 'no longer allow their children to be educated by ideological foes' and that they should therefore withdraw their children from religious instruction in the schools. The *Kreisleiter* summoned all Nürtingen party functionaries and the leaders of party formations to a training course on 25 July 1939 to learn about how to proceed in this matter.[84]

There was not always, however, a clear distinction between those whose first allegiance was to the party and those whose was to the church. In the Leonberg local branch, a Methodist preacher had served as party organisation leader until the local branch leader became convinced that 'he had done absolutely and completely nothing' for the party while always having time for his religious activities, which included proselytising among his colleagues in the bank where he worked. The mayor of Gebersheim, too, was a Methodist lay preacher, an activity to which, according to the local branch leader, he devoted much time and energy while making little effort to promote National Socialist policies.[85] On the other hand, the local branch leader was content that the Evangelical church choir in Leonberg was in reliable hands because its leader was a party member. He judged that the choir was 'overwhelmingly unpolitical and exists only for its true purpose, the singing of church songs'.[86] The local branch leader was of the opinion that many party members who continued to send their children for religious instruction and had them confirmed in the church would not do so if the party provided ideological instruction and attractive rituals. It seems, then, that Nazi ceremonies such as name giving and the initiation of youth – introduced to replace Christian baptism and confirmation or first communion – had not been adopted in outlying areas, and that Christian rituals remained, for some perhaps *faute de mieux*, the norm for Württembergers whether or not they were party members.[87]

Both major churches in Württemberg were in a strong position in small towns and villages where the rhythms of communal life had long been determined by the distinctive rituals of the sacraments and Sunday services. The Evangelical Church enjoyed strong support in Württemberg, where its Pietist heritage meant that scriptural texts took precedence over institutional forms and rules. Nevertheless, its structures and communities were both more permeable and more reconcilable with National Socialism than were those of the Catholic Church. Indeed, the introverted, ingrained and constantly reinforced character of the Catholic sub-culture remained a force in some communities until at least the 1970s.[88] Strongly Catholic communes, in particular, were naturally hostile to external influences, which made Nazification at least difficult and at times impossible. When the Catholic priest in Erbach, in Ulm district, refused in 1940 to marry a soldier home on leave to the daughter of an NSDAP block leader, he was clearly indicating his – and possibly also his commune's – perception that the NSDAP was a foreign body whose officers could not expect to enjoy the benefits of belonging to the community. An Evangelical pastor, too, might remain the chief figure of authority in a commune. This was the case in Neenstetten, where not only could the party itself make little headway but, in addition, the local branch leader complained that he was treated like an outcast.[89] In some places, then, something similar to the Nazis' policy of excluding alleged 'aliens' from their 'ethnic people's community' was used against party functionaries when they tried to subvert and dominate communities which long predated the party's emergence.

SD reports in the 1930s and 1940s regularly demonstrate the difficulties which the NSDAP had in replacing Catholic rituals, festivals and allegiances with their own. In summer 1939, for example, the celebration of the solstice was said to have been better attended than previously, especially in Evangelical communes, whereas in most Catholic villages the festivities had been muted, with the SS and the Hitler Youth the main participants, while in other Catholic villages the ceremony was said to have been 'sabotaged'. The events mounted by the Labour Front's 'Strength through Joy' leisure project encountered similar obstacles. Trying to recreate traditional customs and costumes – and sometimes inventing traditions – they were faced with opposition from groups or communities which had long nurtured local traditions: 'the folklore groups insist on their good old traditions and reject anything new and any kind of influence', reported the SD. It was possible for the party to play the leading role in major festivals such as the National Garden Show in Stuttgart, but, by contrast, the annual meeting of the traditional Württemberg militias was heavily dominated by the militias' close links with the Catholic Church. The SD complained that, during the militias' rally, some individual militia groups went to church two or three times while much of the rest of the time was taken up with drinking sessions.[90]

If many adults were regarded as incorrigible, the party hoped for more success with the young. Yet here, too, it faced difficulties at local level. In July 1939, the SD reported that confessional youth organisations were 'now very active again, especially in Catholic areas'. In some places, the strength of Catholic youth groups meant that the HJ could not function effectively, and in Söflingen, in Ulm district, the Catholic youth group had actually attacked the local HJ. In other places, Catholic groups were so strong that the HJ had simply given up trying to function in them.[91] In Evangelical Leonberg, it seemed that little could be done to ensure that HJ members did their duty. When they were summoned to sing at the Nazified Christmas service in 1938, only one HJ member and three BDM members attended. One Evangelical pastor in Leonberg was said to have particular success in attracting boys from the HJ to his small bible study groups. The local HJ leaders left him unmolested, saying that there was nothing they could do about it because they 'couldn't offer the young anything better'.[92]

Removing young men from their local communities was one way of breaking their ties to their church. With the introduction of compulsory military service and Labour Service for young men in 1935, the churches became concerned about losing the allegiance of young men who were conscripted. The army's traditional *Land*-based military units had been replaced by a truly national *Wehrmacht*, making contact between the churches in Württemberg and their conscripted parishioners less straightforward.[93] The Catholic Church in Württemberg instituted a system of lay liaison officers who contacted individual conscripts before and after their period of service in order to keep them in touch with the clergy.[94] This, however, was a preoccupation of the party as well as of the churches, and it mirrored the concern expressed by the SD about the way in which young men lost their connection with Nazi organisations through conscription into the *Wehrmacht* and Labour Service, leaving the HJ on enlistment but not returning to membership of the NSDAP or any of its formations after the completion of their period of service.[95] In some cases at least, young men whose experience of military service and Labour Service broadened their horizons welcomed the opportunity to break with the stifling conformity of either their church affiliation or the HJ – or perhaps both. Nevertheless, in wartime, with huge numbers of young men conscripted, both churches endeavoured to maintain contact with them by conducting postal correspondence with their parishioners who were in the *Wehrmacht* and by ingeniously 'smuggling church propaganda material' in packages containing Nazi propaganda which were routinely sent to the front.[96]

By 1939, the churches in Württemberg had experienced the full force of Nazi anticlericalism. One reason for this was the position of the Minister President, Mergenthaler as, in addition, *Kultminister*, the minister in charge of both education and church affairs. From 1933, Mergenthaler unleashed a barrage of policies directed at Nazifying education at all levels. Central to this was the deconfessionalisation of Württemberg's state elementary schools, which had been organised on denominational lines since 1909. In keeping with Nazi policy at national level, in August 1935 Mergenthaler introduced the so-called community school, as a non-denominational alternative to confessional elementary schools. Invoking the support of NSDAP *Kreisleiter*, the NSDAP's formations, the heads of schools and mayors of communes, and threatening reprisals against those who obstructed his will, Mergenthaler forced through his reform at speed, with the result that by autumn 1936 few denominational state schools remained, and these were finally replaced by community schools in June 1937.[97] While Mergenthaler embraced this policy with fanatical zeal, it was enforced not only in Württemberg but throughout Germany, with similar results in Bavaria, for example.[98] There remained relatively small numbers of private confessional schools, many of which were run by Catholic religious orders. These were permitted to survive where no alternative provision was available. While in practice this meant that significant numbers of Catholic schools remained in the Bavarian countryside, Mergenthaler's zeal ensured that few private church schools remained in rural Württemberg.[99] In July 1939, the SD reported that almost all confessional and convent schools had been abolished or turned into non-denominational schools.[100]

The deconfessionalising of the schools was imposed with the use of force, threats and blandishments. While the Catholic Church in Württemberg protested about the policy and its implementation, the Evangelical Church authorities quickly succumbed to Mergenthaler's pressure, not least because Württemberg's parents were promised, by the minister as well as by Goebbels, that secularising the schools did not mean the end of religious instruction in them.[101] On the contrary, promised Nazi authorities, religious instruction would be maintained in the new community schools. This was a pledge made to be broken, and soon there was pressure on the clergy to conform by using for instruction only a version of the bible which was acceptable to the regime. In particular, the Nazi authorities were not prepared to allow young people to study material which conflicted with the 'moral feelings of the Germanic people'. This was a clear reference to the Old

Testament.[102] Whereas the churches had ultimately accepted the secularisation of the schools – long a liberal objective – they fought a sustained battle on the issue of religious instruction, a battle which epitomised their attitudes and their tactics. The education of the young in the Christian faith was an issue of such fundamental importance to both churches that they invested in it their major effort of protest against and obstruction of Nazi policies. Nothing mattered more to them than the future of the faith.

The first blow was struck by a Reich law of 1 July 1937 requiring members of the clergy teaching religious instruction in schools to pledge allegiance to the regime. The refusal of some 200 Catholic and 900 Evangelical clergy to do so led in 1937–38 to their being banned from teaching in schools. Lay teachers were enlisted to give religious instruction in their place, leading some clergymen to encourage parents to withdraw their children from these classes and to attend only instruction given out of school hours by members of the clergy. Mergenthaler quickly retaliated by introducing classes in 'Weltanschauungsunterricht' (WAU – 'ideological instruction'), for those who had been withdrawn from religious instruction. The churches protested about this, and the Catholic Church put parents under redoubled pressure by threatening to excommunicate all parents who submitted their children to WAU. There was also the threat of denying such parents a Christian burial.[103] While this undoubtedly had an effect, the slow progress of WAU was especially due to the shortage of teachers who were competent to teach it.[104] By the end of 1938 some 10,000 pupils – out of an elementary school population of around 300,000 – attended classes in WAU. A new offensive was planned for 1939, with the aim of running courses in all schools. Preparation for this had included the training of more teachers in WAU.[105] It was, however, a tall order: the SD reported in April 1939 that opposition to WAU was becoming ever stronger, especially in rural areas.[106]

By July 1939 this issue had galvanised the Catholic Church throughout Württemberg as no other had and probably as no other would. The clergy held additional prayer meetings, while Catholic mothercare courses, the confessional and pamphlets were all used as means of impressing on the Catholic population the need to resist state pressure to enforce attendance at WAU classes. The church's publications, often in the form of calendars, were regarded by the SD as being vehicles for purveying perverted accounts of National Socialist ideas and values.[107] Occasions such as the celebration of first communion and confirmation were also used to promote the church's position, while the clergy visited homes personally to ensure that all parents were apprised of the need to send their children to the church's religious instruction classes. The SD's view was that the Catholic clergy were using the issue 'increasingly to undermine Catholic people's trust in the party's leadership'.

It appeared to work: in July 1939, the SD reported that it had been impossible to introduce WAU in the elementary schools of two overwhelmingly Catholic districts of Württemberg. At the same time, when teachers at a senior school in the Catholic district of Ehingen demanded that forty HJ leaders withdraw from religious instruction and enrol in WAU, only five complied. When pressure was put on the dissidents, their parents told them to resign from their HJ offices.[108] The Nazi women's organisation was enlisted to collaborate with the SD in monitoring the churches' influence on women, not least because mothers were particular targets for Catholic persuasion.[109] In August 1940, the SD reported that the Catholic welfare organisation, *Caritas*, had recently been very active in recruiting mothers and their children for holidays in spiritual retreats and Catholic hostels. Ostensibly, these visits of between two and four weeks were intended for rest and recreation, but the SD was in no doubt that the spiritual guidance provided amounted to propaganda which was at least potentially of an anti-regime character.[110] Although the SD took the view that the Catholic Church was relatively restrained in its opposition to WAU, attributing this to the absence of 'the aggressive Bishop Sproll', the Catholic clergy was highly successful in persuading parents to resist the demand for their children's attendance at WAU classes. They waged an effective campaign at local level and through individual contact, consciously avoiding a public confrontation with the regime at district or *Land* level.

The Evangelical Church's leadership had fewer inhibitions, conducting a high-profile campaign against WAU. The Württemberg church council announced that it would accept classes in education for citizenship, but it could not accept the indoctrination of children with 'antichristian teaching' and the introduction of a Germanic faith religion. A senior member of the Württemberg church council, Reinhold Sautter, was particularly active in holding large assemblies on the theme of 'religious instruction or ideological instruction?' in a manner regarded by the SD as 'detrimental' to the image of party and state. Eventually, in August 1944, Sautter was imprisoned for his outspoken opposition to WAU. Wurm, too, addressed meetings, emphasising the importance of the religious education of the young for the survival of the church. In addition, parents' evenings were held in almost all Evangelical communes, at which the church's message was 'ideological instruction is anti-church, anti-Christian and contrary to the teachings of the bible'. The Evangelical Church appealed not only to its most assiduous members but also to those whose attachment to a church was tenuous, arguing that there was no proper legal basis for the compulsory introduction of ideological instruction and that this move was not regarded favourably by the highest offices of party and state.[111]

If the Reich government had misgivings about the attempt to enforce WAU on Württemberg's youth, it was less because it was out of sympathy with the objective than because it could see tactical disadvantages in it. One official at the

Reich Chancellery commented: 'To choose Württemberg as a field of experiment would seem to be particularly unsuitable, since it has the most active Evangelical Church life, an awake populace and a forceful bishop.'[112] Officers of both party and state, in other *Länder* and centrally, abstained from following this example whose major effect was to alienate both parents and clergy from the regime in Stuttgart. Even *Reichsstatthalter* Murr predicted that forcing the issue would antagonise the population and cause unrest.[113] In September 1939 he issued an order stipulating that WAU could be introduced only 'if there is a particular demand for it (a desire on the part of a majority of parents)'. He added that the churches should not put pressure on those who opted for WAU to renounce it in favour of religious instruction, and that the state should allow pupils a genuinely free choice between WAU and religious instruction. Reich Education Minister Rust approved this arrangement.[114] Hitler's view, echoed by Hess, was that in wartime there should be no acceleration of radical policies in an area that was relatively peripheral.[115]

The stubborn Mergenthaler was, however, not to be deflected, and continued to pursue his campaign for the eradication of religious instruction and the implementation of compulsory WAU. Whereas for both Bavarian Nazis and the Catholic Church in Bavaria the issue of removing the crucifix from classrooms was the defining trial of strength between them, for Mergenthaler, NSDAP radicals and the two main denominations in Württemberg the battle for school children's hearts and minds fulfilled a similar function. On 23 May 1940, the *Kultminister* issued a ban on religious instruction during school hours, which were, in his view, from 7.30 to 12 noon and 1.30 to 6pm, with some of the afternoons reserved for HJ activities. If this made it difficult for the clergy to hold classes in religious instruction on weekdays, Mergenthaler closed a potential loophole by adding that, allegedly on health grounds, children were not permitted to attend religious instruction classes before regular school work began. This attempt to eradicate religious instruction for the young altogether caused alarm beyond Württemberg, with Bishop Bernings of Osnabrück protesting to the government in Stuttgart about it.[116]

Murr's failed attempts to moderate Mergenthaler's policies clearly demonstrated the weakness of the former and the obduracy of the latter.[117] There was a clear division of opinion within the Württemberg NSDAP, with conservatives such as Murr and Jonathan Schmid, the interior minister, confronting Mergenthaler and the district and local party activists. In February 1940, Murr and Schmid agreed that the churches could use appropriate accommodation, such as classrooms, on an *ad hoc* basis and under stringent conditions, because they had had to surrender meeting rooms for wartime purposes. This was said to be causing problems for the religious life of smaller communes.[118] This attempt to appear conciliatory was in line with the Berlin government's posture. In July 1940, Rust pronounced that not only should there be no school classes on the days of legally sanctioned church festivals, but that on other major dates in the churches' calendars, such as Corpus Christi or Reformation Day, individual teachers and pupils could apply to be exempted from school in order to allow them to attend church. In schools where more than half of the pupils were of one or other denomination, classes could be cancelled in whole or in part, depending on what had been customary in the school's locality. In Württemberg this permitted a dignified retreat. Corpus Christi in 1940 had been declared a regular school day; on it, however, Catholic teachers had either failed to give classes or had begun them late in the day, while Catholic children had attended school either late or not at all. On the following Sunday, to which Corpus Christi had been translated by official order, many Catholic members of the HJ had been absent from the Reich sports competition because of 'their religious duties'.[119]

The battle over religious instruction versus WAU turned into a war of attrition, with Wurm directing several of his complaints about Mergenthaler's policies to Rust. His particular concern was about the choice between the two which Mergenthaler was enforcing, contrary to the law and contrary to policy in the rest of Germany. The Evangelical Church in Württemberg, like the Catholic Church, instructed all parents who adhered to its confession to choose religious instruction for their children. Where they were pressured into choosing WAU, the church left open the possibility of their returning to the religious fold. In May 1941, Rust's ministry confirmed that withdrawal from WAU was possible at the end of the school year. This clarification was the result of a petition from Evangelical parents in some of Württemberg's communes who had found that their children were being denied not only school classes in religious instruction but also the right to attend confirmation classes.

As with so much else in Württemberg, conditions varied from district to district, and even between communes in the same district; they were also dependent on the complexion of the local Nazi functionaries. The Evangelical authorities complained in April 1940 about the recruiting methods for WAU adopted by both the NSDAP local branch leader in Ditzingen and activists in four other communes. On the other side, the NSDAP local branch leader in Metzingen openly criticised the Reich ministry's policy of allowing withdrawal from WAU, and other Nazi officers were aghast. Party activists in Ludwigsburg, Heilbronn and elsewhere complained about the church's propaganda for religious instruction. To calm these warring factions, Murr tried, on 24 July 1941, to moderate by once again instructing both the church and the proponents of WAU to desist from canvassing for support. Mergenthaler's defiant response was to introduce compulsory WAU in girls' middle schools in autumn 1941, and to require that those applying to withdraw their children from WAU should do so in writing and give reasons for their decision.[120]

The pressures of war had their effect on this dispute. Several teachers of religious instruction were conscripted, providing a school's head or a local party leader with an excuse for discontinuing religious instruction altogether. Yet that solved only part of the problem. The SD reported in August 1940 that WAU was being very poorly taught, with teachers inadequately prepared and, in many cases, lacking inner conviction about the subject matter. Some of those teaching WAU sent their own children to religious instruction. Most were not party members and many seemed to feel little allegiance to National Socialism. It did not take long, added the SD, for pupils to deduce that some teachers of WAU were very ill-versed in it, while the clergy of both denominations were known to make a practice of priming pupils with questions designed to discomfit teachers.[121] Some local Nazi activists justified their pressure for WAU on the grounds that children should be educated in the ideology for which Germany's soldiers were fighting and dying. Kottmann, Bishop Sproll's deputy, argued heatedly that this was a false premise: 'Our soldiers … are angered when they hear that, while they are away fighting at the front and drawing strength from their faith … this faith is being attacked at home.' He was particularly critical of a teacher in Isny, in Wangen district, who had argued that Christianity's 'love thine enemy' injunction had no place in a country at war with the USSR.[122] No one could, after all, accuse the Catholic Church of being soft on communism.

The conscription by 1942 of 50 per cent of Evangelical pastors, of countless teachers and fathers, and of significant numbers of NSDAP officers meant that many figures of authority both in families and in communes were now absent. The success or failure of the WAU campaign therefore depended increasingly on the disposition of the remaining teachers, whose profession had been purged and 'co-ordinated' as a priority from 1933, with membership of the NSLB (*NS-Lehrerbund* – Nazi Teachers' Association) effectively compulsory.[123] In fact, many teachers were active church members, and, particularly where there was not a fanatical NSDAP local leadership, they continued to provide religious instruction for pupils. Nevertheless, there remained some militantly Nazi teachers – including some female teachers – who vigorously implemented WAU in their classes, frequently in the face of opposition from parents. The latter included, even in summer 1942, some NSDAP members who were continuing to choose religious instruction for their children. In Langenau, in Ulm district, the school's head and the NSDAP local branch leader together felt the need to issue a statement instructing party members and the members of NSDAP formations to ensure that their children were registered for WAU. Similarly, in Stuttgart a woman teacher canvassed vigorously for WAU, especially in cases where the father of a child was a party member.[124] Problems with the teaching profession would not be solved in wartime with a shortage of teachers, an overburdening of those who remained on the home front and the consequent unavoidability of re-employing 'unsuitable teachers who had been pensioned off [and] teachers who have a religious affiliation'.[125]

In their quest for compliance, some local party functionaries targeted wives of conscripted soldiers. Overburdened as these women already were by the pressures of war, if they had chosen religious instruction for their children they might be summoned by the local NSDAP officer to explain themselves or singled out for criticism at a public meeting. In Metzingen, where the contest between party and church was particularly bitter, pregnant wives received house visits from party activists to persuade them to plan for a Nazi 'naming ceremony' for the new child instead of religious baptism. In some places, parents were threatened with sanctions, including discrimination against their children in school and, later, in employment if they chose religious instruction rather than WAU for them. Mothers in Hessental were told that their young children could not receive religious instruction in school because there was no one to teach it. On the other hand, mothers of new school pupils in Stuttgart were asked whether they wished their children to be enrolled in religious instruction or WAU classes. The Evangelical Church's leadership was incensed both by this inconsistency and by the apparent fact that Catholic clergy and teachers were imparting religious instruction in schools in mainly Catholic areas, apparently unmolested.[126]

Confessional solidarity undoubtedly contributed to the relative failure to establish WAU in strongly Catholic areas, although individual teachers there tried to pressure or trick young pupils into opting for WAU. In Laupheim, in Biberach district, they were told that it involved lessons with slide shows. In the end, however, only twenty out of six hundred primary pupils chose WAU. In the senior classes, its rejection was unanimous. In Nordstetten, in Horb district, only one pupil in each of the senior classes opted for WAU. Elsewhere, however, there were attempts to impose WAU on the pretext that there was no one to give religious instruction. In these cases, Catholic priests offered their services. The school authorities in Isny simply dismissed the Catholic religious studies teacher and introduced WAU, warning parents against trying to resist. In January 1942, Kottmann complained in detail to Mergenthaler about this, basing his arguments on Murr's cautious approach which warned against compulsion and on Rust's understanding that no pressure would be exerted to win converts to WAU. In Kottmann's view, 'WAU is nothing more than a campaign against Christianity and in particular against the Catholic Church'.[127] Some parents did resist. In Westerstetten, in Ulm district, where an assiduous NSDAP local branch leader had already alienated the inhabitants, thirty mothers descended on the town hall to demand that they retain their right to choose religious education for their children. They demonstrated their hostility to two teachers who had tried to crush parental resistance to the imposition of WAU on the commune's children by ostracising them, to the extent that the two were obliged to take their meals in a neighbouring commune because no one in Westerstetten was prepared to provide them with food.[128]

The acrimonious battle over WAU was only one indication of how the exigencies of war radicalised Nazi policy towards the churches. Party functionaries at all levels used wartime emergency measures as a pretext for restricting various church activities, including religious festivals and the confirmation of the young. In February 1940, Schirach, as Reich HJ leader, stipulated that all ten to eighteen year olds should perform HJ duty on every second Sunday, under the guise of special war service. No exceptions were permitted; it was specified that those taking preparatory classes for confirmation were not to be exempted.[129] Frequently, with special duties and events, war service expanded into successive Sundays for several weeks at a time. The Evangelical Church authorities made their displeasure known, and, even where there was an assertive Hitler Youth leadership, the pressure on often unwilling young people to attend HJ or BDM activities could be fruitless.[130]

In Waiblingen district, the assiduous HJ leader did his utmost to arrange events for Sundays, importuning Nazi officers to give lectures to his subordinates.[131] When he remonstrated with his junior HJ officers because of the derisory turnout of both leaders and members for 'war service' in Öffingen on a Sunday morning in August 1944, it was not clear whether the absence of forty or fifty boys, out of a possible seventy, in one case, and of around half of a unit of fifty boys in another case, was because they were attending church or because, as he claimed, they were 'loafing'.[132] The venue was, however, Catholic Öffingen, where attachment to the local priest was strong.[133] In the case of a youth in full time work in his father's business, both parents contested the HJ's demand that he at least attend HJ service on a Sunday.[134] This may have been because, as they claimed, he needed a day of rest. On the other hand, it may have been because they preferred that he attend church. In a Catholic village in the Hohenlohe, if there was an HJ meeting on a Sunday morning, the boys who were members of the HJ normally went to church rather than to the meeting, knowing full well that they would be taken to task for their choice.[135]

From spring 1941, the NSDAP waged a campaign – explicitly as part of its mission of *Menschenführung* – to try to discourage or prevent young people from preparing themselves for Evangelical confirmation and to replace it with the HJ's own 'dedication of youth' ceremony. Part of this involved compulsory attendance by HJ members at 'name giving' and Nazi marriage ceremonies, which brought sharp complaints from parents and clergy alike about yet another tactic designed to prevent the churches from nurturing the young and to win their allegiance to National Socialist beliefs and rites by force. The Party Chancellery decreed that the Nazi 'dedication of youth' should become the only ceremony for fourteen year olds, with all other ceremonies – including those of the churches

– banned. Wurm protested vigorously to the Party Chancellery, and his obduracy as well as disregard on the part of many ordinary churchgoers ensured that the party enjoyed limited success. With many of the clergy conscripted, those who remained held preparatory classes for confirmation on weekday afternoons in some communes, with only the deputy *Kreisleiter* of Nürtingen and a head teacher in Notzingen obstructing this.[136] The commune of Bopfingen was undoubtedly typical in continuing to hold confirmation services throughout the war.[137] Where local party zealots could not force the young to observe Nazi rituals, they might try to obstruct those who persisted with religious practices. In the last days of the war, there was relief in Fachsenfeld that, for the first time for years, children were able to take their first communion without party harassment.[138]

While the major battles between the regime and the churches concerned their rival claims to the allegiance of the young, the two were also at odds over other issues in wartime. Ministering to forced foreign workers was one; the seizure of various church assets was another. Catholic priests in several communes invited Polish Catholics and Uniate Ukrainians to regular church services and other religious events, encouraging their flock to take a compassionate attitude towards these co-religionists from an enemy nation. The SD in Stuttgart reported in February 1940 that

> several priests have, without any scruples whatsoever, asked the congregation to take part in religious services with Polish prisoners of war, often in the same pew. Some of them have even been prepared to hold up the 'poor Poles' as an example to German citizens of especial piety. As a consequence of this attitude on the part of the clergy, the people think it appropriate even to accommodate the Poles to the extent of providing them with underwear, food and small luxuries.

Attendance by foreign workers at parochial church services was therefore prohibited in February 1940.[139] As an alternative, provision was made for separate Sunday services to be held for foreign workers.[140] Nevertheless, the SD reported in September 1940 that Polish POWs and civilian forced workers were continuing to attend regular church services, with Catholic priests instructing their congregations to treat them with 'Christian neighbourliness', calling for 'more humane treatment' for them and demanding that they be permitted to attend regular Sunday services. Some priests were said to have encouraged demonstrations of sympathy for the foreign workers, and to have expressed the view that Hitler could not have been aware of the harsh treatment meted out to them by subordinate party functionaries and army officers because he would certainly not have approved of it.[141]

While solidarity with foreign workers was an issue that mainly concerned the Catholic Church, it was not exclusive to it. In Metzingen, near Reutlingen, in the second half of the war, Evangelical pastor Lang noticed at his services some women and girls wearing unusual clothing and headscarves. These, it transpired, were Russians who had belonged to a Protestant sect at home but had been brought to Germany and put to work in a timber concern. Their employer heard about their attendance at church and reported it to the NSDAP local branch leader, who was incensed by this violation of controls over foreign workers. Although he issued a ban on further church attendance by the Russian women, Lang and his fellow pastor Römer said that they neither had nor wished to have control over who attended their services, and that they welcomed all worshippers. Accordingly, the Russians continued to attend, with the result that some of them were apprehended by the authorities and locked in the mayor's office on Sundays as punishment. When pastor Römer complained about this to the Evangelical Church council and also to the civil authorities in Stuttgart, he was summoned by the *Gestapo* to Stuttgart where he was violently berated by an SS officer.[142]

In wartime, with pressure on buildings of all kinds as a result of bombing, migration and evacuation, the regime targeted the substantial premises owned by both churches. Catholic convents and hospitals as well as Evangelical seminaries and deacons' premises were sequestered for a variety of secular purposes, including the accommodation of ethnic Germans from eastern Europe. In April 1941, Cardinal Bertram complained to Lammers at the Reich Chancellery about the seizure of several religious houses, including that of the Benedictines at Kellenried in the Rottenburg diocese.[143] In July 1941, Mergenthaler decreed that Evangelical seminaries in Maulbronn, Blaubeuren, Schöntal and Urach were to be taken over by the *Land* schools' authorities for use as boarding schools for the sons of *Wehrmacht* officers, bureaucrats, senior party officers and, especially, casualties of the war. The Catholic seminary in Rottweil was to be used for the same purpose; that in Ehingen had already been taken over by the *Wehrmacht*. The SD welcomed these moves as finally removing a 'foreign body' from the Nazi school system, arguing that they had caused little concern among the ordinary population although the council of the Evangelical Church, and Wurm in particular, had complained bitterly about them.[144] Yet the Stuttgart State Prosecutor saw it differently, reporting that the seizures had caused 'much ill feeling' among churchgoers of both denominations.[145] In Westerstetten, the threat to close down the local Catholic convent led to the commune's mothers to protest publicly. They had their way, and the convent continued to function as before.[146]

The seizure of church assets extended to the requisitioning of church bells. Determined to utilise Germany's material resources more effectively in this war than the Kaiser's government had done in the previous one, Göring ordered in March 1940 that bells made of bronze and parts of buildings made of copper be identified and that the bells be gathered together for the war effort without delay.[147] There were bells in various locations, including town halls, but the vast majority of bells were in churches large and small. Virtually every commune had at least one church bell, which was rung not only for celebrations but also to signal danger. In some, bells might date from the early 1920s, when replacements had been installed for those surrendered to the state during the First World War.[148] As a concession to popular sentiment, it was decreed in December 1941 that any bell of particular artistic or historic value would be spared, and that, in any event, every parish should be left with at least one. While ceremonies which had been planned to mark the bells' removal – at which the intention was to make a recording of the sound of the requisitioned bells – were banned, it was conceded that reference could be made to their removal in regular church services. As a local official pointed out, yet again, it was essential not to antagonise the population.[149]

The bronze bells which remained in Württemberg's communes by 1940 tended to be of considerable age because they had been exempted in 1914–18 on grounds of their historic value. In spite of undertakings that this would again be a consideration, some bells of evident historic value were seized. In Dalkingen, for example, three bells which had been spared in the First World War, two of which had been cast in 1607 and 1782, were removed in March 1942. In Bopfingen, a bell made of silver alloy and cast in 1496, known as the *Blasiusglocke*, was removed along with two others, one dating from 1648 and another whose age was unknown. The latter two were returned after the war, but not the *Blasiusglocke*. In Suppingen, a bell dating from 1575 – which, it was pointed out, had survived the Thirty Years War and subsequent conflicts – was removed after determined opposition by the villagers. The only concession was that a metal label could be hung round it asking that it be spared.[150] The removal of the bells was widely perceived as a direct attack on religion rather than as a desperate attempt to utilise all available materials for the war effort, although by this time there had been extensive collections of metal, and items like metal door handles would soon be requisitioned.[151] Later, on 16 August 1944, mayor Strölin of Stuttgart announced that organ pipes and wind chests made of any usable metal were to be surrendered.[152]

Yet this has to be seen within the context of several measures which discriminated against the churches and were therefore deeply resented by large sections of the population. Beyond the struggle over religious instruction and WAU, seminaries and religious houses were seized, church kindergartens were forcibly taken over by the NSV from 1936, and in 1941 the churches' remaining press was closed down, on grounds of paper shortage.[153] It was therefore scarcely surprising that the removal of the bells was construed as a further attack on the churches. The issue of the church bells struck a chord of atavistic resentment, and one of the items on the postwar questionnaire about 'the last days of the war' in Württemberg's communes asked whether and when bells had been removed. The replies suggest that no distinction was made between Evangelical and Catholic churches in this matter.[154] The questionnaires also show that, in some cases, bells which had been requisitioned were not melted down but held in store until the end of the war, after which they were returned to the villages. These included the Suppingen bell.[155]

For villagers, church bells and church buildings, along with rituals such as first communion and confirmation and festivals such as Christmas and Easter, were an integral part of their commune's life and its heritage. When nuns in Beuren, in Wangen district, made a house to house collection in June 1941 for funds for the repair of the church's roof, they collected 950 marks, whereas at the same time a state sponsored collection for the Red Cross raised only 271 marks. The SD regarded this as noteworthy when it was merely a normal expression of local loyalty and piety.[156] Similarly, in Gebersheim, when monitored collections were made in 1939 for Nazi purposes, the inhabitants contributed around twenty-five to thirty marks altogether, while collections made by the pastor raised 'seventy marks and even more'. Again, the local branch leader took this as an affront.[157] He seemed not to comprehend that the rural population, particularly, accepted religious faith and observance as part of the fabric of their life and their identity.

When urban Catholics poured into the churches on 6 July 1941 to hear the reading of a letter issued by the Fulda Conference of Catholic bishops, church attendance was said by the SD to be 'extraordinarily good', with the churches filled to overflowing in towns such as Reutlingen, where several NSDAP members were among the congregation. If church attendance on that Sunday was 'normal' on the land, that was because it was already customarily high. The rural population listened quietly to their priest's reading of the letter, unless they fell asleep during it because of exhaustion as a result of the long hours which they worked on their farms in high summer. They heard the message of the letter 'with equanimity and [it] aroused no particular reaction', in marked contrast with the lively interest which it evoked in the towns.[158] This attitude epitomised the rural population's allegiance to their church which was, for the most part, unquestioning, unconditional and, unless they were provoked, distinctly passive. The result was that, when the party attempted to replace traditional functions and festivals with their own version, it met a wall of obstruction. This was not a matter of political opposition, although officers of the regime, for instance those in the SD, tended to regard it as such. On the contrary, it reflected small communes' 'unpolitical parochialism', a stubborn adherence to the traditional and the familiar.[159]

Attempts to manufacture National Socialist harvest festivals at local level foundered on the reluctance of the Württemberg farming community to participate in them, because, the SD explained, on the same Sunday they 'flooded into the churches' harvest thanksgiving services even without confessional propaganda'. This was an ingrained tradition with which rural Württembergers felt at home, which rendered party efforts to displace it ineffectual.[160] The regime's attempts to disrupt the rhythms of the religious calendar were similarly unproductive. Changing the date of Ascension Day in 1941 had, said the SD, 'not entirely produced the desired result'. Part of the rural population, and a few town-dwellers, had celebrated the festival in the traditional way. In some places, including Württemberg, there was substantial attendance at church, and farming families had taken a holiday. They had dressed in their best clothes and gone to the nearest town to shop and to visit acquaintances.[161]

The additional constraints, dangers and tragedies of wartime made retreat into the familiar faith and rituals of a church more comforting than anything the NSDAP could offer, for Christianity promised the life hereafter. Himmler might imagine himself to be the reincarnation of the pre-Christian Henry the Fowler, at whose tomb he held a solemn ceremony in 1936 on the one thousandth anniversary of the king's death.[162] Others might fantasise about Valhalla. Yet, like Marxists in the USSR and elsewhere, the Nazis lacked the churches' trump card of 'victory over death'. This was of vital importance in maintaining stubborn allegiance to the churches in a war with unprecedented numbers of casualties, both at the front and at home. By 1943, the NSDAP's leadership seemed resigned to this. As a report from the Party Chancellery in Munich put it, on 9 April,

> it is in the nature of things that the hardships of war, its sacrifices and all the other material and psychological difficulties connected with it, give the clergy a great opportunity to influence in their own way the spiritual disposition of a large section of the population.

The churches, continued the report, sought out the relatives of soldiers at the front and of those who had been killed, and, 'as if that was not enough', held all manner of church services of intercession or remembrance.[163]

It was scarcely surprising that, with casualties mounting, especially on the eastern front from summer 1941, the clergy's traditional role in a commune, of comforting the bereaved and conducting obsequies for the dead, was greatly enhanced. Yet the NSDAP was anxious that its officers in a fallen soldier's home locality should play the most prominent part in both comforting his family and commemorating him. At the end of July 1941, the SD had instructed its agents to report on whether party ceremonies to commemorate fallen heroes were taking place and what the population's view of them was. Responses showed that party members certainly thought that 'this would give the party an opportunity to make itself popular ... [and] to demonstrate the *Volksgemeinschaft*'s strength of belief in Germany and its future, irrespective of confession'. They hoped that it would enable 'the *Volksgemeinschaft* to find its concrete expression ... so that through these ceremonies it can be affirmed that the entire nation in solidarity together shares in the grief of the relatives'. The chief motive, however, was to steal a march on the churches. Somewhat unrealistically, given both the logistics and the unceasing depletion of civilian officials through conscription, the SD recommended that the postal authorities should inform the relevant party official as soon as a notice of death had been received so that he would be the first to convey to the family the 'sympathy of the entire German people', thus getting his condolences in ahead of the local clergyman's. This kind of petty jockeying for position with the clergy informed the entire issue of paying tribute to fallen soldiers. The party feared that, if the care of the bereaved were left to the clergy, they would undermine people's will to support the war by emphasising both the sadness and pain of the survivors and the promise of the life hereafter.

By September 1941, Nazi commemorations of the fallen had been staged in only six of the party's thirty-six districts in *Gau* Württemberg-Hohenzollern, namely Calw, Leonberg, Schwäbisch Hall, Waiblingen, Sigmaringen and Böblingen. In addition, in a few local branches in *Kreis* Biberach a wreath had been placed at the war memorial after a religious service of remembrance. In Horb and Bad Mergentheim there was little enthusiasm for party involvement in commemorating the dead. Calw was probably the best organised district, its *Kreisleiter* having ordered that party services should be held every month in all of the larger communes, if the number of casualties justified it. In 1940, the party there conducted a burial service for three airmen, while in Wangen a party ceremony was held for an SS officer who had fallen ill on the eastern front and died in hospital. In the towns, these services employed the entire panoply of ceremony, filling a large hall with party formations in uniform and choirs of Hitler Youth or BDM members. There was solemn instrumental music followed by readings from letters either from or about the deceased, and, as the centrepiece, an address by the *Kreisleiter*. The laying of a wreath and the offering of formal condolences to the bereaved completed the ceremony. Such services were reported as being very impressive, apart from the unfortunate occasion in Calw when an army choir had arrived half an hour late and had then sung a Christian hymn. The SD's view was that people were prepared to attend the party's events when they were held, with '*even those strongly attached to a religious confession* taking part, if the invitations are issued tactfully'. The response of those who attended party services was said to have been extremely favourable, with even those with an attachment to a church leaving with a good impression.[164]

Yet it soon transpired that, while impressive party services could be staged in towns at the end of a military campaign, in the countryside few local party branches had the resources to mount an appropriate event. Therefore, in those rural areas where party ceremonies were held, they almost always augmented but did not replace religious services, for four reasons. First, the local church held a funeral service for each individual member of a commune who died, whereas the party's ceremonies generally honoured several casualties of war together. Secondly, the church had appropriate premises for a service, premises which were familiar to churchgoers, so that they felt comfortable at a time when they required sensitivity and personal warmth. Thirdly, in rural areas, holding a religious service for the soul of the departed was, the SD reported, part of 'an old, deep seated Christian faith and tradition' in which the entire commune participated.[165] It tended to be the custom on the land for at least one person from each household in the commune to attend a burial service.[166] Fourthly, the local clergyman was a familiar figure who was generally trusted by his parishioners; he was also an experienced public speaker. In addition, some clergymen devised innovative methods of remembrance. For example, in early 1942, individual 'symbolic graves' were marked with birchwood crosses for fifty-four casualties from the commune of Eislingen whose bodies had not been recovered, with fifty-four candles lit on the Catholic church's 'altar of the slain'. This made a great impression on the population, whose contributions had made possible the decoration of the graves. This practice was followed in other Catholic communes where even those whose family members had left the church were included in the commemoration, giving the priest the chance to meet these relatives who, in most cases, reported the SD, visited the graves and the service of remembrance 'with good results' for the church.[167] The Evangelical Church, too, held commemoration services, such as that in July 1941 in Metzingen, where six of the slain were honoured in the main Evangelical church.

The party faced three problems in trying to organise separate – and competing – commemorations in small communes. First, there tended not to be suitable premises. As a result, in some places party services were held either in locations which were regarded as unsuitable, such as a local tavern, or in the church itself. Secondly, as the SD pointed out, there was the leadership question: 'in small rural communes … the [NSDAP] local branch leader generally does not possess the intellectual capability to mount the kind of events that are impressive and appropriate'.[168] From the rural communes in *Kreis* Tübingen, it was reported that party ceremonies were utterly unimpressive because of the poor quality of the speeches, which might consist simply of the local branch leader reading out a printed statement. In some communes in Württemberg, the party gave up the unequal struggle and dispensed with speeches altogether.[169] In addition, with his many other wartime duties it was also difficult for the local branch leader to arrange an event in time to pre-empt mention of the deceased by the priest or pastor at Sunday church service. Thirdly, the form that party events took in the towns exploited resources which were not available to it in small communes. On the land, the weakness of the local HJ as well as of party formations and affiliates precluded this. In the commune of Buchau, the ceremony – which consisted of one piece of music, a few words of commemoration from the local branch leader and the laying of a wreath – was felt to be 'insufficient'.[170]

However hard the party tried to outdo the churches in honouring the dead and comforting the bereaved, church services of remembrance continued to be held virtually everywhere in Württemberg. The Stuttgart SD's view was that the Catholic Church, 'in spite of the alleged repression and persecution which it has endured', was determined to demonstrate that it could still fulfil its duties to the slain and the bereaved, even in the case of those who had left the church.[171] Even worse, from the party's point of view, as reports from Schwäbisch Gmünd, Ludwigsburg, Göppingen and Crailsheim showed, 'the activities of the clergy have even gone the length of exploiting the immediate grief of relatives of the slain so that *religious funeral services* have been held even for *convinced National Socialists*'. In Göppingen, for example, an Evangelical pastor held a memorial service in the Friedrichskirche for an SA leader and some party members. In Wangen, the father of a dead SS officer insisted on a church service for his son in addition to the service mounted by the party, saying: 'Now he belongs to me again, and I shall do what I believe is right.' In small communes where a church service alone was held for the slain, some were said to be asking why the party did not participate in it, especially if the deceased had supported the NSDAP or worked for it on a voluntary basis. From Ulm it was reported that '*in rural areas, even party functionaries are of the view that the best solution is for the party to take part in church services*', because it gave a poor impression if they did not.[172] In some small communes, then, the party had to concede that the churches possessed superior resources for this purpose, including the allegiance of large sections of the population, and that staying aloof from their services worked only to its own disadvantage.

There can be little doubt that the Nazi regime in Württemberg regarded the churches as adversaries and as obstacles to their objectives of effecting total control over the population and eliciting from it total commitment towards Nazism as both an ideology and a political system. In wartime, the SD reported that the clergy were spreading defeatism and indifference towards the war effort.[173] Individual clergymen and lay Christians who consciously and courageously obstructed party or state could be victimised without much difficulty. That this happened with the exiling of as high profile a figure as Württemberg's leading Catholic clergyman, Bishop Sproll, showed the implacability of the Stuttgart regime towards the Catholic clergy, in particular. In their turn, the Catholic clergy in Württemberg fought tenaciously and successfully to retain the allegiance of their parishioners, especially in rural areas. The Evangelical Church, too, was under pressure, with individual clergymen such as Sautter spending time in gaol, although Wurm was apparently invulnerable after his brief period of house arrest in 1934. Both churches, however, survived in Württemberg's communes, in the basic unit of the parish, as accounts of the last days of the war attest. Clergymen remained influential members of rural communities, with Kottmann claiming in early May 1945 that there were 800 parishes and 1200 priests to minister to around a million Catholics – not counting evacuees – in Württemberg.[174] The celebration of Easter 1945 took place as a matter of course, unless a commune was directly in the firing line as enemy forces closed in on Württemberg.[175]

This can be judged a success, for survival became the churches' major objective in the Third Reich. Their perspective was not that of any one individual's lifetime but rather a long term view which was informed by inherited memories of the Reformation and the Thirty Years War. Ensuring that the institutions remained viable was, from the point of view of the majority of the clergy, the only guarantee that the spiritual needs of the mass of the people would be satisfied in the indefinite future and that they would be guided towards eternal life. For the churches, the suffering and death of those who were targeted for persecution were overshadowed by that consideration, and, above all, by comparison with their conception of the suffering and death of Christ. The inconvenient answer given by Christ to the question 'who is my neighbour?' was at odds with the policy of both major denominations of battening down the hatches and conserving their essential identities.

8

Forced Foreign Workers

Germany's chronic and increasingly damaging shortage of human resources was partially mitigated in wartime by the importation from defeated countries of several million foreign labourers. As non-Germans, and for the most part non-'Aryans', they were axiomatically not members of the *Volksgemeinschaft* and were therefore, in varying degrees, unprivileged inhabitants, some of whom were treated with utterly barbaric cruelty. The conventional figures given for prisoners of war together with some voluntary migrants and many forcibly conscripted civilians show that there were over one million in 1940 and well over seven million in 1944.[1] These annual totals, however, camouflage the true extent of German pillaging of foreign labour, with estimates varying between ten and fifteen million people, including non-Germans in concentration camps within the Greater German Reich. These foreigners were used, and largely abused, by the Nazi authorities to try to compensate for the loss to the German economy of the millions of German men who were conscripted into the armed forces, to say nothing of hundreds of thousands of German civilians who were sent to administer the newly annexed areas of the Reich and occupied territories in both east and west.[2] Foreign workers from western European countries, especially from more 'Aryan' populations such as those of Denmark or Holland, were treated with some humanity, at first at least, and were, for example, often paid wages that were not significantly lower than those paid to Germans performing the same work.[3] This was particularly true of Flemings from Belgium – who were distinguished from Walloons in reports to the SD – who received preferential treatment, in the first half of the war at least. More than half of the almost 400,000 Belgians who went to work in Germany were volunteers, albeit after the military defeat of their country by the *Wehrmacht*. Of major importance was the fact that Belgians received the same wages and social benefits as Germans working alongside them.[4]

Even so, many western Europeans paid with their life after being deported to work for the German war effort. For example, by the end of 1944, out of almost one million French POWs who had remained in Germany after 1940, 21,000 had either met their death or else were counted as 'missing, presumed dead'; in the last year of the war, that total would rise to 37,000.[5] Some western Europeans would be treated with atrocious brutality, especially where they labourered in concentration camps such as Buchenwald or Mauthausen, or in the conglomerate of construction camps at Dora-Mittelbau in Thuringia.[6] For Italian soldiers who fell into the category of 'military internees' after the fall of Mussolini in July 1943 and the Badoglio government's 'treachery' in effectively changing sides, there was 'bestial' treatment from German workers as well as the authorities to contend with, over and above brutal working conditions, inadequate nutrition and arbitrary punishment for low productivity. It has been suggested that 'only Soviet forced workers were treated worse'.[7] In France, which was obliged to make the single biggest contribution of any western European country to Germany's foreign labour resources, some war memorials were in the 1980s and 1990s augmented by marble plaques commemorating the sacrifice of civilian deportees. In the Place Gambetta in Bergerac, in Lalinde (Dordogne) and in Guilliers (Brittany), for example, ashes from camps such as Mauthausen were deposited at the site of the war memorial decades after the end of the war. Yet not all foreigners' deaths were directly due to mistreatment by Germans. For example, 70 per cent of Belgian workers who died in Germany were killed in air raids.[8] Altogether, however, even where they received relatively preferential treatment, workers from western European countries which had been conquered were generally at best second class citizens in Germany.

While western Europeans figured in significant numbers in the German labour force during the war, the overwhelming majority of foreign workers were brought from eastern Europe, chiefly from Poland and the USSR, areas populated, in the Nazi view, by the 'racially worthless', give or take scattered groups of ethnic Germans.[9] Once their armies had been defeated by the *Wehrmacht*, Slavs from eastern Europe were either enticed under pressure, or else simply seized, and brought to Germany to serve as a helot class of 'aliens' who were denied the remaining rights enjoyed by German 'Aryan' citizens in the Third Reich. The advantage, from the point of view of the authorities, was that they could be worked as hard as possible for as little return – in terms of food and remuneration – as possible.[10] Further, they could be physically controlled by being accommodated in camps or barracks in the vicinity of the factories, mines or foundries where many of them worked. Generalisations of this kind mask, however, a multiplicity of conditions, and oversimplify the relationships which developed between, or were imposed on, the foreign workers in their encounters with, on the one hand, representatives of the German state and the Nazi Party, and, on the other hand, ordinary German civilians. Further, the presence of foreign workers in a community also had ramifications for German civilians' attitudes towards state and party authorities, and for these authorities' treatment of civilians.

There was nothing new about the employment of foreigners – especially Poles – in Germany in both industry and agriculture: it had occurred on a significant scale from the later nineteenth century, and was a feature of the German exploitation of occupied countries during the First World War.[11] By the later 1930s, once the catastrophic levels of unemployment contingent on the depression had receded and a shortage of labour became evident in some sectors of the German economy, there was a revival of the recruitment of foreigners. In the countryside, with the renewed flight from the land, German agriculture was clearly 'no longer viable without foreign labour', much as Nazis such as Darré deplored it.[12] For example, agreements in 1937 with both Austria and Fascist Italy – countries where unemployment rates remained stubbornly high – brought some relief. Württemberg and Baden were each to have a share of 2000 Austrians from Vorarlberg, while Italy would provide Germany with 5000 long term workers and over 25,000 seasonal workers under the supervision of the SS and accompanied by a foreman and an interpreter who were both members of the Fascist Party. South-western Germany was one of the major reception areas for Italian agricultural workers.[13]

In addition, in 1937, Württemberg was awarded a share of the six hundred Polish agricultural workers from among those seeking work in Germany allocated to the south west. The advance notice of this warned the employment exchanges against giving specific promises about numbers to potential employers in their area in case 'hopes are raised that cannot be fulfilled'.[14] By mid 1939, there were already 5000 foreigners – including Italians, Slovaks, Bulgars and *Volksdeutsche* (ethnic Germans) from Yugoslavia, as well as Poles – at work in Württemberg, but they were said 'not to suffice for even the most pressing demands'. The SD reported that farmers were 'generally pleased' with Italian workers, although not with the Yugoslav *Volksdeutsche*.[15] By this time, in Germany as a whole 'the influx [was] a veritable invasion', with, 'in the middle of 1939, some 37,000 Italians, 15,000 Yugoslavs, 12,000 Hungarians, 5000 Bulgarians, 4000 Dutch, over 40,000 Slovaks and around the same number of workers from Bohemia-Moravia'.[16] The quota for Polish workers alone, at 60,000 in 1938 and 90,000 in 1939, was breached as unemployed Poles provided much needed recruits for German agriculture. The defeat of Poland in autumn 1939 brought POWs and civilian conscripts to Germany on an increasing scale, with Göring envisaging the importation of one million civilians as early as January 1940.[17]

The policy of importing cheap foreign labour on a large scale was, therefore, not intrinsically distinctively *Nazi* in character: it can plausibly be viewed as an integral phase in the continuity of recent *German* history, from the later nineteenth century through to the *Gastarbeiter* (guest workers) of the later twentieth century, to meet the virtually chronic need for additional labour in Germany. The idiosyncratically Nazi facets of this policy derived rather from the creation of a new racial order where

> the egalitarianism of 1789 was revoked ... Hierarchies were ... declared ... not to be functional and hence conquerable by means of mobility and changes of roles ... they

were enshrined in perpetuity. The ideal was that of the German worker, with his sense of cardinal, 'essential' superiority to his foreign colleagues.[18]

This was a clear indication of the regime's vision of the future, for the importation of foreign workers was recognised as being not merely a wartime 'necessary evil and temporary expedient', but rather the setting of a long term pattern in which 'Aryan' Germans would dominate Europe, and its vanquished peoples would serve the requirements of the 'master race'.[19] One indicator of this was the substantial reduction in January 1940 of the wages of Polish agricultural workers.[20]

For ideologues like Himmler, eastern European 'aliens' in Germany, like their co-nationals under German occupation, were to be worked to death. Moral considerations apart, this ignored the desperate need in the German wartime economy for productive labour, including particularly skilled labour, which could be met only by foreign workers. This was because, from whichever angle it is viewed, there were simply not sufficient Germans for the achievement of the regime's grandiose ambitions. It has been assumed that foreign labour had to be brought in and deployed once Hitler's government had refused to grasp the nettle of conscripting German women, and that victory in the west in 1940 absolved the regime of the need to agonise further about this contentious issue for a couple of years, 'since now prisoners of war and civilian workers from the conquered areas … would be available'.[21] This disregards the fact that by 1939 the available and willing resources of German female labour had already been worked into the economy, compared with, for example, Britain where there continued to be significant levels of female unemployment in 1940, and where the introduction of labour conscription for young women in 1941 was a response to Britain's desperate circumstances in the early years of the war, at a time when Germany was victorious.[22] There was perhaps some potential for recruitment among German single women, almost 90 per cent of whom were in work in 1939.[23] Yet some of the remainder – young, single 'Aryan' women – were already being utilised in various service schemes as inexpensive short-term conscripts in areas which were starved of labour – for example, agriculture – especially from 1938.[24] Some businesses did increase the size of their female workforce in 1939–40, including Daimler-Benz, whose managers preferred unskilled or semi-skilled German women to unskilled foreigners who, they feared, might engage in sabotage of their sophisticated production processes.[25]

The conscription of a million mostly married and largely reluctant German women in 1940 might have obviated the need to deploy foreign workers in industry and agriculture at that time, although the productivity that could have been expected from the untrained and unwilling, against whom harsh and deterrent discipline could hardly be used, would not have been on the level that could be extracted from foreigners working very long hours, often for little reward and under the threat of severe sanctions. Further, alleviating the labour shortage in agriculture by sending married urban middle-class or working-class women into the countryside to work would not have been practicable from any point of view, although there were isolated individual cases where this did happen.[26] Even by the end of 1940, 'German agriculture would no longer have been in a position to maintain food production at the required level without the two million or so foreign men and women working in it'.[27] Beyond that, it would not have been possible to recruit German women in the numbers required in the years 1940–44 to compensate for the millions of foreigners who could be brought in then. As early as October 1941, the SS recognised that 'in spite of bringing in female and foreign workers', and in spite of giving priority to businesses which were essential for the war effort, 'the situation has so far not eased'.[28] Eventually, the regime's concern about the need for ever more labour to replace the recurrent waves of conscripted German men led to attempts to conscript women from January 1943, at a time when there were already over four and a half million foreigners at work in Germany.[29] Conscripting German women and exploiting millions of foreigners were, therefore, not alternatives in the second half of the war: as Germany's fortunes waned, the regime required both.

The racist foundations of Nazism suggested that, even where Himmler's 'work to death' policy was rejected for pragmatic reasons, workers from eastern Europe would be condemned to live and work in inhuman conditions. One indicator of this was the appallingly high death rate among Soviet POWs, in particular, from malnutrition, exposure and disease. In Württemberg, the corpses of Soviet POWs were delivered from POW camps, including that at Heuberg, the site of an early concentration camp, to the anatomy department in Tübingen in and after the autumn of 1941.[30] It has, however, long been argued that there was a marked shift in official policy towards the end of the war, with attempts to soften the 'ideological' stance in the foreigners' favour, to encourage them to be more productive workers.[31] Certainly, there were minor palliative measures in the last year of the war, as, for example in September 1944, when the Reich Minister of Food and Agriculture revoked the provision of his order of 17 August 1944 excluding '*Ostarbeiter*' ('eastern workers', those from the USSR) from a share of a special issue of extra rations.[32]

Yet some mitigation of the initially unremittingly harsh attitude towards eastern Europeans is clearly discernible from the middle years of the war. As early as December 1941, Field Marshal Keitel, acting in Hitler's name, explained the need to improve conditions for Red Army POWs by providing adequate food rations, clothing and heating, as well as eradicating disease among them, in order to render them fit to be productive workers in the armaments industry.[33] Bormann felt that the German people would have to be informed that this was only to improve their productivity.[34] In businesses such as Daimler-Benz, the management recognised in 1942 that Russian workers would not be able to meet production targets on starvation rations. Fritz Sauckel, too, as the head of forced labour recruitment, accepted this, with the result that 'the blanket brutality of the period up to mid 1942 gave way to a more differentiated system of incentive and discipline'.[35] Even the SS admitted in autumn 1941 that 'the care of foreign workers is important to the extent that a contented foreign worker will be the best propaganda for Germany in their homeland'.[36] As the need for labour in the German economy became ever more acute, with, for example, younger farmers who had so far escaped conscription being called up, bringing in foreigners who were reasonably willing was an increasing priority.[37] Nevertheless, it was precisely in the later stages of the war that some foreign workers – including some western Europeans – were treated with unspeakable brutality as Germany's fortunes plummeted and desperate remedies were sought. This was, for example, the case at Dora-Mittelbau.[38] Beyond that, while prescriptions for eastern Europeans were in some respects moderated, in practice 'the gulf between [them] … and the actual living conditions of Russian and Polish forced workers became ever greater in the last two years of the war'.[39]

Even if conditions for a few foreign workers were somewhat improved in order to make them more productive, the fact remains that most foreign workers, and especially eastern Europeans, continued to be treated by the authorities as vassals without fundamental rights, far less privileges, and with lower rations, poorer accommodation and less personal freedom than Germans, all as a matter of both policy and principle. For example, in the spring of 1940 it was decreed that Polish workers were to observe a strict curfew, from 9 p.m. until 5 a.m. in summer and from 8 p.m. until 6 a.m. in winter. They were not permitted to use public transport unless they had express permission from the police. They were prohibited from visiting German cultural, religious or social institutions, and, in particular, restaurants. Separate church services were provided for them, as well as some restaurants 'of a simple kind', although industrial concerns which employed Poles were normally expected to provide them with a canteen.[40] In addition, Poles were forbidden to own bicycles, radios or cameras, or to use public telephones. Where they were permitted to use public transport, they were forbidden to occupy seats in tramcars if there were Germans standing. The detailed repetition of the prohibitions on POWs and Polish civilian workers in November 1941, and the repeated threat that not only Poles but any Germans who colluded with them would be punished, was clear evidence that the restrictions on Poles, in particular, were not being observed and that some Germans were conniving at their violation.[41]

Bringing in large numbers of non-'Aryans' from the start of the war perhaps solved one immediate problem, the shortage of readily available labour in specific sectors of the economy, especially war-related industry and agriculture.

In industry, foreigners accounted for only 3 per cent of the workforce in 1940, but by 1944 this figure had risen to 29 per cent. In agriculture, the comparable figures were 6 per cent and 22 per cent, which meant, in absolute terms, 661,000 and 2,402,000 respectively.[42] Nevertheless, there was an obvious disadvantage: the regime which preached 'racial purity', and whose overriding mission was to rid Germany of all 'racial inferiors', found that its imperial policies necessitated a substantial net inflow of these very *'Untermenschen'* ('sub-humans') on whom the German economy would become uncomfortably dependent. The spectre of 'racial mixing' that haunted zealots such as Himmler and the SS leadership guaranteed that there would be strenuous attempts to minimise contact between the foreigners and ordinary Germans, through billeting them, if possible, in camps or barracks, and by denying them physical mobility, prohibiting them from attending normal social venues and events, and keeping them under close surveillance.[43] With these constraints in place, the foreigners had the particular attraction of being easy to direct and deploy. While there was a welcome influx of western European skilled workers into German industry in 1940, the large majority of workers from the east, whether proletarians or peasants, formed a non-privileged underclass who would serve Germany in the long term. During and after the war, it was envisaged, they would perform the jobs that German proletarians could avoid in time of labour shortage, for wages that Germans despised, while this would obviate the need for taking account of 'all considerations which aimed at a tightening up of labour deployment or the fixing of priorities'.[44]

From the start, with the deployment of Polish POWs in autumn 1939, the host population was given clear and detailed instructions about how to conduct itself vis-à-vis the foreigners, through public notices, the press and verbal warnings by NSDAP officers. Germans were forbidden to approach POWs, to converse or correspond with them; they were also prohibited from passing on letters or parcels sent by third parties. They were instructed neither to give nor to sell writing paper, postage stamps or alcoholic drinks to POWs. They were neither to give money to POWs nor to purchase provisions for them, because POWs were permitted to have only the special currency that was valid only in the camps where they were housed, where they would, it was said, be provided with the essentials which they were deemed to need. Germans were expressly forbidden to invite POWs either to communal events or into their own homes. They were, further, neither to eat with them nor to take them to their church. In sum, POWs were not to be treated as if they were family members or close acquaintances; rather, they were to be shunned as pariahs. Germans who did not observe these regulations would be 'severely punished' and might even be charged with treason.[45] Of particular concern was the possibility of Germans engaging in sexual relationships with Poles. This was a matter of considerable anxiety to the authorities, and Germans, especially German women, were warned against fraternisation of any kind, with instructions about maintaining an appropriate distance from the 'aliens', on pain of punishment up to and including imprisonment.[46] This was no idle threat, with NSDAP *Kreisleiter* (district leaders) on the lookout for violations of these instructions, *Gestapo* agents ready to listen to denunciations accusing women deemed to be in breach of them, and the Stuttgart Special Court prepared to send those convicted to gaol for up to two years, although milder sentences, including fines, were also imposed.[47]

The prescriptions for Germans in their dealings – or absence of dealings – with POWs were soon broadly applied to Germans' conduct towards the foreign civilian workers brought in from Poland from spring 1940 and – in varying measure – to those recruited from western European countries in and after 1940. From 1941, they were applied also to the large numbers brought to Germany from eastern Europe, and especially from the USSR. By 1944 one worker in five was a foreigner, although the ratio was smaller in Württemberg, where by 1944–45 there were some 50,000 to 60,000 foreign workers.[48] Nevertheless, there could hardly have been a German who was not aware of their presence.[49] Indeed, the regime intended that Germans should be aware of the identity of foreigners, especially eastern Europeans. In March 1940, it was decreed that Polish civilian workers should wear a distinguishing badge to be 'securely fixed' on the right hand side of their upper body clothing. The badge was in the form of a yellow square with sides of five centimetres in length, with a half centimetre of 'bright violet' border and a 'violet P two and a half centimetres high'. Failure to wear this badge would be punished with a fine of up to 150 marks or up to six weeks in gaol.[50]

This requirement, along with the prescriptions for Germans in their dealings with foreigners, was transmitted by the Württemberg Ministry of the Interior to the *Landräte*, who would then pass them on to the mayors of communes.[51] A few weeks later, however, the SD in Württemberg reported that 'farm workers from former Poland are refusing … to wear on their clothing the prescribed badge for civilian workers of Polish nationality, on the grounds that they are not Poles but Ukrainians'. It seemed that neither the *Gestapo* nor the *Landräte* were aware that the regulation about the 'violet P' did not apply to those from Poland who were not ethnic Poles, undoubtedly because the decree had not made this clear. New instructions were, accordingly, devised for the depleted police forces to try to ascertain whose claims to Ukrainian nationality were justified.[52] It suited Germany's rulers politically to encourage a separate Ukrainian identity, as a continuation of the regime's prewar policy of undermining the stability of the Polish state.[53] This, along with the balkanisation of eastern Europe as a whole, was also the Nazi regime's motive for publishing, for propaganda purposes, newspapers and books in a variety of foreign languages, including Russian, Ukrainian,

Croatian, Slovak.[54] Nevertheless, the regime's true attitude towards the peoples of the USSR, at least, was evident from autumn 1941, when huge numbers of men and women began to be transported to Germany from the occupied areas of the Soviet Union. These people were deliberately dehumanised and their ethnicity denied by their being obliged to wear a badge bearing the letters 'OST' for *'Ostarbeiter'* ('eastern worker').[55]

Under a dictatorship, and especially in wartime, there seemed to be a good chance of enforcing these rules and injunctions. Meagre rations and the threat, and conspicuous exercise, of terror did much to cow unprivileged foreign workers, particularly at first. Their nationality, representing the enemy whose forces had killed Germans, also made them seem to many at least suspect and often worthy of hostility. Official propaganda about the 'racial inferiority' of Slavs, in particular, was intended to reinforce that hostility. Yet it is probably true that the greatest blow to the official *'Untermensch'* image derived from bringing 'intelligent ... and likeable' eastern European workers into close contact with Germans.[56] There was, then, a noticeable gulf between even the less inhumane versions of official policy and the attitudes of some sections of the population. To the frustration and incomprehension of some officers of the Nazi regime, the ideology of 'master race' versus *'Untermensch'* did not permeate civilian Germans' consciousness to the extent that the regime had intended and expected, in spite of the NSDAP's immense effort from 1933 to fulfil its role of *Menschenführung* and to win ordinary Germans' hearts and minds through 'political education'. This was certainly noticeable in the Württemberg countryside.[57]

Nevertheless, Nazi racist propaganda did enjoy undoubted successes. For example, serving soldiers on the eastern front were systematically imbued with Nazi racism, which does much to explain the appalling brutality visited by members of the *Wehrmacht* and the police, as well as by SS troops, on civilians and soldiers alike in the conquered eastern territories.[58] Equally, the German industrial worker generally accepted and sometimes asserted his favoured position vis-à-vis foreign workers brought to Germany to serve for little reward, turning a blind eye to the degradation of fellow beings whose basic humanity the regime denied.[59] At the same time, public officials consistently helped, by small acts in their everyday life and work, to reinforce that degradation, while large numbers of employers gladly accepted allocations of coerced foreign workers and also the inmates of concentration camps whom they could treat as virtually slave labour.[60] Yet where German civilians spoke in deprecating tones of Poles, for example, what they mostly displayed was less 'racial consciousness' than the xenophobic prejudice visible in virtually any community, then and now, as well as traditional *German* contempt for Poles.[61] Further, in Württemberg, complaints about the conduct of some foreign workers were different in content from, but qualitatively equivalent to, those made of German women evacuees from northern industrial towns, who were also, in effect, 'foreigners' in rural Württemberg.[62]

It was perhaps possible to maintain a system of apartheid between Germans and eastern Europeans in towns, where the 'aliens' worked under supervision in factories and mostly lived together in segregated accommodation, although western European civilian workers might well live in private rented accommodation.[63] Yet the conditions that were imposed reasonably effectively on foreign workers in the towns were much less applicable in the countryside, where Poles were deployed in substantial numbers from the autumn of 1939. At first, it was possible in some places to segregate Polish POWs by having small numbers of them living together in makeshift barracks. In the Friedrichshafen area, for example, one commune's school was taken over to accommodate some twenty Polish POWs who were being deployed as agricultural workers. There remained at this time sufficient manpower to permit guards from either the *Wehrmacht* or police auxiliaries to escort them to and from work on neighbouring farms. At night, they were guarded by the fire service, SA men or members of the Nazi war veterans' association. When, in the summer of 1940, most of the Poles opted for civilian worker status, they were able to leave communal and supervised accommodation in the barracks to live on the individual farms where they worked. The greater personal freedom thus gained was offset by the obligation to work much longer hours than they had done as POWs. While most Polish POWs were changing their status, there was a new influx of POWs, now from vanquished western Europe. By this time, there were also coerced Polish civilian workers on Württemberg's farms. A regulation was introduced prohibiting the employment of POWs and coerced civilians together on the same farm.[64]

The waters were, however, muddied by the arrival in Württemberg of people who were patently Polish but who were classed by Himmler and his SS racial theorists as 'racially valuable', consisting of individuals and families who were allegedly of German stock but had been 'polonised'. These 'could be made German again'.[65] For them, the implications of this were less dire than were the effects of Nazi policy for those classed as 'racially worthless', but they were damaging enough. The aim was to destroy these people's existing identities, to break up families into 'valuable' and 'worthless' elements, and to impose a new, prefabricated identity on them. Some of those chosen for this allegedly favoured treatment became deeply unhappy, having, in some cases, been separated from family members who were deemed to be 'worthless' and who were therefore relegated to living in poverty in occupied Poland. Among the incomers were those who had been reasonably prosperous farmers who now had to work as farm labourers. Some of these had shown unwillingness to work or had even expressed political dissent, which had earned them a four week sojourn in a concentration camp. Others, however, were said to have shown a positive attitude, especially if they were given some responsibility and independence at work.

Nevertheless, although they were mostly described as being 'willing, honourable, thrifty, domesticated and surprisingly clean', they were said to lack initiative. Above all, they mostly did not feel that they were German and, where they had the chance, they associated with Polish workers, whom they regarded as their fellow countrymen. Yet it was a priority with the regime to ensure that they were segregated from foreigners who were 'racially worthless', and, in at least one case, Polish workers in Württemberg regarded a Pole who 'could be made German' as a spy. The adults, then, did not feel that they belonged as Germans but were forced to abandon, or at least conceal, their Polish identity, although a few were outspoken in their refusal both to learn the German language and to give up hope that they would return to Poland.[66] One family in the Friedrichshafen area, where the incomers were put to work in agriculture, managed to give aid and comfort to neighbouring forced Polish workers, in deepest secrecy, and to maintain its own Polish identity, returning to Poland at the end of the war.[67] If some adults posed problems for the German authorities who were shamefully manipulating them, the children were, from the regime's point of view, a better prospect, mixing easily with native village children and quickly learning the Swabian dialect. The SD was both confident that 'the children will be sucked into the German *Volksgemeinschaft*' and satisfied that the majority of the adults would 'distance themselves from workers of foreign origin' – namely, those who, like themselves, were from Poland.[68] Even allowing for the distortions to which they were expected to submit, those who 'could become German' could see how those regarded as Poles were treated. Many must have found the temptation to embrace the undoubtedly contrasting benefits of being regarded as German hard to resist.

In the autumn of 1940, there were more than 17,500 Polish forced workers in Württemberg.[69] Most of the foreign workers on Württemberg's farms were Poles or Ukrainians, although there were both men and women from several other countries. For example, in Crailsheim district there were Czechs, who were said in September 1940 to have become very 'unruly'. Some were taken into police custody while others simply ran away.[70] There were also French, Belgian and Serb POWs. During 1942, however, these were more likely to be withdrawn from the farms and transferred to industry or trades, as renewed waves of conscription made the shortage of labour in these areas critical. Yet conscription had continued to hit farming severely also, with farmers who had originally been exempted called up as the battle of Stalingrad reached its climax.[71] The rural population in Württemberg and elsewhere 'could not understand why agriculture always had to take second place to industry'. The removal of workers who had been on farms for some time created instability on the land, which was bound to affect productivity. This was particularly true when French or Serbian POWs were replaced by Russian POWs or civilians, who were regarded as being of little use on small, unmechanised farms. The problem was that Russians who were familiar with agricultural work could not be used to milk cows or tend animals because, it was said, they were accustomed to the collective farm system and could not adjust to work on a small farm. The farmers, or farmers' wives, were reluctant to provide food and wages for them because 'they had not helped them but had made the work more difficult'.[72]

Authorities of both party and state were aware that it was more difficult to supervise and regulate civilian foreigners' activities in rural areas, as they were often allocated to small farms on an individual basis. For example, in February 1940 officials at the Württemberg Ministry of the Interior admitted that 'the influx of Polish male and female farm workers brings with it a number of difficulties which must ... be overcome if the Reich government's aim of affording agriculture tangible assistance is to be realised'. They had envisaged requiring the Poles to report daily to the local police, but now realised that this was 'impracticable' because of the distance between most farms and the nearest police station. The only solution was to order the Poles not to leave their district, and to ask Poles' employers to report any absences.[73] Yet a farm proprietor who did this risked losing his – or, increasingly, her – Polish labourer if he or she were punished with a custodial sentence, although 'many Poles' were said to 'prefer a spell in a German prison to working'. The Stuttgart State Prosecutor complained in September 1940 about the Poles' attitude to work and their disregard of the conditions which had been imposed on them: 'the longer the war lasts, the more unwillingly they work. They do not abide by the rules and residence restrictions laid down for them'. Disciplining them was rendered more difficult because the 'indifference' of the farmers to these rules and restrictions appeared to give the Poles 'a certain degree of support'.[74]

The reason for this was not hard to find. With the labour shortage on the land acute in Württemberg even before September 1939, the effects of conscription in wartime were potentially disastrous. It was, therefore, not only in Bavaria that foreign workers were regarded as 'saviours in a time of need'.[75] The call up of farmers and labourers in autumn 1939 made both the harvest – which was late because of adverse weather conditions – and the sowing of seed for the following spring extremely difficult. There was patent relief in Türkheim, near Ulm, in November 1939 when 'the conscripted proprietors and farm workers were replaced by [Polish] prisoners of war'. From 1941, Türkheim received an influx of civilian 'Ostarbeiter', to join 'French, Belgian, Italian prisoners of war and Ukrainian, Polish, White Russian and Yugoslav Ostarbeiter [sic]'. An unspecified section of the POWs proved 'very valuable, the equal of the German workers'.[76] As more and more German men were called up, farms, like some businesses, became increasingly dependent on foreign labour. To act as an incentive for increased productivity, and, later in the war, to try to avoid reprisals in the event of German defeat, farmers might improve conditions or overlook absenteeism or thieving on the part of foreign workers. In such cases, many Germans, especially in rural areas, were prepared to defy official injunctions about the treatment of foreign workers, which could bring them into conflict with the authorities.

In Württemberg, this was undoubtedly not (as the SD in Lower Franconia suggested in June 1940 was the case there) a political gesture directed against the Nazi authorities: 'some national comrades express their rejection of the party and state by way of a particularly loving treatment of the Poles'.[77] It is true that, already before the war, there was disaffection with the party and its functionaries, while the failure of the state to mitigate the problems of small-scale agriculture had made positive loyalty to it at best grudging in the countryside.[78] Nevertheless, in their dealings with foreign workers, small farmers and their families reacted pragmatically, sometimes as a matter of instinct and sometimes out of conscious material self-interest. Above all, it is clear that self-gratification, in terms of both instinctual reactions and material motives, often took precedence over obedience to the Nazi regime's prescriptions, and even over fear of the sanctions which it threatened and conspicuously implemented, in a way which undermined official policy without necessarily being a 'political' gesture, either intentionally or unconsciously. It is a commonplace that in the Third Reich the regime defined the 'political' to include virtually any attitude or act of nonconformity with its wishes and precepts. Yet in Württemberg, at least, the legal authorities did not interpret farmers' disobedience as being politically motivated. Even the SD there seems to have regarded individuals' fraternisation with foreign workers as mere delinquence with no political motive, although the attitudes and conduct of members of the Catholic clergy vis-à-vis foreign workers tended to be viewed as highly political.

Certainly, as we have seen, some members of the Catholic clergy gave a clear lead to their flock by welcoming Polish Catholics and Uniate Ukrainians to regular church services and other events, instead of merely providing occasional separate services for them as the authorities had instructed. This was a key point at which the relationship between German civilians and the regime was affected by the presence of the foreigners. For the regime, it vindicated its view of the Catholic Church as an 'opponent' – giving aid and comfort to enemies of Germany – and spiritual comradeship undoubtedly consoled foreign co-religionists in their lonely plight. This example signalled to the Catholic population that POWs and conscripted foreign labourers were to be regarded as fellow communicants and therefore, in effect, as brothers and sisters. German Catholics were, then, at least implicitly encouraged to violate the regime's prescriptions prohibiting association with foreigners and acts of kindness towards them. The result was a renewed ban on Polish POWS attending normal church services and an intensification of SD surveillance of the clergy.[79]

The shortage of labour in rural Württemberg meant especially the shortage of male workers on family farms, with the progressive call up of able-bodied farm hands and farmers virtually complete by mid 1943. Farm proprietors reacted pragmatically to the substitutes which were offered to them. Those who contributed to the maintenance of the farm – or the rural business, in the case of artisans such as millers – were welcomed and treated with some hospitality. Those who did not contribute, for example many urban evacuees in rural areas, and those whose contribution seemed to be more trouble than it was worth, such as young women in service schemes, were treated with some hostility. In the case of young women in service schemes, the limited period of service necessitated the repeated initiation of raw recruits mostly from an urban background. In the women's Labour Service, camp duties and ideological indoctrination ensured that the *Arbeitsmaid*'s (Labour Service girl's) working day was, in the view of the rural population, often laughably short and sometimes almost non-existent.[80] By contrast, most foreign workers were welcomed as a more or less reliable substitute, who, after a day's work, often seemed as deserving as family members, alongside whom they worked, of a meal at the family's table and a good night's rest in something better than a barn.[81]

This kind of fraternisation was explicitly and repeatedly forbidden, and just as insistently continued, in spite of the risk of denunciation and the threat of punishment. Officials of party and state issued regular warnings about the need to maintain a certain distance between 'Aryan' Germans and foreign workers, especially 'inferior' easterners. In February 1940, for instance, the *Tübingen Chronicle* ran the headline 'Not at the same table as a Pole!'[82] Undeterred, Germans in significant numbers continued to treat 'their' foreign workers as fellow humans.[83] In spite of official strictures, in the Friedrichshafen area it was customary for Polish, Ukrainian and Russian workers to eat at the farming family's table, on the principle that 'those who work on the farm eat together'. In some households, a small table was prepared in case an official of some kind arrived without warning; placing it only a small distance from the family's table was a gesture of defiance. As information gatherers such as the SD were well aware, eastern Europeans ate not only at the same table as Germans but even helped themselves from the common bowl of food provided for the household.[84]

The regime's officers recognised that, in rural areas, with Poles coming into close contact with the German population,

> there is the danger that far too close and trusting a relationship can develop ... Each citizen must realise that the Poles belong to an enemy state and to a cultural level far below that of the German rural population. Every farmer and every farmer's wife must take account of this superiority ...

This was an urban perspective – and a skewed one at that – which demonstrated a complete lack of understanding of life on a small south German farm. For example, there was particular official concern about the Poles' 'primitive levels of hygiene', which showed little comprehension of conditions on small Württemberg farms.[85] Many Poles came from farming families and had much in common with Württemberg's farmers. South German farmers might be more prosperous than many of those from Poland, but the experiential background of both was reasonably similar. In the Friedrichshafen area, among others, farming families were mostly, like their Polish workers, Catholic. They appreciated that Polish POWs had been, like their own conscripted menfolk, unwilling soldiers, and that they worried about their families at home. The Poles, in their turn, recognised that their employers had similar worries about family members who were at the front.[86] On farms in Württemberg where there was no piped water, where animals shared the family's accommodation and where the manure piled up in front of the farmer's dwelling was an indication of prosperity, there would be some fellow feeling between rural Württembergers and Poles from a rural background. Certainly, these two groups had more in common than farmers had with most urban dwellers. Beyond that, it became clear during the war that there was more common ground between foreigners – including particularly French POWs – from a rural background and farming families in Württemberg than there was between the latter and evacuees from Ruhr towns, who seemed truly foreign to rural Swabians.

From the start, the authorities were determined to monitor relations between German citizens and foreign civilians and POWs, and this became an increasing part of the *Kreisleiter*'s remit.[87] The general level of morals was to be monitored, especially among the wives of serving soldiers, and women's conduct towards both German soldiers and foreign prisoners noted.[88] Some Germans were punished for the simplest gestures towards foreigners – such as providing food, drink or cigarettes – but this depended on arbitrary and uneven local enforcement which caused both uncertainty and resentment.[89] In January 1940, the senior SS authorities in Württemberg and Baden requested that not only should all 'unseemly behaviour' be reported, but that all instances in which a German 'has not maintained the necessary distance' between himself and a foreigner should also be reported to the SD.[90] One result of this was that instances of sexual relations between Polish men and German women were reported to Himmler, who invariably ordered the death penalty for the man.[91] Nevertheless, there continued to be cases of individuals who had no relationship with a foreign worker – and therefore no immediate vested interest in his wellbeing – providing scraps of food or clothing, or even ration cards.[92] Again, in the Friedrichshafen area from 1942–45, a part-time police photographer developed photographs taken illicitly by a Polish worker who, as a Pole, was forbidden either to own a camera or to buy film. This was a simple act of kindness – if a distinctly risky one – on the part of one photography enthusiast towards another, a connection that overrode considerations of nationality or 'race'.[93]

While it would be misleading to suggest that foreign workers allocated to small farms enjoyed *good* conditions – any more than did German labourers or indeed many farming families, especially during the war – it is clear that their scarcity value often worked to their advantage. A direct correlation is discernible between a farm's need for labour and the extent to which the foreigners were treated favourably rather than brutally. This was particularly obvious in the later stages of the war although it was visible from the start. At the same time, there was a matching correlation between the shortage of labour and the growing self-confidence and assertiveness of at least some foreign workers, as they became aware of their value to farmers and as news of Germany's military reverses reached them.[94] As the foreigners became increasingly indispensable in the countryside, and aware of the possibilities in their surroundings, they could demand better conditions – such as more and better food, to augment their meagre official allocations – and sexual favours. Undoubtedly, there were cases of straightforward sexual attraction, and there were also cases of genuine attachment between a German woman and a foreign man.[95] Sometimes, however, a farmer's wife might embark on a sexual relationship with a foreign worker, or encourage either a daughter or a maid to do so, in order to retain his labour and enhance his motivation. The Stuttgart State Prosecutor reported in May 1943 that 'frequently in court when women admit their guilt they say that they consented so as not to lose the prisoner of war's labour'. He also claimed that, 'in the case of pregnant German women and girls particularly', it seemed that they had engaged in sex with a foreigner out of fear of violence against them if they refused.[96] Giving this impression may have been a matter of special pleading: German women who were found out were probably anxious to prevent or mitigate punishment by the authorities.

The Nazi racist obsession with maintaining the 'purity' of German blood ensured that sexual relationships were the issue involving foreign workers that caused most friction between German civilians and the Nazi authorities. To try to minimise the 'danger' of 'racial mixing', brothels staffed by female foreigners were established 'in almost every larger town and close to every large industrial concern'.[97] In Württemberg, such brothels were opened in Stuttgart, Ulm and Friedrichshafen, although there was local opposition in the latter two towns, and in neither was there the expected volume of trade.[98] This, however, did not address the possibility of relationships developing between foreigners living and working in rural areas and the German 'Aryans', to whom they were often in close proximity. It was here that Nazi attitudes revealed a fatal double standard. A foreign man found to have had sexual intercourse with a German woman was likely to be hanged, while his German lover was often humiliated and pilloried before perhaps being obliged to watch his execution and then being sent to prison.[99] For example, in the commune of Cleeborn, near Heilbronn, in July 1941, a Pole, who had 'befriended a girl with a bad reputation and had sexual intercourse with her, was hanged on the order of the *Reichsführer* SS'. The Stuttgart State Prosecutor estimated that this was the sixth case in Württemberg in which a Pole had been hanged on Himmler's orders for a similar offence.[100] By contrast, in the case of German men and foreign women who were sexual partners there was official displeasure but no consistently applied penalty, although in *Landkreis* Stade, for example, a German man might be arrested and even sent to a concentration camp for having sex with a foreign woman.[101] This was, however, by no means the rule. In Württemberg, most men escaped with a warning.[102]

This double standard was a source of both confusion and disgust to many ordinary civilians. For example, by mid 1941, there were around 800 French and Belgian women renting rooms privately in Württemberg. The local population complained about their attitude in general and their alleged sexual promiscuity in particular. They could not understand why French women, especially, could flaunt their relationships with German men and even teenage boys unmolested, while a German woman found to have a foreign lover might have to endure public humiliation and imprisonment.[103] The SS, in particular, was keen to pillory women who were guilty of 'racial defilement', and Himmler encouraged local party activists to stage the public head shaving of such women and to parade them around their locality bearing a placard detailing their offence.[104] The age old prejudice which judged women more harshly than men in sexual matters was the essential context for reactions to German women's liaisons with foreign men. In both an age and a place where traditional conservative attitudes to sexual morality prevailed, many people felt that lapses, particularly on the part of women, deserved retribution, not least where wives of serving soldiers were consorting with men from enemy countries. The regime played its part by introducing in 1942 a new crime of 'insult of husbands at the front', and then, in March 1943, the possibility of a 'post-mortem divorce', by which the adulterous widow of a dead soldier might have her pension cancelled.[105] The chief issue for Nazis, however, was less the contravening of conventional moral standards than the dual concern of the invasive defilement by a 'racial inferior' of a German woman and the associated risk of a 'polluted' pregnancy.

The rhythms and practices of life on the land made it more likely that foreign workers there would be in close and fairly continuous contact with the natives with whom they worked. Where there were few men left on family farms, as a result of conscription, this meant close and habitual contact between foreign men and German women. In the Friedrichshafen area, for example, those charged with 'racial defilement' were not from the town itself but were overwhelmingly 'farm maids, farmers' wives, farmers' daughters and women from the rural middle class'.[106] By September 1940, twelve women in Württemberg had been accused of 'racial defilement' and pilloried for it. The three who had had French lovers claimed to have believed that the penalties advertised applied only to those who had sex with a Pole. The Stuttgart State Prosecutor was not sympathetic. No doubt a lawyer in Stuttgart was fully conversant with the precise prescriptions governing relations with foreigners, but it is not implausible that women in rural communes were not. Especially at such an early stage in the war, they may not have encountered the warnings given 'in the daily papers and also by political leaders, Landräte and mayors'.[107] Part-time mayors of communes, who had enough difficulty in keeping up with the demands of the War Economy Decree, among much else, may well not have read or passed on every warning about relations with foreigners. Further, the emphasis which had been placed from the start of the war on prohibitions of any kind of personal relationship with a Pole might well have overshadowed other restrictions. Nevertheless, it appears that news of the penalties imposed for 'racial defilement' had its effect. In early 1941, the Stuttgart State Prosecutor attributed the recent decline in the number of prosecutions for this alleged 'crime' to the deterrent effect of well-publicised prison sentences on women convicted of it in 1940.[108] More probably, however, the number of prosecutions decreased because a woman with a Polish lover had learned to be more discreet.

There was widespread disquiet about the ritual public humiliation of German women and girls organised by the party without recourse to the law, a disquiet shared by some law officers. In rural communes such as Meckenbeuren, near Friedrichshafen, the ritual of humiliation, including public head shaving, was carried out by SA men and NSDAP members; the rest of the population regarded it as deeply repugnant.[109] In Denkendorf in 1940 the Esslingen *Kreisleiter*, Eugen Hund, ordered that three women who had consorted with POWs should have their hair shorn, after which the Stuttgart Special Court sentenced them to terms of up to two years in prison. While Hund tried to justify this in terms of Nazi racial policy, the local population found it all 'repellent'. Unrepentant after the war, Hund asserted that 'Females, I would not like to call them women, who in 1940, in time of war, turned a battling and struggling homeland into a whorehouse, had to be treated like whores'. Again, in January 1941, in the commune of Faurndau, a young woman had her hair shorn 'in the presence of various NS functionaries', and was then taken through nearby Göppingen with a placard around her neck stating: 'I went with a Pole and polluted German blood'. She was sent first to prison and then for a short spell in Ravensbrück concentration camp. There were several other instances of this kind of public humiliation of women in Württemberg, with officials of the NSDAP, often including the *Kreisleiter*, taking part.[110] The party's treatment of women who transgressed the racial – rather than the moral – law signalled a coarsening of attitudes on the part of diehard Nazis towards even German 'Aryans'; this became most apparent in the closing stages of the war. Finally, however, on 13 October 1941, Hitler banned vigilante activity, including public head shaving, because of the adverse reactions to publicity about it among Germany's friends and allies abroad.[111]

Nevertheless, the prison sentences and deterrent spells in concentration camps – especially for women deemed to be 'asocial' – continued to be imposed. In February 1943, the criminal court in Rottweil sentenced three young women to between three and eight months in prison for having had 'relationships' with French POWs.[112] Again, in June 1943, the Stuttgart Special Court sentenced a fifty-eight-year-old woman to three years' imprisonment for having 'prohibited relations' with French and Belgian POWs.[113] The SD admitted in January 1944 that sexual relationships with Frenchmen were 'not restricted only to women from feckless or asocial sections [of society], but have for some time embraced also [those from] other circles'. They mentioned the example of a teacher who was a member not only of the NSDAP but also of various formations and affiliates of the party, including the Nazi women's organisation. She, too, had been given a custodial sentence.[114] It was perhaps not surprising that in some cases a pregnant German woman whose relationship with a foreigner had not been detected would claim not to know who was the father of her child, in order both to receive state support and to avoid punishment.[115] Yet, at the same time, members of the Wehrmacht stationed in Württemberg were said to be 'on a very "intimate footing" with foreign women', walking around 'arm in arm even in broad daylight and kissing'. In Reutlingen, there were apparently bars where soldiers – many of them married men – and French women met freely, while in Ulm 'great offence' was caused by the 'shameless manner' in which 'intimate relations were conducted between French women and German soldiers'.[116] The Wehrmacht's leadership washed its hands of the matter, informing the SS that 'there is no reason to prohibit relationships between German officers and French women'.[117]

Similarly, it seemed that there was little that could be done when German civilian men became involved with foreign women. There was particular outrage in Balingen, where youths aged between fifteen and eighteen, most of them Hitler Youth members, were said to follow the foreign women around 'and virtually camp outside their door at night', while the SD in Tübingen reported that seven Hitler Youth members in the commune of Unterjessingen were in the habit of 'going out with Belgian women at night and having sexual intercourse with them'. The women made no secret of their affairs: 'when one of the Belgian women has sexual intercourse, next day she lets fly the most vulgar utterances from her window, regardless of whether there are children of school age in the vicinity'. Like the German soldiers who consorted with French women workers, they seemed not to suffer for their conduct, to the anger of the population who demanded that they be housed in barracks where they could be controlled, instead of privately.[118] In another case, three Hitler Youth members under the age of eighteen, along with a young adult male German and several French women workers, had spent the night together in a ski hut which had one room with several beds. It was a particular cause for concern that two of the women were believed to be venereally diseased. Charges were laid against the three youths under the Youth Protection Order, but no action was taken against the other young man 'because there is no penalty for having sex with foreign women workers, even if they belong to enemy states and it constitutes a major national disgrace', reported the Stuttgart State Prosecutor regretfully. Typically blaming the women rather than the boys, he claimed that 'big city prostitutes' from France and Belgium were at the root of the trouble.[119]

If there was little that could be done about relations between German men and foreign women, it became clear that controlling the conditions under which foreigners lived and worked on individual farms was also problematic. If the foreigners were housed collectively, and if there were sufficient guards, it was easier to prevent them both from forming close relationships with the natives and from absconding or violating official restrictions. Where POWs were accommodated in purpose-built camps, however, time was spent in the morning and evening conveying them to and from their places of work, and driving them around occupied men who could be more usefully employed. Accordingly, in December 1941, it was announced that there would be less supervision of French POWs in order to release manpower, although Germans were still expected to adopt an attitude of 'complete reserve' towards them.[120] Yet, even from the start, maintaining both orderly supervision and observance of the restrictions 'was scarcely achievable in agriculture, where everyone knew everyone else and every worker counted'. In particular, there were foreigners, including French POWs, who lived in their employers' household. In addition, trying to restrict Poles to the commune in which they worked no doubt seemed a tidy arrangement to urban minds, until it became clear that the fields in which they were to work might be outside the commune's boundary. It was still the case that many farmers– and even some mayors of communes – thought in terms of the traditional parish boundaries rather than administrative units. When a female Polish worker was discovered not to be displaying the 'violet P' badge when she visited a relative nearby, the mayor of Ailingen interceded because, he said, firstly, there were no such badges available, and, secondly, it was his fault for not realising that her visit would take her across the commune's boundary. Sometimes employers, and even mayors, connived at the use of bicycles by Poles, for example to make the fortnightly journey to report to the nearest employment office. With a worker's time at a premium, it seemed only sensible.[121]

By the middle of the war, employers might refrain from reporting cases of malicious damage or theft in case they lost the foreigner's labour, and innkeepers were reluctant to turn a foreigner away and thus both lose his custom and risk arousing his anger. As even the overstretched *Gendarmerie* turned a blind eye, foreign workers were often able to disregard the rules circumscribing their mobility and prohibiting them from frequenting the same restaurants, cinemas and dancehalls as Germans. The guards assigned to supervise foreign workers were commonly said to be both 'negligent and lenient' in terms of the latitude which they tolerated. This was, however, a recognition of the realities of wartime conditions. With virtually all fit German men conscripted from rural areas, by mid 1943 there were many farms and rural businesses which could not have operated without the foreigners. For example, a corn mill in Rottweil district was being run solely by a Pole and a Ukrainian. On one farm, whose childless widowed female proprietor had been murdered by a Pole, another Pole was now in charge. Only the intervention of the *Kreisleiter* brought to an end the 'degrading situation' of this Pole's being in authority over a German girl who was employed there. According to the Stuttgart State Prosecutor, rural women now went in fear of the foreigners, especially when the press reported violence and murder perpetrated by them.[122] To the increasing anxiety of the German population, it was reported, 'the foreigners (civilian workers and prisoners of war), day by day [become] more impudent in their behaviour and careless in their work'.[123]

It would be wrong to give the impression that most foreign POWs and forced labourers in Germany during the Second World War were able to make the system work in their favour, and ultimately to control their conditions and their hosts. It is true that some tried to improve their circumstances by asserting their loyalty to Germany: there were cases of both Ukrainians and Russians expressing relief at their liberation from 'Bolshevism'.[124] Others were able to operate on the black market, both amongst themselves and together with Germans, to the consternation of the authorities who regarded it as yet another threat to the maintenance of 'the distance between Germans and foreigners which should above all be upheld'. Goods that were scarce in Germany – either received from their home country or somehow bought with money which they had saved – were bartered, and ration cards were obtained illegally. In some cases in Württemberg, foreigners had been able to obtain bicycles, motor cycles, watches and shaving equipment, which some of them attempted to take back to their home country. Some foreigners, especially Frenchmen, were able to deal in contraband ration cards.[125] Many, however, were far too weakened by starvation and abuse, and far too closely policed, to do more than try to survive.[126] This was especially – but not uniformly – the case in industrial centres, whereas in rural areas, with foreigners often scattered among small farms, as individuals, they were more difficult to control, especially in the later stages of the war when the police were very thin on the ground.

Foreign workers living and working in rural households generally experienced better conditions and less regimentation, and were therefore undoubtedly 'in much better circumstances, than those in factories and towns'.[127] In addition, and crucially, those in the countryside had better access to food supplies. Indeed, particularly if they ate at the family table, they often were better supplied with food than were urban Germans, and they certainly were better nourished than their compatriots back home. The effect of this was that 'the agricultural forced workers broke through a National Socialist "nutritional hierarchy", which was strictly determined by racist principles and therefore condemned "less valuable" people to starvation to the benefit of members of the "higher" race'.[128] The Württemberg farmer who preferred to give his cows' excess milk to his Ukrainian farm workers rather than surrender it to the official depot was clearly far from exceptional.[129] This was partly because farmers resented the whole system of delivery quotas. Yet it was also not least because many in the native rural population simply recognised their foreign workers as fellow humans with personality traits, convictions and a family history, rather than as faceless members of an enemy alien force. Particularly by the later stages of the war, those foreigners who had been there for months or years had become part of the community. It was a failure to appreciate this that led a Nazi local branch leader to complain 'Does it not make a real mockery of our *Weltanschauung* if I enter a German peasant home and there in a German pram lies the child of a Russian woman, sired by a Frenchman and cared for by a German woman?' Even among some of the faithful, there was not always wholehearted acceptance of the implications of Nazi ideology. For example, an assiduous district leader of the Nazi women's organisation in Württemberg, who had grown up in a farming household and 'whose husband was one of the best known Nazis in the area', looked after the young Polish worker who became pregnant by her son in 1944 during her pregnancy, and took care of both her and her child, who was born in February 1945.[130]

The official view of foreign workers from the east remained remorseless, and also uncomprehending. There was irritation that 'these Poles' did not seem to realise that they were not free to move about as they chose, and that they were obliged at all times to wear on their clothing the conspicuous violet coloured 'P' which clearly identified their origin. There was impatience that 'they still simply cannot get used to the restrictions imposed on them'. The irritation and impatience derived from the clear assumption – to which many Poles manifestly did not subscribe – that Poles ought on the one hand to recognise the inferior status to which both their 'race' as Slavs and German victory had relegated them, and ought on the other hand passively to accept the constraints which their enemy's victory had brought. Part of the problem for the authorities, however, was that the individual small employer had far more to worry about than checking up on whether foreign workers were abiding by petty regulations which did not directly affect him, or, increasingly, her. As early as summer 1941, the Stuttgart State Prosecutor recognised that the Poles' employers needed their labour far too much to try to restrain or report them, and that an employer would be as aggrieved as his Polish worker if the Pole were sent to prison for a relatively minor misdemeanour.[131]

With the dissolution of the Nazi system in Württemberg in April 1945, and the arrival of the invading French and American forces, the balance of advantage swung decisively in favour of the newly liberated foreign workers and against German civilians. Both American and French forces tolerated widespread thieving on the part of foreign workers, who in most reported cases were Poles or Russians.[132] Nevertheless, while theft and plundering were widespread, especially where large numbers of foreigners were gathered together, foreign workers in Württemberg seem relatively seldom to have targeted specific individual Germans, in spite of their undoubted euphoria at liberation and, given official Nazi policy at least, good cause for revenge. This suggests that, on the whole, a foreigner who had worked for a small proprietor did not normally have a personal grudge against him or her, although there were doubtless exceptions. Some foreigners even protected their former employers from the soldiers' wrath, while others took a hand in arranging a local ceasefire. When the invading Americans arrested a youth in Oppingen, on suspicion of being an artillery lookout, it was on the intercession of Belgian workers that he was finally released.[133] In Wendelsheim, French POWs immediately reported to their invading countrymen that 'they had been well-treated here during their fifty-eight month stay', and asked that the troops should leave the village unmolested, which they did.[134] When a local notable in Steinenbronn went to surrender the village, on 20 April, three French POWs accompanied him, one of whom went ahead to meet the French forces with a white flag.[135] In Musberg, a French former POW was even installed as civil head of local government, as an interim measure.[136] Thus in a sense the roles were reversed: whereas German civilians had often mediated, and mitigated, the Nazi regime's provisions about the conduct and conditions of foreign workers, with their liberation some foreigners briefly served a similar function between the occupation forces and the vanquished.

These instances, however, all refer to foreigners from western Europe. The eastern Europeans, far larger in number, were generally gathered together in transit camps to await repatriation. Some remained in the camps, but others exercised their new freedom. In Frankenbach, for example, this 'created a real terror in the area, with a great deal stolen during these days'.[137] Poles who were gathered in camps in Ulm and Geislingen returned by night to the villages where they had worked; for a whole week they staged break ins, stealing money and goods.[138]

Some seventy Russians and Poles were still at large in Hüttlingen towards the end of May 1945, while as late as autumn 1945 some Poles in Ulm district, dressed partly in American army uniform, robbed a German couple of money and almost all of their laundry; they were, however, apprehended and part of the haul was returned.[139] In Rohrau, it was said, the former foreign workers there, who had been gathered in a nearby camp, used their local knowledge to help the occupying French troops to plunder the village.[140] There was not, however, invariably cooperation between foreigner workers and the invaders. In Schöckingen, for example, 'the first heroic act' of an advance force of French troops was to shoot in the foot a Pole who failed to answer their enquiry about whether there were German soldiers in the commune.[141] Some foreign workers met a worse fate when enemy forces sought the surrender of a commune. In Entringen, in Tübingen district, a French POW was killed when approaching French soldiers lobbed a grenade into a farmer's house.[142] When German troops tried to defend Niedernhall, two Russians were among those killed by American artillery fire.[143]

Nevertheless, for the most part, theft and looting by the liberated foreigners was, not surprisingly, restricted to the bare necessities of life, although bicycles, which afforded mobility, were much sought after. For example, in Jonathan Schmid's birthplace, Gebersheim, 'under the leadership of Poles who were in service here, there was thieving of bicycles and food'.[144] The clear impression is that, in Württemberg, thieving and looting by foreign workers – by contrast with that perpetrated by the invading forces themselves – were more a desperate attempt to remedy acute material deprivation than a conscious act of retribution or revenge. For example, in Eschenau, in the summer of 1945, some Poles stole a large cow and made off with it in an American car. Three weeks later, twelve armed Poles and Slovenes arrived in the night and killed two pigs and a calf.[145] In Rudersberg, just before the burial of ten casualties of the invasion, a group of Russians broke into a tailor's premises next to the pastor's house and helped themselves to clothing and cloth.[146] German villagers endured these bouts of virtually legalised lawlessness with a combination of anger and resignation; it was a particular source of resentment that they were subject to a curfew but the foreigners were not, which allowed the latter to wander about and pillage at will. In addition, in many places under French occupation each family had to provide a suit, shoes and other items of apparel *in good condition* to afford the liberated foreigners adequate clothing; this was seen by the unwilling donors as a major hardship after years of rationing of clothes and shoes.[147]

By no means all of the foreigners plundered, however, and those who did were not necessarily – and perhaps not often – plundering their former employers. In Wallhausen, some left for a transit camp while others remained at work on the farms 'although they were no longer obliged to work', and 'in general ... the remaining foreigners behaved decently'.[148] In Rohrau some foreign workers protected their own former employers against the 'plague' of looting by other foreigners.[149] In Höfingen, near Leonberg, the threat to Germans came not from the foreign workers but from the invading forces. French troops indulged in an orgy of rape, with only those with a French POW in the household enjoying some immunity: 'on the whole, thanks to the good treatment which they had experienced, the French prisoners of war protected the women and girls'.[150] Much the same was true in Hirschlanden and in Rudersberg, where 'many former French prisoners of war' did their best to protect their former employers from French soldiers on the rampage.[151]

In Württemberg's households, and even in whole villages, peasants had had a vested interest in the wellbeing of 'their' foreign workers even while perhaps remaining prejudiced against 'foreign workers' as a depersonalised category. For example, the way in which the generalised category of 'Poles and Russians' was blamed for thieving and plundering, both during the war and in the first weeks of enemy occupation, suggests a distaste for anonymous 'foreigners' which was entirely consistent with village attitudes towards incomers – including Germans – who did not contribute to the continuing survival of the community, especially if they also brought some kind of trouble with them, as some evacuees did. Further, as one astute state prosecutor suggested in 1944, it was possible that peasants tried to disguise their own violation of wartime economic controls by blaming unidentified 'foreigners'. For example, peasants who were accused of illegally slaughtering pigs might deny that they had done so and, to find a convenient scapegoat, might claim that people from a 'foreigners' camp' had stolen the animals.[152]

By contrast, those foreign workers who had lived and worked in a commune might behave as if they were indeed members of it. For example, in Wallhausen the wife of a farmer who, with his brother, was a POW in the USSR fled with her child shortly before American forces arrived in the village. Her property was cared for by a woman forced worker from Russia.[153] In April 1945 in Hermuthausen the conflagration in the church – after it was hit by the invading forces' incendiaries – was extinguished with the help of 'the Poles and Russians who were still in the village', although 'civilians from Poland and Russia' were also said to have plundered the village.[154] This was perhaps not as paradoxical as it seems: the postwar mayor of Goldburghausen drew a distinction between local foreign workers – 'armed, disciplined Poles' – who in April 1945 reinforced the new police authority which was composed of former French workers, and another group, 'wandering Poles' from elsewhere who plundered the village. In spite of the best efforts of the village's former foreign workers, they could not prevent 'a series of damaging thefts' by these incomers.[155] In Rohrau, it was foreign workers – 'mostly Poles' – who offered to take clothing and food to men from the village who had been seized and imprisoned by invading French soldiers.[156] In Bächlingen, when in April 1945 some villagers approached the American tanks carrying a white flag, 'the Poles who were working here for the farmers went along with them as intermediaries'.[157] It was French POWs who greeted an advance party of French soldiers when they entered Münchingen. They explained that they had been well treated, which apparently did much to spare the commune's members, and especially its women, physical violence. The French POWs' departure for France, on 22 April, was greatly regretted, because 'they would have prevented much unpleasantness' on the part of Polish and Russian civilians. It is not clear whether these civilians had worked in the commune or not.[158]

Western Europeans mostly hastened to return home. Nevertheless, in Oberkochen, 'the warmth with which most of the French, Dutch and also Belgian prisoners took their leave of their hosts was remarkable'.[159] In Lendsiedel, former Belgian POWs, who had been hastily sent to Dachau at the end of March 1945, returned on VE-Day, driving through the village in a horse-drawn vehicle on which a Belgian flag had been hoisted, and stopping to visit the mayor and the farmers. Their former employers put them up for the night before they resumed their journey homewards. It was said, in November 1948, that most of them had kept in touch by letter with their former hosts.[160] Some eastern Europeans, however, were less eager to return home. Conditions in Aalen district at the end of the war were certainly deemed more attractive than those back home by Ukrainian workers who stayed on after French and Polish workers had left.[161] That may not say much, given the treatment of the Ukraine by Stalin during the period of forced collectivisation. In addition, some workers from the Ukraine and Belorussia had gone voluntarily to work in Germany, which gave them good cause for anxiety about returning home. Some now chose to claim that they were Polish, a contrast with the insistence of some Polish citizens in calling themselves Ukrainians in the early stages of the war.[162]

Altogether, it seems clear that many foreign workers, including some eastern Europeans, did develop reasonably cordial relationships with their host families. This was precisely what the Nazi regime was at pains to avoid. Yet it had itself facilitated these relationships by bringing into Germany so many foreigners, especially by dispersing a substantial proportion of these in the countryside, where the household economy persisted. The Stuttgart State Prosecutor spoke in despairing tones in May 1943 about 'the ever increasing number of these foreigners' as if a *deus ex machina* had effected this, and as if it was not an entirely self-inflicted 'problem'.[163] Yet perhaps the chief effect of bringing a wide variety of foreigners into areas, including rural Württemberg, where 'foreigner' had meant a person from outside the commune was, entirely contrary to Nazi purposes, to broaden the perceptions of villagers and to give them some preparation for the influx of strangers who would arrive as refugees at the end of the war.

9

Migrants, Evacuees and Refugees

In the Second World War in Europe large numbers of people were on the move, detached from their normal surroundings and thrust into a new, unfamiliar and often inhospitable environment. The emigration, incarceration or deportation of the Nazi regime's targeted victims not only from Germany but from all over occupied Europe was one of the most obvious instances of this. Beyond that, in all belligerent countries huge numbers of men in roughly the eighteen to forty-five years old age group were conscripted into the armed forces from all kinds of background, regimented and sent far from home. In addition to experiencing the stresses of military combat, some would participate in atrocities against civilians, especially on the eastern front. Many German soldiers ended their days there, fighting in desperate circumstances or being harassed by partisans. Men from the commune of Zipplingen, in Aalen district, died in both Russia and Bosnia, and an airman from the village perished in the last of his many bombing missions on the Mius front in Russia. If they were lucky, German soldiers might find a relatively comfortable niche, policing a quiescent area in Denmark, perhaps, or Norway, in France or the Low Countries, until the western allies' progress after D-Day in June 1944 made them, too, retreating defenders. Nevertheless, pacified western Europe had its hazards: for example, a soldier from Zipplingen died in Norway as a result of a land mine explosion.[1] Equally, soldiers from other nations spent time in Württemberg, some in a prisoner-of-war camp in Ludwigsburg.[2] Others, as allies of Germany, sought temporary refuge in Württemberg: French soldiers loyal to the Vichy leader, Marshal Pétain, having fled from France in late 1944, reformed in Aalen district to prepare for a counterattack against the invading allies.[3] In Neresheim, 'a great stir and confusion was caused by the quartering of the Vlasow army which was passing through' in March 1945. These anti-Bolshevik Russian soldiers offered the inhabitants army horses in return for schnaps.[4] In Hüttlingen, 'war weary soldiers … from the Balkan states came here'.[5]

Civilians, too, were on the move. First, ethnic Germans were 'brought home into the Reich' from eastern Europe after the Molotov–Ribbentrop pact of August 1939, making people from the Baltic States, Poland or Romania refugees in a foreign country which, they were told, was their homeland.[6] Secondly, in any country invaded by German forces, and in Germany itself towards the end of the war, there were refugees fleeing from the fighting front to what they hoped would be safety. Thirdly, as we have seen, military POWs were set to work in Germany while millions of citizens of the occupied countries were sent to Germany, as coerced civilian workers, to serve the German war effort in factories and fields. Fourthly, in any country subjected to aerial bombardment, including Germany, there were civilian refugees from both bombed areas and probable bombing targets. Some moved on their own initiative; others were compulsorily evacuated by government order. In general, urban factory workers were kept at their post, although, where bombing intensified, their works might be relocated to a less vulnerable area. Urban children, especially, were evacuated to the safer countryside. Sometimes they were accompanied by their mothers or their teachers, sometimes not. In Germany, 850,000 ten to fourteen year olds were sent to *Kinderlandverschickung* camps in rural areas where they came under the authority and influence of stalwarts of the Hitler Youth.[7] In Britain, by contrast, smaller numbers than had been expected left the towns as evacuees in 1940, and they soon began to drift back home, leading some to claim that the entire evacuation project was a failure.[8] Nevertheless, it was also observed that many British evacuees remained in the countryside throughout most of the war, and that some of the relationships established then were maintained after the war.[9]

Yet Britain was, as always, a special case. There was perhaps the threat of invasion in 1940, but otherwise what Britons fled from was, simply, the bombing. By contrast, in many continental European countries, there was at some point during 1939–41 the reality of both German bombing and German invasion, followed, in most of eastern Europe in 1944–45, by Soviet invasion. This led the then Polish President, Lech Walesa, to say, fifty years after the event, that VE-Day, on 8 May 1945, could not be considered a day of liberation for his country.[10] By contrast, in western Europe, most citizens undoubtedly greeted the western allies as liberators: in 1993, the Dutch Prime Minister, Ruud Lubbers, could say that people of his generation and older still felt gratitude for the liberation of their country by Canadian and British troops.[11] Even so, the Allied invasion of mainland Europe, following the D-Day landings in June 1944, inflicted serious damage and casualties on the areas and people they were liberating. In recognition of this experience in Argentan, in Normandy, a marble plaque, apparently added to the war memorial there in the 1990s, bears the inscription: 'Hommage aux victimes civiles des bombardements de 1944'. And, following D-Day, there were German atrocities in France: for example, in Pressignac (Dordogne), the war memorial records that 'le 21 juin 1944 ce village fut incendie par l'occupant tuant et fusillant 35 de ses defenseurs'. The most notorious German atrocity in France had already been perpetrated at Oradour-sur-Glane on 10 June 1944.[12] These and similar experiences in continental Europe were markedly different from those of the inhabitants of both Britain and, until the last few months of the war, Germany.

Even so, the pressures of war changed the character of Württemberg's communes from 1939. The conscription of adult males, many of whom would not return, and, as we have seen, an influx of coerced foreign workers altered the balance of the population. Beyond this, there were various German incomers. Some communes received evacuees from Baden's western border areas in 1939–40, and some received groups of ethnic Germans from eastern Europe. Later, from 1943, much larger and less transient groups of people arrived, often with few possessions and in acute distress. In the years 1943–45 there was a massive influx of urban evacuees into Württemberg's rural communes. As well as those escaping from bombing, there were, in the later stages of the war, those fleeing from the invading Red Army in eastern Europe and eastern Germany. To the farming families, they were all – urban Germans, eastern Germans, ethnic Germans from outside the Reich and people of other nationalities – incomers with unfamiliar ways whose merit was judged by the contribution they made to the life of the community which they joined. As we have seen, it was not unusual for a French, Polish or Ukrainian foreign worker to become a valued member of the household because of the useful role played by him or her in the work of the household's business.[13]

On the other hand, fellow Germans, who were supposed to be co-members of the *Volksgemeinschaft*, in which institutions like the Labour Service had allegedly helped to build 'a bridge between town and country', were sometimes at least mutually suspicious and not infrequently mutually hostile.[14] Some Württembergers had, even before the war, had bruising experiences when they had accommodated urban children to afford them a rural holiday. The NSDAP local branch leader in Nürtingen South had great difficulty in 1938 in trying to place 'holiday children' in local homes with farming families. His cell leaders reported that, among those who had previously taken in one or two children, there was outright refusal to do so again.[15] In wartime, rural folk regarded some of the urban migrants and evacuees as greedy and lazy, if not unashamedly promiscuous in addition. The townees, for their part, tended to despise rural people whom they regarded as simple and hidebound. From Aalen it was reported, after young evacuees from Duisburg had left, that:

> They did not leave a good impression. One of the little madams wrote on the school's table: 'We bought everything from the Swabians except their stupidity'. Another accompanied *Kreisleiter* Trefz when he took flight from the approaching Americans in a car.[16]

Yet there were also examples of warmer relationships between evacuees and their hosts, as shared hardships bred a degree of mutual understanding. At the end of the war, and in the ensuing months, an influx of refugees from eastern Germany and eastern Europe was accepted – with or without good grace – as one of the many costs of a lost war and a discredited political system that civilian Germans had to bear.

In the early stages of the war, ethnic Germans from eastern Europe, including Romania, the Baltic States, Galicia and Volhynia, were brought into the Greater German Reich. In the first instance, they were accommodated in transit camps where their 'racial value' was assessed. Those who were found to be 'racially worthless' were abandoned, often being deposited in the 'General Government' area of Poland which was ruled by the merciless Hans Frank. By contrast, those who were judged to be 'Aryan' Germans were settled, many of them on land annexed from Poland and in homes from which Poles – including Polish Jews – had been summarily evicted, while others were brought to Germany.[17] Those who were to be settled in Württemberg were said to have 'mostly returned voluntarily to the Reich', although foreign policy priorities had put them in a position where they had had little choice but to uproot themselves from their home. For many, however, settling in Germany proper was preferable to being obliged to remain on former Polish territory, which was the lot of many. Himmler's office, the *Volksdeutsche Mittelstelle* (Liaison Office for Ethnic Germans), was one of many agencies putting pressure on localities to release accommodation.[18] For Himmler, this served two purposes, first by providing living quarters for 'racially valuable' ethnic German settlers from eastern Europe, and secondly by giving him a pretext for dispossessing religious orders of their convents and hospitals. For example, the Mariahilfe hospital, which belonged to the *Kloster* Untermarchtal in Ehingen, was taken over by the *Volksdeutsche Mittelstelle* in November 1940 to enable it to accommodate ethnic German refugees from eastern Europe.[19] In the same month, the *Sicherheitsdienst* reported that a transport of ethnic Germans from Bessarabia and Bukovina was due to arrive in Württemberg, 'of whom the majority will be accommodated in expropriated convents'.[20] The anticipated influx of ethnic Germans led also to the commandeering of care homes for mentally incapacitated persons; this would, as we have seen, condemn many of them to become victims of the 'euthanasia' programme.

By November 1944, there were some 1800 young settlers in Württemberg, for whom the HJ was expected to provide support. According to one HJ leader, they had arrived with high ideals about Germany, the German people and German institutions, ideals which had promoted significant expectations. Yet 'what they have personally experienced has in most cases had the effect of a cold shower'. It was not their fault, he said, that these boys and girls could hardly speak German: in states such as Hungary, Romania and Russia they and their forebears – who had formed 'a bulwark against the Steppe' – had been forced to adopt a foreign language. Clearly, in the xenophobic atmosphere of Nazi Germany, where, especially in wartime, there were many foreigners who were classed as 'subhuman' and others who were merely suspect, young people who appeared not to be

German experienced prejudice. To counteract this and to make these young people feel welcome, the HJ leadership in Württemberg decreed that its districts should appoint liaison officers to minister to the needs of the young settlers and to ensure that there was cooperation with other relevant agencies, for example the *NS-Frauenschaft* (NSF – Nazi women's organisation). It was, no doubt, a sign of the extent of conscription that officers of the *Bund Deutscher Mädel* (League of German Girls) were considered suitable candidates for the post of liaison officer. To promote both appropriate attitudes and approved methods for providing support, they were to undergo a series of training courses.[21]

Accommodation in Württemberg was already becoming scarce when the first ethnic Germans arrived, because evacuees from Baden were brought in long before area bombing commenced in 1942. In the period of the 'phoney war', or '*drôle de guerre*', from the subjugation of Poland in September 1939 until the *Wehrmacht*'s attack on western European countries in April 1940, the possibility of a French attack on Germany's south-western border seemed a genuine threat. Indeed, a few air raids did occur in Baden during this period. As *Reichsverteidigungskommissar* (RVK – Reich Defence Commissioner) for Army District V, which embraced both Baden and Württemberg, from September 1939 until November 1942, Wilhelm Murr was responsible for security in the border area of Baden. In keeping with plans drawn up by the NSDAP shortly before the war, in autumn 1939, women and children from Baden, in the areas adjacent to France, were sent eastwards to safety in Württemberg, Bavaria and even further afield. Some were accommodated in convents, including that at Untermarchtal.[22] Other evacuees stayed with families in Württemberg to whom they were related, while still others were simply billeted on farms, often for weeks at a time. Sometimes they were positively welcomed: in Zipplingen, farmers hoped that the women evacuees from Rastatt would help with farm work, because many farming families had already lost their male workers, either through pre-war migration or through conscription into the armed forces. However, 'it was soon obvious that there was disappointment on both sides'. The evacuees were accustomed to going regularly to the cinema and the café, neither of which facilities existed in the village, and they were reluctant to become involved in the work of a farm, saying, reportedly, 'You get paid for having us, so we don't need to work!'[23]

Further south, in Ulm district, the tiny commune of Oppingen, with its 160 inhabitants, received thirty refugees from Kehl. They remained for only a matter of weeks because the commune was 'too remote and isolated', and because 'they didn't want to work with the farmers'.[24] In nearby Suppingen, in autumn 1939, forty-eight evacuees from Kehl were at first boarded with villagers in their own homes, but 'later, to stop friction and prevent any more of it, they were put into empty storage buildings on their own'.[25] By contrast, in Urspring, also in Ulm district, the seventy-five evacuees from Kehl were welcomed, and there was palpable regret in the commune when they departed. Some evacuees left for home before the all-clear was given, and, once it was obvious that French forces were not going to invade western Germany, most of those remaining returned home, although those in both Urspring and Suppingen remained until the fall of France in June 1940.[26] To the relief of both parties, the evacuees from Rastatt left Zipplingen before Christmas 1939.[27]

Two factors made Württemberg a key reception centre for migrants, evacuees and refugees, and also for essential war industries which were relocated from areas which were actual or potential bombing targets. As one of the last areas to be invaded and occupied by Allied forces, from late March 1945, it received ever increasing numbers of people from other regions which fell to the enemy in the preceding months. Long before that, however, it was the non-industrial, rural character of much of Württemberg – or, for wartime organisational purposes, *Gau* Württemberg-Hohenzollern – which attracted incomers of various kinds. Not only were small towns and rural communes seen as safe havens for refugees of one kind and another, but, particularly towards the end of the war and in its aftermath, so much of the pre-war urban housing stock in Germany had been destroyed by bombing or, to a lesser extent, artillery fire that most of the available accommodation left intact was in the countryside.[28] By 1943, urban Germans who had been evacuated from northern and western towns and cities were increasingly accommodated in small towns or in rural communes where they were often billeted on farming families, although in some places, and particularly in the first half of the war, there was communal accommodation for evacuees. This might be in a school, but, in additiion, the authorities' seizure of convents, hospitals and care homes for the mentally impaired was sometimes in order to accommodate the influx of evacuees.[29] From 1945, many refugees and expellees from eastern Europe were also housed in southern farming areas.[30]

If there were glitches in the organisation of evacuation and relocation in the early stages of the war, to the extent that there was 'little coordination ... terrible confusion reigned', in comparison with the last year or eighteen months of the war these processes were carried out in relatively good order at first, and even for much of 1943.[31] By 1944–45, however, with the position desperate in many towns and cities, evacuees were increasingly allocated to safe accommodation in a hand-to-mouth manner. For example, in autumn 1944, the authorities in relatively safe Tübingen were said to be helpless in the face of a massive influx of evacuees, the bombed out, workers from relocated industries, staff from relocated civil administrative offices and students. The town's population had increased by 15 per cent since the start of the war, and yet not a single extra house had been built. The rural communes in Tübingen district had also received some 3000 incomers.[32] In Öschingen, for example, fifty-nine people arrived on 12 June 1944. Accommodating and feeding them caused serious problems, not least, it was said, because they were very demanding. Other evacuees arrived in penny numbers, and in February 1945, a further thirty-five people were brought to the commune from Mannheim and housed communally. It was estimated that on 1 April 1945 there were 236 evacuees in the commune.[33]

In the early stages of the war, during 1940–42, Württemberg's rural areas received evacuees from various towns in the Rhineland, as well as from Hamburg, who were more or less voluntary migrants. With the increasing severity of bombing, 1943 was the year in which the capability of party and state for dealing with mass evacuation was put to the test. In July 1943, in response to the growing crisis in industrial centres and ports, the Reich Ministry of the Interior drew up a plan for allocating evacuees from a particularly stricken *Gau* to a number of *Gaue* that seemed relatively safe. While within some *Gaue* – for example, Koblenz-Trier and Westmark – there were rural areas which could accommodate that same *Gau*'s urban evacuees, by contrast *Gau* Düsseldorf required four reception *Gaue* while *Gau* Essen was assigned six, of which the first on the list was Württemberg-Hohenzollern. Nevertheless, this clear division of labour and the apparently orderly chain of command did not prevent bottlenecks from occurring. The proliferation of both responsible offices and written memoranda meant that in the second half of the war it was sometimes difficult for those organising evacuation to see the wood for the trees.[34] In Nuremberg, for instance, the intricacy of bureaucratic structures and the accompanying paper trail increasingly seemed to denote displacement activity and an inability to cope with problems spiralling out of control, as relentless enemy bombing left increasing numbers of families homeless while the options for accommodating them safely nearby were being exhausted.[35] Ultimately, large cities in the north and west of Germany had 40 or perhaps even 45 per cent of their population evacuated, while some 20 to 30 per cent of the inhabitants of smaller towns there were also evacuated.[36]

The allocations from these urban areas were made centrally, with the Reich Ministry of the Interior transmitting instructions to the RVKs. From November 1942, when each *Gauleiter* became the RVK in his region, Wilhelm Murr ceased to be responsible for the RVK's duties in Baden while retaining responsibility for them in Württemberg.[37] The organisation of evacuation on the territorial basis of the *Gau* seemed to give the party, in the form of the NSV (NS People's Welfare), the leading role, making it officially responsible for effecting the evacuation of people from cities as well as their reception and accommodation when they reached their destination. Certainly, the people who were actually dealing with the evacuees on the ground were officers of the NSV in the *Gau* that was sending people to Württemberg, and they therefore liaised with NSV offices in Württemberg-Hohenzollern. This did not always work out in practice. No doubt part of the reason was that Murr, as RVK, tended to act not as *Gauleiter* but in his identity as *Reichsstatthalter*, transmitting the Reich Minister of the Interior's instructions to the Württemberg Minister of the Interior, Jonathan Schmid, who then liaised with the *Landräte*. This sometimes caused offence to the NSV. For example, in Tübingen district, the NSV was angered by the involvement of civil authorities, including the *Landrat* and the mayors, in the reception and organisation of evacuees. The incomers were instructed to report to the local police in the mayor's office, to receive their ration cards and allowance as well as to be allocated to accommodation. Accordingly, where there were problems, the evacuees addressed themselves to the mayor rather than to party authorities, to the chagrin of the latter.[38]

Yet when the going became really tough, in February 1944, the NSV's district office in Ulm abdicated responsibility for ensuring that accommodation was available for evacuees in individual localities. Its leader said that it would simply act as a clearing house, sending evacuees to communes on the assumption that places could be found for them, and that it would be up to local NSV officers to work with the mayor of a commune, and perhaps also with the NSDAP's local branch leader, to accommodate them. The only assistance from the district NSV office would be 'to give notice as early as possible' if a particularly large transport of evacuees was being sent to a locality. The local officials of party and state were therefore left to assume the most unpopular duties. After ascertaining which properties in his locality had rooms to spare – a married couple with one child living in four rooms came within this definition – the local NSV official was, said the Ulm district NSV leader, to report to the mayor which rooms were to be commandeered for evacuees. If a family tried to resist, 'drastic measures' were to be used, for example bringing in the *Gendarmerie* to enforce the quartering of evacuees. Recent experience of billeting several hundred homeless people in small communes had shown that reluctant hosts claimed that there was no legal basis for this. The district NSV leader in Ulm stressed that mayors had been empowered by the *Landrat* in Ulm to requisition rooms as necessary, and that local NSV officers would have to take 'a firm stance' in the face of opposition from residents 'in the interests of caring for the homeless'. This did not mean that life would be easy for evacuees: they were to be restricted to as small a space as possible, because any remaining space would probably be required for new waves of evacuees. It would, said the district NSV leader, be 'completely pointless' for a *Landrat* or mayor to argue in future that it was not possible to accommodate more evacuees. Those who were sent to a locality from the district NSV office would have to be housed: 'It is', he said, 'one of the harsh principles that the war imposes on us.'[39]

The regime failed, however, to maximise resources by ensuring that lines of demarcation and chains of command were clearly defined. In March 1944, the *Landrat* in Ulm observed to his superior, the Württemberg Minister of the

Interior, that while NSDAP local branch leaders as well as mayors in his district had been told by Ulm's NSV office – and, he presumed, the NSDAP *Kreisleiter* had been told by the *Gauleiter* – that further allocations of evacuees were being made to his district and that accommodation had to be arranged for these people, he had not been informed about this. At the same time, he was expected to arrange accommodation for those evacuees whose names had been given to him by the Ministry of the Interior. 'Two authorities', he said, 'are working in parallel to supply the existing housing space for the bombed out or evacuated, without either of them knowing what the other is doing.' He was not able to fulfil his duty to report on the precise numbers accommodated in Ulm district, he said, because he frequently lacked up to date information about who was lodged where. Whereas his local food office, which was responsible for dealing with evacuees' ration cards, had recently informed him that the district of Ulm had accommodated 672 people from Essen and a further 1715 from other *Gaue*, an NSV official had phoned to say that the numbers were greater than these. The *Landrat* added that he was sure of only one thing: that there remained very little spare accommodation in his district, and that it would be difficult enough to house people from the town of Ulm if it was attacked, without taking in any extra evacuees from elsewhere.[40]

On one issue authorities of both party and state could agree: where area bombing became a regular and severe occurrence, removing as many civilians as possible from bombed towns to the countryside and dispersing them there was a priority, as much for the sake of public order in urban areas as to provide safe accommodation for bomb victims. For many evacuees, however, moving away from home to the countryside was a last resort and was sometimes embarked on only under pressure from the authorities or because there really was no alternative. In Cologne in July 1943, where there had already been widespread criticism of the NSV's failure to cope with the numbers of those bombed out, there were renewed complaints about the arrangements for them – with public anger verging on disorder. By this time, some two hundred thousand people were homeless in the city. Many of them had to make do with camping out on the banks of the Rhine, with a network of field kitchens as their only source of food. It was reported that 'there were rumours of large scale disturbances ... People were said to have stormed food shops.'[41]

Some urban dwellers had, then, already experienced rudimentary, shared or cramped accommodation before they arrived in the countryside. For example, after 'Operation Gomorrha' in July-August 1943, one family in Hamburg found itself sharing its three-roomed home with three lodgers. Having, like others, chosen to take in friends or relations so as not to have strangers forced on them, they nevertheless found it 'difficult to avoid conflict. In spite of rotas for using the kitchen and bathroom and a special bell-ring signal for each lodger, the minimal level of private life in this household was unwelcome'. Those who were evacuated sometimes returned home, only to flee to the countryside again when the effects of bombing became intolerable.[42] Yet the demonstrations in Witten in October 1943 showed that popular feeling about the way in which evacuation broke up families ran high, and that some women returned home as much to reunite the family as because of the 'very primitive conditions ... in small villages and rural communes'.[43] Although much was made of those who either refused to be evacuated or returned home after evacuation, the vast majority of those instructed to move to the countryside did so. In all, almost twelve million Germans were evacuated in the course of the war.[44]

With area bombing pulverising industrial cities in the north and west in the years 1943–45, Württemberg, as a 'reception *Gau*', received increasing numbers of evacuees as families, and even whole school classes with their teachers, were moved to apparently safer conditions in rural southern Germany. This could cause resentment. After the war, the head teacher in Auenstein, near Heilbronn, noted critically that, when an entire school class of twenty-five children and their teacher were evacuated to the neighbouring hamlet of Helfenberg, they were in a more favourable position than native Helfenberg children, who still had to travel to a school in the commune's main village of Auenstein.[45] In the remote village of Schöckingen, in Leonberg district, the local people showed their incomprehension of the realities of bombing by claiming that women evacuees from Essen and the Rhineland, who 'did nothing to make themselves popular', had really come for a holiday. To the delight of their hosts, they did not remain for long, preferring to return to the dangers of their urban home than to live in a village where they were not welcome.[46] By the end of 1943, however, even medium-sized and small towns in the north and west were being pre-emptively evacuated, although bombing was increasingly affecting targets in southern Germany also. This led Goebbels to say in January 1944 that 'the whole area of the Reich must be regarded as being more or less in danger of attack from the skies'.[47] The *Landrat* in Ulm was certainly convinced, in March 1944, that it was a matter of when rather than whether Ulm would be be attacked.[48] His worst fears materialised on 17 December 1944, when Ulm was severely bombed.[49]

By the end of February 1944, 44,609 evacuees from Essen had been found accommodation in Württemberg, yet that was far from the end of the story. There were in addition 3272 people from Essen living in temporary family care centres, 683 children from Essen and Düsseldorf in children's camps, and 27,651 workers in relocated factories, together with family members, who had had to be housed. Beyond that, 40,487 people – whose provenance was not given – were lodging with relatives or friends. Some urban Württembergers, too, had been found accommodation away from home before the worst of the bombing struck at their towns. Altogether, taking into account those who had had rooms found for them by the NSV or local authorities, those who were lodging with relatives or friends, children in camps, school children and those in family care centres, the number of Württembergers who had been accommodated away from home and in the countryside amounted to 52,402. No doubt many of those who were lodging with friends or relatives were also from within Württemberg. Thus a significant proportion – and perhaps as many as half – of the 169,104 evacuees in Württemberg in February 1944 were natives.[50]

This figure perhaps gave the impression of leaving a great deal of spare capacity, given that the Reich Minister of the Interior's revised target intake for Württemberg-Hohenzollern – increased from 135,000 at the beginning of 1944 – was 240,000. This obligation was calculated on the basis of utilising 40 per cent rather than the previous 26 per cent of Württemberg-Hohenzollern's households.[51] Accordingly, the monthly reports show an inexorable increase in the numbers accommodated, to a total of 197,591 on 1 April, then 231,042 on 1 May, and 263,417 on 1 June 1944. By 10 August, the figure had risen to 335,650.[52] This was far more of a burden than it perhaps appeared in crude arithmetical terms, for Württemberg's own towns were also increasingly bombing targets: for example, in one raid on Stuttgart on 14 October 1944, 957 people were killed, a thousand were wounded, and fifty thousand were made homeless.[53] Given that Stuttgart accounted for some four hundred thousand of Württemberg's population of almost three million, and that other much smaller but nevertheless substantial towns – especially Heilbronn, Friedrichshafen and Ulm – would also in 1944 have citizens to evacuate, it was clear that the majority of small town and rural homes were being expected to accommodate evacuees, migrants or relocated workers. In March 1944, Interior Minister Schmid referred to the 'often frantic search for space' for evacuees, which was compounded by the complete unavailability of labour to convert attics into rooms or to construct temporary accommodation, because repairing or rebuilding bomb damaged armaments factories had first priority.[54] In this area as in virtually every other one, it was evident that Germany's resources, and in particular its accommodation and human resources, were not sufficient to meet the demands of the Nazi regime's ambitions.

There were, however, attempts to create new housing, in spite of the increasing shortage of both building materials and labour. In a commune near Maulbronn, building warrants were sought in January 1944 to construct three large wooden chalets to accommodate at least some of the workers from a relocated factory. The priority of housing factory workers near their works led two months later to permission being given for Maulbronn to construct two buildings containing sixteen homes each and eight wooden chalets which would, it was estimated, solve the factory workers' accommodation problems. Yet this would depend on the availability of all of the necessary materials, only some of which had been delivered.[55] In Musberg, adjacent to Stuttgart, emergency communal accommodation was built for inhabitants by the Labour Front after a highly destructive bombing raid in March 1944.[56] In Ebnat, near Aalen, however, two hundred evacuees from the Rhineland were all accommodated in emergency shelters.[57] Elsewhere, for example in Auenstein, the evacuees themselves set to work building emergency housing, but, even so, they had in the first instance to be billeted on farming families.[58]

Where materials and labour for building new housing were unavailable, there was nowhere for evacuees to live but with indigenous families in their own homes. Yet in many cases these were scarcely suitable for urban migrants. For example, according to the district leadership of the NSDAP, in the area around Ulm the rural communes were mostly inhabited by farming families whose homes had only one living room that could be heated and bedrooms which might or might not have plastered walls.[59] In Marlach, in Künzelsau district, throughout the war there was no bakery and the villagers baked their own bread, using the commune's plentiful supplies of grain. This left evacuees there dependent on bread being brought in from neighbouring communes in Baden, although after communications systems had been destroyed in April 1945 the mayor released grain from the commune for their use.[60] Again, the *Landrat* in Crailsheim argued that in 'some 90 per cent of the rural communes there is no piped water, and, in particular, there are many small and widely dispersed partial communes without shops for food and other goods'. Accordingly, he said, Crailsheim was less able than almost any other district in Württemberg to take in the proportion of evacuees and others that its number of inhabitants might suggest.[61] Nevertheless, while both central and local authorities in Württemberg argued in desperation that they could not accommodate further consignments of evacuees, they argued in vain.

If there was undoubtedly an element of special pleading by individual local authorities, it certainly seems that the communes which were least likely to be bombed were also those which were most poorly provided with the utilities and facilities to accommodate urban evacuees. In addition, while rural areas were in general safer than urban areas, they were not immune from bombing, especially if there happened to be a rail line or decoy installations nearby. For example, in summer 1940, a decoy airfield was constructed 500 metres to the north of the commune of Rohrau, in Böblingen district, which attracted bombers from September 1940. There were several severe attacks from 1942 onwards, which damaged both Rohrau and neighbouring communes. Nevertheless, evacuees from Stuttgart arrived, especially after the devastating raids there in July 1944 which left a hundred thousand people homeless, with a further fifty thousand losing their homes in the raid on 12 September 1944. Shortly before Christmas 1944 the NSV brought to Rohrau some eighty evacuees from Karlsruhe. All of those evacuated to Rohrau were of the opinion that they had been safer in a town because there at least there were bunkers and shelters, while there was no such protection in this rural commune. Only the more favourable food supply in the countryside kept them there.[62] Even in the last stages of the war, with air raids over Stuttgart continuing, some of the capital's remaining inhabitants were reluctant to move to the countryside because of the absence of air-raid shelters.[63]

Especially after the air raids in July 1944, those who remained in Stuttgart did so in the face of official propaganda to encourage them to leave. Reluctant to introduce a forced evacuation, which might generate acute discontent and even public disorder, the Württemberg *Gau* leadership unleashed a massive campaign in the Nazi press urging those who were not engaged in essential work in Stuttgart to leave, in order to release accommodation for workers in vital industries who had lost their homes. Headlines asked 'Why are you still in Stuttgart?', and urged 'out of the city with the non-employed'. The aim was particularly to provide housing for homeless armaments workers, and appeals to leave were directed especially at older inhabitants. It was recognised that these were the very people who would not want to move into the unknown from a home in which they had lived perhaps for decades. Nevertheless, the overriding priority was to persuade them to leave, and propaganda to this end was relentless. It clearly was also successful, with the population of Stuttgart reduced from around 400,000 in the early war years to some 265,000 by the end of the war.[64] Accordingly, rural communes increasingly found that evacuees from Stuttgart were among those seeking refuge in their midst. In Schöckingen, in Leonberg district, around a hundred women and children arrived from Stuttgart in 1944–45, 'mostly on their own initiative, some because they had been bombed out or had at least suffered air raid damage, some to escape from the nerve-wracking air raids'. Three years after the end of the war, sixty-seven of them were still resident in Schöckingen.[65]

While the *Gau* leadership tried to persuade people to leave stricken Stuttgart in 1944, the mounting pressure on accommodation in rural areas made it reluctant to permit the evacuation of smaller towns which had not been bombed but were nevertheless potential targets. In both Heilbronn and Ulm, the densely inhabited central areas of the old town had little in the way of shelter. At the same time, the narrow streets were likely to obstruct attempts at rescue and assistance in the event of an air raid. In March 1944, the NSDAP's leadership in Ulm asked *Gauleiter* Murr for permission to evacuate children and the infirm, whose presence might obstruct rescue efforts in the event of a raid. In addition, he asked Murr to authorise the necessary requisitioning of accommodation, given that the town's rural hinterland was already earmarked for evacuees from both Essen and Stuttgart.[66] In Heilbronn, an escape route had been prepared in the old town by breaking through cellar walls, but Richard Drauz, as Heilbronn NSDAP *Kreisleiter*, predicted that, in the event of a raid, there would be heavy losses. In March 1944, he drew up a detailed plan for the pre-emptive evacuation of 1974 women and children from the the the old town. Heilbronn's mayor joined him in urging Murr to approve this, but to no avail.[67] The anxiety which motivated the authorities in both Heilbronn and Ulm was tragically vindicated when both towns were attacked in December 1944, with particularly catastrophic results in Heilbronn.[68] In Ulm's case, whatever plans had been made for evacuating people from further afield to the surrounding rural areas, there was no alternative to finding accommodation there for those fleeing the town after that raid and a further severe attack in March 1945. Some ninety people from Ulm were billeted in the commune of Steinberg, while a few found their way to nearby Weiler, along with small numbers of evacuees from Stuttgart, Heilbronn and Frankfurt.[69] Schnürpflingen, like other adjacent communes, received evacuees from Ulm in 1944 and 1945 to add to the children and adults who had been evacuated in progressive waves from the Rhineland from 1943.[70]

As bombing intensified and the pressure of evacuees' numbers increased ineluctably, their allocation became increasingly haphazard. Some communes received penny numbers of evacuees from a wide variety of places. For example, in Ulm district, the commune of Sonderbuch played host to the following: in 1943, three people from Cologne and one person from Stuttgart; in 1944, three people from Augsburg, six from Stuttgart, nineteen from Düsseldorf, two from Wiesbaden and five from Mannheim; in 1945, eighteen people from Ulm and five from East Prussia.[71] Of the approximately 250 evacuees accommodated in nearby Setzingen, people from Ulm joined those who had already arrived from various Rhineland towns, Stuttgart and the area around Königsberg in East Prussia.[72] After the air raid on 18 December, several families from Ulm joined evacuees from Cologne, Duisburg, Essen and Stuttgart in Regglisweiler.[73] Like other communes in Ulm district, Westerstetten had already had to find room for evacuees from the industrial towns of the Rhineland before Ulm itself was bombed. A total of 115 evacuees, including those from Ulm and Stuttgart between autumn and spring 1945, brought the commune's population up to 1070 inhabitants, before a further 235 refugees from eastern Europe joined them.[74]

Some communes were inundated. In Aalen district, Essingen received no evacuees at all until autumn 1944, but thereafter altogether five hundred people – who either had been bombed out of their own homes or else had abandoned them as a pre-emptive measure – descended on it. In the first instance, evacuees came to Essingen 'from every city' because they had friends or relations in the village, but in February 1945 a 'transport from Kaiserslautern' arrived, and later there were also refugees from Silesia.[75] Nearby Neresheim received 611 evacuees and had, in addition, by the end of the war 1033 foreigners of a dozen nationalities living in the commune, the overwhelming majority of whom were refugees from eastern Europe – Slovenes, Russians, Estonians, Latvians.[76] The commune of Marlach, in Künzelsau district, which had had a prewar population of 462, had by the end of the war received between 720 and 730 evacuees and refugees.[77] After the war, Künzelsau district received substantial numbers of ethnic Germans from eastern Europe. In February 1946, an initial transport of 486 arrived from Hungary, and in September and October of that year there were weekly transports of between 250 and 300 people, so that the October census showed that, in Künzelsau town alone, around a thousand of the 5879 inhabitants were refugees.[78] In some communes, evacuees were able to return home before the refugees from eastern Europe arrived, but in others ethnic Germans from the east arrived before evacuees had an urban home to which they could return. In Laibach, where this was the case, it was said that, before the evacuees had left, the door of every house had refugees from the east knocking on it, begging for accommodation.[79]

The arrival of a few hundred evacuees could make a significant difference to the character of a small village. For example, Aufhausen, in Aalen district, had had a population of only 650 before the war, and received 250 evacuees during it – although they were probably not all there at the same time – as well as eighty to a hundred French civilian workers.[80] Again, nearby Oberdorf had nine hundred inhabitants in 1939, but in a count held on 1 October 1948 its numbers had risen to 1620.[81] Further north, in Crailsheim district, Kirchberg, a commune of nine hundred people, received evacuees from the Ruhr and the Karlsruhe area, 'and was in addition a place of refuge for many seeking safety from neighbouring cities such as Nuremberg, Stuttgart, etc.'. By the end of the war it had received two hundred incomers.[82] In nearby Wallhausen, a series of evacuee transports arrived in February 1945, including a family of eight which had to be accommodated in one of the classrooms in the school.[83] Langenburg received evacuees from the Rhineland and also, in 1945, refugees from Bessarabia, Hungary, Siebenbürgen, Sudetenland and Silesia, doubling the size of its prewar population.[84] Leuzendorf found its population increased by 40 per cent with the influx of 193 persons from Stuttgart, Essen, Duisburg, Mannheim, Frankfurt, Heilbronn, Mühlheim, Freiburg, Saarland and 'a few families from Berlin'. These all returned home in the course of the summer of 1945.[85] For Oberspeltach, the arrival of some three hundred people, mainly women and children, from 1943 meant a 75 per cent increase in the size of the commune's population.[86] The fighting in the Crailsheim area in April 1945 brought further incomers to adjacent communes: Marktlustenau was 'flooded' with them.[87] But neighbouring Rossfeld received only 'some thirty-five people' because its own facilities had already suffered as a result of bomb damage in summer 1944.[88]

Beyond the bickering and confusion between different agencies of party and state, the experience of evacuation did more than anything to illustrate the extent to which both living conditions and attitudes in urban areas had diverged from those in rural areas. The incomprehension of urban women even from modest circumstances, who were amazed that country women could live without amenities which they took for granted, was matched by that of rural dwellers who could not understand why townswomen complained so much about the absence of what they regarded as luxuries, and sometimes frivolous ones at that. While farm women regarded the townees as lazy and greedy, the townees viewed the farm women as 'stupid and stubborn' for tolerating a regime of grindingly hard physical work in primitive conditions. In general, relations were better between evacuees from Württemberg's own towns and their rural hosts, some of whom accommodated urban relatives in the countryside. This was probably helped by their shared Swabian identity; at least they had something in common. In addition, some of the more local evacuees may have been familiar with life in the Württemberg countryside through visiting relatives there before the war. Beyond that, there was perhaps more mutual tolerance in the emergency circumstances of the later stages of the war, which was when urban Württembergers, particularly from Stuttgart, were moved in large numbers to the countryside. Particularly after the western Allies had secured air bases in France, in the second half of 1944, air raids on western Germany as a whole became both more comprehensive and more frequent, with rural areas, too, suffering bomb damage in 1944–45. In the first air raid experienced in Essingen, for example, on 7 October 1944, the rail line was hit causing damage that was, however, quickly repaired.[89] This kind of experience at last gave rural inhabitants some insight into what urban dwellers had endured, in some cases since 1940.

The first migrants to the countryside, in 1940–41, tended to be women who had both the freedom and the money to migrate voluntarily from industrial centres further north which were potential bombing targets to southern areas, and particularly to Württemberg's holiday resorts. In summer 1941, resentment developed in the districts of Mergentheim and Backnang, among others, at the way in which these incomers were able to outbid ordinary local people for goods that were becoming scarce. The visitors were said to be offering 'fantastic prices' for fruit when it was in short supply, pricing local people out of the market, regardless of notional price controls. To the tensions between town and country, richer and poorer, was added the further irritant of 'foreign' incomers from other parts of Germany, particularly the north-western regions, who seemed to have 'bottomless purses'. Their extravance was doubly offensive to Württembergers with their reputation – or notoriety – for thrift. The SD believed that the flourishing black market in Württemberg owed much of its success to the presence of women migrants and evacuees from the industrial north, who bought up eggs and other scarce foodstuffs to send home, on the grounds that

Württemberg was much better supplied than Ruhr towns.[90] Nevertheless, as we have seen, Württembergers did not require instruction from northern 'foreigners' in this matter: they were perfectly capable of resorting to black market practices on their own initiative.

In addition to these voluntary migrants, by September 1941 an estimated 2500 women and children had been evacuated to Württemberg from Essen, Düsseldorf and Hamburg. The SD admitted that the figure could well have been higher 'because it is very difficult to give an exact number for the women'. The vast majority were housed communally, in guesthouses or hotels. Most, however, were so disgusted with life in the countryside that, after only six or eight weeks, they took themselves and their children back home – in spite of all attempts at persuasion to the contrary by officers of the NSV – on the grounds that they 'would rather go back to where the bombs are than live here in a village where nothing ever happens'. The indigenous population's response to the incomers suggests that they felt scant sympathy for the evacuees' plight and did little to make them feel welcome. On the contrary, there were mounting complaints about the evacuees' attitudes: 'they were regarded as being very demanding in every respect', and reported as making comments such as 'I don't like this accommodation. I'm used to something better than this. At home I have central heating, hot and cold running water and all kinds of mod cons'. The complaints came from all over Württemberg and were reported assiduously by the SD, who gave every impression of taking the side of the Württembergers against the evacuees. Perhaps natives themselves, they showed little comprehension of the plight of women who had been persuaded to leave a home in the city – possibly with children in tow – for the safety of the southern countryside, which seemed to many evacuees an underdeveloped country where a foreign language, the Swabian dialect (*Schwäbisch*), was spoken, conditions were comparatively primitive and the food, while relatively plentiful, was unfamiliar and sometimes presented in a way that was highly unpalatable to them.

Almost all of the reports from regions of Württemberg spoke of the difficulty which the women had in adjusting to 'south German conditions'. In a small country town in northern Württemberg, 'one woman had scarcely left the train before asking "whether there's a cinema here, because she was used to going to the cinema two or three times a week"'. Most were accommodated in small communes which had alien rhythms and few social facilities. One woman complained that she could not sleep because of the quacking of geese and ducks. It was said that women living in modest guesthouses '"think they should be waited on as if they were in a hotel"'. In one case, it was even "expected that the proprietor should bring coffee out to the swimming pool"'. In the commune of Wüstenrot in Heilbronn district, 'all the women who were staying in a guesthouse refused to eat a traditional Swabian soup'. If there were soldiers stationed nearby, some of the evacuees soon became accustomed to going out with them in the evening, leaving their children unsupervised and expecting their hosts to cope. The result was that scarce NSV personnel had to be enlisted to help out with them. All of this would probably have generated merely minor friction with the natives if only the evacuees had shown some willingness to pull their weight in their new circumstances. Local people were 'incensed that the women wouldn't even do a hand's turn in the house': those billeted in private households showed little inclination to help with routine chores like the washing or mending of clothes. They took the view that, with the NSV paying them an allowance for living away from home, they were in the position of being compensated for the upheaval of moving and certainly did not require to make their circumstances worse than they already were by working for or with inhospitable natives.

The greatest offence felt by the rural host population was that, at a time of dire labour shortage on the land, the evacuees were overwhelmingly not prepared to help with farm work. This speaks volumes for the way in which second or third generation urban dwellers – as many evacuees were bound to be, given the dramatic migration from villages to towns since 1870 – had completely lost touch with the rhythms and demands of life on the land. Undoubtedly, some of the evacuees were genuinely frightened of farm animals, although their children sometimes proved more adventurous in this regard. In September 1941, the SD reported that the natives' complaints about the evacuees 'were increasing rather than diminishing', particularly to the effect that the evacuees were idle and demanding, 'sitting around all day in restaurants and cafés'. Their demeanour toward the natives was 'arrogant'. Those billeted on farms would not think of helping

> our farm women, who have to slave away from early morning until late at night ... We can understand that they are in a difficult position, but it's not unreasonable to expect that, just a few times during their stay, they might make the effort to be useful.[91]

It was undoubtedly the case that the rural population showed little appreciation of the plight in which urban evacuees found themselves. Nevertheless, it was equally apparent that many evacuees did not make the connection between working on the land and securing the food supply for the towns. Those who declared that they would rather return home than 'live here in a village where nothing ever happens' wilfully ignored the reality that what *happened* in Württemberg's villages was that cows were milked, fields were ploughed, seed was sown, manure was collected and spread, crops were harvested and deliveries were made to the towns. If some farming families felt little obligation to work tirelessly to provide food for the towns and observe the controls that were intended to ensure the equitable distribution of foodstuffs, they were matched by some evacuees who felt little responsibility for the work of the farms on which they were billeted. In

August 1943, an order from the Four Year Plan Office referred to how 'harvest work gives those evacuated from bomb-threatened areas to rural districts the opportunity to contribute to safeguarding the food supply by helping with bringing in the harvest'. In an attempt to be even-handed, the author went on to say that the more evacuees were shown some understanding by their hosts, the more ready they would be to work alongside them, concluding optimistically that 'this mutual support can only strengthen the feeling of solidarity'.[92]

Yet even when the situation was critical, in 1943–45, there were problems. As in 1939 women from Kehl had found the tiny commune of Oppingen 'too remote and isolated', so in 1943–44 families from Essen, Duisburg and Dortmund stayed only a short time 'because there was neither a cinema nor a café'.[93] Even the people of Urspring, who had found the early evacuees from Kehl congenial, regarded those from the Rhineland who arrived in 1943 much less favourably. It is not clear if this was because these were northerners while the Kehl evacuees were fellow southerners. The final straw for the Urspring villagers was when, near the end of the war, a transport of people who had lost everything through bombing arrived from the Saarland. The villagers were most unwilling to take them in because they were convinced that the war was lost. This demonstrated their failure to comprehend the predicament of the victims of bomb damage who had no home to return to, whether or not the war came to an end. Only the threat of coercive measures persuaded them to take in the Saarlanders. In particular, households which were in bad odour with the party were threatened by NSDAP officials with arrest and transfer to a concentration camp to get them to take in this new wave of evacuees. Yet the people of Urspring were not inherently inhospitable. Just before as well as after the final collapse of the Third Reich, they showed exemplary kindness to soldiers and civilians who arrived in the village, helping them where they could.[94]

In Essingen, when the first evacuees arrived in autumn 1944, accommodating them was 'very difficult' because the natives did not want to give up any of their space to them. The commune's mayor was put in the invidious position of having to allocate to individual households the 130 twelve to fourteen year olds whose schooling was to take place in a nearby HJ hostel. This caused problems because 'the city children and the farmers had little sympathy for each other at first'. In time, however, the older children began to take the cows out and 'even helped the farmer's wife with the milking'.[95] Nevertheless, with adult women problems persisted. The rural population made plain its resentment at the attitude of evacuees who believed that, 'as "guests of the Führer" they had a right to especial respect and attention'. After the war, the chronicler in Eschenau, in Heilbronn district, admitted that 'the local population here had regrettably little sympathy for the plight of these unfortunate people' from the Rhineland, and that many refused to accommodate mothers with several children until 'a certain amount of police pressure' was exerted.[96] That kind of pressure was guaranteed to inflame rural resentment, and to ensure that it was directed at the regime's officers as well as at individual evacuees. At least one district leader of the NSF in Württemberg became very unpopular in her locality by, among other things, making threats of retribution against those who would not take evacuees into their homes.[97]

Some evacuees were so unsettled in the countryside that they returned home from their temporary refuge, in spite of attempts by the authorities to force them back to the countryside by withdrawing their ration cards.[98] This put them once more in the line of enemy fire. Yet flight to the countryside provided no guarantee of safety from enemy operations, especially in the last stages of the war. During the Allied invasion of Crailsheim district on 10 April 1945, a high explosives bomb killed five people in the commune of Onolzheim, of whom three were locals and two evacuees.[99] A week later, a woman evacuee from Duisburg was one of three people who died in nearby Reubach as a result of artillery fire.[100] Some women who stayed in the countryside were moved about from place to place: one Hamburg woman recalled being in at least five different locations in Bavaria, in central Germany and in Silesia as an evacuee. Another, bombed out in 1943, went to live with relatives where twelve people were housed in a room measuring fifty square metres.[101] Some evacuees found themselves being moved on during the last days of the war as the fighting front approached. For example, those from Essen and Ludwigshafen, who had in the first instance been sent to Crailsheim and Goldbach, were moved to the commune of Wohnstätten in April 1945.[102] Onolzheim received 'several families' from the Rhineland, and then had to take in 'further families' from neighbouring Oberspeltach when that village was destroyed in April 1945, as well as from the nearby town of Crailsheim.[103] In Nufringen, the fifty-one evacuees who arrived from the Duisburg and Düsseldorf areas in July 1943 had to move away after a major air raid on 7–8 October 1943 had made 114 families homeless.[104] But those who had been evacuated from Essen and Oberhausen to Tiefenbach refused to be moved again when the order for this came through on 31 March 1945, because 'a journey into the unknown could bring only death and disaster, or renewed misery'.[105]

By the end of 1944, Württemberg's communes were awash with outsiders. Half a million adults and children were present as evacuees, with, in addition, 82,000 armaments workers who had been relocated with their concerns from more endangered areas. The largest numbers of evacuees were sent to the districts of Heilbronn (which received over 10 per cent of the total), Ludwigsburg and Ravensburg; but most of the other districts each received between ten and twenty thousand of them.[106] By this time, the districts of Calw, Freudenstadt, Horb and Rottweil were regarded as being in the rear of the western front and therefore reserved for military personnel, although they were also under strong pressure from civilians fleeing from Baden. As the Allies began to close in on Germany from both east and west, the country was alive with streams of humanity trying to reach a destination. This had already become a feature of wartime life, with the relocation of some industries and evacuation from towns, but in the second half of 1944 the movement of people into and around Germany began to assume massive proportions, in the west especially once the Allies had established a firm foothold in France. Prisoners from Natzweiler concentration camp in Alsace – which was closed in September 1944 – were transferred eastwards to small and hastily constructed 'outlying camps', of which there were twenty in Württemberg.[107] Some notorious fugitives tried to evade the advancing Allies, with, for example, Marshal Pétain, the erstwhile leader of Vichy France, and some members of his entourage taking refuge in the former Hohenzollern castle at Sigmaringen in 1944.[108] Officers of Pétain's system followed: in January 1945, 757 members of the notorious French *Milice* – a paramilitary police force in Vichy France – were among the 2857 foreigners accommodated in purpose-built camps in Württemberg, while almost as many 'foreign refugees' were 'otherwise accommodated'.[109]

Communes in Württemberg might also be a staging post for German troops leaving France. In some, the troops were billeted in schools and inns, and, if necessary, also in private houses: 'from December 1944, scattered groups of German soldiers came from Alsace, from the Vosges and from the Black Forest. [They] were assembled in the villages and towns between Ulm and Tuttlingen', that is, across southern Württemberg.[110] Particularly after Allied forces had crossed the Rhine, in March 1945, the convergence on Württemberg of a variety of people, both civilian and military, continued as the core of unoccupied Germany shrank inexorably. Some foreign workers, whether POWs or forced labourers, in areas of western Germany still under German control, were moved eastwards, deeper into the central core of the country in the last weeks of the war. For example, some Belgians in Lendsiedel (Crailsheim district) were sent to the concentration camp at Dachau in March 1945, but once hostilities ceased they were able to find their way home.[111] Desperately weak survivors of Germany's extermination and concentration camps in the east were either forced to move westwards, in the brutal death marches, or else they were murdered.[112] Eventually, some of the survivors passed through Württemberg's communes. At Bopfingen 'on Thursday, 19 April, a transport of concentration camp prisoners arrived here from Ellwangen ... People who could go no further, forty-two in total, were shot, beaten to death or hanged'. The remainder were divided into two groups and led away in different directions.[113]

The flight from enemy bombing continued to the end. On 8 April, the village of Berlichingen in Künzelsau district was destroyed by bombing, leaving the neighbouring commune of Schöntal to take in its inhabitants.[114] When Aalen town was seriously bombed in the middle of April, the commune of Fachsenfeld received between three and four hundred refugees. They arrived on 17 April, bringing almost nothing with them, and had to be hastily accommodated in barns and wooden huts. For some, there was not even that degree of rudimentary cover. The NSV nurse who accompanied them was in possession of a document given to her in February 1945 by the district NSV leader to enable her to secure accommodation in the event of an attack on Aalen. It was worthless. By this time, it was said, 'any kind of orderly allocation was no longer possible', while the order had already gone out for the inhabitants of Fachsenfeld to evacuate their commune, although no destination had been specified.[115] In the second half of April 1945, no part of Germany could be considered a safe haven from enemy attack, either on land or from the air.

10

The Last Days of the War

While most Germans had greeted the unleashing of Hitler's war in September 1939 with misgivings, once it was under way they wanted their armed forces to win, and to do so quickly. In the first place, a short war would mean relatively few German casualties, a major preoccupation given the carnage of 1914–18, when around two million men had been killed and many, many more injured.[1] Further, the reversal of the Versailles Treaty, the humbling of both Poland and France, and the victory over 'Bolshevism' that came tantalisingly close in 1941, were all widely welcomed, although even the early victorious stages of the Russian campaign had occasioned significant anxiety at home.[2] But when, after another two or three increasingly agonising years, it became apparent, from mid-1944 especially, that Germany was going to lose, most people wanted defeat to come sooner rather than later. Apart from the terrible casualties in the field, the failure of the *Luftwaffe* to deny enemy bombers access to German air space left towns and cities almost defenceless against attacks from the sky. By 1945, with the promised German *Vergeltung* (retaliation), in the form of new 'wonder weapons', failing to materialise in anything approaching decisive dimensions, the devastation resulting from repeated bombing raids on towns and cities convinced most ordinary civilians – and, increasingly, also some Nazi officials – that unless Germany called a halt, even if it meant 'unconditional surrender', the entire country would be destroyed.[3]

By early 1945, most Germans were looking not for a heroic death but merely for an end to the slaughter at the front and the bombing at home. Any remaining faith in the Nazi leadership, which had inflicted this disaster on them and which seemed increasingly incapable of mitigating its effects, plummeted.[4] The desperate attempt to raise troops for the defence of German cities, towns and villages through the levying of the *Volkssturm* (home guard) from September 1944 was correctly recognised by civilians as illusory. For urban civilians, there was both the fear and the experience of the increasingly frequent bombing which killed people and either damaged or destroyed homes, schools, shops and offices, driving survivors to spend uncomfortable nights in bunkers or cellars. Domestic utilities – gas, electricity and water supplies – as well as other essential services, including transport and telecommunications, were disrupted by air attacks. All in all, by the early months of 1945 most German urban civilians confronted a daily battle for survival, both in the face of an imminent takeover by enemy forces and in negotiating the complex obstacle race which they experienced in getting to work, obtaining essential supplies and seeking refuge from the bombers.[5] Rural inhabitants had for the most part been spared the terror of bombing before autumn 1944, but they increasingly found their homes invaded by urban evacuees and their villages used as emergency quarters for a variety of concerns, including army hospitals and administrative offices. In February 1945, for example, an SS rehabilitation unit for the wounded was moved to the relative safety of Neresheim in Aalen district, along with a branch office of the SD.[6] In the first week of April, an army hospital for sick horses was established in Kerkingen.[7] From October 1944, retreating German troops were billeted in Württemberg's communes. Partly because of this, in the final months and weeks of the war some villagers had their first experience of air raids, while the enemy's ground forces converged on their territory.

It was something of a lottery. Two neighbouring communes in Leonberg district had differing experiences. Schöckingen was exceptional in being attacked from the air in July 1940, for no apparent reason. A small, remote commune which lay far from any rail line or main road, it survived thereafter unscathed by attack from land or air until spring 1945.[8] Hemmingen, however, was close to a rail line. Twelve people were killed there in an air raid on 5 November 1944 which totally destroyed eleven buildings and damaged most of the other houses. Fires raged because the commune's spraying equipment was being repaired elsewhere and there was a delay before extinguishers from other communes arrived.[9] In these two communes, and in many others, by spring 1945 low-flying aircraft were attacking individuals working in the fields. In Suppingen, a male evacuee from nearby Ulm who was helping to plant potatoes was fatally injured in the first air raid on the village on 18 March 1945. Five horses and a cow were killed in the attack, and fifteen sheep which were injured had to be destroyed.[10] In neighbouring Weiler, the first air attacks on the nearby rail line came in mid-April 1945, making it hazardous for the commune's farmers to work in their fields.[11]

It was patently obvious by March 1945 that the western Allies' advance into Germany was irresistible. They could perhaps be somewhat delayed by determined defenders, but, for anyone prepared to be realistic, the ultimate outcome was not in doubt. Nevertheless, German soldiers were bound by army discipline to fight on for as long their commanders ordered. The problem was that, in the increasingly chaotic system of the Third Reich, only Hitler's will counted: he alone could give the order to the armed forces that would bring a halt to the war, while none of the generals, particularly after the failure of the July Plot in 1944, was prepared to surrender unilaterally. Military discipline generally prevailed, not least because of the terror visited upon any considered 'defeatist' – and sometimes on their family as well – and army units fought on to increasingly certain defeat. Even so, 'defeatism' on the part of serving soldiers, mostly manifested through desertion, was growing in 1945, although retribution was swift and harsh.[12] For example, from the end of March until the middle of April 1945, an SS unit under 'SS-General Oberg, the "butcher of Paris" was quartered in Kirchheim a. Ries'. True to form, he established a drumhead court in the mayor's office, where he tried a soldier who had failed to return from leave to the front and had him summarily shot in a nearby wood.[13]

In a last desperate attempt to reverse the tide of invasion, retreating German soldiers were marched to strategic points inside Germany to reform in anticipation of launching counterattacks against the invading forces, as the core of the country still controlled by German troops steadily diminished. In early 1945, some villagers in Crailsheim district saw columns of 'tired and resigned' or 'exhausted' soldiers with inadequate arms or no weapons at all straggling through their area on the way to Rothenburg ob der Tauber, over the Bavarian border.[14] Other communes had troops billeted on them. Schleierhof, in Künzelsau district, found itself playing host to a succession of German forces. First, in early March 1945, soldiers retreating from Mannheim appeared unannounced. The local inhabitants were obliged to find provisions for the sixty-five horses and numerous troops who remained in the commune for a week. Scarcely had they departed than an artillery unit arrived, with its own provisions. After some ten days its members dispersed to join infantry units, blowing up their equipment in a nearby wood. Hard on its heels came SS troops with a company of officer cadets. These thirty or more men, as well as other groups of retreating soldiers, had to be provisioned over Easter. A pig was taken to a neighbouring commune to be slaughtered so that the meat could be distributed to the troops. The SS men seized all the bicycles in the commune, one of their number boxing the ears of a youth who had removed the pump from his. When he refused to surrender it, the SS man threatened to hang both him and his father. In the end, after mediation by a local government official, the pair had to provide the troops with three hundredweight of flour, baked into bread. With the arrival of two companies of American assault troops on 8 April, the SS forces left the commune.[15]

Other communes experienced occupation by German troops who had been ordered to defend their territory against the advancing enemy, whatever the cost. In Marlach, in Künzelsau district, an elite battalion consisting of officer cadets arrived in March 1945 and dug themselves in to defend the commune, to the dismay of the inhabitants. The battalion withdrew only when other German units arrived to take over defensive measures, including blowing up a bridge, which disrupted the commune's power lines.[16] It was all in vain. By early April, Württemberg was being invaded from the north by American forces, with Heilbronn, Mergentheim, Künzelsau, Öhringen and Crailsheim in the front line. French forces were poised to invade south-western Württemberg.[17] In Aalen district, one of the last areas to be invaded, in mid-April 1945 units of both the *Organisation Todt* and the army passed through Bopfingen on their way first to Neresheim and then, further south, to Ulm. For ten days in early April, part of Kesselring's Army Group B was stationed in the commune of Goldburghausen before moving south to Regensburg.[18] In Hüttlingen, as late as 22 April 1945

> thousands upon thousands of scattered soldiers passed through our village by day and by night. They came here, some with handcarts, in disorganised flight. The unspeakable stresses of the battles of the last weeks and days were etched on their features.[19]

The desperate straits to which the regime was reduced are well illustrated by the formation of the *Volkssturm* in autumn 1944, with enemy forces on the point of invading Germany from both east and west. The *Volkssturm* units were hastily-mustered auxiliary troops in each locality who received only rudimentary military training. Nevertheless, they were treated as army conscripts and expected to submit to military discipline.[20] In some communes, men who had been unwillingly drafted into the *Volkssturm* refused to turn out when ordered to do so. One reason may have been that farmers were not prepared to devote time to it when they could have been tending their fields or animals.[21] In addition, the army's high command had misjudged the popular mood, imagining that men would be more prepared to defend their own commune than any other.[22] Yet by the time the Allies had reached south Germany, at least, few believed that they could be stopped. Using ill-equipped and ill-led irregular forces to delay their progress through rural communes would incur damage and destruction which, in the view of most villagers, could be avoided by speedy surrender. In Schöckingen, the *Volkssturm* received orders to join their battalion in Ditzingen, as quickly as possible, on 20 April 1945. Only two of their number complied. The rest saw no point in regarding themselves as soldiers when they possessed only two bazookas and half a dozen outdated rifles. It was an added incentive to abstain from *Volkssturm* activity that a French patrol arrived in the commune on the lookout for German soldiers. Its members seemed satisfied that there was none.[23]

These motley assemblies of men aged between sixteen and sixty, who were axiomatically unfit for service in the *Wehrmacht*, were taken seriously by few in Württemberg's communes. In Musberg, in Böblingen district, it was said that 'the *Volkssturm* was, in terms of organisation, weapons and training, a stillborn child'.[24] The Künzelsau *Volkssturm*, which consisted of 450 men of all age groups, took the oath of allegiance to Hitler in November 1944 and turned out every Sunday thereafter for training by regular soldiers in the use of firearms. But this unit, which possessed only fifteen rifles, small quantities of munitions and a few bazookas, did not see military service. To the relief of the commune's inhabitants, this meant that none of the local *Volkssturm* men was killed, injured or taken prisoner.[25] The situation in Künzelsau, with relatively small numbers of men and even smaller supplies of weapons and ammunition, was representative of that in many of Württemberg's communes. In Grantschen, in Heilbronn district, for example, the entire strength of the *Volkssturm* was fifteen men and seven members of the HJ.[26]

In the village of Bächlingen, in Crailsheim district, the inhabitants, who 'had hardly noticed any direct effect of the war on themselves during the entire six-year period, even from the bombing campaign', were thrust into the cauldron of war in April 1945. As the military front came ever nearer, they could hear explosions and see flames. American fighter-bombers began to attack the area, and some inhabitants were killed, either on the streets or in the fields. Nevertheless, farmers continued to work in the fields, ready to dive to the ground if they heard a plane approaching. The chances of the *Volkssturm* defending them against this kind of attack – or, perhaps, any other – were limited, as the local chronicler observed:

> The *Volkssturm*, an institution of the party under military discipline and under the command of the district leaders and local branch leaders [of the NSDAP], was mobilised. If the order came, [they were] to dig foxholes, to build tank barriers and to offer every kind of resistance to the advancing Allies with weapons and trenches. Bazookas were distributed, guard duties detailed. The men, however, had enough sense to realise the pointlessness of this semi-military and absolutely inadequate outfit, and the so-called leaders of the *Volkssturm*, who were mostly people who had no idea about how to wage war, often had to listen to the blunt views of the farmers, who were mostly veterans of the First World War.[27]

Military plans for defending Aalen's communes depended on the *Volkssturm* making a significant contribution alongside SS troops. These foundered not only because morale in the *Volkssturm* was at rock bottom but – even more crucially – because *Volkssturm* units lacked serviceable heavy weaponry. In Fachsenfeld, in Aalen district, the strength and equipment of the Americans advancing on the commune on 23 April were said to show that 'a comparison with the last German troops who had marched through here in disarray and with scarcely any arms, or with the local *Volkssturm*, was laughable'. The latter's equipment amounted to two bazookas and eight rifles, one of which was German and the others French or Italian; only some of them functioned.[28] Even in Aalen town, the planned five companies of the *Volkssturm*, with 120 men each, were said to exist on paper only. When the summons went out for these companies to assemble, around twenty to twenty-five men reported for duty in each company, in spite of threats that any who did not attend would be shot or hanged. Their unhappy commander was threatened with a court martial, yet he was powerless: he could not, he said, produce anything like the full complement 'by magic'. In neighbouring Wasseralfingen, the picture was much the same.[29]

Similarly, *Volkssturm* units, numbering around 300 men from several communes in Ulm district, were assembled at an inn in Steinberg. When the signal
was given for them to prepare for duty, with American forces approaching, only
a small proportion of the *Volkssturm* men responded because it was clear that
any attempt to halt the enemy would be pointless.[30] The Göppingen *Volkssturm*,
which had been sent to defend villages in Ulm district, dissolved itself on the
night of 21–22 April 1945, and its members dispersed homewards individually.[31]
The twenty-two men and boys of the Grantschen *Volkssturm* were ordered to
march several kilometres to Gmünd on 9 April. Scarcely had they passed the
neighbouring commune of Sulzbach than the seven boys returned home. The
men arrived back in Grantschen on 12 April.[32] In the end, *Volkssturm* men in
Württemberg's communes were used predominantly for digging trenches and
constructing tank barriers.[33] In some places they refused to do even that. In
Brettheim, in Crailsheim district, with American forces in the vicinity in early
April 1945, the *Volkssturm* rank and file effectively mutinied against their leaders,
refusing to defend the commune.[34] In nearby Hausen am Bach, most of the older
Volkssturm men had experienced combat in the First World War and were of the
view that in 1945 any attempt to defend the commune would be pointless and
would only endanger life, limb and property. Accordingly, no tank barriers were
erected in Hausen, and the *Volkssturm* men failed to heed instructions to join up
with *Wehrmacht* units.[35] Ditches were dug in Schöckingen, but they were intended
to protect villagers from low-flying aircraft, not to provide cover for troops.[36] By
April 1945, Oberkessach, in Künzelsau district, had been neither bombed nor
shelled. The local *Volkssturm* leader, who was also the commune's mayor, refused
to implement the order to destroy two bridges over the river Kessach. In addition,
the order to build tank barriers was ignored, without reprisal.[37]

Where *Volkssturm* units mounted resistance to the invader, it was mostly
under duress. In Tailfingen, the *Volkssturm* assembled for service only after
being threatened with summary execution for failure to do so.[38] In Bopfingen,
the *Volkssturm* was placed under the direct command of an SS unit which
arrived in early April from Ellwangen.[39] Elsewhere, *Volkssturm* activity generally
amounted to little more than guarding tank barriers. In Aufhausen, however, a
rash attempt by the *Volkssturm* to halt an American tank led to shooting which
damaged two houses on the edge of the commune.[40] For the most part, when
enemy forces were poised to take a commune the *Volkssturm* dissolved itself. Its
members in Aalen returned to their homes on 23 April.[41] On the departure of the
SS unit from Bopfingen, the local *Volkssturm* leader urged his men to go home
and destroy their uniforms and weapons so as to avoid arrest when the invader
arrived.[42] Outside nearby Oberdorf, some *Volkssturm* men managed, under cover
of darkness, to evade the SS unit whose young leader had demanded that they
face a hero's death. Those who changed into civilian clothes slipped back into the

commune unmolested, but those who remained in uniform were apprehended by American troops.[43]

Despairing of any significant contribution from the *Volkssturm*, some party and military leaders tried to mobilise one group over which they believed they could exert authority, teenage boys. The chief effect of SS attempts in Bavaria to coerce HJ boys of fifteen or sixteen into 'volunteering' for service in the *Waffen-SS* late in March 1945 was to horrify the youths and their families, friends and neighbours, and thus to promote widespread defeatism.[44] Attempts in Honhardt, in Crailsheim district, to recruit boys born in 1928, 1929 and 1930 into HJ military formations were actually prevented by the refusal of their parents to countenance it.[45] In Bopfingen, however, HJ boys born in 1929 were ordered to join the SS, and between twenty and twenty-four of them responded. Force was not used, but peer pressure proved effective, with the reluctant complying when they were stigmatised as cowards. There were also a few volunteers from among those born in 1930.[46] Yet even when youths obeyed orders to report for duty, they did not always reach their destination. Boys from Künzelsau, from the years of birth of 1929 and earlier, were summoned to Schwäbisch Gmünd on 7 April 1945 to join an army unit. Those who set off on foot turned back in Schwäbisch Hall, and those who went by bicycle returned home before Künzelsau was occupied by American forces on 12 April.[47] In Hemmingen, parents protested strenuously when their twelve to fourteen year old sons were conscripted on 3 April 1945 to construct entrenchments in another commune. The boys all returned home on the same evening, but they were taken away again two days later to Maichingen, from where they were sent back because they were considered unfit for service.[48] It was perhaps easier to recruit teenagers who had been evacuated and whose parents were not on hand to object. Among the raggle-taggle forces charged with defending Crailsheim in April 1945, without any tanks of their own, were teenagers from a secondary school in Bad Mergentheim, including some who had been evacuated from Duisburg.[49]

Rallying the *Volkssturm* and trying to conscript youths for military or defensive purposes were one aspect of the radicalisation of the Nazi regime's policies and practices in wartime, with Goebbels referring to the 'unified deployment of the entire people, united in the idea of National Socialism'.[50] The fanatical belief – which Goebbels shared with Hitler – that an entire people could, through its determined will, prevail over invading armies, found its logical conclusion in the last weeks of the war in the attempt by either German military forces or NSDAP officials to assume control over all but the most isolated of communes in the territory which remained under their jurisdiction. In theory, instructions continued to emanate from Berlin, but from early 1945, with Germany increasingly under Allied occupation, the authorities who counted were at *Land*, district or even more local level. Yet, although Hitler may himself have been logistically powerless to control the diminishing area of unoccupied Germany, his writ still ran where there were army or party officers intent on obeying his instructions.[51] Like Winston Churchill in 1940, Hitler was determined that neither he nor his people would ever surrender. Accordingly, his 'Nero decree' of 19 March 1945 demanded that German soldiers and civilians resist to the end, and that a 'scorched earth' policy be followed.[52] This was reinforced on 12 April by Himmler's order that 'No German city will be declared an open city. Every town and every village will be defended at all costs'.[53] For exhausted civilians in the towns, where bombing had taken a heavy toll, this kind of fanaticism was excruciating. For rural dwellers whose territory had been either totally untouched by bombing or only marginally affected, it was incomprehensible.

Whereas life in the larger towns had been entirely transformed in wartime, in many villages there was a degree of normality, even in early 1945. In an increasing number of towns, destruction and dislocation were the rule. For those whose housing remained intact, utilities were disrupted by both bombing and the rationing of supply. In Stuttgart, there were severe restrictions on the use of coal, electricity and gas in the last winter of the war, while public transport ran at much reduced services.[54] Many schools were closed and school children evacuated. Food, clothing and other commodities were nominally rationed but, by 1945, increasingly unavailable even for controlled distribution, although Württemberg was better provided with food supplies than some other parts of the country, once Germans no longer had an empire to pillage. Nevertheless, in Tübingen, by March and April 1945 the daily calorie content of rationed goods for 'normal' 'Aryan' consumers had declined to 1602.[55] The conscription of farmers and rural labourers, with forced foreign workers only a partial substitute, had led increasingly to subsistence production. As a result, there were reports that the evils of 1918 were being reproduced, with farmers selling produce at exorbitant prices or exchanging it for other scarce goods, which only the rich could afford.[56] This was the logical conclusion to the evasive practices to which farmers and rural traders had resorted since the start of the war, and even in the last years of peace.

The countryside, while better provided than the towns, was not immune to scarcity and panic, with evacuees adding greatly to the pressure on communes' food supplies. A diarist in Hofen, in Aalen district, described how, on Saturday, 7 April 1945, the approach of American forces led villagers to besiege food shops in long queues, hoping to exchange their new ration tokens in full for supplies that would see them through the imminent crisis.[57] In other communes, with the enemy approaching, available food supplies were distributed, sometimes without the receipt of ration tokens. The absence of transport to collect milk produced in Grantschen in April 1945 left the commune's inhabitants with an abundant daily supply of 700 litres for themselves.[58] In Hausen, in mid-April, there was clearly some food to spare. Successive *Wehrmacht* units which passed through the commune were plied with bread and coffee, because, it was said, most of them had no provisions of their own.[59] A feeling of solidarity with rank and file German troops persisted, not least, no doubt, because villagers hoped that their own menfolk in the forces would receive similar treatment, wherever they were. In this spirit, villagers in Wendelsheim, in Tübingen district, provided hungry German soldiers who had surrendered to the French with food before they were taken into captivity in April 1945.[60]

By contrast with the towns, in some villages it was possible for schooling to continue until enemy forces arrived, although the conscription of teachers sometimes meant that children of different ages had to be taught in a group together.[61] Even so, in other communes by March and April 1945, schooling was disrupted by the billeting of army units or civil authorities in school buildings.[62] All the schools in Böblingen district were closed at the end of March, because many parents, fearing danger from the air and from enemy artillery, insisted on keeping their children at home.[63] Church services were held as normal, even at the end of March 1945, when the arrival of American forces in Württemberg coincided with Easter. In Fachsenfeld, it was believed that the NSDAP's local branch leader had ordered the digging of defensive ditches on Good Friday deliberately to impress on locals the party's antipathy towards Christianity. The digging continued into the following day, at which point the *Volkssturm* leader suggested that, if work continued until the excavation was complete, they would not need to work on Easter Sunday. Nevertheless, the order went out for work to continue on the Sunday. In the event, no villagers reported until mid-day, presumably to enable them to observe the Christian rites of the day. A week later, several children took their first communion – for once, it was said, without harassment by party officials.[64] In nearby Bopfingen, children born in 1930 had been confirmed on 18 March, and, for good measure, those born in 1931 were confirmed a fortnight later, because of uncertainty about what the future might hold.[65] There can be little doubt that in small communes attachment to a Christian denomination and to the local church persisted, regardless of Nazi attempts to impose their own festivals. While the NSDAP was still able to force villagers in Ditzingen, in Leonberg district, to stage a celebration of Hitler's birthday on 20 April 1945, some communes reported with satisfaction that this was the first time for many years that such a celebration was not held.[66]

To the end, however, there remained in Württemberg ardent Nazis, particularly including SS commanders, who insisted on a last-ditch defence, as well as army officers who were reluctant to flout orders from above to hold out, however much they realised the hopelessness of the cause. Neither the military nor the SS men were native to the communes which they were sent to defend, and they therefore had no vested interest in preserving them from damage.[67] As a result, especially in the final weeks, in March and April 1945, conflict developed in many towns and villages in areas still under German control between the zealots, who were determined to implement the Nazi leadership's orders to the letter, and the majority who became increasingly bold in refusing to stage patently hopeless attempts to block the advancing enemy's inexorable progress. This could be extremely risky because, while the diehards were in an increasingly small minority as the war ground on to its end, they could, as policemen or as NSDAP or SS functionaries, nevertheless be disproportionately influential and punitive even when the regime was breaking up, and they were sometimes still in a position to force reluctant civilians to mount hopeless resistance to a well-armed enemy. In Eschenau, in Heilbronn district, local men removed the tank barriers which had been erected on the orders of an army officer on 12 April 1945. Suddenly, an SS officer arrived by motorcycle, threatened to reduce the commune to ashes if the barriers were not replaced, and sped off. In this case, the order was disobeyed with impunity because the enemy was fast approaching, but in other communes the inhabitants reluctantly undertook defensive measures, well aware that this risked devastation by enemy armour.[68]

Some NSDAP functionaries, notably *Gauleiter*, *Kreisleiter* and SS officers, regarded the wholesale devastation of communes which were forced to resist the enemy as a price worth paying, to demonstrate their unshakable loyalty to the Führer, and to try to avoid both the personal ignominy and the consequences of surrender.[69] Some may have believed, with Hitler and Goebbels, that, contrary to the evidence before them in 1945, the enemy could not sustain his incursions against a people whose determination to resist was galvanised by the fanatical willpower of the Nazi party.[70] *Gauleiter* Murr, for one, remained steadfastly faithful to his leader, urging the people of Württemberg to continue to believe in victory and threatening defeatists with execution, as the enemy closed in on his territory. Determined to implement Hitler's 'Nero decree' to the letter in Württemberg, on 27 March 1945 he loyally relayed to his subordinates a series of watchwords designed to trigger the stages of the Third Reich's ultimate defiance of its foes. The watchword 'Caesar' indicated that enemy forces were within fifty kilometres, and that therefore party papers were to be burned, while civilians were instructed to prepare for the evacuation of their homes and their commune. When the watchword 'Nero' was issued, the evacuation was to commence. Finally, the watchword 'Schwabentreue' was the cue for the destruction of all essential supplies and installations. These were to include all military hardware which German forces could not utilise, transportation links such as bridges, communications systems and industrial plant and equipment, as well as depots with supplies of food and other essentials.[71]

The dying regime's attempt to turn every last town and village into a defensive bastion threatened communes which had so far escaped the bombing raids with the full force of military operations in a fight to the finish. As the Third Reich disintegrated, however, and as communications systems were disrupted by bombing, many communities were reduced to a kind of isolation that left their fate either in their own hands or, if they were unlucky, in the hands of any military or party unit that happened to be in the vicinity. Instructions from superior authorities still reached some district and local NSDAP officials, but because the orders remained the same – to defend German territory unconditionally – the attitude of those in control on the ground was crucial. Most civilians in Württemberg took a characteristically pragmatic view: given that the result of the war was no longer in doubt by early 1945, hostilities should cease forthwith. Sometimes the inhabitants of a town or village decided themselves to surrender before further damage or loss of life was sustained, while in other places a lead was given by people who had clearly been 'politically reliable' enough to prosper in the Third Reich, as mayors or NSDAP officials. Where the local population and its leaders were of this mind and were not coerced by military, police or party forces, the Führer's directives were disregarded, and surrender to an Allied army in the west was speedy and generally bloodless, although there were individual cases of indiscriminate shootings, and more frequent cases of rape, committed by the invading troops.[72] Where, however, external forces were present in a commune, the only alternative to mounting a pointless defence under their authority was disobedience at local level. The disobedience which was manifested in many communes can perhaps scarcely be dignified as 'resistance'. Yet, given the mortal danger in which disobedience of the 'Nero decree' placed individuals and communities, it may be presumptuous to dismiss it as being of lesser value.[73] Even with few civilian policemen to enforce observance of orders from the centre on a disaffected population, the SS or *Gestapo* could be deadly if brought in to investigate allegations of 'defeatism' among civilians.

Few imagined that a loser's peace would be palatable. As one commentator in Crailsheim district put it, 'Even at the beginning of the year [1945], it was obvious to any reasonable person that for our people and country the war's ending would be utterly dreadful'.[74] Yet this has to be seen in relative terms. In Bavaria, it was said in February 1945 that 'as long as the Russians don't come here, we can put up with anything'.[75] Word had by this time obviously reached southern Germany of the fate that befell those who stood in the Red Army's path. From late 1944, the inhabitants of the eastern regions of Germany were compelled by their political masters to engage in a desperate, and ultimately futile, attempt to repel invasion by Soviet forces. Those in towns and villages which were overrun by the Red Army suffered atrocities of a kind for which even Nazi anti-Soviet propaganda had not prepared them. This was only partly in retaliation for the atrocities inflicted on the Soviet Union's western populations by the occupying German forces in and after 1941.[76]

In southern Germany, by contrast, there was news from closer to home, from the western areas of Germany which had been invaded by American and British forces from October 1944. The Württemberg SD reported on 27 March 1945 the popular view that the war was virtually over and that the Americans would reach Stuttgart by Easter, at the end of the month. In anticipation, some citizens took provisions and retreated to bunkers. Many of those who remained in the capital were reluctant to heed renewed calls for those not involved in essential services to evacuate it because of the lack of protective bunkers or tunnels in the countryside, and also because of the ever increasing difficulty of finding accommodation in rural areas which were already overcrowded with evacuees and refugees. With palpable relief, Württemberg's inhabitants predicted that 'it isn't the Russians who are coming but, on the contrary, civilised people, and it's clear from areas already under Allied control that the inhabitants are finding the occupation tolerable'. However much Goebbels deplored the eagerness with which the arrival of American troops was anticipated, the willingness of the population to surrender was evident.[77] Even when it transpired that some parts of Württemberg were being invaded by French forces – including North African troops – the will for peace was stronger than fear of reprisals for what Germans had inflicted on the French during the years of occupation.

The hunger of Württemberg's inhabitants for peace was entirely at odds with *Gauleiter* Murr's insistence that there should be no surrender on his territory. He remained inflexibly true to Hitler's instruction that Germans should fight to the last house and lay waste their country, so that its enemies should not benefit from its remaining assets. On 10 April, with the invader on course to take Stuttgart and calling upon Germans to surrender peacefully, Murr proclaimed: 'Whoever submits to the enemy will face proscription and contempt. Whoever pays heed to the enemy's words forfeits his life.'[78] Two days later, he issued an even more explicit threat: 'Any attempt either to obstruct the closing of a tank barrier, or to open a tank barrier that is closed, will be punished by summary execution. Similarly, anyone who shows a white flag will be executed.' To reinforce this threat, he added that a defeatist's family, too, could 'expect Draconian punishment'. As late as 18, 19 and 20 April 1945, the NSDAP's newspaper in Stuttgart, the *NS-Kurier* insisted that all was not lost, that faith in the *Führer* remained unstinting and that defiance, not cowardice, characterised the popular mood. These, however, were its last editions, and Murr himself fled from the city on 19 April, enabling its Nazi mayor, Karl Strölin, to hand Stuttgart over to the French on 22 April without further bloodshed.[79]

Sparing Stuttgart additional destruction beyond that wrought by Allied bombing was Strölin's prime objective. He could see that inviting further destruction of his city and inflicting additional misery on ordinary citizens who had already endured extreme suffering was indefensible.[80] Strölin had recently been president of the International Association for Housing and Town Planning, and it may be that this interest partly motivated him to surrender his already battered city.[81] On 4 April, he had told Murr that Stuttgart could not be successfully defended against the French and American troops who surrounded it, and he asked that it be declared an open city. Murr refused to countenance this, and so Strölin, having consulted local notables who shared his view, opened negotiations with the Allies on 10 April with a view to handing the city over to them peacefully. Thus Stuttgart was spared the final agony that was inflicted on the town of Heilbronn. The reign of terror there presided over by the NSDAP's district leader, Richard Drauz, saw numerous people summarily shot or hanged for displaying a white flag, and culminated in a week's bitter hand-to-hand fighting before the invader claimed his predictable victory.[82] Other Nazi officers, too, were determined to fight tooth and nail to the death. Seibold, the Tettnang *Kreisleiter*, was intent on having Friedrichshafen defended, if necessary by shooting alleged defeatists and cowards. It was not until he and his entourage had fled, on the night of 28–29 April, that the civil authorities were able to hand heavily-damaged Friedrichshafen over to the French.[83]

Across Württemberg, most district and local Nazi leaderships' response was, following the 'Nero decree', to order villagers to evacuate their communes, to leave remaining German regular or SS troops, and perhaps also *Volkssturm* or HJ units, to mount a patently hopeless defence against a well-armed enemy. They could hardly, by this time, hope to avoid defeat, as many minor party functionaries recognised.[84] In Malmsheim, in Leonberg district, the party's leader made only a half-hearted attempt to persuade villagers to retreat to the Allgäu.[85] Nevertheless, the presence in a town or village of an army unit with orders to defend German territory against the invader at all costs could mean that civilians had no influence over whether their town or village was to be defended or surrendered. This was the case in Wolpertswende, in Ravensburg district, where in April 1945 there remained a German garrison with plentiful equipment. On the arrival of French troops, a battle ensued in which the casualties included a local woman, after which the French took control of the town, burning down three buildings as retribution for the military resistance which they had encountered.[86] Thus local civilians were punished for conduct over which they had had no control.

After the war, the mayor of Zipplingen recorded that, at a public meeting, the Aalen district and local NSDAP leaders had told the commune's inhabitants to prepare themselves to face death. The villagers had responded vehemently that their commune simply could not be defended and that 'it seemed senseless to allow our homeland to be destroyed for a second time'. The first time had been during the Thirty Years War in the seventeenth century, when Zipplingen was totally destroyed, with only two men managing to escape and all the houses burned to the ground by the marauding Swedes. In the Second World War, the villagers felt, there had been two miraculous escapes, first when a local train had been bombed, on 16 December 1944, but none of the Zipplingers among the passengers had been killed – although twenty others had – and secondly when a bomber had jettisoned its remaining bombs in fields just outside the village, on 4 April 1945. After that, the inhabitants were in no mood to court certain disaster by mounting resistance.[87] Folk memory of the catastrophe of the Thirty Years War vividly reminded villagers there and elsewhere of how unacceptably high the price could be. It was recalled that the commune of Oberspeltach, in Crailsheim district, had been all but burned to the ground in 1634.[88] In Heimsheim, in Leonberg district, amid the devastation of the Thirty Years War the church's chancel had survived, only to be destroyed by fire in April 1945.[89]

There can be little doubt that the Zipplingers' reluctance to mount a defence of their commune was the rule rather than the exception. However ordinary members of communes had regarded the NSDAP, its leaders and its policies – whether they had more or less welcomed them, grudgingly tolerated them or heartily disliked them – the one policy that united them against diehard local leaders was that of defending their locality to the last house against vastly superior enemy forces. The Neresheim local branch leader, for one, incurred opprobrium from members of his commune for wanting them to make a last-ditch stand against the approaching Americans.[90] Further south, in Waldsee, where the local branch leader was also mayor, there were a few tense days in April 1945 during which he tried to organise defence of the commune in the face of opposition from its inhabitants. In the end, he took flight.[91] In Unterkirchberg, the commune's men were so incensed by the local branch leader's determination to obey orders to defend the village that they broke in and bundled him out of his house. In the ensuing fight, in which an army unit became involved, a soldier was mortally wounded, three men were shot, three houses were burned down and the local branch leader was injured.[92]

Where there were only token army or SS troops, they might force civilians to construct tank barriers and destroy any bridges which the invader might utilise. But in Steinberg, near Ulm, the villagers refused to cut down lime trees adjacent to the church which were around 150 to 180 years old to serve as tank barriers, perhaps because the army and SS units in the vicinity were 'without vehicles, without heavy weapons, and pretty exhausted'.[93] In these places, units of the *Volkssturm* or the HJ might be the only forces available for defence. If there was no party, SS or army commander to compel them to make a stand, they probably would not do so, regardless of orders issued in Berlin or Stuttgart. If, however, there was a local leader determined to follow his Führer to the end, then a battle of wills was likely to ensue, with the leader using dire threats to terrorise local people into compliance. In Zipplingen, it was the police who ordered the construction of tank barriers, and threatened that anyone refusing to help – or anyone trying to dismantle a barrier – would be executed.[94] Sometimes threats of this kind achieved compliance, but in other cases they did not. Nevertheless, in view of the readiness with which SS officers, in particular, were given to uttering threats of execution, which they did not shrink from carrying out, it is hardly surprising that in many places preparations to resist the enemy were made, albeit with the utmost reluctance.

Where there was a stalemate between German civilians and party, SS or army officers about the course of action, the invader could lose patience. In Bächlingen on 11 April, where the American commander of an advance party anticipated the arrival of German reinforcements, he announced that, unless the inhabitants raised a white flag by the following morning, the commune would be burned down. Sure enough, a flag appeared, but shortly afterwards it was removed by a newly arrived German army unit. Its commander threatened the civilians and refused to meet their request that, to preserve the commune, the soldiers should withdraw from it. The American commander declared a cease-fire for two hours to enable the civilians to flee. But he was so taken with the beauty of the place that he ordered his men to try to avoid damaging buildings which were not in the hands of the defending German soldiers. Nevertheless, two days of bitter close-range fighting were enough to leave the commune's centre devastated; altogether, a third of its houses were destroyed, as well as commercial premises. This disaster befell Bächlingen for two reasons. First, Hitler's insistence that every inch of territory be defended for as long as possible was implemented by the local NSDAP leaders, who supervised the construction of tank barriers and mobilised the *Volkssturm*. Then, the arrival of a German army detachment, small in number and poorly-equipped but with orders to defend the commune, ensured that the civilians' desire to surrender was disregarded. As a result, a place which had been relatively unscathed by bombing found itself unwillingly in the front line – according to the local chronicler, because of 'the arbitrary destruction order of a madman'.[95]

It is not clear whether all of the fanatics genuinely believed that a last-ditch attempt at defence could save the Third Reich. They seem mostly to have been the kind of Nazi or SS criminal whose only options in the spring of 1945 were suicide, arrest followed by either imprisonment or execution, or going down fighting and taking with them not only their own immediate followers but also civilians who wanted no part in the armed conflict. In some places, an SS or army unit did score a temporary success, recapturing a town or village from the invader, only to lose it for good a few days later. Crailsheim endured this kind of struggle, which caused massive destruction.[96] In Nufringen, in Böblingen district, an SS-led force counter-attacked within twenty-four hours of the town's being occupied. There were some casualties on both sides and, as a punishment for the SS assault, French troops burned down a large building in Nufringen. The SS attackers – who were perhaps reminiscent of the *Freikorps* of the immediate post-1918 years – departed in the direction of Tübingen, only to be cut down by enemy artillery.[97] In Oberdorf, in Aalen district, an incident after the Americans had occupied the commune cost the lives of twelve people, as the local chronicler put it, 'in order to prolong the life of a criminal regime by a few days'.[98]

In Waldsee, where tank barriers indicated a readiness to defend the commune, even the local NSDAP leader, who was also mayor, gave up the idea of making a stand because there was strong popular opposition to it. This was confirmed by the large group of citizens who besieged the town hall, demanding immediate surrender and cheering as some of their number raised a white flag. But the local army commander insisted that it be removed; even at this late date, on 23 April, he remained determined to defend Waldsee because he feared that, if he did not, 'he would lose his head'. He was, however, eventually persuaded that saving the commune was what mattered, and he therefore agreed to withdraw his forces into the nearby woods so that it could be surrendered to the French without bloodshed or destruction.[99] On the other hand, a demonstration by several hundred women in front of Sindelfingen town hall, reinforcing the opposition of the mayor to the erecting of a tank barrier, was without effect. The district army commander would not be persuaded to disobey orders to defend this commune, which had been a bombing target on twelve occasions since November 1942 largely because of the presence of a Daimler works.[100]

Army discipline mostly prevailed, with troops generally continuing to fight even when surrounded, heavily outnumbered and outgunned, if ordered to do so by their superiors, whether or not an SS execution squad was in the vicinity. There were also cases of army officers executing 'defeatist' civilians.[101] Where the army's resolve faltered, it might be strengthened by threats of summary execution from party or SS personnel. In Rohrau, where German troops were quartered in April 1945, the local army commander had omitted to order the building of tank barriers. He was instructed to remedy this by a 'rather brusque representative of the [NSDAP's] district leadership', and he complied.[102] In what was probably a rare instance, in Adelmannsfelden, in Aalen district, the army general who arrived on 15 April managed to restrain the SS from enforcing the pointless defence of the commune.[103] Nevertheless, the hopelessness of the German position increasingly led to desertions. In Waldburg, in Ravensburg district, two German soldiers who had deserted were condemned to death by a drumhead court: they were hanged from a nearby tree, and their bodies buried in a gravel pit.[104] By mid-April there was some disarray among the convoys of retreating troops from the western front passing through Württemberg's towns and villages. To the disgust of villagers in Hüttlingen and Öschelbronn, remnants of an army unit seized horses from their stables and made off into the unknown.[105] Other communes had already reluctantly had to surrender horses, carts, motorcycles and bicycles to the retreating army in a more orderly manner.[106]

In the final days of the war, further confusion was caused by attempts by either political leaders or army commanders to persuade both villagers and evacuees to leave their commune for their own safety while a last ditch effort was made to defend it against the advancing enemy. Alternatively, villagers might be told to take cover in cellars. Local people did not welcome either of these alternatives because they implied an anticipation of severe damage to the town or village; most of the time, however, there was little that they could do about it. Murr's order to evacuate Stuttgart and some of Württemberg's northern districts came into force in late March 1945.[107] In the next two or three weeks it would apply throughout Württemberg. The communes which were most likely to suffer damage were those where there was an army or SS unit with adequate arms. In many places the decision to defend a town or village was taken soberly, in the full knowledge of what it would mean for the community. Most villagers, however, refused to move. In many communes, including Leinfelden, in Böblingen district, and Heimerdingen, in Leonberg district, NSDAP officers urged villagers to leave, without success.[108] In Amrichshausen, in Künzelsau district, members of the commune met on 29 March 1945 and decided not to comply with instructions to evacuate it.[109] In Crailsheim district, 'even the *Landrat* made no secret of the fact that he regarded the compulsory evacuation of civilians', before final resistance to the enemy was mounted, 'as a mistake, and as practically unenforceable'.[110]

One reason for this was the refusal of farmers to leave their fields and their livestock. While it was undoubtedly unpleasant, frightening and inconvenient for urban dwellers to leave their homes, those who were employees and their families were more mobile than those whose livelihood derived from the land. In Korntal, in Leonberg district, after the watchwords 'Nero' and 'Schwabentreue' were transmitted by radio on the night of 16–17 April, local farmers made it clear that they had no intention of leaving the commune because there were only between four and six wagons available, whereas forty or fifty wagons would be needed to allow each villager to transport a basic twenty-five kilos of provisions and possessions. After negotiations involving the *Ortsbauernführer,* an army platoon commander and the local *Volkssturm* leader, it was agreed that there would be no evacuation of Korntal.[111] In Eschenau, which was near enough to Heilbronn to feel the effects of attacks on the town, farmers had built bunkers or huts outside the commune where they stored items of value. There remained, however, the problem of ensuring that farm animals were accommodated safely.[112] Beyond that, many farmers tried to carry on working as usual, adhering to the rhythms of the agricultural year, in spite of the increasing risk of bombing and the proximity of the enemy's land forces. In Friolzheim, in Leonberg district, after bombing raids had destroyed four farmers' barns in late March and early April 1945, 'the farmers ventured into the fields only at first light and at nightfall'.[113] The same was the case in Rohrau, where 'with unexpected attacks from the air, farmers very often had to abandon their wagons and take cover from machine-gun fire in ditches and trenches'. The local chronicler regarded it as amazing that farmers had been able to continue to tend their fields in spring 1945 without sustaining any fatalities or the destruction of a single wagon. The Nazi leaders in the area had wanted the villagers to leave Rohrau, taking all of their farm animals with them, but the farming population regarded this suggestion as absurd, and in any case none of the villagers wanted to embark on a journey into the unknown, whatever the risks of remaining.[114]

In Fachsenfeld, preparations for the defence of the commune had been thorough, with women and girls involved in digging trenches alongside the *Volkssturm* men to create a defensive ring around the village. The meaning of the watchwords, 'Caesar' and 'Nero' was explained to villagers, with their implications for the evacuation of the commune by both people and animals. On 7 April, the order to prepare for evacuation came, with the mayor receiving the watchword 'Caesar' from the *Landrat*'s office by telephone. This was passed on to the commune by the ringing of church bells. Enemy forces were approaching, and mourners at a funeral on 11 April had to take cover during the service while bombers flew over the village. Yet no-one could imagine how a complete evacuation of the commune might be effected, and almost no-one made preparations for evacuation. In the mayor's office, only a few important documents were destroyed, contrary to orders for the destruction of all papers relating to the Third Reich. When the watchword 'Nero' was relayed 'by the NSDAP', on 21 April, there was no response. Apart from anything else, there was no information about where the villagers should go or how long they should remain away from the commune.[115] By this time, there was probably no predictably safe destination.

On the whole, mayors of small communes were opposed to attempts by army or SS units to defend their territory, while some NSDAP local branch leaders, too, put the interests of their community before the demands of their political superiors. In Hüttlingen, the local branch leader joined forces with the deputy mayor to prevent the blowing up of the commune's bridge.[116] This was a more heroic act than it perhaps appears: other local officials reluctantly obeyed orders from military or SS units to blow up bridges or construct tank barriers, under threat of execution.[117] The threat was not an idle one, as the mayor and NSDAP local branch leader of Brettheim, in Crailsheim district, discovered to their cost. They were hanged on the orders of the SS for refusing to sign the death warrant of a farmer who had been 'defeatist'.[118] Their grisly fate was soon made known in other communes in the district.[119] Similarly, on 3 April 1945, in Sontheim,

Kreisleiter Drauz had the NSDAP's local branch leader shot for urging that a tank barrier be dismantled – and ordered that his corpse be left lying for a whole day, with a placard stating 'I am a traitor' round its neck.[120]

Others, too, were courageous. In Kocherstetten, in Künzelsau district, two officers from a Bavarian military unit appeared and ordered the *Volkssturm* leader to undertake preparations for blowing up the commune's bridge. When local men refused to do this, the officers ordered two French POWs to take their place. The mayor of Kocherstetten argued strenuously against destroying the bridge and was threatened with arrest. In the end, the bridge was partially destroyed by explosives.[121] In Suppingen, on 22 April 1945, an army officer's threat to hang the mayor for doubting that Germany would be victorious was averted only by the arrival of American tanks. The mayor had distributed bedding from an abandoned air base nearby to villagers taking cover in cellars.[122] On Good Friday, 30 March 1945, an assembly of all the mayors in Crailsheim district had been given instructions about evacuating their communes to enable the military to stage a defence against the approaching Americans. Unanimously, the mayors called this unrealistic.[123] Nevertheless, on 14 April, with his town in the midst of a bitter battle between German and American forces and with the Americans having captured the *Landrat* and then temporarily retreated, Otto Hänle, the Crailsheim *Kreisleiter*, was still at his post, using a partially repaired telephone network to order NSDAP local branch leaders to erect barricades to impede the enemy's advance.[124]

The one event which did most to prevent further destruction of towns and villages in the last days of the war was the sudden flight of a party leader or SS commander who had been trying to enforce Hitler's orders on an unwilling population. With Allied troops bearing down on them, some erstwhile fanatics discovered that, while they might be prepared to bludgeon other Germans into fighting to the death, they were reluctant to mount a last stand themselves. Even SS units were not above abandoning their posts and fleeing after a realistic appraisal of the situation, although many stood and fought. They were at their most tenacious in Bopfingen, where two SS officers with a unit of thirty-five men took command of the local *Volkssturm*, supervised defensive measures and enrolled HJ boys born in 1929 into their ranks. A fierce battle followed which was finally won by American forces, although the fanatical SS commander had to be dissuaded by the Bopfingen *Volkssturm* from launching a counter-attack. He and his men departed towards the Bavarian border, taking the HJ boys with them.[125] In nearby Dalkingen, it was a matter of great relief to the civilian population when, with American forces only a day's march away, the SS unit which had been forcing women, girls and old men to construct defences around the village suddenly left, removing the worst threat to their safety.[126] In Adelmannsfelden, the sight of the head of the Americans' tank column was enough to persuade the remaining SS men in the town to withdraw, thus enabling the Americans to take over 'without incident'.[127]

Nevertheless, many NSDAP leaders at district and local level held on desperately into April 1945, believing either the promises or the threats of their superiors – promises that areas of Germany could still be successfully defended and threats that whoever permitted surrender would pay with his life. When it was clear that the game was up, they tried to escape, usually commandeering the only available transport in the area for their flight. On 22 April, *Kreisleiter* Trefz of Aalen drove off in a car with his adjutant and a schoolgirl evacuee from Duisburg. The *Volkssturm* in Aalen town had dissolved itself, the SS unit stationed in Aalen had been ordered to retreat, and American forces were fast approaching. Happily for the townspeople, 'the whole plan for defending Aalen collapsed like a house of cards'.[128] In fact, Trefz had given up hope almost three weeks earlier. On 3 April 1945, he told a meeting of his local branch leaders that 'we are facing collapse'. The Bopfingen leader, for one, returned to his commune and relayed to a meeting of *Volkssturm* men, political leaders and the commune's council the *Kreisleiter*'s view that 'it is all over and further resistance is pointless'. Then he dissolved the NSDAP in Bopfingen and ordered the destruction of all party documents. This was a little premature, given that the watchword 'Caesar' was not in force there until 7 April.[129] Even so, as we have seen, the SS tried to defend Bopfingen, while the Aalen NSDAP leader had already been obliged to prolong the town's resistance to the enemy because of the presence of the same SS unit. Its twenty-two year old commander ordered local bridges to be blown up and dismissed the mayor of Aalen for representing the view of the majority of citizens that the town could not be defended.[130]

Probably no NSDAP leader was more fanatically active in the last days of the war than Richard Drauz, who wanted to turn 'every commune into a small bastion in order either to halt or to delay the enemy's advance'. At the same time, he ordered the burning of all papers, while many party members, hoping to evade detection, burned their uniforms.[131] In some communes in his district, such as Auenstein, army units carried out desperate defensive operations.[132] In other places, disobedience was possible. For example, in Biberach, tank barriers 'erected on the express order of the infamous *Kreisleiter* Drautz [sic]' were removed a few days later, before the Americans reached the village, while in Bachenau the tank barriers which had been erected by 'party functionaries in their final desperation', were dismantled by the villagers 'in order to protect the village'. In Brettach, tank barriers which had been built on Drauz's orders in early April 1945 were dismantled when the enemy approached. Drauz had ordered the local *Volkssturm* and the HJ to defend Brettach, but they refused.[133] There was nothing that Drauz could do about these acts of disobedience in remote communes, because he was not in Bachenau, Biberach or Brettach, nor were there police or SS forces which could, and undoubtedly would, have enforced his orders.

Drauz was not to be deterred. Having on 6 April closed down the NSDAP's district office in Heilbronn and burned papers and flags, in accordance with the watchword 'Caesar', he toured some of his communes to try to enforce defence to the last ditch.[134] On the evening of 15 April, he arrived in Gronau 'heavily armed and with a large force of heavily armed SS and party adherents'. He berated the mayor of Gronau for failing to have the commune's bridge over the River Bottwar blown up and threatened him with a drumhead court martial. Drauz claimed that Gronau was 'the last commune in his district and it would be defended to the last man. Any of the inhabitants who opposed its defence would be shot'. Then he departed to try to raise army units to reinforce the troops already present in this remaining outpost of his district, leaving the mayor of Gronau free to disobey his orders.[135] Richard Drauz had nothing to lose and remained fanatical until the end. He finally took refuge in a convent, where he was arrested by American forces in June 1945. He was tried and executed in Landsberg in 1946 for having shot an American pilot who had surrendered; he had also caused the death of many Germans in his own district. Whether he can seriously be regarded as a mere 'scapegoat' for the crimes of the NSDAP in Heilbronn is a matter for doubt; he was the leader there, in a system where the 'leadership principle', reinforced by *Gauleiter* Murr's friendship, gave him virtually unlimited power.[136] He set a merciless example which was assiduously followed by some of his subordinates.[137] At the end, at least, however much they had collaborated with him for years, the majority of the party's local branch leaders were no longer prepared to obey him when he demanded that they defend their communes to the death.

Other officers of both party and state took flight.[138] The mayor of Oberkochen, in Aalen district, along with his deputy and a member of the commune's council – apparently all members of the NSDAP – left the commune by car for the south on 22 April, after destroying all the papers generated in his office during the Third Reich.[139] In Wendelsheim, near Tübingen, the local branch leader and his family departed on 17 April, leaving the mayor to deal with the advancing French forces.[140] Two women who had been active in the Schönaich NSDAP local branch, near Böblingen, left the commune in a horse-drawn cart on 5 April along with the local branch leader's family.[141] The *Kreisleiter* of Böblingen and his entourage, having claimed that they could defend their territory, attempted, on 20 April, to flee to Vaihingen, with the result that the NSDAP in the district was deemed to have dissolved itself. The local branch in Musberg had already ceased to function because of the conscription of its 'last local branch leader'.[142] *Gauleiter* Murr retreated from Stuttgart on 19 April 1945 in order to set up an alternative headquarters in southern Württemberg. With the enemy closing in, he changed out of his uniform and into a civilian suit. When he and his wife were apprehended by French forces on 13 May, they posed as evacuees. On the following day, first she and then he took a fatal dose of poison.[143]

With the flight of local Nazi leaders, communes were left to fend for themselves in the face of either German troops or the enemy – or both. Those adjacent to a rail line were in particular jeopardy. Stimpfach, in Crailsheim district, was a case in point. In increasingly intensive air attacks in April 1945, enemy planes derailed a goods train, shot at farmers working in the fields and hit not only Stimpfach rail station but also the commune's bridge and oil mill. On 21 April, enemy planes detected a German military vehicle, which had arrived in the commune with multiple rocket launchers, and fired on it. Some of the grenades in the vehicle exploded, and, together with enemy firing, caused considerable damage to buildings. Then American ground forces approached. SS men who were still in the area fired at their tanks with machine guns, and the tanks returned fire. After about twenty minutes of shooting, a large part of Stimpfach was in flames. Fire spread so quickly that the inhabitants had difficulty in rescuing any of their possessions or animals. Only a cloudburst – which cut communications between the front and the German artillery with the rocket launchers – prevented the complete annihilation of Stimpfach, because the artillery was unable to continue its fire. This was not the end of the damage. Once German resistance had been crushed, huge tanks and heavy vehicles belonging to American forces rolled through Stimpfach, inflicting substantial damage on fields and gardens.[144]

Further west, Abstatt, in Heilbronn district, was in the firing line between German and American forces for a week in mid-April 1945. Ten villagers were killed by artillery fire which penetrated the cellars in which they had taken refuge, and the commune's church was seriously damaged. A farmer was killed by a splinter when a German grenade exploded.[145] By contrast, nearby Affaltrach sustained some damage because the remnants of a *Wehrmacht* unit were on its outskirts and under attack from American forces, but when this unit withdrew, 'peace reigned'.[146] In Leonberg district, although Heimsheim was not itself defended, it sustained fire damage from exchanges in the area between German and French forces. This resulted in the death of four people, around eighty oxen and many smaller animals. Almost 200 families lost their home, farm buildings and all of their possessions. To meet this emergency, a communal kitchen was set up to feed them, every remaining house was packed full with people, and neighbouring communes provided what assistance they could.[147] Erroneously thinking that Friolzheim was defended, French forces bombarded the commune for three days. The local fire brigade did not possess a mechanical water sprinkler, making it difficult to quench the fires which destroyed barns and homes. Eight firefighters were killed and two wounded by a direct hit on the school, which was their headquarters, and five more villagers were killed by enemy fire. On the following day, after the mayor and the priest had handed the commune over to the French, it came under fire from German artillery. There were no fatalities, but some villagers sustained injuries.[148]

Some communes were surrendered to American or French forces without bloodshed. Aschhausen, in Künzelsau district, was one.[149] In nearby Amrichshausen, there was an exchange of fire between SS troops and American forces. In spite of death threats from local Nazis, the inhabitants ran up two white flags on the church tower, and the priest handed the village over to the Americans without incident.[150] Neither Unterdeufstetten nor Tiefenbach, in Leonberg district, had suffered air raids. Unterdeufstetten was fortunate in that a German artillery unit withdrew from the commune as the enemy approached at speed, and therefore it sustained no damage at all.[151] In Tiefenbach, the only damage resulted from the destruction of the commune's bridge, which meant that vehicles had to travel through the fields. The fruit orchards suffered significant damage, because soldiers flattened trees in order to have the optimum field of fire.[152] It is not clear how villagers in Holzgerlingen, in Böblingen district, were able to 'expel our own German soldiers from the commune' in early April, but, while they did so with a heavy heart, they were determined that their commune should not become a battlefield. They felt that they had suffered enough from the terror of air-raid sirens as enemy aircraft overflew the commune. Worse than that, on Easter Sunday, 1 April 1945, houses had been damaged by bombing and two villagers seriously injured by fire from low-flying aircraft. A unit of French forces arrived by motorcycle, along with some tanks, on 19 April, searching houses for German soldiers. A French POW, who had been working in the commune, took a motorcycle and rode through the commune on it in joy at his liberation. This was discovered after a terrifying rumour had spread that someone had stolen a motorcycle, and that the commune would be bombed from the air if it was not returned at once.[153]

With the enemy's advance, many German soldiers became POWs. Over and above those who were captured defending foreign territory which Germans had seized and exploited, thousands of German soldiers became captives in their own country as the Allied noose tightened in early 1945. Two days after the commune of Ebnat was occupied on 24 April by American forces, lorries taking several hundred German soldiers from the front into captivity passed through it.[154] By chance, when a column of German soldiers was led through Hüttlingen on its way to a POW camp in Heilbronn, a local man was recognised. In woods adjacent to the commune, an estimated 10,000 and more German soldiers were held while their captors decided whom to release and whom to investigate further. A few men from Hüttlingen were among those who were released.[155] Others were less fortunate: one of Zipplingen's sons died of pneumonia, as a POW in France.[156] Units of the *Volkssturm*, too, were taken captive. Some from Oberdorf were taken to a prison camp near Ludwigshafen 'where they had to endure seven weeks of awful food and sleeping in the open air'. While some were handed over to the French, others were set to work by the Americans. Some returned home three months later, but others were in captivity for a year.[157] Almost all the men of the Aufhausen Volkssturm spent time in captivity, while members of the Gronau Volkssturm, who were captured in mid-April 1945, spent some time as POWs in France.[158] Prominent members of Württemberg's Nazi elite were not immune. The deputy Gauleiter of Württemberg-Hohenzollern, Friedrich Schmidt, who had become an SS officer, was captured while serving at the front in France in 1944 and taken as a POW to Britain.[159] The diabetic Württemberg Interior and Economics Minister, Jonathan Schmid, having served for a time in the German military administration in France, suffered fatal insulin deprivation in July 1945 in French internment.[160]

Many officials of the Nazi regime who had neither fled nor committed suicide were apprehended and imprisoned to await investigation. Several Kreisleiter and other Nazi functionaries were held and eventually put on trial.[161] The Landrat of Aalen district and the most prominent NSDAP members in Aalen town were captured, amid 'a boom in denunciations', as local people settled old scores.[162] Denunciations by local inhabitants in Wendelsheim led to the arrest in May 1945 of eight men. Two of them were released on the same day, but six were taken by car to a holding camp near Böblingen where two of them died, reportedly in an accident. The remaining four were released after six weeks.[163] At the end of April 1945, it was reported from Aalen district that 'district leaders, local branch leaders and other [NSDAP] officials …were arrested', and that as late as 21 July house searches by the Americans in Neresheim had resulted in the arrest of a few NSDAP functionaries.[164]

Further south, in Regglisweiler, the local branch leader was arrested, along with other NSDAP members, by French soldiers on 24 April 1945 and taken away. It transpired, some weeks later, that he and the local NSDAP business manager had been shot in a wood. This seems to have been because of a counter-attack against French troops by a Werwolf partisan band; 'otherwise, the shooting of German civilians was unknown here'. The local NSDAP training officer had saved his skin by attaching himself to a Red Cross unit, which enabled him to make his escape.[165] The shooting of the deputy mayor of Oberkessach, who was also the NSDAP cell leader, was reported as a private initiative on the part of two American soldiers who broke into his house in search of plunder.[166] Yet it seems too much of a coincidence that he was singled out. More probably, he was denounced to the Americans by villagers. The local branch leader and the mayor of Fachsenfeld received orders from above on 19 April to dress in Volkssturm uniform and leave the village for the south. The former seems to have done this, but the mayor was still in his commune on 23 April when the Americans arrived.

They set up a post in front of his office and lit a fire to keep themselves warm. It was fuelled partly by swastika flags and pictures of Hitler.[167]

Some Nazis who neither fled nor were captured tried to blend into their surroundings. The burning of party uniforms became routine, while the mayor of Hofen, who had habitually worn an NSDAP uniform, changed into army uniform on 22 April.[168] In Bopfingen, when the stones of an anti-tank barrier were being dismantled, 'a whole lot of party badges came to light which had, during the construction, obviously been "lost"'.[169] In some places the occupying power tried systematically to identify former Nazis. In Holzgerlingen, the French authorities instructed all the commune's inhabitants to sign a declaration relating to membership of the party, its formations and affiliates.[170] Postwar German local authorities, too, might conduct a survey of former political activists. In December 1945, the mayor of a commune in Heilbronn reported in detail to his *Landrat* about 'functionaries of the NSDAP and its affiliated formations'. He named four cell leaders, the propaganda leader, ten block officials, the NSV cell leader and five NSV block officials, 'all of whom are resident in this commune'. He added emphatically that none of the block officials of the NSV had been members of the NSDAP.[171] Sometimes, former NSDAP members were detailed to undertake hard labour. In Musberg, between 30 April and 25 July 1945, the French military government issued thirty-four orders, one of which, proclaimed on 4 June, read: 'Labour that is painful or unpleasant shall preferably be performed by the former active members of the NSDAP'. This included clearing up the debris caused by the major air raid on 15 March 1944 which had not yet been removed.[172] In Tailfingen, 'a mass grave of former concentration camp prisoners, mostly Jews, was uncovered' on 1 June 1945. All the men of the commune had to participate in opening the grave and removing the corpses, with non-NSDAP members working until midday on 2 June and former party members until the evening of the same day.[173] In Hemmingen, French forces, observing the traditional sexual division of labour, obliged the wives of former NSDAP members to clean the sports hall, where former Polish forced workers were to be accommodated.[174]

The occupation of Württemberg's communes by either American or French forces lasted for varying lengths of time, for days, weeks or months. Sometimes the invader merely ascertained that there were no German soldiers in a commune and then left. In Grantschen, American troops were in the vicinity, but none was quartered at any time, leaving 'the inhabitants to conduct their agricultural work in peace'.[175] In some villages, the period of military occupation was very brief – as little as either a day or two, or the Americans' four-day sojourn in Hofen.[176] In Heimerdingen, French forces passed through the commune, appropriating radios, cameras and other valuables. A field hospital was set up for a few days, but that was the extent of the occupation there.[177] Sindeldorf, in Künzelsau district, was occupied by American forces from 8 to 11 April, and thereafter experienced

only the occasional passage of military traffic through the village until the middle
of July, when an American infantry company was quartered there for eight
weeks.[178] By contrast, other communes experienced several months' occupation.
The last American troops left Westernhausen on 5 September 1945.[179] French
troops remained in Friolzheim for about three months, until – to the relief
of the inhabitants – they were replaced by American forces.[180] In Crailsheim
district, American troops remained in many places until November 1945. In
both Kirchberg and Stimpfach, it was said that only then did life begin to return
to normal.[181]

There can be no doubt that the American occupiers were less demanding
and less hostile than the French, for understandable reasons. Nevertheless,
most communes reported that the occupiers either requisitioned or plundered
goods. There was a difference between requisitioning and plundering: army
commanders might issue a blanket demand for the surrender of items such as
bicycles, telephones, telescopes, typewriters, radios and cameras.[182] If they were
remaining rather than passing through, they would require some villagers to
move out of their homes to provide accommodation. In Kerkingen it was said
that the Americans seized the best houses.[183] In Sindeldorf, they requisitioned
twenty-three homes in July 1945.[184] If they were lucky, expropriated villagers
moved in with neighbours. In Hermuthausen, however, many displaced families
had to find shelter in cellars and barns after surrendering their homes.[185] In
Stimpfach, it was regarded as a particular hardship that, after many buildings
had been damaged, the Americans requisitioned the only remaining decent
accommodation, giving the owners two hours' notice to move out.[186] Aschhausen
endured 'constant unpleasant quartering' as wave after wave of foreign troops
arrived for a short stay and then moved on.[187]

Some communes were required to provide food for occupying troops in
either their own or a neighbouring area. In Niedernhall, in Künzelsau district,
the commander of an American army unit enlisted two local women to cook for
him and his men.[188] If there was a transit camp for liberated foreign workers
in the area, communes might be required to provide it with food. Further, in
districts invaded by French forces, in the south and west, every household was
required to provide a complete outfit of clothing for distribution to former
foreign workers.[189] This was regarded as a particular hardship after years of
cloth rationing. At the same time, in many places a curfew was imposed which
restricted farmers' work but allowed former foreign workers to roam at will,
to the dismay of some villagers. The occupying forces tolerated, and in some
cases encouraged, this.[190] After Eschenau had been occupied without incident
by American troops on 14 April, there was firing from the neighbouring hamlet
of Wieslensdorf. An American was injured, and several barns were set on fire in
reprisal. In addition, former Polish workers were let loose on the area to plunder

at will. They seized poultry, schnapps and wine, and continued to break into cellars for several weeks, causing terror among the villagers. Yet the fact that the Poles mostly removed foodstuffs – including livestock – suggests that they were, above all, hungry.[191]

Beyond military requisitioning and plundering by former foreign workers, there was also thieving by individual soldiers, although in Hermuthausen the view was that any robbery was less attributable to Americans than to 'civilians from Poland and Russia', the former forced workers.[192] In Stimpfach, however, jewellery, musical instruments, linen and schnapps, among other goods, were seized by American soldiers.[193] In Amrichshausen, it was said that 'the Americans searched the houses for German soldiers, but no less for clocks and fountain pens, of which many were subsequently missing'.[194] French soldiers behaved in similar fashion. In Unterjettingen, in Böblingen district, villagers were ordered to surrender weapons, cameras and telescopes. In complying, some were relieved of their possessions by individual soldiers as they conveyed them to the mayor's office. The soldiers were said to be particularly interested in pocket watches, many of which they stole. Bands of two to four French soldiers conducted house searches on their own initiative, taking whatever they wanted. What turned out to be a spurious order to villagers to surrender their radios was countermanded by a French officer who required only transmitting equipment. A fortnight later, however, a senior officer arrived and sought out the best radios which he removed to his car, although the mayor had received assurances from the French commander in Böblingen that radios could be confiscated only with his express approval. Nevertheless, French soldiers continued to seize radios and typewriters.[195] In Friolzheim, they not only stole from villagers but also wilfully damaged houses.[196]

By contrast, in Adelmannsfelden the conduct of the American occupiers was described as 'correct', and it was even said that relations between them and the villagers were 'good, indeed even to some extent friendly'.[197] In other communes, however, fraternisation was regarded as excessive. In Kirchberg, 'the attitude of mercifully only a few young women elicited justified complaints and must have made an unfavourable impression on even the occupation troops'.[198] A similar complaint came from Matzenbach.[199] In French-occupied areas, the problem was somewhat different. Reports from the communes refer consistently to sexual assault and rape, describing North African troops – routinely referred to as 'the Moroccans' – as the perpetrators. In the first days of the occupation of Mössingen, in Tübingen district, they were said to have raped 220 women and children.[200] In Ditzingen, some 200 women and girls were 'defiled' by soldiers quartered in a neighbouring commune. They returned on evening after evening, leading some women to hide or to seek refuge in the church or in the school, where the Red Cross was quartered. Former French POWs in Ditzingen formed a guard to try to protect villagers from 'the Moroccans'.[201] There was undoubtedly prejudice in Württemberg's communes against 'French colonial troops (Blacks and Moroccans)'.[202] Simply hearing that 'Blacks' were in the area was enough to cause panic among villagers.[203] Nevertheless, the frequency with which rapes, in particular, were attributed to French colonial troops, in numerous communes in different districts which were invaded by the French, lends these reports credence.[204] There were also reported instances of rape by American soldiers, but these seem to have been exceptional.[205]

With NSDAP officials and members mostly taking flight or seeking camouflage in the confused final days of the war, some communes had already chosen new leaders to represent them before hostilities ceased. In Waldsee, the former deputy mayor was elected 'by the mass of the people' to lead negotiations with the German commander with a view to handing over the commune to the enemy.[206] Many mayors of communes had, however, remained at their post. This did not guarantee them either immunity from arrest or continued tenure of office, although the Americans, in particular, were anxious to re-establish structures of German local government as quickly as possible. In many communes, civil officials were either chosen or approved by the occupying power. For example, in Gundelsheim the Americans appointed as mayor a member of the former mayor's staff.[207] In Setzingen, near Ulm, however, the mayor, who had also been local branch leader of the NSDAP, had been sent by American soldiers to the internment camp at Ludwigsburg. His successor as mayor was regarded by the Americans as 'politically tainted', and was therefore replaced by someone of their choice in June 1945. Yet even he turned out 'not to be flawless from the political point of view', leading the military government in Ulm to appoint a 'temporary mayor' for Setzingen in the following month.[208]

Further north, in Neresheim, the Americans dismissed the mayor and appointed a retired *Landrat* as provisional mayor with a legal official as his deputy. As in some other communes, former forced foreign workers were enlisted as armed auxiliary policemen. In Neresheim's case, sixteen French POWs fulfilled this role.[209] In one of Crailsheim's communes, Blaufelden, with the installation of a new mayor on 20 April, '14–15 men from among the so-called unincriminated inhabitants were appointed auxiliary policemen' to enforce order in the commune.[210] In Oberkochen, the vacuum created by the flight of the mayor and his deputy was partially filled when, shortly after their arrival, the Americans appointed 'men…who had not belonged to the NSDAP'. Once an American military government had been established in Aalen district, a former mayor of Oberkochen – who had been displaced in the Third Reich – was reinstated, and 'once again, there was life in the town hall'.[211] While many mayors were replaced, sometimes because they had been NSDAP officials or members and sometimes simply because they had served under the Third Reich, others survived, for a time at least. The wartime mayor of Gronau who – by his own account – had stood up to Drauz, was still in post in 1949.[212] One district, Crailsheim, even chose the heir to the former royal house of Württemberg as its *Landrat*.[213]

Most of Württemberg's communes experienced some degree of damage and disruption during the Second World War. Few were as unscathed as Oberginsbach, in Künzelsau district, which sustained neither bombing nor damage to its bridges; nor does it seem to have received evacuees. Three buildings were slightly damaged in fifteen minutes of firing on 8 April 1945. On the following day, the commune was occupied by American forces, without incident either then or in the weeks that followed. None of the agricultural land, vineyards or fruit trees was damaged. The postwar mayor could think of 'no particular incidents in the village relating to the war'. Like Eschenau, it did not even have its church bells removed.[214] Other communes experienced some damage and disruption from which they recovered relatively quickly. There was a small battle over Aufhausen, which cost eight lives, but there was little other damage. Subsequently, the commune was entirely cut off from the outside world on which it depended for some food supplies, and the curfew from seven at night until seven in the morning was irksome. During the war, church bells which had replaced those surrendered in the First World War had, in their turn, been removed. Both evacuees and French civilian workers had had to be accommodated. Yet the local chronicler could say of the immediate postwar period that, 'after the initial difficulties and the early uncertainty had been overcome, life continued almost in the old way'.[215]

By contrast, other communes were devastated. The disaster that struck Heimsheim from 18 to 20 April 1945 left some farmers with nothing – with houses, barns, stalls and farm implements, as well as livestock, destroyed by fires resulting from French aerial bombing and artillery bombardment. Around eighty per cent of the commune's buildings were destroyed, leaving the homeless to seek shelter in the remainder. They slept on straw mattresses, seven or more to a room. Temporary accommodation was created by dismantling the barracks at Malmsheim airport and transporting them to Heimsheim for reassembly. The school building could not be used because the French occupying force was quartered there until 17 July. On their departure, these troops ransacked the school, removing anything of value.[216] Oberspeltach, too, suffered devastation, with ninety per cent of the population left homeless as a result of American bombing on 21 April. Most livestock and draught animals were destroyed in the flames, along with the mayor's office, the church and the school. Only eight properties were not affected. The rail system was out of service and utilities were out of order. Yet farmers had to tend their fields, somehow obtaining the necessary tools. There was despair in the commune that the work of generations of farmers had been destroyed in a few hours of modern warfare. The local

view was that it would take many years for the wounds of war to be healed in
this commune. It seemed entirely arbitrary that Oberspeltach had experienced
such destruction while some neighbouring communes had been untouched by
military operations.[217]

Whatever their experience during the war, for the rural population the overwhelming concern was to return to as normal a life as possible and, above all, to
resume farm work that had been disrupted during the final days of the war. In
both Belsenberg and Öschingen, after a few days of enforced inactivity while the
occupation forces installed themselves and made demands of the inhabitants,
farmers began to return to their fields. Nevertheless, in Belsenberg finding
passage for a cart along streets that were jammed with military vehicles was so
difficult that they had to make a detour.[218] In Niedernhall, the exercises engaged
in by a substantial American infantry and artillery unit between April and
June 1945 imposed tight restrictions on the farming population's movements.
Only after special pleading by representatives of the commune, via a woman
interpreter, was it possible for farmers to 'hoe their potatoes, bring in green
fodder for their livestock' and tend their fields.[219] Some aspects of normal life
returned only slowly. In Holzgerlingen, the commune's school was closed until
1 October 1945, although each age-group of children had received two hours of
religious instruction each week from the end of May. In the meantime, French
forces purged the school's library of all books which were entirely or even partly
written from a National Socialist standpoint.[220] While some communes, such as
Steinberg, did not have their church bells restored, Suppingen's inhabitants were
able to hold a service of celebration for the return of theirs in September 1947.[221]
Only two of Amrichshausen's four surrendered bells were returned.[222] The two
missing ancient bells of Niedernhall were conveyed from Westphalia by ship to
Heilbronn and then by road and rail in winter 1947–48, to be hung once more
in the church tower on 9 March 1948.[223]

Yet in many places the return to normal could be only partial. In Eschenau,
while the commune had emerged physically unscathed from the war, it had lost
many of its young men. In 1948, several families were left to imagine what had
happened to those whom they had lost. Perhaps they lay in graves in a foreign
country.[224] Perhaps they were POWs in Soviet Russia. In Hermuthausen, while
the size of the population had grown from 249 in 1939 to 413 in 1948, there was
nevertheless a great shortage of labour on the land because residual evacuees and
incoming refugees had neither farming experience nor a desire to become farm
labourers. On larger farms which had previously had three male labourers, there
was in 1948 at best one man, and in some cases none at all.[225] Several factors
converged to ensure that the shortage of labour on the land would remain acute
for many years. Communes' wartime losses, in terms of dead, injured and missing
men, were coupled with reluctance on the part of some who had returned from

the war to submit once more to a life of rural toil. In addition, the forced foreign labourers, on whom Württemberg's agriculture had depended in wartime, were eventually repatriated.[226] The labour problem, which had dogged south German agriculture throughout the war, and for some years before it, would be solved only by the greater mechanisation of farming tasks in the 1950s and 1960s, which, in its turn, provided the impetus for a renewed flight from the land and the increasing dissolution of rural communal society.

11

Conclusion

At the end of the war, rural Württembergers' preoccupations remained largely what they had been before it: family, land, community, church. For most, family life and work had been disrupted during the war by the conscription of able-bodied men. As a result of fatalities, injuries and imprisonment, many of them did not return with the end of hostilities, and some did not return at all. Some communes had experienced additional losses as a result of bombing or invasion – and the Nazi regime's attempts to repel it – in April 1945. These events had also caused damage to land, accommodation for people and animals, and livestock. The desperate attempt by some local party leaders to effect an evacuation of communes by the inhabitants in the face of invasion mostly failed. For Swabians with deep family and communal roots in the soil of their native land, leaving it was inconceivable.[1] It seemed symbolic that the time of final trial for rural Württembergers came at Easter, the season of the ultimate Christian sacrifice. The anticlericalism of the Nazi years had put the faithful in some communes on the defensive – especially where district or local party leaders were positively hostile to one or both churches – but it had not lessened their adherence to their church, which continued to be at the centre of communal life in rural areas. The religious festival of Easter was celebrated in 1945 where hostilities on the ground did not prevent it.

The pressures of war had altered the complexion of communities, with the removal of native men and an influx of strangers, including prisoners of war, forced foreign labourers, evacuees from urban areas and, lastly, ethnic German refugees from eastern Europe. Some foreigners were, contrary to Nazi prescriptions, treated virtually as family members, not least because of the vital contribution they made to the survival of a farm or agricultural trade which might have had to cease operating without them. In Catholic areas, particularly, there was often a bond between native and foreign co-religionists. By contrast, evacuees from Protestant northern areas could feel uncomfortable in a Catholic village. Urban evacuees and refugees were unfamiliar with farm work and often aghast at the primitive conditions of life and work on a labour intensive small farm in a village without modern amenities, from a domestic hot water supply to a cinema. Unwelcome in the crowded home where they were billeted, they sought entertainment outside and found little, unless there was an army barracks nearby. This was particularly true of evacuees from the industrial centres of north-western Germany, whereas families evacuated from Stuttgart, as fellow Swabians, were regarded by farming families as more congenial. There was some compassion for those who arrived penniless as expellees or refugees at the end of the war, many of whom settled in the villages while POWs, forced foreign workers and evacuees returned home. The refugees arrived in the villages because there was no accommodation for them in the bomb-damaged towns. For the same reason, some evacuees remained in rural areas for several months beyond the end of hostilities. It was, however, the refugees who did most to change the character of the villages, adding markedly to their population size and altering their socio-economic profile, in the medium term, at least.[2]

It was not only incomers who altered the complexion of communities. The removal of virtually all fit and healthy native men left women and elderly men to cope with the business of farms and trades, and to cope with the economic controls to which the regime tried to subject them. In 1944–45, even elderly men were liable to conscription into the *Volkssturm*. With women more susceptible to clerical influence than men, conscription had the effect of strengthening the churches' influence in villages vis-à-vis that of the party, which had always had a stronger attraction for men than women.[3] The burdens borne by women were both physical and psychological, leaving them exhausted and exasperated by urban evacuees' attitudes, and receptive to forced foreign workers whose vital contribution to the maintenance of a farm or trade made them attractive. The retribution visited on those found to have had a sexual relationship with a foreigner shocked even those who disapproved on conventional moral grounds. In this, as in other respects, it was clear that the racial ideology of the NSDAP had failed to penetrate villagers' consciousness. With women the great majority of native adults by the end of the war, it was not surprising that they played a significant part in trying to resist the regime's last-ditch attempts at resistance to the invader.[4]

For villagers, at the end of the war a return to something close to normal was easier than it was for townspeople. Damage in rural areas was generally of a lesser order, although some communes suffered substantial destruction, and the imperatives of the agricultural calendar required a resumption of routines which had in many places been disrupted at a crucial point in the early sowing season. Tending fields, vines and, above all, animals was a continuous activity, rendered difficult and even dangerous during the invasion. The advent of peace, even with occupation troops and vehicles remaining in some communes and with the constraints of a curfew, was welcomed as the precondition of the restoration of normality. Nevertheless, the repatriation of forced foreign workers, before a commune's men had returned from war and captivity, enhanced the burdens of cultivation and animal husbandry, leaving them as small scale, largely subsistence activities, providing for family and commune. The disruption of communications meant, in any case, that trying to supply a market was for many hardly practical. In some places, providing sufficient food for the commune was enough of a problem.

Yet the return of peace did not bring an easing of the fundamental problems of agriculture in Württemberg – because they were fundamental. In some communes, there remained shortages of labour on the land even after the return of men from the war.[5] In others, the influx of refugees and expellees seemed to have 'solved' the labour problem, but the issue of wages for agricultural labourers in southern Germany remained a thorny one, with farmers insisting that they could not nearly match the wages paid in recovering industry or trades. Particularly once reconstruction was under way in the towns, there was a renewed flight from the land, with younger people no more prepared to submit to a life of rural toil in the late 1940s and 1950s than they had been in the 1930s.[6] The problems with labour supply on the land and the provision of food for the towns were such that the structures of the *Reichsnährstand* remained in being. At least they provided an organisational framework in a time of chaos and upheaval. Remarkably, they were not disbanded until 1960, remaining the last official reminder of the discredited twelve-year regime which it had outlived by fifteen years.[7]

Nazi institutions and Nazi control had been imposed on Württemberg as a result of Hitler's assumption of power in Berlin. This is not to suggest that Württembergers had given the NSDAP negligible support before 1933, nor that they did not provide numerous collaborators in nefarious Nazi policies. *Gauleiter* Wilhelm Murr was not, however, a charismatic leader who inspired a mass of followers. Only Hitler's delegated authority gave him power in Stuttgart. Although by 1933 the Württemberg NSDAP had both avid supporters and an organisational structure, especially in the towns, in terms of members, sympathisers and capable leaders the party had a weaker infrastructure than in many other parts of Germany, particularly the north and east. In 1933, more than half of Württemberg's rural communes had no local Nazi organisation.[8] There were, however, enough dedicated men – and some women, such as Berta Kiehn in Trossingen – to ensure that Nazism in Württemberg was homegrown.[9] Office-bearers may have been approved and sustained by Hitler and the party's Reich leadership, but they were the product of the Swabian cultural context.

The result was that, for some Württemberg Nazis, the version of National Socialism to which they subscribed was refracted through the lens of their Swabian identity and was, accordingly, conservative rather than radical. This does not mean that they rejected Nazi racial theories. Württemberg's Nazi leaders at central, district and local level subscribed wholeheartedly to the regime's antisemitic world view, as well as to its desire to purge society of 'asocials', Romanies and 'useless eaters'. Some of them, however, regarded National Socialism as a means of safeguarding essentially Swabian traditions and practices against the threat they believed was posed by these diverse groups who did not conform to their ideal of the Swabian identity. Other Württemberg Nazis repudiated their Swabian heritage, seeking to impose radical Nazification on traditional institutions. The Leonberg local branch NSDAP leader, for one, despaired of the local inhabitants' traditional attitudes because they made it difficult to win Leonbergers' hearts and minds for the Nazi cause.[10] Although he was by disposition more conservative than radical, Murr's gratitude for his preferment made him uncompromisingly loyal to Hitler and therefore prepared to accept a massive erosion of the relative autonomy which Württemberg enjoyed up to 1933.[11]

For the party's conservatives, Nazism was a means to reassert and consolidate positions that seemed to have been under threat since the end of the First World War and its aftermath. The determination of men such as Schmid, Waldmann and Stümpfig to maintain professional standards in the bureaucracy and local government, if necessary in the face of attempts by NSDAP activists to erode them, was one manifestation of this. Their collusion in the violence and retribution meted out to communists and socialists – the perceived beneficiaries of the lost war in 1918 and the ensuing crises – in the spring of 1933 was another. As Nazis, these leading men did not question the authority of their Führer; as Württembergers, they interpreted his pronouncements in a manner that took account of local traditions and considerations. They resented the centralising momentum of the Third Reich which they perceived as a clear indication of continuing Prussian aspirations to control non-Prussian areas of Germany.[12] In the eyes of many bureaucrats in Stuttgart, as well as district and local government officials, these leading Nazis' respect for their environment and traditions mitigated their loyalty to the leader of a rather disreputable party. Whether as converts or as opportunists, those central and local government officials who joined the party in and after 1933 were reassured by the Ministry of the Interior's seemingly conservative Swabian leadership which held party activists in check as far as their own professional standards and priorities were concerned. Harsh treatment of communists and socialists, Romanies and 'asocials' accorded rather than conflicted with their priorities. Discrimination against Jews who were 'overrepresented' in desirable professional positions caused them scant concern.

Leading Nazis with radical rather than conservative aims had less regard for Württemberg's traditions. Their acceptance of the fundamental premises of National Socialism, namely that for all 'valuable' Germans their ethnic identity as Germans, together with their blood heritage as 'Aryans', was their primary characteristic transcended the parochial concerns of a *Land* with fewer than three million inhabitants. Within Schmid's Ministry of the Interior, alongside the conservative corps of senior bureaucrats there were men who formulated increasingly radical policies. They regarded themselves as being above all Nazi and German, rather than Swabian. Chief among them were Stähle and Mauthe who, with others, drove the eugenic policies of sterilisation and 'euthanasia' in Württemberg, with terrible consequences for thousands of people. The *Kultminister*, Mergenthaler, in status second only to *Gauleiter* Murr in the Nazi hierarchy, embraced Nazi ideology wholeheartedly and confronted both major churches in a manner not attempted elsewhere in Germany. Abolishing denominational schools was ambitious enough in a *Land* whose people mostly had a strong religious faith and affiliation, but it was in line with government policy nationally. Trying go beyond that, and to replace religious education with ideological instruction in school classrooms, went against the grain of traditional Württemberg society, especially – but by no means only – in rural areas. It was in keeping with Mergenthaler's unbending allegiance to Nazism as a creed and one of many areas where he had differences with Murr.

The narrow-minded Murr could sound and seem radical when he lashed out, yet his temperamental conservatism was symbolised by the wood-panelled farmhouse parlour constructed in his new home in Stuttgart. He would have been content with a 'German Christian' victory in Württemberg, but the fragmentation of the Württemberg 'German Christians' left him vulnerable to anti-church pressure from Ley, for one. His resignation from the autonomous Württemberg Evangelical Church followed in 1942. Murr's unconditional loyalty to the Nazi leadership resulted in his estrangement from his closest adviser, Waldmann, from 1935, and his growing dependence on a group of radical, ambitious party officers; his enduring friendship with the uncompromising *Kreisleiter* Drauz reinforced this. Waldmann wished to safeguard the bureaucracy's jurisdiction by removing purely party functionaries from the central administration's premises. One of his additional suggestions – that the Reich Propaganda Ministry be abolished – predictably enraged Goebbels, the minister. Murr completely dissociated himself from these proposals, and, in wartime, openly castigated Waldmann for expressing misgivings about the wisdom of waging war.[13] Murr's final demonstration of unconditional obedience came in April 1945 when he insisted on trying to enforce Hitler's order that Germans should fight to the last man, whether in Stuttgart or in rural communes.

With the authority of Hitler's government behind them and alternative sources of information largely suppressed by effective censorship, these leading Nazis had enough power to give the impression that Württemberg's society had been truly coordinated. Seeking to control the German population to an unprecedented extent, they introduced new methods of propaganda, surveillance and retribution. They offered – and endeavoured to impose – a perverted ideal based on charismatic leadership and unquestioning obedience to that leadership.[14] This involved a concerted attempt to break the traditional allegiances of individuals and communities to parties, trades unions and churches. Belonging to a movement whose dynamic led them inexorably towards conquest – and therefore towards war – they imposed new pressures and priorities which led to remarkable technological innovation and development. They utilised state-of-the-art scientific, medical and bureaucratic techniques to impose pseudo-scientific priorities concerned with 'cleansing' the race and purging from Germany's physical space those whom they designated as being without 'value'. Together, these policies amounted to a quest for total control of the population. This is a more appropriate description than 'totalitarian', which implies that total control was achieved.

An examination of rural Württemberg under Nazism and in wartime demonstrates that the quest for total control was not achieved and, furthermore, was not realistic. It was one thing to win a degree of consent – even if much of that was frittered away before 1939 by the imposition of policies to the disadvantage of the rural population. It was quite another to win over hearts and minds, the ambitious goal which activist Nazis set themselves, and by which they therefore should be judged. Expecting the mass of the people to accept Nazi priorities wholeheartedly and to reorientate their working, social and family lives to accord with them was to court disappointment. Even ordinary NSDAP members could fail to show the total commitment expected by their leaders. Those who joined the party in and after 1933, or sought to do so in the years of restricted admission, might be enthusiasts but they were more often opportunists seeking job security or advancement. This was a consideration that was more applicable to public employees than to small scale owner-occupiers on the land, although some farmers and rural traders did join the NSDAP – where, in Württemberg, they remained underrepresented – or the SA.

Party members did not necessarily swallow Nazi ideology whole: there were clearly à la carte Nazis who subscribed to some aspects of Nazism but were reluctant to change their habits to accord with the remainder. The continuing attendance of the children of some party members at religious instruction classes rather than ideological instruction is one example. The irritation expressed by local party functionaries at the unwillingness of ordinary members to turn out for party events is another. There were also, as we have seen, party members who had apparently not understood the full implications of Nazi racial policy, with the segregation of Jews and the 'euthanasia' of 'useless eaters' and other vulnerable members of society. The party's claim to the total allegiance of its members was little understood by the many who paid their dues and attended meetings periodically but baulked at the idea of undergoing ideological training.[15] To the frustration of devout activists, only a minority comprehended the total commitment required to a 'movement' that claimed to be entirely different from the political parties and clubs of the previous era. If party members were generally loyal but half-hearted in their efforts, the mass of the rural population of Württemberg was more or less obedient but scarcely enthusiastic about a party whose orientation was in many ways alien to them.

The Nazi obsession with physical exercise and fitness, for example, was a preoccupation of deskbound townees with mechanised transportation on hand – until the exigencies of war starkly reduced its availability. The Nazi obsession with cleanliness and hygiene – to say nothing of aseptic Nazi peasant festivals and art – took no account of the varieties of dirt that were integral to labour intensive, unmechanised farming. The major factor in winning Hitler's regime acceptance in urban areas – recovery from the depression and the creation of jobs on a large scale – barely applied in the countryside. Certainly, there was immediate assistance for indebted farmers. Yet the disadvantages for the countryside of the economic recovery soon outweighed any benefits, as labour was drained away from the land to expanding industries and trades, and as a battery of controls and sanctions was imposed on traditional farming practices and rural relationships. The Hereditary Farm Law, for example, may have been popular in other parts of Germany, but in some small communes in Württemberg it alienated farmers from the regime.[16]

The experience of controls in the 1930s was a foretaste of the pressures of a twentieth century war. It has been argued that one of the unintended consequences of National Socialist rule was 'the revolution of modernity'.[17] Closer inspection reveals that the Nazis were selective in the varieties of modernisation which they embraced – favouring new developments such as advanced military hardware, sophisticated surveillance systems and intrusive medical investigation. For farmers, however, modernisation meant conformity and submission to external urban authorities. It is true that some benefited from piecemeal land improvement schemes, which generally came at a cost. Nevertheless, the empty rhetoric of 'blood and soil' propaganda could not disguise the poverty and primitive living conditions of small farmers in Württemberg's rural communes. One farmer, Alois Wieder, was regarded locally as having represented the hostility of many in Buchau to a visit by 'blood and soil' guru Alfred Rosenberg in 1937. Wieder drove his dung cart, with its leaky barrel of liquid manure, across the festively decorated marketplace shortly before Rosenberg was due to speak. This demonstrated the gulf that persisted between the realities of rural life and the assumptions of Nazi grandees in their smart uniforms. Rosenberg had not even been provided with a glass of water; one of his lackeys eventually procured one, unaware that glass's owner was a Jew. This caused much mirth in Buchau.[18] The gulf between town and country was particularly apparent where modern methods of transport and modern media enabled some rural inhabitants to view – but mostly not to share – the increasingly sophisticated facilities and rising living standards of those who lived and worked in towns such as Stuttgart and Friedrichshafen which benefited considerably from the economic upswing of the 1930s.

It was in the nature of the Nazi system that its objectives – in particular preparation for war – necessitated the kind of modernisation that benefited industry. This did not, however, bring mechanisation and rationalisation to small farms. Producing motorised farm machinery would have diverted industry from its purpose of preparing for war. It would also have been redolent of developments in the Soviet Union, where the production of tractors was accompanied by collectivisation, the peasants' nightmare. Yet the regime might have won support in rural areas had it committed itself to the kind of mechanisation which small farmers would embrace when it became available from the 1950s. Tractors, trucks, threshing machines, and more, relieved those who remained on the land of at least some back-breaking toil. When they became available, after the war, they were clearly the kind of 'progress' that rural people welcomed, where the terrain on which they worked made their use feasible. It would have made more sense for a regime intent on conquest to produce farm machinery which would have provided some compensation for the terrible drain on manpower resulting from conscription. A logical way to ensure that the towns were supplied with food in wartime, to prevent another 'stab-in-the-back', was to modernise and mechanise agriculture. As it was, those working in unmechanised agriculture lost their prime assets, men and, if they had them, horses. As time went on, they also lost chemical fertiliser, metal implements and serviceable shoes. In terms of their living and working conditions, Hitler's war took them backwards rather than forward. This was underscored when many urban evacuees – not entirely unreasonably – refused to help with arduous physical farm work and complained about the absence in farmhouses and in villages of amenities to which they were accustomed in the towns.

In the Third Reich, the uncongenial aspects of modernisation were imposed on rural society without countervailing advantages. Yet the imposition of controls which were intended to be universal and watertight was only partial. This was partly because of a shortage of human resources. Especially in wartime, there were not sufficient policemen or other enforcers of state or party to ensure that government requirements were uniformly observed. It was also the case that some of those in authority connived at – or even participated in – illegal acts that vitiated the regime's attempts to control the production and distribution of food supplies. This was regarded as extremely serious by a regime whose leaders remained obsessed by the memory – or the myth – of the way in which the home front had betrayed the fighting front in the First World War. Although many miscreants were punished in Draconian fashion, some of those in small rural communities received relatively moderate penalties. Most striking was how these derived from the sensitivity of some officers of the regime to their circumstances, as members of a small in-bred community. Yet beyond that lay the fundamental terrifying characteristic of retribution in the Third Reich: even before the uncontrolled violence of the last weeks of the war, it was unpredictable – if one was 'Aryan' and politically unobjectionable. If one was not, it became all too predictable in its brutality.

The arbitrary character of a system where the rule of law was compromised and undermined by the pronouncements of party grandees such as Himmler and Bormann was exacerbated by the authority which even minor NSDAP functionaries arrogated to themselves. With some local government officials unsure about the precise terms of laws issued by proclamation, and with variable penalties for similar offences, the effect was disorienting. The president of the Württemberg supreme court reported in March 1940 that perfectly reasonable people believed that 'in many cases today an offender cannot judge whether he will get away with a fine or whether he is risking his head'. Even NSDAP functionaries and SA leaders had sometimes been taken aback by the harsh penalties sought by prosecutors and sentences passed by judges in the Special Court.[19] The differences between town and country in the outcome for those violating the War Economy Decree were a case in point. For those in the countryside, awareness of the detail of new laws was sketchy, which may help to account for the volume of violations in wartime. For example, some women had understood that they would incur severe penalties if they consorted with Poles, but were shocked to discover that a sexual relationship with a western European man rendered them equally liable to prosecution and punishment.[20]

In terms of laws which tried to inhibit farmers and traders from conducting their business in the traditional manner – slaughtering as they saw fit and bartering with each other, among other practices – it seems clear, however, that there was conscious disobedience. This was piecemeal but widespread, and sometimes involved groups rather than isolated individuals. Some of those involved might be officers of party or state who were in a position to assist or conceal violations of the law. Personal advantage or greed was undoubtedly a motive behind offences involving the production and distribution of food and other supplies in time of shortage and rationing, in Germany as in any other country. As in Britain, many of those involved in black market activities did not feel that they were doing wrong.[21] Yet in Württemberg the scale of it, and the participation or complaisance of officials, reflected a general rejection of a system which was perceived as unjust and uncomprehending – the product of deskbound bureaucrats far beyond Württemberg's borders. The enforcers were local, but their numbers were limited and their empathy with law-breakers was sometimes enough to override their loyalty to the system. As Judge Cuhorst remarked, it could be difficult for those charged with upholding the law in a small community with close ties of kinship.[22]

One of the tools of the arbitrary system was the much discussed use of denunciation. There can be no doubt that this was potentially deadly in the dictatorial system of Nazi Germany, as in Stalinist Russia.[23] It was used against Jews and against those who consorted with Jews or forced foreign workers.[24] This was not, however, the whole story. In an environment of increasing shortages, where a sense of inequity of sacrifice was all-pervasive but there were no formal channels of representation, the denunciation – or tip-off – was used, with official encouragement. It was used by the self-righteous to inform on those perceived to be gaining an unfair advantage, contravening conventional moral standards or creating a public nuisance by breaking the law. In this, Nazi Germany was not markedly different from polities of most kinds, with well-advertised dedicated telephone lines the preferred method of encouraging tip-offs by ordinary citizens in a twenty-first century democracy, such as Britain. Those violating the production and distribution controls of the War Economy Decree were particularly vulnerable, as were women who consorted with POWs or forced foreign workers.[25] Townspeople, including evacuees, denounced farmers for providing foreign workers freely with rationed foodstuffs. Denunciation was also used to settle scores, not least at the end of the war when former Nazis were denounced to the occupation authorities. It was not, therefore, merely – as we are sometimes led to believe – the one-way traffic of those collaborating with a brutal dictatorship. To say that the Gestapo had merely to sit back and wait for denunciations to roll in, obviating the need for it to employ official spies and informers, is an exaggeration. Yet in a brutal dictatorship the risk of denunciation was peculiarly dangerous. Neither the informer nor the victim could be sure whether the penalty for the latter would be a warning or a death sentence.[26]

The Nazi regime could hope to control rural Württembergers up to a point, as far as diminishing human resources permitted. In communes where the party had a presence, open criticism and disobedience were curtailed through fear. As we have seen, farmers who traded with Jewish cattle dealers, women who shopped at Jewish-owned stores and individuals who publicly showed friendship towards Jews risked being punished in some way or pilloried in the scurrilous *Flammenzeichen*. In the disorder of the 1938 November pogrom, physical violence was threatened, and sometimes used, against gentiles who tried to protect Jews. In an environment where trying to attract interest in National Socialism and members to the party brought disappointing returns, antisemitic policy gave local party functionaries and activists a purpose and a rare chance to demonstrate their power. The restraints that fettered their arbitrary instincts in most other areas – laws, policemen, local government officials, even senior party officers – increasingly were ineffective or did not apply in this area where there was almost complete lawlessness by the later 1930s. Yet, even so, in those small communes where outrages against Jews and their property were perpetrated in November 1938, the tormentors were overwhelmingly members of Nazi formations from elsewhere. Causing damage and destruction in one's own commune was clearly something of a taboo.

In most communes, the difficulty in generating enthusiasm for Nazism was disillusioning for activists. The civil authorities' insistence on the maintenance of law and order meant that, after the freelance violence of early 1933, the small bands of local NSDAP leaders and enthusiasts found their room for manoeuvre restricted. They could, often with impunity, bully Jews and dissident individuals, especially those who maintained a commercial or social relationship with Jews; in some communes they harassed churchgoers at religious festivals. The disruption of traditional allegiances was, however, the most the party could hope for. The SD kept both the major churches and smaller sects under surveillance and consistently reported pro-church sentiment in rural areas. In strongly Catholic areas, the Hitler Youth was detailed to daub anti-Catholic slogans or harass young people who were attending Catholic services or activities.[27] Particularly during Mergenthaler's campaign to promote ideological instruction and to discourage young people from preparing for confirmation or first communion, some local party activists harassed those attending the churches' preparatory classes for these rites of passage. In rural areas, however, there was a marked failure to replace church sacraments or ceremonies with Nazi rituals, although the forced celebration of Hitler's birthday continued in some places until the end of the war. The carnage of war presented the churches with new opportunities to bind parishioners to them, in spite of attempts by party activists to muscle in on funerals or services of commemoration. The paucity or absence of party personnel in small communities in wartime made the already slim chances of party rituals replacing the traditional and familiar ones of the churches illusory.

Allegiance to a church impinged on many aspects of village life and was therefore difficult for the party to displace. Committed NSDAP leaders and members earnestly tried to find ways of outbidding the churches in their appeal to ordinary parishioners. At the same time, however, government policies undermined their efforts to wean people away from automatic loyalty to a church. The attempt to impose ideological instruction was one example which aroused the ire of clergy and laity of both main denominations. Another was the requisitioning of church bells, ordered by Göring's Four Year Plan Office on 15 March 1940.[28] This struck at communes' identity, because 'the bells are the voice of the community in both its sacred and secular dimensions'. Their chimes and peals signalled the time of day, summoned villagers to church, celebrated local events and warned of impending danger.[29] Bells were often highly decorated, and the newer ones might also bear religious inscriptions. That on the largest bell in Rutesheim, in Leonberg district, dating from 1903, read: 'I call the living, I mourn the dead, I withstand lightning. O be with us in thy mercy, Lord Jesus Christ!'[30] For Kayh, in Böblingen district, the removal of its only church bell was 'one of the greatest material losses which the commune had to bear, which will not be made good in the foreseeable future'.[31] The commune's chronicler in Tomerdingen, in Ulm district, regarded the removal of two ancient bells – one allegedly the oldest church bell in Württemberg – which had been spared in 1914–18 as the second body blow to the commune, the first being the Hereditary Farm Law. A craftsman who had tried to prevent the bells' removal had been threatened with Dachau.[32]

If this issue – like others that aroused complaint in rural communes in the Third Reich and especially during the war – seems trivial to the urban mind, it was about a matter that was central to communes' identity. Similarly, there were complaints about the manner of conscription. Whereas in the First World War whole age groups had been conscripted together, with the kind of notice that allowed a commune's clergy to arrange a service to mark the occasion, in Hitler's war, individuals were suddenly summoned, piecemeal, which made a communal event impossible. At first rural clergymen were able to stay in touch with conscripted villagers and to send them Christian literature. Then they were told that the provision of literature was the duty of army chaplains. Nevertheless, some priests and pastors managed to maintain contact with their parishioners.[33] The arbitrary manner of conscription caused general ill-feeling predominantly because of its effect on the rural labour supply, especially as the war dragged on and newly eligible young people were removed. Those who remained at home were infuriated by continuous official demands for deliveries of produce, and by 'commissions' who came to inspect stalls and barns to assess the numbers of livestock and estimate a farmer's future production. In Tomerdingen during the war, it was said that 'the spying was intolerable. Therefore: hold your tongue … Little was said. Anyone who talked about anything that might excite the people, even if he was an eyewitness, ran the risk of being arrested.'[34]

This was not special pleading. The Nazi regime unleashed its most fearsome terror on its political and racial enemies, but it was also prepared to terrorise 'valuable Aryans' who obstructed its requirements, particularly in wartime and on a large scale in the last days of the war.[35] Such Germans suffered, as did the many who experienced the necessary evil of Allied bombing. It has become controversial to admit this, especially in the face of claims that 'the Germans' had a collective disposition to favour war-mongering and racial murder. Even those who assert that it was most Germans' indifference that allowed perpetrators to commit barbarous crimes including genocide have been taken to task for neglecting to mention Germans' allegedly unanimous desire to purge their country of Jews, above all.[36] Apart from the pointlessness of ascribing collective traits to an entire nation, this ignores the inherent blinkered self-centredness of most human beings. In wartime, the loss of a commune's men through conscription, the difficulty of maintaining rural businesses without sufficient labour, the influx of strangers, the attacks on their church and, in some, the effects of bombing were enough to occupy their minds and consume their emotions. For those with family members and neighbours who were killed or missing there was – understandably – little sentiment to spare for others' troubles.

The war undoubtedly brought 'a withdrawal into the private sphere' – in Germany as elsewhere – with interest in political affairs at a low ebb.[37] The unavailability of reliable information about the course of the war and the fate of loved ones at the front was no doubt one reason for this.[38] Yet rural Württembergers' main concerns had already revolved around a private sphere of family and land that was largely congruent with their limited public sphere of community and church. Whereas some had been aware of the use of slave labour on government projects in their vicinity, it was only in the last days of the war that others were brought face to face with the worst of the regime's brutality as columns of concentration camp prisoners were driven on through their commune, the weakest of them murdered by their guards. On the night of 15–16 April 1945, prisoners who had been forced labourers at the Schwäbisch Hall airfield were taken through Dirgenheim, in Aalen district, en route to Nördlingen in Bavaria: 'They were completely exhausted from hunger and sickness, many had no shoes, and, as far as one could see in the dark, their clothing looked very poor.' The few villagers out and about at night searched and found a man with two shots to his head. He had no identification of any kind. All the villagers could do was to bury him in their cemetery. This was not an isolated instance.[39]

The complaint customarily made against Germans of any kind or condition is that they did nothing to prevent the murder of Jews. In most of Württemberg's communes there were in 1933 no Jewish inhabitants. By 1939, as a result of discrimination and persecution – with some local people following the lead in this given by the party – Jews emigrated, leaving an incrementally smaller minority of communes where they were still a presence. Once emigration was halted, remaining Jews were concentrated in a very few places, generally not in their native commune and in segregated accommodation. Their deportation from there was organised from the centre in Stuttgart, where they were gathered before being crammed into trains and, with a very few exceptions, sent to their death. It is difficult to see how civilian rural Württembergers could have averted this, far less prevented the genocide that was perpetrated in distant places. A strong lead from even one of the churches in the 1930s might have mobilised popular disquiet, as happened with the 'euthanasia' programme and over the attempt to introduce ideological instruction in schools, but it was not forthcoming. Even so, it was unlikely that the regime's leaders would have been deflected from a policy that was an obsessive priority. By the time deportations began, few rural Jews remained, and fewer still remained in their native commune: in their new surroundings, they were faceless strangers living in segregated accommodation. By moving Jews from their home commune to one where they were strangers, the regime was able to exploit the customary rural attitude of reserving concern and assistance for members of one's own community.

Nevertheless, those who persecuted Jews, and others, in Württemberg were Württembergers. They may have been obeying orders, but many of them did so with a will. Some were NSDAP functionaries, others were medical, legal or local government officials. No doubt there were men from Württemberg serving in the *Wehrmacht* who committed atrocities against the soldiers and civilians of other countries, particularly in eastern Europe. Württembergers were not inherently more virtuous than Germans from other regions. However, those who remained as civilians in small communes during the war overwhelmingly did not participate in atrocities, even if some of them engaged in acts of discrimination and marginalisation. Some adults had positively aligned themselves with the new regime, whether out of conviction or in the hope of gaining some kind of advantage, even if the advantage they sought was merely to be left alone. There were enough who joined party formations, including the SA, and participated in the pogrom of November 1938 – away from their own commune.[40] They were, however, in a small minority. It is true that young people were obliged to join the Hitler Youth, and some became avid supporters of its activities. Others did not, especially in strongly Catholic areas, and in both the male and the female branches of the Hitler Youth concerns about the shortage of suitable leaders persisted. In wartime, the young were easy to direct into war-related tasks while remaining enthusiasts were creamed off into voluntary work – among German settlers, perhaps. Left mainly to foot-draggers, the local organisations functioned at an increasingly low level of activity. The NSDAP had become the new establishment, against which many who were not 'dissident youth' rebels reacted.[41]

The majority of rural Württembergers persisted with their customary ways of conducting their affairs, running a farm or other rural business with few native men and increasing difficulty in wartime. If individuals or groups defied government attempts to get them to change their ways, it was, other than exceptionally, not because they were consciously resisting Nazism. They simply resented and often obstructed orders to change their ways.[42] Much of the resentment was directed at towns, townspeople and, especially, Berlin. This sometimes translated into resentment at Nazism, whose leaders were based in towns and imposed the pressure to change, especially where pressure was exerted on churches and churchgoers. Some, like Alois Wieder in Buchau, were prepared to give a pungent indication of their resentment. There was, however, little that was political and less that was unequivocally noble about most of it. Insisting on continuing to trade with a Jewish cattle dealer – even when NSDAP activists noted names and took photographs of the individuals involved – was generally a matter of self-interested habit reinforced by downright stubbornness. Attending church and sending children to religious instruction classes was not resistance; it was God-fearing habit. Violating the War Economy Decree was mostly a matter of undiluted self-interest, whether in protecting traditional ways or in making a personal gain. Treating forced foreign workers as members of the household was pragmatic and appropriate, given their contribution. Refusing to treat those evacuees who seemed like strangers and contributed nothing as fellow members of the same community demonstrated incomprehension of, rather than opposition to, the idea of a national ethnic community.

These attitudes amount to dissent from official norms, or dissidence in the face of authority.[43] They are worth noting because they testify to the failure of a political party – whose aim was total control and the eliciting of total commitment from the mass of the people – to persuade or intimidate relatively simple people into compliance. These people retained a sense of their traditional values and morality in the face of a dictatorial government with the siren calls of its perverted ideals, with its fearsome terror apparatus and its massive propaganda onslaught. Their achievement was to avoid being colonised by Nazi norms and values. If this seems modest, it contrasts favourably with the way in which many lawyers, doctors and teachers, among others, succumbed to the Nazi appeal. Until the last days of the war, when protection of their commune against nihilist Nazi functionaries was at stake, that was as far as rural Württembergers' 'resistance' generally went. By April 1945, however, as in the Thirty Years War, 'the enemy was war', whoever waged it.[44] The insistence of their self-appointed leaders in waging it to the point where resistance to the invader meant certain destruction forfeited any remaining shreds loyalty to their nation's rulers that rural Württembergers might have harboured.

Abbreviations and Glossary

agrarpolitischer Apparat	Agrarian Policy Apparatus – from 1930–33, the office within the NSDAP charged with spreading party propaganda in rural areas and recruiting farmers to the Nazi cause
AIDA	Arbeitswissenschaftliches Institut der Deutschen Arbeitsfront – the research unit of the German Labour Front
Anschluss	the name given by Hitler's regime to the absorption of Austria into the German Reich in March 1938
Arbeitsmaid	a young woman member of the RAD
'Aryan'	term used by National Socialists to describe the race to which the ideal 'nordic' German allegedly belonged
BA	Bundesarchiv – Federal Archives, formerly in Koblenz and now in Berlin
Bauer	farmer, used as a term of honour by Nazis to describe one who was accepted as an *Erbhofbauer*
BDC	Berlin Document Center – formerly under American control, now part of the Bundesarchiv in Berlin
Blockleiter	leader of a block, a group of houses – normally forty to sixty – which he kept under surveillance on behalf of the NSDAP
Bü	Büschel – folder of documents in Württemberg archives
BDM	(*Bund Deutscher Mädel*) League of German Girls – section of the HJ for girls aged fourteen to eighteen
Bürgermeister	mayor
BWB	*Bauern- und Weingärtnerbund* – Farmers' and Winegrowers' Association, a Württemberg political party, dissolved in summer 1933
Centre Party	political party representing the views of the Catholic Church in Germany
Confessing Church	a group of pastors within the Evangelical Church who opposed the encroachment of the 'German Christians'
Deutsche Gemeindeordnung	law of 30 January 1935 which created a uniform and Nazified political structure of local government
DFW	*Deutsches Frauenwerk* (German Women's Enterprise) the 'mass' organisation of German women under the leadership of the NSF

DNVP	German National People's Party, conservative party in the Weimar Republic which dissolved itself in June 1933
Dorf	village
ehrenamtlich	honorary – used of Nazi functionaries to mean 'unpaid'
Erbhof	hereditary farm – created by the *Reichserbhofgesetz* – normally of between 7.5 and 125 hectares, with single-heir inheritance
Erbhofbauer	hereditary farmer – the proprietor of an *Erbhof*, who had to prove 'Aryan' ancestry
Führer	leader, the title applied *simpliciter* to Hitler
Führerprinzip	leadership principle – a form of line management, with instructions cascading downwards and unquestioning obedience required from below
Führerstaat	state based on the *Führerprinzip*
Gau	region – part of the territorial organisation of the NSDAP
Gauleiter	regional leader – leader of an NSDAP *Gau*
Gemeinde	commune – the smallest administrative unit in Württemberg, consisting of either one village or a small cluster of neighbouring villages
'*Gemeinnutz vor Eigennutz*'	'the common good before self-interest' – the slogan in point 24 of the NSDAP's 1920 programme
Gendarmerie	police units in the *Gemeinden*
'German Christians'	group of pastors within the Evangelical Church who accepted Nazi ideological tenets and aimed for a Nazification of the church
German Labour Front	the largest mass organisation in Nazi Germany, the sham collective substitute for trade unions
Gestapo	secret state police
Glaube und Schönheit	Faith and Beauty, the section of the BDM for young women aged eighteen to twenty-one
Gleichschaltung	co-ordination – the policy pursued by Hitler's government from 1933 of dissolving political parties and trade unions, Nazifying the governments of the *Länder*, and either dissolving or purging the leadership of organisations of all kinds and at all levels and bringing them under the leadership of the NSDAP
gottgläubig	literally, 'believing in a deity', the designation adopted by Nazis who left their church but did not claim to be atheist
HJ	*Hitlerjugend* (Hitler Youth) – both the collective name for the NSDAP's youth organisation for both sexes and the specific name for the section of the youth organisation for boys aged 14 to 18
HStAS	Hauptstaatsarchiv Stuttgart
Jungmädel	section of the HJ for girls aged ten to fourteen

Jungvolk	section of the HJ for boys aged ten to fourteen
Kampfzeit	literally, 'time of struggle' – the period of the NSDAP's existence before Hitler's appointment as Chancellor on 30 January 1933
KBF	*Kreisbauernführer* – district RNS leader, subordinate to the LBF
KBS	*Kreisbauernschaft* – district RNS organisation, subdivision of the LBS
KdF	*Kraft durch Freude* (Strength through Joy) – the German Labour Front's project providing recreational and cultural activities for its members, under Nazi leadership
KPD	*Kommunistische Partei Deutschlands* (German Communist Party), founded in December 1918 and banned in February 1933
Kreis	district – subdivision of a *Gau*, part of the territorial organisation of the NSDAP
Kreisleiter	district leader – leader of an NSDAP *Kreis*
Kreisleitung	district leadership of the NSDAP
Kristallnacht	'night of broken glass' – the pogrom against Jewish persons and property across Germany on 9-10 November 1938
Kultminister	Württemberg Minister for Education and Culture (including the churches), a post held from 1933 to 1945 by Christian Mergenthaler
Kultministerium	Württemberg Ministry for Education and Culture (including the churches)
Kulturkampf	literally, 'cultural struggle' – the campaign (chiefly in Prussia in the 1870s) against the temporal power of the Catholic Church
KZ	*Konzentrationslager* – concentration camp
Land	federal state of the German Reich, e.g., Württemberg, Prussia, Bavaria
Landesbischof	literally, '*Land* bishop', the bishop of the Evangelical Church in an individual *Land* – in Württemberg's case, Theophil Wurm
Landdienst	service scheme placing young people in agricultural work, organised by the HJ
Landeskirchen	the federated *Land* churches (Evangelical church)
Landkreis	rural district
Landrat	(plural *Landräte*) highest civil non-political official in a district within a *Land*
Landtag	representative assembly of a *Land*
Landwirt	farmer – the term used by Nazis to describe farmers who did not qualify for the status of *Erbhofbauer*
LBF	*Landesbauernführer* – leader of the RNS at *Land* level, in Württemberg's case, Alfred Arnold

LBS	*Landesbauernschaft* – the division of the RNS at *Land* level
Machtübernahme	literally, 'takeover of power' – Hitler's assumption of power as Chancellor on 30 January 1933
MadR	*Meldungen aus dem Reich* – the reports of SD agents throughout Germany, 1938–1945
Marktordnung	market regulation – the controls imposed by the RNS in the 1930s on farmers' production, distribution and prices
Menschenführung	literally, 'leading people' – the role of the NSDAP from January 1933 in guiding, exhorting and monitoring the mass of the people
NSDAP	*Nationalsozialistische Deutsche Arbeiterpartei* – National Socialist German Workers' Party, the Nazi Party
NSDFB	National Socialist German Freedom Movement – shortlived *völkisch* group formed when the NSDAP was banned following Hitler's *Putsch* attempt in Munich on 9 November 1923
NSF	*NS-Frauenschaft* – Nazi Women's Group, a formation of the NSDAP
NSKK	*NS-Kraftfahrer Korps* – Nazi Automobile Drivers' Corps, a formation of the NSDAP
NSLB	*NS-Lehrerbund* – Nazi Teachers' League, an affiliated organisation of the NSDAP
NSV	*Nationalsozialistische Volkswohlfahrt* – NS People's Welfare, an affiliated organisation of the NSDAP which provided welfare for needy 'Aryan' Germans; the second largest mass organisation in Nazi Germany
Oberamt	(plural, *Oberämter*), county – the sixty-one units into which *Land* Württemberg was divided before the reform of 1938 created the thirty-seven new districts
Oberpräsident	head of the civil government in a Prussian province
OBF	*Ortsbauernführer* – local RNS official, whose superior was the KBF
Opferbereitschaft	literally, 'readiness for sacrifice', the attitude that Nazi indoctrination was aimed to promote in 'valuable' Germans
Ortsgruppe	local branch - subdivision of a *Kreis*, part of the territorial organisation of the NSDAP
Ortsgruppenleiter	local branch leader – leader of an NSDAP local branch
Pflichtjahr	compulsory year of service in agriculture or domestic work for some women aged under twenty-five, introduced in February 1938
Reichsamt für Agrarpolitik	Central Department for Agricultural Policy in the NSDAP, the successor, in 1933, to the *agrarpolitischer Apparat*
RAD	*Reichsarbeitsdienst* – the Reich Labour Service, into which young men and young women were (separately) encouraged

	and later conscripted, to perform manual work, often in agriculture
Reichsbauernführer	Reich Farmers' Leader, the post held by R. Walther Darré as leader of the RNS from its founding in September 1933
Reichserbhofgesetz	Hereditary Farm Law, enacted on 29 September 1933, which introduced the *Erbhöfe*
Reichsführer-SS	Reich Leader of the SS, the title assumed by Heinrich Himmler in 1929
Reichsstatthalter	civil head of a *Land* from April 1933
RNS	*Reichsnährstand* (Reich Food Estate) – the organisation of which membership was obligatory for growers, processors, wholesalers and retailers of agricultural produce, as well as for those engaged in forestry, fishing, hunting, viticulture and horticulture
RVK	*Reichsverteidigungskommissar* (Reich Defence Commissioner), the title conferred on some *Gauleiter* in September 1939, when they became overlords of all domestic policy in an Army District, and on all *Gauleiter* in November 1942
SA	*Sturmabteilungen* – formation of the NSDAP whose leadership was purged on 30 June-2 July 1934
Schulungsleiter	literally, 'training leader', the NSDAP officer in a division of the territorial organisation who was responsible for 'political education'
Schutzpolizei	(abbrev. *Schupo*) municipal police
Schwäbisch	Swabian – used to describe that which belongs to Württemberg, including landscape, people, character and dialect
Schwarzschlachtung	literally, 'black slaughtering', the illegal slaughtering of farm animals by farmers
SD	*Sicherheitsdienst* – Security Service of the SS, whose functions included monitoring and reporting on the mood and attitude of the German people at district level
Sondergericht	Special Court, established by decree on 21 March 1933 to deal particularly with political offences, in which the rights of the accused were severely restricted
SOPADE	Social Democratic Party in Exile – the SPD leadership based in Prague from spring 1933 and in Paris 1938–40, whose agents in Germany compiled monthly reports on economic and social conditions and on the popular mood in Germany
SPD	*Sozialdemokratische Partei Deutschlands* (German Social Democratic Party), founded in 1875 and banned in June 1933

SS	*Schutzstaffel* – formation of the NSDAP whose leader was Heinrich Himmler
Stahlhelm	literally, 'steel helmet' – the name of the paramilitary organisation associated with the DNVP
StAL	Staatsarchiv Ludwigsburg
StJ	*Statistisches Jahrbuch für das Deutsche Reich* (Statistical Yearbook for the German Reich)
'unermüdlich'	'tireless' – used routinely to describe the efforts of loyal NSDAP activists
'Untermensch'	literally, 'sub-human' – term applied by Nazis to those deemed to be 'racially inferior', in particular Slavs
USHMM	United States Holocaust Memorial Museum, Washington, DC
USSR	Union of Soviet Socialist Republics
Vergeltung	'retaliation', specifically the promised German retaliation for Allied area bombing, using unmanned rockets – the V1 and V2 – against Britain
völkisch	ethnic-nationalist, with mystical and racist connotations
Völkischer Beobachter	the official newspaper of the NSDAP, published in regional editions
Volksdeutsche Mittelstelle	Himmler's Liaison Office for Ethnic Germans
Volksgemeinschaft	'people's ethnic community' – the notional collective body of 'valuable Aryan' Germans
Volksgenossen	literally, 'national comrades' – the term used to describe 'valuable' citizens who were not NSDAP members
Volkskörper	literally, 'racial body' – conceived as the embodiment of the nation's collective racial, physical and mental health
Volkssturm	the home guard levied from among non-combatant men in autumn 1944
Wehrmacht	the armed forces in Nazi Germany
WAU	*Weltanschauungsunterricht* – ideological instruction, specifically the indoctrination of school children with Nazi ideology
Wiedereindeutschungsfähig	literally, 'capable of being made German again' – applied to ethnic Germans who had lived under foreign rule for some time, perhaps for generations, and had allegedly lost their German identity
Winterhilfswerk	Winter Aid Scheme, a charitable venture of the NSV whose funds were in part used to support other Nazi organisations
Zwangswirtschaft	coercive economy – the pejorative term used by many farmers to describe the regime of government requisitioning and price fixing of agricultural produce during and after the First World War

Notes

Notes to Introduction

1 Hans Mommsen, 'The Realisation of the Unthinkable: The "Final Solution of the Jewish Question" in the Third Reich', in Gerhard Hirschfeld (ed.), *The Policies of Genocide* (London, 1986), pp. 97–144.

2 Robert Gellately, *Backing Hitler: Consent and Coercion in Nazi Germany* (Oxford, 2001); Ian Kershaw, *The 'Hitler Myth': Image and Reality in the Third Reich* (Oxford, 1987).

3 See the pioneering work of Edward N. Peterson, *The Limits of Hitler's Power* (Princeton, New Jersey, 1969).

4 Thomas Schnabel, 'Einleitung', in Thomas Schnabel (ed.), *Die Machtergreifung in Südwestdeutschland* (Stuttgart, 1982), p. 11; Mühlberger, p. 50.

5 Eberhard Schanbacher, 'Das Wählervotum und die "Machtergreifung" im Südwesten', in Schnabel, *Die Machtergreifung*, p. 300.

Notes to Chapter 1: Town and Country

1 For example: Lothar Burchardt, 'The Impact of the War Economy on the Civilian Population of Germany during the First and Second World Wars', in Wilhelm Deist (ed.), *The German Military in the Age of Total War* (Leamington Spa, 1985), pp. 40–70; Marie-Luise Recker, *Nationalsozialistische Sozialpolitik im Zweiten Weltkrieg* (Munich, 1985); Jeremy Noakes, 'Germany', in Jeremy Noakes (ed.), *The Civilian in War* (Exeter, 1992), pp. 34–61; Earl R. Beck, *Under the Bombs: The German Home Front, 1942–45* (Lexington, Kentucky, 1986); Terry Charman, *The German Home Front, 1939–45* (London, 1989); Eleanor Hancock, *National Socialist Leadership and Total War, 1941–45* (New York, 1991); Martin Kitchen, *Nazi Germany at War* (London, 1995).

2 Quoted in Manfred J. Enssle, 'The Harsh Discipline of Food Scarcity in Postwar Stuttgart, 1945–1948', *German Studies Review*, 10 (1987), p. 484.

3 Martin K. Sorge, *The Other Price of Hitler's War: German Military and Civilian Losses Resulting from World War II* (Westport, Connecticut, 1986), p. 92; Alan J. Levine, *The Strategic Bombing of Germany, 1940–45* (Westport, Connecticut, 1992), p. 47.

4 Ursula Büttner, *'Gomorrha': Hamburg im Bombenkrieg. Die Wirkung der Luftangriffe auf Bevölkerung und Wirtschaft* (Hamburg, 1993), pp. 20–26. See also Ursula Büttner,

'"Gomorrha" und die Folgen: der Bombenkrieg', in Forschungsstelle für Zeitgeschichte in Hamburg (ed.), *Hamburg im 'Dritten Reich'* (Göttingen, 2005), pp. 613–32; Rainer Hering, '"Operation Gomorrha": Hamburg remembers the Second World War', *German History*, 13 (1995), pp. 91–94.

5 Jose Harris, 'War and Social History: Britain and the Home Front during the Second World War', *Contemporary European History*, 1 (1992), p. 22.

6 Jörg Friedrich, *Der Brand: Deutschland im Bombenkrieg, 1940–1945* (Munich, 2002) gives an impression of the experience of those in bombed towns and cities. See also Joachim Szodrzynski, 'Die "Heimatfront" zwischen Stalingrad und Kriegsende', in Forschungsstelle für Zeitgeschichte in Hamburg, *Hamburg im 'Dritten Reich'*, pp. 640–45, 663–64.

7 Hauptstaatsarchiv Stuttgart (hereafter HStAS), J170: Bü1 (Aalen), Gemeinde Zipplingen; Bü3 (Böblingen), Gemeinde Holzgerlingen; Bü4 (Crailsheim), Gemeinde Oberspeltach; Bü10 (Leonberg), Gemeinde Heimsheim; Bü78 (Tübingen), Gemeinde Entringen.

8 Ibid.: Bü1, 'Die letzten Woche vor un[d] die ersten Wochen nach der Besetzung in Neresheim', n.d. [October/November 1948], p. 1; Bü4: 'Gemeinde Gaggstatt Krs Crailsheim. Geschichtliche Darstellung der letzten Kriegstage', n.d. [October/November 1948], p. 4; 'Geschichtliche Darstellung der letzten Kriegstage', 27 October 1948 (date received by *Landratsamt* Crailsheim), p. 5. See also Neil Gregor, '"Is He Still Alive, or Long Since Dead?": Loss, Absence and Remembrance in Nuremberg, 1945–56', *German History*, 21 (2003), pp. 183–203.

9 Thomas Schnabel, *Württemberg zwischen Weimar und Bonn, 1928–1945/46* (Stuttgart, 1986), p. 574.

10 Jürgen Kocka, *Facing Total War* (Leamington Spa, 1984), pp. 24–60; N.P. Howard, 'The Social and Political Consequences of the Allied Food Blockade of Germany, 1918–19', *German History*, 11 (1993), pp. 161–88; Ute Daniel, *Arbeiterfrauen in der Kriegsgesellschaft* (Göttingen, 1989).

11 Tim Mason, *Social Policy in the Third Reich: The Working Classes and the 'National Community'* (Providence, Rhode Island, and Oxford, 1993), ch. 1, 'The Legacy of 1918 for National Socialism', pp. 19–40. See also the earliest version of this essay in Anthony Nicholls and Erich Matthias (eds), *German Democracy and the Triumph of Hitler: Essays in Recent German History* (London, 1971), pp. 215–39.

12 Ian Kershaw, *Popular Opinion and Political Dissent in the Third Reich: Bavaria, 1933–1945* (Oxford, 1983), pp. 70–110; Tim Mason, 'The Containment of the Working Class in Nazi Germany', in Jane Caplan (ed.), *Nazism, Fascism and the Working Class: Essays by Tim Mason* (Cambridge, 1995), pp. 233–73.

13 On Schleswig-Holstein, see Rudolf Heberle, *Landbevölkerung und Nationalsozialismus: eine soziologische Untersuchung der politischen Willensbildung in Schleswig-Holstein, 1918–1932* (Stuttgart, 1963), pp. 160–71. See also M.R. Lepsius, 'Extremer Nationalismus: Strukturbedingungen vor der nationalsozialistischen Machtergreifung' (first pub. 1970), *Demokratie in Deutschland* (Göttingen, 1993), pp. 62–67; J.E. Farquharson, *The Plough and the Swastika: The NSDAP and Agriculture in Germany, 1928–45* (London, 1976), chs. 2 and 3; Kershaw, *Popular Opinion*, pp. 37–40; Zdenek Zofka, 'Between Bauernbund and National Socialism', in Thomas Childers (ed.), *The Formation of the Nazi Constituency, 1919–1933* (London and Sydney, 1986), pp. 37–63.

14 Avraham Barkai, *Nazi Economics: Ideology, Theory, and Policy*, trans. by Ruth Hadass-Vaschitz (Oxford and New York, 1990), p. 140.

15 Mason, 'The Containment of the Working Class in Nazi Germany ', pp. 234–37, 241–42.

16 David Welch, 'Nazi Propaganda and the *Volksgemeinschaft*: Constructing a People's Community', *Journal of Contemporary History*, 39 (2004), pp. 219–26; Ronald Smelser, *Robert Ley: Hitler's Labour Front Leader* (Oxford, 1988), pp. 281–283; Recker, *Nationalsozialistische Sozialpolitik* (Munich, 1985), pp. 82–87, 125–154. Cf. Michael Prinz, *Vom neuen Mittelstand zum Volksgenossen* (Munich, 1986), pp. 296–321. For a polemical view, see Götz Aly, *Rasse und Klasse: Nachforschungen zum deutschen Wesen* (Frankfurt am Main, 2003), especially pp. 230–44.

17 On Hitler as a charismatic leader, see Ian Kershaw: *Hitler* (London, 1991), pp. 10–14; *Hitler, 1889–1936: Hubris* (London, 1998), pp. xiii, xxvi–xxvii.

18 On 'German socialism', see Gregor Strasser's view, expressed in 1927, quoted in Jeremy Noakes and Geoffrey Pridham (eds), *Nazism, 1919–1945: A Documentary Reader*, i: *The Rise to Power* (Exeter, 1983), pp. 41–42. Hitler claimed, in arguing with Otto Strasser in 1930, that 'I am a Socialist, and a very different kind of Socialist from your rich friend Reventlow', concluding that 'That word "socialism" is the trouble'. Quoted in ibid., pp. 66–67.

19 Hitler: 'One cannot take the false idol of Marxism from the people without giving it a better god.' Quoted in Tim Mason, 'The Legacy of 1918 for National Socialism', in Nicholls and Matthias, *German Democracy and the Triumph of Hitler*, p. 221.

20 Hartmut Berghoff, *Zwischen Kleinstadt und Weltmarkt: Hohner und die Harmonika, 1857–1961* (Paderborn, 1997), p. 454. I am indebted to Frank Bajohr for drawing my attention to this book. See also Kershaw, *Popular Opinion*, pp. 54, 63, 79, 171.

21 Quoted in Kershaw, *Popular Opinion*, p. 54. See also pp. 373–77, 384–85; Tim Mason, 'The Workers' Opposition in Nazi Germany', *History Workshop Journal*, 11 (1981), pp. 120–37; Stephen Salter, 'Structures of Consensus and Coercion: Workers' Morale and the Maintenance of Work Discipline, 1939–1945', in David Welch (ed.), *Nazi Propaganda: The Power and the Limitations* (London, 1983), pp. 88–116. Cf. Norbert Frei, *National Socialist Rule in Germany: The Führer State, 1933–1945* (Oxford, 1993), pp. 77–78, 82–83.

22 Walter Rinderle and Bernard Norling, *The Nazi Impact on a German Village* (Lexington, Kentucky, 1993), p. 155. See also Daniela Münkel, *Nationalsozialistische Agrarpolitik und Bauernalltag* (Frankfurt am Main, 1996), p. 337.

23 'Aus Monatsbericht der Gendarmerie-Station Aufsess, 26.1.41' in M. Broszat, E. Fröhlich and F. Wiesemann (eds), *Bayern in der NS-Zeit*, i, *Soziale Lage und politisches Verhalten der Bevölkerung im Spiegel vertraulicher Berichte* (Munich and Vienna, 1977), p. 145.

24 Point 24 of the Nazi Party Programme, Noakes and Pridham, *Nazism*, i, p. 16.

25 Richard Bessel, *Germany after the First World War* (Oxford, 1993), p. 42; Rinderle and Norling, *The Nazi Impact on a German Village*, pp. 165ff.

26 See, especially, the work of Ina-Maria Zweiniger-Bargielowska on the black market in Britain during the Second World War: Ina Zweiniger-Bargielowska, *Austerity in Britain: Rationing, Controls, and Consumption, 1939–1955* (Oxford, 2000). See also Angus Calder, *The People's War* (London, 1969). On France, see Robert Gildea, *Marianne in*

Chains: In Search of the German Occupation of France, 1940–1945 (London, 2002), pp. 27–28, 113–18. On Poland, see Joanna Hanson, 'Poland', in Noakes, *The Civilian at War*, pp. 150–72.

27 Ian Kershaw: *Hitler, 1889–1936*, pp. 576ff; 'Social Unrest and the Response of the Nazi Regime', in Francis R. Nicosia and Lawrence D. Stokes (eds), *Germans Against Nazism: Nonconformity, Opposition and Resistance in the Third Reich. Essays in Honour of Peter Hoffmann* (New York and Oxford, 1990), pp. 158–68. See also Staatsarchiv Ludwigsburg (hereafter StAL), K110, Bü46, 'Lagebericht des 2. Vierteljahres 1939', 1 July 1939, pp. 33–35.

28 Frei, *National Socialist Rule*, p. 77; see also below, Chapter 2.

29 Statistisches Reichsamt, *Statistisches Jahrbuch für das Deutsche Reich* (hereafter *StJ*): 1880, p. 7; 1907, p. 11. See also Volker Berghahn, 'Demographic growth, industrialisation and social change', in John Breuilly (ed.), *Nineteenth Century Germany* (London, 2001), pp. 185–88. The figures for individual towns are: Ulm, 51,820; Heilbronn, 40,004; Esslingen, 29,172; Ludwigsburg, 22,585; Tübingen, 16,809; Tuttlingen, 14,627; Aalen, 10,442. *StJ*, 1907, pp. 11–12.

30 Paul Sauer, *Erinnerung an Stuttgart in den zwanziger Jahren* (Würzburg, 2000), captions to plates 66, 69–79; Paul Sauer, *Württemberg in der Zeit des Nationalsozialismus* (Ulm, 1975), pp. 101–103.

31 Sauer, *Erinnerung an Stuttgart*, caption to plate 79.

32 HStAS, E382, Bü350, An das Württbg. Wirtschaftsministerium, Abtg. Preisüberwachung, 'Betrifft: Abführungsbescheid. 7 B 23–350', 6 May 1942. For the absence of radios in Bavarian villages – and low newspaper readership – see Edward N. Peterson, *The Limits of Hitler's Power* (Princeton, New Jersey, 1969), p. 418. See also Kershaw, *Popular Opinion and Political Dissent in the Third Reich*, p. 48. More generally, see Daniela Münkel, '"Der Rundfunk geht auf die Dörfer": der Einzug der Massmedien auf dem Lande von den zwanziger bis zu den sechziger Jahren', in Daniela Münkel (ed.), *Der lange Abschied vom Agrarland: Agrarpolitik, Landwirtschaft und ländliche Gesellschaft zwischen Weimar und Bonn* (Göttingen, 2000), pp. 177–98.

33 HStAS, J170, Bü10 (Leonberg), Malmsheim, n.d. [October/November 1948].

34 StAL, Bü45, 'Lagebericht des 2. Vierteljahres 1939', 1 April 1939, p. 22. See also Wolfgang König, *Volkswagen, Volksempfänger, Volksgemeinschaft: 'Volksprodukte' im Dritten Reich. Vom Scheitern einer nationalsozialistischen Konsumgesellschaft* (Paderborn, 2004), pp. 35–99, especially pp. 86–88.

35 Bernd Burkhardt, *Eine Stadt wird braun: die nationalsozialistische Machtergreifung in der Provinz: Eine Fallstudie* (Hamburg, 1980), p. 11; König, *Volkswagen, Volksempfänger, Volksgemeinschaft*, pp. 91–94.

36 StAL, Bü40, Rundschreiben Nr 119/41, 'Betr.: Einführung des Gemeinderundfunks', 12 November 1941.

37 Arbeitswissenschaftliches Institut der Deutschen Arbeitsfront (hereafter AIDA) (ed.), *Die Sozialstruktur des Gaues Württemberg-Hohenzollern: eine sozialgeographische Analyse* (Berlin, 1940), pp. 6, 34–43.

38 StAL, Bü46, p. 38, reports the view of the SD (*Sicherheitsdienst*) that the undervaluing of rural life and the rural contribution to the economy was one of the major reasons

for low morale in farming communities in Württemberg in the later 1930s. See also Theresia Bauer, *Nationalsozialistische Agrarpolitik und bäuerliches Verhalten im Zweiten Weltkrieg: eine Regionalstudie zur ländlichen Gesellschaft in Bayern* (Frankfurt am Main, 1996), p. 201; Münkel, *Nationalsozialistische Agrarpolitik und Bauernalltag*, p. 97.

39   Thomas Schnabel (ed.), *Die Machtergreifung in Südwestdeutschland: das Ende der Weimarer Republik in Baden und Württemberg, 1928–1933* (Stuttgart, 1982), p. 313.

40   The idea of 'integration' is found in David Schoenbaum, *Hitler's Social Revolution: Class and Status in Nazi Germany, 1933–1939* (London, 1967), p. 293.

41   For examples of this elsewhere, see Michael H. Kater, *The Nazi Party: A Social Profile of Members and Leaders, 1919–1945* (Cambridge, Massachusetts, 1983), p. 208.

42   Schnabel, *Württemberg zwischen Weimar und Bonn*, pp. 188–98; Christine Arbogast, *Herrschaftsinstanzen der württembergischen NSDAP: Funktion, Sozialprofil und Lebenswege einer regionalen NS-Elite, 1920–1960* (Munich, 1998), pp. 121–22.

43   Paul Sauer, *Die jüdischen Gemeinden in Württemberg und Hohenzollern: Denkmale, Geschichte, Schicksale* (Stuttgart, 1966), passim.

44   Paul Sauer, 'Staat, Politik, Akteure', in Otto Borst (ed.), *Das Dritte Reich in Baden und Württemberg* (Stuttgart, 1988), p. 26.

45   Paul Sauer, *Wilhelm Murr: Hitlers Statthalter in Württemberg* (Tübingen, 1998), pp. 40–42. See also below, Chapter Three.

46   This could be observed in other areas of Germany during the Third Reich, notably Bavaria. See Peterson, *The Limits of Hitler's Power*, pp. 446–49.

47   Michael Kissener and Joachim Scholtyseck, 'Nationalsozialismus in der Provinz: zur Einführung', in Michael Kissener and Joachim Scholtyseck (eds), *Die Führer der Provinz: NS-Biographien aus Baden und Württemberg* (Konstanz, 1997), p. 23; Terry Weiss, 'Translator's Note', in Landeszentrale für politische Bildung Baden-Württemberg (ed.), *The German Southwest: Baden-Württemberg. History, Politics, Economy and Culture* (Stuttgart, 1991), p. 9

48   George D. Spindler, *Burgbach: Urbanisation and Identity in a German Village* (New York, 1973), p. 19.

49   Kissener and Scholtyseck, *Die Führer der Provinz*, p. 851.

50   On the threat of a 'new *Kulturkampf*', see Thomas Schnabel, 'Das Wahlverhalten der Katholiken in Württemberg, 1928–1933', in Geschichtsverein der Diözese Rottenburg-Stuttgart (ed.), *Kirche im Nationalsozialismus* (Sigmaringen, 1984), pp. 104, 110. Cf. Oded Heilbronner, *Catholicism, Political Culture, and the Countryside: A Social History of the Nazi Party in South Germany* (Ann Arbor, Michigan, 1998), p. 139.

51   See below, Chapters Four and Seven.

52   Schnabel, *Württemberg zwischen Weimar und Bonn*, pp. 18–21. See also Kershaw, *Popular Opinion and Political Dissent in the Third Reich*, pp. 15–16.

53   *StJ*, 1938, pp. 16–18. In the 1933 census, Karlsruhe had 159,926 inhabitants.

54   Tübinger Vereinigung für Volksheilkunde e.V., *Volk und Gesundheit: Heilen und Vernichten im Nationalsozialismus* (Tübingen, 1982), pp. 151, 160–67.

55   Jeremy Noakes and Geoffrey Pridham (eds), *Nazism, 1919–1945: A Documentary Reader*, ii, *State, Economy and Society, 1933–1939* (Exeter, 1986), pp. 457–58.

56 Annette Schäfer, *Zwangsarbeiter und NS-Rassenpolitik: Russische und polnische Arbeitskräfte in Württemberg, 1939–1945* (Stuttgart, 2000), pp. 48–49.

57 HStAS, J170, Bü4, 'Betr. Geschichtliche Darstellung der letzten Kriegstage', Hengstfeld, 20 October 1948, p. 1. The number of communes is given variously as 1825 and 1829, the figure used by the Württemberg Interior Ministry at the time of reorganisation of the districts in 1938. See HStAS, E151/01, Bü652, 'Zweckmässigkeit der Neueinteilung des Landes'.

58 Günter Golde, *Catholics and Protestants: Agricultural Modernisation in Two German Villages* (New York, 1975), pp. 40–41, 115–16, 126ff., 177; Spindler, *Burgbach*, pp. 75, 77.

59 Golde, *Catholics and Protestants*, pp. 92–93. On frugality, see Spindler, *Burgbach*, pp. 19–20.

60 HStAS, J170, Bü18 (Ulm), Türkheim, p. 1.

61 Ibid., Bü10 (Leonberg), 'Kriegs-Chronik der Gemeinde Münchingen verfasst von –, Bauer, Münchingen', n.d.

62 Spindler, *Burgbach*, p. 79.

63 John Alexander Williams, '"The Chords of the German Soul are Tuned to Nature": The Movement to Preserve the Natural *Heimat* from the Kaiserreich to the Third Reich', *Central European History*, 29 (1996), p. 384.

64 Spindler, *Burgbach*, pp. 17, 28, 44; Golde, *Catholics and Protestants*, p. 40.

65 Arnd Bauerkämper, 'Landwirtschaft und ländliche Gesellschaft in der Bundesrepublik in den 50er Jahren', in Axel Schildt and Arnold Sywottek (eds), *Modernisierung im Wiederaufbau: die westdeutsche Gesellschaft der 50er Jahre* (Bonn, 1998, first published in 1993), pp. 188–200; Spindler, *Burgbach*, pp. 24–25, 71, 73.

66 Ibid., passim; Golde, *Catholics and Protestants*, pp. 133–76. This was true also in other areas of Germany, including eastern districts which became part of the German Democratic Republic. See Mary Fulbrook, 'The Limits of Totalitarianism: God, State and Society in the GDR', *Transactions of the Royal Historical Society*, 7 (1997), p. 39. See also the essays in Münkel, *Der lange Abschied vom Agrarland*.

67 Schnabel: *Württemberg zwischen Weimar und Bonn*, pp. 36–48, 73–89, 105–21, 126–47, 160–80; 'Das Wahlverhalten der Katholiken in Württemberg, 1928–1933', pp. 103–14. On electoral results in Württemberg from 1919 to 1933, see Schnabel, *Die Machtergreifung*, pp. 312–13.

68 Schoenbaum, *Hitler's Social Revolution*, pp. 160–61.

69 Johnpeter Horst Grill, *The Nazi Movement in Baden, 1920–1945* (Chapel Hill, North Carolina, 1983), p. 530.

70 Farquharson, *The Plough and the Swastika*, p. 3.

71 See below, Chapter 3, as well as individual essays in Kissener and Scholtyseck, *Die Führer der Provinz*.

72 StAL, K631/I, Bü1625, *Wochenblatt der Landesbauernschaft Württemberg*: 4 May 1935, cover; 11 May 1935 (*Festausgabe*), pp. 10–12, 16, 17; 18 May 1935, p. 764.

73 Heide Fehrenbach, *Cinema in Democratising Germany: Reconstructing National Identity after Hitler* (Chapel Hill, North Carolina, 1995), pp. 32–39, 44–50.

74 StAL, Bü45, p. 23.

75 Ibid., Bü46, pp. 16–17.

76 Martin Wiener, *English Culture and the Decline of the Industrial Spirit, 1850–1980* (Cambridge, 1981). Wiener uses 'English' and 'British' interchangeably.

77 Wolfgang Kaschuba, 'Peasants and Others: The Historical Contours of Village Class Society', in Richard J. Evans and W.R. Lee (eds), *The German Peasantry: Conflict and Community in Rural Society from the Eighteenth to the Twentieth Centuries* (London and Sydney, 1986), p. 236.

78 Utz Jeggle, 'The Rules of the Village: On the Cultural History of the Peasant World in the Last 150 Years', trans. by Richard J. Evans, in Evans and Lee, *The German Peasantry*, p. 284. Cf. Gerhard Wilke and Kurt Wagner, 'Family and Household: Social Structures in a German Village between the Two World Wars', in Richard J. Evans and W.R. Lee (eds), *The German Family* (London, 1981), pp. 126–28, 142.

79 Kaschuba, 'Peasants and Others', p. 248.

80 Jeggle, 'The Rules of the Village', p. 278.

81 There is a huge literature on this. See, among many others, Michael Burleigh and Wolfgang Wippermann, *The Racial State: Germany, 1933–1945* (Cambridge, 1991); Marion A. Kaplan, *Between Dignity and Despair: Jewish Life in Nazi Germany* (New York and Oxford, 1998); Robert N. Proctor, *Racial Hygiene: Medicine under the Nazis* (Cambridge, Massachusetts, 1988); Götz Aly, Peter Chroust and Christian Pross, *Cleansing the Fatherland: Nazi Medicine and Racial Hygiene* (Baltimore, Maryland, 1994).

82 AIDA, *Die Sozialstruktur*, pp. 20–22, 28, 30, 34; StAL, K110: Bü44, 'Lagebericht des 4. Vierteljahres 1938', 1 February 1939, pp. 18–19; Bü46, p. 38.

83 'Bevölkerungspolitik und Rassenpflege auf dem Lande', *Völkischer Beobachter*, 13/14 May 1934 (Racial Hygiene Supplement).

84 John E. Knodel, *Demographic Behaviour in the Past: A Study of Fourteen German Village Populations in the Eighteenth and Nineteenth Centuries* (Cambridge, 1988), p. 455.

85 *StJ*, 1941/42, p. 70. The figures refer to the *Altreich*, Germany by its borders of 1937.

86 StAL, K110, Bü46, p. 13.

87 Ibid., pp. 12–13. On the League of Large Families, see Jill Stephenson, '"Reichsbund der Kinderreichen": The League of Large Families in the Population Policy of Nazi Germany', *European Studies Review* (1979), pp. 350–75.

88 See Bauerkämper, 'Landwirtschaft und ländliche Gesellschaft', pp. 188–200; Golde, *Catholics and Protestants*, pp. 121–26; Spindler, *Burgbach*, p. 14. See also Landesstelle für Museumbetreuung Baden-Württemberg und der Arbeitsgemeinschaft der regionalen Freilichtmuseen Baden-Württemberg (eds), *Zöpfe ab, Hosen an! Die Fünfzigerjahre auf dem Land in Baden-Württemberg* (Tübingen, 2002).

89 Ralf Dahrendorf, *Society and Democracy in Germany* (London, 1968), p. 403.

90 Schoenbaum, *Hitler's Social Revolution*, p. 296, makes this claim. Nevertheless, he also says, on p. 287, that 'The *Gemeinschaft* invoked by Nazi ideology struck genuinely resonant notes in the hearts of a population desperate for authority and sick unto death of conflict. But the real *Gemeinschaft* was no closer to realisation in practice at the end of Nazi rule than it was at the beginning'. Cf. Kershaw, *Popular Opinion and Political Dissent in the Third Reich*, p. 373.

91 Christa Tholander, *Fremdarbeiter, 1939 bis 1945: Ausländische Arbeitskräfte in der Zeppelin-Stadt Friedrichshafen* (Essen, 2001), p. 92.

92 Wilke and Wagner, 'Family and Household', p. 145: 'we must concede these villagers their own "rationality"'.

93 Much the same was true in Britain. See Sadie Ward, *War in the Countryside* (London, 1988), pp. 88–89, 92.

94 HStAS, J170, Bü8 (Heilbronn), Gemeinde Hausen a.d.Z. n.d. [October/November 1948].

95 Michael Geyer, 'Restorative Elites, German Society and the Nazi Pursuit of War', in Richard Bessel (ed.), *Fascist Italy and Nazi Germany: Comparisons and Contrasts* (Cambridge, 1996), pp. 154–55. See also Richard Bessel, *Nazism and War* (New York, 2004), p. 31: 'The transcendent faith that Germans in their millions placed in Nazism and its leader was, at root, a faith in war'.

96 For wise words about this, see Ian Kershaw, *The Nazi Dictatorship* (4th ed. London, 2000), pp. 21, 31–32, 42, 223, and especially chapter 7, 'The Third Reich: "social reaction" or "social revolution"?', pp. 161–82, and 'Nazism and Modernisation', section II of chapter 10, pp. 243–48. See also Mark Roseman, 'National Socialism and Modernisation', in Bessel, *Fascist Italy and Nazi Germany*, pp. 197–229; Jill Stephenson, 'Widerstand gegen soziale Modernisierung am Beispiel Württembergs, 1939–1945', in Michael Prinz and Rainer Zitelmann (eds.), *Nationalsozialismus und Modernisierung* (Darmstadt, 1991), pp. 93–166, and criticisms of this in Bauer, *Nationalsozialistische Agrarpolitik und bäuerliches Verhalten*, p. 201; Münkel, *Nationalsozialistische Agrarpolitik und Bauernalltag*, p. 476.

97 Kershaw, *Hitler, 1889–1936*, p. 577.

98 The burdens imposed on women are discussed in Jill Stephenson, '"Emancipation" and its Problems: War and Society in Württemberg, 1939–1945', *European History Quarterly*, vol. 17 (1987), pp. 351–61. See also Rinderle and Norling, *The Nazi Impact on a German Village*, pp. 164, 166–67, 171; and pp. 64–65 on the First World War. Cf. Wilke and Wagner, 'Family and Household', p. 143.

Notes to Chapter 2: Before the War

1 John Hiden, *Republican and Fascist Germany: Themes and Variations in the History of Weimar and the Third Reich* (London, 1996), p. 152. For the nineteenth century background, see the essays in John Breuilly (ed.), *Nineteenth-Century Germany: Politics, Culture and Society, 1780–1918* (London, 2001): Robert Lee, '"Relative Backwardness" and Long-run Development: Economic, Demographic and Social Changes', pp. 66–95; Volker Berghahn, 'Demographic Growth, Industrialisation and Social Change', pp. 185–98.

2 *Statistisches Jahrbuch für das Deutsche Reich* (hereafter *StJ*): 1927, p. 8, gives the 1871 population as 41,058,792; 1914, p. 5, gives the 1910 population as 64,925,993 (both including Alsace-Lorraine); see also 1941/42, p. 22. A 'town' here means a contiguous community of 2,000 or more inhabitants. On urbanisation in nineteenth-century Germany, see David Blackbourn, *The Fontana History of Germany, 1780–1918: The Long Nineteenth Century* (London, 1997), pp. 198–207, 351–54, 385–99.

3 S.B. Saul, *Industrialisation and De-industrialisation? The Interaction of the German and British Economies before the First World War*, Annual Lecture 1979, German Historical Institute London, pp. 11, 29.

4   *StJ*, 1927, p. 12.

5   Ibid., 1941/42, p. 22.

6   Jürgen Kocka, *Facing Total War* (Leamington Spa, 1984), pp. 24–28, 41–42, 48–53, 58, 116–23; Richard Bessel, *Germany after the First World War* (Oxford, 1993), pp. 15–19, 32–44; N.P. Howard, 'The Social and Political Consequences of the Allied Food Blockade of Germany, 1918–19', *German History*, 11 (1993), pp. 161–88; Walter Rinderle and Bernard Norling, *The Nazi Impact on a German Village* (Lexington, Kentucky, 1993), pp. 60–64.

7   Eric D. Kohler, 'Inflation and Black Marketeering in the Rhenish Agricultural Economy, 1919–1922', *German Studies Review*, 8 (1985), pp. 46, 64. See also Bessel, *Germany after the First World War*, pp. 195–219; Rinderle and Norling, *The Nazi Impact on a German Village*, p. 66; Ian Kershaw, *Popular Opinion and Political Dissent in the Third Reich: Bavaria, 1933–1945* (Oxford, 1983), pp. 34, 36.

8   Thomas Schnabel, *Württemberg zwischen Weimar und Bonn, 1928–1945/46* (Stuttgart, 1986), pp. 24, 47. See also Belinda J. Davis, *Home Fires Burning: Food, Politics and Everyday Life in World War I Berlin* (Chapel Hill, North Carolina, 2000), pp. 132, 274 n. 98.

9   Felix Höffler, 'Kriegserfahrungen in der Heimat: Kriegsverlauf, Kriegsschuld und Kriegsende in württembergischen Stimmungsbildern des Ersten Weltkriegs', in Gerhard Hirschfeld, Gerd Krumeich, Dieter Langewiesche and Hans-Peter Ullmann (eds), *Kriegserfahrungen: Studien zur Sozial- und Mentalitätsgeschichte des Ersten Weltkriegs* (Tübingen, 1997), p. 75. See also Kocka, *Facing Total War*, p. 123. On Bavaria, see Kershaw, *Popular Opinion*, p. 18. See also pp. 36, 47. But by no means all 'Prussians' thought of themselves as such. For example, 'Winzigers identified themselves proudly as Silesians rather than Prussians'. Rita S. Botwinick, *Winzig, Germany, 1933–1946: The History of a Town under the Third Reich* (Westport, Connecticut, 1992), p. 10.

10 Alon Confino, *The Nation as a Local Metaphor: Württemberg, Imperial Germany, and National Memory, 1871–1918* (Chapel Hill, North Carolina, 1997), pp. 16–17, 20–23, 33. The quotation is from p. 17. See also Günter Golde, *Catholics and Protestants: Agricultural Modernisation in Two German Villages* (New York, 1975), p. 13. Cf. George D. Spindler, *Burgbach: Urbanisation and Identity in a German Village* (New York, 1973), p. 12. On post-1918, see Schnabel, *Württemberg zwischen Weimar und Bonn*; p. 42; Michael Kissener and Joachim Scholtyseck, 'Nationalsozialismus in der Provinz', in Michael Kissener and Joachim Scholtyseck (eds), *Die Führer der Provinz. NS-Biographien aus Baden und Württemberg* (Konstanz, 1997), pp. 21, 23. For anti-Prussian sentiment before 1914, see David Blackbourn, *Class, Religion and Local Politics in Wilhelmine Germany: The Centre Party in Württemberg before 1914* (New Haven, Connecticut, and London, 1980), pp. 20, 74–75, 86.

11 From a newspaper article, dated 25 December 1932, quoted in Thomas Schnabel, '"Warum geht es in Schwaben besser?" Württemberg in der Weltwirtschaftskrise 1928–1933', in Thomas Schnabel (ed.), *Die Machtergreifung in Südwestdeutschland* (Stuttgart, 1982), p. 215.

12 Angela Borgstedt, 'Im Zweifelsfall auch mit harter Hand: Jonathan Schmid, Württembergischer Innen-, Justiz- und Wirtschaftsminister', in Kissener and Scholtyseck, *Die Führer der Provinz*, p. 609.

13 Rinderle and Norling, *The Nazi Impact on a German Village*, p. 174. See also pp. 58, 173.

14   Karl Weller and Arnold Weller, *Württembergische Geschichte im südwestdeutschen Raum* (Stuttgart and Aalen, 1975), pp. 207–12, gives the complex detail of this. See also Joachim Whaley, 'The German Lands before 1815', in Breuilly, *Nineteenth-Century Germany*, pp. 24–31; Theodor Eschenburg, 'The Formation of the State of Baden-Württemberg', in Landeszentrale für politische Bildung Baden-Württemberg (ed.), *The German Southwest* (Stuttgart, 1991), pp. 37–40; Confino, *The Nation as a Local Metaphor*, pp. 16–17; Kissener and Scholtyseck, 'Nationalsozialismus in der Provinz', pp. 20–21; Golde, *Catholics and Protestants*, pp. 9–13. On p. 6, Golde shows that Hohenlohe-Franken is largely coterminous with the 1938 reformed districts of Crailsheim, Künzelsau, Mergentheim, Öhringen and Schwäbisch Hall (see below, at n. 41). On the earlier political history of 'old Württemberg' (i.e., pre-1806), see Mary Fulbrook, *Piety and Politics: Religion and the Rise of Absolutism in England, Württemberg and Prussia* (Cambridge, 1983), pp. 66–75.

15   The quotations are, respectively, from Paul Sauer, *Württemberg in der Zeit des Nationalsozialismus* (Ulm, 1975), p. 47, and Golde, *Catholics and Protestants*, p. 9.

16   Michael Geyer, 'Restorative Elites, German Society and the Nazi Pursuit of War', in Richard Bessel (ed.), *Fascist Italy and Nazi Germany* (Cambridge, 1996), pp. 160–61. For longer term background, see Whaley, 'The German lands before 1815', pp. 34–38.

17   Kissener and Scholtyseck, 'Nationalsozialismus in der Provinz', p. 23. Walter Ziegler, 'Gaue und Gauleiter im Dritten Reich', in Horst Möller, Andreas Wirsching and Walter Ziegler (eds), *Nationalsozialismus in der Region: Beiträge zur regionalen und lokalen Forschung und zum internationalen Vergleich* (Munich, 1996), p. 150, argues that in *Das Buch der deutschen Gaue*, the contributions generally reflected the character, culture and traditions of the region rather than the history of the NSDAP within it. Cf. Kissener and Scholtyseck, 'Nationalsozialismus in der Provinz', p. 23, on the contrast between the contributions on Württemberg and Baden.

18   Confino, *The Nation as a Local Metaphor*, p. 188.

19   Geyer, 'Restorative Elites', pp. 155–58; Golde, *Catholics and Protestants*, pp. 34–36.

20   Weller and Weller, *Württembergische Geschichte*, pp. 268–71, 283.

21   *StJ*, 1927, p. 9; Paul Sauer, 'Die jüdischen Gemeinden in Baden und Württemberg von 1933 bis zum Wiederaufbau nach 1945', in Heinz Sproll and Jörg Thierfelder (eds), *Die Religionsgemeinschaften in Baden und Württemberg* (Stuttgart, 1984), p. 190.

22   Schnabel, *Die Machtergreifung in Südwestdeutschland* (Stuttgart, 1982), appendix 8, p. 317. In his introduction, p. 11, the editor refers to 'the two most important social institutions, namely the Evangelical and Catholic churches'.

23   Blackbourn, *The Fontana History of Germany, 1780–1918*, pp. 291–92. On the early history of Pietism in Württemberg, see Fulbrook, *Piety and Politics*, pp. 27–36, 41–42. 98–101, 130–52. See also Weller and Weller, *Württembergische Geschichte*, pp. 249–50.

24   *StJ*: 1941/42, pp. 7, 23; 1938, pp. 13, 19; Arbeitswissenschaftliches Institut der Deutschen Arbeitsfront (hereafter AIDA) (ed.), *Die Sozialstruktur des Gaues Württemberg-Hohenzollern: eine sozialgeographische Analyse* (Berlin, 1940), p. 14.

25   Ibid.; Thomas Schnabel, 'Warum geht es in Schwaben besser?', p. 187.

26   *StJ*, 1941/42, p. 7. The number of inhabitants per square kilometre for a few selected regions at the 1939 census was:

Württemberg	148.5
Bavaria	105.7
Baden	166.1
Saxony	348.9
Hamburg (*Land*)	2,292.8
Berlin (city)	4,910.0
Reich average	136.0

27   AIDA, *Die Sozialstruktur*, pp. 12–16. The seven districts in the north-east were: Aalen, Backnang, Crailsheim, Schwäbisch Hall, Künzelsau, Mergentheim and Öhringen; the six southern central districts were Biberach, Ehingen, Freudenstadt, Horb, Münsingen and Saulgau. In the early 1970s, Esslingen (980) and Munsingen (62) remained the most and the least densely populated districts. Weller and Weller, *Württembergische Geschichte*, p. 344.

28   *StJ*, 1927, p. 52. The 1925 census recorded the following percentages for owner-occupation and rented agricultural land:

	Proprietors	*Tenants*
Württemberg	91.7	6.8
Bavaria	95.4	4.0
Baden	86.4	10.6
East Prussia	91.8	6.8
Reich average	86.6	12.4

See also Jonathan Osmond, 'A Second Agrarian Mobilisation? Peasant Associations in South and West Germany, 1918–24', in Robert Moeller (ed.), *Peasants and Lords in Modern Germany: Recent Studies in Agricultural History* (Boston, Massachusetts, and London, 1986), p. 171.

29   Calculated from figures in *StJ*, 1941/42, p. 59.

30   Sauer, *Württemberg*, p. 286. See also Christa Tholander, *Fremdarbeiter 1939 bis 1945: Ausländische Arbeitskräfte in der Zeppelin-Stadt Friedrichshafen* (Essen, 2001), p. 34.

31   Doreen Warriner, *Economics of Peasant Farming* (London, 1964), p. 159.

32   Spindler, *Burgbach*, p. 79.

33   Thomas Schnabel, 'Warum geht es in Schwaben besser?', pp. 188–89.

34   Calculated from figures in *StJ*, 1941/42, p. 109.

35   Utz Jeggle, 'The Rules of the Village: On the Cultural History of the Peasant World in the Last 150 Years', trans. by Richard J. Evans, in Richard J. Evans and W.R. Lee (eds), *The German Peasantry: Conflict and Community in Rural Society from the Eighteenth to the Twentieth Centuries* (London and Sydney, 1986), p. 272. See also Wolfgang Kaschuba, 'Peasants and Others: The Historical Contours of Village Class Society', in Evans and Lee, *The German Peasantry*, pp. 242, 245. On women as proprietors, according to Daniela Münkel, *Nationalsozialistische Agrarpolitik und Bauernalltag* (Frankfurt, 1996), p. 24, out of 3606 farms (13 per cent) examined in Stade district (Lower Saxony) 474 were in the sole ownership of women in 1933.

36   AIDA, *Die Sozialstruktur*, pp. 22, 24–25, especially the map on p. 24, which shows that the districts of Freudenstadt and Rottweil were exceptions to the rule of partible inheritance in western Württemberg. The term 'single heir inheritance' (*Anerbensitte*) rather than

'primogeniture' (*Erstgeburtsrecht*) is the normal usage. See also Robert Mielke, *Das Deutsche Dorf* (Leipzig and Berlin, 1920), pp. 94–95; Alan Mayhew, *Rural Settlement and Farming in Germany* (London, 1973), pp. 130–32, especially the map on p. 132; Schnabel, 'Warum geht es in Schwaben besser?', p. 189; J.E. Farquharson, *The Plough and the Swastika: The NSDAP and Agriculture in Germany, 1928–45* (London, 1976), p. 64.

37   Blackbourn, *The Fontana History of Germany, 1780–1918*, pp. 192–93; John E. Knodel, *Demographic Behaviour in the Past: A Study of Fourteen German Village Populations in the Eighteenth and Nineteenth Centuries* (Cambridge, 1988), p. 511; Paul Sauer, *Wilhelm Murr: Hitlers Staathalter in Württemberg* (Tübingen, 1998), p. 81.

38   Blackbourn, *The Fontana History of Germany, 1780–1918*, p. 198; Kaschuba, 'Peasants and Others', pp. 241–42.

39   Rudolf Hofsähs, 'Die Abwanderung aus wirtschaftlich zurückgebliebenen Gebieten in Baden-Württemberg', doctoral dissertation for the Wirtschaftshochschule Mannheim, 1957, pp. 26, 28. By 1953, the figure had risen to 503. Württemberg had altogether 1829 communes (excluding the towns of Stuttgart, Heilbronn and Ulm) in 1938. See also Farquharson, *The Plough and the Swastika*, p. 64.

40   Golde, *Catholics and Protestants*, pp. 17–19.

41   Hauptstaatsarchiv Stuttgart (hereafter HStAS), E151/01, Bü673, 'Die Leistungsfähigkeit der Land- und Stadtkreise', pp. 3–5. See also Weller and Weller, *Württembergische Geschichte*, p. 305; Sauer, *Württemberg*, pp. 110–21.

42   Mielke, *Das Deutsche Dorf*, p. 93.

43   Weller and Weller, *Württembergische Geschichte*, p. 344; Klaus Kulinat, 'Regional Planning in Baden-Württemberg', in Landeszentrale für politische Bildung Baden-Württemberg, *The German Southwest*, pp. 158–63. See also Staatsarchiv Ludwigsburg (hereafter StAL), K631/II, Bü75, 'Aktennotiz. Betr.: Besprechung mit dem RAD betr. Einsatz der RAD-Abteilung Walxheim Kreis Aalen', 14 January 1942.

44   From a newspaper article, dated 25 December 1932, reproduced in Schnabel, 'Warum geht es in Schwaben besser?', p. 216.

45   Spindler, *Burgbach*, pp. 17, 77–78.

46   Schnabel, 'Warum geht es in Schwaben besser?', pp. 189–90.

47   HStAS, E151/01, Bü673, pp. 2–5.

48   Schnabel, 'Warum geht es in Schwaben besser?', pp. 189–90.

49   S.H. Franklin, *The European Peasantry: The Final Phase* (London, 1969), pp. 58–60.

50   Kaschuba, 'Peasants and Others', pp. 238–39.

51   Schnabel, 'Warum geht es in Schwaben besser?', p. 191.

52   AIDA, *Die Sozialstruktur*, pp. 21–25, quotation from p. 22.

53   Golde, *Catholics and Protestants*, p. 36.

54   Spindler, *Burgbach*, p. 17.

55   Gerhard Wilke and Kurt Wagner, 'Family and Household: Social Structures in a German Village between the Two World Wars', in Richard J. Evans and W.R. Lee (eds), *The German Family* (London, 1981), p. 122. See also Jeggle, 'Rules of the Village', pp. 284–87. Cf. Kaschuba, 'Peasants and Others', pp. 247–48.

56   Franklin, *The European Peasantry*, p. 56.

57   Jeggle, 'The Rules of the Village', p. 287.

58　Bernd Burkhardt, *Eine Stadt wird braun: die nationalsozialistische Machtergreifung in der Provinz. Eine Fallstudie* (Hamburg, 1980), pp. 11–12.

59　Golde, *Catholics and Protestants*, pp. 17–18.

60　Franklin, *The European Peasantry*, p. 60.

61　Schnabel, 'Warum geht es in Schwaben besser?', p. 186; Schnabel, *Württemberg zwischen Weimar und Bonn*, p. 18.

62　Weller and Weller, *Württembergische Geschichte*, pp. 273, 296; Schnabel, 'Warum geht es in Schwaben besser?', p. 188.

63　From a newspaper article, dated 25 December 1932, reproduced in Schnabel, 'Warum geht es in Schwaben besser?', pp. 216–17. See also Detlef Mühlberger, *Hitler's Followers: Studies in the Sociology of the Nazi Movement* (London, 1991), pp. 51, 54.

64　Schnabel, 'Warum geht es in Schwaben besser?', p. 187.

65　From a newspaper article, dated 25 December 1932, reproduced in Schnabel, 'Warum geht es in Schwaben besser?', p. 214. Cf. Roland Müller, *Stuttgart zur Zeit des Nationalsozialismus* (Stuttgart, 1988), 'Einleitung I: Stuttgart, Oase in der Krise', pp. 3–11.

66　Burkhardt, *Eine Stadt wird braun*, p. 58.

67　Sauer, *Württemberg*, p. 15; Weller and Weller, *Württembergische Geschichte*, p. 296; Kissener and Scholtyseck, 'Nationalsozialismus in der Provinz', p. 21.

68　Burkhardt, *Eine Stadt wird braun*, pp. 13–14.

69　Müller, *Stuttgart zur Zeit des Nationalsozialismus*, p. 8; Hartmut Berghoff, *Zwischen Kleinstadt und Weltmarkt: Hohner und die Harmonika, 1857–1961* (Paderborn, 1997), pp. 420–21. I am indebted to Frank Bajohr for bringing this book to my attention.

70　AIDA, *Die Sozialstruktur*, p. 25; Kaschuba, 'Peasants and Others', pp. 240, 249. The quotation is from p. 240. See also Franklin, *The European Peasantry*, p. 54, on the 'famous "Puffer" or cushion argument', that worker peasants could withdraw from industrial employment to their farm in time of high unemployment.

71　HStAS, E151/03, Bü968: Der Landrat (Ulm) an den Herrn Innenminister, 'Betreff: Verteilung der Wohnungen; hier: Unterbringung der Umquartierten aus Stuttgart und Essen', 10 March 1944; Der Landrat (Crailsheim) an den Herrn Württ. Innenminister, 'Betreff: Unterbringung von Luftkriegsbetroffenen im Kreis Crailsheim', 16 March 1944.

72　Burkhardt, *Eine Stadt wird braun*, p. 11.

73　Golde, *Catholics and Protestants*, p. 26; Kaschuba, 'Peasants and Others', p. 238.

74　Kurt Leipner (ed.), *Chronik der Stadt Stuttgart, 1933–1945* (Stuttgart, 1982), p. 99.

75　StAL, K110, Bü47, SD 'Lagebericht,' 15 July 1941, pp. 18–19, 22–23.

76　AIDA, *Die Sozialstruktur*, pp. 11–12.

77　Neil Gregor, *Daimler-Benz in the Third Reich* (New Haven, Connecticut, and London, 1998), pp. 21–26, 36–42; Willi A. Boelcke, 'Wirtschaft und Sozialsituation', in Otto Borst (ed.), *Das Dritte Reich in Baden und Württemberg* (Stuttgart, 1988), pp. 30–31.

78　AIDA, *Die Sozialstruktur*, pp. 11–12.

79　Sauer, *Wilhelm Murr*, p. 101.

80　HStAS, E151/1, Bü3960, 'Geschäftsbericht des Technischen Landesamts über die Zeit vom 1. April bis 30. Juni 1939'.

81　Golde, *Catholics and Protestants*, p. 26; Spindler, *Burgbach*, p. 79.

82　AIDA, *Die Sozialstruktur*, p. 12; Boelcke, 'Wirtschaft und Sozialsituation', p. 30.

83   David Schoenbaum, *Hitler's Social Revolution: Class and Status in Nazi Germany, 1933–39* (London, 1967), pp. 174–75; J.E. Farquharson, *The Plough and the Swastika: The NSDAP and Agriculture in Germany, 1928–1945* (London, 1976), p. 42. See also Daniela Münkel, '"Der Runkdfunk geht auf die Dörfer": der Einzug der Massmedien auf dem Lande von den zwanziger bis zu den sechziger Jahren', in Daniela Münkel (ed.), *Der lange Abschied vom Agrarland: Agrarpolitik, Landwirtschaft und ländliche Gesellschaft zwischen Weimar und Bonn* (Göttingen, 2000), pp. 184–92.

84   Quoted in Lionel Kochan, *Russia in Revolution* (London, 1970), p. 64.

85   StAL, K110: the first quotation is from Bü44, 'Lagebericht des 4. Vierteljahres 1938', 1 February, 1939, p. 11; the second quotation is from Bü45, 'Lagebericht des 1. Vierteljahres 1939, 1 April, 1939, p. 22. See also Schoenbaum, *Hitler's Social Revolution*, p. 162. Cf. Detlev J.K. Peukert, *Inside Nazi Germany: Conformity, Opposition and Racism in Everyday Life*, trans. Richard Deveson (London, 1987), pp. 99–100.

86   Bessel, *Germany After the First World War*, pp. 212–19; Kohler, 'Inflation and Black Marketeering in the Rhenish Agricultural Economy', pp. 49–64; Farquharson, *The Plough and the Swastika*, p. 14; Kershaw, *Popular Opinion*, pp. 36–37.

87   Jeremy Noakes and Geoffrey Pridham (eds), *Nazism, 1919–1945: A Documentary Reader*, i: *The Rise to Power* (Exeter, 1983), pp. 15, 61. See also Farquharson, *The Plough and the Swastika*, pp. 1–3, 13; Thomas Childers, *The Nazi Voter: The Social Foundations of Fascism in Germany, 1919–1933* (Chapel Hill, North Carolina, 1983), pp. 150–51; Michael H. Kater, *The Nazi Party: A Social Profile of Members and Leaders, 1919–1945* (Cambridge, Massachusetts, 1983), pp. 39–41; Geoffrey Pridham, *Hitler's Rise to Power: The Nazi Movement in Bavaria, 1923–33* (London, 1973), pp. 116–17.

88   Schoenbaum, *Hitler's Social Revolution*, p. 163. Cf. Ursula Büttner, '"Volksgemeinschaft" oder Heimatbindung: Zentralismus und regionale Eigenständigkeit beim Aufstieg der NSDAP, 1925–1933', in Horst Möller, Andreas Wirsching and Walter Ziegler (eds), *Nationalsozialismus in der Region: Beiträge zur regionalen und lokalen Forschung und zum internationalen Vergleich* (Munich, 1996), pp. 88ff. See also Johnpeter Horst Grill, *The Nazi Movement in Baden, 1920–1945* (Chapel Hill, North Carolina, 1983), pp. 144–50. Oded Heilbronner, *Catholicism, Political Culture, and the Countryside: A Social History of the Nazi Party in South Germany* (Ann Arbor, Michigan, 1998), is devoted to this subject. See also the work of Daniela Münkel: *Bauern und Nationalsozialismus: der Landkreis Celle im Dritten Reich* (Bielefeld, 1991), pp. 32, 36–51; *Nationalsozialistische Agrarpolitik und Bauernalltag*, pp. 68–85.

89   Ibid., pp. 136–40; Kershaw, *Popular Opinion*, p. 37; Pridham, *Hitler's Rise to Power*, pp. 117–18; Jeremy Noakes, *The Nazi Party in Lower Saxony, 1921–1933* (Oxford, 1971), pp. 109–11.

90   Farquharson, *The Plough and the Swastika*, pp. 4–12, 25–36. The quotation is from p. 30.

91   Ibid., pp. 15–24. The quotation is from p. 19. See also Childers, *The Nazi Voter*, pp. 151, 215–16; cf. Heilbronner, *Catholicism, Political Culture, and the Countryside*, pp. 150–54.

92   Kershaw, *Popular Opinion*, p. 38.

93   Childers, *The Nazi Voter*, pp. 215–16; Kershaw, *Popular Opinion*, p. 37; Grill, *The Nazi Movement in Baden*, pp. 229–30; Pridham, *Hitler's Rise to Power*, pp. 121–23. Cf. Gustavo Corni, 'Richard Walther Darré – The "Blut-und-Boden" Ideologe', in Ronald Smelser and

Rainer Zitelmann (eds), *Die Braune Elite I: 22 biographische Skizzen* (Darmstadt, 1989), pp. 18–19.

94   Thomas Schnabel, 'Die NSDAP in Württemberg, 1928–1933: die Schwäche einer regionalen Parteiorganisation', in Schnabel, *Die Machtergreifung in Südwestdeutschland*, p. 49. See also Wolfram Pyta, 'Ländlich-evangelisches Milieu und Nationalsozialismus bis 1933', in Möller, Wirsching and Ziegler, *Nationalsozialismus in der Region*, pp. 199–212. Pyta focuses overwhelmingly on northern and eastern Germany. In *Landkreis* Celle, e.g., over 90 per cent of the inhabitants were Evangelical. See Münkel, *Bauern und Nationalsozialismus*, p. 32.

95   Kissener and Scholtyseck, 'Nationalsozialismus in der Provinz', p. 22.

96   Ibid., pp. 20–21. See also Sauer, *Wilhelm Murr*, pp. 12–19; Arbogast, *Herrschaftsinstanzen der württembergischen NSDAP*, pp. 22–26; Müller, *Stuttgart zur Zeit des Nationalsozialismus*, pp. 21–22; Schönhagen, *Tübingen unterm Hakenkreuz*, pp. 42–45; Mühlberger, *Hitler's Followers*, pp. 55–56.

97   Büttner, '"Volksgemeinschaft" oder Heimatbindung', p. 90.

98   Schnabel, *Württemberg zwischen Weimar und Bonn*, pp. 29–30, 42–43, 112–13; Weller and Weller, *Württembergische Geschichte*, pp. 269–70. Schnabel, 'Die NSDAP in Württemberg, 1928–1933', p. 57; Burkhardt, *Eine Stadt wird braun*, pp. 66, 69, 94, 96–97.

99   Thomas Schnabel, 'Das Wahlverhalten der Katholiken in Württemberg, 1928–1933', in Geschichtsverein der Diözese Rottenburg-Stuttgart (ed.), *Kirche im Nationalsozialismus* (Sigmaringen, 1984), p. 104.

100   Schnabel, *Die Machtergreifung in Südwestdeutschland*, appendix 4, pp. 312–13.

101   Ibid., p. 313; Eberhard Schanbacher, 'Das Wählervotum und die "Machtergreifung" im deutschen Südwesten', in Schnabel, *Die Machtergreifung in Südwestdeutschland*, pp. 299–304.

102   Schnabel, 'Das Wahlverhalten der Katholiken in Württemberg', p. 104.

103   Schnabel, *Württemberg zwischen Weimar und Bonn*, pp. 39–40.

104   Childers, *The Nazi Voter*, pp. 148, 319 n. 106.

105   Schnabel, 'Die NSDAP in Württemberg, 1928–1933', pp. 58–59, and Appendix 4, pp. 312–13.

106   Schnabel, *Württemberg zwischen Weimar und Bonn*, p. 34.

107   Schnabel, 'Die NSDAP in Württemberg, 1928–1933', pp. 66–68. The quotation is from p. 67.

108   Schnabel, *Die Machtergreifung in Südwestdeutschland*, pp. 312–313; Schnabel, *Württemberg zwischen Weimar und Bonn*, pp. 116–22. The quotations are from p. 118.

109   Müller, *Stuttgart zur Zeit des Nationalsozialismus*, p. 13; Noakes and Pridham, *Nazism*, i, p. 83.

110   Schanbacher, 'Das Wählervotum', pp. 306–07.

111   Münkel, *Nationalsozialistische Agrarpolitik*, p. 522.

112   Schnabel, *Die Machtergreifung in Südwestdeutschland*, p. 313.

113   Schnabel, 'Die NSDAP in Württemberg, 1928–1933', p. 59; Schanbacher, 'Das Wählervotum', p. 307. Cf. electoral patterns in Bavaria in Kershaw, *Popular Opinion*, pp. 18–27; Pridham, *Hitler's Rise to Power*, pp. 282–84, 290.

114   Mühlberger, *Hitler's Followers*, p. 50; Schanbacher, 'Das Wählervotum', p. 300.

115   Sauer, *Wilhelm Murr*, p. 25.

116   Schnabel, 'Das Wahlverhalten der Katholiken in Württemberg', p. 110.

117   Mühlberger, *Hitler's Followers*, p. 50.

118 Kissener and Scholtyseck, 'Nationalsozialismus in der Provinz', p. 21: 'der Südwesten Deutschlands [war] eine "erste Hochburg des Liberalismus"'.

119 Mühlberger, *Hitler's Followers*, p. 55.

120 Schnabel, 'Die NSDAP in Württemberg, 1928–1933', p. 49.

121 For a brief discussion of the 'middle-class thesis' in electoral terms, see: John Hiden and John Farquharson, *Explaining Hitler's Germany: Historians and the Third Reich* (2nd edn, London, 1989), pp. 86–91; Jürgen Falter, '"Anfälligkeit" der Angestellten – "Immunität" der Arbeiter? Mythen über die Wähler der NSDAP', in U. Backes, E. Jesse and R. Zitelmann (eds), *Die Schatten der Vergangenheit: Impulse zur Historisierung des Nationalsozialismus* (Frankfurt and Berlin, 1990), pp. 272–82. See also Thomas Childers and Jane Caplan, 'Introduction', in T. Childers and J. Caplan (eds), *Reevaluating the Third Reich* (New York, 1993), p. 14, n. 6.

122 Müller, *Stuttgart zur Zeit des Nationalsozialismus*, p. 17; Benigna Schönhagen, *Tübingen unterm Hakenkreuz: eine Universitätsstadt in der Zeit des Nationalsozialismus* (Stuttgart, 1991), p. 39; Barbara Hachmann, 'Der "Degen": Dietrich von Jagow, SA-Obergruppenführer', in Kissener and Scholtyseck, *Die Führer der Provinz*, pp. 271–73; Christine Arbogast, *Herrschaftsinstanzen der württembergischen NSDAP: Funktion, Sozialprofil und Lebenswege einer regionalen NS-Elite, 1920–1960* (Munich, 1998), pp. 20–24. Cf. ibid., p. 10: 'Obwohl Württemberg in den frühen 20er Jahren als nationalsozialistische Hochburg galt …'

123 Gunther Mai, *Die Geislinger Metallarbeiterbewegung* (Düsseldorf, 1984), pp. 54–55.

124 Schnabel, 'Die NSDAP in Württemberg, 1928–1933', pp. 52–53; Arbogast, *Herrschaftsinstanzen der württembergischen NSDAP*, pp. 22–27. Dietrich Orlow, *The History of the Nazi Party, 1919–1933* (Newton Abbot, 1971), p. 97, says: 'Hitler and Goebbels travelled to Stuttgart to receive Mergenthaler personally' into the NSDAP. See also Sauer, *Wilhelm Murr*, p. 13.

125 Arbogast, *Herrschaftsinstanzen der württembergischen NSDAP*, p. 29. Cf. the discussion in Heilbronner, *Catholicism, Political Culture, and the Countryside*, pp. 78–80.

126 Schnabel, 'Die NSDAP in Württemberg, 1928–1933', p. 66. The counties were Biberach, Ehingen, Laupheim and Riedlingen.

127 Mühlberger, *Hitler's Followers*, pp. 62–65, 78–79.

128 Kater, *The Nazi Party*, p. 25.

129 Joachim Scholtyseck, '"Der Mann aus dem Volk": Wilhelm Murr, Gauleiter und Reichsstatthalter in Württemberg-Hohenzollern', in Kissener and Scholtyseck, *Die Führer der Provinz*, p. 483.

130 Reichsorganisationsleiter (ed.), *NSDAP Partei-Statistik* (Munich, 1935), i, p. 150. Cf., on Bavaria, Kershaw, *Popular Opinion*, pp. 27–28.

131 Jill Stephenson, *The Nazi Organisation of Women* (London, 1981), pp. 53–54. See also Arbogast, *Herrschaftsinstanzen der württembergischen NSDAP*, pp. 27–28.

132 Hubert Roser, 'Vom Dorfschultheiss zum hohen Ministerialbeamten: Georg Stümpfig, Kanzleidirektor im Württembergischen Innenministerium und Gauamtsleiter für Kommunalpolitik', in Kissener and Scholtyseck, *Die Führer der Provinz*, p. 687.

133 Berghoff, *Zwischen Kleinstadt und Weltmarkt*, pp. 424–30; Hartmut Berghoff and Cornelia Rauh-Kühne, *Fritz K.: Ein deutsches Leben im zwanzigsten Jahrhundert* (Stuttgart and Munich, 2000), pp. 10, 47–49. The quotation is from p. 47. I am indebted to Frank Bajohr for drawing my attention to this book.

134 Burkhardt, *Eine Stadt wird braun*, p. 130. There were minority governments also in Bavaria, Hesse, Saxony and Hamburg. On this and its consequences, see Martin Broszat, *The Hitler State: The Foundations and Development of the Internal Structure of the Third Reich*, trans. John W. Hiden (London, 1981), pp. 97–100.

135 Schnabel, *Die Machtergreifung in Südwestdeutschland*, pp. 312–313; Schnabel, 'Die NSDAP in Württemberg, 1928–1933', p. 72; Roser, 'Vom Dorfschultheiss zum hohen Ministerialbeamten', p. 687.

136 Sauer, *Württemberg*, pp. 14–28; Schnabel, *Württemberg zwischen Weimar und Bonn*, pp. 161–87; Hachmann, 'Der "Degen": Dietrich von Jagow', pp. 278–79. See also Broszat, *The Hitler State*, pp. 101–104; Burkhardt, *Eine Stadt wird braun*, pp. 137–46; Berghoff, *Zwischen Kleinstadt und Weltmarkt*, p. 430.

137 Sauer, *Wilhelm Murr*, pp. 34–36.

138 Noakes and Pridham, *Nazism*, i, p. 167; Leipner, *Chronik der Stadt Stuttgart*, p. 54.

139 Weller and Weller, *Württembergische Geschichte*, p. 304; Sauer, *Württemberg*, pp. 38, 50, 58–62; Borgstedt, 'Im Zweifelsfall auch mit harter Hand', p. 609.

140 Sauer, *Wilhelm Murr*, pp. 36–39; Scholtyseck, 'Der Mann aus dem Volk', p. 487.

141 On Germany from 1918 to 1933, see especially Richard J. Evans, *The Coming of the Third Reich* (London, 2003); Bessel, *Germany After the First World War*; Detlev J.K. Peukert, *The Weimar Republic: The Crisis of Classical Modernity*, trans. Richard Deveson (London, 1992); Eberhard Kolb, *The Weimar Republic*, trans. P.S. Falla (London, 1988); Harold James, *The German Slump: Politics and Economics, 1924–1936* (Oxford, 1986); Timothy W. Mason, *Sozialpolitik im Dritten Reich: Arbeiterklasse und Volksgemeinschaft* (Opladen, 1977), chapters 1 and 2. English edition: Tim Mason, *Social Policy in the Third Reich: The Working Class and the 'National Community'* (Providence, Rhode Island, and Oxford, 1993), ed. Jane Caplan; trans. John Broadwin.

142 Schnabel, *Württemberg zwischen Weimar und Bonn*, pp. 533–36. On farmers' relations with Jewish livestock traders, see below, Chapter 4.

143 Jeremy Noakes and Geoffrey Pridham (eds), *Nazism, 1919–1945: A Documentary Reader*, ii, *State, Economy and Society, 1933–39* (Exeter, 1986), pp. 223–25, 523–25.

144 Ibid., pp. 534–37.

145 Schnabel, *Württemberg zwischen Weimar und Bonn*, p. 565.

146 For 'the SA of Jesus Christ', see Karl Dietrich Bracher, *The German Dictatorship: The Origins, Structure, and Effects of National Socialism*, trans. Jean Steinberg (London, 1971), p. 471. For the 'Aryan paragraph', see Ernst Christian Helmreich, *The German Churches under Hitler: Background, Struggle, and Epilogue* (Detroit, Michigan, 1979), p. 144. On the German Christians, see Doris L. Bergen, *Twisted Cross: The German Christian Movement in the Third Reich* (Chapel Hill, North Carolina, 1996).

147 On the Confessing Church, see Helmreich, *The German Churches under Hitler*, passim; Richard Steigmann-Gall, *The Holy Reich: Nazi Conceptions of Christianity, 1919–45* (Cambridge, 2003), pp. 171–87.

148 In Bavaria, after 1918 the Centre was known as the Bavarian People's Party. On the negotiations for the Concordat, see John Cornwell, *Hitler's Pope: The Secret History of Pius XII* (London, 2000), pp. 141–50.

149 Schnabel, *Württemberg zwischen Weimar und Bonn*, pp. 268–69.

150   Schönhagen, *Tübingen unterm Hakenkreuz*, p. 166.

151   Schnabel, *Württemberg zwischen Weimar und Bonn*, pp. 268–69, 404–5, 408, 410–12, 469–70.

152   Kyle Jantzen, 'Propaganda, Perseverance and Protest: Strategies for Clerical Survival amid the German Church Struggle', *Church History: Studies in Christianity and Culture*, 70 (2001), pp. 296–97. I am indebted to John J. Delaney for giving me a copy of this journal.

153   Berghoff, *Zwischen Kleinstadt und Weltmarkt*, p. 452.

154   Schönhagen, *Tübingen unterm Hakenkreuz*, pp. 169–71.

155   Joachim Köhler, 'Die katholische Kirche in Baden und Württemberg in der Endphase der Weimarer Republik und zu Beginn des Dritten Reiches', in Schnabel, *Die Machtergreifung in Südwestdeutschland*, p. 26; Jörg Thierfelder, 'Die Kirchen', in Otto Borst (ed.), *Das Dritte Reich in Baden und Württemberg* (Stuttgart, 1988), p. 83.

156   'Ich habe versucht, dem Wort Gottes gehorsam zu sein: Interview mit Alfred Leikam', in Bettina Wenke, *Interviews mit Überlebenden: Verfolgung und Widerstand in Südwestdeutschland* (Stuttgart, 1980), pp. 123–24; Thierfelder, 'Die Kirchen', p. 84.

157   Sauer, *Württemberg*, p. 198.

158   'Ich habe versucht, dem Wort Gottes gehorsam zu sein', pp. 123–24; Georg May, *Kirchenkampf oder Katholikenverfolgung? Ein Beitrag zu dem gegenseitigen Verhältnis von Nationalsozialismus und christlichen Bekenntnissen* (Stein am Rhein, 1991), p. 443.

159   Paul Kopf, 'Buchau am Federsee in nationalsozialistischer Zeit: die Ereignisse der Jahre 1934 bis 1938', in Geschichtsverein der Diözese Rottenburg-Stuttgart, *Kirche im Nationalsozialismus*, pp. 274–78; Rudolf Renz, 'Kirchenkampf in Ellwangen: Bericht eines Zeitgenossen', in ibid., pp. 264–66.

160   The quotation is from Avraham Barkai, *Nazi Economics: Ideology, Theory, and Policy*, trans. by Ruth Hadass-Vaschitz (Oxford and Providence, Rhode Island, 1990), p. 139.

161   Noakes and Pridham, *Nazism*, ii, p. 317.

162   Mason, *Sozialpolitik im Dritten Reich*, pp. 136–50, 159–62.

163   Gustavo Corni and Horst Gies, *Brot, Butter, Kanonen: die Ernährungswirtschaft in Deutschland unter der Diktatur Hitlers* (Berlin, 1997), pp. 201–9, 266, 274–80, 399–406.

164   Leipner, *Chronik der Stadt Stuttgart*, p. 54.

165   Münkel, *Bauern und Nationalsozialismus*, pp. 61–62; Kershaw, *Popular Opinion*, pp. 40–41; Farquharson, *The Plough and the Swastika*, pp. 75–85; Theresia Bauer, *Nationalsozialistische Agrarpolitik und bäuerliches Verhalten im Zweiten Weltkrieg: eine Regionalstudie zur ländlichen Gesellschaft in Bayern* (Frankfurt am Main, 1996), pp. 184–85.

166   Sauer, *Württemberg*, p. 279. See also Schnabel, *Württemberg zwischen Weimar und Bonn*, pp. 227–28; Farquharson, *The Plough and the Swastika*, p. 61.

167   Michael Rademacher, *Handbuch der NSDAP-Gaue, 1928–1945: die Amtsträger der NSDAP und ihrer Organisationen auf Gau- und Kreisebene in Deutschland und Österreich sowie in den Reichsgauen Danzig-Westpreussen, Sudetenland und Warthegau* (Vechta, 2000), pp. 330–31. On the many jurisdictional conflicts involving the RNS, see Corni and Gies, *Brot, Butter, Kanonen*, pp. 170–248.

168   Farquharson, *The Plough and the Swastika*, pp. 92, 97, 188–89; Stephenson, *The Nazi Organisation of Women*, pp. 132, 140–41, 162; Barkai, *Nazi Economics*, p. 151.

169 StAL: K631/I, 'Wochenblatt der Landesbauernschaft Württemberg', 11 May 1935, p. 5; K631/II, Bü83, 'Verzeichnis der Kreisbauernschaften', 20 June 1939 names the twenty as Biberach, Bietigheim, Calw, Crailsheim, Ehingen, Hall, Hechingen (Hohenzollern), Heidenheim, Heilbronn, Künzelsau, Leutkirche, Ravensburg, Reutlingen, Rottweil, Saulgau, Sigmaringen (Hohenzollern), Stuttgart, Tübingen, Ulm, Waiblingen.

170 Ibid., K631/II, Bü70, Landesbauernschaft Württemberg: Vorläufige Geschäftsordnung, 30 January 1936, pp. 1–17. The quotation is from p. 6.

171 Ibid., Landesbauernschaft Württemberg, Geschäfts-Verteilungsplan des Verwaltungsamtes, 28 January 1936.

172 Ibid., Bü84: 'Geschäfts – Verteilungs – Plan des Viehwirtschaftsverbandes Württemberg', 15 October 1938; 'Geschäftsverteilungsplan des Viehwirtschaftsverbandes Württemberg mit Wirkung vom 1. April 1941', 1 April 1941; Der Landesbauernführer an den Viehwirtschaftsverband Württemberg, 'Betr.: Beirat der Marktgemeinschaft Stuttgart', 17 July 1936.

173 Ibid., Der Landesbauernführer an den Viehwirtschaftsverband Württemberg, 'Betr.: Beirat der Marktgemeinschaft Stuttgart', 8 February 1938.

174 Ibid., 'Verbindungsleute', 1943.

175 Bauer, Nationalsozialistische Agrarpolitik und bäuerliches Verhalten, p. 24.

176 Schnabel, Württemberg zwischen Weimar und Bonn, pp. 216–17. The quotation is from p. 217. See also Leipner, Chronik der Stadt Stuttgart, p. 227; Boelcke, 'Wirtschaft und Sozialsituation', p. 37. More generally, see Farquharson, The Plough and the Swastika, pp. 66–67; Barkai, Nazi Economics, p. 144.

177 Noakes and Pridham, Nazism, ii, pp. 319–20, gives the text of the Reichserbhofgesetz of 29 September 1933. See also Farquharson, The Plough and the Swastika, chapter 8, 'The Erbhof Law', pp. 107–23, and passim; Münkel, Bauern und Nationalsozialismus, pp. 114–31; Corni, 'Richard Walther Darré', pp. 21–22. On women as farm proprietors, see Münkel, Nationalsozialistische Agrarpolitik und Bauernalltag, pp. 452–63.

178 Rinderle and Norling, The Nazi Impact on a German Village, p. 145.

179 Kershaw, Popular Opinion, pp. 42–44; Noakes and Pridham, Nazism, ii, pp. 320–21.

180 Farquharson, The Plough and the Swastika, p. 267.

181 Ibid., p. 115.

182 StAL, K631/I, Bü1642, 'Liste die Erbhöfe der KBsch Stuttgart betreffend (7.7.39)'.

183 HStAS, E397, Bü37, 'Abschrift. Sondergericht für den Oberlandesgerichtsbezirk Stuttgart in Stuttgart, SL.Nr.523–526/42. I 22 SJs.1313–16/42.', 24 November 1942.

184 Günter Neliba, 'Führerprinzip', in Wolfgang Benz, Hermann Graml and Hermann Weiss (eds), Enzyklopädie des Nationalsozialismus (Munich, 1997), p. 475.

185 Hiden, Republican and Fascist Germany, pp. 158–59. See also Farquharson, The Plough and the Swastika, pp. 43–49; Corni and Gies, Brot, Butter, Kanonen, pp. 79–99, 212–28.

186 Münkel, Nationalsozialistische Agrarpolitik und Bauernalltag, p. 129.

187 StAL, PL504/22, Bü6, Der Ortsgruppenleiter Nürtingen an die NS-Formationen der Ortsgruppe, 24 May 1935.

188 StAL, K110, Bü45, pp. 12–13.

189 Ibid., K631/II, Bü29, Gesch.-Z. II C 240/1/39, 'Betr.: Hohenloher Wasserversorgungsgruppe', 13 October 1939.

190 HStAS, E151/03, Bü968, Der Landrat (Crailsheim) an den Herrn Württ. Innenminister, 'Betreff: Unterbringung von Luftkriegsbetroffenen im Kreis Crailsheim', 16 March 1944.

191 StAL, K631/II, Bü39, 'Gutachten für das Dränung in Schnaitbach, Gemeinde Laupertshausen, Kreis Biberach/Riss', 26 January 1939.

192 Ibid., 'Gutachten – Dürnachverbesserung mit Dränung in Ringschnait, Kreis Biberach/Riss, 20 March 1939. There are other examples of this in the same Büschel.

193 Ibid., K631/I, Bü1625, Heinrich Kaul, 'Kunder erbeingesessenen Bauerntums', 7 July 1936, pp. 1–5.

194 Ibid., Landesbauernschaft Württemberg an die Vertreter der zur Auszeichnung kommenden alteingesessenen Bauerngeschlechter, 13 April 1935.

195 Ibid., Bü1645: two letters of 26 June 1935; 'Betr.: Erster Erntewagen', 18 July 1935; Landesbauernschaft Württemberg to the Ortsbauernführer Ruppertshofen, Kreis Gaildorf, 19 July 1935; Landesbauernschaft Württemberg internal memo I B 10625/35, 21 August 1935; Bü1625, 'Betr.: Ehrung alteingesessener Bauerngeschlechter', 9 May 1935. Brach (archaic) = fallow; Heu = hay; Ernte = harvest; Mond (archaic) = month.

196 Ibid.: NS-Gemeinschaft Kraft durch Freude, 'Betr: Sonderzug zum Staatsakt auf dem Bückeberg am 6.10.1935', 11 September 1935; 'An das Kreisamt der DAF … Wangen i.A.', 19 September 1935; Kreisbauernschaft Alb an die Landesbauernschaft Württemberg, 18 January 1936; Landesbauernschaft Württemberg internal memo, 23 January 1936. 'Sonnenwendfeier' is also rendered as 'Sonnwendfeier'.

197 Ibid., 'Betr.: Erster Erntewagen', 18 July 1935. There are several letters and postcards on the same subject in this file. See also Wolfgang Kashuba, 'Peasants and Others: The Historical Contours of Village Class Society', in Evans and Lee, The German Peasantry, p. 236.

198 Berghoff and Rauh-Kühne, Fritz K., pp. 158–59.

199 BBC2, People's Century, 1900–1999, 'Master Race', 1995.

200 Barkai, Nazi Economics, p. 145. The Zwangswirtschaft was either implicitly or explicitly referred to in complaints about the new system, for example, Kershaw, Popular Opinion, p. 46.

201 Münkel, Nationalsozialistische Agrarpolitik und Bauernalltag, p. 328.

202 StAL, K110: Bü44, p. 19; Bü46, 'Lagebericht des 2. Vierteljahres 1939', 1 July 1939, p. 37; HStAS, E151/01cII, Bü434, Kommandeur der Gendarmerie des Landes Württemberg an den Württ. Innenminister, 'Tätigkeitsbericht für das Jahr 1939', 1 February 1940, p. 9; Kershaw, Popular Opinion, pp. 45–46, 47 n.52, 54; Münkel, Nationalsozialistische Agrarpolitik und Bauernalltag, pp. 106–12.

203 Schnabel, Württemberg zwischen Weimar und Bonn, pp. 214–18.

204 Boelcke, 'Wirtschaft und Sozialsituation', p. 43. See also StAL, K110, Bü46, p. 37; Kershaw, Popular Opinion, p. 283.

205 AIDA, Die Sozialstruktur, pp. 18–22; StAL, K110: Bü44, pp. 18–19; Bü46, pp. 35, 42; Münkel, Bauern und Nationalsozialismus, pp. 84–90; Kershaw, Popular Opinion, pp. 55–63.

206 Boelcke, 'Wirtschaft und Sozialsituation', pp. 30–35.

207 HStAS, E151/01, Bü3596.

208 Leipner, Chronik der Stadt Stuttgart, p. 121.

209 StAL, K110, Bü44, pp. 22–23.

210 AIDA, *Die Sozialstruktur*, pp. 14–21; Staatsarchiv Ludwigsburg (StAL), K110, Bü36, Sicherheitsdienst RFSS, Unterabschnitt Württ.-Hohenz., II/236 Ha/Sc, Rundschr. Nr.83/39, 'Betr.: Störungen des planmäßigen Arbeitseinsatzes', 19 May 1939. See also Kershaw, *Popular Opinion*, pp. 59–60.

211 HStAS, E151/01, Bü3596, 'Betrifft: Arbeitseinsatz der Jugendlichen', 28 July 1936.

212 Ibid., E151/01, Bü3596, An den Herrn Ministerialdirektor, 8 April 1937.

213 *Deutschland-Berichte der Sozialdemokratischen Partei Deutschlands* (Paris), 1939, no. 6, 12 July 1939, pp. A59–61. The quotation is from p. A60.

214 AIDA, *Die Sozialstruktur*, pp. 6, 27–29.

215 StAL, K110, Bü45, p. 34.

216 Ibid., Bü46, p. 25.

217 *Deutschland-Berichte*, 1939, no. 6, 12 July 1939, p. A65.

218 StAL, K110, Bü46, p. 25.

219 Anecdotal information from a friend who was a teenager at the time.

220 StAL, K110, Bü44, 1 February 1939, pp. 18–19.

221 Ibid., Bü45, pp. 45–46.

222 Ibid., Bü46, p. 42. See also Jill Stephenson, 'Women's Labor Service in Nazi Germany', *Central European History*, 15 (1982), pp. 258–59.

223 *Deutschland-Berichte*, 1939, no. 6, 12 July 1939, pp. A63–64; Tholander, *Fremdarbeiter, 1939 bis 1945*, p. 34.

224 AIDA, *Die Sozialstruktur*, pp. 20–21.

225 Franklin, *The European Peasantry*, pp. 41–42.

226 AIDA, *Die Sozialstruktur*, p. 28; StAL, K110, Bü45, pp. 43–45; 'Bevölkerungspolitik und Rassenpflege auf dem Lande', *Völkischer Beobachter*, 13/14 May 1934 (Racial Hygiene supplement); Lore Kleiber, '"Wo ihr seid, da soll die Sonne scheinen!" – Der Frauenarbeitsdienst am Ende der Weimarer Republik und im Nationalsozialismus', in Frauengruppe Faschismusforschung (ed.), *Mutterkreuz und Arbeitsbuch* (Frankfurt am Main, 1981), pp. 208–9; Münkel, *Nationalsozialistische Agrarpolitik und Bauernalltag*, pp. 439–65; Münkel, *Bauern und Nationalsozialismus*, pp. 88–89.

227 Schnabel, *Württemberg zwischen Weimar und Bonn*, p. 574.

228 Barkai, *Nazi Economics*, pp. 156–57.

229 StAL, K110, Bü45, 1 April 1939, p. 12.

230 Ibid., p. 43.

231 AIDA, *Die Sozialstruktur*, pp. 28–29.

232 Sauer, *Württemberg*, pp. 183–84; Thierfelder, 'Die Kirchen', p. 83.

233 Sauer, *Württemberg*, pp. 203–4; Scholtyseck, 'Der Mann aus dem Volk', p. 492; Guenter Lewy, *The Catholic Church and Nazi Germany* (London, 1964), pp. 217–18.

234 Sauer, *Wilhelm Murr*, pp. 90–91; Scholtyseck, 'Der Mann aus dem Volk', pp. 492–93; Arbogast, *Herrschaftsinstanzen der württembergischen NSDAP*, p. 212.

235 Conway, *The Nazi Persecution of the Churches*, p. 224.

236 Sauer, *Württemberg*, pp. 198–203; Sabine Schmidt, 'Vom Hilfsarbeiter zum Kreisleiter: Eugen Maier, NSDAP-Kreisleiter von Ulm', in Kissener and Scholtyseck, *Die Führer der Provinz*, p. 383. I am grateful to Dr Kevin Spicer for information about sexual abuse in the Catholic Church.

237   StAL, Bü46, p. 37.

238   Ibid., Bü44, p. 23; HStAS, E151/01, Bü652, 'Zweckmässigkeit der Neueinteilung des Landes', n.d. (1938), p. 2.

239   StAL, Bü44, p. 19.

240   Ibid., Bü45, p. 43.

241   Ibid., Bü46, p. 36.

242   HStAS, E151cII, Bü394a, Der Innenminister [Württemberg], Nr III A 5450/17W, 'Betreff: Einstellung von Hilfspolizeibeamten zur Bekämpfung der Maul- und Klauenseuche', 4 March 1939.

243   Ibid., 'Verzeichnis der von der Maul- und Klauenseuche stärker betroffenen Kreise. Stand vom 10. Januar 1939'.

244   Ibid.: Der Innenminister [Württemberg], 4 March 1939; Der Landrat (Ulm) an den Herrn Württ. Innenminister, 'Betreff: Seuchenüberwachung; hier: Anstellung des Oberlandjägers a.D ... in Beimerstetten, 3 February 1939.

245   Ibid.: Der Reichsführer SS und der Chef der Deutschen Polizei im Reichsministerium des Innern an den Herrn Württembergischen Innenminister, O-VuR.Org.5134 III/38, 20 March 1939; Der Kommandeur der Gendarmerie des Landes Württemberg an den Herrn Württ. Innenminister, Nr R 784/38, 'Betreff: Einstellung von Hilfspolizeibeamten für die Überwachung der zur Bekämpfung der Maul- und Klauenseuche getroffenen Massnahmen', 8 June 1939.

246   StAL, Bü46, p. 38.

247   Ibid., p. 37.

248   HStAS, E151/01, Bü3596, Der Landesbauernführer an die Kreisbauernschaften, Sonderrundschreiben, Gesch.Z: I B 21156/39, 31 May 1939.

249   StAL, Bü46, p. 38.

250   Ibid., pp. 37–38.

251   StAL: Bü44, p. 19; Bü46, p. 13. See also *Deutschland-Berichte*, 1939, no. 6, 12 July 1939, p. A61.

252   StAL, Bü45, p. 44.

253   Ibid., Bü44, p. 19.

Notes to Chapter 3: Party and State

1   Jeremy Noakes and Geoffrey Pridham (eds), *Nazism, 1919–1945: A Documentary Reader*, i, *The Rise to Power, 1919–1934* (Exeter, 1983), p. 167.

2   Ronald Smelser, *Robert Ley: Hitler's Labour Front Leader* (Oxford and New York, 1988), pp. 16, 30–31. The quotation is from Jeremy Noakes and Geoffrey Pridham (eds), *Nazism, 1919–1945: A Documentary Reader*, ii, *State, Economy and Society, 1933–1939* (Exeter, 1984), 'Decree of the Führer on the Nature and Goals of the German Labour Front', 24 October 1934, p. 344.

3   Jürgen Schuhladen-Krämer, 'Die Exekutoren des Terrors: Hermann Mattheiss, Walther Stahlecker, Friedrich Mussgay, Leiter der Geheimen Staatspolizeileitstelle Stuttgart', in Michael Kissener and Joachim Scholtyseck (eds), *Die Führer der Provinz: NS-Biographien aus Baden und Württemberg* (Konstanz, 1997), pp. 409–16. See also Hartmut Berghoff and

Cornelia Rauh-Kühne, *Fritz K.: ein deutsches Leben im zwanzigsten Jahrhundert* (Stuttgart and Munich, 2000), pp. 70–78.

4 Short biographies of these leading Nazis and others may be found in Ronald Smelser, Enrico Syring and Rainer Zitelmann (eds): *Die Braune Elite, i, 22 biographische Skizzen, Die Braune Elite, ii, 21 weitere biographische Skizzen* (Darmstadt, 1999).

5 Jeremy Noakes 'Leaders of the People? The Nazi Party and German Society', *Journal of Contemporary History*, 39 (2004), pp. 190–91. See Noakes and Pridham, *Nazism*, i, pp. 148–51, 167–81, on the SA's response to the seizure of power and the purge of the SA in summer 1934.

6 On the USSR, see Lewis H. Siegelbaum, *Soviet State and Society between Revolutions, 1918–1929* (Cambridge, 1992), pp. 22–25, 38–45, 87–92, 190–203; Ronald Grigor Suny, 'Stalin and his Stalinism: Power and Authority in the Soviet Union, 1930–1953', pp. 30–40, and Moshe Lewin, 'Bureaucracy and the Stalinist State', pp. 56–62, 67–71, both in Ian Kershaw and Moshe Lewin (eds), *Stalinism and Nazism: Dictatorships in Comparison* (Cambridge, 1997).

7 On consent for the police state, see Robert Gellately, *Backing Hitler: Consent and Coercion in Nazi Germany* (Oxford, 2001).

8 On the state of development of the Italian Fascist Party in the years 1919–22, see Adrian Lyttelton, *The Seizure of Power: Fascism in Italy, 1919–1929* (London, 1973), pp. 35–76. On instability within the party after the 'seizure of power', see pp. 166–70, 175–78, 183–88. On the party's weakness in the south, see pp. 188–201.

9 See, e.g., the reports on NSDAP activity and support in the area of Mainz, Koblenz and Trier before 1933 in Franz Josef Heyen (ed.), *Nationalsozialismus im Alltag: Quellen zur Geschichte des Nationalsozialismus vornehmlich im Raum Mainz – Koblenz – Trier* (Boppard, 1967).

10 Thomas Schnabel, 'Die NSDAP in Württemberg, 1928–1933: die Schwäche einer regionalen Parteiorganisation', in Thomas Schnabel (ed.), *Die Machtergreifung in Südwestdeutschland* (Stuttgart, 1982), pp. 49–80. On Schleswig-Holstein, see, e.g., Institut für Zeitgeschichte archive, MA138, frame 300886, 'Arbeitsbericht der Gaufrauenschaftsleiterin', Schleswig-Holstein, 29 November 1941.

11 Jill Stephenson, *The Nazi Organisation of Women* (London, 1981), pp. 34, 36–37, 72–74. This was true also of other political parties: on the greater activity of women in the DVP (German People's Party) and DNVP (German National People's Party) in urban than in rural areas during the Weimar Republic, see Raffael Scheck, *Mothers of the Nation: Right-Wing Women in Weimar Germany* (Oxford, 2003).

12 Literally, 'leading people'. On *Menschenführung*, see Peter Hüttenberger, *Die Gauleiter: Studie zum Wandel des Machtgefüges in der NSDAP* (Stuttgart, 1969), pp. 118ff; Eberhard Laux, 'Führung und Verwaltung in der Rechtslehre des Nationalsozialismus', in Dieter Rebentisch and Karl Teppe (eds), *Verwaltung contra Menschenführung: Studien zum politisch-administrativen System* (Göttingen, 1986), pp. 40–43; Noakes, 'Leaders of the People?', pp. 189, 197–206. See also Hitler on the tasks of the NSDAP in Noakes and Pridham, *Nazism*, ii, pp. 234–36.

13 A '*Märzveilchen*' (March violet) or, literally, 'March casualty' (*Märzgefallener*), was one whose opportunism had led him or her to apply for party membership soon after the *Reichstag* election of 5 March 1933 which gave the NSDAP and its allies a small majority.

14   Dietrich Orlow, *The History of the Nazi Party, 1933–45* (Newton Abbot, 1973), pp. 48–50, 202–7.

15   See Noakes and Pridham, *Nazism*, ii, pp. 233–34, 244–46, on the alleged 'unity of party and state'.

16   Staatsarchiv Ludwigsburg (StAL), PL501/45, NSDAP Kreis Stuttgart, p. 70275, Rundschreiben Nr 39/39, 'Betr.: Fragebogen der SA zur Erfassung der Wehrmannschafts-Dienstpflichtigen', 9 August 1939; p. 70254, Rundschreiben Nr 48/39, 'Betr.: Künftige Verteilung der Lebensmittelkarten', 5 September 1939.

17   Ibid., K110, Bü44, 'Lagebericht des 4. Vierteljahres 1938', 1 February 1939, p. 17.

18   Horst Matzerath, *Nationalsozialismus und kommunale Selbstverwaltung* (Stuttgart, 1970), pp. 90–91; Martin Broszat, *The Hitler State: The Foundation and Development of the Internal Structure of the Third Reich* (London and New York, 1981), pp. 104–11.

19   The quotation is from Thomas Schnabel, *Württemberg zwischen Weimar und Bonn, 1928–1945/46* (Stuttgart, 1986), p. 187. See also Broszat, *The Hitler State*, pp. 62–67, 72–74, 86, 96–97.

20   On the *Gauleiter* assuming the role of *Reichsstatthalter*, see Hüttenberger, *Die Gauleiter*, pp. 74–80

21   Ibid., pp. 199–200. The quotation is from Michael Ruck, 'Zentralismus und Regionalgewalten im Herrschaftsgefüge des NS-Staates', in Horst Möller, Andreas Wirsching and Walter Ziegler (eds), *Nationalsozialismus in der Region: Beiträge zur regionalen und lokalen Forschung und zum internationalen Vergleich* (Munich, 1996), p. 119.

22   Paul Sauer, *Württemberg in der Zeit des Nationalsozialismus* (Ulm, 1975), p. 495.

23   Berlin Document Center (BDC), personnel file on Wilhelm Murr: 'Wilhelm Murr: 10 Jahre Gauleiter in Württemberg', *Völkischer Beobachter*, n.d. (1935); 'Reichsstatthalter Gauleiter Murr 50 Jahre alt', *Völkischer Beobachter*, 16 December 1938. See also Paul Sauer, *Wilhelm Murr: Hitlers Statthalter in Württemberg* (Tübingen, 1998), p. 46, and photographs on pp. 21, 28, 41, 57, 67, 68, 76, 86, 107, and in Berghoff and Rauh-Kühne, *Fritz K.*, p. 157.

24   For example, Orlow, *The History of the Nazi Party, 1933–1945*. While thirty-six *Gauleiter* and a number of deputy *Gauleiter* appear in Orlow's list of 'Less Familiar Nazi Leaders' on pp. 499–503, Murr does not. On Kube, see p. 181. See also Noakes, 'Leaders of the People?', pp. 189–212; Jay W. Baird, 'Julius Streicher: Der Berufsantisemit', in Smelser, Syring and Zitelmann, *Die Braune Elite*, ii, pp. 231–40; Ludger Syré, 'Der Führer vom Oberrhein: Robert Wagner, Gauleiter, Reichsstatthalter in Baden und Chef der Zivilverwaltung in Elsass', in Kissener and Scholtyseck, *Die Führer der Provinz*, pp. 756–59; Sauer, *Wilhelm Murr*, p. 69. For an example of Murr's antisemitic expression, see Kurt Leipner (ed.), *Chronik der Stadt Stuttgart, 1933–1945* (Stuttgart, 1982), p. 976 (23 July 1944).

25   On Nazi leaders and corruption, see Frank Bajohr, *Parvenüs und Profiteure: Korruption in der NS-Zeit* (Frankfurt am Main, 2001). The single mention of Murr is on p. 113, while Kaufmann and Koch, for example, figure prominently. The quotation is from Orlow, *The History of the Nazi Party, 1933–1945*, p. 124. For a critical account of Kaufmann's career, see Frank Bajohr, 'Hamburgs "Führer": zur Person und Tätigkeit des Hamburger NSDAP-Gauleiters Karl Kaufmann (1900–1969)', in Frank Bajohr and Joachim Szodrzynski (eds), *Hamburg in der NS-Zeit: Ergebnisse neuerer Forschung* (Hamburg, 1995), pp. 59–91.

26   Jeremy Noakes (ed.), *Nazism, 1919–1945: A Documentary Reader*, iv, *The German Home Front in World War II* (Exeter, 1998), pp. 355–56.

27   Broszat, *The Hitler State*, p. 109.

28   Sauer, *Wilhelm Murr*, gives a detailed account of Murr's life and career. See also Joachim Scholtyseck, '"Der Mann aus dem Volk": Wilhelm Murr, Gauleiter und Reichsstatthalter in Württemberg-Hohenzollern', in Kissener and Scholtyseck, *Die Führer der Provinz*, pp. 477–502. The quotation is from p. 486. On the position of RVK, see Hüttenberger, *Die Gauleiter*, pp. 156–57; Syré, 'Der Führer vom Oberrhein', p. 733.

29   BDC, Murr, letter from Kerber, Gauamtsleiter für Kommunalpolitik (Baden), to the Hauptamt für Kommunalpolitik, München, 13 January 1940. The quotation is from *The German Southwest*, p. 38. On rivalry between Baden and Württemberg, see Johnpeter Horst Grill, *The Nazi Movement in Baden, 1920–1945* (Chapel Hill, North Carolina, 1983), pp. 48–51, 259–60; Syré, 'Der Führer vom Oberrhein', p. 755. The sentiment was reciprocated, with Murr bitter when Baden Gauleiter Wagner became Statthalter in Alsace in 1940. Sauer, *Wilhelm Murr*, pp. 116–17.

30   On Heilbronn, see Chapter 5, p. 160. On Stuttgart, see Sauer, *Württemberg*, pp. 489–95.

31   Paul Sauer, 'Staat, Politik, Akteure', in Otto Borst (ed.), *Das Dritte Reich in Baden und Württemberg* (Stuttgart, 1988), p. 26.

32   Sauer, *Württemberg*, p. 494; Beck, *Under the Bombs*, pp. 189–90. See also Chapter 9, below.

33   This statement was made to a gathering of Württemberg's *Landtag* and *Reichstag* deputies together with the NSDAP's district leaders in *Gau* Württemberg-Hohenzollern. Leipner, *Chronik der Stadt Stuttgart*, p. 70.

34   Waldemar Besson, *Württemberg und die deutsche Staatskrise: eine Studie zur Auflösung der Weimarer Republik* (Stuttgart, 1959), p. 352; Sauer, *Württemberg*, p. 30; Sauer, *Wilhelm Murr*, pp. 37–38; Benigna Schönhagen, 'Zwischen Verweigerung und Agitation: Landtagspolitik der NSDAP in Württemberg 1928/29–1933', in Thomas Schnabel (ed.), *Die Machtergreifung in Südwestdeutschland: das Ende der Weimarer Republik in Baden und Württemberg, 1928–1933* (Stuttgart, 1982), p. 125; Jörg Thierfelder and Eberhard Röhm, 'Die evangelischen Landeskirchen von Baden und Württemberg in der Spätphase der Weimarer Republik und zu Beginn des Dritten Reiches', in ibid., p. 238.

35   Michael Stolle, 'Der schwäbische Schulmeister: Christian Mergenthaler, Württembergische Ministerpräsident, Justiz- und Kultminister', in Kissener and Scholtyseck, *Die Führer der Provinz*, pp. 445–75. See also Besson, *Württemberg und die deutsche Staatskrise*, pp. 260, 269, 324, 337, 348–50.

36   Sauer, *Wilhelm Murr*, pp. 36–39.

37   Thomas Schnabel, 'Die NSDAP in Württemberg 1928–1933: die Schwäche einer regionalen Parteiorganisation', in Schnabel, *Die Machtergreifung in Südwestdeutschland*, pp. 73–74. See also, e.g., the case of Stahlecker in Schuhladen-Krämer, 'Die Exekutoren des Terrors', pp. 414, 421–22.

38   Sauer, 'Staat, Politik, Akteure', p. 27.

39   Hüttenberger, *Die Gauleiter*, pp. 89–90.

40   Wolfgang Benz, *The Holocaust: A Short History* (London, 2000), pp. 90, 92–93; Dieter Pohl, 'Die Ermordung der Juden im Generalgouvernement', in Ulrich Herbert (ed.),

Nationalsozialistische Vernichtungspolitik, 1939–1945: Neue Forschungen und Kontroversen (Frankfurt am Main, 1998), pp. 101–7, 113, 117; Jeremy Noakes and Geoffrey Pridham (eds), *Nazism, 1919–1945: A Documentary Reader*, iii, *Foreign Policy, War and Racial Extermination* (Exeter, 2001), pp. 446–47, 462–63, 551, 554–59, 562.

41   BDC, personnel file on Friedrich Schmidt, gives the information on Schmidt in this and the preceding paragraph.

42   Sauer, 'Staat, Politik, Akteure', p. 27. On Schmid as relatively conciliatory, see the example in Besson, *Württemberg und die deutsche Staatskrise*, p. 351; Angela Borgstedt, 'Im Zweifelsfall auch mit harter Hand. Jonathan Schmid, Württembergischer Innen-, Justiz- und Wirtschaftsminister', in Kissener and Scholtyseck, *Die Führer der Provinz*, p. 596.

43   Ibid., pp. 595–620; Michael Kissener and Joachim Scholtyseck, 'Nationalsozialismus in der Provinz', in Kissener and Scholtyseck, *Die Führer der Provinz*, p. 23.

44   Sauer, *Württemberg*, pp. 97–99.

45   Sauer, 'Staat, Politik, Akteure', pp. 23–24. Cf. the pressure successfully exerted by Hitler on his Foreign Minister, Neurath, first to join the NSDAP and then to join the SS as an honorary member. John L. Heinemann, *Hitler's First Foreign Minister* (Berkeley and Los Angeles, California, 1979), pp. 84–85.

46   Annette Roser, '"Beamter aus Berufung": Karl Wilhelm Waldmann, Württembergischer Staatssekretär', in Kissener and Scholtyseck, *Die Führer der Provinz*, pp. 781–802, provides the material on Waldmann. The quotation is from p. 795. See also Kissener and Scholtyseck, 'Nationalsozialismus in der Provinz', pp. 23–24.

47   Matzerath, *Nationalsozialismus und kommunale Selbstverwaltung*, pp. 232–33.

48   Hubert Roser, 'Vom Dorfschultheiss zum hohen Ministerialbeamten', in Kissener and Scholtyseck, *Die Führer der Provinz*, pp. 683–702, provides the material on Stümpfig. Cf. Michael Ruck, *Korpsgeist und Staatsbewusstsein: Beamte im deutschen Südwesten, 1928 bis 1972* (Munich, 1996), pp. 117–18.

49   Sauer, 'Staat, Politik, Akteure', p. 24. On the other hand, the NSDAP group in the Württemberg *Landtag* in 1932 was on average some ten years younger. Schönhagen, 'Zwischen Verweigerung und Agitation', p. 121.

50   BDC: personnel file on Eugen Stähle, NSDAP membership card; personnel file on Karl Strölin, NSDAP membership card and Führerfragebogen (SA), 12 March 1934.

51   Christine Arbogast, *Herrschaftsinstanzen der württembergischen NSDAP: Funktion, Sozialprofil und Lebenswege einer regionalen NS-Elite, 1920–1960* (Munich, 1998), p. 46.

52   BDC, personnel file on Adolf Mauer, NSDAP membership card and Führerfragebogen (SA), 12 March 1934.

53   Roland Müller, *Stuttgart zur Zeit des Nationalsozialismus* (Stuttgart, 1988), pp. 193, 279.

54   Susanne Schlösser, '"Was sich in den Weg stellt, mit Vernichtung schlagen": Richard Drauz, NSDAP-Kreisleiter von Heilbronn', in Kissener and Scholtyseck, *Die Führer der Provinz*, p. 143.

55   BDC, Stähle.

56   Ibid., Schmidt, letters and telegrammes dated 13, 17 and 18 May 1944, 21 September 1944, 27 December 1944.

57   BDC, Mauer.

58   A. Roser, 'Beamter aus Berufung', p. 781; H. Roser, 'Vom Dorfschultheiss zum hohen Ministerialbeamten', p. 683; Stolle, 'Der schwäbische Schulmeister', p. 445; Scholtyseck, 'Der Mann aus dem Volk', p. 477. But Waldmann also had a daughter who died in infancy in 1918. On the eleven siblings, pp. 685, 783.

59   BDC, Strölin; Angela Borgstedt, 'Im Zweifelsfall auch mit harter Hand', p. 595.

60   Arbogast, *Herrschaftsinstanzen der württembergischen NSDAP*, pp. 139, 178.

61   Sauer, *Wilhelm Murr*, pp. 13–19, 23–24, 34–36; Arbogast, *Herrschaftsinstanzen der württembergischen NSDAP*, pp. 22–23, 25, 42–49, 176, 181, 187, 195–96; Detlef Mühlberger, *Hitler's Followers: Studies in the Sociology of the Nazi Movement* (London, 1991), pp. 56–57; Sauer, *Württemberg*, p. 29; Scholtyseck, 'Der Mann aus dem Volk', pp. 481–85, 487–88; Barbara Hachmann, 'Der "Degen": Dietrich von Jagow', in Kissener and Scholtyseck, *Die Führer der Provinz*, pp. 279–80; Stolle, 'Der schwäbische Schulmeister', pp. 457–59, 461. On particular instances, see: BDC, Murr, letter from Murr to the NSDAP Reichsleitung, 'Betr. Uschla', 14 November 1930; StAL, K110, Bü45, 'Lagebericht des 1. Vierteljahres 1939', p. 16. See also, at more local level, Berghoff and Rauh-Kühne, *Fritz K.*, pp. 63–64, 166. On 'pig-headed Swabians', see above, Chapter 2.

62   Ruck, *Korpsgeist und Staatsbewusstsein*, pp. 31–32.

63   Frank Raberg, 'Das Aushängeschild der Hitler-Regierung: Konstantin Freiherr von Neurath, Aussenminister des Deutschen Reiches', in Kissener and Scholtyseck, *Die Führer der Provinz*, pp. 503–538; Heinemann, *Hitler's First Foreign Minister;* Joachim Scholtyseck, 'Der "Schwabenherzog": Gottlob Berger, SS-Obergruppenführer', in Kissener and Scholtyseck, *Die Führer der Provinz*, pp. 77–110; Hüttenberger, *Die Gauleiter*, pp. 220, 223.

64   Arbogast, *Herrschaftsinstanzen der württembergischen NSDAP*, p. 140.

65   Borgstedt, 'Im Zweifelsfall auch mit harter Hand', p. 609. Cf. Sauer, 'Staat, Politik, Akteure', p. 27: 'Although it can hardly be doubted that he did not approve of much of what Berlin required, he accepted it essentially passively and carried it out without protest'.

66   Hauptstaatsarchiv Stuttgart (HStAS), E151/01, Bü3960, Der Württ. Innenminister an den Herrn Reichsstatthalter in Württemberg, 'Betreff: Tätigkeitsbericht für die Monate April bis Juni 1939', 24 July 1939, p. 2.

67   Hüttenberger, *Die Gauleiter*, pp. 147–52. See also Lothar Kettenacker, 'Die Chefs der Zivilverwaltung im Zweiten Weltkrieg', in Rebentisch and Teppe, *Verwaltung contra Menschenführung*, pp. 396–417.

68   Scholtyseck, 'Der Mann aus dem Volk', p. 477.

69   BDC, Murr, letter from SS-Gruppenführer [illegible], Stuttgart, to the Reichsführer-SS, 5 June 1934.

70   StAL, K110, Bü46, SD 'Lagebericht des 2. Vierteljahres 1939', 1 July 1939, pp. 28, 32.

71   Ruck, *Korpsgeist und Staatsbewusstsein*, pp. 94–100. The quotation is from p. 97, emphasis in the original. Until 1934, the senior administrator in the provinces was the *Oberamtsvorstand* (county council chairman). From 1934, the Prussian term *Landrat* (district governor) was imposed in Württemberg by order of the central government. See Karl Weller and Arnold Weller, *Württembergische Geschichte im südwestdeutschen Raum* (Stuttgart and Aalen, 1975), p. 305; Sauer, *Württemberg*, pp. 110–21.

72   Berghoff and Rauh-Kühne, *Fritz K.*, pp. 170–72. The quotation is from p. 172.

73   H. Roser, 'Vom Dorfschultheiss zum hohen Ministerialbeamten', pp. 696, 700.

74 Michael Ruck, 'Administrative Eliten in Demokratie und Diktatur: Beamtenkarrieren in Baden und Württemberg von den zwanziger Jahren bis in die Nachkriegszeit', in Cornelia Rauh-Kühne and Michael Ruck (eds), *Regionale Eliten zwischen Diktatur und Demokratie: Baden und Württemberg, 1930–1952* (Munich, 1993), pp. 44–46, 49–52, 64–66.

75 Reichsorganisationsleiter (ed.), *NSDAP Partei-Statistik* (Munich, 1935), i, p. 252; Schnabel, *Württemberg zwischen Weimar und Bonn*, pp. 324–25.

76 Ruck, *Korpsgeist und Staatsbewusstsein*, pp. 94–96. See also, A. Roser, 'Beamter aus Berufung', pp. 791–92.

77 Ibid., p. 92. Cf. Göring's address to Prussian civil servants, 25 April 1933, in Noakes and Pridham, *Nazism*, ii, pp. 225–27. See also Matzerath, *Nationalsozialismus und kommunale Selbstverwaltung*, p. 249.

78 Berghoff and Rauh-Kühne, *Fritz K.*, p. 172.

79 Ruck, *Korpsgeist und Staatsbewusstsein*, pp. 304–5.

80 H. Roser, 'Vom Dorfschultheiss zum hohen Ministerialbeamten', pp. 691–94. On 'personal union', see Matzerath, *Nationalsozialismus und kommunale Selbstverwaltung*, pp. 237–38; Ruck, *Korpsgeist und Staatsbewusstsein*, pp. 162–65.

81 Matzerath, *Nationalsozialismus und kommunale Selbstverwaltung*, p. 238 n. 49, gives *Gau* Düsseldorf at 4.7 per cent and, at the other end of the scale, *Gau* Danzig at 52.2 per cent and *Gau* Bayerische Ostmark at 34.3 per cent. For Hesse, p. 132. See also pp. 88–90.

82 Ruck, *Korpsgeist und Staatsbewusstsein*, pp. 155–57. See also Arbogast, *Herrschaftsinstanzen der württembergischen NSDAP*, p. 167.

83 Ruck, *Korpsgeist und Staatsbewusstsein*, pp. 164–65, 188, 191, 194–95; Kurt Düwell, 'Gauleiter und Kreisleiter als regionale Gewalten des NS-Staates', in Möller, Wirsching and Ziegler, *Nationalsozialismus in der Region*, pp. 167–68; H. Roser, 'Vom Dorfschultheiss zum hohen Ministerialbeamten', p. 699.

84 Schnabel, *Württemberg zwischen Weimar und Bonn*, pp. 279, 327–28.

85 Michael Ruck, 'Kollaboration – Loyalität – Resistenz: Administrative Eliten und NS-Regime am Beispiel der südwestdeutsschen Innenverwaltung', in Landeszentrale für politische Bildung und Haus der Geschichte (ed.), *Formen des Widerstandes im Südwesten, 1933–1945* (Ulm, 1994), p. 131.

86 Christine Arbogast and Bettina Gall, 'Aufgaben und Funktionen des Gauinspekteurs, der Kreisleitung und der Kreisgerichtsbarkeit der NSDAP in Württemberg', in Rauh-Kühne and Ruck, *Regionale Eliten zwischen Diktatur und Demokratie*, pp. 156–57.

87 Arbogast, *Herrschaftsinstanzen der württembergischen NSDAP*, pp. 43, 54–56.

88 HStAS, E151/01, Bü3168: letter from the Württemberg Interior Minister to the Reich Ministry of the Interior, Nr I 2568, 26 September 1939; Württemberg Interior Ministry, Nr I 627, 'Betreff: Kreiskommunale Bezüge der Landräte', 28 March 1940; Reichsminister der Finanzen, *Reichshaushalts- und Besoldungsblatt*, Nr 11, 19 March 1940, p. 103; Württemberg Interior Ministry to the Reichswirtschaftsminister, 23 April 1940.

89 Ruck, *Korpsgeist und Staatsbewusstsein*, pp. 156–57.

90 HStAS, E151/01, Bü620, 'Geschäftsverteilungsplan des Landratsamts Böblingen (Stand vom 30.12.1940)'.

91 Ibid., Bü652, 'Zweckmässigkeit der Neueinteilung des Landes', n.d. (1938).

92 Ibid., Bü615 to Bü645, gives the office plans of most of the new districts. See also

Carl-Wilhelm Reibel, *Das Fundament der Diktatur: die NSDAP-Ortsgruppen, 1932–1945* (Paderborn, 2002), p. 335.

93 HStAS, E151/01cII, Bü434, Kommandeur der Gendarmerie des Landes Württemberg an den Württ. Innenminister, 'Tätigkeitsbericht für das Jahr 1939', 1 February 1940, pp. 3, 10–11.

94 Hüttenberger, *Die Gauleiter*, pp. 91ff.

95 Sauer, *Württemberg*, pp. 90, 104.

96 Schnabel, *Württemberg zwischen Weimar und Bonn*, pp. 187ff. The quotation is from p. 189. Cf. Rinderle and Norling, *The Nazi Impact on a German Village*, p. 155, who report that, in Oberschopfheim, with two exceptions, 'the NSDAP merely selected current village leaders to serve as Party functionaries, mayor and local officials'. See also pp. 112–13.

97 HStAS, J170, Bü18 (Ulm), 'Geschichtliche Darstellung der letzten Tage und Wochen des zweiten Weltkrieges 1939–1945', Weinstetten, 13 October 1948.

98 Matzerath, *Nationalsozialismus und kommunale Selbstverwaltung*, pp. 88–90. See also Schnabel, *Württemberg zwischen Weimar und Bonn*, p. 198. On pensioning off, see Jeremy Noakes, 'Nationalsozialismus in der Provinz: Kleine und mittlere Städte im Dritten Reich, 1933–1945', in Möller, Wirsching and Ziegler, *Nationalsozialismus in der Region*, p. 240.

99 Klaus-Dietmar Henke, *Die amerikanische Besetzung Deutschlands* (Munich, 1995), p. 786.

100 HStAS, J170, Bü1 (Aalen), 'Auszüge aus dem Kriegstagebuch 1945 u.ff. von –, Gewerbeschulrat a.D. geschrieben in Hofen Krs Aalen', p. 7, entry for 22 April 1945.

101 StAL, PL504/18, Bü18, An die Kreisleitung der NSDAP Leonberg, 'Ratsherren', 21 November 1938.

102 Ibid., NSDAP Kreisleitung Leonberg an Ortsgruppenleiter Pg. –, Leonberg, 'Gemeinderäte', 9 February 1939.

103 Ibid., PL504/5, Bü6, 'Betrifft: Einsatzorganisation bei Luftangriffen', n.d.

104 Noakes, 'Nationalsozialismus in der Provinz', p. 241.

105 Christa Tholander, *Fremdarbeiter, 1939 bis 1945: Ausländische Arbeitskräfte in der Zeppelin-Stadt Friedrichshafen* (Essen, 2001), p. 44, H3tA3, J170. Bü65 (Ravensburg), 'Waldsee vor der unmittelbaren Besetzung durch den Feind!', 18 July 1945; Bü18, Gemeinde Setzingen, Kreis Ulm, 'Geschichtliche Darstellung der letzten Kriegstage', n.d.; Arbogast, *Herrschaftsinstanzen der württembergischen NSDAP*, p. 122.

106 *Partei-Statistik*, p. 290. See also Matzerath, *Nationalsozialismus und kommunale Selbstverwaltung*, pp. 249–53. Specifically on Württemberg, see Arbogast, *Herrschaftsinstanzen der württembergischen NSDAP*, p. 122.

107 Noakes, 'Nationalsozialismus in der Provinz', p. 241.

108 *Partei-Statistik*, pp. 260–62, 264. The quotation is from p. 261; italics in the original. See also Arbogast, *Herrschaftsinstanzen der württembergischen NSDAP*, p. 122.

109 HStAS, E397, Bü5, Sondergericht für den Oberlandesgerichtsbezirk Stuttgart in Stuttgart, SL, 121–149/42. SL, 219–220/42, 6 July 1942, pp. 9–10; Württembergisches Statistisches Landesamt, *Staatshandbuch für Württemberg – Ortschaftsverzeichnis* (Stuttgart, 1936), p. 11. On the mayor of Untermarchtal, see below, Chapter 6.

110 HStAS, E397, Bü37, 'Abschrift. Sondergericht für den Oberlandesgerichtsbezirk Stuttgart in Stuttgart, SL, Nr 523–526/42. I 22 SJs 1313–16/42', 24 November 1942, p. 2.

111   Noakes, 'Nationalsozialismus in der Provinz', p. 241.

112   Arbogast, *Herrschaftsinstanzen der württembergischen NSDAP*, pp. 56–57.

113   StAL, PL504/22, Bü1, Kreisleitung Nürtingen an den Stützpunktleiter der NSDAP, 'Betreff: Bürgermeister –, Aich', 10 September 1937. For other examples of such friction, see Schnabel, *Württemberg zwischen Weimar und Bonn*, pp. 200–1.

114   Arbogast, *Herrschaftsinstanzen der württembergischen NSDAP*, p. 120.

115   Schnabel, *Württemberg zwischen Weimar und Bonn*, pp. 188–90, 198, 202; Arbogast, *Herrschaftsinstanzen der württembergischen NSDAP*, pp. 120–21.

116   Ruck, 'Administrative Eliten und Diktatur', p. 42. See also Ruck, 'Kollaboration – Loyalität – Resistenz', ibid., p. 126.

117   Berghoff and Rauh-Kühne, *Fritz K.*, pp. 60, 155, 171. The quotations are from pp. 60 and 155.

118   StAL, K110, Bü45, 'Lagebericht des 1. Vierteljahres 1939', 1 April 1939, p. 38.

119   Arbogast, *Herrschaftsinstanzen der württembergischen NSDAP*, p. 121.

120   Matzerath, *Nationalsozialismus und kommunale Selbstverwaltung*, p. 249; Arbogast, *Herrschaftsinstanzen der württembergischen NSDAP*, pp. 42–47, 121–23. Technical skills, too, might be lacking. See Reibel, *Das Fundament der Diktatur*, p. 117.

121   BDC, Richard Drauz, 'Fragebogen für die Beauftragten der NSDAP, Stuttgart, 7.1.1936'; Arbogast, *Herrschaftsinstanzen der württembergischen NSDAP*, pp. 38–40.

122   Michael Rademacher, *Handbuch der Gaue, 1928–1945: die Amtsträger der NSDAP und ihrer Organisationen auf Gau- und Kreisebene in Deutschland und Österreich sowie in den Reichsgauen Danzig-Westpreussen, Sudetenland und Wartheland* (Vechta, 2000), pp. 331–43.

123   StAL, K110, Bü46, pp. 27, 36.

124   Arbogast, *Herrschaftsinstanzen der württembergischen NSDAP*, pp. 41, 158, 163.

125   StAL, K110, Bü48, 1 September 1941, pp. 11, 13, 18.

126   Schnabel, *Württemberg zwischen Weimar und Bonn*, pp. 199–202.

127   Arbogast, *Herrschaftsinstanzen der württembergischen NSDAP*, p. 121.

128   StAL, K110, Bü44, p. 17.

129   See below, Chapter 4.

130   Schnabel, *Württemberg zwischen Weimar und Bonn*, pp. 201–2.

131   Ibid., p. 418.

132   Berghoff, *Zwischen Kleinstadt und Weltmarkt*, pp. 452–53. On the NSDAP in elections in Trossingen, see pp. 424–30; see also the table in Berghoff and Rauh-Kühne, *Fritz K.*, p. 48. For outward conformity elsewhere, see Schnabel, *Württemberg zwischen Weimar und Bonn*, pp. 417–18.

133   George D. Spindler, *Burgbach: Urbanisation and Identity in a German Village* (New York, 1973), p. 12.

134   Günter Golde, *Catholics and Protestants: Agricultural Modernisation in Two German Villages* (New York, 1975), pp. 146–47.

135   Albert Ilien and Utz Jeggle, *Leben auf dem Dorf: zur Sozialgeschichte des Dorfes und Sozialpsychologie seiner Bewohner* (Opladen, 1978), pp. 119, 122.

136   See below, Chapter 7, at notes 105, 106. Cf. Franz Josef Heyen (ed.), *Nationalsozialismus im Alltag: Quellen zur Geschichte des Nationalsozialismus vornehmlich im Raum Mainz – Koblenz – Trier* (Boppard, 1967), pp. 133–35.

137   StAL, PL501/46, pp. 70383–85, Kreis Freudenstadt, Rundschreiben Folge 09/36, 'Betr.: Block- und Zellen-Neuordnung der NSDAP 1936', 15 June 1936.

138   Golde, *Catholics and Protestants*, pp. 146–47; Ilien and Jeggle, *Leben auf dem Dorf*, pp. 119, 122–23, 126–27; HStAS, J170, Bü18, 'Chronikale Aufzeichnungen über die Gemeinde Tomerdingen, Kreis Ulm (aus der Pfarrchronik), n.d. [October/November 1948], p. 2.

139   Ibid., E151/01cII, Bü434, 1 February 1940, pp. 12–13.

140   Schnabel, *Württemberg zwischen Weimar und Bonn*, pp. 202–203. See also William Sheridan Allen, *The Nazi Seizure of Power: The Experience of a Single German Town, 1922–45* (London, 1989), pp. 25–34; Stephenson, *The Nazi Organisation of Women*, pp. 27–33.

141   Gunther Mai, *Die Geislinger Metallarbeiterbewegung* (Düsseldorf, 1984), pp. 50–54, 59 Berghoff and Rauh-Kühne, *Fritz K.*, pp. 36–86.

142   H. Roser, 'Vom Dorfschultheiss zum hohen Ministerialbeamten', pp. 686–87.

143   StAL, PL504/18, Bü12, 'Lage- und Stimmungsbericht der Ortsgruppe Leonberg für das Jahr 1938 bis 1. März 1939'.

144   Schnabel, *Württemberg zwischen Weimar und Bonn*, p. 419.

145   Ibid., PL504/18, Bü6, 'Ortsgruppe Leonberg – Mitgliederstand per 29.2.36'.

146   Ibid., Bü12, 'Lage- und Stimmungsbericht der Ortsgruppe Leonberg für das Jahr 1938 bis 1. März 1939'.

147   Ibid., PL502/34, Bü51, Ortsgruppe Schondorf, Kreis Waiblingen, 'Liste der Parteimitglieder', 1942.

148   Ibid., PL502/16, G4730, 'H-Böckingen', membership list with entries up to and including 1944.

149   Ibid., G1416, membership list of the Brettach SA in July 1935, dated 13 August 1935. The final number is also given as 137.

150   StAL, PL504/18, Bü12, 'Lage- und Stimmungsbericht der Ortsgruppe Leonberg für das Jahr 1938 bis 1. März 1939', pp. 3–4.

151   Berghoff, *Zwischen Kleinstadt und Weltmarkt*, p. 453.

152   StAL, K110, Bü44, p. 15.

153   Ibid., Bü46, p. 44.

154   Berghoff, *Zwischen Kleinstadt und Weltmarkt*, p. 452.

155   StAL, PL504/18, Bü12, p. 5.

156   StAL, K110, Bü40, 24 November 1941, 'Betr.: Kriegswinterhilfswerk'.

157   Ian Kershaw, *The 'Hitler Myth': Image and Reality in the Third Reich* (Oxford, 1987), pp. 93–103. See also Berghoff, *Zwischen Kleinstadt und Weltmarkt*, p. 437.

158   Arbogast, *Herrschaftsinstanzen der württembergischen NSDAP*, p. 58.

159   For examples of this from the Rhineland, see Heyen, *Nationalsozialismus im Alltag*, pp. 256–57.

160   StAL, PL504/34, Bü13, 'Block-Fragebogen. Feststellung über die Zugehörigkeit der Bevölkerung zur NSDAP, ihre Gliederungen u. angeschl. Verbänden. Termin 1. Oktober 1938'.

161   Ibid., PL502/16, G4737, 'Meldung der Funktionäre von der NSDAP u. ihrer angeschlossenen Gliederungen', 14 December 1945.

162   Ibid., PL502/34, Bü40, 'Ortsgruppe-Fragebogen', Beinstein, 31 July 1945.

163   Ibid., PL502/16, G4730, 'H-Böckingen'.

164   Stephenson, *The Nazi Organisation of Women*, pp. 17–19, 121, 124, 141–42, 152.

165   Berghoff and Rauh-Kühne, *Fritz K.*, pp. 58, 158–60.

166   StAL, PL504/34, Bü14, An den Kreispresseamtsleiter, 'Bericht', 13 September 1940.

167   Arbogast, *Herrschaftsinstanzen der württembergischen NSDAP*, p. 85.

168   StAL, K631/II, Bü83, NSF-DFW: 'Anschriften der Kreisfrauenschaftsleiterinnen', 18 November 1942; 'Anschriften der Kreisabteilungsleiterinnen Volkswirtschaft-Hauswirtschaft', 17 November 1942.

169   Arbogast, *Herrschaftsinstanzen der württembergischen NSDAP*, p. 85.

170   NSDAP Hauptarchiv, reel 13, folder 253, 'Rundschreiben Nr F 118/41', 4 October 1941.

171   StAL, PL501/45, p. 70473, Kreis Stuttgart, Rundschreiben Nr 30/37, 'Betr.: Blockhelfer', p. 2, 15 February 1937. See also Benigna Schönhagen, *Tübingen unterm Hakenkreuz: eine Universitätsstadt in der Zeit des Nationalsozialismus* (Stuttgart, 1991), pp. 180–81.

172   Quoted in Noakes, *Nazism*, iv, p. 98. Italics in the original.

173   StAL, PL504/18, Bü12.

174   StAL, PL504/34, Bü13, 'Rundschreiben', 24 June 1937.

175   Ibid., Bü28, NSDAP card from Ortsgruppe Oberurbach i.R., Kreis Leonberg.

176   Ibid., Bü 20, NSDAP book from Ortsgruppe Grunbach i.R., Kreis Leonberg.

177   Ibid., Bü13: 'Rundschreiben', 24 June 1937; attendance list, 1939–40.

178   Ibid., PL504/22, Bü16, Ortsgruppe Nürtingen-Süd, 'Rundschreiben', 28 January 1939. See also ibid., Bü11, NSDAP Ortsgruppe Nürtingen-Süd an alle Zellen- und Blockleiter, Blockwalter der DAF u. NSV sowie die Werkscharmänner, 'Betr.: Dienst am Sonntag 30. Juni 1940', 27 June 1940.

179   Ibid., Bü40, Ortsgruppe Nürtingen-Süd, 'Betreff: Metallsammlung, Soldatenadressen, Kameradschaftsabend', 18 April 1940.

180   Ibid., PL504/18, Bü4, '*Schwarzes Brett*', *Leonberger Tageblatt*, 12 July 1940.

181   Ibid., Bü26, '*NS-Frauenschaft, DF. u. JG. Eltingen*', *Leonberger Tageblatt*, 2 July 1940.

182   Arbogast, *Herrschaftsinstanzen der württembergischen NSDAP*, p. 78.

183   StAL, PL504/22, Bü13, 'Arbeitsplan der NS Frauenschaft – Februar', 28 February 1938.

184   Ibid., 'Arbeitsplan für den Monat Oktober', 10 October 1938.

185   Ibid., Bü7, 'Arbeitsplan für den Monat Februar 1938', 21 January 1938.

186   Ibid., Bü11, Kreisleiter Nürtingen an die Ortsgruppenleitungen der NSDAP, 11 September 1940.

187   Ibid., 16 September 1940.

188   Ibid., Kreisleitung Nürtingen an die Ortsgruppenleitung der NSDAP Nürtingen-Süd, n.d.

189   Ibid., PL502/16: G, 'Geschäftsbericht auf 15. Dez. 1937', 8 January 1938; G1411, 'Betrifft den Tätigkeitsbericht', 8 July 1938.

190   Ibid., G1393, NSDAP Ortsgruppe Kirchhausen an die NSDAP, Kreiskulturhauptstelle Heilbronn, 'Betreff: Tätigkeitsbericht', 8 July 1938.

191   Ibid., PL501, Bü14, Ortsgruppe Nürtingen-Süd an die Zellenleiter der Ortsgruppe, 'Betr.: Feststellung der NSV Mitglieder', 15 June 1938.

192   Ibid., Propagandaleiter (Nürtingen-Süd) an die Kreisleitung der NSDAP, 'Mitgliederwerbung für die NSV', 18 June 1938.

193 Ibid., Propagandaleiter (Nürtingen-Süd) an die Ortsamtsleitung der NSV, 'Werbung von NSV-Mitgliedern', 17 June 1938.

194 Ibid., NSDAP Ortsgruppe Nürtingen-Süd an die Zellenleiter der Ortsgruppe, 'Betr.: 'Mitgliederwerbung für die NSV', 28 May 1938.

195 Recurrent cash benefits were paid from 1936 to low income 'valuable' families for the fifth and subsequent children. From 1938, the third and fourth children in a low income family also qualified. Jill Stephenson, *Women in Nazi Germany* (London, 2001), p. 30.

196 StAL, PL501, Bü14, Kreisleitung Nürtingen an den Ortsgruppenleiter der NSDAP, Nürtingen-Süd, 'Betreff: NSV-Mitgliederwerbung', 7 September 1939.

197 Ibid., PL504/35, Zellenleiter, Zelle 1, an den Ortsgruppenleiter der NSDAP (Nürtingen-Süd), 19 August 1938.

198 Ibid.: report by the leader of block 3, 19 August 1938; report by the leader of cell 4, n.d.

199 Ibid., PL504/34, Bü17, Gauschatzmeister an den Kassenleiter der NSDAP Geradstetten, 'Entrümpelung von Landschaft und Dorf. Mein Rundschreiben Folge 13 vom 25.6.37', 31 May 1938.

200 Ibid., 'Entrümpelung von Landschaft und Dorf', 1 June 1938.

201 Ibid., PL504/22, Bü40, NSDAP Kreisleitung Nürtingen, 'Betr.: Neue Schrottsammelaktion', 10 July 1939.

202 Ibid., PL504/18, Bü10, Leonberg local branch leader to the Leonberg district NSDAP office, 21 January 1938.

203 Ibid., K631/II, Bü87, letter of 25 October 1937.

204 Ibid., Bü84, letter of 25 March 1936.

205 Ibid., Der Landesbauernführer an den Viehwirtschaftsverband Württemberg, 'Betr.: Beirat der Marktgemeinschaft Stuttgart', letters of 17 July 1936 and 8 February 1938.

206 Ibid., 'Beirat der Marktgemeinschaft', 1 October 1940.

207 Ibid., Bü99, an den Kreisleiter Leonberg, 23 May 1939.

208 Ibid., PL501/15, 330533, NSDAP Kreisleitung Stuttgart an die NSDAP Gauleitung Württemberg-Hohenzollern, 20 November 1942.

209 Ibid., PL502/16, G1375: Die Ortsfrauenschaftsleiterin Böckingen-Nord an die NSDAP-Gauleitung der NS-Frauenschaft, 23 March 1939; Die Ortsfrauenschaftsleiterin an die NSDAP Kreisleitung der NS-Frauenschaft, 9 June 1939.

210 Ibid., PL502/16, G4732, 'Betr.: Anerkennung als Lehrbetriebe für die Ausbildung von ländl. Hauswirtschaftslehrlingen', 24 August 1944.

211 Ibid., PL503/34, Kreisgericht Waiblingen (n.d.).

212 StAL, K110, Bü45, p. 38.

213 Noakes, *Nazism*, iv, p. 409.

214 StAL, K110: Bü44, pp. 13, 18, 23–26. The quotation is from p. 24; Bü46, pp. 20–22.

215 Schuhladen-Krämer, 'Die Exekutoren des Terrors', p. 414.

216 StAL, PL504/18, Bü12, 'Lage- und Stimmungsbericht der Ortsgruppe Leonberg für das Jahr 1938 bis 1. März 1939', pp. 2, 6.

217 StAL, K110, Bü44, pp. 14–15. On church youth groups in the Rhineland, see Heyen, *Nationalsozialismus im Alltag*, pp. 183–85.

218 Gerhard Rempel, *Hitler's Children: The Hitler Youth and the SS* (Chapel Hill, North Carolina, 1989), pp. 10–11, 268.

219 Wolfgang Benz, Hermann Graml and Hermann Weiss (eds), *Enzyklopädie des Nationalsozialismus* (Munich, 1997), p. 513.

220 Mark Roseman, 'National Socialism and Modernisation', in Richard Bessel (ed.), *Fascist Italy and Nazi Germany: Comparisons and Contrasts* (Cambridge, 1996), p. 224.

221 StAL, K110, Bü44, p. 14.

222 Golde, *Catholics and Protestants*, pp. 149–50.

223 StAL, K110, Bü44, p. 14.

224 Ibid., p. 17.

225 Ibid., p. 14.

226 Stephenson, *The Nazi Organisation of Women*, pp. 83–92.

227 Stephenson, *Women in Nazi Germany*, pp. 77–78, 90–91.

228 Karl Schneider, 'Schule und Erziehung', in Otto Borst (ed.), *Das Dritte Reich in Baden und Württemberg* (Stuttgart, 1988), p. 133.

229 Dagmar Reese, *Straff, aber nicht stramm – herb, aber nicht derb: zur Vergesellschaftung von Mädchen durch den Bund Deutscher Mädel im sozialkulturellen Vergleich zweier Milieus* (Weinheim and Basel, 1989), pp. 72–84.

230 E.g., Noakes, *Nazism*, iv, p. 409.

231 Rempel, *Hitler's Children*, pp. 141–72; Michael H. Kater, *Hitler Youth* (Cambridge, Massachusetts, and London, 2004), pp. 44–48, 86–91; Elizabeth Harvey, *Women and the Nazi East: Agents and Witnesses of Germanisation* (New Haven, Connecticut, and London, 2003), pp. 87–89, 92–104, 120, 128–29, 138–39, 142, 147–53, 162–69, 191–211, 238–45; Nicholas Stargardt, *Witnesses of War: Children's Lives under the Nazis* (London, 2005), pp. 51–54

232 On the increasing demands on the local branches in wartime, see Reibel, *Das Fundament der Diktatur*, pp. 333, 344–51; Arbogast, *Herrschaftsinstanzen der württembergischen NSDAP*, p. 83.

233 StAL, K110, Bü48, 'Betr.: Allgemeine Stimmung und Lage', 1 September 1941, 'Bezeichnende Ausführungen eines Aussenstellen-Mitarbeiters zur Lageberichterstattung', p. 5.

234 Ibid., 'Betr.: Allgemeine Stimmung und Lage', p. 38.

235 BA, R22/3387, Der Oberlandesgerichtspräsident an den Herrn Reichsminister der Justiz, 'Betreff: Bericht über die allgemeine Lage', 6 November 1940.

236 HStAS, E151/01, Bü3168, letters of 4 June 1940, 11 December 1940, 26 May 1941.

237 Ibid., memorandum Nr I 2568 from the Württemberg Interior Ministry to the Reich Ministry of the Interior, 28 March 1940; letter of 24 April 1940; Reichshaushalts- und Besoldungsblatt, Nr 11, p. 103.

238 Ibid., letters of 7 June 1940, 11 June 1940, 27 July 1940.

239 Ibid., Bü450, D3dJ/113, letter from Murr to the Minister of the Interior, 8 June 1943.

240 Reibel, *Das Fundament der Diktatur*, pp. 333–37.

241 StAL, PL504/22, Bü17, Nürtingen district, circulars of 3 April 1940 and 15 July 1940.

242 Arbogast, *Herrschaftsinstanzen der württembergischen NSDAP*, p. 144.

243 StAL, PL509, Bü91, an die NSDAP – Hitlerjugend Bann 'Waiblinger' 364 'Betr.: Sonderrundschreiben v. 13.1.42', 24 January 1942. See also Noakes, *Nazism*, iv, p. 402.

244 StAL, K110, Bü48, pp. 13, 18.

245 Ibid., PL509: Bü66, Reutlinger to Frau –, Jugendherberge Schorndorf, 27 May 1943; Bü64: – to the Bannführer, 29 October 1944; Reutlinger to Mädelhauptgruppenführerin

–, 6 January 1943; Reutlinger to the editor, *Waiblinger Kreiszeitung*, 29 January 1942 and 27 May 1944. There are other similar documents in PL509. He was only following orders: see the Hitler Youth War Service Plan for 1940 quoted in Noakes, *Nazism*, iv, pp. 399–402. 'Reutlinger' is a pseudonym used to maintain anonymity.

246 Ibid.: Bü89, Reutlinger to Scharführer –, 30 November 1944; letters of 2 October 1942, 8 October 1942; Bü90, 'Reutlinger' to –, Führer des Standortes 7/364, 'Betr.: Führerauslese', 8 June 1944.

247 Ibid., Reutlinger: 'Betr.: Führerdienst am 23.5.1943', 14 May 1943.

248 Ibid., Bü90, Reutlinger to a subordinate, 'Betr.: Dienstschluss der Schar Hegnach', 4 March 1943.

249 Ibid., Bü92, letter of 12 October 1942.

250 Ibid., Der Hauptstammführer an den Führer der Gefolgschaft 10/364, 'Betr.: Dienstaufforderungen, 30 April 1943.

251 Ibid., Bü87: Reutlinger to –, 'Betr.: Kriegseinsatz in Öffingen am vergangenen Sonntag', 7 August 1944; Reutlinger to Führer des Standorts Waiblingen der HJ, 'Betr.: Kriegseinsatz in Öffingen am vergangenen Sonntag', 8 August 1944.

252 Ibid., Bü89, Reutlinger to –, 'Betr.: Bannsportfest 1944', 27 June 1944.

253 See, e.g., ibid., letters of 3 May 1944, 8 June 1944, 31 August 1944, 30 November 1944.

254 StAL, PL509, Bü67: Der Bannführer, 4 November 1944; 'Schlussmeldung zur Kriegsfreiwilligenaktion', 9 October 1944. See also 'Kriegsfreiwilligenmeldung des Jahrganges 1928 nach dem Stand vom 18 September 1944'.

255 Ibid., Bü68, letter from Reutlinger to Frau –, 25 August 1943.

256 Ibid., Bü89, letter of 22 June 1943.

257 Ibid.: letter from Reutlinger to –, Führer des Standortes 7/364, 17 June 1944.

258 Ibid., letter from Reutlinger to –, 1 June 1944.

259 Ibid., letter of 10 November 1944.

260 Quoted in Marlis G. Steinert, *Hitlers Krieg und die Deutschen* (Düsseldorf, 1970), p. 401.

261 Leipner, *Chronik der Stadt Stuttgart*, passim; Müller, *Stuttgart zur Zeit des Nationalsozialismus*, pp. 274–81.

262 On the local branches and evacuees and the bombed out, see Reibel, *Das Fundament der Diktatur*, pp. 348–51.

263 BA, R22/3387, Der Generalstaatsanwalt an den Herrn Reichsminister der Justiz, Nr 420b – 36, 31 January 1942.

264 Kershaw, *The 'Hitler Myth'*, pp. 166–68, 180–86. See also the jokes about 'the person of the Führer' in BA, R55/601 [date in 1944], pp. 128–29.

265 HStAS, J170, Bü1 (Aalen), 'Die letzten Kriegstage von Aalen', n.d. (October 1948), pp. 1, 12.

266 Ibid., 'Auszüge aus dem Kriegstagebuch 1945 u.ff. von –, Gewerbeschulrat a.D. geschrieben in Hofen Krs Aalen'.

267 Ibid., E397, Bü14: Der Reichsminister für Ernährung und Landwirtschaft an die Landesernährungsämter, Abt B, 25 May 1944; Gauleitung Württemberg-Hohenzollern, NS-Frauenschaft, Abt. Volksw.-Hausw., 'Betreff: Lebensmittelkontingent des Deutschen Frauenwerkes, Abt. V.-H.', 13 March 1945; Nr D.K. 947, 'Auf Ihr Schreiben vom 13. März 1945', 23 March 1945.

268   Ibid., J170, Bü1 (Aalen), 'Bopfingen im Zweiten Weltkrieg', n.d. [October/November 1948], p. 4.

269   Ibid., Bü4 (Crailsheim), Satteldorf, 'Geschichtliche Darstellung der letzten Kriegstage', 11 November 1948, p. 4.

270   Arbogast, *Herrschaftsinstanzen der württembergischen NSDAP*, pp. 66, 241.

Notes to Chapter 4: Racial Health and Persecution

1   'Aryan' (deriving from the Sanskrit *'arya'* – noble) was adopted, in a spurious form, by Nazi racial theorists to describe Germans whose antecedents did not include non-Europeans, Jews, Romanies, Slavs or Latins. These Germans 'of pure blood', allegedly deriving from nordic ancestors, were described as culturally the most highly developed people, the supreme people. Others to whom nordic ancestry was ascribed – mostly Scandinavians, Dutch and Belgian Flemings – were 'of related blood' and therefore 'racially valuable'. The rest were, in varying degrees, 'of lesser value' or 'worthless', with Jews at the bottom of the racial hierarchy. Jews and Slavs, particularly, were designated 'racial enemies' whose alleged aim was to destroy the 'Aryan race'.

2   Paul Weindling, *Health, Race and German Politics between National Unification and Nazism, 1870–1945* (Cambridge, 1989), pp. 489–503, 514–30; Michael Burleigh and Wolfgang Wippermann, *The Racial State: Germany, 1933–45* (Cambridge, 1991); Robert N. Proctor, *Racial Hygiene: Medicine under the Nazis* (Cambridge, Massachusetts, 1988); Marion A. Kaplan, *Between Dignity and Despair: Jewish Life in Nazi Germany* (New York and Oxford, 1998); Götz Aly, *'Final Solution': Nazi Population Policy and the Murder of the European Jews*, trans. Belinda Cooper and Allison Brown (London, 1999). See also the essays in Omer Bartov (ed.), *The Holocaust: Origins, Implementation, Aftermath. Rewriting Histories* (London and New York, 2000).

3   Guenter Lewy, *The Nazi Persecution of the Gypsies* (Oxford, 2000), pp. 102–104, 135–40.

4   Gisela Bock, *Zwangssterilisation im Nationalsozialismus: Studien zur Rassenpolitik und Frauenpolitik* (Opladen, 1986); Angelika Ebbinghaus (ed.), *Opfer und Täterinnen: Frauenbiographien des Nationalsozialismus* (Frankfurt am Main, 1996); Elizabeth D. Heineman, *What Difference Does a Husband Make? Women and Marital Status in Nazi and Postwar Germany* (Berkeley and Los Angeles, California, 1999).

5   Proctor, *Racial Hygiene*, pp. 97–101; Nancy L. Gallagher, *Breeding Better Vermonters: The Eugenics Project in the Green Mountain State* (Hanover, New Hampshire, 1999); Gunnar Broberg and Nils Roll-Hansen (eds), *Eugenics and the Welfare State: Sterilisation Policy in Denmark, Sweden, Norway, and Finland* (East Lancing, Michigan, 1996).

6   Zygmunt Bauman, *Modernity and the Holocaust* (New York, 1991), pp. 13, 18, 70, 91–93, 113–14.

7   Tübinger Vereinigung für Volksheilkunde e.V., *Volk und Gesundheit: Heilen und Vernichten im Nationalsozialismus* (Tübingen, 1982), pp. 160–65, 169. See also Götz Aly, 'Pure and Tainted Progress', in Götz Aly, Peter Chroust and Christian Pross, *Cleansing the Fatherland: Nazi Medicine and Racial Hygiene*, trans. Belinda Cooper (Baltimore, Maryland, and London, 1994), pp. 156–237; Weindling, *Health, Race and German Politics*, pp. 464–84.

8   Lewy, *The Nazi Persecution of the Gypsies*, p. 6.

9   Panikos Panayi, *Ethnic Minorities in Nineteenth- and Twentieth-Century Germany: Jews, Gypsies, Poles, Turks and Others* (London, 2000), pp. 144–45; Sybil H. Milton, '"Gypsies" as Social Outsiders in Nazi Germany', in Robert Gellately and Nathan Stoltzfus (eds), *Social Outsiders in Nazi Germany* (Princeton, New Jersey, and Oxford, 2001), pp. 213–15.

10   Tübinger Vereinigung für Volksheilkunde e.V., *Volk und Gesundheit*, p. 165; Lewy, *The Nazi Persecution of the Gypsies*, pp. 43–49. On p. 16, Lewy explains that the Jenische were 'Gypsy-like itinerants, the so-called white Gypsies ... of German origin [who] lived and conducted themselves like Gypsies'.

11   Gallagher, *Breeding Better Vermonters*, p. 124. See also the essays in Broberg and Roll-Hansen, *Eugenics and the Welfare State*: Bent Sigurd Hansen, 'Something Rotten in the State of Denmark: Eugenics and the Ascent of the Welfare State', pp. 37–43, 57; Gunnar Broberg and Mattias Tydén, 'Eugenics in Sweden: Efficient Care', pp. 102–3; Nils Roll-Hansen, 'Norwegian Eugenics: Sterilisation as Social Reform', pp. 173–76; Marjatta Hietala, 'From Race Hygiene to Sterilisation: The Eugenics Movement in Finland', pp. 232–33.

12   Jeremy Noakes and Geoffrey Pridham (eds.), *Nazism, 1919–1945: A Documentary Reader*, ii, *State, Economy and Society, 1933–1939* (Exeter, 1986), p. 457.

13   Tübinger Vereinigung für Volksheilkunde e.V., *Volk und Gesundheit*, p. 151.

14   Lisa Pine, *Nazi Family Policy, 1933–1945* (Oxford and New York, 1997), pp. 117–46; Heineman, *What Difference Does a Husband Make?*, pp. 26–31.

15   Wolfgang Ayass, *'Asoziale' im Nationalsozialismus* (Stuttgart, 1995), pp. 165–209.

16   Walter Wuttke, 'Medizin, Ärzte, Gesundheitspolitik', in Otto Borst (ed.), *Das Dritte Reich in Baden und Württemberg* (Stuttgart, 1988), pp. 216–17, 224; Michael Burleigh, 'Saving Money, Spending Lives: Psychiatry, Society and the "Euthanasia" Programme', in Michael Burleigh (ed.), *Confronting the Nazi Past: New Debates on Modern German History* (London, 1996), pp. 98–111; Götz Aly, 'Medicine Against the Useless', in Aly, Chroust and Pross, *Cleansing the Fatherland*, pp. 23, 25.

17   Proctor, *Racial Hygiene*, pp. 99–100; Hansen, 'Something Rotten in the State of Denmark', pp. 45–46; Hietala, 'From Race Hygiene to Sterilisation', pp. 219–22, 230.

18   Annette Schäfer, *Zwangsarbeiter und NS-Rassenpolitik: russische und polnische Arbeitskräfte in Württemberg, 1939–1945* (Stuttgart, 2000), pp. 44–52; 206–20; Kaplan, *Between Dignity and Despair*, p. 151.

19   Proctor, *Racial Hygiene*, pp. 181–82; Beate Meyer, *'Goldfasane' und 'Nazissen': die NSDAP im ehemals 'roten' Stadtteil Hamburg-Eimsbüttel* (Hamburg, 2002), p. 103.

20   Bronwyn Rebekah McFarland-Icke, *Nurses in Nazi Germany: Moral Choice in History* (Princeton, New Jersey, 1999), pp. 33–41, 63–64, 135–38, 179–81, 211.

21   Wuttke, 'Medizin, Ärzte, Gesundheitspolitik', pp. 231–32.

22   Weindling, *Health, Race and German Politics*, pp. 441–49; Pine, *Nazi Family Policy*, p. 95; Kurt Leipner, *Chronik der Stadt Stuttgart, 1933–1945* (Stuttgart, 1982), p. 139; Jill Stephenson, '"Reichsbund der Kinderreichen": The League of Large Families in the Population Policy of Nazi Germany', *European Studies Review*, 9 (1979), pp. 356–63.

23   Staatsarchiv Ludwigsburg (StAL), K110, Bü46, 'Lagebericht des 2. Vierteljahres 1939', 1 July 1939, p. 13.

24 Ayass, 'Asoziale' im Nationalsozialismus, pp. 20–41, 71–102, 139–65, 169; Roland Müller, Stuttgart zur Zeit des Nationalsozialismus (Stuttgart, 1988), pp. 83–89, 111.

25 StAL, Bü46, p. 19.

26 Ayass, 'Asoziale' im Nationalsozialismus, pp. 86–87.

27 Hauptstaatsarchiv Stuttgart (HStAS), E151cII, Bü434, Kommandeur der Gendarmerie des Landes Württemberg an den Württ. Innenminister, 'Tätigkeitsbericht für das Jahr 1939', 1 February 1940, p. 14.

28 Jörg Schadt, 'Verfolgung und Widerstand', in Borst, Das Dritte Reich in Baden und Württemberg, p. 118.

29 Lewy, The Nazi Persecution of the Gypsies, pp. 39–41, 187–93.

30 Schadt, 'Verfolgung und Widerstand', p. 118.

31 Lewy, The Nazi Persecution of the Gypsies, pp. 72, 146, 181. Schadt, 'Verfolgung und Widerstand', p. 119, gives the numbers as forty transported and two survivors.

32 StAL, K110: Bü45, 'Lagebericht des 1. Vierteljahres 1939', 1 April 1939, p. 18; Bü46, pp. 14–15; HStAS, E151cII, Bü434, 1 February 1940, p. 14.

33 Robert N. Proctor: 'The Nazi War on Tobacco: Ideology, Evidence, and Possible Cancer Consequences', Bulletin of the History of Medicine, 71 (1997), pp. 435–88; The Nazi War on Cancer (Princeton, New Jersey, 1999), pp. 173–247. Robert Mackay, The Test of War: Inside Britain, 1939–1945 (London, 1999), pp. 156–57, shows that tobacco was not rationed in wartime Britain because it was regarded as morale-boosting.

34 StAL, Bü46, pp. 13–14.

35 HStAS, E151kVI, Bü221, Der Württ. Wirtschaftsminister an den Herrn Württ. Innenminister, 'Betreff: Reichseinheitliche Regelung für den Einkauf von Tabakwaren', 15 October 1942.

36 StAL, Bü38, SD Rundschreiben Nr 186, 'Betr.: Lageberichterstattung', 8 December 1940; HStAS, E151kVI, Bü221: Der Amtsarzt, Schwäbisch Gmünd, dem Herrn Innenminister, 'Betr.: Bekämpfung gesundheitsschädlicher Genussmittel (Hier: Nikotin)', 16 April 1942; Der Amtsarzt, Friedrichshafen, an den Bürgermeister der Stadtgemeinde Friedrichshafen, 'Betrifft: Rauchen im Krankenhaus', 18 July 1942.

37 Ibid., 'Betr. Lebensmittelversorgung für Juden', 19 November 1941.

38 Ibid., NSDAP Reichsleitung an die Gauleiter der NSDAP zur Kenntnis, an die Gauamtsleiter der NSDAP, Leiter der Ämter für Volkswohlfahrt, Rundschreiben Nr. V 28/39, 13 November 1939.

39 Ibid., Staatliches Gesundheitsamt Tuttlingen an den Herrn Württ. Innenminister, 'Betreff: Gefährdung der Säuglingsernährung', 10 March 1942.

40 Ibid., NSDAP Kreisleitung Freudenstadt an die Gaupropagandaleitung der NSDAP, 15 September 1943.

41 See below, Chapter 5.

42 HStAS, E151kVI, Bü221, letter to Stähle, 13 December 1942.

43 Ibid.: letters of 12 September 1941, 7 November 1941, 13 June 1942, 17 June 1942, 31 August 1942, 15 September 1942, 30 September 1942.

44 Mackay, The Test of War, p. 156.

45 HStAS, E151kVI, Bü221, Der Württ. Innenminister an den Wehrkreisarzt V, 'Betreff: Aufgabenerweiterung der staatlichen Gesundheitsämter während des Krieges', 11 December 1940, p. 1.

46 Ibid., pp. 1–2. On Stähle's theories, including that of 'racial smell', see Proctor, *Racial Hygiene*, pp. 78–79.

47 Ibid., E151kVI, Bü221, Staatliches Gesundheitsamt Böblingen an den Herrn Württ. Innenminister, 'Betr.: Zusatzseife fur Offentuberkulöse', 30 October 1940.

48 Ibid., E151kVII, Bü2412, 'Betr.: Beratungsstelle für Geschlechtskranke', 3 April 1943.

49 See below, Chapters 8 and 9.

50 HStAS, E151kVII, Bü2412, Staatliches Gesundheitsamt Backnang dem Herrn Württ. Innenminister: 5 October 1943 and 11 April 1944.

51 Ibid., Staatliches Gesundheitsamt Ehingen (Donau) an den Herrn Württ. Innenminister, 23 March 1942. See also ibid., Staatliches Gesundheitsamt Friedrichshafen, der Amtsarzt an den Herrn Württ. Innenminister, 27 March 1942.

52 Ibid., Staatliches Gesundheitsamt des Landkreises Göppingen an den Herrn Württ. Innenminister, 1 September 1942.

53 Ibid., Nr. X 1713, 'Betreff: Bekämpfung der Geschlechtskrankheiten', 27 May 1943.

54 Noakes and Pridham, *Nazism*, ii, pp. 457–58.

55 Jeremy Noakes and Geoffrey Pridham (eds), *Nazism, 1919–1945: A Documentary Reader*, i, *The Rise to Power, 1919–1934* (Exeter, 1983), p. 167.

56 Michael Burleigh, *Death and Deliverance: 'Euthanasia' in Germany, 1900–1945* (Cambridge, 1994), pp. 41–42; Richard Steigmann-Gall, *The Holy Reich: Nazi Conceptions of Christianity, 1919–1945* (Cambridge and New York, 2003), pp. 192–95; Tübinger Vereinigung für Volksheilkunde e.V., *Volk und Gesundheit*, p. 151.

57 Paul Sauer, *Württemberg in der Zeit des Nationalsozialismus* (Ulm, 1975), p. 147.

58 Bock, *Zwangssterilisation im Nationalsozialismus*, pp. 247–53.

59 Björn Marnau, '"…empfinde ich das Urteil als hart und unrichtig": Zwangssterilisation im Kreis Steinburg/Holstein', in Michael Salewski and Guntram Schulze-Wegener (eds), *Kriegsjahr 1944: Im Grossen und im Kleinen* (Stuttgart, 1995), p. 320.

60 Sauer, *Württemberg in der Zeit des Nationalsozialismus*, p. 149.

61 Benigna Schönhagen, *Tübingen unterm Hakenkreuz: eine Universitätsstadt in der Zeit des Nationalsozialismus* (Stuttgart, 1991), p. 148.

62 Tübinger Vereinigung für Volksheilkunde e.V., *Volk und Gesundheit*, p. 150.

63 HStAS, E151cII, Bü434, 1 February 1940, p. 14.

64 Bock, *Zwangssterilisation im Nationalsozialismus*, pp. 247–48; Marnau, '"…empfinde ich das Urteil als hart und unrichtig"', p. 321.

65 Sauer, *Württemberg in der Zeit des Nationalsozialismus*, pp. 151–52, 407; Thomas Schnabel, *Württemberg zwischen Weimar und Bonn, 1928–1945/46* (Stuttgart, 1986), p. 452; Tübinger Vereinigung für Volksheilkunde e.V., *Volk und Gesundheit*, p. 166.

66 HStAS, E151bII, Bü474, 'Bericht zum Antrag auf Befreiung von den Vorschriften des Ehegesundheitsgesetzes', 18 July 1942.

67 Ibid.: Staatliches Gesundheitsamt Waiblingen an den Herrn Württ. Innenminister, 11 December 1942; Der Bürgermeister, Gemeinde Oppelsbohm, Kreis Waiblingen, an das Staatl. Gesundheitsamt Waiblingen, 7 December 1942.

68 Ibid., 'Bericht zum Antrag auf Befreiung von den Vorschriften des Ehegesundheitsgesetzes', 29 June 1943.

69 Lewy, *The Nazi Persecution of the Gypsies*, p. 192.

70 Tübinger Vereinigung für Volksheilkunde e.V., *Volk und Gesundheit*, p. 149; Sauer, *Württemberg in der Zeit des Nationalsozialismus*, pp. 149–50; Schönhagen, *Tübingen unterm Hakenkreuz*, pp. 149–50.

71 Utz Jeggle, 'The Rules of the Village: On the Cultural History of the Peasant World in the Last 150 Years' (trans. by Richard J. Evans), in Richard J. Evans and W.R. Lee (eds), *The German Peasantry: Conflict and Community in Rural Society from the Eighteenth to the Twentieth Centuries* (London and Sydney, 1986), pp. 278–81.

72 Claus Mühlfeld and Friedrich Schönweiss, *Nationalsozialistische Familienpolitik: Familiensoziologische Analyse der nationalsozialistischen Familienpolitik* (Stuttgart, 1989), pp. 176–87; Jill Stephenson, *Women in Nazi Society* (London, 1975), p. 41.

73 Heineman, *What Difference Does a Husband Make?*, pp. 22–25. Cf. Henry Friedlander, 'The Exclusion and Murder of the Disabled', in Gellately and Stoltzfus, *Social Outsiders in Nazi Germany*, p. 150. See also 'Unfruchtbar gemacht', in Uli Rothfuss, *Die Hitlerfahn' muss weg! Zwanzig dramatische Stationen in einer schwäbischen Kleinstadt* (Tübingen, 1998), pp. 59–62.

74 Stephenson, *Women in Nazi Society*, pp. 44–45.

75 Jeremy Noakes (ed.), *Nazism, 1919–1945: A Documentary Reader*, iv, *The German Home Front in World War II* (Exeter, 1998), p. 373.

76 HStAS, E151bII, Bü474, 'Bericht zum Antrag auf Befreiung von den Vorschriften des Ehegesundheitsgesetzes', 16 October 1942.

77 Ibid.: 'Bericht zum Antrag auf Befreiung von den Vorschriften des Ehegesundheitsgesetzes', 16 March 1943; 'Nr. II B 1271/6', 29 April 1943.

78 Ibid., 'Bericht zum Antrag auf Befreiung von den Vorschriften des Ehegesundheitsgesetzes', 22 June 1943.

79 Bock, *Zwangssterilisation im Nationalsozialismus*, p. 377.

80 StAL, K110, Bü38, 'Betr. Unterbringung von Bessarabiendeutschen', 14 November 1940.

81 Ernst Klee, *'Euthanasie' im NS-Staat: die 'Vernichtung lebensunwerten Lebens'* (Frankfurt am Main, 1983), pp. 15–33, 61–85; Gerhard Schäfer, *Landesbischof D. Wurm und der nationalsozialistische Staat, 1940–1945* (Stuttgart, 1968), p. 113; Michael Burleigh, 'Psychiatry, German Society and the Nazi "Euthanasia" Programme', in Bartov, *The Holocaust: Origins, Implementation, Aftermath*, pp. 45–54.

82 Leipner, *Chronik der Stadt Stuttgart*, p. 246.

83 Wuttke, 'Medizin, Ärzte, Gesundheitspolitik', pp. 210–18, 230–31; Jeremy Noakes and Geoffrey Pridham (eds), *Nazism, 1919–1945. iii, Foreign Policy, War and Racial Extermination* (Exeter, 2001), chapter 36, 'The Euthanasia Programme, 1939–1945', pp. 389–93.

84 Klee, *'Euthanasie' im NS-Staat*, pp. 89, 94–98, 294–95; Ernst Klee (ed.), *Dokumente zur 'Euthanasie'* (Frankfurt am Main, 1985), pp. 238–45; Burleigh, *Death and Deliverance*, pp. 93–121.

85 Ibid., pp. 130–32; McFarland-Icke, *Nurses in Nazi Germany*, pp. 220–22; Noakes and Pridham, *Nazism 1919–1945. iii*, pp. 412, 545.

86 Klee, *'Euthanasie' im NS-Staat*, pp. 100–101.

87 Sauer, *Württemberg in der Zeit des Nationalsozialismus*, p. 408. Cf. Klee, *'Euthanasie' im NS-Staat*, p. 340, who gives a figure of 9839. Wuttke, 'Medizin, Ärzte, Gesundheitspolitik', p. 229, says 'over 10,000'. On Grafeneck, see Klee, *'Euthanasie' im NS-Staat*, pp. 135–65.

88 Klee, *Dokumente zur 'Euthanasie'*, p. 154.

89 Schäfer, *Landesbischof D. Wurm und der nationalsozialistische Staat*, p. 116. For evacuees from Baden in Württemberg in 1939–40, see Chapter 9.

90 Klee, *'Euthanasie' im NS-Staat*, pp. 130, 132; Muller, *Stuttgart zur Zeit des Nationalsozialismus*, pp. 388–89.

91 Klee, *'Euthanasie' im NS-Staat*, p. 120; Bundesarchiv (BA), R22/4209, Der Generalstaatsanwalt an den Herrn Reichsminister der Justiz, 'Betreff: Unnatürlicher Tod von Anstaltsinsassen', 12 October 1940.

92 Klee, *'Euthanasie' im NS-Staat*, p. 252.

93 Schnabel, *Württemberg zwischen Weimar und Bonn*, p. 454.

94 Klee, *'Euthanasie' im NS-Staat*, p. 208.

95 BA, R22/3387, Der Oberlandesgerichtspräsident an den Herrn Reichsminister der Justiz, 31 August 1940.

96 Wuttke, 'Medizin, Ärzte, Gesundheitspolitik', pp. 231–33.

97 Klee, *'Euthanasie' im NS-Staat*, pp. 89–90, 131, 134, 189–90; Schnabel, *Württemberg zwischen Weimar und Bonn*, p. 450.

98 Michael Ruck, *Korpsgeist und Staatsbewusstsein: Beamte im deutschen Südwesten 1928 bis 1972* (Munich, 1996), pp. 101, 208–9.

99 Wuttke, 'Medizin, Ärzte, Gesundheitspolitik', pp. 226, 231–34.

100 Burleigh, *Death and Deliverance*, p. 142; Klee, *'Euthanasie' im NS-Staat*, pp. 269–72.

101 Müller, *Stuttgart zur Zeit des Nationalsozialismus*, p. 391.

102 Angela Borgstedt, 'Im Zweifelsfall auch mit harter Hand: Jonathan Schmid, Württembergischer Innen-, Justiz- und Wirtschaftsminister', in Michael Kissener and Joachim Scholtyseck (eds), *Die Führer der Provinz: NS-Biographien aus Baden und Württemberg* (Konstanz, 1997), pp. 607–8.

103 Schnabel, *Württemberg zwischen Weimar und Bonn*, p. 451.

104 Borgstedt, 'Im Zweifelsfall auch mit harter Hand', p. 608.

105 BA, R22/4209, Der Generalstaatsanwalt an den Herrn Reichsminister der Justiz, 15 July 1940.

106 Klee, *'Euthanasie' im NS-Staat*, pp. 269–72.

107 Burleigh, *Death and Deliverance*, pp. 139–40.

108 Klee, *Dokumente zur 'Euthanasie'*, pp. 99–100.

109 Tübinger Vereinigung für Volksheilkunde e.V., *Volk und Gesundheit*, p. 180; Schnabel, *Württemberg zwischen Weimar und Bonn*, pp. 452–53; Burleigh, 'Psychiatry, German Society and the Nazi "Euthanasia" Programme', pp. 52–53, 55; Noakes and Pridham, *Nazism*, iii, p. 421.

110 BA, R22/4209, 8 July 1940.

111 Ibid., R22/3387, 6 November 1940.

112 Klee, *Dokumente zur 'Euthanasie'*, pp. 211–12.

113 Sauer, *Württemberg in der Zeit des Nationalsozialismus*, pp. 406–7; Müller, *Stuttgart zur Zeit des Nationalsozialismus*, p. 386.

114 Schäfer, *Landesbischof D. Wurm und der nationalsozialistische Staat*, p. 117.

115 Schnabel, *Württemberg zwischen Weimar und Bonn*, p. 451.

116 Schäfer, *Landesbischof D. Wurm und der nationalsozialistische Staat*, p. 119.

117   Klee, '*Euthanasie*' *im NS-Staat*, pp. 184–89; Friedlander, 'The Exclusion and Murder of the Disabled', p. 156; McFarland-Icke, *Nurses in Nazi Germany*, p. 220; Noakes and Pridham, *Nazism*, iii, pp. 415–16, 422.

118   Schäfer, *Landesbischof D. Wurm und der nationalsozialistische Staat*, pp. 115–16, gives a list of these, and of the number of patients from each who were murdered.

119   Klee, *Dokumente zur 'Euthanasie'*, p. 212.

120   Schnabel, *Württemberg zwischen Weimar und Bonn*, p. 456.

121   Ludwig Volk (ed.), *Akten deutscher Bischöfe über die Lage der Kirche, 1933–1945*, v, *1940–1942* (Mainz, 1983): document 572, Gröber and Kottmann to Lammers, 1 August 1940, pp. 81–82; document 575, 5 August 1940, p. 86; document 616, 1 December 1940, p. 281. On protests in Bavaria about 'euthanasia', and the Catholic Church's response, see Ian Kershaw, *Popular Opinion and Political Dissent in the Third Reich: Bavaria, 1933–1945* (Oxford, 1983), pp. 334–40.

122   Volk, *Akten deutscher Bischöfe*, document 591, Ordinariat Rottenburg to Schmid, 5 October 1940, pp. 205–9.

123   Klee, *Dokumente zur 'Euthanasie'*, pp. 151–62.

124   Cf. Kershaw, *Popular Opinion and Political Dissent in the Third Reich*, p. 335; Steigmann-Gall, *The Holy Reich*, pp. 201–2.

125   Schäfer, *Landesbischof D. Wurm und der nationalsozialistische Staat*, pp. 119–24, 125–26.

126   Volk, *Akten deutscher Bischöfe*, pp. 81–82.

127   Schäfer, *Landesbischof D. Wurm und der nationalsozialistische Staat*, pp. 118, 125.

128   Klee, *Dokumente zur 'Euthanasie'*, p. 212.

129   StAL, Bü45, p. 16.

130   Klee, '*Euthanasie*' *im NS-Staat*, pp. 177–78.

131   Klee, *Dokumente zur 'Euthanasie'*, pp. 222–25.

132   Klee, '*Euthanasie*' *im NS-Staat*, pp. 289–90.

133   BA, R22/4209, 12 October 1940.

134   Klee, '*Euthanasie*' *im NS-Staat*, pp. 189–90.

135   Ibid., pp. 291–93; Hans Franke, *Geschichte und Schicksal der Juden in Heilbronn: vom Mittelalter bis zur Zeit der nationalsozialistischen Verfolgungen, 1050–1945* (Heilbronn, 1963), pp. 346, 352; Paul Sauer, *Die jüdischen Gemeinden in Württemberg und Hohenzollern: Denkmale, Geschichte, Schicksale* (Stuttgart, 1966), pp. 100, 131; Paul Sauer, *Die Schicksale der Jüdischen Bürger Baden-Württembergs während der nationalsozialistischen Verfolgungszeit, 1933–1945* (Stuttgart, 1969), pp. 264–65.

136   Tübinger Vereinigung für Volksheilkunde e.V., *Volk und Gesundheit*, p. 183.

137   Klee, '*Euthanasie*' *im NS-Staat*, pp. 452–56, 61.

138   Sauer, *Die jüdischen Gemeinden*, p. 22; Resi Weglein, 'Ich streichelte jeden Schrank und jeden Stuhl', in Barbara Bronnen (ed.), *Geschichte vom Überleben: Frauentagebücher aus der NS-Zeit* (Munich, 1998), pp. 108–9; Noakes and Pridham, *Nazism*, iii, pp. 521–23, 530.

139   Franke, *Geschichte und Schicksal der Juden in Heilbronn*, p. 180.

140   Resi Weglein, *Als Krankenschwester im KZ Theresienstadt*, ed. and intro. Silvester Lechner and Alfred Moos (Stuttgart, 1988), pp. 216–17.

141   Sauer, *Württemberg in der Zeit des Nationalsozialismus*, p. 414.

142   Christhard Hoffmann, 'Verfolgung und Alltagsleben der Landjuden im nationalsozial-istischen Deutschland', in Monika Richarz and Reinhard Rürup (eds), *Jüdisches Leben auf dem Lande: Studien zur deutsch-jüdischen Geschichte* (Tübingen, 1997), p. 387; Herman Dicker, *Creativity, Holocaust, Reconstruction: Jewish life in Württemberg, Past and Present* (New York, c1984), pp. 178–83.

143   United States Holocaust Memorial Museum archive, results of the German Minority Census of 17 May 1939, sample of returns from Württemberg's communes.

144   See the brief accounts of individual communes in Sauer, *Die jüdischen Gemeinden*, pp. 25–192. For a similar picture in Bavaria, see Kershaw, *Popular Opinion and Political Dissent in the Third Reich*, pp. 225–28.

145   Württembergisches Statistisches Landesamt, *Staatshandbuch Württemberg – Ortschaftsverzeichnis* (Stuttgart, 1936), pp. 147–53.

146   Felix Sutschek, 'Die jüdische Landgemeinde Oberdorf am Ipf in der Zeit des National-sozialismus', in Michael Kissener (ed.), *Widerstand gegen die Judenverfolgung* (Konstanz, 1996), p. 129.

147   Sauer, *Die jüdischen Gemeinden*, pp. 73, 110–11.

148   Ibid., p. 20; Walter Strauss, *Signs of Life, Jews from Württemberg: Reports for the Period after 1933 in Letters and Descriptions* (New York, 1982), map.

149   StAL, Bü46, p. 1; Paul Kopf, 'Buchau am Federsee in nationalsozialistischer Zeit: die Ereignisse der Jahre 1934 bis 1938', in Geschichtsverein der Diözese Rottenburg-Stuttgart (ed.), *Kirche im Nationalsozialismus* (Sigmaringen, 1984), p. 291.

150   David Blackbourn, *Class Religion and Local Politics in Wilhelmine Germany: The Centre Party in Württemberg before 1914* (New Haven, Connecticut, and London, 1980), pp. 88, 96–97, 106, 155, 182, 199–200, 223; Weglein, *Als Krankenschwester im KZ Theresienstadt*, p. 122; Hoffmann, 'Verfolgung und Alltagsleben der Landjuden im nationalsozialistischen Deutschland', p. 381.

151   Sauer, *Die jüdischen Gemeinden*, pp. 69, 142–43, 177.

152   Sauer, *Die jüdischen Gemeinden*, pp. 35, 46, 57, 71, 94, 108, 111, 119, 122, 125, 128, 135, 145, 148, 158, 160, 190. Cf. Hoffmann, 'Verfolgung und Alltagsleben der Landjuden im nationalsozialistischen Deutschland', p. 398, who refers to 'the few places in which relations between Christians and Jews were traditionally good'. This refers to Germany as a whole.

153   Sauer, *Die jüdischen Gemeinden*, pp. 50, 51, 71, 77, 86, 89, 94, 142, 152, among others.

154   Schnabel, *Württemberg zwischen Weimar und Bonn*, pp. 535–36.

155   Sauer, *Die jüdischen Gemeinden*, pp. 57, 108, 119, 135, 190; Sutschek, 'Die jüdische Landgemeinde Oberdorf am Ipf', pp. 141, 143.

156   Utz Jeggle, *Judendörfer in Württemberg* (Tübingen, 1969), pp. 224–27, 229–30.

157   Sauer, *Die Schicksale der Jüdischen Bürger*, p. 111.

158   Schnabel, *Württemberg zwischen Weimar und Bonn*, pp. 536–37, 546. On similar reactions in Bavaria, see Kershaw, *Popular Opinion and Political Dissent in the Third Reich*, pp. 231–32.

159   Noakes and Pridham, *Nazism*, ii, 'The Law for the Restoration of the Professional Civil Service', 7 April 1933, pp. 223–25.

160   Paul Sauer (ed.), *Dokumente über die Verfolgung der jüdischen Bürger in Baden-Württemberg durch das nationalsozialistischen Regime, 1933–1945* (Stuttgart, 1966), document 139, p. 163.

161   Sauer, *Die jüdischen Gemeinden*, p. 156.

162   Sauer, *Dokumente über die Verfolgung der jüdischen Bürger*: document 146, p. 171; document 145, pp. 169–70. On maintaining order and restraining Nazi party activists, see Christine Arbogast, *Herrschaftsinstanzen der württembergischen NSDAP: Funktion, Sozialprofil und Lebenswege einer regionalen NS-Elite 1920–1960* (Munich, 1998), pp. 124–25.

163   Schnabel, *Württemberg zwischen Weimar und Bonn*, p. 536. Cf. pp. 546, 548.

164   Jeggle, *Judendörfer in Württemberg*, pp. 229–30.

165   Sutschek, 'Die jüdische Landgemeinde Oberdorf am Ipf', pp. 141–42.

166   Hoffmann, 'Verfolgung und Alltagsleben der Landjuden im nationalsozialistischen Deutschland', p. 376, makes this claim.

167   Schnabel, *Württemberg zwischen Weimar und Bonn*, p. 536.

168   Sauer, *Die jüdischen Gemeinden*, pp. 94, 110, 112, 135, 147, 160, 175.

169   Sutschek, 'Die jüdische Landgemeinde Oberdorf am Ipf', pp. 141–43, 149–50.

170   Franke, *Geschichte und Schicksal der Juden in Heilbronn*, p. 180.

171   Sauer, *Die jüdischen Gemeinden*, p. 57.

172   Harmut Berghoff and Cornelia Rauh-Kühne, *Fritz K.: ein deutsches Leben im zwangzigsten Jahrhundert* (Stuttgart and Munich, 2000), pp. 178–79.

173   Noakes and Pridham, *Nazism*, ii: 'The Law for the Protection of German Blood and Honour'; 'The Reich Citizenship Law', pp. 535–37.

174   Franke, *Geschichte und Schicksal der Juden in Heilbronn*, p. 178.

175   Jeggle, *Judendörfer in Württemberg*, pp. 224–25.

176   Sutschek, 'Die jüdische Landgemeinde Oberdorf am Ipf', p. 142. See also Schnabel, *Württemberg zwischen Weimar und Bonn*, p. 552.

177   Sauer, *Die jüdischen Gemeinden*, p. 123. On the *Flammenzeichen*, see Gabriele Blum, '"Wirtschaft am Pranger": Die Berichterstattung des württembergischen "Kampfblatts" "Flammenzeichen" über unangepasstes Verhalten von Gewerbetreibenden', in Cornelia Rauh-Kühne and Michael Ruck (eds), *Regionale Eliten zwischen Diktatur und Demokratie: Baden und Württemberg, 1930–1952* (Munich, 1993), pp. 247–62.

178   Sauer, *Die jüdischen Gemeinden*, pp. 115, 125.

179   Sauer, *Dokumente über die Verfolgung der jüdischen Bürger*, document 156, p. 185.

180   Sutschek, 'Die jüdische Landgemeinde Oberdorf am Ipf', pp. 142–43.

181   Sauer, *Dokumente über die Verfolgung der jüdischen Bürger*, document 136, p. 161.

182   Schnabel, *Württemberg zwischen Weimar und Bonn*, pp. 546–47.

183   Sauer, *Dokumente über die Verfolgung der jüdischen Bürger*, document 135, pp. 160–61.

184   Ibid.: document 130, pp. 150–51; document 131, pp. 151–52.

185   Sauer, *Die jüdischen Gemeinden*, p. 163; Leipner, *Chronik der Stadt Stuttgart*, p. 538.

186   Schnabel, *Württemberg zwischen Weimar und Bonn*, pp. 546, 548–49.

187   Sauer, *Dokumente über die Verfolgung der jüdischen Bürger*, document 133b, p. 158.

188   Leipner, *Chronik der Stadt Stuttgart*, p. 538; Sauer, *Dokumente über die Verfolgung der jüdischen Bürger*, p. 146. For Bavaria, see Kershaw, *Popular Opinion and Political Dissent in the Third Reich*, p. 245.

189   Schnabel, *Württemberg zwischen Weimar und Bonn*, p. 548; Sauer, *Dokumente über die Verfolgung der jüdischen Bürger*: document 129, pp. 149–50; document 134b, p. 159. On problems with 'Aryan' cattle dealers in Bavaria, see Kershaw, *Popular Opinion and Political Dissent in the Third Reich*, pp. 241–42.

190 Sauer, *Dokumente über die Verfolgung der jüdischen Bürger*, document 134b, p. 159.

191 Sauer, *Dokumente über die Verfolgung der jüdischen Bürger*: documents 133a and 133b, p. 158; document 134a, p. 159.

192 Sutschek, 'Die judische Landgemeinde Oberdorf am Ipf', pp. 144–45. Cf. Sauer, *Dokumente über die Verfolgung der jüdischen Bürger*, p. 146.

193 Ibid., p. 147 and document 179e, pp. 217–19.

194 On orders from the centre, see Sauer, *Dokumente über die Verfolgung der jüdischen Bürger*, document 177, pp. 210–13. On 'Aryanisation', see Schnabel, *Württemberg zwischen Weimar und Bonn*, pp. 562ff.

195 Sauer, *Die jüdischen Gemeinden*, pp. 152–53; Hoffmann, 'Verfolgung und Alltagsleben der Landjuden im nationalsozialistischen Deutschland', p. 395.

196 Sauer, *Die Schicksale der jüdischen Bürger*, pp. 146–49, gives detailed figures for Württemberg and Baden together. Sauer, *Die jüdischen Gemeinden*, gives figures for many individual communes.

197 Franke, *Geschichte und Schicksal der Juden in Heilbronn*, p. 370.

198 Sutschek, 'Die jüdische Landgemeinde Oberdorf am Ipf', pp. 144–45.

199 Sauer, *Dokumente über die Verfolgung der jüdischen Bürger*: document 148, pp. 172–73; document 149, pp. 174–75. See also Schnabel, *Württemberg zwischen Weimar und Bonn*, p. 561.

200 Arbeitswissenschaftliches Institut der Deutschen Arbeitsfront (hereafter AIDA) (ed.), *Die Sozialstruktur des Gaues Württemberg-Hohenzollern: eine sozialgeographische Analyse* (Berlin, 1940), pp. 30–43.

201 Sauer, *Die jüdischen Gemeinden*, pp. 57, 143, 148, 160, 177, 190–91, 192.

202 Ibid., pp. 123, 147, 163, 184.

203 Ibid., pp. 57–58. Cf. Hoffmann, 'Verfolgung und Alltagsleben der Landjuden im nationalsozialistischen Deutschland', pp. 389ff.

204 Sutschek, 'Die jüdische Landgemeinde Oberdorf am Ipf', pp. 145–48.

205 Sauer, *Die jüdischen Gemeinden*, pp. 48, 50, 54, 81, 90, 131, 145.

206 Kopf, 'Buchau am Federsee in nationalsozialistischer Zeit', pp. 288–90.

207 Franke, *Geschichte und Schicksal der Juden in Heilbronn*, p. 178.

208 Sauer, *Die jüdischen Gemeinden*, p. 175.

209 StAL, K110, Bü45, p. 41.

210 Schnabel, *Württemberg zwischen Weimar und Bonn*, p. 558.

211 StAL, K110, Bü44, pp. 1–2, 4–6.

212 Ibid., Bü45, pp. 2–3.

213 Ibid., Bü46, p. 1.

214 Sauer, *Die jüdischen Gemeinden*, p. 172.

215 Kopf, 'Buchau am Federsee in nationalsozialistischer Zeit', p. 291.

216 HStAS, E151/01, Bü3134, 'Volkszählung 1939', provisional results, p. 52.

217 Schnabel, *Württemberg zwischen Weimar und Bonn*, p. 565.

218 Franke, *Geschichte und Schicksal der Juden in Heilbronn*, p. 344; Sauer, *Die jüdischen Gemeinden*, p. 58.

219 Franke, *Geschichte und Schicksal der Juden in Heilbronn*, pp. 176–77.

220 Sauer, *Die jüdischen Gemeinden*, pp. 46, 124f, 158.

221   Franke, *Geschichte und Schicksal der Juden in Heilbronn*, pp. 176–77, 347.

222   Sauer, *Die jüdischen Gemeinden*, p. 21.

223   Sutschek, 'Die jüdische Landgemeinde Oberdorf am Ipf', pp. 148–49.

224   Franke, *Geschichte und Schicksal der Juden in Heilbronn*, pp. 344–52.

225   Sauer, *Die jüdischen Gemeinden*, pp. 66, 90, 105, 144, 176, 191.

226   Franke, *Geschichte und Schicksal der Juden in Heilbronn*, p. 344.

227   Sauer, *Die jüdischen Gemeinden*, pp. 46, 124f, 158.

228   Sauer, *Die Schicksale der Jüdischen Bürger*, pp. 258–60.

229   Sauer, *Die jüdischen Gemeinden*, pp. 22, 90; Schadt, 'Verfolgung und Widerstand', pp. 116–17.

230   Rothfuss, *Die Hitlerfahn' muss weg!*, pp. 70–73; Kopf, 'Buchau am Federsee in nationalsozialistischer Zeit', p. 291 n. 65.

231   Sauer, *Die jüdischen Gemeinden*, p. 22; Noakes and Pridham, *Nazism*, iii, pp. 523–24, 527, 528.

232   Weglein, *Als Krankenschwester im KZ Theresienstadt*, pp. 15, 18–19.

233   Kopf, 'Buchau am Federsee in nationalsozialistischer Zeit', p. 291 n. 65.

234   Stadtarchiv Göppingen (ed.), *Jüdisches Museum Göppingen* (Memmingen, 1992), pp. 106–7; Noakes and Pridham, *Nazism*, iii, p. 530; Weglein, *Als Krankenschwester im KZ Theresienstadt*, pp. 19–23.

235   Stadtarchiv Göppingen, *Jüdisches Museum Göppingen*, pp. 98, 107.

236   Franke, *Geschichte und Schicksal der Juden in Heilbronn*, pp. 179–80. See also Hoffmann, 'Verfolgung und Alltagsleben der Landjuden im nationalsozialistischen Deutschland', p. 397.

237   Sauer, *Die jüdischen Gemeinden*, pp. 125, 128.

238   Ibid., pp. 145, 148, 175.

239   Ursula Büttner, 'Von der Kirche verlassen: die deutschen Protestanten und die Verfolgung der Juden und Christen jüdischer Herkunft im "Dritten Reich"', in Ursula Büttner and Martin Greschat (eds), *Die verlassenen Kinder der Kirche: der Umgang mit Christen jüdischer Herkunft im 'Dritten Reich'* (Göttingen, 1998), p. 40.

240   Schäfer, *Landesbischof D. Wurm und der nationalsozialistische Staat*, pp. 149–51.

241   Guenter Lewy, *The Catholic Church and Nazi Germany* (London, 1964), pp. 277, 294.

242   Joachim Köhler and Jörg Thierfelder, 'Anpassung oder Widerstand? Die Kirchen im Bann der "Machtergreifung" Hitlers', in Landeszentrale für politische Bildung und Haus der Geschichte (ed.), *Formen des Widerstandes im Südwesten: Scheitern und Nachwirken*, edited by the Landeszentrale für politische Bildung Baden-Württemberg und vom Haus der Geschichte Baden-Württemberg durch Thomas Schnabel unter Mitarbeit von Angelika Hauser-Hauswirth (Ulm, 1994), pp. 80–81.

243   Schäfer, *Landesbischof D. Wurm und der nationalsozialistische Staat*, pp. 151, 158–65.

244   For a trenchant exposition of this view, see Götz Aly, *Hitlers Volksstaat: Raub, Rassenkrieg und nationaler Sozialismus* (Frankfurt am Main, 2005), especially 'Die Früchte des Bösen', pp. 311–27.

245   Sauer, *Dokumente über die Verfolgung der jüdischen Bürger*, document 183c, p. 227.

Notes to Chapter 5: The Impact of War

1 Bundesarchiv (BA), R55/601, 'Tätigkeitsbericht (Stichtag: 2. Oktober 1944)', p. 151: 'Germany is for practical purposes on its own and can no longer expect much from its allies'.

2 On 'total war', see Peter Longerich, 'Joseph Goebbels und der totale Krieg: eine unbekannte Denkschrift des Propagandaministers vom 18. Juli 1944', *Vierteljahrshefte für Zeitgeschichte*, 35 (1987), pp. 290–92; Roger Chickering, Stig Förster and Bernd Greiner (eds), *A World at Total War: Global Conflict and the Politics of Destruction, 1937–1945*, Publications of the German Historical Institute, Washington, DC (Cambridge, 2005). See also Michael Geyer, 'Restorative Elites, German Society and the Nazi Pursuit of War', in Richard Bessel (ed.), *Fascist Italy and Nazi Germany* (Cambridge, 1996), pp. 151–54.

3 The quotation is from ibid., p. 157.

4 For a brief but excellent summary of the effects of the war on British society, see Jose Harris, 'War and Social History: Britain and the Home Front during the Second World War', *Contemporary European History*, 1 (1992), pp. 17–35. For a comprehensive account that is rich in fascinating detail, see Angus Calder, *The People's War: Britain, 1939–1945* (London, 1971). For a more recent illuminating account, see Ina Zweiniger-Bargielowska, *Austerity in Britain: Rationing, Controls, and Consumption, 1939–1955* (Oxford, 2000).

5 Benigna Schönhagen, *Tübingen unterm Hakenkreuz: eine Universitätsstadt in der Zeit des Nationalsozialismus* (Stuttgart, 1991), pp. 309–10; Gerda Szepansky, *'Blitzmädel', 'Heldenmutter', 'Kriegerwitwe': Frauenleben im Zweiten Weltkrieg* (Frankfurt am Main, 1986), p. 13; cf. Walter Rinderle and Bernard Norling, *The Nazi Impact on a German Village* (Lexington, Kentucky, 1993), p. 166; *Deutschland-Berichte der Sozialdemokratische Partei Deutschlands*, 1939, no. 8, p. A6. See also Thames Television, *The World at War* (1973), part 16, 'Inside the Reich, 1940–1944'.

6 On the military course of the war in Europe, see John Keegan, *The Second World War* (London, 1989). On Stalingrad, Earl R. Beck, *Under the Bombs: The German Home Front, 1942–1945* (Lexington, Kentucky, 1986), pp. 33–38. On 'black radio', see Michael Balfour, *Propaganda in War, 1939–1945: Organisations, Policies and Publics in Britain and Germany* (London, 1979), pp. 96, 125, 207, 323, 353, 390, 439, 466.

7 BA, R22/3387, Der Generalstaatsanwalt an den Herrn Reichsminister der Justiz, Nr 3130 – 1a – 2, 31 May 1943.

8 Hauptstaatsarchiv Stuttgart (HStAS), J170, Bü18 (Ulm), Gemeinde Tomerdingen, 'Chronikale Aufzeichnungen über die Gemeinde Tomerdingen, Kreis Ulm (aus der Pfarrchronik)', n.d. [October/November 1948], p. 1.

9 Ibid., Bü4 (Crailsheim), 'Geschichtliche Darstellung der letzten Kriegstage', 27 October 1948 (date received by *Landratsamt* Crailsheim), p. 5.

10 Ibid., Bü1 (Aalen), 'Die letzten Woche vor un[d] die ersten Wochen nach der Besetzung in Neresheim', n.d. [October/November 1948], p. 1.

11 Jürgen Förster, 'From "Blitzkrieg" to "Total War": Germany's War in Europe', in Chickering, Förster and Greiner, *A World at Total War*, p. 102.

12 Alan J. Levine, *The Strategic Bombing of Germany, 1940–1945* (Westport, Connecticut, 1992), pp. 25–29, 31–32, 44–48. See also Martin K. Sorge, *The Other Price of Hitler's*

War (Westport, Connecticut, 1986), pp. 90–112. See also Beck, *Under the Bombs*. For an excellent case study, see Neil Gregor, 'A *Schicksalgemeinschaft*? Allied Bombing, Civilian Morale, and Social Dissolution in Nuremberg, 1942–1945', *Historical Journal*, 43 (2000), pp. 1051–70.

13   Schönhagen, *Tübingen unterm Hakenkreuz*, pp. 360–61.

14   Martin Kitchen, *Nazi Germany at War* (London, 1995), p. 97.

15   Charles Eade (compiler), *The War Speeches of the Rt Hon. Winston S. Churchill, OM, CH, PC, MP* (London, 1951), 'The Finest Hour. A Speech Delivered First to the House of Commons and Then Broadcast, June 18, 1940', p. 206: 'Hitler knows that he will have to break us in this island or lose the war. If we can stand up to him, all Europe may be free and the life of the world may move forward into broad, sunlit uplands ...'

16   For a brief account of this in several countries, see Jeremy Noakes (ed.), *The Civilian in War: The Home Front in Europe, Japan and the USA in World War II* (Exeter, 1992).

17   Edward R. Zilbert, *Albert Speer and the Nazi Ministry of Arms* (London, 1981), gives the figure of eleven and a half million. Förster, 'From "Blitzkrieg" to "Total War"', p. 102: 'Altogether, some 18.3 million soldiers (*Wehrmacht* and *Waffen-SS*) were mobilised'. Not all of these were German nationals. On secondments, see, e.g., HStAS: E151/01, Bü1167: Der Oberbürgermeister der Stadt der Auslandsdeutschen an den Herrn Württ. Innenminister, 'Auf den Randerlass vom 18.7.1940, Nr I 1625', 13 August 1940; 'Aufstellung der für Norwegen-Einsatz abgestellten NSKK-Männer NSKK-Motorgruppen Nord und Nordmark – Württemberg', n.d.; Bezirks- und öffentlicher Notar i.R., Ehingen (Donau) an den Herrn Reichsminister des Innern, 'Betreff: Entscheidung über die Richtigkeit einer Notdienstverpflichtung', 5 May 1940; R22/3387, Der Generalstaatsanwalt Stuttgart an den Herrn Reichsminister der Justiz, Nr. 420 b-25, 1 April 1940. On women's burdens, see Daniela Münkel, *Nationalsozialistische Agrarpolitik und Bauernalltag* (Frankfurt am Main, 1996), pp. 440–51; Jill Stephenson: '"Total War" on the Home Front: Women in Germany and Britain in World War II', in Chickering, Förster and Greiner, *A World at Total War*, pp. 226–29; '"Emancipation" and its Problems: War and Society in Württemberg, 1939–1945', *European History Quarterly*, 17 (1987), pp. 345–65.

18   Bernhard R. Kroener, 'Squaring the Circle: Blitzkrieg Strategy and Manpower Shortage, 1939–1942', in Wilhelm Deist (ed.), *The German Military in the Age of Total War* (Leamington Spa, 1985), pp. 282–303; Marie-Luise Recker, *Nationalsozialistische Sozialpolitik im Zweiten Weltkrieg* (Munich, 1985), pp. 58–81, 266–75. For prewar 'combing out', see StAL, Bü46, 'Lagebericht des 2. Vierteljahres 1939', 1 July 1939, pp. 37–38.

19   Staatsarchiv Ludwigsburg (StAL), K110, Bü46, Sicherheitsdienst RFSS – SD Leitabschnitt Stuttgart, 'Betr.: Allgemeine Stimmung und Lage', 1 July 1939, p. 36; Timothy W. Mason, *Sozialpolitik im Dritten Reich* (Opladen, 1977), pp. 218, 228, 289–90.

20   See Kroener, 'Squaring the Circle', on recruitment problems, pp. 286–87, 296–97. Cf. Förster, 'From "Blitzkrieg" to "Total War"', pp. 100–1. See also above, Chapter 3.

21   For the ten million figure, Uwe Kaminsky, '"Vergessene Opfer" – Zwangssterilisierte, "Asoziale", Deserteure, Fremdarbeiter', in Sybille Baumbach, Uwe Kaminsky, Alfons Kenkmann and Beate Meyer, *Rückblenden: Lebensgeschichtliche Interviews mit Verfolgten des NS-Regimes in Hamburg* (Hamburg, 1999), p. 348. For the rest, Ulrich Herbert, *Hitler's*

Foreign Workers: Enforced Foreign Labour in Germany under the Third Reich (Cambridge and New York, 1997), pp. 194, 296–98.

22 On foreign workers in industry in Württemberg, see Neil Gregor, *Daimler-Benz in the Third Reich* (New Haven, Connecticut, and London), 1998), pp. 176–94, passim; Christa Tholander, *Fremdarbeiter, 1939 bis 1945: Ausländische Arbeitskräfte in der Zeppelin-Stadt Friedrichshafen* (Essen, 2001); Annette Schäfer, *Zwangsarbeiter und NS-Rassenpolitik: Russische und polnische Arbeitskräfte in Württemberg, 1939–1945* (Stuttgart, 2000).

23 See the brief discussion of women's work during the war in Jill Stephenson, *Women in Nazi Germany* (London, 2001), pp. 55–58, 156–57. On Jewish women, see Marion A. Kaplan, *Between Dignity and Despair: Jewish Life in Nazi Germany* (New York and Oxford, 1998), pp. 173–78.

24 Kurt Leipner (ed.), *Chronik der Stadt Stuttgart, 1933–1945* (Stuttgart, 1982), p. 937. See also Christine Arbogast, *Herrschaftsinstanzen der württembergischen NSDAP: Funktion, Sozialprofil und Lebenswege einer regionalen NS-Elite, 1920–1960* (Munich, 1998), p. 111.

25 These issues will be discussed in more detail in later chapters of this book.

26 The only fighting on German soil in the First World War was immediately after the Russian invasion of East Prussia in August 1914. On the bombing of German towns and cities generally in the Second World War, see Jörg Friedrich, *Der Brand: Deutschland im Bombenkrieg, 1940–1945* (Munich, 2002); Beck, *Under the Bombs*, passim; Klaus Rainer Röhl, *Verbotene Trauer: Ende der deutschen Tabus* (Munich, 2002), pp. 100–32.

27 BA, R22/3364, Der Oberlandesgerichtspräsident an den Herrn Reichsminister der Justiz, 'Bericht über die allgemeine Lage im Oberlandesgerichtsbezirk Frankfurt a.M.', 26 June 1940.

28 Quotation from Levine, *The Strategic Bombing of Germany*, p. 24. See also Sorge, *The Other Price*, pp. 90–94; Max Hastings, *Bomber Command* (London, 1981), pp. 111–12, 147, 230–31, 268.

29 HStAS, J170, Bü3 (Böblingen), Gemeinde Rohrau.

30 Paul Sauer, *Württemberg in der Zeit des Nationalsozialismus* (Ulm, 1975), p. 346.

31 Leipner, *Chronik der Stadt Stuttgart*, pp. 780, 783; Heinz Bardua, *Stuttgart im Luftkrieg, 1939 1945* (Stuttgart, 1967), p. 21. On other instances of Allied bombers missing their target in southern Germany, see Beck, *Under the Bombs*, pp. 110–11.

32 Bardua, *Stuttgart im Luftkrieg*, p. 28.

33 Gregor, *Daimler-Benz in the Third Reich*, pp. 218–37. On the dispersal of industry in the Landsberg area (Bavaria), see Martin Paulus, Edith Raim and Gerhard Zelger, *Ein Ort wie jeder andere: Bilder aus einer deutschen Kleinstadt. Landsberg, 1923–1958* (Reinbek bei Hamburg, 1995), pp. 18–19.

34 Levine, *The Strategic Bombing of Germany*, pp. 46, 58, 67, 85–86, 102, 125, 131, 133–34, 159, 196, 199. Quotations on pp. 58 and 134, respectively. See also Sorge, *The Other Price*, pp. 95, 97–98; Tholander, *Fremdarbeiter, 1939 bis 1945*, pp. 105–7.

35 Hastings, *Bomber Command*, p. 269; Levine, *The Strategic Bombing of Germany*, pp. 114–16.

36 The first quotation is from Jeremy Noakes (ed.), *Nazism, 1919–1945: A Documentary Reader*, iv, *The German Home Front in World War II* (Exeter, 1998), p. 185; the second quotation is from Gregor, *Daimler-Benz in the Third Reich*, p. 219. See also, more generally, Beck, *Under the Bombs*, p. 86.

37 BA, R22/3387, Der Generalstaatsanwalt Stuttgart an den Herrn Reichsminister der Justiz, Nr 420b – 28, 'Betreff: Lagebericht', 30 September 1940.

38 StAL, PL501/45, Kreis Stuttgart, p. 70237, Rundschreiben Nr. 55/39, 'Betr.: Luftschutz-Rettungsstellen', 20 September 1939.

39 Bardua, *Stuttgart im Luftkrieg*, pp. 34–35; Leipner, *Chronik der Stadt Stuttgart*, pp. 675, 693, 828. The quotation is from p. 675.

40 Sauer, *Württemberg*, pp. 346–47.

41 Peter Hüttenberger, *Die Gauleiter: Studie zum Wandel des Machtgefüges in der NSDAP* (Stuttgart, 1969), p. 170 n. 95.

42 Bardua, *Stuttgart im Luftkrieg*, pp. 57–62.

43 Müller, *Stuttgart zur Zeit des Nationalsozialismus*, pp. 465–67, quotation on p. 466; Bardua, *Stuttgart im Luftkrieg*, pp. 90–122; Leipner, *Chronik der Stadt Stuttgart*, pp. 977–81, 984–85.

44 Beck, *Under the Bombs*, pp. 133–34.

45 BDC, personnel file on Adolf Mauer, letters: from the Landesleiter für Musik to the President of the Reichskulturkammer, 28 February 1944; from the Landesleiter für Schriftum to the Reichsschriftumskammer, 29 March 1944; from the Government Library in the Württemberg Ministry of the Interior to the Landeskulturwalter Württemberg, 6 April 1944; from the Landeskulturwalter to the President of the Reichskulturkammer, 11 April 1944; and from the Landeskulturwalter to the President of the Reichskulturkammer, 15 September 1944. See also Bardua, *Stuttgart im Luftkrieg*, pp. 68–73.

46 StAL, K100/10, Kriminalpolizeileitstelle Stuttgart, 'Betr.: Sofortunterbringung der Kriminalpolizeileitstelle Stuttgart', 14 September 1944.

47 BDC, personnel file on Friedrich Schmidt, letter from the Munich Adjutant on the Personal Staff of the Reichsführer-SS to Dr Brandt, Personal Staff of the Reichsführer-SS, Berlin, 13 May 1944.

48 Leipner, *Chronik der Stadt Stuttgart*, pp. 991, 993–94, 1000–1, 1003. See also Bardua, *Stuttgart im Luftkrieg*, pp. 122–24, 137–40, 143, 165.

49 HStAS, E397, Bü10, 'Im Gebiet des Landwirtschaftsamts Württemberg. Nährmittel-bevölkerung für die 72. Zuteilungsperiod vom 5.2.1945 bis 4.3.1945'.

50 Leipner, *Chronik der Stadt Stuttgart*, pp. 1011, 1022, 1024. The quotation is from p. 1011.

51 HStAS, J170, Bü77 (Tettnang), 'Aktennotiz: Luftangriffe auf Friedrichshafen im 2. Weltkrieg', 26 October 1953.

52 Ibid., 'Friedrichshafen', Sonderdruck aus der Zeitschrift 'Der Städtetag', no. 3, 1957, p. 2; Beck, *Under the Bombs*, p. 111.

53 Sauer, *Württemberg*, p. 357; Schnabel, *Württemberg zwischen Weimar und Bonn*, p. 586; HStAS, J170, Bü18, Gemeinde Tomerdingen, p. 3.

54 Ibid., E151/03, Bü968, Kreisleitung Heilbronn, der Kreisleiter an die Gauleitung der NSDAP, 'Betreff: Räumung des Altstadtkernes der Stadt Heilbronn', 27 March 1944.

55 Sauer, *Württemberg*, pp. 355–56; Schnabel, *Württemberg zwischen Weimar und Bonn*, pp. 585–86; Susanne Schlösser, '"Was sich in den Weg stellt, mit Vernichtung schlagen": Richard Drauz, NSDAP-Kreisleiter von Heilbronn', in Michael Kissener and Joachim Scholtyseck (eds), *Die Führer der Provinz: NS-Biographien aus Baden und Württemberg* (Konstanz, 1997), p. 156.

56 Sauer, *Württemberg*, p. 357.

57 Hartmut Berghoff and Cornelia Rauh-Kühne, *Fritz K. Ein deutsches Leben im zwanzigsten Jahrhundert* (Stuttgart and Munich, 2000), pp. 202, 204.

58 HStAS, J170, Bü8 (Heilbronn), 'Betrifft: Geschichtliche Darstellung der letzten Kriegstage. [F]ür das Württ. Stattistische [sic] Landesamt-Stuttgart', Gundelsheim a.N., 8 September 1948, p. 1.

59 Schönhagen, *Tübingen unterm Hakenkreuz*, p. 360.

60 HStAS, J170, Bü78 (Tübingen), Paul Sting, 'Der große Szenenwechsel. Tübingen in Niemandsland', *Schwäbisches Tageblatt*, 19 April 1955.

61 Ibid., Bü3 (Böblingen), Gemeinde Sindelfingen; Gregor, *Daimler-Benz in the Third Reich*, pp. 229ff.

62 Schönhagen, *Tübingen unterm Hakenkreuz*, pp. 361–62, 367–68.

63 Leipner, *Chronik der Stadt Stuttgart*, p. 985. The quotation is from Schnabel, *Württemberg zwischen Weimar und Bonn*, p. 584. Cf. Beck, *Under the Bombs*, p. 134.

64 Sauer, *Wilhelm Murr*, p. 135.

65 HStAS, E151/03, Bü968, Kreisleitung Ulm, der Kreisleiter an den Gauleiter der NSDAP, 'Betr.: Umquartierung', 23 March 1944.

66 Ibid., J170, Bü3 (Böblingen), 'Geschichte der letzten Kriegstage des Zweiten Weltkriegs in Musberg', 18 October 1948, pp. 1–15. The quotation is from p. 7.

67 For a sense of what it was like, see Friedrich, *Der Brand*, pp. 493–514. See also Beck, *Under the Bombs*, pp. 57–197.

68 Gregor, 'A *Schicksalgemeinschaft*?', pp. 1056, 1061, 1063–64, 1067; Leipner, *Chronik der Stadt Stuttgart*, pp. 898–99, 930, 977, 995. See, by contrast, the optimistic view from *Gau Baden-Elsass*, *Völkischer Beobachter*, 7 June 1944, reproduced in Stephenson, *Women in Nazi Germany*, pp. 169–71.

69 HStAS, J170, Bü3, Musberg, pp. 4–5.

70 Ibid., E397, Bü14.

71 Leipner, *Chronik der Stadt Stuttgart*, pp. 992, 996, 999, 1005–6, 1009.

72 HStAS, E151/01, Bü3872: Der Reichsminister für Volksaufklärung und Propaganda an alle Obersten Reichsbehörde, 21 July 1943; Nr I 1128, 'Betreff: Filmapparate für die Bevölkerung luftbedrohter Gebiete', 16 August 1943; correspondence of 18 August 1943 and 25 August 1943; Der Oberbürgermeister der Stadt der Auslandsdeutschen an die Ministerialabteilung für Bezirks- und Körperschaftsverwaltung, B23/5/2, 24 August 1943.

73 Levine, *The Strategic Bombing of Germany*, pp. 39–40. On p. 30, Levine refers to 'Lord Cherwell, Churchill's clever if erratic scientific adviser'.

74 Quoted in Manfred J. Enssle, 'The Harsh Discipline of Food Scarcity in Postwar Stuttgart, 1945–1948', *German Studies Review*, 10 (1987), p. 484.

75 Schnabel, *Württemberg zwischen Weimar und Bonn*, p. 587. There are accounts of the damage inflicted on various communes in the HStAS, J170 files.

76 Schönhagen, *Tübingen unterm Hakenkreuz*, p. 360.

77 Sauer, *Württemberg*, p. 354.

78 HStAS, J170, Bü4, Gemeinde Rossfeld.

79 Ibid., Gemeinde Rot am See.

80 Ibid., Gemeinde Stimpfach.

81 Ibid., Gemeinde Oberspeltach.

82   Ibid., Bü3: Gemeinde Nufringen; Gemeinde Herrenberg.

83   Ibid., Bü1, Gemeinde Zipplingen.

84   Ibid., Bü8 (Heilbronn), 'Geschichtliche Darstellung der letzten Kriegstage', Abstatt, 25 November 1948. For 'satellite communes' (*Teilgemeinde* – partial communes), see above, Chapter 1, pp. 12–13.

85   Ibid., 'Geschichtliche Darstellung der letzten Kriegstage', Biberach, 9 November 1948.

86   Ibid., 'Darstellung der letzten Kriegstage des Weltkrieges 1939–1945 in der Gemeinde Eberstadt (Kreis Heilbronn)', 26 October 1948.

87   Ibid., Bü10 (Leonberg), 'Kriegs-chronik der Gemeinde Münchingen', verfasst von –, Bauer, Münchingen, n.d., pp. 1–2.

88   Ibid., Bü18, Gemeinde Tomerdingen.

89   Schnabel, *Württemberg zwischen Weimar und Bonn*, p. 587.

90   Rudolf Hofsähs, 'Die Abwanderung aus wirtschaftlich zurückgebliebenen Gebieten in Baden-Württemberg', doctoral dissertation for the Wirtschaftshochschule (Mannheim, 1957), pp. 38, 43 and appendix IX pp. 1–2. Cf. Schnabel, *Württemberg zwischen Weimar und Bonn*, pp. 586–87.

91   StAL, K110, Bü46, pp. 33–35. See also Willi A. Boelcke, 'Wirtschaft und Sozialsituation', in Otto Borst (ed.), *Das Dritte Reich in Baden und Württemberg* (Stuttgart, 1988), p. 43.

92   Jeremy Noakes and Geoffrey Pridham (eds), *Nazism, 1919–1945: A Documentary Reader*, iii, *Foreign Policy, War and Racial Extermination*, pp. 266, 302; Lothar Burchardt, 'The Impact of the War Economy on the Civilian Population of Germany during the First and Second World Wars', in Deist, *The German Military in the Age of Total War*, pp. 50–52; Misha Glenny, *The Balkans, 1804–1999: Nationalism, War and the Great Powers* (London, 2000), pp. 479–506; Cornelia Fuykshot, *Hunger in Holland: Life During the Nazi Occupation* (Amherst, Massachusetts, 1995), especially pp. 99–108, 124–42, 149–50; BBC 2, *Timewatch* film, 'The Hunger Winter', (undated). See also Götz Aly, *Hitlers Volksstaat: Raub, Rassenkrieg und Nationaler Sozialismus* (Frankfurt am Main, 2005), pp. 195–206, 275–80.

93   StAL, K110, Bü47, 'Betr.: Allgemeine Stimmung und Lage', 15 July 1941, p. 2.

94   Gernot Wiese, 'Die Versorgungslage in Deutschland', in Michael Salewski and Guntram Schulze-Wegener (eds), *Kriegsjahr 1944: im Großen und im Kleinen*, (Stuttgart, 1995), pp. 240–50; Leipner, *Chronik der Stadt Stuttgart*, pp. 981, 995. On the problem of food scarcity in Germany in the era of the two world wars, see Manfred J. Enssle, 'Five Theses on German Everyday Life after World War II', *Central European History*, 26 (1993), pp. 7–14.

95   Michael Karl, 'Landwirtschaft und Ernährung im Deutschen Reich', in Salewski and Schulze-Wegener, *Kriegsjahr 1944*, pp. 260–61; Burchardt, 'Impact of the War Economy', pp. 47–54, 62–64; Sauer, *Württemberg*, p. 367; Willi Schefold, 'Landwirtschaft und Ernährung', in Max Gögler and Gregor Richter (eds), *Das Land Württemberg-Hohenzollern, 1945–1952* (Sigmaringen, 1982), p. 327; Kershaw, *Popular Opinion*, p. 314.

96   Enssle, 'The Harsh Discipline of Food Scarcity', pp. 481–502; Paul Sauer, *Demokratischer Neubeginn in Not und Elend: das Land Württemberg-Baden von 1945 bis 1952* (Ulm, 1978), pp. 16, 18, 30, 280–311; Schefold, 'Landwirtschaft und Ernährung', pp. 327–31.

97   J.E. Farquharson, *The Plough and the Swastika: The NSDAP and Agriculture in Germany, 1928–1945* (London, 1976), pp. 176–179.

98   Jill Stephenson, 'Propaganda, Autarky and the German Housewife', in David Welch

(ed.), *Nazi Propaganda: The Power and the Limitations*, (London, 1983), pp. 121, 126–138; Nancy R. Reagin, 'Marktordnung and Autarkic Housekeeping: Housewives and Private Consumption under the Four-Year Plan, 1936–39', *German History*, 19 (2001), pp. 162–84.

99   Karl, 'Landwirtschaft und Ernährung', p. 259.

100 Stephenson, 'Propaganda, Autarky', pp. 117–38; Kate Lacey, *Feminine Frequencies: Gender, German Radio and the Public Sphere* (Ann Arbor, Michigan, 1996), pp. 174–90.

101 See below, in this chapter.

102 Burchardt, 'The Impact of the War Economy', pp. 63–64.

103 Farquharson, *The Plough and the Swastika*, pp. 221–22; Noakes, *Nazism*, iv, pp. 511–15.

104 StAL, K110, Bü48, 'Betr.: Allgemeine Stimmung und Lage', 1 September 1941, 'Bezeichnende Ausführungen eines Aussenstellen-Mitarbeiters zur Lageberichterstattung', p. 6.

105 Leipner, *Chronik der Stadt Stuttgart*, pp. 605, 643.

106 StAL, K110, Bü47, pp. 21–22.

107 Leipner, *Chronik der Stadt Stuttgart*, p. 605.

108 HStAS, E397, Bü37, Deutsches Frauenwerk, Gaustelle Württemberg-Hohenzollern, to Landesernährungsamt B, Stuttgart, 9 August 1940.

109 StAL, K110, Bü48, SD 'Lagebericht', 1 September 1941, pp. 34, 36.

110 On illicit slaughtering, see below, Chapter 6.

111 Boberach, *Meldungen aus dem Reich*, p. 146. German women were not alone in being reluctant to undertake work for the war effort, whatever may be alleged about British women's willingness to accept conscription into factory work. See Harold L. Smith, 'The Effect of the War on the Status of Women', in Harold L. Smith (ed.), *War and Social Change: British Society in the Second World War* (Manchester, 1986), pp. 211–14. Cf. Tim Mason, 'Women in Germany, 1925–1940', reprinted in Jane Caplan (ed.), *Nazism, Fascism and the Working Class: Essays by Tim Mason* (Cambridge, 1995), pp. 202–3. See also Noakes, 'Germany', pp. 41–43; Stephenson, '"Total War" on the Home Front', pp. 226–29.

112 Stephenson, *Women in Nazi Germany*, pp. 55–58.

113 BA, R22/3387, Der Generalstaatsanwalt Stuttgart an den Herrn Reichsminister der Justiz, 10 July 1940.

114 StAL, K110, Bü47, p. 19.

115 Schönhagen, *Tübingen unterm Hakenkreuz*, pp. 317–18.

116 For examples, see HStAS, E397, Bü37.

117 Leipner, *Chronik der Stadt Stuttgart*, pp. 605, 618 and 636.

118 HStAS, E397, Bü83 gives the instructions for the distribution periods throughout the war. Here, Der Reichsminister für Ernährung und Landwirtschaft an die Landesregierungen, 'Betrifft: Durchführung des Kartensystems für Lebensmittel für die 55. Zuteilungsperiode vom 18. Oktober bis 14. November 1943', 12 September 1943.

119 Boberach, *Meldungen aus dem Reich*, p. 222.

120 StAL, K110, Bü47, p. 1; Balfour, *Propaganda in War*, p. 193.

121 Sauer, *Württemberg*, p. 366; Leipner, *Chronik der Stadt Stuttgart*, pp. 981, 989. See also the periodic ration allocations in HStAS, E397: Bü1, Bü83. More generally, see Burchardt, 'The Impact of the War Economy', p. 49.

122 See the tables detailing food ration allocations in Noakes, *Nazism*, iv, pp. 511–21, and

especially those on pp. 519–21 showing comparisons between the First and Second World Wars.

123 Ian Ousby, *Occupation: The Ordeal of France, 1940–1944* (London, 1999), pp. 116–31. The quotations are from pp. 117, 120. See also Robert Gildea, *Marianne in Chains: In Search of the German Occupation of France, 1940–1945* (London, 2002), pp. 109–13; Julian Jackson, *France: The Dark Years, 1940–1944* (Oxford, 2001), pp. 276–77.

124 Gildea, *Marianne in Chains*, pp. 27–28, 113–18, 126–32.

125 Joanna Hanson, 'Poland', in Noakes, *The Civilian at War*, pp. 150–72. The quotation is from p. 153.

126 Jeremy Noakes and Geoffrey Pridham (eds), *Nazism, 1919–1945*, iii, *Foreign Policy, War and Racial Extermination* (Exeter, 1988), pp. 900–18. The quotations are from pp. 900–1, 916 and 901, respectively. On the USSR's experience of the war, see John Barber and Mark Harrison, *The Soviet Home Front, 1941–1945* (London, 1991).

127 Lisa Pine, *Nazi Family Policy, 1933–1945* (Oxford, 1997), pp. 167–68.

128 Kaplan, *Between Dignity and Despair*, pp. 150–54. The quotation is on p. 151.

129 Victor Klemperer, *I Shall Bear Witness: The Diaries of Victor Klemperer, 1933–1941* (London, 1999), pp. 391–92.

130 Kaplan, *Between Dignity and Despair*, pp. 151–53, 192; Pine, *Nazi Family Policy*, p. 174.

131 HStAS, E397, Bü37, Der Landrat, Ernährungsamt Abt. B an den Viehwirtschaftsverband, 'Betr.: Bezug von Pferdefleisch für russische Kriegsgefangene', n.d. [34th rationing period, 1942]. See also Klemperer, *I Shall Bear Witness*, p. 547.

132 Ibid.: Der Landrat in Rottweil an den Württ. Wirtschaftsminister, Landesernährungsamt, 'Betreff: Tausch und Handel mit Bedarfsnachweisen durch ausländische Zivilarbeiter', 27 April 1944; Reichskriminalpolizeiamt, Berlin, 'Betr.: Schwarzhandel mit Brotmarken – Fehldrucken', 14 October 1944; Der Landrat (Freudenstadt) an den Württ. Wirtschaftsminister, Landesernährungsamt, 'Betreff: Städt. Walfinspektion Freudenstadt; Zuwiderhandlung gegen VRStVO', 21 December 1944; Der Württ. Wirtschaftsminister, Dienststelle Schwäbisch Gmünd, Runderlass Nr 11/45, 'Betreff: Erfassung von Altpapier – Massnahmen zur Verhütung ungesetzlicher Verwertung von Bezugskarten, Bezugscheinen und Abschnitten, Fehldrucken und Makulatur derselben', 10 January 1945. See also Leipner, *Chronik der Stadt Stuttgart*, p. 905; Heinz Boberach (ed.), *Meldungen aus dem Reich* (Herrsching, 1984), vol. 15, 'SD-Berichte zu Inlandsfragen vom 1. November 1943', p. 5954.

133 Noakes, *Nazism*, iv, p. 522; Ulrich Herbert, *Fremdarbeiter: Politik und Praxis des "Ausländer-Einsatzes" in der Kriegswirtschaft des Dritten Reiches* (Berlin and Bonn, 1986), pp. 122, 166–67, 170–71, 286–98. The rations allocated to different categories of inhabitant in Württemberg can be found in HStAS, E397, Bü1.

134 Nikolaus Wachsmann, *Hitler's Prisons: Legal Terror in Nazi Germany* (New Haven, Connecticut, and London, 2004), pp. 83–101, 106–11, 227–56; Michael Burleigh, *Death and Deliverance: 'Euthanasia' in Germany, 1900–1945* (Cambridge, 1994), pp. 261–63.

135 See above, Chapter 1.

136 StAL, K110, Bü47, p. 21.

137 BA, R22/3387, Der Oberlandesgerichtspräsident an den Herrn Reichsminister der Justiz, 'Betreff: Bericht über die allgemeine Lage', 3 July 1941.

138 StAL, K110, Bü47, p. 20; Müller, *Stuttgart zur Zeit des Nationalsozialismus*, p. 336. See also Wiese, 'Die Versorgungslage in Deutschland', p. 244; Jill Stephenson, *The Nazi Organisation of Women* (London, 1981), pp. 187–88.

139 StAL, K110, Bü37, 'Rundschreiben Nr 13/1940 – Betr. Lebensmittel Pakete aus dem Ausland,' 12 February 1940.

140 Ibid., Bü47, pp. 21–22.

141 Ibid., Bü48, pp. 38–39.

142 Ibid., Bü47, p. 18.

143 Ibid., p. 1.

144 Ibid., Bü40, 'III B – La/GS. Rundschreiben Nr 133/41', 29 November 1941, p. 3. On the killing of Red Army POWs, see Noakes and Pridham, *Nazism*, iii, p. 915.

145 Ibid., Bü47, p. 9.

146 Ibid., p. 19.

147 Ibid., Bü48, pp. 36–37. See also BA, R22/3387, 3 July 1941.

148 Ibid., Bü37, SD 'Lagebericht', 25 January 1940.

149 Ibid., Bü47, pp. 20, 22–23.

150 HStAS, E151/1cII, Bü434, Kommandeur der Gendarmerie des Landes Württemberg an den Württ. Innenminister, 'Tätigkeitsbericht für das Jahr 1939', 1 February 1940, pp. 3–5, 7.

151 BA, R22/3387, Der Generalstaatsanwalt Stuttgart an den Herrn Reichsminister der Justiz, Nr. 420b – 25, 'Betrifft: Lagebericht', 1 April 1940.

152 HStAS, E151/1cII, Bü434, 1 February 1940, p. 4.

153 StAL, K110, Bü40, 'III A 3 – Ra./Ab. Rundschr. – Nr 88/41', 18 August 1941.

154 HStAS, E151/1cII, Bü434, 1 February 1940, pp. 4–5.

155 StAL, K110, Bü48, 'Bezeichnende Ausführungen eines Aussenstellen-Mitarbeiters zur Lageberichterstattung', p. 3.

156 HStAS, E397, Bü37, Der Reichsführer SS und Chef der Deutschen Polizei an die Regierungspräsidenten und Landesregierungen, S-V B 2 Nr. 1013/42, 'Betrifft: Polizeiliches Einschreiten zur Bekämpfung der Verstösse gegen die Kriegswirtschaftsbestimmungen', 13 April 1942, p. 1.

157 E.g., Leipner, *Chronik der Stadt Stuttgart*, pp. 868–69, 883.

158 BA, R22/3387, Der Generalstaatsanwalt an den Herrn Reichsminister der Justiz, Nr 420b – 33, 1 August 1941.

159 Ibid., 3 July 1941.

160 Ibid., R22/5005: Der Reichsminister der Justiz, 28 October 1941, p. 193; Der Reichsminister für Ernährung und Landwirtschaft, 18 May 1942, p. 202. The quotation is from p. 193.

161 Ibid., R22/3387, 1 August 1941.

162 Ibid., Der Oberlandesgerichtspräsident an den Herrn Reichsminister der Justiz, 'Betreff: Bericht über die allgemeine Lage', 7 May 1940.

163 Ibid., Der Generalstaatsanwalt an den Herrn Reichsminister der Justiz, Nr 420b-27, 1 August 1940.

164 George D. Spindler, *Burgbach: Urbanisation and Identity in a German Village* (New York, 1973), pp. 44, 77; Günter Golde, *Catholics and Protestants: Agricultural Modernisation in Two German Villages* (New York, 1975), pp. 41–43.

165 HStAS, E151/01, Bü3621: 'Jeder Abfall ist noch was wert', *NS-Kurier*, 22 October 1936; 'Vorbildliche Erfassung des Altmaterials', and 'Es gibt keine wertlosen Abfälle im Betrieb!', both in *NS-Kurier*, 25 February 1937.

166 Ibid., Der Württ. Wirtschaftsminister an den Herrn Reichs- und Preussischen Minister des Innern, Nr B II 2403, 3 May 1937.

167 StAL, PL504/22, Bü40, NSDAP Kreis Nürtingen, 'Betr.: Neue Schrottsammelaktion', 10 July 1939.

168 HStAS, E151/01, Bü3621: Ministerpräsident Generalfeldmarschall Göring, Beauftragter für den Vierjahresplan an die Herren Reichsminister, VP 3656, 23 February 1940; Der Württ. Wirtschaftsminister, Runderlass Nr 197/40, 'Betreff: I, Metallsammlung der Behörden; II, Metallspende des Deutschen Volkes zum Geburtstag des Führers im Kriegsjahr 1940', 20 March 1940.

169 Ibid., Der Württ. Wirtschaftsminister, Runderlass Nr 245/40, 'Betreff: Metallspende des Deutschen Volkes', 13 April 1940.

170 StAL, PL504/22, Bü40, NSDAP Kreis Nürtingen, Ortsgruppe Nürtingen-Süd, 'Betreff: Metallsammlung, Soldatenadressen, Kameradschaftsabend', 18 April 1940.

171 HStAS, E151/01, Bü3621: Der Polizeiamtsvorstand in Schramberg an den Reichsführer-SS, 'Betreff: Erfassung von Metallgegenständen', 11 April 1940 and 29 May 1940; Der Polizeidirektor in Heilbronn an den Reichsführer-SS, 'Betreff: Metallsamlung [sic] bei den Behörden', 12 April 1940; Der Polizeiamtsvorstand in Heidenheim an den Reichsführer-SS, 'Betrifft: Erfassung von Metallgegenständen', 2 April 1940.

172 Ibid.: Der Württ. Wirtschaftsminister, Runderlass Nr 288/40, 27 April 1940; Der Polizeiamts-vorstand in Esslingen am Neckar an den Reichsführer-SS, 'Betreff: Ablieferung von Metallgegenständen', 4 May 1940.

173 Ibid.: Der Landrat (Ludwigsburg) an den Herrn Württ. Innenminister, 'Betreff: Erfassung von Metallgegenständen bei den Behörden', 16 April 1940; Der Landrat (Böblingen) an den Herrn Württ. Innenminister, 'Betreff: Metallsammlung der Behörden', 9 April 1940; 'Erlass an den Herrn Landrat in Böblingen', 18 April 1940.

174 Ibid., 'Ergänzungsrichtlinien v. 11.9.42', II EM 3204/42III.

175 Ibid., Württ. Finanzministerium/Bauabteilung, order of 9 July 1943.

176 Ibid., J170, Bü1 (Aalen): Gemeinde Dalkingen; Gemeinde Bopfingen.

177 Ibid., Bü18 (Ulm), Gemeinde Suppingen.

178 Ibid., E397, Bü37: Sondergericht für den Oberlandesgerichtsbezirk Stuttgart in Stuttgart, SL, Nr 3–4/1943; oKLs. Nr 165–66/43.

179 Ibid., Nr D.K.2136, 6039/42 W, 15 June 1943.

180 Ibid.: Der Landrat, Heilbronn, an den Herrn Württ. Wirtschaftsminister, Nr 4615, 21 February 1942; copy of a denunciation to the criminal police, 4 March 1942.

181 Ibid., Ernährungsamt Öhringen to the Kriminalpolizeileitstelle in Stuttgart, 21 April 1943.

182 Ibid., Sondergericht für den Oberlandesgerichtsbezirk Stuttgart in Stuttgart, SoKLs 236/43.

183 Leipner, *Chronik der Stadt Stuttgart*, p. 610.

184 StAL, K110, Bü47, p. 25.

185 There are numerous examples of this in the HStAS, E382 files.

186   Ibid., Bü358, letters to the Württemberg Wirtschaftsminister, Preisüberwachungsstelle (hereafter, WW/P), ref. 36B14/358: 10 December 1941, 29 June 1942, and 2 August 1942.

187   Ibid., letter from a coal merchant to the WW/P, ref. 16F29/358, 29 December 1941.

188   Renate Bridenthal, 'Beyond *Kinder, Küche, Kirche*: Weimar Women at Work', *Central European History*, 6 (1973), pp. 150–51. See also the employment categories in *StJ*.

189   HStAS, E382, Bü350, N.7, letter to the WW/P, ref. 53 0 22–350 (Bsch), 8 May 1942.

190   Ibid., letter from the WW/P, ref. 53 0 22–350 (Sp), 4 June 1942.

191   Ibid., letters to the WW/P, ref. 2 0 208–350: 19 December 1941; 21 August 1942.

192   Ibid.: letters to the WW/P, ref. 2 0 206–350, 10 August 1942 and 27 March 1943; letters from the WW/P, ref. 2 0 206–350 (Pi), 3 September 1942, and 2 0 206–350 (Pt), 3 April 1943.

193   Ibid., letter from the proprietor of a food and tobacco store to the WW/P, ref. 32D8/350 (Ba), 1 June 1942.

194   Ibid., letter to the Landratsamt, Münsingen, 30 December 1941.

195   Schönhagen, *Tübingen unterm Hakenkreuz*, pp. 316–17; Kitchen, *Nazi Germany at War*, pp. 100–1.

196   HStAS, E397: Bü37, Staatliche Kriminalpolizei, Kriminalpolizeileitstelle Stuttgart an das Landesernährungsamt, Nr D.K.4695, 5 October 1942; Bü14, letter of 10 June 1940.

197   HStAS, E397, Bü14: Nationalpolitische Erziehungsanstalt Backnang an das Landesernährungsamt, 'Betr.: Zusätzliche Ernährung', 30 November 1939; NSDAP Hitler-Jugend, Gebiet Württemberg (20) an das Landesernährungsamt, 'Betr.: Lebensmittelversorgung der Jugendlichen in Gemeinschaftseinrichtungen', 16 March 1943'; Der Landrat an den Herrn Württ. Wirtschaftsminister, Landesernährungsamt, 'Betreff: Versorgung der Nationalpolitischen Erziehungsanstalt Backnang', 24 March, 1943.

198   Ibid., Der Höhere SS- und Polizeiführer bei den Reichsstatthaltern in Württemberg und Baden an das Landesernährungsamt Stuttgart, 'Betr.: Zusatzverpflegung für die Jungmannen der National-Politischen Erziehungsanstalten und Deutschen Heimschulen', 16 November 1943.

199   Ibid., E151kVI, Bü221: letters of 12 September 1941, 7 November 1941, 13 June 1942, 17 June 1942, 31 August 1942, 15 September 1942, 30 September 1942. See also Robert Mackay, *The Test of War: Inside Britain, 1939–1945* (London, 1999), p. 156.

200   Ibid., E397, Bü14, letter of 20 February 1942.

201   Ibid.: Die Leiterin der Lehrerinnenbildungsanstalt Freudenstadt an das Wirtschaftsamt, Ernährungsamt, 25 February 1942; Nr 4092.03 (6) an die Lehrerinnenbildungsanstalt Freudenstadt, 'Betreff: Sonderzulagen in Brot und Milch', 26 February 1942.

202   Ibid.: Die Direktorin der Lehrerinnenbildungsanstalt Haigerloch, Hohenzollern, an das Landesernährungsamt, 1 February 1943; Nr D.K. 499 dem Landrat in Hechingen, 18 Februar 1943.

203   Ibid., Der Reichsminister für Ernährung und Landwirtschaft an alle Landesernährungsämter, II B 2 a – 59, 15 February 1945.

204   These can be found in the HStAS, E382 files.

205   'Joseph Goebbels propagiert den totalen Krieg, 18.2.1943', in Wolfgang Michalka (ed.), *Das Dritte Reich*, ii, *Weltmachtanspruch und nationaler Zusammenbruch, 1939–1945* (Munich, 1985), p. 297.

206   BA, R22/5005, pp. 41–47, Der Polizeipräsident, Berlin, 15 March 1943.

207 Ibid., p. 170, Der Reichsminister der Justiz, 29 March 1943. See also Frank Bajohr, *Parvenüs und Profiteure: Korruption in der NS-Zeit* (Frankfurt am Main, 2001); Kershaw, *The 'Hitler Myth'*, pp. 163–65; Steinert, *Hitler's War and the Germans*, pp. 154–55.

208 BA, R22/3381, Der Generalstaatsanwalt an den Herrn Reichsminister der Justiz, Nr 506/42 (2), 'Betrifft: Lagebericht', 5 June 1942, p. 110.

209 Boberach, *MadR*, vol. 13: no. 360 (18 February 1943); no. 366 (11 March 1943); vol. 13, 'MadR' no. 372, 1 April 1943, pp. 5040–44.

210 Eleanor Hancock, *National Socialist Leadership and Total War, 1941–1945* (New York, 1991), p. 74.

211 From a newspaper article, dated 25 December 1932, quoted in Thomas Schnabel, '"Warum geht es in Schwaben besser?" Württemberg in der Weltwirtschaftskrise, 1928–1933', in Thomas Schnabel (ed.), *Die Machtergreifung in Südwestdeutschland* (Stuttgart, 1982), p. 215.

212 Peter Hüttenberger, *Die Gauleiter. Studie zum Wandel des Machtgefüges in der NSDAP* (Stuttgart, 1969), p. 185; Sauer, *Wilhelm Murr*, p. 132.

213 Schönhagen, *Tübingen unterm Hakenkreuz*, p. 316.

214 Boberach, *MadR*, 17, SD-Bericht zu Inlandsfrage, 26 June 1944, pp. 6608–9.

215 The quotation is from Geyer, 'Restorative Elites, German Society and the Nazi Pursuit of War', p. 161.

216 Stephenson, *The Nazi Organisation of Women*, pp. 199–200.

217 See below, Chapter 9.

218 Schönhagen, *Tübingen unterm Hakenkreuz*, p. 316; Hancock, *National Socialist Leadership and Total War*, p. 97.

219 HStAS, E397, Bü83, 'Merkblatt über die Sammlung, Erfassung, Behandlung und Ablieferung von Bucheckern der Ernte 1942 für die Oelgewinnung'.

220 Ibid.: Der Reichsminister für Ernährung und Landwirtschaft, 'Betr: Ölgewinnung aus Bucheckern', 13 September 1944; Der Reichsminister für Ernährung und Landwirtschaft, 'Betrifft: Ölgewinnung aus Bucheckern', 29 September, 1944.

221 Ibid., Milch-, Fett- und Eierwirtschaftsverband Württemberg, Geradstetten Kr. Waiblingen, 'Betrifft: Sammeln von Bucheckern der Ernte 1944', 19 October 1944.

222 Ibid., E151bIII, Bü8705, 'Regierungs-Anzeiger für Württemberg', 9 March 1945.

223 Ibid., E397, Bü37, Schreiben an die Wirtschaftsgruppe Einzelhandel, Fachgruppe Nahrungs- und Genussmittel, 'Betreff: Diebstähle von Lebensmittelbedarfsnachweisen', 28 February 1945.

224 Ibid., Wirtschaftsgruppe Einzelhandel, Fachgruppe Nahrungs- und Genussmittel an das Landesernährungsamt, 'Betr. Diebstähle von Lebensmittelmarken', 6 March 1945.

225 E.g. Arbogast, *Herrschaftsinstanzen der württembergischen NSDAP*, pp. 110–11; StAL, K110, Bü58, SD report, n.d. [March 1945].

226 BA, R22/3387, Der Generalstaatsanwalt an den Herrn Reichsminister der Justiz, Nr. 420b – 25, 1 April 1940.

227 Ibid., Der Oberlandesgerichtspräsident an den Herrn Reichsminister der Justiz, 'Betreff: Bericht über die allgemeine Lage', 10 July 1940.

228 Ibid., 30 September 1940.

229 Ibid., Der Oberlandesgerichtspräsident an den Herrn Reichsminister der Justiz, 'Betreff: Bericht über die allgemeine Lage', 6 November 1940.

230 Ibid., 3 July 1941.

231 Ibid.: Der Generalstaatsanwalt an den Herrn Reichsminister der Justiz, Nr 420b – 33, 1 August 1941; Der Oberlandesgerichtspräsident an den Herrn Reichsminister der Justiz, Nr 3130, 'Betreff: Bericht über die allgemeine Lage', 5 September 1941.

232 Ibid., Der Generalstaatsanwalt an den Herrn Reichsminister der Justiz, Nr 420b – 34, 30 September 1941.

233 StAL, K110, Bü47, pp. 1, 8.

234 Ibid., Bü48, p. 1.

235 BA, R22/3387, Der Generalstaatsanwalt an den Herrn Reichsminister der Justiz, Nr 420b – 34, 30 September 1941.

236 Ibid., Der Generalstaatsanwalt an den Herrn Reichsminister der Justiz, Nr 420b – 35, 1 December 1941.

237 Ibid.: Der Generalstaatsanwalt an den Herrn Reichsminister der Justiz, Nr 420b – 36, 31 January, 1942; Der Oberlandesgerichtspräsident an den Herrn Reichsminister der Justiz, 'Betreff: Bericht über die allgemeine Lage', 3 March 1942. Also, Schnabel, *Württemberg zwischen Weimar und Bonn*, p. 579.

238 BA, R22/3387, Der Generalstaatsanwalt an den Herrn Reichsminister der Justiz, Nr 420b – 37, 4 April 1942.

239 Steinert, *Hitler's War and the Germans*, p. 161.

240 BA, R22/3387, Der Generalstaatsanwalt an den Herrn Reichsminister der Justiz, Nr 420b – 38, 1 June 1942.

241 Ibid., Der Oberlandesgerichtspräsident an den Herrn Reichsminister der Justiz, 'Betreff: Bericht über die allgemeine Lage', 30 November 1942.

242 Steinert, *Hitler's War and the Germans*, p. 166.

243 On 'unconditional surrender', see Richard Overy, *Why the Allies Won* (New York and London, 1995), pp. 117, 295. On Goebbels' 'total war' speech, see Michalka, *Das Dritte Reich*, ii, pp. 295–97.

244 United States Holocaust Memorial Museum archive (USHMM), NS6/414, Partei-Kanzlei, II B 4, 'Auszüge aus Berichten der Gaue u.a. Dienststellen, Zeitraum 31.1. – 13.2.43', pp. 4–5.

245 Ibid.: 'Auszüge aus Berichten der Gaue u.a. Dienststellen Zeitraum 21.2. – 27.2.43', pp. 3–4; 'Auszüge aus Berichten der Gaue u.a. Dienststellen Zeitraum 11.4.43 – 17.4.43', p. 3; 'Auszüge aus Berichten der Gaue u.a. Dienststellen Zeitraum 18.4.43 – 24.4.43', p. 4.

246 Ibid., 'Auszüge aus Berichten der Gaue u.a. Dienststellen Zeitraum 21.2. – 27.2.43', p. 6. See also Robert Gellately, *Backing Hitler: Consent and Coercion in Nazi Germany* (Oxford, 2001), p. 185.

247 USHMM, NS6/414, Partei-Kanzlei, II B 4, 'Auszüge aus Berichten der Gaue u.a. Dienststellen Zeitraum 11.4. – 17.4.43', p. 3.

248 Ibid., 'Auszüge aus Berichten der Gaue u.a. Dienststellen Zeitraum 21.2. – 27.2.43', p. 6.

249 Balfour, *Propaganda in War*, pp. 335–38.

250 BA, R22/3387, Der Generalstaatsanwalt an den Herrn Reichsminister der Justiz, Nr 3130 – Ia – 2, 31 May 1943.

251 Ibid., R55/601, 'Tätigkeitsbericht (Stichtag: 21 November 1944), p. 231.

252 Ibid., R55/569, p. 56, 'Rundfunkgenehmigungen am 1. Oktober 1940'. On reduced paper supplies, see BA, R22/3387, 3 July 1941; Schnabel, *Württemberg zwischen Weimar und Bonn*, p. 580.

253 BA, R22/3387, 1 December 1941; Gellately, *Backing Hitler*, pp. 186–87, 238. See also Daniela Münkel, '"Der Runkdfunk geht auf die Dörfer": der Einzug der Massmedien auf dem Lande von den zwanziger bis zu den sechziger Jahren', in Daniela Münkel (ed.), *Der lange Abschied vom Agrarland: Agrarpolitik, Landwirtschaft und ländliche Gesellschaft zwischen Weimar und Bonn* (Göttingen, 2000), p. 192.

254 StAL, K110, Bü55, RSHA, 'Meldungen aus den SD-(Leit)-Abschnittsbereichen', 30 July 1943, pp. 14105. See also BA, R55/601, 'Tätigkeitsbericht (Stichtag: 30. Oktober 1944)', pp. 198–99.

255 StAL, K110, Bü55, 8 July 1943, p. 14062.

256 Ibid., 15 July 1943, p. 14074.

257 Ibid., 22 July 1943, p. 14091.

258 Ibid., 30 July 1943, p. 14114. See also Aristotle A. Kallis, *Nazi Propaganda and the Second World War* (Basingstoke, 2005), p.178.

259 Ibid., 22 July 1943 p. 14091.

260 Ibid.: 30 July 1943: the first quotation is from p. 14104; the remainder are from p. 14114.

261 Ibid., 'Meldungen über die Entwicklung in der öffentlichen Meinungsbildung', 8 June 1944, pp. 13906, 13916.

262 Ibid., 30 July, p. 13917.

263 BA, R55/601, 'Tätigkeitsbericht (Stichtag: 2. Oktober 1944)', p. 150.

264 Ibid., 'Tätigkeitsbericht (Stichtag: 14 November 1944)', p. 215.

265 Quoted in Kershaw, *The 'Hitler Myth'*, p. 220.

266 StAL, K110, Bü55: 'Allgemein', 10 June 1944, p. 13923; 'Invasion', 10 June 1944, p. 13924.

267 Ibid., 30 July, p. 13921. See also BA, R55/601: 'Tätigkeitsbericht (Stichtag: 2. Oktober 1944)', pp. 143, 145; 'Tätigkeitsbericht (Stichtag: 30. Oktober 1944)', p. 196.

268 BA, R55/601, 'Tätigkeitsbericht (Stichtag: 21 November 1944)', pp. 226–29. See also Gerald Kirwin, 'Waiting for Retaliation: A Study in Nazi Propaganda Behaviour and German Civilian Morale', *Journal of Contemporary History*, 16 (1981), pp. 565–83.

269 Keegan, *The Second World War*, pp. 581–82; Overy, *Why the Allies Won*, pp. 239–40.

270 David K. Yelton, *Hitler's Volkssturm: The Nazi Militia and the Fall of Germany, 1944–1945* (Lawrence, Kansas, 2002), pp. 7, 80, 86, 98, 133.

271 StAL, K110, Bü59, 'Betrifft: Stimmen zum Erlass des Führers über die Bildung des Deutschen Volkssturmes', 8 November 1944, pp. 1–2. See also Yelton, *Hitler's Volkssturm*, pp. 111–13.

272 BA, R55/601, 'Tätigkeitsbericht (Stichtag: 7 November 1944), p. 208.

273 StAL, Bü59, pp. 1–2.

274 Overy, *Why the Allies Won*, p. 132.

275 HStAS, J170, Bü8 (Heilbronn), Gemeinde Hausen a.d.Z. n.d. [October/November 1948].

Notes to Chapter 6: War in the Countryside

1 The quotation is from Roland Müller, *Stuttgart zur Zeit des Nationalsozialismus* (Stuttgart, 1988), p. 336.

2   Heinz Boberach, *Meldungen aus dem Reich (MadR)*, (Herrsching, 1984), 13, no. 372, 1 April 1943, p. 5048. Also quoted in Thomas Schnabel, *Württemberg zwischen Weimar und Bonn, 1928–1945/46* (Stuttgart, 1986), p. 574.

3   Ian Kershaw, *Popular Opinion and Political Dissent in Germany, 1933–1945: Bavaria in the Third Reich* (Oxford, 1983), p. 285. See also Theresia Bauer, *Nationalsozialistische Agrarpolitik und bäuerliches Verhalten im Zweiten Weltkrieg: eine Regionalstudie zur ländlichen Gesellschaft in Bayern* (Frankfurt am Main, 1996), p. 89.

4   Gustavo Corni and Horst Gies, *Brot – Butter – Kanonen: die Ernährungswirtschaft in Deutschland unter der Diktatur Hitlers* (Berlin, 1997), pp. 434, 437–38.

5   HStAS, E151/1cII, Bü434, Kommandeur der Gendarmerie des Landes Württemberg an den Württ. Innenminister, 'Tätigkeitsbericht für das Jahr 1939', 1 February 1940, p. 9. See also Martin Broszat, Elke Fröhlich, Falk Wiesemann and Anton Grossmann (eds), *Bayern in der NS-Zeit*, i, *Soziale Lage und politisches Verhalten der Bevölkerung im Spiegel vertraulicher Berichte* (Munich, 1977): 'Aus Monatsbericht des Bezirksamts, 30.9.1939', p. 134; 'Aus Monatsbericht der Gendarmerie-Station Aufsess, 26.11.1939', p. 135.

6   HStAS, J170, Bü18 (Ulm), 'Bericht über den Verlauf der letzten Kriegstage in der Gemeinde Türkheim Krs. Ulm', n.d. (received 20 April 1949), p. 1.

7   Schönhagen, *Tübingen unterm Hakenkreuz*, pp. 316–17.

8   Staatsarchiv Ludwigsburg (StAL), K631/II, Bü39, gives instances of grants for land improvement. On the wartime shortage of farm labour in Germany, see Corni and Gies, *Brot – Butter – Kanonen*, pp. 433–68.

9   HStAS, E151/1cII, Bü434, 1 February 1940, p. 9. See also 'Aus Monatsbericht der Gendarmerie-Station Muggendorf, 26.9.1939', in Broszat, Fröhlich and Wiesemann, *Bayern in der NS-Zeit*, i, p. 133.

10 Ibid., J170, Bü18, Türkheim, p. 1.

11 Ibid., Bü10 (Leonberg), 'Kriegs-Chronik der Gemeinde Münchingen verfasst von –, Bauer, Münchingen', n.d.

12 Günter Golde, *Catholics and Protestants: Agricultural Modernisation in Two German Villages* (New York, 1975), pp. 56, 92–93. The quotation is from p. 56.

13 HStAS, J170, Bü3 (Böblingen), Öschelbronn, 'Betreff: Geschichtliche Darstellung der letzten Kriegstage', 29 October 1948.

14 StAL, K110, Bü47, SD 'Lagebericht', 15 July 1941, pp. 15–16; Kurt Leipner (ed.), *Chronik der Stadt Stuttgart, 1933–1945* (Stuttgart, 1982), pp. 1010–11.

15 Walter Rinderle and Bernard Norling, *The Nazi Impact on a German Village* (Lexington, Kentucky, 1993), pp. 169–72; J.E. Farquharson, *The Plough and the Swastika: The NSDAP and Agriculture in Germany, 1928–1945* (London, 1976), pp. 221–23; Jill Stephenson, 'War and Society in Württemberg, 1939–1945: Beating the System', *German Studies Review*, 8 (1985), pp. 92–93, 96, 98.

16 Bundesarchiv (BA), R22/3387, Der Generalstaatsanwalt Stuttgart an den Herrn Reichsminister der Justiz: 1 August 1940; Nr. 420b – 28, 'Betrifft: Lagebericht', 30 September 1940, p. 1; 31 May 1941; StAL, Bü47, pp. 15–16. This was not peculiar to Württemberg; on the contrary, it was widespread. See Corni and Gies, *Brot – Butter – Kanonen*, pp. 495–97.

17 Leipner, *Chronik der Stadt Stuttgart*, p. 866.

18 HStAS, E397, Bü5, Der Landrat (Ehingen) an den Herrn Württ. Wirtschaftsminister, 'Betreff: Anzeige gegen – wegen Vergehens im Sinne der Verbrauchsregelungsstrafordnung vom 6.4.1940', 23 May 1941.

19 Marlis G. Steinert, *Hitler's War and the Germans*, ed. and trans. Thomas E.J. de Witt, (Athens, Ohio, 1977), pp. 31, 33, 64, 207; Dörte Winkler, *Frauenarbeit im 'Dritten Reich'* (Hamburg, 1977), p. 80.

20 StAL, K110, Bü37, 'Rundschreiben Nr 49 – Betr. Pauschwirtschaftsbeihilfe für einberufene Bauern und Landwirte', 22 April 1940.

21 Birthe Kundrus, *Kriegerfrauen: Familienpolitik und Geschlechterverhältnisse im Ersten und Zweiten Weltkrieg* (Hamburg, 1995), pp. 261, 271. The quotation is from p. 271. See also Schönhagen, *Tübingen unterm Hakenkreuz*, pp. 315–16; 'Aus Monatsbericht der Gendarmerie-Station Aufsess, 26.12.1939', in Broszat, Fröhlich and Wiesemann, *Bayern in der NS-Zeit*, i, p. 136; 'Aus Monatsbericht der Gendarmerie-Station Kreisführers, 30.12.1939', in ibid., p. 136.

22 Rinderle and Norling, *The Nazi Impact on a German Village*, p. 170, claim that 'despite much official praise of peasants … after 1938 the Nazi regime reduced them to a state close to serfdom …' See also David Schoenbaum, *Hitler's Social Revolution: Class and Status in Nazi Germany 1933–39* (London, 1967), pp. 171–79, 184–86; Johnpeter Horst Grill, *The Nazi Movement in Baden, 1920–1945* (Chapel Hill, North Carolina, 1983), pp. 300–4.

23 Christa Tholander, *Fremdarbeiter, 1939 bis 1945: Ausländische Arbeitskräfte in der Zeppelin-Stadt Friedrichshafen* (Essen, 2001), p. 104. See also Boberach, *MadR*, 9, 'Anlage zu den "Meldungen aus dem Reich" v. 26.3.42', p. 3534; Corni and Gies, *Brot – Butter – Kanonen*, p. 466.

24 George D. Spindler, *Burgbach: Urbanisation and Identity in a German Village* (New York, 1973), p. 78.

25 Mary Buckley, 'Relations between Individual and System under Stalinism', paper delivered at the International Congress for Russian/Soviet History, Sigriswil, Switzerland, 1–4 October 2003, p. 3, refers to the limited penetration of the Stalinist political system in the countryside. I am indebted to Mary Buckley for sending me copy of this paper. See also her '*Krest'yanskaya gazeta* and Rural Stakhanovism', *Europe-Asia Studies*, 46 (1994), pp. 1388–93, 1398–99, 1402–3.

26 Farquharson, *The Plough and the Swastika*, pp. 63, 69–70. Cf. Bauer, *Nationalsozialistische Agrarpolitik*, pp. 146–47, on rumours and fears in Bavaria in wartime about collectivisation.

27 On the failure of the *Volksgemeinschaft* ideal, see Kershaw, *Popular Opinion*, pp. 373–74.

28 HStAS, J170, Bü18, Gemeinde Tomerdingen, 'Chronikale Aufzeichnungen über die Gemeinde Tomerdingen, Kreis Ulm (aus der Pfarrchronik)', n.d. [October/November 1948].

29 Boberach, *MadR*, 9, pp. 3531–33.

30 BA, R22/3387, Der Generalstaatsanwalt Stuttgart an den Herrn Reichsminister der Justiz, Nr. 420b – 37, 'Betrifft: Lagebericht', 4 April 1942.

31 Boberach, *MadR*, 13, no. 372, 1 April 1943, pp. 5046–48. See also Broszat, Fröhlich and Wiesemann, *Bayern in der NS-Zeit*, i, pp. 154–56

32 HStAS, J170, Bü18, Gemeinde Tomerdingen, p. 1.

33 Schönhagen, *Tübingen unterm Hakenkreuz*, p. 317.

34 Corni and Gies, *Brot – Butter – Kanonen*, pp. 434–35, 442; Michael H. Kater, *Hitler Youth* (Cambridge, Massachusetts, and London, 2004), pp. 84–86, 193–95; Jill Stephenson,

'Women's Labor Service in Nazi Germany', *Central European History*, 15 (1982), pp. 243–44, 252–53, 258–60; Tholander, *Fremdarbeiter, 1939 bis 1945*, pp. 34, 70.

35 See, e.g., 'Inge D.', in Gerda Szepansky, *'Blitzmädel', 'Heldenmutter', 'Kriegerwitwe': Frauenleben im Zweiten Weltkrieg* (Frankfurt am Main, 1986), p. 51; cf. Claus Larass, *Der Zug der Kinder: KLV. Die Evakuierung 5 Millionen deutscher Kinder im 2. Weltkrieg* (Frankfurt am Main, 1992), p. 76.

36 HStAS, E151/01, Bü3168, *Reichsgesetzblatt*, 1942, part 1, 'Verordnung über den Einsatz zusätzlicher Arbeitskräfte für die Ernährungssicherung des Deutschen Volkes', 7 March 1942.

37 BA, R22/3387, Der Generalstaatsanwalt Stuttgart an den Herrn Reichsminister der Justiz, Nr. 420b – 28, 'Betrifft: Lagebericht', 30 September 1940.

38 Boberach, *MadR*, 9, pp. 3533–34.

39 Leipner, *Chronik der Stadt Stuttgart*, p. 620. See also Steinert, *Hitler's War and the Germans*, p. 65; Broszat, Fröhlich and Wiesemann, *Bayern in der NS-Zeit*, i: 'Aus Monatsbericht des Gendarmerie-Kreisführers, 30.12.39', p. 136; 'Aus Monatsberichten des Landrats, 31.8. und 2.9.40', p. 143. The quotation is from StAL, K110, Bü47, p. 24.

40 Jeremy Noakes (ed.), *Nazism, 1919–1945: A Documentary Reader*, iv, *The German Home Front in World War II* (Exeter, 1998), pp. 525–26; Boberach, *MadR*, 16, SD-Berichte zu Inlandsfragen, 24 January 1944, pp. 6281–84.

41 *Deutschland-Berichte der Sozialdemokratischen Partei Deutschlands*, 1939, no. 7, 5 August 1939, p. 61.

42 Boberach, *MadR*, 16, 'SD-Berichte zu Inlandsfragen', 24 January 1944, pp. 6281–84. See also Broszat, Fröhlich and Wiesemann, *Bayern in der NS-Zeit*, i, 'Aus Monatsberichten des Landrats, 31.8 und 2.9.1940', p. 143.

43 Boberach, *MadR*, 9, pp. 3538–41; Golde, *Catholics and Protestants*, pp. 40–41, 121–22. On problems with fertiliser and farm machines, see Corni and Gies, *Brot – Butter – Kanonen*, pp. 423–33.

44 HStAS, E151/1cII, Bü434, Kommandeur der Gendarmerie des Landes Württemberg an den Württ. Innenminister, 'Tätigkeitsbericht für das Jahr 1939', 1 February 1940, p. 18.

45 BA, R22/3387, Der Generalstaatsanwalt an den Herrn Reichsminister der Justiz, Nr 420b – 37, 'Betrifft: Lagebericht', 1 December 1941. See also HStAS, E151/1cII, Bü434, 1 February 1940, p. 17. Similar complaints were made elsewhere, for example, in Schleswig-Holstein: Institut für Zeitgeschichte Archiv, MA138, frame 300883, Gauleitung Schleswig-Holstein/ NS-Frauenschaft, 'Arbeitsbericht der Gaufrauenschaftsleiterin. Monat Oktober 1941', 29 November 1941.

46 StAL, K110, Bü48, SD 'Lagebericht', 1 September 1941, pp. 41–42.

47 BA, R22/3387, 1 December 1941.

48 HStAS, E151/1cII, Bü434, 1 February 1940, p. 18.

49 StAL, K110, Bü47, pp. 18–19.

50 Ibid., Bü48, p. 42. Cf. Bauer, *Nationalsozialistische Agrarpolitik und bäuerliches Verhalten*, pp. 93–96.

51 Ibid.; Boberach, *MadR*, 9, pp. 3533–41.

52 StAL, K631/II, Bü75, 'Aktennotiz. Betr.: Besprechung mit dem RAD betr. Einsatz der RAD-Abteilung Walxheim Kreis Aalen', 14 January 1942.

53   Ibid., Bü41, 'Gutachten des Reichsnährstandes – Wirtschaftswegebau', Münsingen, 18 May 1942.

54   Ibid., Kbsch. Ehingen, 'Übersichtsbogen zu dem Entwurf für die Entwässerung – Obermarchtal und Untermarchtal (Ehingen)', 28 August 1944.

55   Ibid., K110, Bü47, p. 15.

56   HStAS, E397, Bü37, 5 December 1943, p. 1.

57   Ibid., letters of 11, 12 and 27 March 1940, and deposition of 12 March 1940.

58   StAL, K110, Bü47, pp. 18–19, 24.

59   Ibid., Bü48, pp. 41–42.

60   Spindler, *Burgbach*, p. 78, shows that this remained normal practice there around 1970.

61   HStAS, E397, Bü37, 'Anzeige gegen –', 31 March 1940.

62   Ibid., Der Landrat, Horb am Neckar, an den Milch- und Fettwirtschaftsverband Württemberg, 'Betrifft: Milchablieferungspflicht in der Gemeinde Ahldorf', 31 January 1940.

63   Ibid., 'Zweifelsfragen bezüglich der Zuständigkeit zu Abrügung von kriegswirtschaftlichen Verfehlungen', 22 December 1939.

64   Hans Mommsen, 'National Socialism: Continuity and Change', in Walter Laqueur (ed.), *Fascism: A Reader's Guide. Analyses, Interpretation, Bibliography* (London, 1976), p. 190, refers to 'a political style in which all options remained open and decisions were dealt with ad hoc'.

65   HStAS, E397, Bü37, Der Oberstaatsanwalt bei dem Landgericht Rottweil an den Herrn Württ. Wirtschaftsminister – Landesernährungsamt – Abt. B, 29, 'Betr.: Strafbestimmungen gegen Fleischhamstern, Schwarzschlachten und dergl.', November 1939.

66   Ibid., Der Landrat in Rottweil an den Herrn Württ. Wirtschaftsminister, 'Betreff: Strafsache gegen … Gaststättenpächter in Schramberg vom 28 November 1939', 12 December 1939.

67   Ibid., E151/1cII, Bü434, 1 February 1940, p. 17.

68   Ibid., E397, Bü37, Der Oberstaatsanwalt bei dem Landgericht Rottweil an den Herrn Württ. Wirtschaftsminister Landesernährungsamt Württ. Abt. B, 'Betr.: Anzeigesache gegen Mathias [sic] Hohner in Trossingen wegen Vergehens gegen die Milchbewirtschaftung', 27 December 1939.

69   Hartmut Berghoff and Cornelia Rauh-Kühne, *Fritz K.: Ein deutsches Leben im zwanzigsten Jahrhundert* (Stuttgart and Munich, 2000), pp. 170–71.

70   StAL, K110, Bü38, SD Rundschreiben Nr 150/1940, 'Betr: Fleischverknappung', 11 September 1940.

71   HStAS, E397, Bü37, Nr D.K.4679. Niederschrift über die am 6. Oktober 1942 beim Württ. Wirtschaftsministerium, Abteilung für Landwirtschaft, abgehaltene Besprechung über die Bekämpfung von Schwarzschlachtungen', 24 November 1942.

72   Rinderle and Norling, *The Nazi Impact on a German Village*, p. 172.

73   Golde, *Catholics and Protestants*, pp. 41–43, gives an account of the slaughtering of a pig.

74   HStAS, E397, Bü37, 'Abschrift. Sondergericht für den Oberlandesgerichtsbezirk Stuttgart in Stuttgart, SL, Nr 523–526/42. I 22 SJs.1313–16/42', 24 November 1942.

75   HStAS, E397, Bü37: the quotation is from Der Reichsminister für Ernährung und Landwirtschaft II B 6 – 5343, an die Landesregierungen, die Preussischen Oberpräsidenten, 'Betr.: Schwarzschlachtungen', 17 September 1941; Der Württ. Innenminister, Nr XI 1537.

An die Regierungsveterinärräte und den beamteten Tierarzt für den Bereich des Städt. Vieh- und Schlachthofs in Stuttgart. 'Betreff: Schwarzschlachtungen', 23 Oktober 1941.

76   StAL, K110, Bü40, III D – Stä. Rundschr. Nr 122/41, 'Betr.: Überhandnahme der Schwarzschlachtungen und ihre Bekämpfung', 18 November 1941.

77   HStAS, E397, Bü37, Der Reichsminister für Ernährung und Landwirtschaft II A 12 – 1050 RfEuL an die Landesregierungen (Reichsstatthalter) und die Preussischen Oberpräsidenten, 'Betrifft: Bekämpfung von Schwarzschlachtungen nach Aufhebung des Schlachtsteuergesetzes', 21 August 1942.

78   Ibid., Nr D.K.4679, 24 November 1942.

79   The quotation is from BA, R22/3387, 1 December 1941.

80   Ibid., J170, Bü18, Gemeinde Tomerdingen, p. 2.

81   StAL, K110, Bü47, pp. 15–16.

82   Lev Kopelev in 'Class Warriors', an episode in the series *Red Empire*, Yorkshire Television, 1990. See also Sheila Fitzpatrick, *Everyday Stalinism: Ordinary Life in Extraordinary Times. Soviet Russia in the 1930s* (New York and Oxford, 1999), pp. 134–35, 207–9. For lists of conscripted bureaucrats and vacant posts, see StAL, K631/II, Bü83, Ernährungsamt Stuttgart, 9 November 1942, pp. 2–14. Other bureaucrats from this office and other districts were seconded to Berlin, Posen and Wartheland.

83   HStAS, E397, Bü37, Der Leiter der Amtsanwaltschaft an das Württ. Wirtschaftsministerium Landesernährungsamt Abt. B, Nr D.K.3989, 'Betr. Vergehen gegen das Viehzählungsgesetz wegen Nichtangabe von Hühnern', 26 August 1942.

84   Ibid.: Der Reichsführer SS und Chef der Deutschen Polizei an die Regierungspräsidenten und Landesregierungen, S-V B 2 Nr 1013/42, 'Betrifft: Polizeiliches Einschreiten zur Bekämpfung der Verstösse gegen die Kriegswirtschaftsbestimmungen', 13 April 1942, p. 1; Staatliche Kriminalpolizei, Kriminalpolizeileitstelle Stuttgart, Nr 3.K., 'Betrifft: Bekämpfung der Verstösse gegen die Kriegswirtschaftsbestimmungen', 14 May 1942.

85   Ibid., Staatliche Kriminalpolizei, Kriminalpolizeileitstelle Stuttgart an das Landesernährungsamt, Nr D.K.4695, 5 October 1942.

86   BA, R22/3387, 1 December 1941.

87   Ibid., Nr 420 –b – 36, 31 January 1942.

88   There are numerous cases of this in the HStAS, E397, Bü37 files.

89   Ibid., Ministerialabteilung für Bezirks- und Körperschaftsverwaltung, 275, Nr 15, an Herrn Bürgermeister –, 'Betreff: Dienstverfahren gegen Sie', 25 August 1943.

90   Ibid., 'Zusammenstellung einiger Strafsachen und Dienststrafsachen auf dem Gebiet der Kriegsernährungswirtschaft, von denen das Landesernährungsamt Kenntnis erhalten hat, nach dem Stand vom 1. Januar 1943'.

91   BA, R22/3387, Der Generalstaatsanwalt an den Herrn Reichsminister der Justiz: 1 August 1940, 31 May 1941, 1 August 1941, 1 June 1941, 28 January 1943.

92   Ibid., 31 May 1943.

93   HStAS, E151/1cII, Bü434, 1 February 1940, pp. 10, 13.

94   BA, R22/3387, 31 May 1943.

95   HStAS, E397, Bü37, Sondergericht für den Oberlandesgerichtsbezirk Stuttgart in Stuttgart, SL, Nr 276–277/1942. I 9 SJs. 714–15/1941, 72/1942, 13 January 1943.

96   Ibid., letter from Borman to the Minister of Economics, III/07 – WB, 8 December 1940.

97 Stefan Baur, 'Rechtsprechung im nationalsozialistischen Geist: Hermann Albert Cuhorst, Senatspräsident und Vorsitzender des Sondergerichts Stuttgart', in Michael Kissener and Joachim Scholtyseck (eds), *Die Führer der Provinz: NS-Biographien aus Baden und Württemberg* (Konstanz, 1997), pp. 112–13, 120–25; Paul Sauer, *Württemberg in der Zeit des Nationalsozialismus* (Ulm, 1975), p. 343; Dietmut Majer, 'Richter und Rechtswesen', in Otto Borst (ed.), *Das Dritte Reich in Baden und Württemberg* (Stuttgart, 1988), p. 71.

98 HStAS, E397, Bü37, Der Reichsführer SS, S-V B 2 Nr 1013/42, 13 April 1942.

99 Baur, 'Rechtsprechung im nationalsozialistischen Geist', p. 123.

100 HStAS, E397, Bü37, 'Abschrift. Sondergericht für den Oberlandesgerichtsbezirk Stuttgart in Stuttgart, SL, Nr 523–526/42. I 22 SJs.1313–16/42.', 24 November 1942. The observations in the quotation accord with the description of a Protestant village in the Hohenlohe c.1970 in Golde, *Catholics and Protestants*, p. 148: 'Some of the villagers see the fact that so many of them are related to each other [as] a means of keeping a check on too much strife … "If it quakes at one end of the village, it rattles at the other end, too – kinshipwise, that is – even though relations may span several generations … You'll find that the whole village is related to each other".'

101 Baur, 'Rechtsprechung im nationalsozialistischen Geist', p. 111.

102 Majer, 'Richter und Rechtswesen', p. 71.

103 Leipner, *Chronik der Stadt Stuttgart*, pp. 868–69, 883. The quotation is from p. 869.

104 The files of the Stuttgart Special Court were destroyed in the war. This means that 'a reconstruction of [Judge Cuhorst's] conduct of trials is not possible'. Majer, 'Richter und Rechtswesen', p. 71. The records of the two trials outlined above may therefore be exceptional survivors, as copies in the records of the Food Office in the Württemberg Economics Ministry.

105 HStAS, E397, Bü37, Der Reichsführer SS, S-V B 2 Nr 1013/42, 13 April 1942. See also Baur, 'Rechtsprechung im nationalsozialistischen Geist', p. 122, on 'cases with greater public interest'.

106 HStAS, E397, Bü37, Der Landrat in Rottweil an den Herrn Württ. Wirtschaftsminister, 'Betreff: Strafsache gegen … Gaststättenpächter in Schramberg vom 28. November 1939', 12 December 1939.

107 Ibid., Der Landrat an den Milch- und Fettwirtschaftsverband Württemberg, 'Unter Bezugnahme auf Ihr Schreiben vom 16.ds.Mts., Ad.2434.39 Dr.M/Bch. Betrifft: Milchablieferungspflicht in der Gemeinde …', 31 January 1940.

108 Ibid., II/232 – PA: 21435 – Schi/Gr., An die Staatl. Kriminalpolizei, Kriminalpolizeileitstelle z.Hd.v. Herrn Kriminalpolizeirat Boxler, 22 May 1940.

109 On the 'euthanasia' of children, see Michael Burleigh, *Death and Deliverance: 'Euthanasia' in Germany, 1900–1945* (Cambridge, 1994), chapter 3, '"Wheels Must Roll for Victory!" Children's "Euthanasia" and "Aktion T-4"', pp. 93–129. On 'asocial' young women, see especially Elizabeth D. Heineman, *What Difference Does a Husband Make? Women and Marital Status in Nazi and Postwar Germany* (Berkeley and Los Angeles, California, 1999), pp. 26–31.

110 See above, Chapter 2. The biographies in Kissener and Scholtyscheck, *Die Führer der Provinz*, give details about this.

111 HStAS, E397, Bü37, Der Reichsstatthalter in Württemberg an den Herrn Württ.

Innenminister, Nr K 6 iI/446, 'Betr.: Beschlagnahme des Klosters Untermarchtal', 27 June 1941. On perceptions of his motives, see BA, R22/3387, Der Oberlandesgerichtspräsident an den Herrn Reichsminister der Justiz, Nr 3130, 'Betreff: Bericht über die allgemeine Lage', 5 September 1941.

112 HStAS, E397, Bü5, Sondergericht für den Oberlandesgerichtsbezirk Stuttgart in Stuttgart, SL, 121–149/42; SL, 219–220/42, 6 July 1942, pp. 1–37.

113 Ibid., Der Landrat (Ehingen) an den Württ. Wirtschaftsminister, 'Auf den Erl. v. 5.5.1941 Nr D.K.1393', 23 May 1941.

114 Ibid., Sondergericht, 6 July 1942, pp. 37–44.

115 Ibid., pp. 48–56.

116 Ibid., Bü37, Ministerialabteilung für Bezirks- und Körperschaftsverwaltung an den Herrn Wirtschaftsminister, 'Betreff: Strafsache gegen den früheren Bürgermeister – in Untermarchtal und Gen. wegen Kriegswirtschaftsverbrechens u.a.', 18 June 1943.

117 HStAS, E397, Bü37: Der Landrat (Ulm) an das Landeswirtschaftsamt, Nr III/4608, 'Betreff: Zuwiderhandlung des Landwirts – in Nellingen gegen die Milchablieferungspflicht', 24 February 1942; Der Württ. Wirtschaftsminister, Landeswirtschaftsamt für den Wehrwirtschaft Va an den Herrn Württ. Wirtschaftsminister Abteilung B, Landesernährungsamt, Nr I S 228/2, 7 August 1941; Der Landrat (Heidenheim) an den Herrn Württ. Wirtschaftsminister, 'Betr.: Vergehen gegen Verbrauchsregelungsstrafverordnung', 21 May 1942. These constitute a very small sample of the offences that were reported.

118 Ibid., An den Herrn Wirtschaftsminister, 'Betreff: Beschwerde gegen eine Strafverfügung des Landrats in Waiblingen beabsichtigter unentgeldlicher Abgabe von Brestlingen an Verwundete und Kranke', 25 July 1942.

119 Ibid., Der Landrat (Heidenheim), an den Herrn Württ. Wirtschaftsminister, Nr D.K.4944, 'Betr.: Strafsache gegen – Bauersfrau in Niederstotzingen, wegen Urkundenfälschung', 14 October 1942.

120 Ibid., Der Landrat (Nürtingen) an das Landesernährungsamt, Nr D.K.2518, 'Betreff: Strafanzeige gegen – und –', 26 May 1942.

121 Ibid., Der Landrat (Rottweil) to the Württemberg Wirtschaftsminister, 18 May 1944.

122 StAL, K110, Bü40, 'Betr.: Bestechungsversuche bei Behörden', 11 October 1941.

123 HStAS, E397, Bü37, 'Betr.: Schwarzhandel auf dem Lande, besonders auch im Kartoffelhandel', 5 December 1943.

124 Ibid., Nr D.K. 4986, 9 December 1943.

125 Ibid., 'Strafbefehl', 12 April 1944.

126 See above, Chapter 5. Also, StAL, K631/II, Bü75, Aktennotiz. Betr.: Besprechung mit dem RAD betr. Einsatz der RAD-Abteilung Walxheim Kreis Aalen', 14 January 1942; Jill Stephenson, *The Nazi Organisation of Women* (London, 1981), p. 184.

127 Bauer, *Nationalsozialistische Agrarpolitik und bäuerliches Verhalten*, pp. 87–89.

128 HStAS, J170, Bü3 (Böblingen), 'Geschichtliche Darstellung der letzten Kriegstage in der Gemeinde Steinenbronn', 18 October 1949, p. 1.

129 Ibid., Gemeinde Musberg, p. 6.

130 Ibid., Bü4, 'Gemeinde Gaggstatt Krs Crailsheim. Geschichtliche Darstellung der letzten Kriegstage', n.d. [October/November 1948], p. 4.

Notes to Chapter 7: Party and Church

1   John S. Conway, *The Nazi Persecution of the Churches* (London, 1968); Günther van Norden, 'Die Barmer Theologische Erklärung und ihr historischer Ort in der Widerstandsgeschichte', in Peter Steinbach and Johannes Tuchel (eds.), *Widerstand gegen den Nationalsozialismus* (Bonn, 1994), pp. 179–81; Beate Ruhm von Oppen, 'Revisionism and Counterrevisionism in the Historiography of the Church Struggle', in Franklin H. Littell and Hubert G. Locke (eds), *The German Church Struggle and the Holocaust* (Detroit, Michigan, 1974), pp. 56–68. Cf. Guenter Lewy, *The Catholic Church and Nazi Germany* (London, 1964); Georg May, *Kirchenkampf oder Katholikenverfolgung: ein Beitrag zu dem gegenseitigen Verhältnis von Nationalsozialismus und christlichen Bekenntnissen* (Stein am Rhein, 1991); Karl Dietrich Bracher, *The German Dictatorship: The Origins, Structure, and Effects of National Socialism*, trans. Jean Steinberg (London, 1971), pp. 469–83. On the brutal treatment of a Württemberg pastor, see Conway, *The Nazi Persecution of the Churches*, pp. 375–76, 434 n. 46.

2   Martin Broszat, *The Hitler State: The Foundation and Development of the Internal Structure of the Third Reich*, trans. John W. Hiden (London, 1981), pp. 222–27. On the German Christians, see Doris L. Bergen, *Twisted Cross: The German Christian Movement in the Third Reich* (Chapel Hill, North Carolina, 1996).

3   John Cornwell, *Hitler's Pope: The Secret History of Pius XII* (London, 2000). Cf. Michael Phayer, 'The Priority of Diplomacy: Pius XII and the Holocaust during the Second World War', in Donald J. Dietrich (ed.), *Christian Responses to the Holocaust: Moral and Ethical Issues* (Syracuse, New York, 2003), pp. 87–98. See also Ernst Christian Helmreich, *The German Churches under Hitler: Background, Struggle, and Epilogue* (Detroit, Michigan, 1979), pp. 99, 240–56, 300, 364–65, 451; Lewy, *The Catholic Church and Nazi Germany*, pp. 328–29; John S. Conway, 'Coming to Terms with the Past: Interpreting the German Church Struggles, 1933–1990', *German History*, 16 (1998), pp. 384–88.

4   Karl Weller and Arnold Weller, *Württembergische Geschichte in südwestdeutschen Raum* (Stuttgart and Aalen, 1975), p. 297.

5   Jeremy Noakes and Geoffrey Pridham (eds), *Nazism, 1919–1945: A Documentary Reader*, i, *The Rise to Power*, p. 16; Lewy, *The Catholic Church and Nazi Germany*, pp. 328–29; Ursula Büttner, '"The Jewish Problem Becomes a Christian Problem": German Protestants and the Persecution of the Jews in the Third Reich', in David Bankier (ed.), *Probing the Depths of German Antisemitism: German Society and the Persecution of the Jews* (Jerusalem, 2000), p. 434.

6   Paul Sauer, *Wilhelm Murr: Hitlers Staathalter in Württemberg* (Tübingen, 1998), p. 38; Jörg Thierfelder, 'Die Kirchen', in Otto Borst (ed.), *Das Dritte Reich in Baden und Württemberg* (Stuttgart, 1988), pp. 77–78; Jörg Thierfelder and Eberhard Röhm, 'Die evangelischen Landeskirchen von Baden und Württemberg in der Spätphase der Weimarer Republik und zu Beginn des Dritten Reiches', in Thomas Schnabel (ed.), *Die Machtergreifung in Südwestdeutschland: das Ende der Weimarer Republik in Baden und Württemberg, 1928–1933* (Stuttgart, 1982), pp. 225, 236, 238–39; Joachim Köhler, 'Die katholische Kirche in Baden und Württemberg in der Endphase der Weimarer Republik und zu Beginn des Dritten Reiches', in ibid., pp. 262, 278.

7   Kurt Leipner (ed.), *Chronik der Stadt Stuttgart, 1933–1945* (Stuttgart, 1983), p. 152.

8   Michael Balfour and Julian Frisby, *Helmuth von Moltke: A Leader against Hitler* (London, 1972), letter from Moltke to his wife, 11 January 1945, p. 326.

9   On France, see especially Maurice Larkin, *Church and State after the Dreyfus Affair: The Separation Issue in France* (London, 1974).

10 David Blackbourn, *The Fontana History of Germany, 1780–1918: The Long Nineteenth Century* (London, 1997), pp. 197–98. On the nineteenth century Catholic revival and anticlericalism, see pp. 213, 224–27; Katharine A. Lerman, 'Bismarckian Germany and the Structure of the German Empire', in John Breuilly (ed.), *19th Century Germany: Politics, Culture and Society, 1780–1918* (London, 2001), pp. 176–77, 181; Volker Berghahn, 'Demographic Growth, Industrialisation and Social Change', in ibid., pp. 193–94.

11 Cornwell, *Hitler's Pope*, pp. 186, 194.

12 Franz Sonnenberger, 'Historisch-politische Bewertung des Schulkampfes im Dritten Reich', in Martin Broszat, Elke Fröhlich, Falk Wiesemann and Anton Grossmann (eds), *Bayern in der NS-Zeit*, iii, *Herrschaft und Gesellschaft im Konflikt* (Munich and Vienna, 1981), pp. 324–27. On the Soviet Union, see Sheila Fitzpatrick, *Everyday Stalinism: Ordinary Life in Extraordinary Times. Soviet Russia in the 1930s* (New York and Oxford, 1999), pp. 118–20, 128.

13 Richard Steigmann-Gall, *The Holy Reich: Nazi Conceptions of Christianity, 1919–1945* (Cambridge, 2003) argues this case. See, e.g., p. 12.

14 Kurt Nowak, 'Kirchen und Religion', in Wolfgang Benz, Hermann Graml and Hermann Weiss (eds), *Enzyclopädie des Nationalsozialismus* (Munich, 1998), p. 193; Mario Zeck, *Das Schwarze Korps: Geschichte und Gestalt des Organs der Reichsführung SS* (Tübingen, 2002), pp. 168–97; Wolfgang Dierker, *Himmlers Glaubenskrieger: Der Sicherheitsdienst der SS und seine Religionspolitik, 1993–1941* (Paderborn, 2002). Cf. Claus-Ekkehard Bärsch, *Die politische Religion des Nationalsozialismus* (Munich, 2002), pp. 171–73.

15 Christine Arbogast, *Herrschaftsinstanzen der württembergischen NSDAP: Funktion, Sozialprofil und Lebenswege einer regionalen NS-Elite, 1920–1960* (Munich, 1998), p. 75.

16 Staatsarchiv Ludwigsburg (StAL), PL501/46, Nr. 83/Sch. 70375, NSDAP Kreisleitung Balingen-Hechingen, Rundschreiben Folge K 25/38, 'Betr.: Aktion zur seelsorgerischen Betreuung der Familien', 30 September 1938, pp. 3–4.

17 StAL, PL504/18, Bü12, 'Lage- und Stimmungsbericht der Ortsgruppe Leonberg für das Jahr 1938 bis 1. März 1939', pp. 3–4. The quotation is from Franz Josef Heyen (ed.), *Nationalsozialismus im Alltag: Quellen zur Geschichte des Nationalsozialismus vornehmlich im Raum Mainz-Koblenz-Trier* (Boppard, 1967), pp. 170–71. See also Bärsch, *Die politische Religion des Nationalsozialismus.*

18 Thierfelder and Röhm, 'Die evangelischen Landeskirchen von Baden und Württemberg', p. 237. See also Joachim Köhler, 'Das Bistum Rottenburg von der Gründung bis zur Zeit nach dem Zweiten Weltkrieg', in Heinz Sproll and Jörg Thierfelder (eds), *Die Religionsgemeinschaften in Baden-Württemberg* (Stuttgart, 1984), pp. 106–10.

19 Perry Willson, *Peasant Women and Politics in Fascist Italy: The 'Massaie Rurale'* (London, 2002), pp. 185–87.

20 StAL, K110, Bü44, 'Lagebericht des 4. Vierteljahres 1938', 1 February 1939, p. 4.

21 See, for example, StAL, PL504/18, Bü19, Ortsgruppenleiter Leonberg an die Kreisleitung

der NSDAP, Leonberg, 'Gottesdienst am Sonntag, den 12.2.39 in Leonberg', 12 February 1939. See also Ian Kershaw, *Popular Opinion and Political Dissent in the Third Reich: Bavaria, 1933–1945* (Oxford, 1983), pp. 183–84.

22   Broszat, *The Hitler State*, p. 222; Zeck, *Das Schwarze Korps*, pp. 168–97.

23   StAL, K110, Bü38, 'Betr.: Ausstattung von Amtsräumen mit Kruzifixen und anderem kirchlichen Wandschmuck', 1 December 1940. On the crucifix struggle, see: Helmreich, *The German Churches under Hitler*, pp. 289–90, 292, 529, n. 83; Edward N. Peterson, *The Limits of Hitler's Power* (Princeton, New Jersey, 1969), pp. 216–21; Kershaw, *Popular Opinion and Political Dissent in the Third Reich*, pp. 205–208, 340–57; Jeremy Noakes, 'The Oldenburg Crucifix Struggle of November 1936: A Case Study of Opposition in the Third Reich', in Peter D. Stachura (ed.), *The Shaping of the Nazi State* (London, 1978), pp. 210–233; Heyen, *Nationalsozialismus im Alltag*, pp. 240–55.

24   See above, Chapter Four.

25   Bracher, *The German Dictatorship*, p. 483; Conway, *The Nazi Persecution of the Churches*, pp. 223, 262.

26   Benigna Schönhagen, *Tübingen unterm Hakenkreuz: eine Universitätsstadt in der Zeit des Nationalsozialismus* (Stuttgart, 1991), p. 167.

27   Büttner, 'The Jewish Problem Becomes a Christian Problem', pp. 446–58; Hans A. Schmitt, *Quakers and Nazis: Inner Light in Outer Darkness* (Columbia, Missouri, 1997), pp. 40–41.

28   Arbogast, *Herrschaftsinstanzen der württembergischen NSDAP*, pp. 67, 140, 151; Sabine Schmidt, 'Vom Hilfsarbeiter zum Kreisleiter: Eugen Maier, NSDAP-Kreisleiter von Ulm', in Michael Kissener and Joachim Scholtyseck (eds), *Die Führer der Provinz: NS-Biographien aus Baden und Württemberg* (Konstanz, 1997), p. 361. Maier died in 1940. Ibid., pp. 361, 399–400.

29   Arbogast, *Herrschaftsinstanzen der württembergischen NSDAP*, pp. 47, 68, 168–69.

30   Joachim Scholtyseck, '"Der Mann aus dem Volk": Wilhelm Murr, Gauleiter und Reichsstatthalter in Württemberg-Hohenzollern', in Kissener and Scholtyseck, *Die Führer der Provinz*, pp. 89–91. See also Berlin Document Center (BDC), personnel file on Wilhelm Murr, Akten des Obersten Parteigerichts, W53, letter of 26 June 1930.

31   HStAS, E397, Bü37, Der Reichsstatthalter in Württemberg an den Herrn Württ. Innenminister, Nr K 6 iI/446, 'Betr.: Beschlagnahme des Klosters Untermarchtal', 27 June 1941. On perceptions of his motives, see Bundesarchiv (BA), R22/3387, Der Oberlandesgerichtspräsident an den Herrn Reichsminister der Justiz, Nr 3130, 'Betreff: Bericht über die allgemeine Lage', 5 September 1941.

32   BDC, personnel file on Wilhelm Murr, Reichsführer-SS Personal-Akte, n.d. (1942).

33   Heinz Boberach (ed.), *Meldungen aus dem Reich* (Herrsching, 1977), 8, 'Meldungen aus dem Reich' (MadR), 6 October 1941, p. 2843.

34   StAL, K110, Bü40, 'Betr.: Kirchenaustritte von Angehöriger der Sicherheitspolizei und des SD', 20 September 1941.

35   Kissener and Scholtyseck, *Die Führer der Provinz*: Annette Roser, '"Beamter aus Berufung": Karl Wilhelm Waldmann, Württembergischer Staatssekretär', p. 781; Hubert Roser, 'Vom Dorfschultheiss zum hohen Ministerialbeamten: Georg Stümpfig, Kanzleidirektor im Württembergischen Innenministerium und Gauamtsleiter für Kommunalpolitik',

p. 683; Barbara Hachmann, 'Der "Degen": Dietrich von Jagow', p. 267; Susanne Schlösser, '"Was sich in den Weg stellt, mit Vernichtung schlagen": Richard Drauz, NSDAP-Kreisleiter von Heilbronn', p. 143; Michael Stolle, 'Der schwäbische Schulmeister: Christian Mergenthaler, Württembergische Ministerpräsident, Justiz- und Kultminister', pp. 445, 467 n. 122; Scholtyseck, 'Der Mann aus dem Volk', p. 477; Angela Borgstedt, 'Im Zweifelsfall auch mit harter Hand: Jonathan Schmid, Württembergischer Innen-, Justiz- und Wirtschaftsminister', p. 595.

36   Arbogast, *Herrschaftsinstanzen der württembergischen NSDAP*, p. 140.

37   Hartmut Berghoff and Cornelia Rauh-Kühne, *Fritz K.: ein deutsches Leben im zwanzigsten Jahrhundert* (Stuttgart and Munich, 2000), pp. 162, 166; Hartmut Berghoff, *Zwischen Kleinstadt und Weltmarkt: Hohner und die Harmonika, 1857–1961* (Paderborn, 1997), p. 452.

38   Steigmann-Gall, *The Holy Reich*, p. 222.

39   Sauer, *Wilhelm Murr*, p. 75.

40   BDC, personnel file on Friedrich Schmidt, orange party card dated 13 February 1944; Gordon C. Zahn, 'Catholic Resistance? A Yes and a No', in Littell and Locke, *The German Church Struggle and the Holocaust*, pp. 228–29. On 'gottgläubig', see Steigmann-Gall, *The Holy Reich*, pp. 218–60.

41   'Die Broschüre des Reichsschulungsleiters Friedrich Schmidt über "Das Reich als Aufgabe" (Sommer 1941)', printed in Heinrich Hermelink (ed.), *Kirche im Kampf: Dokumente des Widerstands und des Aufbaus in der evangelischen Kirche Deutschlands von 1933 bis 1945* (Tübingen and Stuttgart, 1950), pp. 504–505.

42   BDC, personnel file on Murr, Reichsführer-SS Personal-Akte, n.d. (1942).

43   Scholtyseck, 'Der Mann aus dem Volk', p. 493; Thomas Schnabel, *Württemberg zwischen Weimar und Bonn, 1928–1945/46* (Stuttgart, 1986), p. 434.

44   StAL, PL504/18, Bü12, p. 4. See also Cornelia Rauh-Kühne, *Katholisches Milieu und Kleinstadtgesellschaft: Ettlingen, 1918–1939* (Sigmaringen, 1991), p. 392.

45   Arbogast, *Herrschaftsinstanzen der württembergischen NSDAP*, pp. 67, 119.

46   StAL, K110: Bü44, p. 4; Bü45, 'Lagebericht des 1. Vierteljahres 1939', 1 April 1939, p. 7; Bü46, 'Lagebericht des 2. Vierteljahres 1939', 1 July 1939, p. 5.

47   Kyle Jantzen, 'Propaganda, Perseverance and Protest: Strategies for Clerical Survival Amid the German Church Struggle', *Church History: Studies in Christianity and Culture*, 70 (2001), pp. 297–305. I am indebted to John J. Delaney for giving me a copy of this journal.

48   Sauer, *Wilhelm Murr*, pp. 92–96.

49   F.K.M. Hillenbrand, *Underground Humour in Nazi Germany, 1933–1945* (London, 1995), pp. 102 and 265, n. 94: 'This is an unfortunately untranslatable play on the surnames Wurm ("worm") and Murr (from murren, meaning "to grumble" or "to rebel").'

50   Jonathan Wright, *'Above Parties': The Political Attitudes of the German Protestant Church Leadership, 1918–1933* (Oxford, 1974), pp. 159–60; Schnabel, *Württemberg zwischen Weimar und Bonn*, pp. 432–33; Sauer, *Wilhelm Murr*, pp. 94–95.

51   Leipner, *Chronik der Stadt Stuttgart*, pp. 927–28. See also Schnabel, *Württemberg zwischen Weimar und Bonn*, pp. 412–16.

52   Balfour and Frisby, *Helmuth von Moltke*, pp. 196, 234.

53　Leipner, *Chronik der Stadt Stuttgart*, pp. 924, 928.

54　Balfour and Frisby, *Helmuth von Moltke*, p. 196.

55　StAL, K110, Bü44, p. 3; Thierfelder, 'Die Kirchen', p. 90; Lewy, *The Catholic Church and Nazi Germany*, p. 383 n. 157.

56　Conway, *The Nazi Persecution of the Churches*, p. 224; Sauer, *Württemberg*, pp. 178–79, 203–204.

57　StAL, Bü44, p. 3.

58　Schmitt, *Quakers and Nazis*, p. 41. See also Conway, *The Nazi Persecution of the Churches*, pp. 196–98.

59　Detlef Garbe and Bruno Knöller, 'Die Bibel, das Gewissen und der Widerstand: Die Familie Knöller im "Dritten Reich"', in Hubert Roser (ed.), *Widerstand als Bekenntnis: die Zeugen Jehovas und das NS-Regime in Baden und Württemberg* (Konstanz, 1999), pp. 228–29, 235–36.

60　StAL, K110, Bü44, p. 5.

61　Ibid.: Bü45, p. 9; Bü46, p. 5.

62　Dietrich von Raumer, 'Zeugen Jehovas als Kriegsdienstverweigerer: ein trauriges Kapitel der Wehrmachtjustiz', in Roser, *Widerstand als Bekenntnis*, pp. 182–206; Silvester Lechner, *Das KZ Oberer Kuhberg und die NS-Zeit in der Region Ulm/Neu-Ulm* (Stuttgart, 1988), pp. 88–89.

63　'Ich habe versucht, dem Wort Gottes gehorsam zu sein: Interview mit Alfred Leikam', in Bettina Wenke, *Interviews mit Überlebenden: Verfolgung und Widerstand in Südwestdeutschland* (Stuttgart, 1980), p. 124; Sauer, *Württemberg*, pp. 181, 184, 190; Schnabel, *Württemberg zwischen Weimar und Bonn*, pp. 412–13.

64　Thierfelder, 'Die Kirchen', p. 83.

65　StAL, K110, Bü44, p. 4.

66　Ibid., Bü45, p. 7.

67　Ibid., pp. 5–6. See also Heyen, *Nationalsozialismus im Alltag*, pp. 258–59.

68　Ibid., Bü37, 'Betr.: Jugendarbeit beider Konfessionen', 29 April 1940.

69　Ibid., 'Betr.: Evang. konfessionelle Jugendverbände – Zersetzungsversuche', 4 March 1940.

70　Ibid., Bü38, 'Betr.: Organisierung einer weltanschaulichen Gegnerbeobachtung in der HJ', 31 August 1940.

71　Jeremy Noakes, *Nazism, 1919–1945: A Documentary Reader*, iv: *The German Home Front in World War II* (Exeter, 1998), pp. 408–9. See also Cornelia Rauh-Kühne, 'Katholisches Sozialmilieu, Region und Nationalsozialismus', in Horst Möller, Andreas Wirsching and Walter Ziegler (eds), *Nationalsozialismus in der Region: Beiträge zur regionalen und lokalen Forschung und zum internationalen Vergleich* (Munich, 1996), p. 228.

72　Ruhm von Oppen, 'Revisionism and Counterrevisionism in the Historiography of the Church Struggle', p. 63; Conway, *The Nazi Persecution of the Churches*, pp. 375–76, 434 n. 46.

73　Arbogast, *Herrschaftsinstanzen der württembergischen NSDAP*, pp. 68, 168, 171.

74　Lechner, *Das KZ Oberer Kuhberg*, pp. 20–21.

75　Hauptstaatsarchiv Stuttgart (HStAS), J170, Bü8 (Heilbronn), Gundelsheim.

76　'Die Konfessionsgliederung der deutschen Südwestens nach der Volkszählung von 1933', in Schnabel, *Die Machtergreifung in Südwestdeutschland,* appendix 8, p. 317.

77 Günter Golde, *Catholics and Protestants: Agricultural Modernisation in Two German Villages* (New York, 1975), pp. 2–3, 12, 159–60

78 StAL, K110, Bü46, p. 3. See also Rauh-Kühne, 'Katholisches Sozialmilieu, Region und Nationalsozialismus', p. 229.

79 Arbogast, *Herrschaftsinstanzen der württembergischen NSDAP,* pp. 68–69, 75.

80 Schnabel, *Württemberg zwischen Weimar und Bonn,* pp. 417–19.

81 StAL, PL504/18, Bü19, NSDAP Kreis Leonberg, 'Rundschreiben an sämtliche Ortsgruppenleiter des Kreises Leonberg', 3 January 1939.

82 Ibid., NSDAP Kreis Leonberg, Kreispropagandaleiter – an Ortsgruppenleiter –, 'Methodisten-200-Jahrfeier', 22 June 1938.

83 Ibid., PL504/18, Bü12, pp. 3–4.

84 Ibid., PL504/221, Bü31, Der Kreisleiter an die Hoheitsträger, die Kreisamtsleiter und die Führer und Führerinnen der Gliederungen der NSDAP im Kreis Nürtingen', 13 June 1939.

85 Ibid., PL504/18, Bü12, pp. 3–4, 8.

86 Ibid., Bü19, Der Ortsgruppenleiter an die Kreisleitung der NSDAP Leonberg, 'Evang. Kirchenchor', 2 June 1938.

87 Ibid., Bü12, p. 4.

88 Golde, *Catholics and Protestants,* pp. 133–84; Rauh-Kühne, 'Katholisches Sozialmilieu, Region und Nationalsozialismus', pp. 220, 229.

89 Arbogast, *Herrschaftsinstanzen der württembergischen NSDAP,* p. 76. See also Schnabel, *Württemberg zwischen Weimar und Bonn,* p. 418.

90 StAL, K110, Bü46, pp. 9–10.

91 Ibid., p. 27. See also Heyen, *Nationalsozialismus im Alltag,* pp. 211–15; Gerhard Rempel, *Hitler's Children: The Hitler Youth and the SS* (Chapel Hill, North Carolina, 1989), pp. 48–49.

92 StAL, PL504/18, Bü12, pp. 4, 7.

93 Weller and Weller, *Württembergische Geschichte im südwestdeutschen Raum,* p. 306.

94 StAL, K110, Bü45, p. 6.

95 Ibid., Bü44, p. 14.

96 Ibid., Bü37: 'Betr.: Jugendarbeit beider Konfessionen', 29 April 1940; 'Betr.: Versendung von kirchlichem Propagandamaterial an die Front durch Einschmuggelung in Sendungen der NSDAP', 2 March 1940.

97 Karl Schneider, 'Schule und Erziehung', in Borst, *Das Dritte Reich in Baden und Württemberg,* pp. 125–30; Roland Müller, *Stuttgart zur Zeit des Nationalsozialismus* (Stuttgart, 1988), p. 137.

98 Kershaw, *Popular Opinion and Political Dissent in the Third Reich,* pp. 209–10; Conway, *The Nazi Persecution of the Churches,* p. 179.

99 Schneider, 'Schule und Erziehung', p. 130; Sonnenberger, 'Historisch-politische Bewertung des Schulkampfes im Dritten Reich', p. 327. Cf. Kershaw, *Popular Opinion and Political Dissent in the Third Reich,* pp. 210–13.

100 StAL, Bü46, p. 23.

101 Conway, *The Nazi Persecution of the Churches,* pp. 180, 183; Thierfelder, 'Die Kirchen', p. 89;

Gerhard Schäfer, *Landesbischof D. Wurm und der nationalsozialistische Staat, 1940–1945* (Stuttgart, 1968), p. 76; Kershaw, *Popular Opinion and Political Dissent in the Third Reich*, pp. 213–17. See also Schnabel, *Württemberg zwischen Weimar und Bonn*, pp. 425–26.

102   StAL, K110, Bü45, p. 5; Thierfelder, 'Die Kirchen', p. 89.

103   Ibid., Bü36, 'Betr.: Kampf der Kirchen gegen den weltanschaulichen Unterricht in Württemberg', 26 May 1939, pp. 1–2. See also StAL, PL504/18, Bü19, NSDAP Kreisleitung Leonberg an Ortsgruppenleiter Pg –, 'Betreff: 1. Kath. Religionsunterricht. 2. Gründung einer "Kirchlichen Jugendgemeinschaft"', 29 July 1938.

104   StAL, K110, Bü46, p. 22.

105   Ibid., Bü44, p. 14; Sauer, *Württemberg*, pp. 217, 219.

106   Ibid., Bü45, p. 28.

107   Ibid., Bü38, 5 September 1940.

108   Ibid.: Bü46, pp. 2–3, 21–22. The quotation is from pp. 2–3; Bü36, 26 May 1939, p. 2.

109   Ibid., 'Betr.: Beobachtung der konfessionellen Frauenarbeit', 30 June 1939.

110   Ibid., Bü38, 'Betr.: Ferienverschickung von Kinder und Müttererholung durch die Caritas', 27 August 1940.

111   Ibid.: Bü36, 'Betr.: Kampf der Kirchen gegen den weltanschaulichen Unterricht in Württemberg', 26 May 1939, pp. 3–7; Bü46, p. 4; Leipner, *Chronik der Stadt Stuttgart*, pp. 988, 1011.

112   Quoted in Conway, *The Nazi Persecution of the Churches*, p. 190.

113   Schäfer, *Landesbischof D. Wurm und der nationalsozialistische Staat*, p. 44.

114   Ludwig Volk (ed.), *Akten deutscher Bischöfe über die Lage der Kirche, 1933–1945, v, 1940–42* (Mainz, 1983), document 739, Kottmann to Mergenthaler, p. 670.

115   Conway, *The Nazi Persecution of the Churches*, p. 190.

116   Volk, *Akten deutscher Bischöfe über die Lage der Kirche*, document 578/lia, 21 August 1940, pp. 118, 164.

117   Sauer, *Wilhelm Murr*, p. 112.

118   StAL, K110, Bü37, 'Betr.: Benützung von gemeindeeigenen Räumen für die Zwecke der Kirchen', 11 March 1940. On anti-church party radicals in Bavaria, see Ian Kershaw, *The 'Hitler Myth': Image and Reality in the Third Reich* (Oxford, 1987), pp. 118–19.

119   StAL, K110, Bü38, 'Betr.: Schulbefreiung an kirchlichen Feiertagen', 11 November 1940.

120   Schäfer, *Landesbischof D. Wurm und der nationalsozialistische Staat*, pp. 45–90.

121   StAL, K110, Bü38, 'Betr.: Beurteilung der Lehrer, die den Weltanschauungsunterricht erteilen', 30 August 1940.

122   Volk, *Akten deutscher Bischöfe über die Lage der Kirche*, document 739, p. 671.

123   Jill Stephenson, *Women in Nazi Society* (London, 1975), pp. 159–60.

124   Schäfer, *Landesbischof D. Wurm und der nationalsozialistische Staat*, pp. 70–74.

125   StAL, K110, Bü38, 'Betr.: Berichterstattung auf dem Gebiete der Jugenderziehung und des Schulwesens', 7 October 1940.

126   Schäfer, *Landesbischof D. Wurm und der nationalsozialistische Staat*, p. 72.

127   Volk, *Akten deutscher Bischöfe über die Lage der Kirche*, document 739, pp. 669, 671.

128   HStAS, J170, Bü18 (Ulm), 'Betreff: Geschichtliche Darstellung der letzten Kriegstage', Westerstetten, 20 September 1948.

129   StAL, K110, Bü38, Rundschreiben Nr. 14/40, 25 November 1940.

130 Schäfer, *Landesbischof D. Wurm und der nationalsozialistische Staat*, pp. 90–92.
131 StAL, PL509, Bü66, letters of 8 April 1943 and 14 May 1943.
132 Ibid.: Bü87, 'Betr.: Kriegseinsatz in Öffingen am vergangenen Sonntag', 8 August 1944; Bü89, 'Betr.: Kriegseinsatz in Öffingen am vergangenen Sonntag', 7 August 1944.
133 Arbogast, *Herrschaftsinstanzen der württembergischen NSDAP*, p. 68.
134 StAL, PL509, Bü87, letters of 2 October 1942 and 8 October 1942.
135 Golde, *Catholics and Protestants*, pp. 149–50.
136 Schäfer, *Landesbischof D. Wurm und der nationalsozialistische Staat*, pp. 92–99.
137 HStAS, J170, Bü1, (Aalen), Bopfingen, p. 4.
138 Ibid., Fachsenfeld, pp. 1–2.
139 StAL, K110, Bü37, 'Betr.: Verhalten der Geistlichen gegenüber polnischen Kriegsgefangenen', 9 February 1940.
140 Ibid., 'Betr.: Geistliche Betreuung der Kriegsgefangenen', 8 March 1940.
141 Ibid., Bü38: 'Betr.: Kirchenbesuch von Kriegsgefangenen und polnischen Zivilarbeitskräften', 4 September 1940; 'Betr.: Vergehen von Geistlichen gegen das Heimtückegesetz', 5 September 1940. On a popular view that Hitler did not know, and would not have approved of, actions of lowly Nazi functionaries, see Kershaw, *The 'Hitler Myth'*, pp. 96–104, 178–79.
142 Schäfer, *Landesbischof D. Wurm und der nationalsozialistische Staat*, p. 447.
143 Volk, *Akten deutscher Bischöfe über die Lage der Kirche, 1933–1945*, document 649, Bertram to Lammers, 22 April 1941, pp. 345–46.
144 StAL, K110, Bü48, 'Betr.: Allgemeine Stimmung und Lage', 1 September 1941, pp. 4–9.
145 BA, R22/3387: Der Generalstaatsanwalt an den Herrn Reichsminister der Justiz, Nr 420b – 34, 30 September 1941; Der Oberlandesgerichtspräsident an den Herrn Reichsminister der Justiz, Nr 3130, 'Betreff: Bericht über die allgemeine Lage', 5 September 1941.
146 HStAS, J170, Bü18, Westerstetten, 20 September 1948.
147 StAL, K110, Bü37, 'Betr.: Erfassung von Kirchenglocken', 10 April 1940.
148 See, for example, HStAS, J170: Bü1 (Aalen), Aufhausen; Bü3 (Böblingen), Unterjettingen; Bü4 (Crailsheim), Jagstheim; Bü10 (Leonberg): Ditzingen; Flacht, 27 October 1948.
149 Ibid., E151/01, Bü3621: 9 August 1941, 15 August 1941, 27 November 1941, 9 December 1941, 20 December 1941.
150 Ibid., J170: Bü1, Bopfingen, Dalkingen; Bü18, Suppingen.
151 Ibid., E151/01, Bü3621: 29 March 1938, 23 February 1940, 20 March 1940, 9 April 1940, 4 May 1940, 29 May 1940, 31 July 1940, 25 October 1940, 8 August 1942, 17 August 1942, 27 April 1943, 4 May 1943, 21 May 1943, 21 October 1944. On opposition to the removal of church bells in Bavaria, see 'Aus Monatsbericht des Landrats, 1.5.1942', in Martin Broszat, Elke Fröhlich and Falk Wiesemann (eds), *Bayern in der NS-Zeit. i: Soziale Lage und politisches Verhalten der Bevölkerung im Spiegel vertraulicher Berichte* (Munich and Vienna, 1977), p. 157.
152 Leipner, *Chronik der Stadt Stuttgart*, p. 988.
153 BA, R22/3387, Der Generalstaatsanwalt an den Herrn Reichsminister der Justiz: Nr 420b – 34, 30 September 1941; Nr 420b – 37, 4 April 1942; Schnabel, *Württemberg zwischen Weimar und Bonn*, pp. 421–26.
154 HStAS, J170, Bü8 (Heilbronn): Affaltrach, 22 November 1948, p. 2; Biberach, 9 November 1948, p. 2; Gundelsheim, 8 September 1948, p. 3. See also the description of a teacher's

lesson (c.1970) about 'the history of the four great bells in the tower of the [Evangelical] church in Schönhausen ... when they were cast, when melted down for armaments, when and by whom recast, and what tones they produce', in George D. Spindler, *Burgbach: Urbanisation and Identity in a German Village* (New York, 1973), p. 110. On the significance of church bells in rural society, see Alain Corbin, *Village Bells: Sound and Meaning in the Nineteenth-century French Countryside* (London, 1998), especially pp. 86–93.

155   HStAS, J170, Bü18, Suppingen.

156   StAL, K110, Bü47, 'Betr.: Allgemeine Stimmung und Lage', 15 July 1941, p. 6.

157   Ibid., PL504/18, Bü12, p. 8.

158   Ibid., K110, Bü47, pp. 3–4.

159   Rauh-Kühne, 'Katholisches Sozialmilieu, Region und Nationalsozialismus', p. 232. See also Robert Gellately, *The Gestapo and German Society: Enforcing Racial Policy, 1933–1945* (Oxford, 1990), p. 237.

160   Boberach, *Meldungen aus dem Reich*, 12, MadR, pp. 4538–4541. The quotation is from p. 4541.

161   Heinz Boberach (ed.), *Berichte des SD und der Gestapo über Kirchen und Kirchenvolk in Deutschland, 1934–1944* (Mainz, 1971), 'Meldungen aus dem Reich', no. 189, 26 May 1941, p. 320

162   Josef Ackermann, 'Heinrich Himmler – "Reichsführer-SS"', in Ronald Smelser, Enrico Syring and Rainer Zitelmann (eds), *Die Braune Elite I: 22 biographische Skizzen* (Darmstadt, 1999), p. 125. See also Josef Ackermann, *Himmler als Ideologe* (Göttingen, 1970).

163   United States Holocaust Memorial Museum archive, NS6/414, II B 4, 'Aktivität der Kirche', 9 April 1943, pp. 11–16. The quotation is from p. 11.

164   StAL, Bü48, pp. 10–13, 18–19. The quotations are from pp. 10 and 12. Emphasis in the original. See also Earl R. Beck, *Under the Bombs: The German Home Front, 1942–1945* (Lexington, KY, 1986), pp. 22–23.

165   Boberach, *Meldungen aus dem Reich*, 13, MadR, 1 March 1943, p. 4878. See also 'Aus Monatsbericht des Gendarmerie-Kreisführers, 29.3.1940', in Broszat, Fröhlich and Wiesemann, *Bayern in der NS-Zeit*, i, p. 138.

166   StAL, Bü48, p. 15.

167   Boberach, *Meldungen aus dem Reich*, 13, pp. 4876–77.

168   StAL, Bü48, pp. 13, 18.

169   Boberach, *Meldungen aus dem Reich*, 10, MadR, 15 June 1942, p. 3834.

170   StAL, Bü48, pp. 12–13.

171   Boberach, *Meldungen aus dem Reich*, 13, p. 4877.

172   StAL, Bü48, pp. 14–18. The quotation is from p. 15. Emphasis in the original.

173   Ibid., Bü38, 5 September 1940.

174   Ludwig Volk (ed.), *Akten deutscher Bischöfe über die Lage der Kirche, 1933–1945*, vi, *1943–1945* (Mainz, 1985), document 975, Kottmann to Schwartz, 7 May 1945, p. 471.

175   HStAS, J170, reports from the communes.

Notes to Chapter 8: Forced Foreign Workers

1   Jeremy Noakes and Geoffrey Pridham (eds), *Nazism 1919–1945: A Documentary Reader,*

iii, *Foreign Policy, War and Racial Extermination* (Exeter, 2001), document 638, p. 300. A version of this chapter was published as 'Triangle: Foreign Workers, German Civilians, and the Nazi Regime. War and Society in Württemberg, 1939–1945', *German Studies Review*, 15 (1992), pp. 339–59.

2 Mark Spoerer and Jochen Fleischhacker, 'Forced Laborers in Nazi Germany: Categories, Numbers and Survivors', *Journal of Interdisciplinary History*, 33 (2002), pp. 171–204.

3 Edward L. Homze, *Foreign Labor in Nazi Germany* (Princeton, 1967), pp. 49–55; Jeremy Noakes (ed.), *Nazism 1919–1945: A Documentary Reader*, iv, *The German Home Front in World War II* (Exeter, 1998), p. 247.

4 David Watts, 'German Forced Labor Policy in Belgium, 1916–1917 and 1942–1944', presentation at the Summer Research Workshop on 'Forced Foreign Laborers, POWs, and Jewish Slave Workers in the Third Reich: Regional Studies and New Research', at the Center for Advanced Holocaust Studies (CAHS), United States Holocaust Memorial Museum, 15 August 2003; Staatsarchiv Ludwigsburg (StAL), K110, Bü38, 'Betr.: Belgische Kriegsgefangene', 25 September 1940.

5 Helga Bories-Sawala, *Franzosen im 'Reichseinsatz': Deportation, Zwangsarbeit, Alltag. Erfahrungen und Erinnerungen von Kriegsgefangenen und Zivilarbeitern* (Frankfurt am Main, 1996), pp. 221–22.

6 Michael Petersen, 'Utilisation of Jewish and Non-Jewish Slave Labor in V-2 Rocket Production', presentation at the Summer Research Workshop, CAHS, 14 August 2003.

7 Ralf Lang, *Italienische 'Fremdarbeiter' im nationalsozialistischen Deutschland, 1937–1945* (Frankfurt am Main, 1996), pp. 92–93. See also Ulrich Herbert, *Hitler's Foreign Workers: Enforced Foreign Labor in Germany under the Third Reich* (Cambridge and New York, 1997), pp. 282–86. Cf. Neil Gregor, *Daimler-Benz in the Third Reich* (New Haven, Connecticut, and London, 1998), p. 192.

8 Watts, 'German Forced Labor Policy in Belgium'.

9 See the tables for foreign workers in Germany in Spoerer and Fleischhacker, 'Forced Laborers in Nazi Germany', pp. 187, 189 and 194.

10 On the conditions and treatment of foreign workers in wartime Germany, see especially: Ulrich Herbert, *Fremdarbeiter: Politik und Praxis des 'Ausländer-Einsatzes' in der Kriegswirtschaft des Dritten Reiches* (Berlin and Bonn, 1985) and the English edition, *Hitler's Foreign Workers*; Homze, *Foreign Labor*; Marie-Luise Recker, *Nationalsozialistische Sozialpolitik im Zweiten Weltkrieg* (Munich, 1985), pp. 79–81, 155–76; Detlev J.K. Peukert, *Inside Nazi Germany: Conformity, Opposition and Racism in Everyday Life* (London, 1987), pp. 125–44; Robert Gellately, *The Gestapo and German Society: Enforcing Racial Policy, 1933–1945* (Oxford, 1990), pp. 215–52; Noakes, *Nazism*, iv, pp. 240–49, 257, 261, 304, 325–30, 384–85, 387, 389, 539–40, 589, 639–40.

11 Spoerer and Fleischhacker, 'Forced Laborers in Nazi Germany', p. 170. On foreign workers in German regions before 1918, see Karl Marten Barfuss, *'Gastarbeiter' in Nordwestdeutschland, 1884–1918* (Bremen, 1986); Herbert, *Hitler's Foreign Workers*, pp. 13–26; Richard Charles Murphy, *Guestworkers in the German Reich: A Polish Community in Wilhelmian Germany* (New York, 1983); Watts, 'German Forced Labor Policy in Belgium'.

12 Hans-Erich Volkmann, 'Die NS-Wirtschaft in Vorbereitung des Krieges', in Wilhelm Deist, Manfred Messerschmidt, Hans-Erich Volkmann, Wolfram Wette, *Ursachen und*

Voraussetzungen des Zweiten Weltkrieges (Stuttgart, 1989), p. 430. Daniela Münkel, *National-sozialistische Agrarpolitik und Bauernalltag* (Frankfurt am Main, 1996), pp. 392–403, comments on this problem in *Landkreis* Stade.

13 On Austrians, see Hauptstaatsarchiv Stuttgart (HStAS), E151/01, Bü3596, An den Herrn Ministerialdirektor, 8 April 1937. On Italians, see Lang, *Italienische 'Fremdarbeiter' im nationalsozialistischen Deutschland*, pp. 40–42.

14 StAL, K310, Bü124, Der Präsident des Landesarbeitsamts Südwestdeutschland an die Herren Vorsitzenden der Arbeitsämter (Runderlass Nr 737 Württ.), 19 June 1937, p. 2.

15 StAL, K110, Bü46, 'Lagebericht des 2. Vierteljahres 1939', 1 July 1939, p. 36.

16 The first quotation is from John E. Farquharson, *The Plough and the Swastika: The NSDAP and Agriculture, 1928–1945* (London, 1976), p. 198. The second quotation is from Volkmann, 'Die NS-Wirtschaft', p. 430. See also: Klaus J. Bade, *Auswanderer – Wanderarbeiter – Gastarbeiter: Bevölkerung, Arbeitsmarkt und Wanderung in Deutschland seit der Mitte des 19. Jahrhunderts*, 2 vols, (Ostfildern, 1984); Ulrich Herbert, *Geschichte der Ausländerbeschäftigung in Deutschland, 1880 bis 1980: Saisonarbeiter, Zwangsarbeiter, Gastarbeiter* (Berlin and Bonn, 1986); Herbert, *Fremdarbeiter*, pp. 24–66, especially table 5, 'Ausländische Arbeitskräfte in Deutschland nach Staatsangehörigkeit, 1936 bis 1938', p. 58; Johann Woydt, *Ausländische Arbeitskräfte in Deutschland: vom Kaiserreich bis zur Bundesrepublik* (Heilbronn, 1987), p. 54, table 5, 'Ausländische Arbeiter in Deutschland, 1923 bis 1938'.

17 Noakes and Pridham, *Nazism*, iii, document 678, p. 353.

18 Peukert, *Inside Nazi Germany*, p. 128.

19 Gellately, *The Gestapo and German Society*, p. 250. See also Robert Gellately, *Backing Hitler: Consent and Coercion in Nazi Germany* (Oxford, 2001), pp. 151–82.

20 Theresia Bauer, *Nationalsozialistische Agrarpolitik und bäuerliches Verhalten im Zweiten Weltkrieg: eine Regionalstudie zur ländlichen Gesellschaft in Bayern* (Frankfurt am Main, 1996), pp. 157–58.

21 Recker, *NS Sozialpolitik*, p. 79. See also Roland Müller, *Stuttgart zur Zeit des National-sozialismus* (Stuttgart, 1988), p. 412.

22 Jill Stephenson, 'The Home Front in "Total War": Women in Germany and Britain in the Second World War', in Roger Chickering, Stig Förster and Bernd Greiner (eds), *A World at Total War: Global Conflict and the Politics of Destruction, 1939–1945*, Publications of the German Historical Institute, Washington D.C. (Cambridge, 2005), pp. 224–29.

23 Richard Overy, '"Blitzkriegwirtschaft"? Finanzpolitik, Lebensstandard und Arbeitseinsatz in Deutschland, 1939–1942', *Vierteljahrshefte für Zeitgeschichte* (1988), p. 426.

24 Jill Stephenson, *Women in Nazi Germany* (London, 2001), pp. 79–82; Elizabeth D. Heineman, *What Difference Does a Husband Make?* (Berkeley and Los Angeles, California, 1999), p. 64

25 Gregor, *Daimler-Benz in the Third Reich*, pp. 153–56, 175–76.

26 E.g., HStAS, E397, Bü37, Der Landrat (Nürtingen) an das Landesernährungsamt, Nr D.K.2518, 'Betreff: Strafanzeige gegen – und –', 26 May 1942.

27 Herbert, *Fremdarbeiter*, p. 11.

28 StAL, K110, Bü40, Rundschreiben Nr 107/41, 'Betr.: Unzulänglichkeiten bei der Lenkung des Arbeitseinsatzes', 20 October 1941.

29 Herbert, *Hitler's Foreign Workers*, p. 194. For a local view, see Tobias Weger, *National-sozialistischer 'Fremdarbeitereinsatz' in einer bayerischen Gemeinde, 1939–1945: das Beispiel Olching (Landkreis Fürstenfeldbruck)* (Frankfurt am Main, 1998), pp. 99–104. I am indebted to Professor H.G. Hockerts for giving me a copy of this book.

30 Annette Schäfer, *Zwangsarbeiter und NS-Rassenpolitik: Russische und polnische Arbeitskräfte in Württemberg, 1939–1945* (Stuttgart, 2000), pp. 48–49.

31 Homze, *Foreign Labor*, pp. 264–89, especially pp. 264, 276. Homze does, however, show how little practical difference it made to foreign workers' conditions. Cf. Earl R. Beck, *Under the Bombs: The German Home Front, 1942–1945* (Lexington, Kentucky, 1986), pp. 79–80, 142–43; Ronald Smelser, *Robert Ley: Hitler's Labour Front Leader* (Oxford and New York, 1988), pp. 269–72.

32 HStAS, E397, Bü10, Reichsminister für Ernährungs- und Landwirtschaft, '68./69. Zuteilungsperioden, 29. September 1944, Dritter Abschnitt: Ostarbeiter', p. 7.

33 United States Holocaust Memorial Museum archive (USHMM), NS6/337: pp. 12216–17, Oberkommando der Wehrmacht, 'Betr.: Herstellung und Erhaltung der Arbeitsfähigkeit der sowjet. Kr.Gef', 18 December 1941; pp. 12213–14, Der Chef des Oberkommando der Wehrmacht, 24 December 1941; pp. 12218–19, 'Merkblatt für den Arbeitseinsatz der sowjet Kr.Gef., Hier: Massnahmen zur Wiederherstellung der vollen Arbeitsfähigkeit', n.d.

34 Ibid., p. 12215, Rundschreiben Nr 5/42, 10 January 1942.

35 Gregor, *Daimler-Benz in the Third Reich*, pp. 186–87. See also Herbert, *Hitler's Foreign Workers*, pp. 156–57, 172–87; Gerd Wysocki, *Arbeit für den Krieg: Herrschaftsmechanismen in der Rüstungsindustrie des 'Dritten Reiches'* (Limbach, 1992). See also Müller, *Stuttgart zur Zeit des Nationalsozialismus*, pp. 420–21.

36 StAL, K110, Bü40, Rundschreiben Nr 133/41, 'Betr.: Berichterstattung für das Gebiet Volkstum', 29 November 1941, p. 2.

37 Christa Tholander, *Fremdarbeiter, 1939 bis 1945: Ausländische Arbeitskräfte in der Zeppelin-Stadt Friedrichshafen* (Essen, 2001), p. 67.

38 Petersen, 'Utilisation of Jewish and Non-Jewish Slave Labor in V-2 Rocket Production'.

39 Schäfer, *Zwangsarbeiter und NS-Rassenpolitik*, pp. 99–100, 255.

40 HStAS, E151/01, Bü3596, Der Württ. Innenminister, Nr P.P. 685/245, 'Betreff: Behandlung der im Reich eingesetzten Zivilarbeiter und- arbeiterinnen poln. Volkstums', 18 April 1940.

41 StAL, K110, Bü40, Rdschr.-Nr 126/41, 'Betr.: Merkblatt für den Arbeitseinsatz von Kriegsgefangenen, polnischen Zivil-Arbeitern und Arbeiterinnen', 13 November 1941, pp. 1–4. See also Bauer, *Nationalsozialistische Agrarpolitik und bäuerliches Verhalten*, p. 156; Münkel, *Bauernalltag*, pp. 403–6.

42 Noakes and Pridham, *Nazism*, iii, document 638, pp. 300–301.

43 Ibid., document 697, p. 377; Gellately, *The Gestapo and German Society*, pp. 219–52; Peukert, *Inside Nazi Germany*, pp. 126–29; Anton Grossmann, 'Fremd- und Zwangsarbeiter in Bayern, 1939–1945', in Bade, *Auswanderer*, pp. 593–97; Bauer, *Nationalsozialistische Agrarpolitik und bäuerliches Verhalten*, pp. 163–64; Paul Sauer, *Württemberg in der Zeit des Nationalsozialismus* (Ulm, 1975), pp. 417–24; StAL, K110, Bü40: 'Betr. Merkblatt für den Arbeitseinsatz von Kriegsgefangenen, polnischen Zivil-Arbeitern und Arbeiterinnen', 13 November 1941, pp. 1–4; 'Rdchr.-Nr 127/41', 20 November 1941, pp. 1–4; Müller,

Stuttgart zur Zeit des Nationalsozialismus, pp. 411–25. In December 1942, 'around 50 per cent' of the 55,000 foreign workers in Hamburg were housed in camps. BA, R55/1211, Inspektion Pro/RP, 22 December 1942.

44 Recker, *Nationalsozialistische Sozialpolitik*, p. 161.

45 StAL, PL504/22, Bü23, 'Zehn Gebote im Umgang mit Kriegsgefangenen', n.d. [autumn 1939].

46 Woydt, *Ausländische Arbeitskräfte*, p. 115, quotes 'Verhaltensmassregeln für die deutsche Bevölkerung'; StAL, K110: Bü37, 'Betr. Probleme und Fragen zur Bearbeitung des Sachgebiets Rasse und Volksgesundheit', 28 March 1940, p. 6.

47 Christine Arbogast, *Herrschaftsinstanzen der württembergischen NSDAP* (Munich, 1998), pp. 63–64; Thomas Schnabel, *Württemberg zwischen Weimar und Bonn, 1928–1945/46* (Stuttgart, 1986), p. 570; Müller, *Stuttgart zur Zeit des Nationalsozialismus*, pp. 423–24. Elsewhere, harsh sentences were sometimes imposed. See, e.g., Münkel, *Bauernalltag*, pp. 412–14.

48 HStAS, E397, Bü10, 'Im Gebiet des Landeswirtschaftsamts Württemberg. Nährmittel-bevölkerung', for the food ration allocation periods: 58 (10 January to 6 February 1944); 61 (3 April to 30 April 1944); 62 (1 May to 28 May 1944); 66 (21 August to 17 September 1944); 67 (18 September to 15 October 1944); 70 (11 December 1944 to 7 January 1945); 71 (8 January 1945 to 4 February 1945); 72 (5 February to 4 March 1945).

49 Noakes and Pridham, *Nazism*, iii, document 638; Herbert, *Fremdarbeiter*, p. 11.

50 StAL, K110, Bü37, 'Betr.: Kenntlichmachung der im Reich eingesetzten polnischen Landarbeiter und Landarbeiterinnen', 10 April 1940.

51 HStAS, E151/01, Bü3596, Der Württ. Innenminister, Nr P.P. 685/245, 'Betreff: Behandlung der im Reich eingesetzten Zivilarbeiter und- arbeiterinnen poln. Volkstums', 18 April 1940.

52 StAL, K110, Bü37, 'Betr.: Ukrainische Arbeitskräfte', 27 May 1940. This issue was never entirely resolved. In October 2003, there was a debate about distinguishing insignia for Ukrainian workers on the website: www.ns-zwangsarbeit@hclist.de.

53 StAL, K110: Bü37, 'Betr.: Ukrainische Arbeitskräfte', 27 May 1940 Bü45, pp. 11–12, 15.

54 Homze, *Foreign Labor*, p. 288.

55 Herbert, *Hitler's Foreign Workers*, pp. 165–66; Tholander, *Fremdarbeiter, 1939 bis 1945*, p. 301.

56 Steinert, *Hitler's War*, p. 333. Also, Gellately, *The Gestapo and German Society*, pp. 239–40, 248–49; Ian Kershaw, *Popular Opinion and Political Dissent in the Third Reich: Bavaria, 1933–1945* (Oxford, 1983), p. 288; Sauer, *Württemberg*, pp. 417, 419–22; Müller, *Stuttgart zur Zeit des Nationalsozialismus*, pp. 412–13; Smelser, *Robert Ley*, p. 271; Noakes, *Nazism*, iv, document no. 1292, pp. 539–40.

57 Schäfer, *Zwangsarbeiter und NS-Rassenpolitik*, p. 28; Tholander, *Fremdarbeiter, 1939 bis 1945*, pp. 60–63. Cf. Herbert, *Hitler's Foreign Workers*, p. 141.

58 Omer Bartov, *Hitler's Army: Soldiers, Nazis, and War in the Third Reich* (Oxford, 1992). See also his *The Eastern Front, 1941–45: German Troops and the Barbarisation of Warfare* (London, 1985).

59 Peukert, *Inside Nazi Germany*, pp. 142–44; Kershaw, *Popular Opinion*, pp. 300, 313–14.

60 Herbert, *Fremdarbeiter*, p. 18. See Gellately, *The Gestapo and German Society*, p. 235, on

a doctor who informed on a patient who had a sexual liaison with a Pole; the latter was executed. See also Annette Schäfer, 'Zwangsarbeit in den Kommunen: "Ausländereinsatz" in Württemberg, 1939–1945', *Vierteljahrshefte für Zeitgeschichte*, 49, (2001), pp. 53–75; Schäfer, *Zwangsarbeiter und NS-Rassenpolitik*, pp. 239–52; Gregor, *Daimler-Benz in the Third Reich*, pp. 175–217.

61 Tholander, *Fremdarbeiter, 1939 bis 1945*, p. 45; Jill Stephenson, *The Nazi Organisation of Women* (London, 1981), p. 193.

62 StAL, K110, Bü48, 'Betr.: Allgemeine Stimmung und Lage', 1 September 1941, pp. 43–48; Bundesarchiv (BA), R22/3387, 1 August 1941; HStAS, J170: Bü1 (Aalen), Zipplingen, p. 2; Bü8 (Heilbronn), Hausen a.d.Z.; Bü18 (Ulm), Urspring, 19 October 1948, p. 2. See also Jill Stephenson, '"Emancipation" and its Problems: War and Society in Württemberg, 1939–45', *European History Quarterly*, 17 (1987), pp. 358–59.

63 StAL, K110, Bü47, 'Betr.: Allgemeine Stimmung und Lage', 15 July 1941, p. 10.

64 Tholander, *Fremdarbeiter, 1939 bis 1945*, pp. 39–43, 74; Schäfer, *Zwangsarbeiter und NS-Rassenpolitik*, p. 28.

65 Ibid., pp. 174–75; Tholander, *Fremdarbeiter, 1939 bis 1945*, pp. 84–86. 'Capable of being made German again' was 'Wiedereindeutschungsfähig'.

66 StAL, K110, Bü48, pp. 24–29.

67 Tholander, *Fremdarbeiter, 1939 bis 1945*, pp. 87–91.

68 StAL, Bü48, pp. 28–29.

69 Müller, *Stuttgart zur Zeit des Nationalsozialismus*, p. 411.

70 BA, R22/3387, 30 September 1940.

71 Tholander, *Fremdarbeiter, 1939 bis 1945*, p. 71.

72 Heinz Boberach (ed.), *Meldungen aus dem Reich* (Herrsching, 1984), 9, 'Anlage zu den "Meldungen aus dem Reich" v. 26.3.1942', pp. 3531–35. The quotations are from pp. 3534 and 3535 respectively.

73 StAL, K110, Bü37, 'Betr.: Beschäftigung polnischer Landarbeiter', 1 March 1940. On the regulations governing Poles' conduct, see Schäfer, *Zwangsarbeiter und NS-Rassenpolitik*, pp. 28–37; Tholander, *Fremdarbeiter, 1939 bis 1945*, pp. 50–57.

74 BA, R22/3387, Der Generalstaatsanwalt an den Herrn Reichsminister der Justiz, Nr 420b – 28, 'Betrifft: Lagebericht', 30 September 1940.

75 Kershaw, *Popular Opinion*, p. 286.

76 HStAS, J170, Bü18 (Ulm), Türkheim, 20 April 1949, p. 1.

77 Gellately, *The Gestapo and German Society*, p. 237. See also Bauer, *Nationalsozialistische Agrarpolitik und bäuerliches Verhalten*, p. 166.

78 StAL, K110: Bü44, 1 February 1939, pp. 18–19; Bü45, 1 April 1939, pp. 43–44. See also Jill Stephenson, 'War and Society in Württemberg, 1939–1945: Beating the System', *German Studies Review*, 8 (1985), p. 104.

79 StAL, K110, Bü37, 9 February 1940. Cf. Tholander, *Fremdarbeiter, 1939 bis 1945*, pp. 54–56. See also Schnabel, *Württemberg zwischen Weimar und Bonn*, p. 570; Bauer, *Nationalsozialistische Agrarpolitik und bäuerliches Verhalten*, pp. 165, 170–72, 176. Cf. Grossmann, 'Fremd- und Zwangsarbeiter', pp. 614–18; Boberach, *MadR*, 3, 'Meldungen aus dem Reich (Nr. 62)', 6 March 1940, pp. 844–45; John J. Delaney: 'Sowing *Volksgemeinschaft* in Bavaria's Stony Village Soil: Catholic Peasant Rejection of Anti-Polish Racial Policy,

1939–1945', in Donald J. Dietrich, *Christian Responses to the Holocaust: Moral and Ethical Issues* (Syracuse, New York, 2003), pp. 80–82; 'Racial Values vs. Religious Values: Clerical Opposition to Nazi Anti-Polish Racial Policy', *Church History*, 70 (2001), pp. 271–84. On priests in Berlin ministering to Catholic forced foreign workers, see Kevin P. Spicer, *Resisting the Third Reich: The Catholic Clergy in Hitler's Berlin* (DeKalb, Illinois, 2004), pp. 106–14. On the employment of foreign workers by the Evangelical Church in Württemberg, see Inga Bing-von Häfen, 'Zwangsarbeit in Diensten der Evangelischen Landeskirche und ihrer Diakonie in Württemberg', in Jochen-Christoph Kaiser (ed.), *Zwangsarbeit in Diakonie und Kirche, 1939–45* (Stuttgart, 2005), pp. 385–418.

80   Jill Stephenson, 'Women's Labor Service in Nazi Germany', *Central European History*, 15 (1982), pp. 257–61. A former *Arbeitsmaid*, has, however, told me that, in her experience, Labour Service women had worked hard. See also Tholander, *Fremdarbeiter, 1939 bis 1945*, p. 70.

81   Benigna Schönhagen, *Tübingen unterm Hakenkreuz* (Stuttgart, 1991), p. 356. See also Delaney, 'Sowing *Volksgemeinschaft* in Bavaria's Stony Village Soil', pp. 73–86.

82   Schönhagen, *Tübingen unterm Hakenkreuz*, p. 457, n. 460. See also Delaney, 'Racial Values vs. Religious Values', p. 286.

83   Grossmann, 'Fremd- und Zwangsarbeiter', p. 597; Herbert, *Fremdarbeiter*, p. 94; Gellately, *The Gestapo and German Society*, pp. 227–32; Bauer, *Nationalsozialistische Agrarpolitik und bäuerliches Verhalten*, pp. 164–66, 168–69; Schnabel, *Württemberg zwischen Weimar und Bonn*, p. 603; Beatrix Herlemann, '*Der Bauer klebt am Hergebrachten': Bäuerliche Verhaltensweisen unterm Nationalsozialismus auf dem Gebiet des heutigen Landes Niedersachsen* (Hanover, 1993), p. 321; Delaney, 'Racial Values vs. Religious Values', pp. 284–94.

84   Tholander, *Fremdarbeiter, 1939 bis 1945*, p. 92. See also Jill Stephenson, 'Germans, Slavs and the burden of work in rural southern Germany during the Second World War', in Neil Gregor (ed.), *Nazism, War, Genocide: Essays in Honour of Jeremy Noakes* (Exeter, 2005), pp. 104–5.

85   StAL, K110, Bü37, 1 March 1940.

86   Tholander, *Fremdarbeiter, 1939 bis 1945*, p. 91. See also Uwe Kaminsky, '"Vergessene Opfer": Zwangssterilisierte, "Asoziale", Deserteure, Fremdarbeiter', in Sybille Baumbach, Uwe Kaminsky, Alfons Kenkmann, Beate Meyer, *Rückblenden: Lebensgeschichtliche Interviews mit Verfolgten des NS-Regimes in Hamburg*, (Hamburg, 1999), pp. 348–55.

87   Arbogast, *Herrschaftsinstanzen der württembergischen NSDAP*, p. 65.

88   StAL, K110, Bü37, 28 March 1940.

89   Sauer, *Württemberg*, p. 423; Müller, *Stuttgart zur Zeit des Nationalsozialismus*, p. 414; Delaney, 'Racial Values vs. Religious Values', pp. 289–91; Beck, *Under the Bombs*, p. 97; Gellately, *The Gestapo and German Society*, pp. 227–28; BA, R22/3387: 2 February 1940, 31 May 1941. Also, Herbert, *Fremdarbeiter*, pp. 122–24.

90   StAL, K110, Bü37, 25 January 1940.

91   BA, R22/3387, 1 August 1941.

92   Sauer, *Württemberg*, pp. 420–21; Schnabel, *Württemberg zwischen Weimar und Bonn*, p. 570; Beck, *Under the Bombs*, pp. 97, 123–24; Christoph U. Schminck-Gustavus (ed.), *Hungern für Hitler: Erinnerungen polnischer Zwangsarbeiter im deutschen Reich, 1940–1945* (Hamburg, 1984), pp. 57–58.

93 Tholander, *Fremdarbeiter, 1939 bis 1945*, p. 89.

94 BA, R22/3387, Der Generalstaatsanwalt an den Herrn Reichsminister der Justiz, Nr 3130 – Ia – 2, 31 May 1943; Boberach, *MadR*, vol. 16, 'SD-Berichte zu Inlandsfragen', 24 January 1944, p. 6278; Beck, *Under the Bombs*, pp. 79–80; Stephenson, '"Emancipation" and its Problems', pp. 357–58; Kershaw, *Popular Opinion*, pp. 294–95. Bauer, *Nationalsozialistische Agrarpolitik und bäuerliches Verhalten*, pp. 159–60, argues that in Bavaria farmers sometimes paid Polish workers above the standard wage rate to attract or retain them, and that farmers who mistreated a Polish worker during the war had in the past similarly mistreated German hired hands and indeed family members.

95 Tholander, *Fremdarbeiter, 1939 bis 1945*, pp. 61–63.

96 BA, R22/3387, 31 May 1943; Münkel, *Bauernalltag*, pp. 412–13.

97 Herbert, *Fremdarbeiter*, p. 127.

98 Schäfer, *Zwangsarbeiter und NS-Rassenpolitik*, pp. 153–58.

99 Schnabel, *Württemberg zwischen Weimar und Bonn*, pp. 570–71; Gellately, *The Gestapo and German Society*, p. 238. For an instance of a German girl, attired in a sack, being forced to attend her Polish lover's execution, see Schminck-Gustavus, *Hungern für Hitler*, p. 26.

100 BA, R22/3387, Der Generalstaatsanwalt an den Herrn Reichsminister der Justiz, Nr 420b – 33, 1 August 1941.

101 Münkel, *Bauernalltag*, p. 414. A German man who had sex with a Polish woman was intended by the authorities to be sent to a concentration camp for three months, as the minimum penalty, but this prescription was not always enforced. See Gellately, *The Gestapo and German Society*, pp. 233–34.

102 Arbogast, *Herrschaftsinstanzen der württembergischen NSDAP*, p. 63. See also Tholander, *Fremdarbeiter, 1939 bis 1945*, p. 60.

103 StAL, K110, Bü47, pp. 13–14.

104 Woydt, *Ausländische Arbeitskräfte*, pp. 116–17.

105 Birthe Kundrus, *Kriegerfrauen: Familienpolitik und Geschlechterverhältnisse im Ersten und Zweiten Weltkrieg* (Hamburg, 1995), pp. 391–93.

106 Tholander, *Fremdarbeiter, 1939 bis 1945*, pp. 60–61.

107 BA, R22/3387, 30 September 1940. See also Herlemann, *'Der Bauer klebt am Hergebrachten'*, p. 321.

108 BA, R22/3387: Der Generalstaatsanwalt: 420 b – 30, 3 February 1941; 3130 I a 1746, 31 May 1941. See, further, Stephenson, 'Triangle: Foreign Workers, German Civilians and the Nazi State', pp. 344, 349–50.

109 Tholander, *Fremdarbeiter, 1939 bis 1945*, pp. 60–61.

110 Arbogast, *Herrschaftsinstanzen der württembergischen NSDAP*, pp. 63–64, 239.

111 StAL, K110, Bü40, Rdschr. Nr 132/41, 'Betr.: Umgang Deutscher mit Kriegsgefangenen und fremdvölkischen Zivilarbeitskräften', 27 November 1941.

112 Sauer, *Württemberg*, p. 423.

113 Leipner, *Chronik der Stadt Stuttgart*, p. 967.

114 Boberach, *MadR*, 16, 24 January 1944, p. 6279.

115 StAL, K110, Bü58, SD report from early 1945 (undated).

116 Ibid., Bü47, pp. 11–12. See also Homze, *Foreign Labor*, pp. 55–56. Cf. Herbert, *Fremdarbeiter*, pp. 124–27.

117   StAL, K110, Bü40, Rundschreiben Nr 133/41, 29 November 1941, p. 2.

118   Ibid., Bü47, pp. 13–14.

119   BA, R22/3387, 1 August 1941; Schnabel, *Württemberg zwischen Weimar und Bonn*, p. 571.

120   USHMM, NS6/337: p. 13, Oberkommando der Wehrmacht, 'Betr.: Auflockerung der Bewachung kriegsgefangener Franzosen', 22 December 1941; p. 12, Der Leiter der Partei-Kanzlei, Rundschreiben Nr 4/42, 7 January 1942.

121   Tholander, *Fremdarbeiter, 1939 bis 1945*, pp. 51–52, 74.

122   BA, R22/3387, 31 May 1943. See also Tholander, *Fremdarbeiter, 1939 bis 1945*, pp. 73–75.

123   Ibid., R55/601, 'Tätigkeitsbericht (Stichtag: 4. September 1944), p. 7. See also Noakes, *Nazism*, iv, document 1368, p. 639.

124   StAL, K110, Bü58, statements of 11 and 12 October 1942.

125   Boberach, *MadR*: 'SD-Berichte zu Inlandsfragen vom 1. November 1943', pp. 5954–55; 24 January 1944, pp. 6278–79. The quotation is from p. 5954.

126   Herbert, *Fremdarbeiter*, passim; Herbert, *Geschichte der Ausländerbeschäftigung*, pp. 148–53, 159–63; Woydt, *Ausländische Arbeitskräfte*, pp. 113–34; Schäfer, *Zwangsarbeiter und NS-Rassenpolitik*, pp. 44–52, 101–24; Tholander, *Fremdarbeiter, 1939 bis 1945*, pp. 300–70, 486–91. See also the reminiscences in Schminck-Gustavus, *Hungern für Hitler*.

127   Herbert, *Fremdarbeiter*, p. 342. Also, Schnabel, *Württemberg zwischen Weimar und Bonn*, pp. 572–73, 602–3; Schönhagen, *Tübingen unterm Hakenkreuz*, p. 355; Bing-von Häfen, 'Zwangsarbeit in Diensten der Evangelischen Landeskirche', p. 417.

128   Bauer, *Nationalsozialistische Agrarpolitik und bäuerliches Verhalten*, p. 165.

129   HStAS, E397, Bü37, 'Betr.: Schwarzhandel auf dem Lande, besonders auch im Kartoffelhandel', 5 December 1943.

130   Arbogast, *Herrschaftsinstanzen der württembergischen NSDAP*, pp. 82, 182–83. Arbogast draws a different conclusion from the first case here, arguing that the local branch leader was reflecting the racist prejudice of the population by describing this 'mockery'.

131   BA, R22/3387, 31 May 1941; Schnabel, *Württemberg zwischen Weimar und Bonn*, p. 572.

132   HStAS, J170: Bü1 (Aalen): Kerkingen, 15 January 1950, p. 3; Dankoltsweiler, 6 February 1949, p. 4; Neresheim, n.d. (post-1945) p. 2; Kirchheim am Ries, n.d. (post-1945); Bü3 (Böblingen): Rohrau, 5 February 1951; Rudersberg, 6 February 1950, p. 5; Holzgerlingen, 26 August 1948, p. 4; Unterjettingen, 11 October 1948, p. 2; Bü4 (Crailsheim), Wallhausen, p. 11; Bü8 (Heilbronn), Dürrenzimmern, 1 September 1948, p. 2; Bü18 (Ulm), Tomerdingen, p. 5; Bü65 (Ravensburg): Waldsee, 5 March 1946, pp. 1–2; Michelwinnaden, 9 November 1960; Bü78 (Tübingen): Mössingen, 21 November 1960, pp. 1–2; Äschingen, 8 November 1960, pp. 1–2; Entringen, 10 January 1961, p. 1. See also Schnabel, *Württemberg zwischen Weimar und Bonn*, p. 572. Cf. Herbert, *Fremdarbeiter*, pp. 342–44, who concentrates on independent 'displaced person criminality' in towns which worried, and sometimes disgusted, the occupying powers.

133   HStAS, J170, Bü18, Oppingen, 8 October 1948, p. 1.

134   Ibid., Bü78, Wendelsheim. See also Bü3, Musberg, 18 October 1948, p. 13; Schnabel, *Württemberg zwischen Weimar und Bonn*, p. 603. See Hanna Diamond, *Women and the Second World War in France, 1939–1948: Choices and Constraints* (London, 1999), p. 158, on a French POW returning home.

135   HStAS, J170, Bü3, Steinenbronn, 18 October 1949, p. 2.

136   Ibid., Musberg.

137   Ibid., Bü8, Frankenbach, December 1948, p. 8.

138   Ibid., Bü18, Tomerdingen.

139   Ibid.: Bü1, Hüttlingen, n.d. (post-1945), Bernhard Irtenkauf, 'Aufzeichnungen aus meinem Tagebuch', p. 4; Bü18, Regglisweiler, 3 November 1948, p. 2.

140   Ibid., Bü3, Rohrau, p. 14.

141   Ibid., Bü10 (Leonberg), Schöckingen, 'Betr.: Geschichtliche Darstellung der letzten Kriegstage', 13 September 1948, pp. 3–4.

142   Ibid., Bü78, Gemeinde Entringen, 'Betr.: Ausmass der Zerstörungen im Zweiten Weltkrieg in den einzelnen Gemeinden unseres Landes', 10 January 1961, p. 1.

143   Ibid., Bü9 (Künzelsau), 'Niedernhall in den letzten Kriegstagen', n.d. [October/November 1948], p. 1.

144   Ibid., Bü10, Gebersheim, 'Geschichtliche Darstellung der letzten Kriegstage', 6 May 1949, p. 2.

145   Ibid., Bü8, Eschenau, pp. 4–5.

146   Ibid., Bü3, Rudersberg, p. 5.

147   Ibid., Rohrau, p. 16; Musberg, p. 14; Bü9, Laibach; Bü78, Entringen, p. 2.

148   Ibid.: Bü4, 'Orts-Chronik von Wallhausen, 1945', pp. 11–12. See also: Bü1, Oberkochen; Bü3, Unterjettingen, p. 2.

149   Ibid., Bü3, Rohrau.

150   Ibid., Bü10, 'Gemeinde Höfingen/Kreis Leonberg. Geschichtliches zum Kriegsgeschehen 1939/45', 8 September 1948, p. 3.

151   Ibid., Bü3, Rudersberg, p. 5.

152   BA, R22/3364, Der Generalstaatsanwalt (Frankfurt), 3131 E-34, 'Lagebericht Nr 47', 28 September 1944.

153   HStAS, J170, Bü4, Wallhausen, p. 5.

154   Ibid., Bü9, 'Bericht über die Geschehnisse in den letzten Kriegstagen in der Gemeinde Hermuthausen', 19 December 1948.

155   Ibid., Bü1, Bürgermeisteramt Goldburghausen, 'Geschichtliche Darstellung der letzten Kriegsjahre', 7 January 1950.

156   Ibid., Bü3, Rohrau, p. 13.

157   Ibid., Bü4, Bächlingen.

158   Ibid., Bü10, 'Kriegschronik der Gemeinde Münchingen, verfasst von –, Bauer, Münchingen', n.d., pp. 3–4. See also 'Gemeinde Ditzingen. Kurzgefasste geschichtliche Darstellung der letzten Kriegstage 1945', n.d. (1948/49), p. 3; Hirschlanden, 'Betreff: Geschichtliche Darstellung der letzten Kriegstage', n.d. (received 5 May 1949).

159   Ibid., Bü1, 'Geschichtliche Darstellung der letzten Kriegstage in Oberkochen. Verfasst und geschildert nach eigenem Erleben und den Erlebnissen hiesiger Mitbürger und Augenzeugen von Oberlehrer –', 5 November 1948, p. 4.

160   Ibid., Bü4, Lendsiedel, 3 November 1948, pp. 2–3.

161   Ibid., Bü1, Zipplingen. Also, Schnabel, *Württemberg zwischen Weimar und Bonn*, p. 602.

162   Tholander, *Fremdarbeiter, 1939 bis 1945*, pp. 470–74.

163   BA, R22/3387, 31 May 1943.

Notes to Chapter 9: Migrants, Evacuees and Refugees

Some of the source material for this chapter is to be found in the Hauptstaatsarchiv Stuttgart (HStAS), J170 files, which contain responses to a questionnaire circulated to every commune in 1948 about 'the last days of the war'. Most use the heading 'Geschichtliche Darstellung der letzten Kriegstage', or something very similar. Where this is not the case, the heading is quoted. References contain the *Büschel* number, referring to the district, which is named on first mention, and the name of the *Gemeinde* (commune).

1   Hauptstaatsarchiv Stuttgart (HStAS), J170, Bül (Aalen), 'Kriegsereignisse in der Gemeinde Zipplingen Kreis Aalen', 24 October 1948, pp. 1–2. On the Mius front (1943) see, briefly, Alan Clark, *Barbarossa: The Russian-German Conflict* (London, 1966), pp. 386–88. On the massive movement and different categories of people involved, see Michael Krause, *Flucht vor dem Bombenkrieg: 'Umquartierungen' im Zweiten Weltkrieg und die Wiedereingliederung der Evakuierten in Deutschland, 1943–1963* (Düsseldorf, 1997), pp. 38ff.

2   HStAS, Bül, 'Die letzten Wochen vor un[d] die ersten Wochen nach der Besatzung in Neresheim', n.d. [October/November 1948], p. 2.

3   Ibid., Hüttlingen, n.d. [October/November 1948], p. 1.

4   Ibid., Neresheim, p. 1. There is also reference to 'German soldiers (Wlassowkämpfer)' being quartered in Türkheim in Bü18 (Ulm), Türkheim, n.d. [April 1949].

5   Ibid., Hüttlingen, p. 4.

6   Joseph B. Schechtman, *European Population Transfers, 1939–1945* (New York, 1946), pp. 272–80; Robert L. Koehl, *RKFDV: German Resettlement and Population Policy, 1939–1945* (Cambridge, Massachusetts, 1957), pp. 49–88, 104–10; Jill Stephenson, *The Nazi Organisation of Women* (London, 1981), pp. 178, 191.

7   Gerhard Kock, *Die Kinderlandverschickung im Zweiten Weltkrieg* (Paderborn, 1997), p. 11. A journalist's account, Claus Larass, *Der Zug der Kinder: KLV – die Evakuierung 5 Millionen deutscher Kinder im 2. Weltkrieg* (Frankfurt and Berlin, 1992), paints evocative pictures.

8   Angus Calder, *The People's War: Britain 1939–1945* (London, 1971), pp. 51–54. See also John Macnicol, 'The Evacuation of Schoolchildren', in Harold L. Smith (ed.), *War and Social Change: British Society in the Second World War* (Manchester, 1986), pp. 5–31.

9   Sadie Ward, *War in the Countryside, 1939–1945* (London, 1988), p. 106.

10 Jill Stephenson, 'Anniversaries, Memory and the Neighbours: The German Question in Recent History', *German Politics*, 5 (1996), p. 55.

11 Ruud Lubbers, 'Europe: A Continent of Traditions', the William and Mary Lecture, Cambridge, 16 February 1993.

12 Ian Ousby, *Occupation: The Ordeal of France, 1940–1944* (London, 1997), pp. 287–88. See also Robert Gildea, *Marianne in Chains: In Search of the German Occupation of France, 1940–45* (London, 2002), pp. 326–28; Alan J. Levine, *The Strategic Bombing of Germany, 1940–1945* (Westport, Connecticut, 1992), pp. 139–41.

13 See above Chapter 8. See also Theresia Bauer, *Nationalsozialistische Agrarpolitik und bäuerliches Verhalten im Zweiten Weltkrieg: eine Regionalstudie zur ländlichen Gesellschaft in Bayern* (Frankfurt am Main, 1996), pp. 164–65; John J. Delaney, 'Sowing the

Volksgemeinschaft in Bavaria's Stony Village Soil: Catholic Peasant Rejection of Anti-Polish Racial Policy, 1939–1945', in Donald J. Dietrich (ed.), *Christian Responses to the Holocaust: Moral and Ethical Issues* (Syracuse, New York, 2003), pp. 77–78.

14 'Der Arbeitsdienst wurde zur Brücke zwischen Stadt und Land', *Völkischer Beobachter*, 8 September 1933.

15 Staatsarchiv Ludwigsburg (StAL), PL504/22, Bü33, letters of 8 and 12 March 1938, 'Betreff: Jugenderholungspflege'.

16 HStAS, J170, Bü1, Aalen, n.d. [October 1948]. Comments about rural 'stupidity' seem to have been common. See, e.g., Jeremy Noakes (ed.), *Nazism, 1919–1945: A Documentary Reader*, iv, *The German Home Front* (Exeter, 1998), p. 359, document 1152, in which a townee says to a Bavarian shopkeeper, 'I'll buy anything off you but not your Bavarian stupidity'.

17 See especially Elizabeth Harvey, *Women and the Nazi East: Agents and Witnesses of Germanisation* (New Haven, Connecticut, and London, 2003). Also, Stephenson, *Nazi Organisation of Women*, pp. 191–92, 196–99.

18 Schechtman, *European Population Transfers, 1939–1945*, pp. 272–80; Koehl, *RKFDV*, pp. 49–88, 104–10.

19 HStAS, E397, Bü5, Sondergericht für den Oberlandesgerichtsbezirk Stuttgart, SL121–149/42, SL219–220/42, 11 June 1942, p. 7.

20 StAL, K110, Bü38, 'Betr.: Unterbringung und Betreuung von Bessarabiendeutschen', 14 November 1940.

21 Ibid., PL509, Bü61, NSDAP-Hitlerjugend, Gebiet Württemberg an den Führer des Bannes 364, Waiblingen, 16 November 1944.

22 HStAS, E397, Bü5, p. 7.

23 Ibid., J170, Bü1, Zipplingen. For complaints about Saarlanders who had been evacuated to Bavarian villages, see: 'Aus Monatsbericht des Bezirksamts, 30.9.1939'; 'Aus Monatsbericht des Gendarmerie-Kreisführers, 31.7.1940', in Martin Broszat, Elke Fröhlich, Falk Wiesemann (eds), *Bayern in der NS-Zeit*, i, *Soziale Lage und politisches Verhalten der Bevölkerung im Spiegel vertraulicher Berichte*, pp. 134, 141–42.

24 Ibid., Bü18 (Ulm), Oppingen, 5 October 1948.

25 Ibid., Suppingen, 8 November 1949.

26 Ibid.: Urspring, 19 October 1948; Suppingen. See also Marlis G. Steinert, *Hitler's War and the Germans: Public Mood and Attitude during the Second World War*, ed. and trans. Thomas E. J. De Witt (Athens, Ohio, 1977), p. 63. For similar circumstances in Britain, see Ward, *War in the Countryside*, p. 88.

27 Ibid., Bü1, Zipplingen.

28 Martin Kitchen, *Nazi Germany at War* (London, 1995), pp. 95, 113–14; Frank Bajohr, 'Schlussbetrachtung: Meister der Zerstörung', in Forschungsstelle für Zeitgeschichte in Hamburg (ed.), *Hamburg im 'Dritten Reich'* (Göttingen, 2005), pp. 687–88.

29 See above, Chapters 4 and 7. See also HStAS, J170, Bü78 (Tübingen), Öschingen, 'Auszug aus der Ortschronik', 8 November 1960, p. 1.

30 Günter Golde, *Catholics and Protestants: Agricultural Modernisation in Two German Villages* (New York, 1975), pp. 68, 150; George D. Spindler, *Burgbach: Urbanisation and Identity in a German Village* (New York, 1973), pp. 13–14, 19.

31 Steinert, *Hitler's War*, p. 62.

32 Benigna Schönhagen, *Tübingen unterm Hakenkreuz: eine Universitätsstadt in der Zeit des Nationalsozialismus* (Stuttgart, 1991), p. 367 (emphasis in the original).

33 HStAS, J170, Bü78, Öschingen, p. 1.

34 Peter Hüttenberger, *Die Gauleiter: Studie zum Wandel des Machtgefüges in der NSDAP* (Stuttgart, 1969), pp. 169–72. See also Krause, *Flucht vor dem Bombenkrieg*, pp. 92–106.

35 Neil Gregor, 'A *Schicksalgemeinschaft*? Allied Bombing, Civilian Morale, and Social Dissolution in Nuremberg, 1942–1945', *Historical Journal*, 43 (2000), pp. 1063–67.

36 Krause, *Flucht vor dem Bombenkrieg*, pp. 98–101.

37 Hüttenberger, *Die Gauleiter*, pp. 153–57.

38 Schönhagen, *Tübingen unterm Hakenkreuz*, p. 368. Cf. Hans Mommsen, 'The Dissolution of the Third Reich: Crisis Management and Collapse, 1943–1945', *Bulletin of the German Historical Institute* (Washington), 27 (2000), p. 15.

39 HStAS, E151/03, Bü968, Kreis Ulm/D. Amt für Volkswohlfahrt an die Ortsgruppenleiter für Volkswohlfahrt des Landkreises Ulm, 'Betr.: Umquartierung. Regelung der künftigen Zuweisung von evakuierten Personen in die Ortsgruppen des Landkreises Ulm', 29 February 1944.

40 Ibid., Der Landrat (Ulm) an den Herrn Innenminister, 'Betreff: Verteilung der Wohnungen; hier: Unterbringung der Umquartierten aus Stuttgart und Essen', 10 March 1944.

41 StAL, K110, Bü55, RSHA, 'Meldungen aus den SD-(Leit)-Abschnittsbereichen, 15 July 1943, p. 14078.

42 Doris Foitzik, *Jugend ohne Schwung? Jugendkultur und Jugendpolitik in Hamburg, 1945–1949*, (Hamburg, 2002), pp. 29, 32.

43 Heinz Boberach (ed.), *Meldungen aus dem Reich* (Munich, 1968), pp. 365–70. The quotation is from p. 365. On Witten, see Julia S. Torrie, 'Testing Totalitarianism at War: The Witten Demonstration and German Civilian Evacuations, 1939–45', Transatlantic Doctoral Seminar, 25–28 April, 2001. I am indebted to Roger Chickering for bringing this to my attention.

44 Krause, *Flucht vor dem Bombenkrieg*, p. 100.

45 HStAS, J170, Bü8 (Heilbronn), 'Gemeinde Auenstein mit Teilort Helfenberg u. Abstetterhof', 1 November 1948, p. 1.

46 Ibid., Bü10 (Leonberg), Schöckingen, 13 September 1948, p. 3.

47 Ibid., E151/03, Bü968, Der Reichsminister für Volksaufklärung und Propaganda an alle Gauleiter, 'Betrifft: Reichsinspektion zur Durchführung ziviler Luftkriegsmassnahmen', 28 January 1944.

48 Ibid., Der Landrat (Ulm) an den Herrn Innenminister, 'Betreff: Verteilung der Wohnungen; hier: Unterbringung der Umquartierten aus Stuttgart und Essen', 10 March 1944.

49 Paul Sauer, *Württemberg in der Zeit des Nationalsozialismus* (Ulm, 1975), p. 357; Thomas Schnabel, *Württemberg zwischen Weimar und Bonn, 1928–1945/46* (Stuttgart, 1986), p. 586; HStAS, J170, Bü18, Tomerdingen, n.d. [October/November 1948], p. 3.

50 Ibid., E151/03, Bü968, 'Übersicht über den Stand der Umquartierungen. Stichtag: 25 Februar 1944', 23 March 1944.

51 Ibid., Der Reichsminister des Innern an den Herrn Reichsverteidigungskommissar für den RV-Bezirk Württemberg, 'Betrifft: Umquartierung und Erhöhung des Aufnahmesolls', 4 February 1944.

52 Ibid.: 'Übersicht über den Stand der Umquartierungen. Stichtag: 1. April 1944', 28 April 1944; 'Übersicht über den Stand der Umquartierungen. Stichtag: 1. Mai 1944', n.d.; 'Übersicht über den Stand der Umquartierungen. Stichtag: 1. Juni 1944', 21 June 1944; 'Übersicht über den Stand der Umquartierungen. Stichtag: 10. August 1944', 15 September 1944.

53 Martin K. Sorge, *The Other Price of Hitler's War: German Military and Civilian Losses Resulting from World War II* (Westport, Connecticut, 1986), p. 98.

54 HStAS, E151/03, Bü968, Der Württ. Innenminister an den Herrn Reichsstatthalter in Württemberg, 'Betreff: Ausgleich auf dem Gebiete des Raumbedarfs', 23 March 1944.

55 Ibid., letter from the mayor of Maulbronn to an architect in Pforzheim, 7 January 1944.

56 Ibid., J170, Bü3 (Böblingen), Musberg, p. 10.

57 Ibid., Bü1, Ebnat, p. 1.

58 Ibid., Bü8, 'Gemeinde Auenstein', p. 1.

59 Ibid., E151/03, Bü968, Der Landrat (Ulm) an den Herrn Innenminister, 'Betreff: Verteilung der Wohnungen; hier: Unterbringung der Umquartierten aus Stuttgart und Essen', 10 March 1944.

60 Ibid., J170, Bü9 (Künzelsau), Marlach, 'Betreff: Geschichtliche Darstellung der letzten Kriegstage', 27 October 1948, p. 1.

61 Ibid., E151/03, Bü968, Der Landrat (Crailsheim) an den Herrn Württ. Innenminister, 'Betreff: Unterbringung von Luftkriegsbetroffenen im Kreis Crailsheim', 16 March 1944.

62 Ibid, J170, Bü3, Bürgermeisteramt Rohrau, 5 February 1951, pp. 1–4. See also Kock, *Die Kinderlandverschickung im Zweiten Weltkrieg*, p. 247.

63 StAL, K110, Bü58, 'Betrifft: Stimmung und Meinungsbildung', 27 March 1945.

64 Krause, *Flucht vor dem Bombenkrieg*, pp. 162–64, 200. See also above, Chapter 5.

65 HStAS, J170, Bü10, Schöckingen, p. 3.

66 Ibid., E151/03, Bü968, '*Betr.*: Umquartierung', 23 March 1944.

67 Ibid., 'Betreff: Räumung des Altstadtkernes der Stadt Heilbronn', 27 March, 1944.

68 Sauer, *Württemberg*, pp. 355–57.

69 HStAS, J170, Bü18: Steinberg, 31 December 1948; Weiler, 18 August 1948.

70 Ibid., Schnürpflingen, 20 October 1948.

71 Ibid., Bü18, 'Geschichtliche Darstellung der letzten Kriegstage in Sonderbuch', 18 October 1948.

72 Ibid., Setzingen, n.d. [1948].

73 Ibid., Regglisweiler, 3 November 1948.

74 Ibid., Westerstetten, 20 September 1948.

75 Ibid., Bü1, 'Angaben über Kriegsereignisse in der Gemeinde Essingen', 29 November 1948, p. 1.

76 Ibid., 'Die letzten Wochen vor und die ersten Wochen nach der Besetzung in Neresheim', n.d. [October/November 1948], pp. 1, 3.

77 Ibid., Bü9, Marlach, p. 1.

78 Ibid., Künzelsau, 'Anlage zu Bgm. Amt Künzelsau Reg. Nr 5640 vom 7.9.1949 (Geschichtliche Darstellung der letzten Kriegstage)', 15 September 1949, pp. 9–10.

79 Ibid., Laibach, 'Auszug aus der Pfarrchronik Laibach'.

80 Ibid., Bü1, Aufhausen.

81 Ibid., Oberdorf.

82 Ibid., Bü4 (Crailsheim), Kirchberg, p. 4.

83 Ibid., 'Orts-Chronik von Wallhausen 1945', p. 1.

84 Ibid., Langenburg, p. 8.

85 Ibid., Leuzendorf, p. 4.

86 Ibid., Oberspeltach, p. 3.

87 Ibid., Marktlustenau, 3 November 1948, p. 1.

88 Ibid., Rossfeld, n.d.

89 Ibid., Bü1, Essingen, p. 1.

90 StAL, K110, Bü47, SD 'Lagebericht', 15 July 1941, pp. 21–22. See also Kristin Semmens, *Seeing Hitler's Germany: Tourism in the Third Reich* (Basingstoke, 2005), pp.182–84.

91 StAL, K110, Bü48, SD 'Lagebericht', 1 September 1941, pp. 43–48.

92 HStAS, E151/01, Bü3596, orders of 12 August 1943 and 15 September 1943.

93 Ibid., J170, Bü18, 'Betrifft: Geschichtliche Darstellung der letzten Kriegstage in der Gemeinde Oppingen Kreis Ulm-Do', 5 October 1948. For the expectations of evacuees from Hamburg in Bavaria, see 'Aus Monatsbericht des Landrats, 1.9.1943'; 'Aus Monatsbericht des Gendarmerie-Kreisführers, 29.9.1943', in Broszat, Fröhlich and Wiesemann, *Bayern in der NS-Zeit*, i, p. 175.

94 Ibid., Bü18, Urspring, 19 October 1948.

95 Ibid., Bü1, Essingen, p. 1.

96 Ibid., Bü8, Eschenau, 25 October 1948, p. 3. See also Earl R. Beck, *Under the Bombs: The German Home Front, 1942–1945* (Kentucky, 1986), p. 25.

97 Christine Arbogast, *Herrschaftsinstanzen der württembergischen NSDAP: Funktion, Sozialprofil und Lebenswege einer regionalen NS-Elite, 1920–1960* (Munich, 1998), p. 188.

98 Boberach, *Meldungen aus dem Reich*, pp. 366–70; Torrie, 'Testing Totalitarianism at War'. See also Joachim Szodrzynski, 'Das Ende der "Volksgemeinschaft"? Die Hamburger Bevölkerung in der "Trummergesellschaft" ab 1943', in Frank Bajohr and Joachim Szodrzynski (eds), *Hamburg in der NS-Zeit: Ergebnisse neuerer Forschung* (Hamburg, 1995), pp. 295–96.

99 HStAS, J170, Bü4, 'Über das Geschehen während der letzten Kriegstage', Onolzheim, 8 October 1948.

100 Ibid., Reubach, 15 October 1948.

101 Foitzik, *Jugend ohne Schwung?*, p. 36.

102 HStAS, J170, Bü4, Wohnstätten, n.d., p. 1.

103 Ibid., Onolzheim, 8 October 1948, p. 1.

104 Ibid., Bü3, Nufringen, 20 October 1948.

105 Ibid., Bü10, Tiefenbach, 15 September 1948, p. 2.

106 Ibid., E151/03, Bü936, 'Statistik Stand 25.12.1944'.

107 Sauer, *Württemberg*, p. 360; Sauer, *Wilhelm Murr*, p. 143. See also Julian Jackson, *France: The Dark Years, 1940–1944* (Oxford, 2001), 'Vichy-Sigmaringen: From One Spa to Another', pp. 567–69.

108 Schnabel, *Württemberg zwischen Weimar und Bonn*, p. 588.

109 HStAS, E151/03, Bü936, 'Übersicht über den Stand der Umquartierung. Stichtag: 25 Januar 1945', 16 February 1945. The number of those 'otherwise accommodated' was 2763.

110 Ibid., J170, Bü18, Tomerdingen.
111 HStAS, J170, Bü4, Lendsiedel.
112 See an eye-witness report in ibid., Bü1, Josef Schneele, 'Bericht über die letzten Tage des Krieges 1945 in der Gemeinde Dirgenheim', p. 1.
113 Ibid., Bü1, Bopfingen, p. 8. See also ibid., Bü1: Dalkingen, 9 November 1948, p. 1; Kerkingen, 15 January 1950, p. 1.
114 Ibid., Bü9, Schöntal, 24 October 1948.
115 Ibid., Bü1, Fachsenfeld, 'Kriegsgeschehen um die Zeit des Einmarsches der Amerikaner in Fachsenfeld', n.d. [October/November 1948], p. 3.

Notes to Chapter 10: The Last Days of the War

The main source material for this chapter is to be found in the Hauptstaatsarchiv Stuttgart (HStAS), J170 files, which contain responses to a questionnaire circulated to every commune in 1948 about 'the last days of the war'. Most use the heading 'Geschichtliche Darstellung der letzten Kriegstage', or something very similar. Where this is not the case, the heading is quoted. References contain the *Büschel* number, referring to the district, which is named on first mention, and the name of the *Gemeinde* (commune).

1 Richard Bessel, *Germany after the First World War* (Oxford, 1993), pp. 6–11, 45–46. See also Niall Ferguson, *The Pity of War* (London, 1998), pp. 294–302.
2 Heinz Boberach (ed.), *Meldungen aus dem Reich* (Munich, 1968), pp. 271, 319, 419; Norbert Frei, 'People's Community and War: Hitler's Popular Support', in Hans Mommsen (ed.), *The Third Reich between Vision and Reality: New Perspectives on German History, 1918–1945* (Oxford and New York, 2001), pp. 66–67, 72.
3 The formula of the 'unconditional surrender' of Germany, as the requirement for peace with the Allies, was adopted by Roosevelt and Churchill at the Casablanca conference on 24 January 1943. On 'retaliation' see Gerald Kirwin, 'Waiting for Retaliation: A Study in Nazi Propaganda Behaviour and German Civilian Morale', *Journal of Contemporary History*, 16 (1981), pp. 565–83; Klaus-Dietmar Henke, *Die amerikanische Besetzung Deutschlands* (Munich, 1995), pp. 816–20; 'V1 gegen England!', *Illustrierter Beobachter*, 10 August 1944; 'V1–Kurs London: eine deutsche Geheimwaffe lüftet ihr Geheimnis', *Berliner Illustrierter Zeitung*, 10 August 1944.
4 See above, Chapter 5. Cf. Michael Geyer, 'Restorative Elites, German Society and the Nazi Pursuit of War', in Richard Bessel (ed.), *Fascist Italy and Nazi Germany: Comparisons and Contrasts* (Cambridge, 1996), pp. 154–55. For criticism of the NSV's efforts to mitigate problems, see HStAS, J170, Bü1 (Aalen), 'Kriegsereignisse in der Gemeinde Zipplingen Kreis Aalen', 24 October 1948. Cf. Mommsen, 'The Dissolution of the Third Reich: Crisis Management and Collapse, 1943–1945', *Bulletin of the German Historical Institute* (Washington), 27 (2000), p. 15; Henke, *Die amerikanische Besetzung Deutschlands*, pp. 814, 820–21.
5 Earl R. Beck, *Under the Bombs: The German Home Front, 1942–1945* (Lexington, Kentucky, 1986), passim, and especially pp. 177–86; Joachim Szodrzynski, 'Die "Heimatfront" zwischen Stalingrad und Kriegsende', in Forschungsstelle für Zeitgeschichte in Hamburg

(ed.), *Hamburg im 'Dritten Reich'* (Göttingen, 2005), pp. 633–85.

6   HStAS, J170, Bü1, Neresheim, p. 1.

7   Ibid., Kerkingen, 15 January 1950, p. 1.

8   Ibid., Bü10 (Leonberg), Schöckingen, 13 September 1948.

9   Ibid., Hemmingen, 9 October 1948.

10   Ibid., Bü18 (Ulm), Suppingen, 8 November 1949, p. 1.

11   Ibid., Weiler, 18 August 1948.

12   Mommsen, 'The Dissolution of the Third Reich', pp. 9–10, 19–20; Gerd R. Überschar, 'Krieg auf dem deutschen Boden: der Vormarsch der Alliierten im Südwesten', in Rolf-Dieter Müller, Gerd R. Überschar and Wolfram Wette, *Kriegsalltag und Kriegsende in Südwestdeutschland, 1944/45* (Freiburg i.Br., 1985), p. 61.

13   HStAS, J170, Bü1, 'Bopfingen im Zweiten Weltkrieg', n.d. [October/November 1948], p. 8. On Oberg, see Jackson, *France: The Dark Years*, pp. 215–19; Gildea, *Marianne in Chains*, pp. 265–66, 271.

14   HStAS, J170, Bü4 (Crailsheim): Langenburg, 15 October 1948; Kirchberg, n.d. [October/November 1948].

15   Ibid., Bü9 (Künzelsau), Schleierhof, 15 March 1949.

16   Ibid., Marlach, 27 October 1948, p. 1.

17   Paul Sauer, *Württemberg in der Zeit des Nationalsozialismus* (Ulm, 1975), p. 489; Thomas Schnabel, *Württemberg zwischen Weimar und Bonn, 1928–1945/46* (Stuttgart, 1986), pp. 590–91; Henke, *Die amerikanische Besetzung Deutschlands*, pp. 778–86.

18   Ibid., Bü1, Bopfingen, p. 8.

19   Ibid., Hüttlingen, n.d. [October/November 1948], p. 1.

20   David K. Yelton, *Hitler's Volkssturm: The Nazi Militia and the Fall of Germany, 1944–1945* (Lawrence, Kansas, 2002). On the *Volkssturm* in Württemberg, see Sauer, *Württemberg in der Zeit des Nationalsozialismus*, pp. 475–77.

21   Yelton, *Hitler's Volkssturm*, pp. 85–86, discusses the adverse effect of *Volkssturm* activity on agricultural work.

22   Überschar, 'Krieg auf dem deutschen Boden', p. 64.

23   HStAS, J170, Bü10, Schöckingen, pp. 3–4.

24   Ibid., Bü3 (Böblingen), Musberg, 18 October 1948, p. 11. See also StAL, K110, Bü59, 'Betrifft: Stimmen zum Erlass des Führers über die Bildung des Deutschen Volkssturmes', 8 November 1944, pp. 109117–109122; Benigna Schönhagen, *Tübingen unterm Hakenkreuz: Eine Universitätsstadt in der Zeit des Nationalsozialismus* (Stuttgart, 1991), pp. 369–70.

25   HStAS, J170, Bü9, Künzelsau, 'Anlage zu Bgm. Amt Künzelsau Reg. Nr. 5640 vom 7.9.1949 (Geschichtliche Darstellung der letzten Kriegstage)', 15 September 1949, p. 1.

26   Ibid., Bü8 (Heilbronn), Grantschen, 8 November 1948, p. 1. For problems in raising *Volkssturm* units in Stuttgart, see Roland Müller, *Stuttgart zur Zeit des Nationalsozialismus* (Stuttgart, 1988), pp. 520–22.

27   HStAS, J170, Bü4, 'Die Kämpfe um Bächlingen im April 1945'.

28   Ibid., Bü1 (Aalen), 'Kriegsgeschehen um die Zeit des Einmarches der Amerikaner in Fachsenfeld 1945', n.d. [October/November 1948], p. 7.

29   Ibid., Aalen, 9 October, 1948, pp. 10, 12.

30 Ibid., Bü18, Steinberg, 31 December 1948.

31 Ibid., Türkheim, n.d. [received on 20 April 1949].

32 Ibid., Bü8, Grantschen, pp. 1–2.

33 Ibid.: Bü1, Dalkingen; Bü9, Künzelsau, p. 1.

34 Ibid., Bü4, Brettheim, n.d. [October/November 1948], p. 1.

35 Ibid., Hausen am Bach, n.d. [October/November 1948], p. 2.

36 Ibid., Bü10, Schöckingen, p. 2.

37 Ibid., Bü9, Oberkessach, 14 September 1948.

38 Ibid., Bü3, Bürgermeisteramt Tailfingen an das Württ. Statistische Landesamt, 12 October 1948.

39 Ibid., Bü1, Bopfingen, pp. 9, 12, 17.

40 Ibid., Bü1, Aufhausen, n.d. [October/November 1948], p. 1.

41 Ibid., Aalen, p. 12.

42 Ibid., Bopfingen, p. 18

43 Ibid., Oberdorf, p. 7.

44 Martin Broszat, Elke Fröhlich and Falk Wiesemann (eds), *Bayern in der NS-Zeit*, i, *Soziale Lage und politisches Verhalten der Bevölkerung im Spiegel vertraulicher Berichte* (Munich and Vienna, 1977), 'Aus Bericht der Gendarmerie-Station Feldkirchen, Kreis Bad Aibling/Rosenheim, 24.3.1945', p. 683. See also Johnpeter Horst Grill, *The Nazi Movement in Baden, 1920–1945* (Chapel Hill, North Carolina, 1983), p. 457.

45 HStAS, Bü4, Honhardt, 29 October 1948. See also ibid., Bü1, Adelmannsfelden, n.d. [October/November 1948].

46 Ibid., Bopfingen, p. 7. Cf. p. 4.

47 Ibid., Bü9, Künzelsau, pp. 2, 6.

48 Ibid., Bü10, Hemmingen, p. 2.

49 Henke, *Die amerikanische Besetzung Deutschlands*, p. 783.

50 Quoted in Mommsen, 'The Dissolution of the Third Reich', p. 18. On 'cumulative radicalisation', see Hans Mommsen, 'Cumulative Radicalisation and Progressive Self-Destruction as Structural Determinants of the Nazi Dictatorship', in Ian Kershaw and Moshe Lewin (eds), *Stalinism and Nazism: Dictatorships in Comparison* (Cambridge, 1997), pp. 75–87. See also Henke, *Die amerikanische Besetzung Deutschlands*, pp. 802, 823.

51 Mommsen, 'The Dissolution of the Third Reich', pp. 14–17.

52 Beck, *Under the Bombs*, pp. 187–88; Thomas Schnabel, '"Die Leute wollten nicht einer verlorenen Sache ihre Heimat opfern"', in Landeszentrale für politische Bildung und Haus der Geschichte (ed.), *Formen des Widerstandes im Südwesten: Scheitern und Nachwirken*, edited by the Landeszentrale für politische Bildung Baden-Württemberg und vom Haus der Geschichte Baden-Württemberg durch Thomas Schnabel unter Mitarbeit von Angelika Hauser-Hauswirth (Ulm, 1994), pp. 165–66. I am indebted to Thomas Schnabel for sending me a copy of this book. On 'scorched earth', see Henke, *Die amerikanische Besetzung Deutschlands*, pp. 421–35.

53 Müller, *Stuttgart zur Zeit des Nationalsozialismus*, p. 533.

54 Ibid., pp. 524–26.

55 Schönhagen, *Tübingen unterm Hakenkreuz*, p. 370.

56 HStAS, J170, Bü1, Oberdorf, pp. 7–8.

57 Ibid., Hofen, 'Auszüge aus dem *Kriegstagebuch* 1945 u.ff. von A– H–', p. 3.

58 Ibid., Bü8, Grantschen, p. 1.

59 Ibid., Bü4, Hausen am Bach, p. 4.

60 Ibid., Bü78, 'Einmarsch der franz. Truppen in Wendelsheim und Ereignisse' (Verhandelt mit dem Gemeinderat am 1. August 1946), 10 January 1961, p. 3. See also ibid., Bü8, Eschenau, 25 October 1948, p. 5.

61 Ibid.

62 Ibid: Bü9, Schleierhof; Bü78, Öschingen, 'Auszug aus der Ortschronik', 8 November 1960, p. 1; Schnabel, *Württemberg zwischen Weimar und Bonn*, p. 590.

63 Ibid., Bü3, 'Die Zeit von Januar bis Juli 1945 in Holzgerlingen', 26 August 1948, p. 2.

64 Ibid., Bü1, Fachsenfeld, pp. 1–2.

65 Ibid., Bopfingen, p. 4.

66 Ibid.: Bü10, Ditzingen, n.d. [October/November 1948], p. 3; Bü1, Fachsenfeld, p. 4. Cf. Henke, *Die amerikanische Besetzung Deutschlands*, p. 833.

67 Schnabel, 'Die Leute wollten nicht', p. 169. His view is that 'army units were rather more prepared to surrender than SS units', although there were exceptions, p. 170. Cf. Mommsen, 'The Dissolution of the Third Reich', pp. 19–20.

68 HStAS, J170, Bü8, Eschenau, pp. 2–3.

69 Beck, *Under the Bombs*, pp. 189–95; Broszat, Fröhlich and Wiesemann, *Bayern in der NS-Zeit*, i, pp. 682–83 (7 March 1945); 685–86 (7 April 1945); 686–88 (17 April 1945); Henke, *Die amerikanische Besetzung Deutschlands*, pp. 833–34.

70 Mommsen, 'The Dissolution of the Third Reich', pp. 16–18; Paul Sauer, *Wilhelm Murr: Hitlers Statthalter in Württemberg* (Tübingen, 1998), pp. 146–47, 149.

71 Sauer, *Württemberg in der Zeit des Nationalsozialismus*, p. 489; Schnabel, 'Die Leute wollten nicht', pp. 165–66. See also HStAS, J170: Bü1: Bopfingen, p. 6, Fachsenfeld, pp. 1, 4–5; Bü8, Grantschen, p. 1. On Murr, see Sauer, *Wilhelm Murr*, pp. 146–48.

72 Schnabel, 'Die Leute wollten nicht', pp. 167–69. The reports from the communes suggest that cases of rape were almost exclusively in areas invaded by French troops.

73 Cf. Thomas Schnabel: 'Einleitung', in Landeszentrale für politische Bildung und Haus der Geschichte, *Formen des Widerstandes*, pp. 11–15; 'Die Leute wollten nicht', in ibid., p. 166.

74 HStAS, J170, Bü4, Bächlingen, p. 1.

75 Broszat, Fröhlich and Wiesemann, *Bayern in der NS-Zeit*, i, p. 682 (24 February 1945).

76 Bundesarchiv (BA), R55/601, 'Tätigkeitsbericht (Stichtag: 2. Oktober 1944)', pp. 146–49; Rita S. Botwinick, *Winzig, Germany, 1933–1946: The History of a Town under the Third Reich* (Westport, Connecticut, 1992), pp. 90–102; Alison Owings, *Frauen: German Women Recall the Third Reich* (New Brunswick, New Jersey, 1994), pp. 80, 146, 278, 405, 434, 447–48, 465; Marlis G. Steinert, *Hitler's War and the Germans: Public Mood and Attitude during the Second World War*, ed. and trans. Thomas E.J. De Witt (Athens, Ohio, 1977), pp. 287, 294, 299; Beck, *Under the Bombs*, pp. 137, 159, 171; Bessel, *Nazism and War*, pp. 188–189.

77 StAL, K110, Bü58, 'Betrifft: Stimmung und Meinungsbildung', 27 March 1945, p. 1.

78 HStAS, J170, Bü78 (Tübingen), Paul Sting, 'Der grosse Szenenwechsel: Tübingen in Niemandsland', *Schwäbisches Tageblatt*, 19 April 1955.

79 Sauer, *Württemberg in der Zeit des Nationalsozialismus*, pp. 490–91; Sauer, *Wilhelm Murr*, pp. 152–54; Schnabel, 'Die Leute wollten nicht', pp. 166–67.

80 Müller, *Stuttgart zur Zeit des Nationalsozialismus*, pp. 529ff.

81 Berlin Document Center (BDC), personnel file on Karl Strölin, letter from Strölin to Martin Bormann, 10 November 1941. See also Peter Steinbach and Johannes Tuchel (eds), *Widerstand gegen den Nationalsozialismus* (Bonn, 1994), p. 547.

82 Kurt Leipner (ed.), *Chronik der Stadt Stuttgart, 1933–1945* (Stuttgart, 1982), pp. 1021–24; Sauer, *Württemberg in der Zeit des Nationalsozialismus*, pp. 491–94; Schnabel, 'Die Leute wollten nicht', pp. 167, 169; Henke, *Die amerikanische Besetzung Deutschlands*, p. 782.

83 HStAS, J170, Bü77 (Tettnang), 'Walter Bärlin, früherer Bürgermeister der Stadt Friedrichshafen, Die Übergabe der Stadt Friedrichshafen und ihre Vorgeschichte', 9 April 1946, pp. 1–5; Dr Gmelin, 'Wie es zur Übergabe der Stadt Friedrichshafen kam', n.d.

84 StAL, K110, Bü58, pp. 3–5.

85 Ibid., Bü10, Malmsheim, n.d. [October/November 1948], p. 3.

86 Ibid., Bü65 (Ravensburg), Wolpertswende, 18 November 1960.

87 HStAS, J170, Bü1, Zipplingen.

88 Ibid., Bü4, Oberspeltach. See also ibid., Bü78, Bürgermeisteramt Entringen, 10 January 1961, p. 1.

89 Ibid., Bü10, Heimsheim, August 1948. See also John E. Knodel, *Demographic Behaviour in the Past: A Study of Fourteen German Village Populations in the Eighteenth and Nineteenth Centuries* (Cambridge, 1988), p. 28; Albert Ilien and Utz Jeggle, *Leben auf dem Dorf: zur Sozialgeschichte des Dorfes und Sozialpsychologie seiner Bewohner* (Opladen, 1978), pp. 37–38, 41.

90 HStAS, J170, Bü1, Neresheim, p. 2.

91 Ibid., Bü65, 'Waldsee vor der unmittelbaren Besetzung durch den Feind!', 18 July 1945.

92 Ibid., Bü18, Unterkirchberg, 18 October 1948; Schnabel, 'Die Leute wollten nicht', p. 172.

93 HStAS, J170, Bü18, Steinberg, 31 December 1948.

94 Ibid., Bü1, Zipplingen.

95 Ibid., Bü4, Bächlingen.

96 Sauer, *Württemberg*, pp. 489–90, 493.

97 HStAS, Bü3, Nufringen, 20 October 1948. Cf. Perry Biddiscombe, 'The End of the Freebooter Tradition: The Forgotten Freikorps Movement of 1944/45', *Central European History*, 32 (1999), pp. 53–90.

98 HStAS, J170, Bü1, Oberdorf.

99 Ibid., Bü65, Waldsee.

100 Ibid., Bü3, Sindelfingen, n.d. [October 1948], pp. 1–5.

101 Schnabel, 'Die Leute wollten nicht', pp. 170–71.

102 HStAS, J170, Bü3, Rohrau, p. 6.

103 Ibid., Bü1, Adelmannsfelden.

104 Ibid., Bü65, 'Ausmaß der Zerstörungen im zweiten Weltkrieg in den einzelnen Gemeinden', Waldburg, 5 December 1960.

105 Ibid.: Bü1, Hüttlingen, p. 1; Bü3, Öschelbronn, 29 October 1948, p. 1.

106 Ibid, Bü4, Hausen am Bach, p. 4.

107   Sauer, *Württemberg in der Zeit des Nationalsozialismus*, p. 489. On evacuation, see Henke, *Die amerikanische Besetzung Deutschlands*, pp. 821–22.

108   HStAS, J170: Bü3, Leinfelden, 20 December 1948, p. 2; Bü10, Heimerdingen, 7 August 1948.

109   Ibid., Bü9, Amrichshausen, 10 September 1948.

110   Ibid., Bü4, Langenberg, pp. 2–3.

111   Ibid., Bü10, Korntal, 'Vereitelte Evakuierung Korntals', n.d. [autumn 1948].

112   Ibid., Bü8, Eschenau, pp. 1–2.

113   Ibid., Bü10, Friolzheim, 28 November 1948.

114   Ibid., Bü3, Rohrau, p. 5.

115   Ibid., Bü1, Fachsenfeld, pp. 1–4.

116   Ibid., Bü1, Hüttlingen, p. 1. See also Schnabel, 'Die Leute wollten nicht', p. 174.

117   See, e.g., HStAS, J170, Bü1: Aalen, pp. 10–12; Bopfingen, pp. 2–7; Kerkingen, 15 January 1950, p. 2; Oberdorf, p. 7; Bü4, Hausen am Bach, pp. 2–3.

118   Ibid., Bü4, Brettheim, n.d. [October/November 1948], p. 1. See also Manfred Messerschmidt, 'Verweigerung in der Endphase des Krieges', in Landeszentrale für politische Bildung und Haus der Geschichte, *Formen des Widerstandes*, p. 162.

119   HStAS, J170, Hausen am Bach, p. 3.

120   Ibid., Bü8, Sontheim. The victim is named as 'deputy local branch leader … Karl Taubenberger' in Susanne Schlösser, '"Was sich in den Weg stellt, mit Vernichtung schlagen": Richard Drauz, NSDAP-Kreisleiter von Heilbronn', in Michael Kissener and Joachim Scholtyseck (eds), *Die Führer der Provinz: NS-Biographien aus Baden und Württemberg* (Constance, 1997), p. 156. See also Schnabel, 'Die Leute wollten nicht', p. 171.

121   HStAS, J170, Bü9, Kocherstetten, 22 February 1950, p. 1.

122   Ibid., Bü18, Suppingen, p. 3.

123   Ibid., Bü4, Hausen am Bach, p. 1.

124   Ibid., 'Orts-Chronik von Wallhausen 1945'.

125   Ibid., Bü1, Bopfingen, pp. 6–7, 9–18.

126   Ibid., Dalkingen, 5 November 1948.

127   Ibid., Adelmannsfelden.

128   Ibid., Aalen, pp. 1, 12.

129   Ibid., Bopfingen, pp. 4, 6.

130   Ibid., Aalen, p. 11.

131   Ibid., Bü8, Eschenau, 25 October 1948, pp. 1, 3. See also Henke, *Die amerikanische Besetzung Deutschlands*, pp. 835–36.

132   HStAS, J170, Bü8, Auenstein, 1 November 1948, p. 1.

133   Ibid., Biberach, Bachenau, Brettach.

134   Schlösser, 'Was sich in den Weg stellt, mit Vernichtung schlagen', p. 156.

135   HStAS, J170, Bü8, Gronau, 7 December 1949, pp. 3–4.

136   Schlösser, 'Was sich in den Weg stellt, mit Vernichtung schlagen', pp. 156–58.

137   Henke, *Die amerikanische Besetzung Deutschlands*, pp. 847–50.

138   Ibid., pp. 824–27.

139   HStAS, J170, Bü1, Oberkochen, 5 November 1948, p. 3.

140   Ibid., Bü78, Wendelsheim, pp. 1–2.

141 Ibid., Bü3, Bürgermeisteramt Schönaich, 14 October 1948.
142 Ibid., Bü3, Musberg, 18 October 1948, p. 13.
143 Sauer, *Wilhelm Murr*, pp. 155–56.
144 IIStAS, J170, Bü4, Stimpfach.
145 Ibid., Bü8, Abstatt, 25 November 1948, pp. 1–2.
146 Ibid., Bü1, Affaltrach, 22 November 1948, p. 2.
147 Ibid., Bü10, Heimsheim, p. 1.
148 Ibid., Friolzheim, pp. 1–2.
149 Ibid., Bü9, Aschhausen.
150 Ibid., Amrichshausen.
151 Ibid., Bü10, Unterdeufstetten.
152 Ibid., Tiefenbach.
153 Ibid., Bü3, 'Die Zeit von Januar bis Juli 1945 in Holzgerlingen', pp. 1–3.
154 Ibid., Bü1, Ebnat, 30 November 1948, p. 1.
155 Ibid., Hüttlingen, p. 4.
156 Ibid., Zipplingen.
157 Ibid., Oberdorf, p. 7.
158 Ibid.: Bü1, Aufhausen, p. 2; Bü8, Gronau, p. 4.
159 BDC, personnel file on Friedrich Schmidt, letter from Schnitzler, personal staff of the Reichsführer-SS (Munich office), to Berg, personal staff of the Reichsführer-SS (Berlin office), 'Betrifft: Betreuung d. Familie des in engl. Gefangenschaft befindlichen SS-Brigdf. Schmidt, Gut Thansau', 9 November 1944.
160 Angela Borgstedt, 'Im Zweifelsfall auch mit harter Hand: Jonathan Schmid, Württembergischer Innen-, Justiz- und Wirtschaftsminister', in Kissener and Scholtyseck, *Die Führer der Provinz*, p. 619.
161 Arbogast, *Herrschaftsinstanzen der württembergischen NSDAP*, pp. 199–241.
162 HStAS, J170, Bü1, Aalen, p. 13.
163 Ibid., Bü78, Wendelsheim, pp. 3–4.
164 Ibid., Bü1, Neresheim, pp. 3–4.
165 Ibid., Bü18, Regglisweiler, 3 November 1948, p. 2.
166 Ibid., Bü9, Oberkessach.
167 Ibid., Bü1, Fachsenfeld, pp. 4, 6–7.
168 Ibid., Hofen, p. 7. See also ibid., Bü8, Eschenau, p. 1.
169 Ibid., Bü1, Bopfingen, p. 21.
170 Ibid., Bü3, Holzgerlingen, p. 12.
171 StAL, PL502/16, G4737, 'Meldung der Funktionäre von der NSDAP u. ihrer angeschlossenen Gliederungen', 14 December 1945.
172 HStAS, J170, Bü3, Musberg, pp. 10 and 13.
173 Ibid., Bürgermeisteramt Tailfingen, 12 October 1948.
174 Ibid., Bü10, Hemmingen, p. 3.
175 Ibid. Bü8, Grantschen.
176 Ibid., Bü1, Hofen, p. 13.
177 Ibid., Bü10, Heimerdingen.
178 Ibid., Bü9, Sindeldorf, 'Antwort', 30 December 1948.

179   Ibid., Westernhausen, 'Beantwortung der umseitigen Fragen bezgl. der letzten Tagen des Krieges', n.d. (received by the Künzelsau *Landrat* on 29 October 1948).

180   Ibid., Bü10, Friolzheim, p. 2.

181   Ibid., Bü4: Kirchberg, Stimpfach.

182   Ibid.: Bü3, Oberjettingen, 13 September 1948; Kuppingen, 4 October 1948, p. 1.

183   Ibid., Bü1, Kerkingen.

184   Ibid., Bü9, Sindeldorf.

185   Ibid., Hermuthausen, p. 2.

186   Ibid., Bü4, Stimpfach.

187   Ibid., Bü9, Aschhausen.

188   Ibid., Niedernhall, n.d. [October/November 1948], p. 5.

189   Ibid.: Bü3, Kuppingen, p. 2; Maichingen, n.d. [September/October 1948]; Mönchberg, 29 October 1948; Unterjettingen, 11 October 1948, p. 2; Waldenbuch, 14 September 1948; Bü10, Hemmingen, p. 2; Hirschlanden, 4 May 1949.

190   For more on liberated foreign workers, see above, Chapter 8.

191   HStAS, J170, Bü8, Eschenau, pp. 4–5.

192   Ibid., Hermuthausen.

193   Ibid., Bü4, Stimpfach.

194   Ibid., Bü9, Amrichshausen.

195   Ibid., Bü3, Unterjettingen, p. 2.

196   Ibid., Bü10, Friolzheim.

197   Ibid., Bü1, Adelmannsfelden.

198   Ibid., Bü4, Kirchberg.

199   Ibid., Matzenbach.

200   Ibid., Bü78, Mössingen, 'II. Weltkrieg, Zerstörungen und besondere Vorkommnisse', 21 November 1960, p. 2.

201   Ibid., Bü10, Ditzingen, p. 3.

202   Ibid.: Flacht, Hirschlanden.

203   Ibid., Bü9, Hermuthausen, p. 2.

204   Ibid.: Bü3, Holzgerlingen, p. 4; Kuppingen, p. 2; Mönchberg; Oberjettingen; Weil im Schönbuch, 21 March 1951, p. 2; Bü10, Merklingen a.W., 11 October 1948; Bü78, Öschingen, p. 1.

205   Ibid., Bü9, Vogelsberg, 27 September 1948. Cf. Owings, *Frauen*, pp. 30, 97, 146 n. 2, 230.

206   HStAS, J170, Bü65, Waldsee.

207   Ibid., Bü8, Gundelsheim, p. 2. See also Schnabel, *Württemberg zwischen Weimar und Bonn*, pp. 594–96.

208   HStAS, J170, Bü18, Setzingen, n.d. [October/November 1948].

209   Ibid., Bü1, Neresheim, p. 2. See also ibid., Bü78, Wendelsheim, p. 2.

210   Ibid., Blaufelden, n.d. [October/November 1948], p. 14.

211   Ibid., Bü1, Oberkochen, p. 3.

212   Ibid., Bü8, Gronau, p. 8.

213   Ibid., Bü4, Langenberg, p. 7.

214   Ibid.: Bü9, Oberginsbach, An das Landratsamt Künzelsau, 13 October 1948; Bü8, Eschenau, p. 5. Cf. Owings, *Frauen*, p. 30: 'The war ended quietly in the countryside', referring to the Schwäbisch Hall area.

215 HStAS, J170, Bü1, Aufhausen, pp. 2–3.
216 Ibid., Bü10, Heimsheim, pp. 1–2.
217 Ibid., Bü4, Oberspeltach.
218 Ibid.: Bü9, Belsenberg; Bü78, Öschingen, p. 1.
219 Ibid., Niedernhall, p. 5.
220 Ibid., Bü3, Holzgerlingen, p. 6.
221 Ibid., Bü18: Steinberg, p. 2; Suppingen, p. 4.
222 Ibid., Bü9, Amrichshausen.
223 Ibid., Niedernhall, p. 5.
224 Ibid., Bü8, Eschenau, p. 5.
225 Ibid., Bü9, Hermuthausen.
226 Schnabel, *Württemberg zwischen Weimar und Bonn*, pp. 602–604.

Notes to Chapter Eleven: Conclusion

1 Hauptstaatsarchiv Stuttgart (HStAS), J170, Bü3, Leinfelden, 'Geschichtliche Darstellung der letzten Kriegstage', 20 December 1948.

2 Günter Golde, *Catholics and Protestants: Agricultural Modernisation in Two German Villages* (New York, 1975), pp. 68, 150; George D. Spindler, *Burgbach: Urbanisation and Identity in a German Village* (New York, 1973), pp. 13–14, 18–20, 31–33.

3 Jill Stephenson, *The Nazi Organisation of Women* (London, 1981), pp. 169–72.

4 Thomas Schnabel, '"Die Leute wollten nicht einer verlorenen Sache ihre Heimat opfern"', in Landeszentrale für politische Bildung und Haus der Geschichte (ed.), *Formen des Widerstandes im Südwesten: Scheitern und Nachwirken* (Ulm, 1994), pp. 175–77.

5 HStAS, J170, Bü9, Bürgermeisteramt Hermuthausen, 19 December 1948, p. 2; Thomas Schnabel, *Württemberg zwischen Weimar und Bonn, 1928–1945/46* (Stuttgart, 1986), pp. 602, 604.

6 Forschungsstelle für Zeitgeschichte in Hamburg archive, 226.0, A10n 15ª Sm17: 'Die Landarbeiterfrage', *Wirtschafts-und Finanz-Zeitung*, 11 February 1949; 'Landarbeiter klagen an', *Der Bund* (Nordmark-Ausgabe), 30 March 1949; 'Freiwilliger Landdienst gegen Landarbeitermangel', report from Stuttgart, *Die Neue Zeitung*, 18 March 1952; 'Jugendliche Arbeitskräfte für die Landwirtschaft', report from Stuttgart, 17 December 1952; 'Agrarproduktion durch Kräftemangel und unzureichende Preise bedroht', report from Ravensburg, *VWD* Frankfurt a. Main, no. 117 (Landwirtschaft u. Ernährung), 25 May 1953.

7 Ibid., 936–4, Reichsnährstand-Auflösung, 1947–1960: 'Der Reichsnährstand wird abgewickelt', *Deutsche Zeitung* (Stuttgart), 8 April 1959; Der Bundesminister für Ernährung, Landwirtschaft und Forsten, 'Bekanntmachung über die Bestellung eines Landestreuhänders für die Abwicklung des Reichsnährstandsvermögens im Regierungsbezirk Nordwürttemberg. Vom 12. November 1959', *Bundes-Anzeiger* (Köln), 12 November 1959; 'Behördentod', *Die Welt* (Hamburg), 10 December 1960.

8 After two years of Nazi rule, only half of Württemberg's communes had an NSDAP presence. Schnabel, *Württemberg zwischen Weimar und Bonn*, pp. 201–2.

 9 Hartmut Berghoff and Cornelia Rauh-Kühne, *Fritz K.: ein deutsches Leben im zwanzigsten Jahrhundert* (Stuttgart and Munich, 2000), pp. 58, 158–60.

10 Staatsarchiv Ludwigsburg (StAL), PL504/18, Bü12, 'Lage- und Stimmungsbericht der Ortsgruppe Leonberg für das Jahr 1938 bis 1. März 1939'.

11 Paul Sauer, *Wilhelm Murr: Hitlers Statthalter in Württemberg* (Tübingen, 1998), p. 40.

12 Annette Roser, '"Beamter aus Berufung": Karl Wilhelm Waldmann, Württembergischer Staatssekretär', in Michael Kissener and Joachim Scholtyseck (eds), *Die Führer der Provinz: NS-Biographien aus Baden und Württemberg* (Konstanz, 1997), pp. 794–95.

13 Sauer, *Wilhelm Murr*, pp. 158–59; Roser, 'Beamter aus Berufung', pp. 798–99.

14 On Hitler as 'charismatic leader', see especially Ian Kershaw: *Hitler* (London, 1991), pp. 10–14; *Hitler, 1889–1936: Hubris* (London, 1998), pp. xxvi-xxix.

15 StAL, K110, Bü45, p. 16; Stephenson, *The Nazi Organisation of Women*, pp. 159–61.

16 HStAS, J170, Bü18, 'Chronikale Aufzeichnungen über die Gemeinde Tomerdingen, Kreis Ulm (aus der Pfarrchronik), n.d. [October/November 1948], p. 1.

17 Ralf Dahrendorf, *Gesellschaft und Demokratie in Deutschland* (Munich, 1965), pp. 432–441.

18 Paul Kopf, 'Buchau am Federsee in nationalsozialistischer Zeit: die Ereignisse der Jahre 1934 bis 1938', in Geschichtsverein der Diözese Rottenburg-Stuttgart (ed.), *Kirche im Nationalsozialismus* (Sigmaringen, 1984), p. 286.

19 Bundesarchiv (BA), R22/3387, Der Oberlandesgerichtspräsident an den Herrn Reichsminister der Justiz, 'Betreff: Bericht über die allgemeine Lage', 2 March 1940.

20 Ibid., Der Generalstaatsanwalt an den Herrn Reichsminister der Justiz, Nr 420b – 28, 'Betrifft: Lagebericht', 30 September 1940.

21 Jill Stephenson, 'The Home Front in "Total War": Women in Germany and Britain in the Second World War', in Roger Chickering, Stig Förster and Bernd Greiner (eds), *A World at Total War: Global Conflict and the Politics of Destruction, 1937–1945*, Publications of the German Historical Institute, Washington, DC (Cambridge, 2005), pp. 223–24. On Britain, see Ina Zweiniger-Bargielowska, *Austerity in Britain: Rationing, Controls, and Consumption, 1939–1955* (Oxford, 2000).

22 HStAS, E397, Bü37, 'Abschrift. Sondergericht für den Oberlandesgerichtsbezirk Stuttgart in Stuttgart, SL, Nr 523–526/42. I 22 SJs.1313–16/42.', 24 November 1942.

23 See selected essays in Sheila Fitzpatrick and Robert Gellately (eds), *Accusatory Practices: Denunciation in Modern European History, 1789–1989* (Chicago, Illinois, and London, 1997).

24 See especially Robert Gellately, *The Gestapo and German Society: Enforcing Racial Policy, 1933–1945* (Oxford, 1990); Eric Johnson, *The Nazi Terror: Gestapo, Jews and Ordinary Germans* (London, 2000). On Württemberg, see Christine Arbogast: 'Von Spitzeln, "Greifern" und Verrätern: Denunziantentum im Dritten Reich', in Landeszentrale für politische Bildung und Haus der Geschichte, *Formen des Widerstandes*, pp. 205–21; *Herrschaftsinstanzen der württembergischen NSDAP: Funktion, Sozialprofil und Lebenswege einer regionalen NS-Elite, 1920–1960* (Munich, 1998), pp. 101–11.

25 See, e.g., the unsigned denunciation attached to HStAS, E397, Bü37, Der Landrat, Heilbronn, an den Herrn Württ. Wirtschaftsminister, 'Betreff: Wiederverwendung von Lebensmittelkarten', 21 February 1942.

26 Arbogast, 'Von Spitzeln, "Greifern" und Verrätern', pp. 205, 215.

27　Kopf, 'Buchau am Federsee in nationalsozialistischer Zeit', pp. 274–78.

28　StAL, K110, Bü37, 'Betr.: Erfassung von Kirchenglocken', 10 April 1940.

29　Spindler, *Burgbach*, p. 110.

30　HStAS, J170, Bü10, Rutesheim, 'Abnahme der Glocken und kirchliche Betreuung der Kriegsteilnehmer', n.d. [1948].

31　Ibid., Bü3, Kayh, 2 September 1948.

32　Ibid., Bü18, Tomerdingen, p. 1.

33　Ibid., Bü10, Rutesheim.

34　Ibid., Bü18, Tomerdingen, pp. 1–2.

35　Cf. Johnson, *The Nazi Terror*, p. 485: 'The overwhelming majority of ordinary German citizens, however, never became targets of the terror…'

36　See James M. Glass, *'Life Unworthy of Life': Racial Phobia and Mass Murder in Hitler's Germany* (New York, 1997), pp. 3–5, 85, 118, 162, who criticises Ian Kershaw's carefully argued view of 'indifference' in *Popular Opinion and Political Dissent in the Third Reich: Bavaria, 1933–1945* (Oxford, 1983), pp. 273–77, 368–72. Glass accepts uncritically the flawed arguments of Daniel J. Goldhagen, *Hitler's Willing Executioners: Ordinary Germans and the Holocaust* (New York, 1996), about Germans' alleged 'eliminationist antisemitism', pp. 87–88, 444–50. Cf. Ian Kershaw, *The 'Hitler-Myth': Image and Reality in the Third Reich* (Oxford, 1987), pp. 229–30, 239–40, 241, 244–50.

37　Marlis G. Steinert, *Hitlers Krieg und die Deutschen* (Düsseldorf, 1970), p. 242.

38　See above, Chapter 5.

39　HStAS, J170, Bü1, Dirgenheim, n.d. [October/November 1948]. See also Bü1, 'Die letzten Kriegstage von Aalen', 9 October 1948, p. 4.

40　See above, Chapter 4. Cf. Goldhagen, *Hitler's Willing Executioners*, pp. 100–1.

41　Steinert, *Hitlers Krieg und die Deutschen*, pp. 400–5.

42　Martin Broszat's much-criticised use of *Resistenz* has some applicability here, but only up to a point. In particular, the imperviousness of some areas of society to Nazi penetration is important, especially given the regime's pretensions. *Resistenz* does not, however, adequately reflect the self-interest that informed this imperviousness. See Martin Broszat, 'Resistenz und Widerstand', in Martin Broszat, Elke Fröhlich, Falk Wiesemann and Anton Grossmann (eds), *Bayern in der NS-Zeit*, iv, *Herrschaft und Gesellschaft im Konflikt* (Munich and Vienna, 1981), pp. 691–709.

43　See the discussion in Ian Kershaw, *The Nazi Dictatorship: Problems and Perspectives of Interpretation* (London, 2000), 'Resistance Without the People?', pp. 194–207.

44　Albert Ilien and Utz Jeggle, *Leben auf dem Dorf: zur Sozialgeschichte des Dorfes und Sozialpsychologie seiner Bewohner* (Opladen, 1978), p. 38.

Bibliography

ARCHIVAL SOURCES

HAUPTSTAATSARCHIV STUTTGART

E151/01: Bü 450, 615–45, 652, 673, 1167, 3134, 3168, 3596, 3621, 3872, 3960
E151/01cII: Bü 394a, 434
E151/03: Bü 936, 968
E151bII: Bü 474
E151bIII: Bü 8705
E151kVI: Bü 221
E151kVII: Bü 2412
E382: Bü 350, 358
E397: Bü 5, 10, 14, 37, 83
J170: Bü 1 (Aalen), 3 (Böblingen), 4 (Crailsheim), 8 (Heilbronn), 9
  (Künzelsau), 10 (Leonberg), 18 (Ulm), 65 (Ravensburg), 77 (Tettnang), 78
  (Tübingen)

STAATSARCHIV LUDWIGSBURG

K100/10
K110: Bü 36, 37, 38, 40, 44, 45, 46, 47, 48, 55, 58, 59
K310: Bü 124
K631/I: Bü 1625, 1642, 1645
K631/II: Bü 29, 39, 41, 70, 75, 83, 84, 87, 99
PL501: Bü 14
PL501/15
PL501/45
PL501/46
PL502/16: G, G1375, G1393, G1411, G1416, G4730, G4732, G4737
PL502/34: Bü 40, 51
PL503/34

PL504/5: Bü 6
PL504/18: Bü 4, 6, 10, 12, 18, 19, 26
PL504/22: Bü 1, 6, 7, 11, 13, 16, 17, 23, 33, 40
PL504/34: Bü 13, 14, 17, 20, 28
PL504/35
PL504/221: Bü 31
PL509: Bü 61, 64, 66, 67, 68, 87, 89, 90, 91, 92

BUNDESARCHIV

R22: 3364; 3381; 3387; 4209; 5005
R55: 569; 601; 1211

BERLIN DOCUMENT CENTER

Personnel files: Richard Drauz, Adolf Mauer, Wilhelm Murr, Friedrich
Schmidt, Eugen Stähle, Karl Strölin

UNITED STATES HOLOCAUST MEMORIAL MUSEUM ARCHIVE

NS6/414, NS6/337
Results of the German Minority Census of 17 May 1939

INSTITUT FÜR ZEITGESCHICHTE ARCHIVE

MA138

NSDAP HAUPTARCHIV

Reel 13, folder 253

BOOKS, ESSAYS AND ARTICLES

Ackermann, Josef, *Himmler als Ideologe* (Göttingen, 1970)
Ackermann, Josef, 'Heinrich Himmler – "Reichsführer-SS"', in Smelser, Syring
and Zitelmann, *Die Braune Elite*
Allen, William Sheridan, *The Nazi Seizure of Power: The Experience of a Single
German Town, 1922–45* (London, 1989)
Aly, Götz, Chroust, Peter, and Pross, Christian, *Cleansing the Fatherland: Nazi
Medicine and Racial Hygiene* (Baltimore, Maryland, 1994)

Aly, Götz, 'Pure and Tainted Progress', in Aly, Chroust and Pross, *Cleansing the Fatherland*

Aly, Götz, 'Medicine Against the Useless', in Aly, Chroust and Pross, *Cleansing the Fatherland*

Aly, Götz, *Rasse und Klasse: Nachforschungen zum deutschen Wesen* (Frankfurt am Main, 2003)

Aly, Götz, *Hitlers Volksstaat: Raub, Rassenkrieg und Nationaler Sozialismus* (Frankfurt am Main, 2005)

Arbeitswissenschaftliches Institut der Deutschen Arbeitsfront (ed.), *Die Sozialstruktur des Gaues Württemberg-Hohenzollern: eine sozialgeographische Analyse* (Berlin, 1940)

Arbogast, Christine, and Gall, Bettina, 'Aufgaben und Funktionen des Gauinspekteurs, der Kreisleitung und der Kreisgerichtsbarkeit der NSDAP in Württemberg', in Rauh-Kühne and Ruck, *Regionale Eliten zwischen Diktatur und Demokratie*

Arbogast, Christine, 'Von Spitzeln, "Greifern" und Verrätern: Denunziantentum im Dritten Reich', in Landeszentrale für politische Bildung und Haus der Geschichte, *Formen des Widerstandes im Südwesten*

Arbogast, Christine, *Herrschaftsinstanzen der württembergischen NSDAP: Funktion, Sozialprofil und Lebenswege einer regionalen NS-Elite, 1920–1960* (Munich, 1998)

Ayass, Wolfgang, *'Asoziale' im Nationalsozialismus* (Stuttgart, 1995)

Bade, Klaus J., *Auswanderer – Wanderarbeiter – Gastarbeiter: Bevölkerung, Arbeitsmarkt und Wanderung in Deutschland seit der Mitte des 19. Jahrhunderts*, 2 vols, (Ostfildern, 1984)

Baird, Jay W., 'Julius Streicher: Der Berufsantisemit', in Smelser, Syring and Zitelmann, *Die Braune Elite*

Bajohr, Frank, and Szodrzynski, Joachim, (eds), *Hamburg in der NS-Zeit: Ergebnisse neuerer Forschung* (Hamburg, 1995)

Bajohr, Frank, 'Hamburgs "Führer": zur Person und Tätigkeit des Hamburger NSDAP-Gauleiters Karl Kaufmann (1900–1969)', in Bajohr and Szodrzynski, *Hamburg in der NS-Zeit*

Bajohr, Frank, *Parvenüs und Profiteure: Korruption in der NS-Zeit* (Frankfurt am Main, 2001)

Bajohr, Frank, 'Schlussbetrachtung: Meister der Zerstörung', in Forschungsstelle für Zeitgeschichte in Hamburg, *Hamburg im 'Dritten Reich'*

Balfour, Michael, and Frisby, Julian, *Helmuth von Moltke: A Leader against Hitler* (London, 1972)

Balfour, Michael, *Propaganda in War, 1939–1945: Organisations, Policies and Publics in Britain and Germany* (London, 1979)

Barber, John, and Harrison, Mark, *The Soviet Home Front, 1941–1945* (London, 1991)

Bardua, Heinz, *Stuttgart im Luftkrieg, 1939–1945* (Stuttgart, 1967)

Barfuss, Karl Marten, *'Gastarbeiter' in Nordwestdeutschland, 1884–1918* (Bremen, 1986)

Barkai, Avraham, *Nazi Economics: Ideology, Theory, and Policy*, trans. by Ruth Hadass-Vaschitz (Oxford and New York, 1990)

Bärsch, Claus-Ekkehard, *Die politische Religion des Nationalsozialismus* (Munich, 2002)

Bartov, Omer, *The Eastern Front, 1941–45: German Troops and the Barbarisation of Warfare* (London, 1985)

Bartov, Omer, *Hitler's Army: Soldiers, Nazis and War in the Third Reich* (Oxford, 1992)

Bartov, Omer, (ed.), *The Holocaust: Origins, Implementation, Aftermath: Rewriting Histories* (London and New York, 2000)

Bauer, Theresia, *Nationalsozialistische Agrarpolitik und bäuerliches Verhalten im Zweiten Weltkrieg: eine Regionalstudie zur ländlichen Gesellschaft in Bayern* (Frankfurt am Main, 1996)

Bauerkämper, Arnd, 'Landwirtschaft und ländliche Gesellschaft in der Bundesrepublik in den 50er Jahren', in Axel Schildt and Arnold Sywottek (eds), *Modernisierung im Wiederaufbau: die westdeutsche Gesellschaft der 50er Jahre* (Bonn, 1998, first published in 1993)

Bauman, Zygmunt, *Modernity and the Holocaust* (New York, 1991)

Baur, Stefan, 'Rechtsprechung im nationalsozialistischen Geist: Hermann Albert Cuhorst, Senatspräsident und Vorsitzender des Sondergerichts Stuttgart', in Kissener and Scholtyseck, *Die Führer der Provinz*

BBC 2, *Timewatch* film, 'The Hunger Winter' (undated)

Beck, Earl R., *Under the Bombs: The German Home Front, 1942–45* (Lexington, Kentucky, 1986)

Benz, Wolfgang, Graml, Hermann, and Weiss, Hermann, (eds), *Enzyklopädie des Nationalsozialismus* (Munich, 1997)

Benz, Wolfgang, *The Holocaust: A Short History* (London, 2000)

Berghahn, Volker, 'Demographic growth, industrialisation and social change', in Breuilly, *Nineteenth Century Germany*

Bergen, Doris L., *Twisted Cross: The German Christian Movement in the Third Reich* (Chapel Hill, North Carolina, 1996)

Berghoff, Hartmut, *Zwischen Kleinstadt und Weltmarkt: Hohner und die Harmonika, 1857–1961* (Paderborn, 1997)

Berghoff, Hartmut, and Rauh-Kühne, Cornelia, *Fritz K.: ein deutsches Leben im zwanzigsten Jahrhundert* (Stuttgart and Munich, 2000)

Berliner Illustrierter Zeitung, 10 August 1944, 'V1-Kurs London: eine deutsche Geheimwaffe lüftet ihr Geheimnis'

Bessel, Richard, *Germany after the First World War* (Oxford, 1993)

Bessel, Richard, (ed.), *Fascist Italy and Nazi Germany: Comparisons and Contrasts* (Cambridge, 1996)

Bessel, Richard, *Nazism and War* (New York, 2004)

Besson, Waldemar, *Württemberg und die deutsche Staatskrise: eine Studie zur Auflösung der Weimarer Republik* (Stuttgart, 1959)

Biddiscombe, Perry, 'The End of the Freebooter Tradition: The Forgotten Freikorps Movement of 1944/45', *Central European History*, 32 (1999)

Bing-von Häfen, Inga, 'Zwangsarbeit in Diensten der Evangelischen Landeskirche und ihrer Diakonie in Württemberg', in Jochen-Christoph Kaiser (ed.), *Zwangsarbeit in Diakonie und Kirche, 1939–45* (Stuttgart, 2005)

Blackbourn, David, *Class, Religion and Local Politics in Wilhelmine Germany: The Centre Party in Württemberg before 1914* (New Haven, Connecticut, and London, 1980)

Blackbourn, David, *The Fontana History of Germany, 1780–1918: The Long Nineteenth Century* (London, 1997)

Blum, Gabriele, '"Wirtschaft am Pranger": Die Berichterstattung des württembergischen "Kampfblatts" "Flammenzeichen" über unangepasstes Verhalten von Gewerbetreibenden', in Rauh-Kühne and Ruck, *Regionale Eliten zwischen Diktatur und Demokratie*

Boberach, Heinz, (ed.), *Meldungen aus dem Reich* (Munich, 1968)

Boberach, Heinz, (ed.), *Berichte des SD und der Gestapo über Kirchen und Kirchenvolk in Deutschland, 1934–1944* (Mainz, 1971)

Boberach, Heinz, (ed.), *Meldungen aus dem Reich* (Herrsching, 1984), 17 vols.

Bock, Gisela, *Zwangssterilisation im Nationalsozialismus: Studien zur Rassenpolitik und Frauenpolitik* (Opladen, 1986)

Boelcke, Willi A., 'Wirtschaft und Sozialsituation', in Borst, *Das Dritte Reich in Baden und Württemberg*

Borgstedt, Angela, 'Im Zweifelsfall auch mit harter Hand: Jonathan Schmid, Württembergischer Innen-, Justiz- und Wirtschaftsminister', in Kissener and Scholtyseck, *Die Führer der Provinz*

Bories-Sawala, Helga, *Franzosen im 'Reichseinsatz': Deportation, Zwangsarbeit, Alltag. Erfahrungen und Erinnerungen von Kriegsgefangenen und Zivilarbeitern* (Frankfurt am Main, 1996)

Borst, Otto, (ed.), *Das Dritte Reich in Baden und Württemberg* (Stuttgart, 1988)

Botwinick, Rita S., *Winzig, Germany, 1933–1946: The History of a Town under the Third Reich* (Westport, Connecticut, 1992)

Bracher, Karl Dietrich, *The German Dictatorship: The Origins, Structure, and Effects of National Socialism*, trans. Jean Steinberg (London, 1971)

Breuilly, John, (ed.), *Nineteenth-Century Germany: Politics, Culture and Society, 1780–1918* (London, 2001)

Bridenthal, Renate, 'Beyond *Kinder, Küche, Kirche*: Weimar Women at Work', *Central European History*, 6 (1973)

Broberg, Gunnar, and Roll-Hansen, Nils, (eds), *Eugenics and the Welfare State: Sterilisation Policy in Denmark, Sweden, Norway and Finland* (East Lancing, Michigan, 1996)

Broberg, Gunnar, and Tydén, Mattias, 'Eugenics in Sweden: Efficient Care', in Broberg and Roll-Hansen, *Eugenics and the Welfare State*

Broszat, Martin, Fröhlich, Elke, and Wiesemann, Falk, (eds), *Bayern in der NS-Zeit*, i: *Soziale Lage und politisches Verhalten der Bevölkerung im Spiegel vertraulicher Berichte* (Munich and Vienna, 1977)

Broszat, Martin, 'Resistenz und Widerstand', in Martin Broszat, Elke Fröhlich, Falk Wiesemann and Anton Grossmann (eds), *Bayern in der NS-Zeit*, iv: *Herrschaft und Gesellschaft im Konflikt* (Munich and Vienna, 1981)

Broszat, Martin, *The Hitler State: The Foundations and Development of the Internal Structure of the Third Reich*, trans. John W. Hiden (London, 1981)

Buckley, Mary, '*Krest'yanskaya gazeta* and Rural Stakhanovism', *Europe-Asia Studies*, 46 (1994)

Buckley, Mary, 'Relations between Individual and System under Stalinism', paper delivered at the International Congress for Russian/Soviet History, Sigriswil, Switzerland, 1–4 October 2003

Burchardt, Lothar, 'The Impact of the War Economy on the Civilian Population of Germany during the First and Second World Wars', in Deist, *The German Military in the Age of Total War*

Burkhardt, Bernd, *Eine Stadt wird braun: die nationalsozialistische Machtergreifung in der Provinz. Eine Fallstudie* (Hamburg, 1980)

Burleigh, Michael, and Wippermann, Wolfgang, *The Racial State: Germany, 1933–1945* (Cambridge, 1991)

Burleigh, Michael, *Death and Deliverance: 'Euthanasia' in Germany, 1900–1945* (Cambridge, 1994)

Burleigh, Michael, 'Saving Money, Spending Lives: Psychiatry, Society and the "Euthanasia" Programme', in Michael Burleigh (ed.), *Confronting the Nazi Past: New Debates on Modern German History* (London, 1996)

Burleigh, Michael, 'Psychiatry, German Society and the Nazi "Euthanasia" Programme', in Bartov, *The Holocaust: Origins, Implementation, Aftermath*

Büttner, Ursula, '*Gomorrha': Hamburg im Bombenkrieg. Die Wirkung der Luftangriffe auf Bevölkerung und Wirtschaft* (Hamburg, 1993)

Büttner, Ursula, '"Volksgemeinschaft" oder Heimatbindung: Zentralismus und regionale Eigenständigkeit beim Aufstieg der NSDAP, 1925–1933', in Möller, Wirsching and Ziegler, *Nationalsozialismus in der Region*

Büttner, Ursula, 'Von der Kirche verlassen: die deutschen Protestanten und die Verfolgung der Juden und Christen jüdischer Herkunft im "Dritten Reich"', in Ursula Büttner and Martin Greschat (eds), *Die verlassenen Kinder der Kirche: der Umgang mit Christen jüdischer Herkunft im 'Dritten Reich'* (Göttingen, 1998)

Büttner, Ursula, '"The Jewish Problem Becomes a Christian Problem": German Protestants and the Persecution of the Jews in the Third Reich', in David Bankier (ed.), *Probing the Depths of German Antisemitism: German Society and the Persecution of the Jews* (Jerusalem, 2000)

Büttner, Ursula, '"Gomorrha" und die Folgen: der Bombenkrieg', in Forschungsstelle für Zeitgeschichte in Hamburg, *Hamburg im 'Dritten Reich'*

Calder, Angus, *The People's War* (London, 1969)

Caplan, Jane, (ed.), *Nazism, Fascism and the Working Class: Essays by Tim Mason* (Cambridge, 1995)

Charman, Terry, *The German Home Front, 1939–45* (London, 1989)

Chickering, Roger, Förster, Stig, and Greiner, Bernd, (eds), *A World at Total War: Global Conflict and the Politics of Destruction, 1937–1945* (Cambridge, 2005)

Childers, Thomas, *The Nazi Voter: The Social Foundations of Fascism in Germany, 1919–1933* (Chapel Hill, North Carolina, 1983)

Childers, Thomas, and Caplan, Jane, 'Introduction', in Thomas Childers and Jane Caplan (eds), *Reevaluating the Third Reich* (New York, 1993)

Clark, Alan, *Barbarossa: The Russian-German Conflict* (London, 1966)

Confino, Alon, *The Nation as a Local Metaphor: Württemberg, Imperial Germany, and National Memory, 1871–1918* (Chapel Hill, North Carolina, 1997)

Conway, John S., *The Nazi Persecution of the Churches* (London, 1968)

Conway, John S., 'Coming to Terms with the Past: Interpreting the German Church Struggles, 1933–1990', *German History*, 16 (1998)

Corbin, Alain, *Village Bells: Sound and Meaning in the Nineteenth-century French Countryside* (London, 1998)

Corni, Gustavo, 'Richard Walther Darré – The "Blut-und-Boden" Ideologe', in Smelser and Zitelmann, *Die Braune Elite*

Corni, Gustavo, and Gies, Horst, *Brot, Butter, Kanonen: die Ernährungswirtschaft in Deutschland unter der Diktatur Hitlers* (Berlin, 1997)

Cornwell, John, *Hitler's Pope: The Secret History of Pius XII* (London, 2000)

Dahrendorf, Ralf, *Society and Democracy in Germany* (London, 1968)

Daniel, Ute, *Arbeiterfrauen in der Kriegsgesellschaft* (Göttingen, 1989)

Davis, Belinda J., *Home Fires Burning: Food, Politics and Everyday Life in World War I Berlin* (Chapel Hill, North Carolina, 2000)

Deist, Wilhelm, (ed.), *The German Military in the Age of Total War* (Leamington Spa, 1985)

Delaney, John J., 'Racial Values vs. Religious Values: Clerical Opposition to Nazi Anti-Polish Racial Policy', *Church History*, 70 (2001)

Delaney, John J., 'Sowing *Volksgemeinschaft* in Bavaria's Stony Village Soil: Catholic Peasant Rejection of Anti-Polish Racial Policy, 1939–1945', in Dietrich, *Christian Responses to the Holocaust*

Deutschland-Berichte der Sozialdemokratischen Partei Deutschlands (Paris, 1939)

Diamond, Hanna, *Women and the Second World War in France, 1939–1948: Choices and Constraints* (London, 1999)

Dicker, Herman, *Creativity, Holocaust, Reconstruction: Jewish life in Württemberg, Past and Present* (New York, c1984)

Dierker, Wolfgang, *Himmlers Glaubenskrieger: Der Sicherheitsdienst der SS und seine Religonspolitik, 1933–1941* (Paderborn, 2002)

Dietrich, Donald J., *Christian Responses to the Holocaust: Moral and Ethical Issues* (Syracuse, New York, 2003)

Düwell, Kurt, 'Gauleiter und Kreisleiter als regionale Gewalten des NS-Staates', in Möller, Wirsching and Ziegler, *Nationalsozialismus in der Region*

Eade, Charles, (compiler), *The War Speeches of the Rt Hon. Winston S. Churchill, OM, CH, PC, MP* (London, 1951)

Ebbinghaus, Angelika (ed.), *Opfer und Täterinnen: Frauenbiographien des Nationalsozialismus* (Frankfurt am Main, 1996)

Enssle, Manfred J., 'The Harsh Discipline of Food Scarcity in Postwar Stuttgart, 1945–1948', *German Studies Review*, 10 (1987)

Enssle, Manfred J., 'Five Theses on German Everyday Life after World War II', *Central European History*, 26 (1993)

Eschenburg, Theodor, 'The Formation of the State of Baden-Württemberg', in Landeszentrale für politische Bildung Baden-Württemberg, *The German Southwest*

Evans, Richard J., and Lee, W.R., (eds), *The German Peasantry: Conflict and Community in Rural Society from the Eighteenth to the Twentieth Centuries* (London and Sydney, 1986)

Evans, Richard J., *The Coming of the Third Reich* (London, 2003)

Falter, Jürgen, '"Anfälligkeit" der Angestellten – "Immunität" der Arbeiter? Mythen über die Wähler der NSDAP', in U. Backes, E. Jesse and R. Zitelmann (eds), *Die Schatten der Vergangenheit: Impulse zur Historisierung des Nationalsozialismus* (Frankfurt and Berlin, 1990)

Farquharson, J.E., *The Plough and the Swastika: The NSDAP and Agriculture in Germany, 1928–45* (London, 1976)

Fehrenbach, Heide, *Cinema in Democratising Germany: Reconstructing National Identity after Hitler* (Chapel Hill, North Carolina, 1995)

Ferguson, Niall, *The Pity of War* (London, 1998)

Fitzpatrick, Sheila, and Gellately, Robert, (eds), *Accusatory Practices: Denunciation in Modern European History, 1789–1989* (Chicago, Illinois, and London, 1997)

Fitzpatrick, Sheila, *Everyday Stalinism: Ordinary Life in Extraordinary Times. Soviet Russia in the 1930s* (New York and Oxford, 1999)

Foitzik, Doris, *Jugend ohne Schwung? Jugendkultur und Jugendpolitik in Hamburg, 1945–1949*, (Hamburg, 2002)

Forschungsstelle für Zeitgeschichte in Hamburg (ed.), *Hamburg im 'Dritten Reich'* (Göttingen, 2005)

Franke, Hans, *Geschichte und Schicksal der Juden in Heilbronn: vom Mittelalter bis zur Zeit der nationalsozialistischen Verfolgungen, 1050–1945* (Heilbronn, 1963)

Franklin, S.H., *The European Peasantry: The Final Phase* (London, 1969)

Frei, Norbert, *National Socialist Rule in Germany: The Führer State, 1933–1945* (Oxford, 1993)

Frei, Norbert, 'People's Community and War: Hitler's Popular Support', in Hans Mommsen (ed.), *The Third Reich between Vision and Reality: New Perspectives on German History, 1918–1945* (Oxford and New York, 2001)

Friedlander, Henry, 'The Exclusion and Murder of the Disabled', in Gellately and Stoltzfus, *Social Outsiders in Nazi Germany*

Friedrich, Jörg, *Der Brand: Deutschland im Bombenkrieg, 1940–1945* (Munich, 2002)

Fulbrook, Mary, *Piety and Politics: Religion and the Rise of Absolutism in England, Württemberg and Prussia* (Cambridge, 1983)

Fulbrook, Mary, 'The Limits of Totalitarianism: God, State and Society in the GDR', *Transactions of the Royal Historical Society*, 7 (1997)

Fuykshot, Cornelia, *Hunger in Holland: Life During the Nazi Occupation* (Amherst, Massachusetts, 1995)

Gallagher, Nancy L., *Breeding Better Vermonters: The Eugenics Project in the Green Mountain State* (Hanover, New Hampshire, 1999)

Garbe, Detlef, and Knöller, Bruno, 'Die Bibel, das Gewissen und der Widerstand: Die Familie Knöller im "Dritten Reich"', in Roser, *Widerstand als Bekenntnis*

Gellately, Robert, *The Gestapo and German Society: Enforcing Racial Policy, 1933–1945* (Oxford, 1990)

Gellately, Robert, *Backing Hitler: Consent and Coercion in Nazi Germany* (Oxford, 2001)

Gellately, Robert, and Stoltzfus, Nathan, (eds), *Social Outsiders in Nazi Germany* (Princeton, New Jersey, and Oxford, 2001)

Geschichtsverein der Diözese Rottenburg-Stuttgart (ed.), *Kirche im Nationalsozialismus* (Sigmaringen, 1984)

Geyer, Michael, 'Restorative Elites, German Society and the Nazi Pursuit of War', in Bessel, *Fascist Italy and Nazi Germany*

Gildea, Robert, *Marianne in Chains: In Search of the German Occupation of France, 1940–1945* (London, 2002)

Glass, James M., *'Life Unworthy of Life': Racial Phobia and Mass Murder in Hitler's Germany* (New York, 1997)

Glenny, Misha, *The Balkans, 1804–1999: Nationalism, War and the Great Powers* (London, 2000)

Golde, Günter, *Catholics and Protestants: Agricultural Modernisation in Two German Villages* (New York, 1975)

Goldhagen, Daniel J., *Hitler's Willing Executioners: Ordinary Germans and the Holocaust* (New York, 1996)

Gregor, Neil, *Daimler-Benz in the Third Reich* (New Haven, Connecticut, and London, 1998)

Gregor, Neil, 'A *Schicksalgemeinschaft*? Allied Bombing, Civilian Morale, and Social Dissolution in Nuremberg, 1942–1945', *Historical Journal*, 43 (2000)

Gregor, Neil, '"Is He Still Alive, or Long Since Dead?": Loss, Absence and Remembrance in Nuremberg, 1945–56', *German History*, 21 (2003)

Grill, Johnpeter Horst, *The Nazi Movement in Baden, 1920–1945* (Chapel Hill, North Carolina, 1983)

Grossmann, Anton, 'Fremd- und Zwangsarbeiter in Bayern, 1939–1945', in Bade, *Auswanderer*

Hachmann, Barbara, 'Der "Degen": Dietrich von Jagow, SA-Obergruppenführer', in Kissener and Scholtyseck, *Die Führer der Provinz*

Hancock, Eleanor, *National Socialist Leadership and Total War, 1941–45* (New York, 1991)

Hansen, Bent Sigurd, 'Something Rotten in the State of Denmark: Eugenics and the Ascent of the Welfare State', in Broberg and Roll-Hansen, *Eugenics and the Welfare State*

Hanson, Joanna, 'Poland', in Noakes, *The Civilian in War*

Harris, Jose, 'War and Social History: Britain and the Home Front during the Second World War', *Contemporary European History*, 1 (1992)

Harvey, Elizabeth, *Women and the Nazi East: Agents and Witnesses of Germanisation* (New Haven, Connecticut, and London, 2003)

Hastings, Max, *Bomber Command* (London, 1981)

Heberle, Rudolf, *Landbevölkerung und Nationalsozialismus: eine soziologische Untersuchung der politischen Willensbildung in Schleswig-Holstein, 1918–1932* (Stuttgart, 1963)

Heilbronner, Oded, *Catholicism, Political Culture, and the Countryside: A Social History of the Nazi Party in South Germany* (Ann Arbor, Michigan, 1998)

Heineman, Elizabeth D., *What Difference Does a Husband Make? Women and Marital Status in Nazi and Postwar Germany* (Berkeley and Los Angeles, California, 1999)

Heinemann, John L., *Hitler's First Foreign Minister* (Berkeley and Los Angeles, California, 1979)

Helmreich, Ernst Christian, *The German Churches under Hitler: Background, Struggle, and Epilogue* (Detroit, Michigan, 1979)

Henke, Klaus-Dietmar, *Die amerikanische Besetzung Deutschlands* (Munich, 1995)

Herbert, Ulrich, *Fremdarbeiter: Politik und Praxis des "Ausländer-Einsatzes" in der Kriegswirtschaft des Dritten Reiches* (Berlin and Bonn, 1986)

Herbert, Ulrich, *Geschichte der Ausländerbeschäftigung in Deutschland, 1880 bis 1980: Saisonarbeiter, Zwangsarbeiter, Gastarbeiter* (Berlin and Bonn, 1986)

Herbert, Ulrich, *Hitler's Foreign Workers: Enforced Foreign Labour in Germany under the Third Reich* (Cambridge and New York, 1997)

Hering, Rainer, '"Operation Gomorrha": Hamburg Remembers the Second World War', *German History*, 13 (1995)

Herlemann, Beatrix, *'Der Bauer klebt am Hergebrachten': Bäuerliche Verhaltensweisen unterm Nationalsozialismus auf dem Gebiet des heutigen Landes Niedersachsen* (Hanover, 1993)

Hermelink, Heinrich, (ed.), *Kirche im Kampf: Dokumente des Widerstands und des Aufbaus in der evangelischen Kirche Deutschlands von 1933 bis 1945* (Tübingen and Stuttgart, 1950)

Heyen, Franz Josef (ed.), *Nationalsozialismus im Alltag: Quellen zur Geschichte des Nationalsozialismus vornehmlich im Raum Mainz – Koblenz – Trier* (Boppard, 1967)

Hiden, John, *Republican and Fascist Germany: Themes and Variations in the History of Weimar and the Third Reich* (London, 1996)

Hiden, John, and Farquharson, John, *Explaining Hitler's Germany: Historians and the Third Reich* (2nd edn, London, 1989)

Hietala, Marjatta, 'From Race Hygiene to Sterilisation: The Eugenics Movement in Finland', in Broberg and Roll-Hansen, *Eugenics and the Welfare State*

Hillenbrand, F.K.M., *Underground Humour in Nazi Germany, 1933–1945* (London, 1995)

Höffler, Felix, 'Kriegserfahrungen in der Heimat: Kriegsverlauf, Kriegsschuld und Kriegsende in württembergischen Stimmungsbildern des Ersten Weltkriegs', in Gerhard Hirschfeld, Gerd Krumeich, Dieter Langewiesche and Hans-Peter Ullmann (eds), *Kriegserfahrungen: Studien zur Sozial- und Mentalitätsgeschichte des Ersten Weltkriegs* (Tübingen, 1997)

Hoffmann, Christhard, 'Verfolgung und Alltagsleben der Landjuden im nationalsozialistischen Deutschland', in Monika Richarz and Reinhard

Rürup (eds), *Jüdisches Leben auf dem Lande: Studien zur deutsch-jüdischen Geschichte* (Tübingen, 1997)

Hofsähs, Rudolf, 'Die Abwanderung aus wirtschaftlich zurückgebliebenen Gebieten in Baden-Württemberg', doctoral dissertation for the Wirtschaftshochschule Mannheim, 1957

Homze, Edward L., *Foreign Labor in Nazi Germany* (Princeton, 1967)

Howard, N.P., 'The Social and Political Consequences of the Allied Food Blockade of Germany, 1918–19', *German History*, 11 (1993)

Hüttenberger, Peter, *Die Gauleiter: Studie zum Wandel des Machtgefüges in der NSDAP* (Stuttgart, 1969)

Ilien, Albert, and Jeggle, Utz, *Leben auf dem Dorf: zur Sozialgeschichte des Dorfes und Sozialpsychologie seiner Bewohner* (Opladen, 1978)

Illustrierter Beobachter, 10 August 1944, 'V1 gegen England!'

Jackson, Julian, *France: The Dark Years, 1940–1944* (Oxford, 2001)

James, Harold, *The German Slump: Politics and Economics, 1924–1936* (Oxford, 1986)

Jantzen, Kyle, 'Propaganda, Perseverance and Protest: Strategies for Clerical Survival amid the German Church Struggle', *Church History: Studies in Christianity and Culture*, 70 (2001)

Jeggle, Utz, 'The Rules of the Village: On the Cultural History of the Peasant World in the Last 150 Years', trans. by Richard J. Evans, in Evans and Lee, *The German Peasantry*

Jeggle, Utz, *Judendörfer in Württemberg* (Tübingen, 1969)

Johnson, Eric, *The Nazi Terror: Gestapo, Jews and Ordinary Germans* (London, 2000)

Kallis, Aristotle A., *Nazi Propaganda and the Second World War* (Basingstoke, 2005)

Kaminsky, Uwe, '"Vergessene Opfer" – Zwangssterilisierte, "Asoziale", Deserteure, Fremdarbeiter', in Sybille Baumbach, Uwe Kaminsky, Alfons Kenkmann and Beate Meyer, *Rückblenden: Lebensgeschichtliche Interviews mit Verfolgten des NS-Regimes in Hamburg* (Hamburg, 1999)

Kaplan, Marion A., *Between Dignity and Despair: Jewish Life in Nazi Germany* (New York and Oxford, 1998)

Karl, Michael, 'Landwirtschaft und Ernährung im Deutschen Reich', in Salewski and Schulze-Wegener, *Kriegsjahr 1944*

Kaschuba, Wolfgang, 'Peasants and Others: The Historical Contours of Village Class Society', in Evans and Lee, *The German Peasantry*

Kater, Michael H., *The Nazi Party: A Social Profile of Members and Leaders, 1919–1945* (Cambridge, Massachusetts, 1983)

Kater, Michael H., *Hitler Youth* (Cambridge, Massachusetts, and London, 2004)

Keegan, John, *The Second World War* (London, 1989)

Kershaw, Ian, *Popular Opinion and Political Dissent in the Third Reich: Bavaria, 1933–1945* (Oxford, 1983)

Kershaw, Ian, *The 'Hitler Myth': Image and Reality in the Third Reich* (Oxford, 1987)

Kershaw, Ian, 'Social Unrest and the Response of the Nazi Regime', in Francis R. Nicosia and Lawrence D. Stokes (eds), *Germans Against Nazism: Nonconformity, Opposition and Resistance in the Third Reich. Essays in Honour of Peter Hoffmann* (New York and Oxford, 1990)

Kershaw, Ian, *Hitler* (London, 1991)

Kershaw, Ian, *Hitler, 1889–1936: Hubris* (London, 1998)

Kershaw, Ian, *The Nazi Dictatorship* (4th ed. London, 2000)

Kershaw, Ian, and Lewin, Moshe, (eds), *Stalinism and Nazism: Dictatorships in Comparison* (Cambridge, 1997)

Kettenacker, Lothar, 'Die Chefs der Zivilverwaltung im Zweiten Weltkrieg', in Rebentisch and Teppe, *Verwaltung contra Menschenführung*

Kirwin, Gerald, 'Waiting for Retaliation: A Study in Nazi Propaganda Behaviour and German Civilian Morale', *Journal of Contemporary History*, 16 (1981)

Kissener, Michael, and Scholtyseck, Joachim, (eds), *Die Führer der Provinz: NS-Biographien aus Baden und Württemberg* (Konstanz, 1997)

Kissener, Michael, and Scholtyseck, Joachim, 'Nationalsozialismus in der Provinz: zur Einführung', in Kissener and Scholtyseck, *Die Führer der Provinz*

Kitchen, Martin, *Nazi Germany at War* (London, 1995)

Klee, Ernst, *'Euthanasie' im NS-Staat: die 'Vernichtung lebensunwerten Lebens'* (Frankfurt am Main, 1983)

Klee, Ernst (ed.), *Dokumente zur 'Euthanasie'* (Frankfurt am Main, 1985)

Kleiber, Lore, '"Wo ihr seid, da soll die Sonne scheinen!" – Der Frauenarbeitsdienst am Ende der Weimarer Republik und im Nationalsozialismus', in Frauengruppe Faschismusforschung (ed.), *Mutterkreuz und Arbeitsbuch* (Frankfurt am Main, 1981)

Klemperer, Victor, *I Shall Bear Witness: The Diaries of Victor Klemperer, 1933–1941* (London, 1999)

Knodel, John E., *Demographic Behaviour in the Past: A Study of Fourteen German Village Populations in the Eighteenth and Nineteenth Centuries* (Cambridge, 1988)

Kochan, Lionel, *Russia in Revolution* (London, 1970)

Kock, Gerhard, *Die Kinderlandverschickung im Zweiten Weltkrieg* (Paderborn, 1997)

Kocka, Jürgen, *Facing Total War* (Leamington Spa, 1984)

Koehl, Robert L., *RKFDV: German Resettlement and Population Policy, 1939–1945* (Cambridge, Massachusetts, 1957)

Kohler, Eric D., 'Inflation and Black Marketeering in the Rhenish Agricultural
    Economy, 1919–1922', *German Studies Review*, 8 (1985)
Köhler, Joachim, 'Die katholische Kirche in Baden und Württemberg in der
    Endphase der Weimarer Republik und zu Beginn des Dritten Reiches', in
    Schnabel, *Die Machtergreifung in Südwestdeutschland*
Köhler, Joachim, 'Das Bistum Rottenburg von der Gründung bis zur
    Zeit nach dem Zweiten Weltkrieg', in Sproll and Thierfelder, *Die
    Religionsgemeinschaften in Baden und Württemberg*
Köhler, Joachim, and Thierfelder, Jörg, 'Anpassung oder Widerstand? Die
    Kirchen im Bann der "Machtergreifung" Hitlers', in Landeszentrale für
    politische Bildung und Haus der Geschichte, *Formen des Widerstandes im
    Südwesten*
Kolb, Eberhard, *The Weimar Republic*, trans. P.S. Falla (London, 1988)
König, Wolfgang, *Volkswagen, Volksempfänger, Volksgemeinschaft:
    'Volksprodukte' im Dritten Reich. Vom Scheitern einer nationalsozialistischen
    Konsumgesellschaft* (Paderborn, 2004)
Kopf, Paul, 'Buchau am Federsee in nationalsozialistischer Zeit: die Ereignisse
    der Jahre 1934 bis 1938', in Geschichtsverein der Diözese Rottenburg-
    Stuttgart, *Kirche im Nationalsozialismus*
Krause, Michael, *Flucht vor dem Bombenkrieg: 'Umquartierungen' im Zweiten
    Weltkrieg und die Wiedereingliederung der Evakuierten in Deutschland,
    1943–1963* (Düsseldorf, 1997)
Kroener, Bernhard R., 'Squaring the Circle: Blitzkrieg Strategy and Manpower
    Shortage, 1939–1942', in Deist, *The German Military in the Age of Total War*
Kulinat, Klaus, 'Regional Planning in Baden-Württemberg', in Landeszentrale
    für politische Bildung Baden-Württemberg, *The German Southwest*
Kundrus, Birthe, *Kriegerfrauen: Familienpolitik und Geschlechterverhältnisse im
    Ersten und Zweiten Weltkrieg* (Hamburg, 1995)
Lacey, Kate, *Feminine Frequencies: Gender, German Radio and the Public Sphere*
    (Ann Arbor, Michigan, 1996)
Landestelle für Museumbetreuung Baden-Württemberg und der
    Arbeitsgemeinschaft der regionalen Freilichtmuseen Baden-Württemberg
    (eds), *Zöpfe ab, Hosen an! Die Fünfzigerjahre auf dem Land in Baden-
    Württemberg* (Tübingen, 2002)
Landeszentrale für politische Bildung Baden-Württemberg (ed.), *The German
    Southwest: Baden-Württemberg. History, Politics, Economy and Culture*
    (Stuttgart, 1991)
Landeszentrale für politische Bildung und Haus der Geschichte (ed.), *Formen
    des Widerstandes im Südwesten, 1933–1945* (Ulm, 1994)
Lang, Ralf, *Italienische 'Fremdarbeiter' im nationalsozialistischen Deutschland,
    1937–1945* (Frankfurt am Main, 1996)

Larass, Claus, *Der Zug der Kinder: KLV. Die Evakuierung 5 Millionen deutscher Kinder im 2. Weltkrieg* (Frankfurt am Main, 1992)

Larkin, Maurice, *Church and State after the Dreyfus Affair: The Separation Issue in France* (London, 1974)

Laux, Eberhard, 'Führung und Verwaltung in der Rechtslehre des Nationalsozialismus', in Rebentisch and Teppe, *Verwaltung contra Menschenführung*

Lechner, Silvester, *Das KZ Oberer Kuhberg und die NS-Zeit in der Region Ulm/Neu-Ulm* (Stuttgart, 1988)

Lee, Robert, '"Relative Backwardness" and Long-run Development: Economic, Demographic and Social Changes', in Breuilly, *Nineteenth-Century Germany*

Leipner, Kurt, (ed.), *Chronik der Stadt Stuttgart, 1933–1945* (Stuttgart, 1982)

Lepsius, M.R., 'Extremer Nationalismus: Strukturbedingungen vor der nationalsozialistischen Machtergreifung' (first pub. 1970), in M.R. Lepsius, *Demokratie in Deutschland* (Göttingen, 1993)

Lerman, Katharine A., 'Bismarckian Germany and the Structure of the German Empire', in Breuilly, *Nineteenth-Century Germany*

Levine, Alan J., *The Strategic Bombing of Germany, 1940–45* (Westport, Connecticut, 1992)

Lewin, Moshe, 'Bureaucracy and the Stalinist State', in Kershaw and Lewin, *Stalinism and Nazism*

Lewy, Guenter, *The Catholic Church and Nazi Germany* (London, 1964)

Lewy, Guenter, *The Nazi Persecution of the Gypsies* (Oxford, 2000)

Littell, Franklin H., and Locke, Hubert G., (eds), *The German Church Struggle and the Holocaust* (Detroit, Michigan, 1974)

Longerich, Peter, 'Joseph Goebbels und der totale Krieg: eine unbekannte Denkschrift des Propagandaministers vom 18. Juli 1944', *Vierteljahrshefte für Zeitgeschichte*, 35 (1987)

Lubbers, Ruud, 'Europe: A Continent of Traditions', the William and Mary Lecture, Cambridge, 16 February 1993

Lyttelton, Adrian, *The Seizure of Power: Fascism in Italy, 1919–1929* (London, 1973)

Mackay, Robert, *The Test of War: Inside Britain, 1939–1945* (London, 1999)

Macnicol, John, 'The Evacuation of Schoolchildren', in Smith, *War and Social Change*

Mai, Gunther, *Die Geislinger Metallarbeiterbewegung* (Düsseldorf, 1984)

Majer, Dietmut, 'Richter und Rechtswesen', in Borst, *Das Dritte Reich in Baden und Württemberg*

Marnau, Björn, '"…empfinde ich das Urteil als hart und unrichtig": Zwangssterilisation im Kreis Steinburg/Holstein', in Salewski and Schulze-Wegener, *Kriegsjahr 1944*

Mason, Tim, 'The Legacy of 1918 for National Socialism', in Anthony Nicholls and Erich Matthias (eds), *German Democracy and the Triumph of Hitler: Essays in Recent German History* (London, 1971)

Mason, Timothy W., *Sozialpolitik im Dritten Reich: Arbeiterklasse und Volksgemeinschaft* (Opladen, 1977)

Mason, Tim, 'The Workers' Opposition in Nazi Germany', *History Workshop Journal*, 11 (1981)

Mason, Tim, *Social Policy in the Third Reich: The Working Class and the 'National Community'* (Providence, Rhode Island, and Oxford, 1993), ed. Jane Caplan; trans. John Broadwin

Mason, Tim, 'The Containment of the Working Class in Nazi Germany', in Caplan, *Nazism, Fascism and the Working Class*

Mason, Tim, 'Women in Germany, 1925–1940', reprinted in Caplan, *Nazism, Fascism and the Working Class*

Matzerath, Horst, *Nationalsozialismus und kommunale Selbstverwaltung* (Stuttgart, 1970)

May, Georg, *Kirchenkampf oder Katholikenverfolgung? Ein Beitrag zu dem gegenseitigen Verhältnis von Nationalsozialismus und christlichen Bekenntnissen* (Stein am Rhein, 1991)

Mayhew, Alan, *Rural Settlement and Farming in Germany* (London, 1973)

McFarland-Icke, Bronwyn Rebekah, *Nurses in Nazi Germany: Moral Choice in History* (Princeton, New Jersey, 1999)

Meyer, Beate, *'Goldfasane' und 'Nazissen': die NSDAP im ehemals 'roten' Stadtteil Hamburg-Eimsbüttel* (Hamburg, 2002)

Messerschmidt, Manfred, 'Verweigerung in der Endphase des Krieges', in Landeszentrale für politische Bildung und Haus der Geschichte, *Formen des Widerstandes im Südwesten*

Michalka, Wolfgang, (ed.), *Das Dritte Reich*, ii, *Weltmachtanspruch und nationaler Zusammenbruch, 1939–1945* (Munich, 1985)

Mielke, Robert, *Das Deutsche Dorf* (Leipzig and Berlin, 1920)

Milton, Sybil H., '"Gypsies" as Social Outsiders in Nazi Germany', in Gellately and Stoltzfus, *Social Outsiders in Nazi Germany*

Möller, Horst, Wirsching, Andreas, and Ziegler, Walter, (eds), *Nationalsozialismus in der Region: Beiträge zur regionalen und lokalen Forschung und zum internationalen Vergleich* (Munich, 1996)

Mommsen, Hans, 'National Socialism: Continuity and Change', in Walter Laqueur (ed.), *Fascism: A Reader's Guide. Analyses, Interpretation, Bibliography* (London, 1976)

Mommsen, Hans, 'Cumulative Radicalisation and Progressive Self-Destruction as Structural Determinants of the Nazi Dictatorship', in Kershaw and Lewin, *Stalinism and Nazism*

Mommsen, Hans, 'The Dissolution of the Third Reich: Crisis Management and Collapse, 1943–1945', *Bulletin of the German Historical Institute* (Washington), 27 (2000)

Mühlberger, Detlef, *Hitler's Followers: Studies in the Sociology of the Nazi Movement* (London, 1991)

Mühlfeld, Claus, and Schönweiss, Friedrich, *Nationalsozialistische Familienpolitik: Familiensoziologische Analyse der nationalsozialistischen Familienpolitik* (Stuttgart, 1989)

Müller, Roland, *Stuttgart zur Zeit des Nationalsozialismus* (Stuttgart, 1988)

Münkel, Daniela, *Bauern und Nationalsozialismus: der Landkreis Celle im Dritten Reich* (Bielefeld, 1991)

Münkel, Daniela, *Nationalsozialistische Agrarpolitik und Bauernalltag* (Frankfurt am Main, 1996)

Münkel, Daniela, (ed.), *Der lange Abschied vom Agrarland: Agrarpolitik, Landwirtschaft und ländliche Gesellschaft zwischen Weimar und Bonn* (Göttingen, 2000)

Münkel, Daniela, '"Der Rundfunk geht auf die Dörfer": der Einzug der Massmedien auf dem Lande von den zwanziger bis zu den sechziger Jahren', in Münkel, *Der lange Abschied vom Agrarland*

Murphy, Richard Charles, *Guestworkers in the German Reich: A Polish Community in Wilhelmian Germany* (New York, 1983)

Neliba, Günter, 'Führerprinzip', in Benz, Graml and Weiss, *Enzyklopädie des Nationalsozialismus*

Noakes, Jeremy, *The Nazi Party in Lower Saxony, 1921–1933* (Oxford, 1971)

Noakes, Jeremy, 'The Oldenburg Crucifix Struggle of November 1936: A Case Study of Opposition in the Third Reich', in Peter D. Stachura (ed.), *The Shaping of the Nazi State* (London, 1978)

Noakes, Jeremy, (ed.), *The Civilian in War* (Exeter, 1992)

Noakes, Jeremy, 'Germany', in Jeremy Noakes (ed.), *The Civilian in War* (Exeter, 1992)

Noakes, Jeremy, 'Nationalsozialismus in der Provinz: Kleine und mittlere Städte im Dritten Reich, 1933–1945', in Möller, Wirsching and Ziegler, *Nationalsozialismus in der Region*

Noakes, Jeremy, and Pridham, Geoffrey, (eds), *Nazism, 1919–1945: A Documentary Reader*, i, *The Rise to Power* (Exeter, 1983)

Noakes, Jeremy, and Pridham, Geoffrey, (eds), *Nazism, 1919–1945: A Documentary Reader*, ii, *State, Economy and Society, 1933–1939* (Exeter, 1986)

Noakes, Jeremy, and Pridham, Geoffrey, (eds), *Nazism, 1919–1945*, iii, *Foreign Policy, War and Racial Extermination* (Exeter, 1988; new ed. 2001)

Noakes, Jeremy, (ed.), *Nazism, 1919–1945: A Documentary Reader*, iv, *The German Home Front in World War II* (Exeter, 1998)

Noakes, Jeremy, 'Leaders of the People? The Nazi Party and German Society', *Journal of Contemporary History*, 39 (2004)

Norden, Günther van, 'Die Barmer Theologische Erklärung und ihr historischer Ort in der Widerstandsgeschichte', in Peter Steinbach and Johannes Tuchel (eds.), *Widerstand gegen den Nationalsozialismus* (Bonn, 1994)

Nowak, Kurt, 'Kirchen und Religion', in Benz, Graml and Weiss, *Enzyklopädie des Nationalsozialismus*

Oppen, Beate Ruhm von, 'Revisionism and Counterrevisionism in the Historiography of the Church Struggle', in Littell and Locke, *The German Church Struggle and the Holocaust*

Orlow, Dietrich, *The History of the Nazi Party, 1919–1933* (Newton Abbot, 1971)

Orlow, Dietrich, *The History of the Nazi Party, 1933–1945* (Newton Abbot, 1973)

Osmond, Jonathan, 'A Second Agrarian Mobilisation? Peasant Associations in South and West Germany, 1918–24', in Robert Moeller (ed.), *Peasants and Lords in Modern Germany: Recent Studies in Agricultural History* (Boston, Massachusetts, and London, 1986)

Ousby, Ian, *Occupation: The Ordeal of France, 1940–1944* (London, 1999)

Overy, Richard, '"Blitzkriegwirtschaft"? Finanzpolitik, Lebensstandard und Arbeitseinsatz in Deutschland, 1939–1942', *Vierteljahrshefte für Zeitgeschichte* 36 (1988)

Overy, Richard, *Why the Allies Won* (New York and London, 1995)

Owings, Alison, *Frauen: German Women Recall the Third Reich* (New Brunswick, New Jersey, 1994)

Panayi, Panikos, *Ethnic Minorities in Nineteenth- and Twentieth-Century Germany: Jews, Gypsies, Poles, Turks and Others* (London, 2000)

Paulus, Martin, Raim, Edith, and Zelger, Gerhard, *Ein Ort wie jeder andere: Bilder aus einer deutschen Kleinstadt. Landsberg, 1923–1958* (Reinbek bei Hamburg, 1995)

Petersen, Michael, 'Utilisation of Jewish and Non-Jewish Slave Labor in V-2 Rocket Production', presentation at the Summer Research Workshop on 'Forced Foreign Laborers, POWs, and Jewish Slave Workers in the Third Reich: Regional Studies and New Research', at the Center for Advanced Holocaust Studies, United States Holocaust Memorial Museum, 15 August 2003

Peterson, Edward N., *The Limits of Hitler's Power* (Princeton, New Jersey, 1969)

Peukert, Detlev J.K., *Inside Nazi Germany: Conformity, Opposition and Racism in Everyday Life*, trans. Richard Deveson (London, 1987)

Peukert, Detlev J.K., *The Weimar Republic: The Crisis of Classical Modernity*, trans. Richard Deveson (London, 1992)

Phayer, Michael, 'The Priority of Diplomacy: Pius XII and the Holocaust during the Second World War', in Dietrich, *Christian Responses to the Holocaust*

Pine, Lisa, *Nazi Family Policy, 1933–1945* (Oxford, 1997)

Pohl, Dieter, 'Die Ermordung der Juden im Generalgouvernement', in Ulrich Herbert (ed.), *Nationalsozialistische Vernichtungspolitik, 1939–1945: Neue Forschungen und Kontroversen* (Frankfurt am Main, 1998)

Pridham, Geoffrey, *Hitler's Rise to Power: The Nazi Movement in Bavaria, 1923–33* (London, 1973)

Prinz, Michael, *Vom neuen Mittelstand zum Volksgenossen* (Munich, 1986)

Proctor, Robert N., *Racial Hygiene: Medicine under the Nazis* (Cambridge, Massachusetts, 1988)

Proctor, Robert N., 'The Nazi War on Tobacco: Ideology, Evidence, and Possible Cancer Consequences', *Bulletin of the History of Medicine*, 71 (1997)

Proctor, Robert N., *The Nazi War on Cancer* (Princeton, New Jersey, 1999)

Pyta, Wolfram, 'Ländlich-evangelisches Milieu und Nationalsozialismus bis 1933', in Möller, Wirsching and Ziegler, *Nationalsozialismus in der Region*

Raberg, Frank, 'Das Aushängeschild der Hitler-Regierung: Konstantin Freiherr von Neurath, Aussenminister des Deutschen Reiches', in Kissener and Scholtyseck, *Die Führer der Provinz*

Rademacher, Michael, *Handbuch der NSDAP-Gaue, 1928–1945: die Amtsträger der NSDAP und ihrer Organisationen auf Gau- und Kreisebene in Deutschland und Österreich sowie in den Reichsgauen Danzig-Westpreussen, Sudetenland und Warthegau* (Vechta, 2000)

Rauh-Kühne, Cornelia, *Katholisches Milieu und Kleinstadtgesellschaft: Ettlingen, 1918–1939* (Sigmaringen, 1991)

Rauh-Kühne, Cornelia, 'Katholisches Sozialmilieu, Region und Nationalsozialismus', in Möller, Wirsching and Ziegler, *Nationalsozialismus in der Region*

Rauh-Kühne, Cornelia, and Ruck, Michael, (eds), *Regionale Eliten zwischen Diktatur und Demokratie: Baden und Württemberg, 1930–1952* (Munich, 1993)

Raumer, Dietrich von, 'Zeugen Jehovas als Kriegsdienstverweigerer: ein trauriges Kapitel der Wehrmachtjustiz', in Roser, *Widerstand als Bekenntnis*

Reagin, Nancy R., 'Marktordnung and Autarkic Housekeeping: Housewives and Private Consumption under the Four-Year Plan, 1936–39', *German History*, 19 (2001)

Rebentisch, Dieter, and Teppe, Karl, (eds), *Verwaltung contra Menschenführung: Studien zum politisch-administrativen System* (Göttingen, 1986)

Recker, Marie-Luise, *Nationalsozialistische Sozialpolitik im Zweiten Weltkrieg* (Munich, 1985)

Reese, Dagmar, *Straff, aber nicht stramm – herb, aber nicht derb: zur Vergesellschaftung von Mädchen durch den Bund Deutscher Mädel im sozialkulturellen Vergleich zweier Milieus* (Weinheim and Basel, 1989)

Reibel, Carl-Wilhelm, *Das Fundament der Diktatur: die NSDAP-Ortsgruppen, 1932–1945* (Paderborn, 2002)

Reichsorganisationsleiter (ed.), *NSDAP Partei-Statistik* (Munich, 1935)

Rempel, Gerhard, *Hitler's Children: The Hitler Youth and the SS* (Chapel Hill, North Carolina, 1989)

Renz, Rudolf, 'Kirchenkampf in Ellwangen: Bericht eines Zeitgenossen', in Geschichtsverein der Diözese Rottenburg-Stuttgart, *Kirche im Nationalsozialismus*

Rinderle, Walter, and Norling, Bernard, *The Nazi Impact on a German Village* (Lexington, Kentucky, 1993)

Röhl, Klaus Rainer, *Verbotene Trauer: Ende der deutschen Tabus* (Munich, 2002)

Roll-Hansen, Nils, 'Norwegian Eugenics: Sterilisation as Social Reform', in Broberg and Roll-Hansen, *Eugenics and the Welfare State*

Roseman, Mark, 'National Socialism and Modernisation', in Bessel, *Fascist Italy and Nazi Germany*

Roser, Annette, '"Beamter aus Berufung": Karl Wilhelm Waldmann, Württembergischer Staatssekretär', in Kissener and Scholtyseck, *Die Führer der Provinz*

Roser, Hubert, 'Vom Dorfschultheiss zum hohen Ministerialbeamten: Georg Stümpfig, Kanzleidirektor im Württembergischen Innenministerium und Gauamtsleiter für Kommunalpolitik', in Kissener and Scholtyseck, *Die Führer der Provinz*

Roser, Hubert, (ed.), *Widerstand als Bekenntnis: die Zeugen Jehovas und das NS-Regime in Baden und Württemberg* (Konstanz, 1999)

Rothfuss, Uli, *Die Hitlerfahn' muss weg! Zwanzig dramatische Stationen in einer schwäbischen Kleinstadt* (Tübingen, 1998)

Ruck, Michael, 'Administrative Eliten in Demokratie und Diktatur: Beamtenkarrieren in Baden und Württemberg von den zwanziger Jahren bis in die Nachkriegszeit', in Rauh-Kühne and Ruck, *Regionale Eliten zwischen Diktatur und Demokratie*

Ruck, Michael, 'Kollaboration – Loyalität – Resistenz: Administrative Eliten und NS-Regime am Beispiel der südwestdeutsschen Innenverwaltung', in Landeszentrale für politische Bildung und Haus der Geschichte, *Formen des Widerstandes im Südwesten*

Ruck, Michael, 'Zentralismus und Regionalgewalten im Herrschaftsgefüge des NS-Staates', in Möller, Wirsching and Ziegler, *Nationalsozialismus in der Region*

Ruck, Michael, *Korpsgeist und Staatsbewusstsein: Beamte im deutschen Südwesten, 1928 bis 1972* (Munich, 1996)

Salewski, Michael, and Schulze-Wegener, Guntram, (eds), *Kriegsjahr 1944: im Großen und im Kleinen*, (Stuttgart, 1995)

Salter, Stephen, 'Structures of Consensus and Coercion: Workers' Morale and the Maintenance of Work Discipline, 1939–1945', in Welch, *Nazi Propaganda*

Sauer, Paul, *Die jüdischen Gemeinden in Württemberg und Hohenzollern: Denkmale, Geschichte, Schicksale* (Stuttgart, 1966)

Sauer, Paul, (ed.), *Dokumente über die Verfolgung der jüdischen Bürger in Baden-Württemberg durch das nationalsozialistischen Regime, 1933–1945* (Stuttgart, 1966)

Sauer, Paul, *Die Schicksale der Jüdischen Bürger Baden-Württembergs während der nationalsozialistischen Verfolgungszeit, 1933–1945* (Stuttgart, 1969)

Sauer, Paul, *Württemberg in der Zeit des Nationalsozialismus* (Ulm, 1975)

Sauer, Paul, *Demokratischer Neubeginn in Not und Elend: das Land Württemberg-Baden von 1945 bis 1952* (Ulm, 1978)

Sauer, Paul, 'Die jüdischen Gemeinden in Baden und Württemberg von 1933 bis zum Wiederaufbau nach 1945', in Sproll and Thierfelder, *Die Religionsgemeinschaften in Baden und Württemberg*

Sauer, Paul, 'Staat, Politik, Akteure', in Borst, *Das Dritte Reich in Baden und Württemberg*

Sauer, Paul, *Wilhelm Murr: Hitlers Statthalter in Württemberg* (Tübingen, 1998)

Sauer, Paul, *Erinnerung an Stuttgart in den zwanziger Jahren* (Würzburg, 2000)

Saul, S.B., *Industrialisation and De-industrialisation? The Interaction of the German and British Economies before the First World War*, Annual Lecture 1979, German Historical Institute London

Schadt, Jörg, 'Verfolgung und Widerstand', in Borst, *Das Dritte Reich in Baden und Württemberg*

Schäfer, Annette, *Zwangsarbeiter und NS-Rassenpolitik: Russische und polnische Arbeitskräfte in Württemberg, 1939–1945* (Stuttgart, 2000)

Schäfer, Annette, 'Zwangsarbeit in den Kommunen: "Ausländereinsatz" in Württemberg, 1939–1945', *Vierteljahrshefte für Zeitgeschichte*, 49, (2001)

Schäfer, Gerhard, *Landesbischof D. Wurm und der nationalsozialistische Staat, 1940–1945* (Stuttgart, 1968)

Schanbacher, Eberhard, 'Das Wählervotum und die "Machtergreifung" im deutschen Südwesten', in Schnabel, *Die Machtergreifung in Südwestdeutschland*

Schechtman, Joseph B., *European Population Transfers, 1939–1945* (New York, 1946)

Scheck, Raffael, *Mothers of the Nation: Right-Wing Women in Weimar Germany* (Oxford, 2003)

Schefold, Willi, 'Landwirtschaft und Ernährung', in Max Gögler and Gregor Richter (eds), *Das Land Württemberg-Hohenzollern, 1945–52* (Sigmaringen, 1982)

Schlösser, Susanne, '"Was sich in den Weg stellt, mit Vernichtung schlagen": Richard Drauz, NSDAP-Kreisleiter von Heilbronn', in Kissener and Scholtyseck, *Die Führer der Provinz*

Schmidt, Sabine, 'Vom Hilfsarbeiter zum Kreisleiter: Eugen Maier, NSDAP-Kreisleiter von Ulm', in Kissener and Scholtyseck, *Die Führer der Provinz*

Schminck-Gustavus, Christoph U., (ed.), *Hungern für Hitler: Erinnerungen polnischer Zwangsarbeiter im deutschen Reich, 1940–1945* (Hamburg, 1984)

Schmitt, Hans A., *Quakers and Nazis: Inner Light in Outer Darkness* (Columbia, Missouri, 1997)

Schnabel, Thomas (ed.), *Die Machtergreifung in Südwestdeutschland: das Ende der Weimarer Republik in Baden und Württemberg, 1928–1933* (Stuttgart, 1982)

Schnabel, Thomas, 'Die NSDAP in Württemberg, 1928–1933: die Schwäche einer regionalen Parteiorganisation', in Schnabel, *Die Machtergreifung in Südwestdeutschland*

Schnabel, Thomas, '"Warum geht es in Schwaben besser?" Württemberg in der Weltwirtschaftskrise 1928–1933', in Schnabel, *Die Machtergreifung in Südwestdeutschland*

Schnabel, Thomas, 'Das Wahlverhalten der Katholiken in Württemberg, 1928–1933', in Geschichtsverein der Diözese Rottenburg-Stuttgart, *Kirche im Nationalsozialismus*

Schnabel, Thomas, *Württemberg zwischen Weimar und Bonn, 1928–1945/46* (Stuttgart, 1986)

Schnabel, Thomas, 'Einleitung', in Landeszentrale für politische Bildung und Haus der Geschichte, *Formen des Widerstandes im Südwesten*

Schnabel, Thomas, '"Die Leute wollten nicht einer verlorenen Sache ihre Heimat opfern"', in Landeszentrale für politische Bildung und Haus der Geschichte, *Formen des Widerstandes im Südwesten*

Schneider, Karl, 'Schule und Erziehung', in Borst, *Das Dritte Reich in Baden und Württemberg*

Schoenbaum, David, *Hitler's Social Revolution: Class and Status in Nazi Germany, 1933–1939* (London, 1967)

Scholtyseck, Joachim, 'Der "Schwabenherzog": Gottlob Berger, SS-Obergruppenführer', in Kissener and Scholtyseck, *Die Führer der Provinz*

Scholtyseck, Joachim, '"Der Mann aus dem Volk": Wilhelm Murr, Gauleiter und Reichsstatthalter in Württemberg-Hohenzollern', in Kissener and Scholtyseck, *Die Führer der Provinz*

Schönhagen, Benigna, 'Zwischen Verweigerung und Agitation: Landtagspolitik der NSDAP in Württemberg 1928/29–1933', in Schnabel, *Die Machtergreifung in Südwestdeutschland*

Schönhagen, Benigna, *Tübingen unterm Hakenkreuz: eine Universitätsstadt in der Zeit des Nationalsozialismus* (Stuttgart, 1991)

Schuhladen-Krämer, Jürgen, 'Die Exekutoren des Terrors: Hermann Mattheiss, Walther Stahlecker, Friedrich Mussgay, Leiter der Geheimen Staatspolizeileitstelle Stuttgart', in Kissener and Scholtyseck, *Die Führer der Provinz*

Semmens, Kristin, *Seeing Hitler's Germany: Tourism in the Third Reich* (Basingstoke, 2005)

Siegelbaum, Lewis H., *Soviet State and Society between Revolutions, 1918–1929* (Cambridge, 1992)

Smelser, Ronald, *Robert Ley: Hitler's Labour Front Leader* (Oxford, 1988)

Smelser, Ronald, Syring, Enrico, and Zitelmann, Rainer, (eds): *Die Braune Elite, i: 22 biographische Skizzen; Die Braune Elite, ii: 21 weitere biographische Skizzen* (Darmstadt, 1999)

Smith, Harold L., (ed.), *War and Social Change: British Society in the Second World War* (Manchester, 1986)

Smith, Harold L., 'The Effect of the War on the Status of Women', in Smith, *War and Social Change*

Sonnenberger, Franz, 'Historisch-politische Bewertung des Schulkampfes im Dritten Reich', in Martin Broszat, Elke Fröhlich, Falk Wiesemann and Anton Grossmann (eds), *Bayern in der NS-Zeit*, iii: *Herrschaft und Gesellschaft im Konflikt* (Munich and Vienna, 1981)

Sorge, Martin K., *The Other Price of Hitler's War: German Military and Civilian Losses Resulting from World War II* (Westport, Connecticut, 1986)

Spicer, Kevin P., *Resisting the Third Reich: The Catholic Clergy in Hitler's Berlin* (DeKalb, Illinois, 2004)

Spindler, George D., *Burgbach: Urbanisation and Identity in a German Village* (New York, 1973)

Spoerer, Mark, and Fleischhacker, Jochen, 'Forced Laborers in Nazi Germany: Categories, Numbers and Survivors', *Journal of Interdisciplinary History*, 33 (2002)

Sproll, Heinz, and Thierfelder, Jörg, (eds), *Die Religionsgemeinschaften in Baden und Württemberg* (Stuttgart, 1984)

Stadtarchiv Göppingen (ed.), *Jüdisches Museum Göppingen* (Memmingen, 1992)

Stargardt, Nicholas, *Witnesses of War: Children's Lives under the Nazis* (London, 2005)

Statistisches Reichsamt (ed.), *Statistisches Jahrbuch für das Deutsche Reich*

Steigmann-Gall, Richard, *The Holy Reich: Nazi Conceptions of Christianity, 1919–45* (Cambridge, 2003)

Steinbach, Peter, and Tuchel, Johannes, (eds), *Widerstand gegen den Nationalsozialismus* (Bonn, 1994)

Steinert, Marlis G., *Hitlers Krieg und die Deutschen* (Düsseldorf, 1970)

Steinert, Marlis G., *Hitler's War and the Germans*, ed. and trans. Thomas E.J. de Witt (Ohio, 1977)

Stephenson, Jill, *Women in Nazi Society* (London, 1975)

Stephenson, Jill, '"Reichsbund der Kinderreichen": The League of Large Families in the Population Policy of Nazi Germany', *European Studies Review* (1979)

Stephenson, Jill, *The Nazi Organisation of Women* (London, 1981)

Stephenson, Jill, 'Women's Labor Service in Nazi Germany', *Central European History*, 15 (1982)

Stephenson, Jill, 'Propaganda, Autarky and the German Housewife,' in Welch, *Nazi Propaganda*

Stephenson, Jill, 'War and Society in Württemberg, 1939–1945: Beating the System', *German Studies Review*, 8 (1985)

Stephenson, Jill, '"Emancipation" and its Problems: War and Society in Württemberg, 1939–1945', *European History Quarterly*, 17 (1987)

Stephenson, Jill, 'Widerstand gegen soziale Modernisierung am Beispiel Württembergs, 1939–1945', in Michael Prinz and Rainer Zitelmann (eds.), *Nationalsozialismus und Modernisierung* (Darmstadt, 1991)

Stephenson, Jill, 'Triangle: Foreign Workers, German Civilians, and the Nazi Regime. War and Society in Württemberg, 1939–1945', *German Studies Review*, 15 (1992)

Stephenson, Jill, 'Anniversaries, Memory and the Neighbours: The German Question in Recent History', *German Politics*, 5 (1996)

Stephenson, Jill, *Women in Nazi Germany* (London, 2001)

Stephenson, Jill, 'The Home Front in "Total War": Women in Germany and Britain in the Second World War', in Chickering, Förster and Greiner, *A World at Total War*

Stephenson, Jill, 'Germans, Slavs and the Burden of Work in Rural Southern Germany during the Second World War', in Neil Gregor (ed.), *Nazism, War, Genocide: Essays in Honour of Jeremy Noakes* (Exeter, 2005)

Stolle, Michael, 'Der schwäbische Schulmeister: Christian Mergenthaler, Württembergische Ministerpräsident, Justiz- und Kultminister', in Kissener and Scholtyseck, *Die Führer der Provinz*

Strauss, Walter, *Signs of Life, Jews from Württemberg: Reports for the Period after 1933 in Letters and Descriptions* (New York, 1982)

Suny, Ronald Grigor, 'Stalin and his Stalinism: Power and Authority in the Soviet Union, 1930–1953', in Kershaw and Lewin, *Stalinism and Nazism*

Sutschek, Felix, 'Die jüdische Landgemeinde Oberdorf am Ipf in der Zeit des Nationalsozialismus', in Michael Kissener (ed.), *Widerstand gegen die Judenverfolgung* (Konstanz, 1996)

Syré, Ludger, 'Der Führer vom Oberrhein: Robert Wagner, Gauleiter, Reichsstatthalter in Baden und Chef der Zivilverwaltung in Elsass', in Kissener and Scholtyseck, *Die Führer der Provinz*

Szepansky, Gerda, *'Blitzmädel', 'Heldenmutter', 'Kriegerwitwe': Frauenleben im Zweiten Weltkrieg* (Frankfurt am Main, 1986)

Szodrzynski, Joachim, 'Das Ende der "Volksgemeinschaft"? Die Hamburger Bevölkerung in der "Trummergesellschaft" ab 1943', in Bajohr and Szodrzynski, *Hamburg in der NS-Zeit*

Szodrzynski, Joachim, 'Die "Heimatfront" zwischen Stalingrad und Kriegsende', in Forschungsstelle für Zeitgeschichte in Hamburg, *Hamburg im 'Dritten Reich'*

Thames Television, *The World at War* (1973), part 16, 'Inside the Reich, 1940–1944'

Thierfelder, Jörg, and Röhm, Eberhard, 'Die evangelischen Landeskirchen von Baden und Württemberg in der Spätphase der Weimarer Republik und zu Beginn des Dritten Reiches', in Schnabel, *Die Machtergreifung in Südwestdeutschland*

Thierfelder, Jörg, 'Die Kirchen', in Borst, *Das Dritte Reich in Baden und Württemberg*

Tholander, Christa, *Fremdarbeiter, 1939 bis 1945: Ausländische Arbeitskräfte in der Zeppelin-Stadt Friedrichshafen* (Essen, 2001)

Torrie, Julia S., 'Testing Totalitarianism at War: The Witten Demonstration and German Civilian Evacuations, 1939–45', Transatlantic Doctoral Seminar, 25–28 April 2001

Tübinger Vereinigung für Volksheilkunde e.V., *Volk und Gesundheit: Heilen und Vernichten im Nationalsozialismus* (Tübingen, 1982)

Überschar, Gerd R., 'Krieg auf dem deutschen Boden: der Vormarsch der Alliierten im Südwesten', in Rolf-Dieter Müller, Gerd R. Überschar and Wolfram Wette, *Kriegsalltag und Kriegsende in Südwestdeutschland, 1944/45* (Freiburg i.Br., 1985)

Volk, Ludwig, (ed.), *Akten deutscher Bischöfe über die Lage der Kirche, 1933–1945, v, 1940–1942* (Mainz, 1983)

Volk, Ludwig, (ed.), *Akten deutscher Bischöfe über die Lage der Kirche, 1933–1945, vi, 1943–1945* (Mainz, 1985)

Völkischer Beobachter, 1933, 1934, 1935, 1938

Volkmann, Hans-Erich, 'Die NS-Wirtschaft in Vorbereitung des Krieges', in Wilhelm Deist, Manfred Messerschmidt, Hans-Erich Volkmann, Wolfram Wette, *Ursachen und Voraussetzungen des Zweiten Weltkrieges* (Stuttgart, 1989)

Wachsmann, Nikolaus, *Hitler's Prisons: Legal Terror in Nazi Germany* (New Haven, Connecticut, and London, 2004)

Ward, Sadie, *War in the Countryside* (London, 1988)

Warriner, Doreen, *Economics of Peasant Farming* (London, 1964)

Watts, David, 'German Forced Labor Policy in Belgium, 1916–1917 and 1942–1944', presentation at the Summer Research Workshop on 'Forced Foreign Laborers, POWs, and Jewish Slave Workers in the Third Reich: Regional Studies and New Research', at the Center for Advanced Holocaust Studies, United States Holocaust Memorial Museum, 15 August 2003

Weger, Tobias, *Nationalsozialistischer 'Fremdarbeitereinsatz' in einer bayerischen Gemeinde, 1939–1945: das Beispiel Olching (Landkreis Fürstenfeldbruck)* (Frankfurt am Main, 1998)

Weglein, Resi, *Als Krankenschwester im KZ Theresienstadt*, ed. and intro. Silvester Lechner and Alfred Moos (Stuttgart, 1988)

Weglein, Resi, 'Ich streichelte jeden Schrank und jeden Stuhl', in Barbara Bronnen (ed.), *Geschichte vom Überleben: Frauentagebücher aus der NS-Zeit* (Munich, 1998)

Weindling, Paul, *Health, Race and German Politics between National Unification and Nazism, 1870–1945* (Cambridge, 1989)

Weiss, Terry, 'Translator's Note', Landeszentrale für politische Bildung Baden-Württemberg, *The German Southwest*

Welch, David, (ed.), *Nazi Propaganda: The Power and the Limitations* (London, 1983)

Welch, David, 'Nazi Propoganda and the *Volksgemeinschaft*: Constructing a People's Community', *Journal of Contemporary History*, 39 (2004)

Weller, Karl, and Weller, Arnold, *Württembergische Geschichte im südwestdeutschen Raum* (Stuttgart and Aalen, 1975)

Wenke, Bettina, *Interviews mit Überlebenden: Verfolgung und Widerstand in Südwestdeutschland* (Stuttgart, 1980), 'Ich habe versucht, dem Wort Gottes gehorsam zu sein: Interview mit Alfred Leikam'

Whaley, Joachim, 'The German Lands before 1815', in Breuilly, *Nineteenth-Century Germany*

Wiener, Martin, *English Culture and the Decline of the Industrial Spirit, 1850–1980* (Cambridge, 1981)

Wiese, Gernot, 'Die Versorgungslage in Deutschland', in Salewski and Wegener, *Kriegsjahr 1944*

Wilke, Gerhard, and Wagner, Kurt, 'Family and Household: Social Structures in a German Village between the Two World Wars', in Richard J. Evans and W.R. Lee (eds), *The German Family* (London, 1981)

Williams, John Alexander, '"The Chords of the German Soul are Tuned to Nature": The Movement to Preserve the Natural *Heimat* from the Kaiserreich to the Third Reich', *Central European History*, 29 (1996)

Willson, Perry, *Peasant Women and Politics in Fascist Italy: The 'Massaie Rurale'* (London, 2002)

Winkler, Dörte, *Frauenarbeit im 'Dritten Reich'* (Hamburg, 1977)

Woydt, Johann, *Ausländische Arbeitskräfte in Deutschland: vom Kaiserreich bis zur Bundesrepublik* (Heilbronn, 1987)

Wright, Jonathan, *'Above Parties': The Political Attitudes of the German Protestant Church Leadership, 1918–1933* (Oxford, 1974)

Württembergisches Statistisches Landesamt, *Staatshandbuch für Württemberg – Ortschaftsverzeichnis* (Stuttgart, 1936)

Wuttke, Walter, 'Medizin, Ärzte, Gesundheitspolitik', in Borst, *Das Dritte Reich in Baden und Württemberg*

Wysocki, Gerd, *Arbeit für den Krieg: Herrschaftsmechanismen in der Rüstungsindustrie des 'Dritten Reiches'* (Limbach, 1992)

Yelton, David K., *Hitler's Volkssturm: The Nazi Militia and the Fall of Germany, 1944–1945* (Lawrence, Kansas, 2002)

Yorkshire Television, *Red Empire*, 1990: 'Class Warriors'

Zahn, Gordon C., 'Catholic Resistance? A Yes and a No', in Littell and Locke, *The German Church Struggle and the Holocaust*

Zeck, Mario, *Das Schwarze Korps: Geschichte und Gestalt des Organs der Reichsführung SS* (Tübingen, 2002)

Ziegler, Walter, 'Gaue und Gauleiter im Dritten Reich', in Möller, Wirsching and Ziegler, *Nationalsozialismus in der Region*

Zilbert, Edward R., *Albert Speer and the Nazi Ministry of Arms* (London, 1981)

Zofka, Zdenek, 'Between Bauernbund and National Socialism', in Thomas Childers (ed.), *The Formation of the Nazi Constituency, 1919–1933* (London and Sydney, 1986)

Zweiniger-Bargielowska, Ina, *Austerity in Britain: Rationing, Controls, and Consumption, 1939–1955* (Oxford, 2000)

Index